THE COMPLETE VICTORIA CROSS

*A Full Chronological Record of All Holders
of Britain's Highest Award for Gallantry*

Revised and Updated Paperback Edition

KEVIN BRAZIER

Foreword by
KEITH PAYNE VC

Pen & Sword
MILITARY

First published in Great Britain in 2010
Published in this format in 2015 by
Pen & Sword Military
an imprint of
Pen & Sword Books Ltd
47 Church Street
Barnsley
South Yorkshire
S70 2AS

ISBN 978 1 47384 351 6

Typeset in Times by
Malcolm Bates, Auldgirth, Dumfriesshire

Printed and bound in England by
CPI Group (UK) Ltd, Croydon,CR0 4YY

Pen & Sword Books Ltd incorporates the imprints of Pen & Sword Archaeology,
Atlas, Aviation, Battleground, Discovery, Family History, History, Maritime,
Military, Naval, Politics, Railways, Select, Social History, Transport, True
Crime, and Claymore Press, Frontline Books, Leo Cooper, Praetorian Press,
Remember When, Seaforth Publishing and Wharncliffe.

For a complete list of Pen & Sword titles please contact
PEN & SWORD BOOKS LIMITED
47 Church Street, Barnsley, South Yorkshire, S70 2AS, England
E-mail: enquiries@pen-and-sword.co.uk
Website: www.pen-and-sword.co.uk

CONTENTS

Ballad of the Victoria Cross

I am the pride of the valiant Brave:

I am the shame of the coward knave:

Look through the world – is there prouder need

Than the plain bronze Cross of the golden deed.

Harold Begbie

ACKNOWLEDGEMENTS

My initial thanks must go to my friends who have helped and supported me throughout this project; they are: David Brown, Joe Dever, Richard Jackson, Lance Renetzke for his knowledge of Indian Army rankings, Andrew Cross for his knowledge of naval rankings and for checking cemeteries in Scotland and the north of England, Frank Jones for checking cemeteries in the south of England and Jill Sugden for her many hours of research.

I would also like to thank Barry Nelms for introducing me to the Union Jack Club, and Martin Murphy of the Union Jack Club for his help in the early days of my research. My thanks also go to Colin Godley for his help with information on his grandfather Sidney Godley VC.

Brian Best BA and Tom Johnson BEM of the Victoria Cross Society have given me a great deal of assistance, and their help has been invaluable. I must thank Kyle Nappi for putting me in touch with Edward Kenna VC and Ian Fraser VC, and likewise Didy Grahame OBE, MVO of the VC and GC Association for her help and for putting me in touch with Willie Apiata VC, Johnson Beharry VC, John Cruickshank VC, Mark Donaldson VC, Lachhiman Gurung VC, Keith Payne VC, Rambahadur Limbu VC, William Speakman VC, Tulbahadur Pun VC and Eric Wilson VC.

Three websites have proved to be of great help: Brian Best's at www.Victoriacrosssociety.com, Mike Chapman's at www.victoriacross.net and Iain Stewart's at www.victoriacross.org.uk/vcross.htm. I am most grateful also to the Photographic Department of the Imperial War Museum, the Trustees of the Army Medical Corps Museum and the Victoria Cross Society for allowing me to reproduce some of their photographs for this book.

I must thank the staff at the many cemeteries I have visited, or spoken to on the phone, who have been very helpful in finding the exact location of a great many VC holders. Also my gratitude is due to the staff at many of the museums I have been in contact with, but special thanks go to the Coins and Medals Department of the Fitzwilliam Museum, Cambridge; to Geoff Preece, Museum and Galleries Manager of the Museum & Art Gallery, Doncaster; to Chris Griffiths, Deputy Curator of the Royal Engineers Museum, Gillingham; to Tina Pittock, Curator of the Airborne Forces Museum, Aldershot (now at Duxford); to Derek Marrison, Curator of the Army Medical Corps Museum, Mytchett; to Gary Gibbs, Assistant Curator of the Guards Museum, London; to Mark Smith, Regimental Historical Secretary and Curator of the Royal Artillery Historical Trust, Woolwich; to Fergus Read, Head of Department of the Imperial War Museum, London; and to Lesley Smurthwaite, Department of Uniforms, Badges and Medals of the National Army Museum, Chelsea.

I must thank my editor, Sarah Cook, for guiding me through the publishing process, and my very special thanks go to Keith Payne VC for writing the Foreword. Last, but by no means least, is my wife, Teresa: thanks for putting up with all those nights and weekends without me while I was locked away working.

Thanks to all those who have contacted me with new, updated or correct information for this revised edition, especially Mark Green, whose help has been most useful.

FOREWORD

by Keith Payne VC

The Victoria Cross is a very special subject, so when I was asked to write this Foreword I felt immensely proud. Proud to be asked and proud of all the remarkable men on whom the award has been bestowed over the last 150 years, some of whom I've been lucky enough to have known.

The men who have been awarded the VC exemplify all the qualities we hold dear: duty, loyalty, humility and sacrifice. For many of these men it did not bring them fame or fortune, nor did they seek it. In fact, in many cases it was a millstone around their neck: it did not guarantee them work when the fighting was over, it did not feed their families when they were hungry and it did not guarantee them happiness.

For the first time this work has brought together the three things that I believe a book about the VC should have: complete lists of all VC holders, the locations of every known VC and the last resting-places of all VC holders. The list of VC holders in chronological order is one of the most innovative ideas I've seen in a very long time. This book should stand as one of the best works on the subject and is a must for any military enthusiast.

I was surprised to learn that 75 VC holders are still buried in unmarked graves, and the author is right to ask anyone finding one to try to do something about it. It is a sad but inevitable fact that the number of living VC holders is dwindling, but I am privileged to count myself as one of these 'happy few'. This work will be a lasting memorial to all VC holders, living and dead. I am delighted to write this short Foreword as I feel this is a book worth reading and I wish it every success.

PREFACE

As a small boy growing up in the 1960s, there was only one thing that really interested me, that being anything to do with the military. War books, comics, films and models were at the top of my list. Being dyslexic, however, meant that my appreciation of books and comics was limited mostly to looking at the pictures. So when I found out that my father had actually served in the Merchant Navy in the Second World War, he assumed a new greatness in my mind. But it was a subject he did not like to talk about, much to my dissatisfaction. It was only as I got older that he would tell me the odd story. My happiest memory of him is when we both sat down to watch *Das Boot* together. He was shocked to see how bad things were for the Germans serving in U-boats, and I think slightly surprised at my knowledge of the subject. We talked almost continually throughout, until the part where the merchant ship is torpedoed and set on fire. Suddenly he went very quiet, and I remembered him telling me once about a time when men who had been in the water were brought aboard his ship and they all died a very painful death, having swallowed sea water mixed with oil.

After leaving school at the age of 16, barely able to read and write, I surprised everyone by not joining the army. Instead I got a very mundane job in a post room. But I had not lost my passion for the military and I started trying to read all the books on the Second World War I could find – a most difficult thing to do when your reading ability is that of a 10-year-old.

I first became aware of the Victoria Cross when I saw the film *Zulu* as a small boy, but my real interest in it was sparked during a trip to the Imperial War Museum in 1977 where I saw First Class Boy John Cornwell's VC, which was awarded to him when he was just one year younger than I was at the time. Like most people, I had very little idea how many VCs had been awarded, and knew little about the many great deeds performed since its introduction in 1856.

I kept up a passing interest in the VC over the years and in 2006 my passion was rekindled when I went to a talk by Johnson Beharry VC, who at the time was the most recent recipient. Like many VC holders, he does not believe he did anything other than his duty. After this, I started looking at all the VC-related books I could get my hands on, and found they have one thing in common: they all list VC holders alphabetically. So I started a project to see if I could list them in chronological order, as it seemed to me that no one had done this before. During the process I started to think about writing this book. If I had known then how much work was involved, I would never have started! So, if you are thinking of writing a book, take my advice: don't think about it too much, just get on with it.

Once the decision was taken to write the book, I started collecting more information on who should be included and who should not, as it had not originally been my intention to write up every VC story, but just to concentrate on the bravest of the brave. But as time went on, I found it difficult to decide who should go in and more importantly who should be left out. So once again I found myself going down a path I had not intended.

Note that foreign names and locations have various spellings, and that both local and anglicised versions have been used. Every effort has been made to check facts, dates and names, but errors are bound to creep in. The responsibility for them is entirely mine. Should you find any errors, please contact me with details at kib1856@yahoo.co.uk or find me on Facebook: search for Kevin Brazier Author.

I have been very lucky during my research and had the good fortune to meet several VC holders, and I will never forget the first time I held a VC in my hand - what a privilege. If I have learnt nothing else during the writing of this book, it is that all VC holders have in common their humility, selflessness, courage and determination.

AUTHOR'S NOTE

In Chapters 4 to 13 all VC holders are listed in order of campaign, and within each campaign they are listed chronologically. The occurrence of several 'overlapping' wars meant it was not possible to keep them all in strict chronological order, so some wars may be slightly out of sequence in order to keep the VC actions in the right order. There is not the space in this book for more than a brief summary of each campaign, but interested readers can find more detail elsewhere.

In some cases not much is known about the VC action or the recipient, so some entries have only a few lines. Once again, the three VCs and Bars have been listed twice, the first entry for the VC action and the second for the Bar action. From the start of the First World War I have stopped giving the names of retitled units, as the merging of regiments that went on from that time makes the process very complicated.

Chapter One

A SHORT HISTORY OF THE VICTORIA CROSS

It was Queen Victoria herself who recognised that the bravery of her 'ordinary' soldiers and sailors went largely unrewarded, and she suggested a new medal for all ranks who conducted themselves with unusual bravery. Until then the government and military leaders had only felt the need to reward officers for their courage. Even the Duke of Wellington had believed that serving king and country was reward enough for any low-ranking soldier. The injustice of this state of affairs was exacerbated by the situation abroad, where since the early nineteenth century the junior grades of the French Legion of Honour (instituted in 1803) and the German Iron Cross (instituted in 1813) had been available to all ranks.

The terms of the new medal stipulated that it would be awarded not for 'rank, nor long service, nor wounds, nor any other circumstance or condition whatsoever', but only for 'merit or conspicuous bravery'; this was the key clause and perhaps best describes the unrestricted nature of the award.

The Victoria Cross came into being when the queen signed the royal warrant on 29 January 1856. It takes the shape of a cross pattée (from the French for 'with feet' or 'paws', referring to the spreading ends) rather than a Maltese Cross, as described in the original warrant. The Cross is 1.375 inches across and weighs around 0.87 ounces with the suspension bar and link. The front bears the royal crest (a crown surmounted by a lion), with the words 'For Valour'. (Originally it was intended to read 'For Bravery', but Queen Victoria did not like this as it implied that those who were not awarded it were not brave.) The suspension bar is deco-rated with laurel leaves and has a small 'V' to attach it to the cross. The ribbon is 1.5 inches wide, and was red for the army and blue for the navy until 1918, when crimson was adopted for all services. All living naval recipients were supposed to give up their blue ribbon for the new crimson, but not many did.

All the medals are made by Hancocks & Co., and always have been. Each cross is cast, then chased and finished by hand, then the medal, suspension bar and link are treated with chemicals to give them an overall dull brown colour, which is darker in some issues than others. The reverse is inscribed with the recipient's name, rank and regiment, with the date of the deed engraved in the centre of the circle. In most cases only the initials are given, but the first name has been used on a few occasions. What makes the VC (and later the George Cross) unique is that each medal can be precisely identified in terms of its recipient: no other bravery award does this.

Much has been said about the metal for the first medals being taken from the cascabels (the balls found at the rear of cannon barrels) of two guns of Chinese origin captured in the Crimea. However, there is no real evidence that the Chinese guns in the Woolwich Arsenal had ever been near the Crimea. But there is evidence that they were captured from the Taku Forts in the Third China War. Historical records and scientific analysis, including X-rays, show that the cascabels were not used until 1924, 68 years after the first VCs were made. Also during the Second World War the cascabels disappeared for a time, and different metal was used between 1942 and 1945.

Awards of the VC have always been announced in the pages of the *London Gazette*. This is known as being 'gazetted'. A recommendation for the VC is normally issued by an officer at regimental level and has to be supported by three witnesses, although this is not always the case. The recommendation is then passed up the military hierarchy until it reaches the Secretary of State for War (now the Secretary of State for Defence) and then the monarch. Royal assent is still required and all VCs are presented by the monarch.

The first award ceremony was held in Hyde Park on 26 June 1857. Preparations for the day were made in something of a hurry, the final list of recipients not being published until 22 June, and the staff at Hancocks had to work around the clock to engrave all the crosses in time. Queen Victoria caused some dismay by electing to stay on horseback throughout the ceremony, while awarding the 62 recipients with their crosses. The queen pinned on the entire batch in just 10–15 minutes, and the whole parade went off extremely well, to the rapturous applause of the public. There is, however, one story that the queen, leaning forward to pin the medal on Commander Raby, accidentally stabbed him in the chest. True to the spirit in which he had earned his cross, he stood unflinching.

There is a widespread myth that it is statutory for all ranks to salute the bearer of a VC. There is no official requirement for this in the royal warrant, nor in Queen's Regulations & Orders (QROs). Yet tradition dictates that this occurs, and thus even the Chiefs of Staff will salute a private soldier awarded the VC.

To date (March 2015) a total of 1,363 VCs have been awarded to 1,360 people. Three men have been awarded it twice: Noel Chavasse and Arthur Martin-Leake, both for saving wounded men, and Charles Upham for combat in Crete and North Africa. In 1921 the award was given to the Unknown American Soldier of the First World War. The recipients also include five Americans, four civilians, three Danes, two Germans, a Belgian, a Fijian, a Swede, a Swiss, a Ukrainian and a Grenadian. Six men under the age of 18 have been awarded

it, with a similar number over the age of 50.

There is one VC that is not counted in any official records. In 1856 Queen Victoria laid a VC beneath the foundation stone of Netley Military Hospital. When the hospital was demolished in 1966, this cross, known as the 'Netley VC', was recovered and is now on display at the Army Medical Services Museum, Mytchett.

Women are eligible for the medal, but to date none has been awarded it. However, a gold replica of the cross, but with no inscription on the reverse, was presented to Mrs Webber Harris, the wife of the commanding officer of the 104th Bengal Fusiliers. She received her award from the officers of the regiment for her 'indomitable pluck' while nursing the men through an outbreak of cholera during the Indian Mutiny.

Eight men have forfeited their awards under Rule Fifteen of the warrant. There is a widespread belief that the forfeited VCs were reinstated, but in fact none was ever removed from the VC register. All eight were subject to a Forfeiture Warrant signed by the sovereign and should have returned their medals, but not all of them did. So if none were removed from the register, none could be reinstated. George V was concerned by the prospect of future forfeits as it was declared: 'The King feels so strongly that, no matter the crime committed by anyone on whom the VC has been conferred, the decoration should not be forfeited. Even were a VC [holder] sentenced to be hanged for murder, he should be allowed to wear his VC on the scaffold.'

The largest number of VCs awarded in a single day was 23, on 16 November 1857, at the relief of Lucknow during the Indian Mutiny (but this figure also includes 4 VCs awarded for the period 14–22 November). The largest number awarded for a single action was 11, on 22/23 January 1879, at Rorke's Drift during the Zulu War, and the largest number awarded for a single conflict was 629 for the First World War, nearly half of all VCs awarded. A total of 182 VCs were awarded in both the Indian Mutiny and the Second World War, 111 were awarded in the Crimean War, 78 in the Second

Boer War and 23 in the Zulu War. Assistant Surgeon William Manley remains the only man to have received both the VC for his actions in the Waikato-Haubau Maori War of 1864 and the German Iron Cross for tending the wounded in the Franco-Prussian War of 1870–71. Flying Officer Lloyd Trigg has the distinction of being the only man ever to be awarded a VC solely on evidence provided by the enemy, for an action where there were no surviving Allied witnesses. Six men under the age of 18 have been awarded the Cross, while a similar number have been awarded it while over the age of 50. The two youngest men to be awarded the Cross were Thomas Flynn and Andrew Fitzgibbon, both aged just 15 years and 3 months. The oldest was William Raynor, just 2 months short of his 62nd birthday.

In recent years some Commonwealth countries have introduced their own honours system, separate from the British Honours System. This began with the partition of India in 1947, when the new countries of India and Pakistan introduced their own awards scheme and replaced the VC with the Param Vir Chakra (PVR) in India and the Nishan-e-Haider in Pakistan. However, both countries continue to permit holders of British awards to wear their medals. Australia was the first Commonwealth country to create its own VC in 1991. Although it is a separate award, its appearance is identical to its British counterpart. Canada followed suit in 1993, creating the Canadian VC, which is similar to the British version but bears the Latin words PRO VALORE. New Zealand was next to adapt the VC into its own honours system in 1999. Australia has also set up a committee to investigate any claims or recommendations for a VC that may have been overlooked in the past. While all these are technically separate awards, the decoration in all cases is identical to the British design with the exception of the Canadian motto. They will even be made from the same metal as British VCs and made by Hancocks. The first person to be awarded one of these is Willie Apiata from New Zealand.

Chapter Two

THE TERMS OF THE 1856 VICTORIA CROSS WARRANT, AND ITS AMENDMENTS

WHERAS WE, taking into Our Royal consideration that there exists no means of adequately rewarding the individual gallant services either of officers of the lower grades in our Naval and Military Service, or of warrant and petty officers, seamen and marines in Our Navy, and non-commissioned officers and soldiers in Our Army; And wheras the Third Class of Our Most Honourable Order of the Bath is limited, except in very rare cases, to the higher ranks of both Services, and the granting of medals, both in Our Navy and Army, is only awarded for long service or meritorious conduct, rather than for bravery in action or distinction before an enemy, such cases alone excepted where a general medal is granted for a particular action or campaign, or a clasp added to the medal for some special engagement, in both of which cases all share equally in the boon, and those who by their valour have particularly signalised themselves remain undistinguished from their comrades; Now, for the purpose of attaining an end so desirable as that of rewarding individual instances of merit and valour, We have instituted and created, and by these present, for Us, Our Heirs and Successors, institute and create a New Naval and Military decoration, which We are desirous should be highly prized and eagerly sought after by the officers and men of Our Naval and Military Services, and are graciously pleased to make, ordain, and establish the following rules and ordinances for the government of the same, which shall from henceforth be inviolably observed and kept.

Firstly. – It is ordained, that the distinction shall be styled and designated 'The Victoria Cross', and shall consist of a Maltese Cross of Bronze with Our Royal Crest in the Centre, and underneath which an escroll bearing this inscription, 'For Valour'.

Secondly. – It is ordained, that the Cross shall be suspended from the left breast, by a blue riband for the Navy, and by a red riband for the Army.

Thirdly. – It is ordained, that the names of those upon whom We may be pleased to confer the decoration shall be published in the *London Gazette*, and a registry thereof kept in the office of Our Secretary of State for War.

Fourthly. – It is ordained, that anyone who, after having received the Cross, shall again perform an act of bravery, which if he had not received such Cross would have entitled him to it, such further act shall be recorded by a Bar attached to the riband by which the Cross is suspended, and for every additional act of bravery an additional Bar may be added.

Fifthly. – It is ordained, that the Cross shall only be awarded to those officers and men who have served Us in the presence of the enemy, and shall have then performed some signal act of valour, or devotion to their country.

Sixthly. – It is ordained, with a view to place all persons on a perfectly equal footing in relation to eligibility for the Decoration, that neither rank, nor long service, nor wounds, nor any other circumstance or condition whatsoever, save the merit of conspicuous bravery, shall be held to establish a sufficient claim to the honour.

Seventhly. – It is ordained, that the Decoration may be conferred on the spot where the act to be rewarded by the grant of such Decoration has been performed, under the following circumstances:

I. When the Fleet or Army in which such act has been performed, is under the eye and command of an Admiral or General officer commanding the forces.

II. Where the naval or military force is under the eye and command of an Admiral or Commodore commanding a squadron or detached naval force, or of a General commanding a corps, or division or brigade on a distinct and detached service, when such Admiral, Commodore, or General Officer shall have the power of conferring the decoration on the spot, subject to confirmation by Us.

Eighthly. – It is ordained, where such act shall not have been performed in sight of a commanding officer as aforesaid, then the claimant for the honour shall prove the act to the satisfaction of the captain or officer commanding his ship, or to the officer commanding the regiment to which the claimant belongs, and such captain or commanding officer shall report the same through the usual channel to the Admiral or Commodore commanding the forces employed on the service, or to the officer commanding the forces in the field, who shall call for such description and attestation of the act as he may think requisite, and on approval shall recommend the grant of the Decoration.

Ninthly. – It is ordained that every person selected for the Cross, under rule seven, shall be publicly decorated before the naval military force or body to which he belongs, and with which the act of bravery for which he is to be rewarded shall have been performed, and his name shall be recorded in a General Order,

together with the cause of his special distinction.

Tenthly. – It is ordained that every person selected under rule eight shall receive his Decoration as soon as possible, and his name shall likewise appear in a General Order as above required, such General Order to be issued by the naval or military commander of the forces employed on the service.

Eleventhly. – It is ordained that the General Orders above referred to shall from time to time be transmitted to Our Secretary of State for War, to be laid before us, and shall be by him registered.

Twelfthly. – It is ordained that as cases may arise not falling within the rules above specified, or in which a claim, though well founded, may not have been established on the spot, We will, on the joint submission of Our Secretary of State for War, and of Our Commander-in-Chief of Our Army, or on that of Our Lord High Admiral or Lords Commissioners of the Admiralty in the case of the Navy, confer the decoration, but never without conclusive proof of the performance of the act of bravery for which the claim is made.

Thirteenthly. – It is ordained that, in the event of a gallant and daring act having been performed by a squadron, ship's company, a detached body of seamen or marines, not under fifty in number, or by a brigade, regiment, troop, or company, in which the Admiral, General, or officer commanding such forces, may deem that all are equally brave and distinguished, and that no special selection can be made by them, then in such case the Admiral, General, or other officer commanding may direct that for any such body of seamen and marines, or for every troop or company of soldiers, one officer shall be selected by the officers engaged for the Decoration; and in like manner one petty officer or non-commissioned officer shall be selected by the petty officers and non-commissioned officers engaged; and two seamen or private soldiers or marines shall be selected by the seamen, or private soldiers, or marines engaged respectively, for the Decoration; and the names of those selected shall be transmitted by the senior officer in command of the naval force, brigade, regiment, troop, or company, to the Admiral or General Officer commanding, who shall in due manner confer the Decoration as if the acts were done under his own eye.

Fourteenthly. – It is ordained that every warrant officer, petty officer, seaman, or marine, or non-commissioned officer or soldier, who shall have received the Cross, shall, from the date of the act by which the Decoration has been gained, be entitled to a Special Pension of Ten Pounds a year, and each additional Bar conferred under rule four on such warrant or petty officers, or non-commissioned officers or men, shall carry with it an additional pension of Five Pounds per annum.

Fifteenthly. – In order to make such additional provision as shall effectually preserve pure this most honourable distinction, it is ordained, that if any person on whom such distinction shall be conferred, be convicted of treason, cowardice, felony, or of any infamous crime, or if he is accused of any such offence and doth not after reasonable time surrender himself to be tried for same, his name shall forthwith be erased from the registry of individuals upon whom the said Decoration shall have been conferred by an especial Warrant under Our Royal Sign Manual, and the pension conferred under rule fourteen shall cease and determine from the date of such Warrant. It is hereby further declared that We, Our Heirs and Successors, shall be the sole judges of the circumstance demanding such expulsion; moreover, We shall at times have power to restore such persons as may at any time have been expelled both to the enjoyment

of the Decoration and pension.

Given at Our Court at Buckingham Palace, this twenty-ninth day of January, in the nineteenth year of Our reign, and in the year of Our Lord one thousand eight hundred and fifty-six.

By Her Majesty's Command.

Amendments and Changes to the Warrant, 1858–1919

Over the years several amendments have been made to the original warrant, but the basic principle – that the medal is to be awarded for conspicuous bravery – has remained to this day. The first amendment came a year after the first awards were made. A royal warrant of 1858 extended the medal to 'non-military persons', and also allowed the medal to be given for 'acts of conspicuous courage and bravery under circumstances of extreme danger, such as the occurrence of a fire on board ship, or the foundering of a vessel at sea, or under any other circumstances in which, through the courage and devotion displayed, life or public property might be saved'.

A royal warrant dated 1 January 1867 stated that eligibility for a VC was to be extended to include members of local forces in New Zealand and in the colonies and their dependencies serving with imperial troops under command of a 'general or other officer'. A further royal warrant of 23 April 1881 declared unequivocally that the VC should be awarded for 'conspicuous bravery or devotion to the country in the presence of the enemy'.

On 6 August 1881 another warrant was issued extending the award to members of the Indian ecclesiastical establishments on the grounds that if they were attached to an army in the field they would be required to perform the same role as military chaplains. On 21 October 1911 this warrant was extended to include native officers, NCOs and men of the Indian Army, and new guidelines were introduced relating to their special pensions.

In 1918 it was decided that crimson ribbons

should be adopted by all services, including the newly formed Royal Air Force (RAF), and in 1920 it was decided to have a wholesale shake-up of the initial 1856 regulations. The new royal warrant used simpler language, and the 1856 rules were renumbered to incorporate all the amendments to date.

Terms of the 1920 Victoria Cross Warrant

WHERAS Her late Majesty Queen Victoria, by a Warrant under Her Royal Sign Manual dated 29th January 1856, did create a Naval and Military Decoration to be styled and designed 'The Victoria Cross,' and did express Her desire that this decoration should be highly prized and eagerly sought after by the Officers and Men of Her Naval and Military Services.

AND WHERAS by divers subsequent Warrants other Officers and Men were admitted to and made eligible for the decoration, and certain amendments were made to the Rules and Ordinances attaching thereto.

AND WHERAS We deem it expedient that the said Warrant and subsequent Warrants before referred to, as also the Rules and Ordinances affecting the same, shall be consolidated, varied and extended.

NOW, THEREFORE, We do hereby declare that the said Warrants, and Rules and Ordinances heretofore in force for the Government of the said Decoration, shall for that purpose be amended, varied, modified and extended; and in substitution thereof We by these presents, for Us, Our Heirs and Successors, are graciously pleased to make, ordain and establish the following Rules and Ordinances for the Government of the same which shall from henceforth be inviolably observed and kept:-

Firstly. – It is ordained, that the distinction shall be styled and designated 'The Victoria Cross,' and shall consist of a Maltese Cross of Bronze with our Royal Crest in the Centre, and underneath it an escroll bearing this inscription: 'For Valour'.

Secondly. – It is ordained, that the Cross shall be suspended from the left breast by a red riband, and on those occasions when only the riband is worn a replica of the Cross in miniature shall be affixed to the centre of the riband.

Thirdly. – It is ordained that the Cross shall only be awarded for the most conspicuous bravery or some daring or pre-eminent act of valour or self-sacrifice or extreme devotion to duty in the presence of the enemy.

Fourthly. – It is ordained that the Cross may be awarded posthumously.

[*Frederick Roberts had been given a posthumous VC in 1900 for his action of 1899 (probably due to his family connections), and in 1902 Edward VII approved the award of six posthumous VCs. Another six were approved in 1907 for actions between 1859 and 1897.*]

Fifthly. – It is ordained that the names of all those persons upon or on account of whom We may be pleased to confer or present the decoration shall be published in the *London Gazette*, and a Registry thereof kept in the Office of Our Secretary of State for War.

Sixthly. – It is ordained that:-

(1) Officers, Warrant Officers and subordinate Officers hereinafter referred to as officers, Chief Petty Officers and Petty Officers hereinafter referred to as Petty Officers, men and boys hereinafter referred to as Seamen, serving in — (a) our Navy or in ships of any description for the time being under Naval Command; (b) our Indian Marine Service; (c) Navies or Marine Services of our Dominions, Colonies, Dependencies or Protectorates; and (d) our Mercantile Marine whilst serving under Naval or Military Authority, or who in the course of their duties may become subject to enemy action;

(2) Officers, Warrant Officers, Non-Commissioned Officers, men and boys hereinafter referred to as Marines, serving in our Marines;

(3) Officers, Warrant Officers (Classes I

and II), Non-Commissioned Officers, Men and boys hereinafter referred to as Privates, of all ranks serving in our Army, our Army Reserve, our Territorial or other forces, and the Forces of our Dominions, Colonies, Dependencies or Protectorates;

(4) Officers, Warrant Officers, Non-Commissioned Officers, and Airmen in the ranks of our Air Force, or the Air Forces of our Dominions, Colonies, Dependencies or Protectorates;

(5) British and Indian Officers and men of all ranks of our Indian Army, the Imperial Service Troops of the Native States of India, or any other Forces there serving under the command, guidance, or direction of any British or Indian Officer, or of a Political Officer attached to such Forces on Our behalf, and

(6) Matrons, sisters, nurses and the staff of the Nursing Services and other Services pertaining to Hospitals and Nursing, and Civilians of either sex serving regularly or temporarily under the Orders, direction or supervision of any of the above mentioned Forces shall be eligible for the decoration of the Cross.

Seventhly. – It is ordained that if any recipient of the Cross shall again perform such an act of bravery, as would have made him or her eligible to receive the Cross, such further act of bravery shall be recorded by a Bar to be attached to the Riband by which the Cross is suspended, and for every such additional act of bravery, an additional Bar shall be added, and any such Bar or Bars may be awarded posthumously. For every Bar awarded a replica of the Cross in miniature shall be added to the riband when worn alone.

Eighthly. – It is ordained that every recommendation for the award of the decoration of the Cross shall be made and reported through the usual channels to the Senior Naval, Military or Air Force Officer Commanding the Force, who shall call for such description, conclusive proof as far as the circumstances of the case will

allow, and attestation of the act as he may think requisite, and if he approve he shall recommend the grant of the decoration to Our Lords Commissioners of the Admiralty, Our Secretary of State for War and the Royal Air Force as the case may be, who shall submit to Us the names of every one so recommended whom they shall consider worthy; in the case of there being no British or Indian Officer, then the Political Officer attached to the Force shall, after obtaining conclusive proof of the act of bravery as far as is possible, if he approve, submit the recommendation to Us through the proper channels.

Ninthly. – It is ordained that in the event of any unit of our Naval, Military or Air Forces, consisting in the case of our Navy of a squadron, flotilla or ship's company, or of a detached body of seamen or marines; or in the case of our Army of a regiment, squadron, battery or company, or of a detached body of soldiers; or in the case of our Air Force of a Squadron or other body of airmen, having distinguished itself collectively by the performance of an act of heroic gallantry or daring in the presence of the enemy in such a way that the Admiral, General or other Officer in Command of the Force to which such a unit belongs, is unable to single out any individual as specially pre-eminent in the gallantry or daring, then one or more of the officers, warrant officers, petty officers, non-commissioned officers, seamen, marines, private soldiers or airmen in the ranks comprising the unit shall be selected to be recommended to Us for the award of the Victoria Cross in the following manner:-

(a) When the total personnel of the unit does not exceed 100, then one officer shall be selected for the decoration by the officers engaged; and in like manner one warrant officer or petty officer or non-commissioned officer of the unit shall be selected by the warrant officers, petty officers or non-commissioned officers engaged, and one seaman, marine, private soldier or airman in the ranks shall be selected by the seamen, marines, private soldiers or airmen in the ranks engaged.

(b) When the total personnel of the unit exceeds 100 but does not exceed 200, then the number of seamen, marines, private soldiers or airmen in the ranks to be selected in the manner described in (a) shall be increased to two.

(c) When the total personnel of the unit exceeds 200 in number, the number of Crosses to be awarded in accordance with these provisions shall be the subject of special consideration by Our Lords Commissioners of the Admiralty or by one of Our Secretaries of State for submission to Us.

(d) The selection to be by a secret ballot in such a manner as shall be determined in accordance with the foregoing provisions by the Officer directing the selection to be made.

(e) The death of any person engaged shall not be a bar to his selection.

(f) The names of the persons recommended in accordance with these provisions shall be submitted to Us in the manner laid down in Rule 8.

Tenthly. – It is ordained that every recipient of the Cross, not being nor ranking as a Commissioned Officer nor in the case of Our Navy, being or ranking with a warrant officer, nor coming within Rule 11, shall from the date of the act by which the decoration has been gained, be entitled to a special pension of Ten Pounds a year, and each additional Bar conferred under Rule 7 on such recipient shall carry with it an additional pension of Five Pounds per annum.

Eleventhly. – Every Indian Officer of Our Indian Army of rank junior to that of Second Lieutenant who shall have received the Cross shall, from the date of the act by which the decoration has been gained, be entitled to a special pension of Five hundred and twenty-five rupees a year, and each additional Bar conferred on such Indian Officers shall carry with it an

additional pension of One hundred and fifty rupees a year. In the case of a Warrant or Non-Commissioned Officer or soldier of Our Indian Army aforesaid We ordain and award a special pension of One hundred and fifty rupees, with Seventy-five rupees additional for each additional Bar. On the death of these recipients of the Cross these pensions shall be continued to his widow until her death or remarriage.

Twelfthly. – In order to make such additional provision as shall effectually maintain pure this most honourable distinction, it is ordained that if any person on whom such distinction shall be conferred be convicted of treason, cowardice, felony, or of any infamous crime, or if he or she be accused of any such offence and doth not after a reasonable time surrender himself or herself to be tried for the same, his or her name shall, by an especial Warrant under Our Royal Sign Manual, forthwith be erased from the registry of individuals upon whom the said decoration shall have been conferred and the pension conferred under Rules 10 and 11 shall cease and be determined from the date of such Warrant. It is hereby further declared that We, Our Heirs and Successors, shall be the sole judges of the circumstance demanding such expulsion; moreover, We shall at all times have power to restore such persons as may at any time have been expelled, both to the enjoyment of the decoration and pension, and notice thereof of expulsion or restoration in every case shall be published in the *London Gazette*.

Given at Our Court of St James's this 22nd day of May, in the eleventh year of Our reign, and in the year of Our Lord one thousand nine hundred and twenty.

By His Majesty's Command.

Amendments and Changes to the Warrant, 1931–95

Since 1920 only minor changes have been made to the regulations. A royal warrant of 5 February 1931 gave permission for half-sized replicas to be worn 'on certain occasions'. It also provided that forfeiture of a VC and any restoration of it should be entirely discretionary. This rule came from a recommendation by the Rewards Committee that gallantry awards should be considered irrevocable, except in extreme cases of infamy.

The next amendments were the result of changes to the make-up of the British armed forces, international borders and the Commonwealth in the twentieth century. A warrant dated 9 May 1938 enabled members of the Burmese military to be entitled to the VC. This was done because Burma had stopped being part of India in 1937. A warrant was issued on 24 January 1941 making eligible all ranks of the newly formed Indian Air Force. Another warrant was issued on 31 December 1941 extending eligibility to the Home Guard, the Women's Auxiliary Services and the paramilitary forces of India and Burma.

Constitutional changes to the Commonwealth led to the royal warrant of 30 September 1961 which made all servicemen and women eligible provided the government of each country was prepared to agree to the terms of the warrant. Another royal warrant was issued on 24 March 1964 to transfer responsibilities relating to the VC from the Secretary of State for War to the Secretary of State for Defence.

The first VC awards allowed a special pension of £10 a year, plus £5 for each additional award of the Cross. From 1898 this could be increased, at discretion, to £50, then to £75. Only in 1959 was the pension granted to all ranks and raised to £100. In 1995 it was raised to £1,000. In 2002 it was raised again, this time to £1,495.

Chapter Three

ROLL OF HONOUR: COMPLETE CHRONOLOGICAL LIST OF ALL VICTORIA CROSS HOLDERS

The following is a complete chronological list of all Victoria Cross holders. Where two or more have been awarded for the same day I have put them in order of rank, unless the time of day is known. This has occurred at the start of the First World War for numbers 524 and 525, and for number 715 on 1 July 1916. Where the rank has been the same, I have put them in alphabetical order. Although used extensively locally, the terms Trooper and Rifleman did not officially come into being until 1923, while 'Captain of the Mast' (or Foretop, Forecastle or Afterguard) is a position and not a rank, usually held by a Boatswain. If the award was for an extended period of time I have used the start date for the position in the list. As the VC granted to the Unknown American Soldier of the First World War was not the result of action in the field but was rather a political award made in 1921 (in return for the British unknown soldier being awarded the Medal of Honor), I have put him at the end of the First World War. Multiple VCs and Bars are listed twice, with a note locating its pair.

Each entry starts with its number in the list, followed by the recipient's rank or position (all ranks given are as at the time of the VC action), and his name, all in **bold**. (With Indian and Nepalese names the surname is all-important, and is always written first.) This is followed by the date of the VC action. Next comes the burial location; if this is not known I have indicated where they died, but 'killed' does not necessarily mean they were killed during the VC action. Also note that 'near' can mean up to 5 miles away. I have tried to give as much detail as I can about the burial location in order to make finding each grave easier. However, this is not always possible and if anyone can help to improve this, please write to me at the email address given below. An unmarked grave does not mean that you cannot visit, as most churches/cemeteries should have a record of the grave location on their register. Graves are in England unless otherwise specified. Last but not least is the present location of the VC, in *italics*. 'Not publicly held' means that the VC is either still with the recipient's family or in a private collection. The Ashcroft Collection is now on permanent display at the Imperial War Museum, London.

Amazingly there are about 70 VC holders buried in unmarked graves, 40 of them in the UK and Ireland. So if you live nearby, or are descended from a VC holder who is buried in an unmarked grave, why not start a campaign to raise money for a headstone? Write to your local authority, your MP, the recipient's regiment and your local newspaper. Try to persuade them to put a headstone on the grave. This has worked in many cases, not only for unmarked graves but for badly damaged headstones too. The VC & GC Association memorial appeal was set up to look into the replacing of headstones and can be contacted at Horse Guards, London, SW1A 2AX. After all, we should honour our heroes. If you are successful, I would very much like to hear from you. I can be contacted at kib1856@yahoo.co.uk or via Facebook.

1. Boatswains Mate CHARLES LUCAS, 21 June 1854, buried St Lawrence's Churchyard, The Street, Mereworth, Kent. *VC location: original left on a train by Lucas and never seen again. The official replacement is on loan from the National Maritime Museum, Greenwich, London, to the National Museum of Ireland, Dublin.*

2. Lieutenant JOHN BYTHESEA, 9–12 August 1854, buried Bath Abbey Cemetery, Section 3, K 19–20; Widcombe, Bath, Avon. *VC location: Ashcroft Collection.*

3. Stoker WILLIAM (enlisted and served as **JOHN**) **JOHNSTONE**, 9–12 August 1854, buried at sea in the St Vincent Passage, Caribbean Sea. *VC location: County Museum of Natural History, Los Angeles, California.*

4. Captain EDWARD BELL, 20 September 1854, buried St Mary's Churchyard, near yew tree in SW corner; Kempsey, Worcestershire. *VC location: Royal Welch Fusiliers Museum, Caernarfon Castle, Gwynedd, Wales.*

5. Sergeant JAMES McKECHNIE, 20 September 1854, buried Eastern Necropolis, Gallowgate, Glasgow, Scotland. *VC location: Royal Scots Guards RHQ, Wellington Barracks, London.*

6. Private WILLIAM REYNOLDS, 20 September 1854, buried Brookwood Cemetery, Plot 119, Grave 48232; Cemetery Pales, Woking, Surrey. *VC location: Royal Scots Guards RHQ, Wellington Barracks, London.*

7. Senior Subaltern ROBERT LINDSAY (later **LOYD-LINDSAY**), 20 September and 5 November 1854, buried in family vault at Ardington Church, Wantage, Oxfordshire. *VC location: not publicly held.*

8. Sergeant JOHN PARK, 20 September, 5 November 1854 and 19 April 1855, buried in unmarked grave, Allahabad Cemetery, Church of Scotland Section; India. *VC location: Newarke House Museum, Leicester.*

9. Sergeant JOHN KNOX, 20 September 1854 and 18 June 1855, buried Cheltenham Cemetery, Section N, Grave 17085; Bouncers Lane, Gloucestershire. *VC location: not publicly held.*

10. Sergeant LUKE O'CONNOR, 20 September 1854 and 8 September 1855, buried St Mary's RC Cemetery, Plot 1100; Harrow Road, Kensal Rise, London. *VC location: Royal Welch Fusiliers Museum, Caernarfon Castle, Gwynedd, Wales.*

11. Private FRANCIS WHEATLEY, 12 October 1854, buried Brompton Cemetery, Compartment B, Grave 41396; Old Brompton Road, London. *VC location: Royal Green Jackets Museum, Winchester, Hampshire.*

12. Lieutenant Colonel COLLINGWOOD DICKSON, 17 October 1854, buried Kensal Green Cemetery, Square 112/2, Plot 34633; Harrow Road, London. *VC location: Royal Artillery Museum, Woolwich, London.*

13. Private THOMAS GRADY, 18 October and 22 November 1854, buried Melbourne General Cemetery, RC Section, Block S, Grave 891 (in cemetery register as O'Grady); Springvale, Victoria, Australia. *VC location: Australian War Memorial, Canberra, Australia.*

14. Captain WILLIAM PEEL, 18 October, 5 November 1854 and 18 June 1855, buried in unmarked grave, Old British Cemetery, Cawnpore, India. *VC location: National Maritime Museum, Greenwich, London.*

15. Midshipman EDWARD DANIEL, 18 October, 5 November 1854 and 18 June 1855, buried Hokitika Municipal Cemetery, Block 27, Grave 851; South Island, New Zealand. *VC location: Ashcroft Collection.*

16. Sergeant WILLIAM McWHEENEY (aka **MAWHINNEY**), 20 October and 5 November 1854, buried St James' Cemetery, Consecrated Section R, No. 1–11; Old Charlton Road, Dover, Kent. *VC location: Essex Regiment Museum, Chelmsford, Essex.*

17. Lieutenant ALEXANDER DUNN, 25 October 1854, buried Military Cemetery, Senafe, Eritrea. There are plans to move his remains back to Canada. *VC location: Canadian War Museum, Ottawa, Ontario, Canada.*

18. Sergeant Major JOHN GRIEVE, 25 October 1854, buried St Michael's Churchyard, Inveresk, Midlothian, Scotland.

VC location: Art Gallery of South Australia, Adelaide, Australia.

19. Sergeant JOHN BERRYMAN, 25 October 1854, buried St Agatha's Churchyard, Woldingham, Surrey. *VC location: not publicly held.*

20. Sergeant JOHN FARRELL, 25 October 1854, buried in unmarked grave, Secunderadad Cemetery, India. *VC location: not publicly held.*

21. Lance Sergeant JOSEPH MALONE, 25 October 1854, buried St Andrew's Churchyard, Pinetown, Natal, South Africa. *VC location: 13th/18th Hussars Museum, Barnsley, Yorkshire.*

22. Private SAMUEL PARKES, 25 October 1854, buried Brompton Cemetery, Compartment R, Grave 39265; Old Brompton Road, London. *VC location: Queen's Royal Hussars RHQ, London.*

23. Surgeon JAMES MOUAT, 26 October 1854, buried Kensal Green Cemetery, Square 154/PS, Plot 28837; Harrow Road, London. *VC location: Army Medical Services Museum, Mytchett, Surrey.*

24. Lieutenant JOHN CONOLLY, 26 October 1854, buried Mount Jerome Cemetery, Section B-88, Grove 163-6921; Harold's Cross, Dublin 6, Ireland. *VC location: Coldstream Guards RHQ, Wellington Barracks, London.*

25. Sergeant Major AMBROSE MADDEN, 26 October 1854, buried Up Park Military Camp Cemetery, Jamaica. *VC location: Welch Regiment Museum, Cardiff Castle, Cardiff, Wales.*

26. Sergeant HENRY RAMAGE, 26 October 1854, buried in unmarked grave, Newbridge Cemetery, Co. Kildare, Ireland. *VC location: Scots Greys Museum, Edinburgh Castle, Scotland.*

27. Sergeant CHARLES WOODEN, 26 October 1854, buried St James' Cemetery, Section KG, Grave 8-C; Old Charlton Road, Dover, Kent. *VC location: Queen's Royal Lancers Museum, Belvoir Castle, Grantham, Leicestershire.*

28. Private WILLIAM STANLAKE (**STANLOCK** in *London Gazette*), 26 October 1854, buried Camberwell Old Cemetery, Section 62, Grave 19075; Forest Hill Road, London. *VC location: Coldstream Guards RHQ, Wellington Barracks, London.*

29. Lieutenant WILLIAM 'BULLY' HEWETT, 26 October and 5 November 1854, buried Highland Road Cemetery, Section U, 2nd Plot, Row 2, Grave 33; Highland Road, Southsea, Portsmouth, Hampshire. *VC location: National Maritime Museum, Greenwich, London.*

30. Brevet Major GERALD GOODLAKE, 28 October and November 1854, buried St Mary the Virgin Churchyard, Harefield, Middlesex. *VC location: Coldstream Guards RHQ, Wellington Barracks, London.*

31. Corporal JAMES OWENS, 30 October 1854, buried Christchurch Cemetery, Section E, Grave 146; Lorne Road, Brentwood, Essex. *VC location: Royal Gloucestershire, Berkshire and Wiltshire Regiment Museum, Salisbury, Wiltshire.*

32. Colonel HENRY PERCY, 5 November 1854, buried St Nicholas Chapel (Northumberland Vault), Westminster Abbey, Dean's Yard, London. *VC location: Royal Northumberland Fusiliers Museum, Alnwick Castle, Alnwick.*

33. Brevet Major CHARLES RUSSELL, 5 November 1854, buried in vault at All Saints Church, Swallowfield, Berkshire. *VC location: Grenadier Guards RHQ, Wellington Barracks, London.*

34. Captain HUGH ROWLANDS, 5 November 1854, buried St Michael's Churchyard, Llanrug, Caernarvonshire, Wales. *VC location: Welch Regiment Museum, Cardiff, Wales.*

35. Lieutenant HENRY CLIFFORD, 5 November 1854, buried in family vault St Cyprian's Chapel, Ugbrooke House, Chudleigh, Devon. *VC location: unknown. A replica is on display at Ugbrooke House, Chudleigh, Devon.*

36. Lieutenant FREDERICK MILLER, 5 November 1854, buried Ossuary Garden of Remembrance, Observatory, Cape Town, South Africa. *VC location: Ashcroft Collection.*

37. Lieutenant MARK WALKER,
5 November 1854, buried Cheriton Road
Cemetery, Consecrated Section, Section 18,
Grave 1259-A; Cheriton Road, Folkestone,
Kent. *VC location: Ashcroft Collection..*

38. Sergeant ANDREW HENRY,
5 November 1854, buried Ford Park
Cemetery, Section F, Grave 35/R2; Ford
Park Road, Plymouth, Devon. *VC location:
Royal Artillery Museum, Woolwich, London.*

39. Sergeant GEORGE WALTERS,
5 November 1854, buried City of Westminster
Cemetery (aka East Finchley Cemetery),
Grave E 10/55 (headstone reads 'with others');
East End Road, London. *VC location: Royal
Gloucestershire, Berkshire and Wiltshire
Regiment Museum, Salisbury, Wiltshire.*

40. Corporal JOHN PRETTYJOHNS
(sometimes spelt **PRETTYJOHN**),
5 November 1854, buried Southern Cemetery,
C of E Section L, Grave 642; Barlow Moor
Road, Manchester. *VC location: Royal
Marines Museum, Southsea, Hampshire.*

41. Able Seaman THOMAS REEVES,
5 November 1854, buried in unmarked grave,
Portsea General Cemetery, Plot 701, Grave
57 (in Mile End Gardens, part of the P&O
ferry terminal), Portsmouth, Hampshire.
VC location: Ashcroft Collection.

42. Private THOMAS BEACH, 5 November
1854, buried in unmarked grave, Eastern
Necropolis, Section H, Grave 857; Arbroath
Road, Dundee, Scotland. *VC location: Sheesh
Mahal Museum, Patiala, Punjab, India.*

43. Private JOHN McDERMOND (spelt
McDIARMID in cemetery register),
5 November 1854, buried in unmarked grave,
Woodside Cemetery (Paisley Old Cemetery),
Section 26; Paisley, Glasgow, Scotland.
VC location: not publicly held.

44. Private ANTHONY PALMER,
5 November 1854, buried Heywood
Cemetery, Section E, Grave 183; Rochdale
Road East, Rochdale, Lancashire. *VC
location: Grenadier Guards RHQ, Wellington
Barracks, London.*

45. Seaman MARK SCHOLEFIELD,
5 November 1854, buried at sea. *VC location:
Ashcroft Collection.*

46. Seaman JAMES GORMAN, 5 November
1854, buried C of E Cemetery, Norton Street,
Balmaine, Sydney, New South Wales,
Australia. *VC location: not publicly held.*

47. Private JOHN BYRNE, 5 November
1854 and 11 May 1855, buried St Woolo's
Cemetery, RC Section, Block 14, E15;
Bassaleg Road, Newport, Monmouthshire,
Wales. *VC location: unknown. May have been
buried with him.*

48. Lieutenant CLAUD BOURCHIER,
20 November 1854, buried St Andrew's
Churchyard, Buxton, Norfolk. *VC location:
Royal Green Jackets Museum, Winchester,
Hampshire.*

**49. Lieutenant WILLIAM
CUNNINGHAME**, 20 November 1854,
buried Kirkmichael Churchyard, Ayr,
Scotland. *VC location: Royal Green Jackets
Museum, Winchester, Hampshire.*

50. Lieutenant WILBRAHAM LENNOX,
20 November 1854, buried Brighton Extra-
Mural Cemetery (aka Lewis Road Parochial
Cemetery), Plot FF, Grave 47/48/49; Lewis
Road, Brighton, Sussex. *VC location: Royal
Engineers Museum, Gillingham, Kent.*

51. Private WILLIAM NORMAN,
19 December 1854, buried Weaste Cemetery,
C of E section; Cemetery Road, Salford,
Lancashire. *VC location: Royal Fusiliers
Museum, Tower of London.*

52. Corporal WILLIAM LENDRIM
(**LENDRUM**), 14 February, 11 and 20 April
1855, buried Royal Military Academy
Cemetery, Grave 182; Haig Road,
Camberley, Surrey. *VC location: Royal
Engineers Museum, Gillingham, Kent.*

53. Private ALEXANDER WRIGHT,
22 March and 19 April 1855, no known
grave, died at Calcutta, India. *VC location:
Prince of Wales Royal Regiment & Queen's
Regiment RHQ, Canterbury, Kent.*

54. Sergeant GEORGE GARDINER,
22 March and 18 June 1855, buried Clouleigh
Churchyard, Lifford, Co. Donegal, Ireland.
*VC location: Princess of Wales Royal
Regiment & Queen's Regiment RHQ,
Canterbury, Kent.*

55. Private WILLIAM COFFEY, 29 March

1855, buried Spittal Cemetery, RC section, Grave 10657; Chesterfield, Derbyshire. *VC location: Border Regiment Museum, Carlisle, Cumbria.*

56. Brevet Major FREDERICK ELTON, 29 March, 7 June and 4 August 1855, buried St Andrew's Parish Churchyard, Whitestaunton, Somerset. *VC location: Border Regiment Museum, Carlisle, Cumbria.*

57. Boatswains Mate JOHN SULLIVAN, 10 April 1855, believed to be buried in unmarked grave, Glasnevin Cemetery, Finglas Road, Dublin, Ireland. *VC location: not publicly held.*

58. Private SAMUEL EVANS, 13 April 1855, buried Piershill Cemetery, Piershill Terrace, Edinburgh, Scotland. *VC location: Green Howards Museum, Richmond, Yorkshire.*

59. Captain MATTHEW DIXON, 17 April 1855, buried Kensal Green Cemetery, Square 103/2, Plot 22977; Harrow Road, London. *VC location: with recipient's family.*

60. Colour Sergeant HENRY MacDONALD, 19 April 1855, buried Western Necropolis, Section K, Lair 957; Tresta Road, Glasgow, Scotland. *VC location: Glasgow Museums Resource Centre, Glasgow, Scotland.*

61. Private JOSEPH BRADSHAW, 22 April 1855, no known grave but references indicate buried at St John's, Co. Limerick, Ireland. *VC location: Royal Green Jackets Museum, Winchester, Hampshire.*

62. Private ROBERT HUMPSTON (spelt **HEMPSTON** in cemetery register), 22 April 1855, buried Nottingham General Cemetery, Grave 0276; Nottingham. *VC location: Royal Green Jackets Museum, Winchester, Hampshire.*

63. Private RODERICK McGREGOR, 22 April and July 1855, buried St Mary's Churchyard (also known as Old Kilmore Churchyard), Drumnadrochit, near Urquhart, Highland Region, Scotland. *VC location: Royal Green Jackets Museum, Winchester, Hampshire.*

64. Captain THOMAS HAMILTON, 11 May 1855, buried Cheltenham Cemetery, Section L, Grave 1143; Bouncers Lane,

Gloucestershire. *VC location: with recipient's family.*

65. Lieutenant HUGH BURGOYNE, 29 May 1855, no known grave, drowned at sea, off Cape Finisterre, Bay of Biscay. *VC location: not publicly held.*

66. Gunner JOHN ROBARTS, 29 May 1855, Highland Road Cemetery, 1st Row, Grave 14; Highland Road, Southsea, Portsmouth, Hampshire. *VC location: not publicly held.*

67. Lieutenant CECIL BUCKLEY, 29 May and 3 June 1855, buried British Cemetery, Grave 459; Funchal, Madeira. *VC location: Royal Collection, Windsor Castle, Berkshire.*

68. Boatswain HENRY COOPER, 29 May and 3 June 1855, buried St Mary & St James Churchyard, Anthony, Torpoint, Cornwall. *VC location: Ashcroft Collection.*

69. Sergeant GEORGE SYMONS, 6 June 1855, buried in unmarked grave, St Mary the Virgin, Burlington Priory Churchyard, Yorkshire. *VC location: HQ RLC Museum, Princess Royal Barracks, Deepcut, Surrey.*

70. Captain HENRY JONES, 7 June 1855, buried Ocklynge Old Cemetery, Grave X-10; Willingdon Road, Eastbourne, Sussex. *VC location: Victoria Barracks, Sydney, New South Wales, Australia.*

71. Bombardier THOMAS WILKINSON, 7 June 1855, buried York Cemetery, Cemetery Road, York. *VC location: Royal Marine Museum, Southsea, Portsmouth, Hampshire.*

72. Gunner THOMAS ARTHUR (real name **McARTHUR**), 7 and 18 June 1855, buried Cadley Churchyard (now private), near Savernake, Wiltshire. *VC location: Royal Artillery Museum, Woolwich, London.*

73. Private MATTHEW HUGHES, 7 and 18 June 1855, buried Undercliffe Cemetery, Consecrated Section N, Grave 388; Bradford, Yorkshire. *VC location: Royal Fusiliers Museum, Tower of London.*

74. Private JOHN LYONS, 10 June 1855, burial location unknown, died at Naas, Co. Kildare, Ireland. *VC location: Green Howards Museum, Richmond, Yorkshire.*

75. Private JOSEPH PROSSER, 16 June 1855, buried Liverpool Cemetery (formerly

Anfield Cemetery), Section 14, Grave 589; Liverpool. *VC location: Royal Scots Regiment Museum, Edinburgh, Scotland.*

76. Lieutenant HOWARD ELPHINSTONE, 18 June 1855, drowned at sea, near Ushant, Bay of Biscay, France. *VC location: Ashcroft Collection.*

77. Lieutenant WILLIAM HOPE, 18 June 1855, buried Brompton Cemetery, Compartment E, 142' x 110'; Old Brompton Road, London. *VC location: Royal Fusiliers Museum, Tower of London.*

78. Lieutenant GERALD GRAHAM, 18 June 1855, buried East-the-Water Cemetery, Section C, Grave 523; Bideford, Devon. *VC location: Royal Engineers Museum, Gillingham, Kent.*

79. Lieutenant HENRY RABY, 18 June 1855, buried Highland Road Cemetery, Central Section, near path; Highland Road, Southsea, Portsmouth, Hampshire. *VC location: Ashcroft Collection..*

80. Colour Sergeant PETER LEITCH, 18 June 1855, buried in unmarked grave, Margravine Road Cemetery, Grave 7 - H - 18; Margravine Road, Hammersmith, London. *VC location: Royal Engineers Museum, Gillingham, Kent.*

81. Corporal FELIX SMITH, 18 June 1855, buried Glasnevin Cemetery, St Briget's Section, Grave TH/113-1/2 (headstone bears the name Scully); Finglas Road, Dublin, Ireland. *VC location: Royal Leicestershire Regiment Museum, Leicester.*

82. Boatswains Mate HENRY CURTIS, 18 June 1855, buried Kingston Cemetery, Lights 88, Block 10, Grave 22; St Mary's Road, Portsmouth, Hampshire. *VC location: Ashcroft Collection.*

83. Captain of the Forecastle JOHN TAYLOR, 18 June 1855, buried Woolwich Cemetery, Section D, Grave 510; Kings Highway, London. *VC location: Sheesh Mahal Museum, Patiala, Punjab, India.*

84. Private JOHN SIMS, 18 June 1855, buried in unmarked grave, City of London Cemetery, Square 311, No. 46112; Aldersbrook Road, Manor Park, London. *VC location: unknown.*

85. Sapper JOHN PERIE (spelt **PIRRIE** in cemetery register), 18 June 1855, buried in unmarked grave, St Peter's Cemetery, Strangers Ground, Section 1, Grave 43; King Street, Aberdeen, Scotland. *VC location: Royal Engineers Museum, Gillingham, Kent.*

86. Captain THOMAS ESMONDE, 18 and 20 June 1855, buried Town Cemetery, Plot 4, Grave 55; Bruges, Belgium. *VC location: on loan to the Imperial War Museum, London.*

87. Private JOHN ALEXANDER, 18 June and 6 September 1855, no known grave, presumed buried where he fell, killed at Alumbagh, Lucknow, India. *VC location: National War Museum of Scotland, Edinburgh Castle, Scotland.*

88. Private CHARLES McCORRIE (aka **McCURRY**), 23 June 1855, buried Msida Bastion Cemetery, Valletta, Malta. *VC location: not publicly held.*

89. Seaman JOSEPH TREWAVAS, 3 July 1855, buried in unmarked grave, Old School Cemetery (grave is in the corner behind the school); Paul Village, Mousehole, Cornwall. *VC location: Penlee House Gallery and Museum, Penzance, Cornwall. It is not generally on display, but can be viewed by appointment.*

90. Lieutenant GEORGE DOWELL, 13 July 1855, buried Purewa Cemetery, Grave 4385-B; St John's, Auckland, New Zealand. *VC location: Royal Marines Museum, Southsea, Portsmouth, Hampshire.*

91. Captain GEORGE INGOUVILLE, 13 July 1855, no known grave, drowned at sea. Supposedly washed ashore near Hyeres, France, but there is no record of his burial. *VC location: Maritime Museum, New North Quay, St Helier, Jersey, Channel Islands.*

92. Boatswains Mate JOHN SHEPPARD (or **SHEPHERD**), 15 July and 16 August 1855, buried Padstow Cemetery, Cornwall. *VC location: National Maritime Museum, Greenwich, London.*

93. Corporal JOHN ROSS, 21 July, 23 August and 8 September 1855, buried in St Pancras & Islington Cemetery, Block 2, Section 2, Grave 9765; High Road, East Finchley, London. *VC location: Royal*

Engineers Museum, Gillingham, Kent.

94. Sergeant JOHN COLEMAN, 30 August 1855, no known grave, died at Lucknow, India. *VC location: Queen's Own Royal West Kent Regiment Museum, Maidstone, Kent.*

95. Boatswain Third Class JOSEPH KELLAWAY, 31 August 1855, buried Maidstone Road Cemetery, Section N, Grave 579; Chatham, Kent. *VC location: not publicly held.*

96. Private ALFRED ABLETT, 2 September 1855, buried in unmarked grave, St Andrew's Parish Churchyard, grave on west side of church; Weybread, Suffolk. *VC location: Grenadier Guards RHQ, Wellington Barracks, London.*

97. Colour Sergeant JAMES CRAIG, 6 September 1855, buried St Mary's Cemetery, Valley Road, South End, Port Elizabeth, Cape Province, South Africa. *VC location: Scots Guards RHQ, Wellington Barracks, London.*

98. Brevet Lieutenant Colonel FREDERICK MAUDE, 8 September 1855, buried Brompton Cemetery, Compartment 2 West, 198' x 30'; Old Brompton Road, London. *VC location: not publicly held.*

99. Assistant Surgeon THOMAS HALE, 8 September 1855, buried Acton Parish Churchyard, near Nantwich, Cheshire. *VC location: Army Medical Services Museum, Mytchett, Surrey.*

100. Captain GRONOW DAVIS, 8 September 1855, buried Arnos Vale Cemetery, Bath Road, Knowle, Bristol. *VC location: Royal Artillery Museum, Woolwich, London.*

101. Captain CHARLES LUMLEY, 8 September 1855, buried Brecon Cathedral Churchyard, Powys, Wales. *VC location: Queen's Own Royal West Kent Regiment Museum, Maidstone, Kent.*

102. Sergeant ANDREW MOYNIHAN, 8 September 1855, buried Ta Braxia International Cemetery, Section S, Grave 182; Malta. *VC location: Cameronians Museum, Hamilton, Lanarkshire, Scotland.*

103. Corporal ROBERT SHIELDS, 8 September 1855, buried in unmarked grave, St Thomas's Cathedral, in Back Bay Section; Bombay, India. *VC location: not publicly held.*

104. Bombardier DANIEL CAMBRIDGE, 8 September 1855, buried in unmarked grave, St Nicholas Parish Churchyard, Plumstead, London. *VC location: Royal Artillery Museum, Woolwich, London.*

105. Private JOHN CONNORS, 8 September 1855, buried British Cemetery, Corfu Town, Corfu. *VC location: reported destroyed.*

106. Assistant Surgeon WILLIAM SYLVESTER, 8 and 18 September 1855, buried Paignton Cemetery, Grave 2614; Colley End Road, Paignton, Devon. *VC location: Army Medical Services Museum, Mytchett, Surrey.*

107. Lieutenant GEORGE DAY, 17 and 21 September 1855, buried Weston-super-Mare Cemetery, Consecrated Section, Grave 2397 (grave bears the name Caroline Foster); Ebdon Road, Worke, Avon. *VC location: Sheesh Mahal Museum, Patiala, Punjab, India.*

108. Private GEORGE STRONG, 25–30 September 1855, buried Church of the Holy Cross Churchyard, Sherston, near Malmesbury, Wiltshire. *VC location: Coldstream Guards RHQ, Wellington Barracks, London.*

109. Lieutenant CHRISTOPHER TEESDALE, 29 September 1855, buried St Mary Magdalene Churchyard, South Berstead, Sussex. *VC location: Ashcroft Collection.*

110. Commander JOHN COMMERELL, 11 October 1855, buried Cheriton Road Cemetery, Consecrated Section, Section 22, Grave 3237-4; Cheriton Road, Folkestone, Kent. *VC location: Ashcroft Collection.*

111. Quartermaster WILLIAM RICKARD, 11 October 1855, buried Town Cemetery, Old Section, Grave 2456; West Street, Ryde, Isle of Wight. *VC location: Ashcroft Collection.*

112. Captain JOHN WOOD, 9 December 1856, buried St Mary's Churchyard, under the name Augustus John Wood; Poona, India. *VC location: believed to be held by the 2nd Rajputana Rifles, India.*

113. Lieutenant JOHN MALCOLMSON,

8 February 1857, buried Kensal Green Cemetery, Square 99/RS, family vault; Harrow Road, London. *VC location: held by the 2nd Rajputana Rifles, India.*

114. Lieutenant ARTHUR MOORE, 8 February 1857, buried Mount Jerome Cemetery, Section C-156, No. 14036; Harold's Cross, Dublin 6, Ireland. *VC location: not publicly held.*

115. Captain DIGHTON PROBYN, 1857 to 1858, buried Kensal Green Cemetery, Square 117/2, Grave 21487; Harrow Road, London. *VC location: not publicly held.*

116. Deputy Assistant Commissary of Ordnance JOHN BUCKLEY, 11 May 1857, buried Tower Hamlets Cemetery; Southern Grove, London. *VC location: RLC Museum, Camberley, Surrey.*

117. Lieutenant GEORGE FORREST, 11 May 1857, buried Dehra Dun Cemetery, India. *VC location: not publicly held.*

118. Lieutenant WILLIAM RAYNOR, 11 May 1857, buried Ferozepore Civil Cemetery, Plot 358; India. *VC location: RLC Museum, Camberley, Surrey.*

119. Ensign EVERARD LISLE-PHILLIPPS, 30 May–18 September 1857, buried in unmarked grave, Old Delhi Military Cemetery (the Nicholson Cemetery), India. *VC location: Ashcroft Collection.*

120. Lieutenant ALFRED HEATHCOTE, June to September 1857, buried St James Anglican Churchyard (Bowral Cemetery), grave to the left of the entrance; New South Wales, Australia. *VC location: Victoria Barracks, Sydney, New South Wales, Australia.*

121. Sergeant Major PETER GILL, 4 June 1857, buried in unmarked grave, Artillery Lines Cemetery, Gwalior, India. *VC location: not publicly held.*

122. Sergeant Major MATTHEW ROSAMUND, 4 June 1857, buried at sea, Red Sea. *VC location: not publicly held.*

123. Private JOHN KIRK, 4 June 1857, buried Liverpool Cemetery (formerly Anfield Cemetery), Grave CH - 14 - 2318; Liverpool. *VC location: Museum of Lincolnshire Life, Lincoln.*

124. Colour Sergeant CORNELIUS

COUGHLAN (aka **COGHLAN**), 8 June and 18 July 1857, buried Westport Old Cemetery, Co. Mayo, Ireland. *VC location: National War Museum of Scotland, Edinburgh Castle, Scotland.*

125. Lieutenant ALFRED JONES, 8 June and 10 October 1857, buried St James Churchyard, Section R, Finchampstead, Berkshire. *VC location: not publicly held.*

126. Pensioned Sergeant HENRY HARTIGAN, 8 June and 10 October 1857, buried in unmarked grave, Barrackpore New Cemetery, Calcutta, India. *VC location: Newcastle-under-Lyne Museum. (Hancocks now say it appears this medal is not an authentic VC).*

127. Lieutenant THOMAS CADELL, 12 June 1857, buried Tranent Parish Churchyard, family vault; East Edinburgh, Scotland. *VC location: not publicly held.*

128. Private THOMAS HANCOCK, 19 June 1857, buried Brompton Cemetery, Compartment AG, 306' 9" x 18' 3"; Old Brompton Road, London. *VC location: not publicly held.*

129. Private JOHN PURCELL, 19 June 1857, buried in unmarked grave, Old Delhi Military Cemetery (the Nicholson Cemetery), India. *VC location: not publicly held.*

130. Private SAMUEL TURNER, 19 June 1857, buried in unmarked grave, St John's Cemetery, Meerut Cantonment, India. *VC location: not publicly held.*

131. Colour Sergeant STEPHEN GARVIN, 23 June 1857, buried St Andrew's Churchyard, Church Street, Chesterton, Cambridgeshire. *VC location: not publicly held.*

132. Private JOHN McGOVERN (aka **McGOWAN**), 23 June 1857, buried Holy Sepulchre Cemetery, Section E, Lot 53; Hamilton, Ontario, Canada. *VC location: National Army Museum, London.*

133. Lieutenant WILLIAM CUBITT, 30 June 1857, buried St Peter's Churchyard, Frimley, Surrey. *VC location: not publicly held.*

134. Corporal WILLIAM OXENHAM, 30 June 1857, buried Higher Cemetery, Dissenters Section B, Div. 126, Grave 126; Pinhoe Road, Exeter, Devon. *VC location:*

Duke of Cornwall's Light Infantry Museum, Bodmin, Cornwall.

135. Lieutenant ROBERT AITKEN, 30 June–22 November 1857, buried Eastern Cemetery, St Andrews, Fife, Scotland. *VC location: National Army Museum, London.*

136. Colonel JAMES TRAVERS, July 1857, buried in unmarked grave, New Cemetery, remains placed in Municipal Ossuary, Pallanza, Italy. *VC location: not publicly held.*

137. Private WILLIAM DOWLING, 4 and 9 July and 27 September 1857, buried in unmarked grave, Ford Cemetery, Gorsey Lane, Litherland, Liverpool. *VC location: Duke of Cornwall's Light Infantry Museum, Bodmin, Cornwall.*

138. Gunner WILLIAM CONNOLLY, 7 July 1857, buried in Kirkdale Cemetery, Section 17, Grave 220, headstone not on the exact place of burial; Longmoor Lane, Walton, Liverpool. *VC location: unknown. A copy is on display at the British in India Museum, Colne, Lancashire.*

139. Lieutenant SAMUEL LAWRENCE, 7 July and 26 September 1857, buried British Cemetery, Avenue General Rivera, Montevideo, Uruguay. *VC location: Duke of Cornwall's Light Infantry Museum, Bodmin, Cornwall.*

140. Major HENRY TOMBS, 9 July 1857, buried Carisbrooke Cemetery, Section B, Grave 113; Whitcomb Road, Newport, Isle of Wight. *VC location: Royal Artillery Museum, Woolwich, London.*

141. Second Lieutenant JAMES HILLS (later **HILLS-JOHNES**), 9 July 1857, buried in vault in Caio Churchyard, Dyfed, Wales. *VC location: Royal Artillery Museum, Woolwich, London.*

142. Private JAMES THOMPSON, 9 July 1857, buried in unmarked grave, Queen Street Cemetery (also known as Old Cemetery), Walsall, Staffordshire. *VC location: Royal Green Jackets Museum, Winchester, Hampshire.*

143. Lieutenant WILLIAM KERR, 10 July 1857, buried Cheriton Road Cemetery, Consecrated Section, Grave 3911-A; Cheriton Road, Folkestone, Kent. *VC location:*

Ashcroft Collection.

144. Lance Corporal ABRAHAM BOULGER, 12 July–25 September 1857, buried Ballymore RC Churchyard, Co. Kildare, Ireland. *VC location: York and Lancaster Regiment Museum, Rotherham, Yorkshire.*

145. Private PATRICK MYLOTT, 12 July–25 September and 17 November 1857, buried in Liverpool Cemetery (formerly Anfield Cemetery), RC Section, No. 21, Grave 1743; headstone reads 'within this cemetery'; Liverpool. *VC location: not publicly held.*

146. Lieutenant HENRY HAVELOCK (later **HAVELOCK-ALLAN**), 16 July 1857, buried Harley Street Cemetery, Rawalpindi, India. *VC location: unknown; believed to have gone missing during his lifetime.*

147. Lieutenant RICHARD WADESON, 18 July 1857, buried Brompton Cemetery, Compartment E, 118' x 158'; Old Brompton Road, London. *VC location: Gordon Highlanders Museum, Aberdeen, Scotland.*

148. Lieutenant ANDREW BOGLE, 29 July 1857, ashes interred at St Lawrence's Churchyard, Effingham, Surrey. *VC location: Highlanders Museum, Fort George, Ardersier, Inverness-shire, Scotland.*

149. Sergeant Major GEORGE LAMBERT, 29 July, 16 August and 25 September 1857, buried Wardsend Cemetery (aka St Philip's Burial Ground), headstone lying broken in overgrown section of cemetery; Club Mill Road, Sheffield, Yorkshire. *VC location: York and Lancaster Regiment Museum, Rotherham, Yorkshire.*

150. Civilian ROSS MANGLES, 30 July 1857, buried Brookwood Cemetery, Plot 31, Grave 154820; Cemetery Pales, Woking, Surrey. *VC location: National Army Museum, London.*

151. Civilian WILLIAM McDONELL, 30 July 1857, buried St Peter's Churchyard, Leckhampton, Gloucestershire. *VC location: unknown. Original stolen; an official replacement was issued in 1878 which is now in the Ashcroft Collection.*

152. Bugler WILLIAM SUTTON, 2 August

and 13 September 1857, buried in unmarked grave, St Peter's Parish Churchyard (broken kerb on approximate site); Ightham, Kent. *VC location: Royal Green Jackets Museum, Winchester, Hampshire.*

153. Lieutenant JOSEPH CROWE, 12 August 1857, buried Old Anglican Cemetery, Old Moths Section, Grave 132/133, near Garden of Remembrance; Uitenhage, South Africa. *VC location: destroyed in a fire at his sister's farm. It is not known if an official replacement was issued.*

154. Captain JAMES BLAIR, 12 August and 23 October 1857, buried Trinity Churchyard, Melrose, Roxburghshire, Scotland. *VC location: not publicly held.*

155. Private DENIS DEMPSEY, 12 August 1857 and 14 March 1858, buried St Michael's Cemetery, Plot I, Grave 88 (RC); Toronto, Ontario, Canada. *VC location: not publicly held.*

156. Major CHARLES GOUGH, 15 and 18 August 1857, 27 January and 23 February 1858, buried St Patrick's Cemetery, Clonmel, Co. Tipperary, Ireland. *VC location: Ashcroft Collection.*

157. Captain HENRY GORE-BROWNE, 21 August 1857, buried St Mary the Virgin Churchyard, Newport Road, Brook, near Shanklin, Isle of Wight. *VC location: Duke of Cornwall's Light Infantry Museum, Bodmin, Cornwall.*

158. Private JOHN DIVANE (aka **DEVINE**), 10 September 1857, buried St Clare's Churchyard (Penzance Cemetery), Section M-3, Grave 18; Cornwall. *VC location: not publicly held.*

159. Private PATRICK GREEN, 11 September 1857, buried Aghada Cemetery (several cemeteries are known by this name, exact cemetery not identified); Co. Cork, Ireland. *VC location: not publicly held.*

160. Lieutenant DUNCAN HOME, 14 September 1857, buried Bolandsharh Cemetery, large tomb; near Aligarh, India. *VC location: unknown. Believed to have been lost by children in the 1920s when playing 'soldiers' in a field.*

161. Lieutenant PHILIP SALKELD, 14 September 1857, buried in unmarked grave, Old Delhi Military Cemetery (the Nicholson Cemetery), India. *VC location: not publicly held.*

162. Lieutenant ROBERT SHEBBEARE, 14 September 1857, buried at sea, south of Shanghai, East China Sea. *VC location: with recipient's family.*

163. Sergeant JAMES McGUIRE (sometimes spelt **MAGUIRE**), 14 September 1857, possibly buried in unmarked grave (under his wife's maiden name, Patrick Donnelly), Donagh Cemetery; near Lisnaskea, Co. Fermanagh, Northern Ireland. *VC location: National Army Museum, London.*

164. Sergeant JOHN SMITH, 14 September 1857, buried Artillery Cemetery, Jullundar, India. *VC location: not publicly held.*

165. Lance Corporal HENRY SMITH, 14 September 1857, buried in unmarked grave, Gwalior Cemetery (interred in mass grave with other cholera victims); India. *VC location: Royal Green Jackets Museum, Winchester, Hampshire.*

166. Bugler ROBERT HAWTHORNE, 14 September 1857, buried in unmarked grave, Ardwick Cemetery, Plot I, Grave 32291; Manchester. *VC location: Royal Green Jackets Museum, Winchester, Hampshire.*

167. Drummer MILES RYAN, 14 September 1857, no known grave, possibly died at Bengal, India. *VC location: not publicly held.*

168. Surgeon HERBERT READE, 14 and 16 September 1857, buried Locksbrook Cemetery, Section H, Grave 1687; Upper Bristol Road, Bath, Avon. *VC location: Soldiers of Gloucestershire Museum, Gloucester.*

169. Lieutenant GEORGE WALLER, 14 and 18 September 1857, buried Holy Trinity Parish Churchyard, Grave D-48, near his mother's headstone; Hurstpierpoint, Sussex. *VC location: Royal Green Jackets Museum, Winchester, Hampshire.*

170. Lieutenant GEORGE RENNY, 16 September 1857, buried Locksbrook Cemetery, Section FJ, Grave 864; Upper Bristol Road, Bath, Avon. *VC location: stolen* *in 1978, it was found by a man using a metal detector on Sheen Common in 1983 and returned to the family, it is now in the Ashcroft Collection.*

171. Second Lieutenant EDWARD THACKERAY, 16 September 1857, buried English Cemetery, Grave 228; Bordighera, Italy. *VC location: National Museum of Military History, Johannesburg, South Africa.*

172. Sergeant PATRICK MAHONEY, 21 September 1857, no known grave, died at Lucknow, India. *VC location: British Library, London.*

173. Lieutenant WILLIAM RENNIE, 21 and 25 September 1857, buried Elgin Cemetery, Lair H-96; Moray, Scotland. *VC location: Cameronians Museum, Hamilton, Lanarkshire, Scotland.*

174. Sergeant ROBERT GRANT, 24 September 1857, buried Highgate Cemetery (East Side), Plot 89, Grave 15054; Swains Lane, London. *VC location: Royal Northumberland Fusiliers Museum, Alnwick Castle, Alnwick, Northumberland.*

175. Surgeon JOSEPH JEE, 25 September 1857, buried Ratcliffe RC College Cemetery, small cemetery at rear of college grounds; Queniborough, Leicestershire. *VC location: Army Medical Services Museum, Mytchett, Surrey.*

176. Assistant Surgeon VALENTINE McMASTER, 25 September 1857, buried City Cemetery, Plot 2, Grave 318; Falls Road, Belfast, Northern Ireland. *VC location: National War Museum of Scotland, Edinburgh Castle, Scotland.*

177. Captain FRANCIS MAUDE, 25 September 1857, buried Windsor Town Cemetery, St Leonards Road, Windsor, Berkshire. *VC location: not publicly held.*

178. Captain WILLIAM OLPHERTS, 25 September 1857, buried Richmond Cemetery, Section N, Grave 1953; Lower Grove Road, Richmond-upon-Thames, Surrey. *VC location: Royal Artillery Museum, Woolwich, London.*

179. Lieutenant HERBERT MacPHERSON, 25 September 1857, buried Yay Way Cemetery, Truck Road, North Okalapa,

Noka, north of Rangoon, Burma. *VC location: Highlanders Museum, Fort George, Ardersier, Inverness-shire, Scotland.*

180. Private JOEL HOLMES, 25 September 1857, buried in unmarked grave, All Souls' Cemetery, Halifax, Yorkshire. *VC location: York and Lancaster Regiment Museum, Rotherham, Yorkshire.*

181. Private HENRY WARD, 25/26 September 1857, buried Great Malvern Cemetery, Malvern, Worcestershire. *VC location: Highlanders Museum, Fort George, Ardersier, Inverness-shire, Scotland.*

182. Surgeon ANTHONY HOME, 26 September 1857, buried Highgate Cemetery (West Side), Square 49, Grave 16593; Swains Lane, London. *VC location: Army Medical Services Museum, Mytchett, Surrey.*

183. Assistant Surgeon WILLIAM BRADSHAW, 26 September 1857, buried St Mary's Church of Ireland Churchyard, Thurles, Co. Tipperary, Ireland. *VC location: Army Medical Services Museum, Mytchett, Surrey.*

184. Colour Sergeant STEWART McPHERSON, 26 September 1857, buried Culross Abbey Cemetery, Dunfermline, Fife, Scotland. *VC location: Highlanders Museum, Fort George, Ardersier, Inverness-shire, Scotland.*

185. Private THOMAS DUFFY, 26 September 1857, buried in unmarked grave, Glasnevin Cemetery, Section Z-B, Grave 8 1/2; Finglas Road, Dublin, Ireland. *VC location: National Army Museum, London.*

186. Private JAMES HOLLOWELL (aka **HOLLIWELL**, spelt **HULLOWAY** in the cemetery register), 26 September 1857, buried Brookwood Cemetery, Corps of Commissionaires Plot, Grave 70067; Cemetery Pales, Woking, Surrey. *VC location: Highlanders Museum, Fort George, Ardersier, Inverness-shire, Scotland.*

187. Private PETER McMANUS, 26 September 1857, no known grave, died Allahabad, India. *VC location: Royal Northumberland Fusiliers Museum, Alnwick*

Castle, Alnwick, Northumberland.
188. Private JOHN RYAN, 26 September
1857, buried in unmarked grave, Old British
Cemetery, Cawnpore, India. *VC location:*
National Army Museum, London.
189. Bombardier JACOB THOMAS,
27 September 1857, buried in unmarked
grave, Bandel Churchyard, Hooghly, near
Darjeeling, India. *VC location: Royal*
Artillery Museum, Woolwich, London.
190. Lieutenant ROBERT BLAIR, 28
September 1857, buried in unmarked grave
(a headstone erected for him is now missing),
Old British Cemetery, Cawnpore, India.
VC location: Queen's Dragoon Guards
Museum, Cardiff, Wales.
191. Sergeant BERNARD DIAMOND,
28 September 1857, buried Masterton
Cemetery, Block P, Row 3; New Zealand.
VC location: National Army Museum, State
Highway 1, Waiouru, New Zealand.
192. Lance Corporal ROBERT KELLS,
28 September 1857, buried Lambeth
Cemetery, Section F2, Grave 391 (now has
the name McDougal on headstone);
Blackshaw Road, London. *VC location:*
9th/12th Royal Lancers Regiment Museum,
The Strand, Derby.
193. Private PATRICK DONOHOE,
28 September 1857, buried in unmarked
grave, Donaghmore RC Churchyard, near
Ashbourne, Co. Meath, Ireland. *VC location:*
private collection in Canada.
194. Gunner RICHARD FITZGERALD,
28 September 1857, no known grave, died in
Ghaziabad, India. *VC location: Bristol*
Museum and Art Gallery, Bristol.
195. Private JAMES ROBERTS,
28 September 1857, buried in unmarked
grave, Paddington Old Cemetery, Section B,
Common 3rd Ground; Willesden Lane,
London. *VC location: 9th/12th Royal Lancers*
Regiment Museum, The Strand, Derby.
196. Captain AUGUSTUS ANSON,
28 September and 16 November 1857, buried
Cimetiere Protestant du Grand-Jus, Grave in
4th Allee; Avenue du Grasse, Cannes, France.
VC location: Shugborough Estate, near
Stafford.

197. Corporal DENIS DYNON, 2 October
1857, no known grave, died in Dublin,
Ireland. *VC location: Ashcroft Collection.*
198. Lieutenant JOHN DAUNT, 2 October
and 2 November 1857, buried Redland Green
Chapel Graveyard (a headstone said to exist,
but area totally overgrown); Bristol.
VC location: Ashcroft Collection.
199. Private PATRICK McHALE, 2 October
and 22 December 1857, buried Shorncliffe
Military Cemetery (aka Garrison Cemetery),
Section I – Upper Right; on the B2063,
Folkestone, Kent. *VC location: Royal*
Northumberland Fusiliers Museum, Alnwick
Castle, Alnwick, Northumberland.
200. Lance Corporal JOHN SINNOTT,
6 October 1857, buried Morden Cemetery, RC
Section, Grave H-10; Lower Morden Lane,
Surrey. *VC location: York and Lancaster*
Regiment Museum, Rotherham, Yorkshire.
201. Private JOHN FREEMAN, 10 October
1857, buried Abney Park Cemetery, Plot I-3,
Grave 11724; Stoke Newington High Street,
London. *VC location: Ashcroft Collection.*
202. Conductor JAMES MILLER,
28 October 1857, buried in unmarked grave,
Simla Churchyard, India. *VC location: not*
publicly held.
203. Civilian THOMAS KAVANAGH,
9 November 1857, buried North Front
Cemetery, Grave 4567; Gibraltar, Spain.
VC location: not publicly held.
204. Lieutenant HUGH GOUGH,
12 November 1857 and 25 February 1858,
buried Kensal Green Cemetery, Square
175/RS, Grave 42112; Harrow Road,
London. *VC location: not publicly held.*
205. Lieutenant JOHN WATSON,
14 November 1857, buried St James
Churchyard, Finchampstead, Berkshire.
VC location: Ashcroft Collection.
206. Lieutenant HASTINGS HARINGTON,
14–22 November 1857, buried Agra Cemetery,
India. *VC location: not publicly held.*
207. Rough Rider EDWARD JENNINGS,
14–22 November 1857, buried Preston
Cemetery, RC Section, Block J, Grave 328;
Walton Avenue, North Shields,
Northumberland. *VC location: Royal*

Artillery Museum, Woolwich, London.
208. Gunner THOMAS LAUGHNAN, 14–22 November 1857, burial location unknown, died Kilmadaugh, Co. Galway, Ireland. *VC location: Royal Artillery Museum, Woolwich, London.*
209. Gunner HUGH McINNES (spelt **McINNIS** in cemetery register), 14–22 November 1857, buried in unmarked grave, Dalberth Cemetery, London Road, Glasgow, Scotland. *VC location: Royal Engineers Museum, Gillingham, Kent.*
210. Gunner JAMES PARK, 14–22 November 1857, no known grave, died at Lucknow, India. *VC location: not publicly held.*
211. Captain WILLIAM STEUART (sometimes spelt **STEWART**), 16 November 1857, buried in family vault, St Mary's Church, Grandtully, Perth, Scotland. *VC location: not publicly held.*
212. Lieutenant FRANCIS BROWN, 16 November 1857, buried West Hill Cemetery, St James' Lane, Winchester, Hampshire. *VC location: Wellington College, Crowthorne, Berkshire.*
213. Lieutenant ALFRED FFRENCH, 16 November 1857, buried Brompton Cemetery, Compartment AD, 8' x 104'6", Grave 69995; Old Brompton Road, London. *VC location: King's Shropshire Light Infantry Museum, Shrewsbury, Shropshire.*
214. Lieutenant NOWELL SALMON, 16 November 1857, buried St Peter's Churchyard, Curdridge, Hampshire. *VC location: Ashcroft Collection.*
215. Lieutenant THOMAS YOUNG, 16 November 1857, buried Protestant Cemetery, Rue du Magasin a Poudre, Caen, France. *VC location: National Maritime Museum, Greenwich, London.*
216. Colour Sergeant JAMES MUNRO, 16 November 1857, buried Graigdunin Cemetery (cemetery in woods behind hospital); near Inverness, Scotland. *VC location: Argyll and Sutherland Highlanders Museum, Stirling, Scotland.*
217. Sergeant JOHN PATON, 16 November 1857, buried Rookwood Cemetery, C of E

Section, AAA - 414; Strathfield, West Sydney, New South Wales, Australia. *VC location: Argyll and Sutherland Highlanders Museum, Stirling, Scotland.*
218. Lance Corporal JOHN DUNLAY (aka **DUNLEY** or **DUNLEA**), 16 November 1857, burial location unknown, died in Cork, Ireland. *VC location: Sheesh Mahal Museum, Patiala, Punjab, India.*
219. Private PETER GRANT, 16 November 1857, buried in unmarked grave, Eastern Necropolis, Section S (now part section of N & O), Lair 309; Arbroath Road, Dundee, Scotland. *VC location: not publicly held.*
220. Private CHARLES IRWIN, 16 November 1857, buried St Mark's Church of Ireland Churchyard (name on headstone is that of his brother Edward, his own name being illegible); Agfhadrumsee, Magheraveely, Co. Fermanagh, Northern Ireland. *VC location: King's Shropshire Light Infantry Museum, Shrewsbury, Shropshire.*
221. Private JAMES KENNY, 16 November 1857, buried in unmarked grave, Mooltan Cemetery, India. *VC location: not publicly held.*
222. Private DAVID MacKAY, 16 November 1857, buried in Lesmahagow Cemetery, Paupers Section (headstone erected near his grave); Strathaven Road, Lanarkshire, Scotland. *VC location: unknown. He sold it during his lifetime and it was auctioned around 1910.*
223. Private JOHN SMITH, 16 November 1857, buried in unmarked grave, Taujore Cemetery, Trichinopoly, India. *VC location: not publicly held.*
224. Leading Seaman JOHN HARRISON, 16 November 1857, buried Brompton Cemetery, Compartment O, 22' x 25'. His headstone may have been removed. Old Brompton Road, London. *VC location: National Maritime Museum, Greenwich, London.*
225. Able Seaman WILLIAM HALL, 16 November 1857, buried Hantsport Baptist Church Cemetery, Nova Scotia, Canada. *VC location: Nova Scotia Museum, Canada.*
226. Major JOHN GUISE, 16/17 November

1857, buried Gorey Churchyard, Co. Wexford, Ireland. *VC location: Ashcroft Collection.*

227. Sergeant SAMUEL HILL, 16/17 November 1857, buried in unmarked grave, St John's Cemetery, Meerut, India. *VC location: Tolson Memorial Museum, Huddersfield, Yorkshire.*

228. Sergeant Major CHARLES PYE, 17 November 1857, buried Tower Hill Cemetery, Koroit, Victoria, Australia. *VC location: Auckland War Memorial Museum, Auckland, New Zealand.*

229. Private PATRICK GRAHAM, 17 November 1857, buried in unmarked grave, Arbour Hill Cemetery (exact location unknown, cemetery records destroyed); Arbour Hill, Stoneybatter, Dublin, Ireland. *VC location: Cameronians Museum, Hamilton, Lanarkshire, Scotland.*

230. Lieutenant THOMAS HACKETT, 18 November 1857, buried Lockeen Churchyard, in the 'Marshall' family plot; near Riverstown, Co. Tipperary, Ireland. *VC location: Ashcroft Collection.*

231. Private GEORGE MONGER, 18 November 1857, buried Hastings Borough Cemetery, Section H, Grave E-18; The Ridge, Sussex. *VC location: Royal Welch Fusiliers Museum, Caernarfon Castle, Gwynedd, Wales.*

232. Lieutenant HARRY PRENDERGAST, 21 November 1857, buried Richmond Cemetery, Section M, Grave 1502; Lower Grove Road, Richmond-upon-Thames, Surrey. *VC location: Royal Engineers Museum, Gillingham, Kent.*

233. Midshipman ARTHUR MAYO, 22 November 1857, buried East Cemetery, Section K-4, Grave 207; Gloucester Road, Boscombe, Bournemouth, Dorset. *VC location: thought to have been left to the Museum of Bombay, India, but this was not the case and its whereabouts are unknown.*

234. Drummer THOMAS FLYNN (incorrectly spelt **FLINN** on his citation), 28 November 1857, buried Cornamagh RC Cemetery (aka Athlone Old Cemetery), Casey family headstone on grave; 3 miles from Athlone, Co. Westmeath, Ireland. *VC location: not publicly held.*

235. Lieutenant FREDERICK ROBERTS, 2 January 1858, buried St Paul's Cathedral Crypt, Ludgate Hill, London. *VC location: National Army Museum, London.*

236. Private BERNARD McQUIRT (spelt **McCOURT** in cemetery register), 6 January 1858, buried City Cemetery, Public Section J, Grave 233; Falls Road, Belfast, Northern Ireland. *VC location: not publicly held.*

237. Troop Sergeant Major DAVID SPENCE, 17 January 1858, buried in Section A2 General, Grave 175; Lambeth Cemetery, Blackshaw Road, London. *VC location: 9th/12th Royal Lancers Regiment Museum, The Strand, Derby.*

238. Lieutenant JOHN TYTLER, 10 February 1858, buried Kohat Cemetery, India. *VC location: Gurkha Museum, Winchester, Hampshire.*

239. Lieutenant JAMES INNES, 23 February 1858, buried City Cemetery (aka Newmarket Road Cemetery), Section 8, Grave 3704; Newmarket Road, Cambridge, Cambridgeshire. *VC location: Royal Engineers Museum, Gillingham, Kent.*

240. Lieutenant FREDERICK AIKMAN, 1 March 1858, buried Kensal Green Cemetery, Square 76/RS, Grave 4627, large mausoleum; Harrow Road, London. *VC location: not publicly held.*

241. Lance Corporal WILLIAM GOATE (sometimes spelt **GOAT**), 6 March 1858, buried Highland Road Cemetery, Section E, Row 5, Grave 20; Highland Road, Southsea, Portsmouth, Hampshire. *VC location: 9th/12th Royal Lancers Regiment Museum, The Strand, Derby.*

242. Lieutenant THOMAS BUTLER, 9 March 1858, buried St Michael's Churchyard, Camberley, Surrey. *VC location: Royal Military Academy, Sandhurst, Berkshire.*

243. Lieutenant FRANCIS FARQUHARSON, 9 March 1858, buried Harberton Parish Churchyard, Devon. *VC location: Black Watch Museum, Balhousie Castle, Perth, Scotland.*

244. Captain HENRY WILMOT, 11 March

1858, buried St Mary's Churchyard, Chaddesden, Derbyshire. *VC location: Royal Green Jackets Museum, Winchester, Hampshire.*

245. Lieutenant WILLIAM McBEAN, 11 March 1858, buried Grange Cemetery, Section I, Lair 91-92; Edinburgh, Scotland. *VC location: Argyll and Sutherland Highlanders Museum, Stirling, Scotland.*

246. Corporal WILLIAM NASH, 11 March 1858, buried in unmarked grave, St John's Churchyard, Lower Clapton Road, Hackney, London. *VC location: not publicly held.*

247. Private DAVID HAWKES, 11 March 1858, no known grave, died at Fyazabad, India. *VC location: Fitzwilliam Museum, Cambridge.*

248. Able Seaman EDWARD ROBINSON, 13 March 1858, buried St Peter & St Andrew's Churchyard, Old Windsor Cemetery, Berkshire. *VC location: National Maritime Museum, Greenwich, London.*

249. Major RICHARD KEATINGE, 17 March 1858, buried Hills Street Cemetery, RH Section; Horsham, Sussex. *VC location: not publicly held.*

250. Troop Sergeant Major DAVID RUSHE, 19 March 1858, buried in unmarked grave, Marlow Parish Churchyard, Marlow, Buckinghamshire. *VC location: on loan to the Derby Museum & Art Gallery.*

251. Cornet WILLIAM BANKES, 19 March 1858, no known grave, killed at Lucknow, India. *VC location: Queen's Own Hussars Museum, Warwick.*

252. Private ROBERT NEWELL, 19 March 1858, buried in unmarked grave, Umballa Cemetery, India. *VC location: Ashcroft Collection.*

253. Lieutenant AYLMER CAMERON, 30 March 1858, buried St Mark's Churchyard, Highcliffe, Christchurch, Dorset. *VC location: Highlanders Museum, Fort George, Ardersier, Inverness-shire, Scotland.*

254. Lieutenant HUGH COCHRANE, 1 April 1858, buried Highland Road Cemetery, Section U, 2nd Central, Row 2, Grave 3; Highland Road, Southsea, Portsmouth, Hampshire. *VC location: not publicly held.*

255. Lieutenant JAMES LEITH, 1 April 1858, buried Towie Churchyard, near Glenkindie, Grampian Region, Scotland. *VC location: 14th/20th Hussars Museum, Preston, Lancashire.*

256. Corporal MICHAEL SLEAVON (spelt **SLEVIN** on his death certificate), 3 April 1858, buried Bannagh RC Churchyard, in Slevin family grave but not named; Turbird, near Ederney, Co. Fermanagh, Northern Ireland. *VC location: not publicly held.*

257. Bombardier JOSEPH BRENNAN, 3 April 1858, buried Shorncliffe Military Cemetery (aka Garrison Cemetery), Section F; on the B2063, Folkestone, Kent. *VC location: not publicly held.*

258. Private JAMES BYRNE, 3 April 1858, buried Glasnevin Cemetery, Section J-F, Grave 236; Finglas Road, Dublin, Ireland. *VC location: original stolen from his son in Uganda; replacement in the Royal Ulster Rifles Museum, Belfast, Northern Ireland.*

259. Private JAMES PEARSON, 3 April 1858, no known grave, died at Madras, India. *VC location: not publicly held.*

260. Private FREDERICK WHIRLPOOL (born **CONKER** but later changed to **JAMES**), 3 April and 6 May 1858, buried in unmarked grave, General Presbyterian Cemetery, McGrath's Hill, New South Wales, Australia. *VC location: Australian War Memorial, Canberra, Australia.*

261. Captain HENRY JEROME, 3 April and 28 May 1858, buried Lansdown Cemetery, Lansdown Walk, Bath, Avon. *VC location: Ashcroft Collection.*

262. Sergeant WILLIAM NAPIER, 6 April 1858, buried Bendigo General Cemetery, Rochester, Victoria, Australia. *VC location: Somerset Light Infantry Museum, Taunton, Somerset.*

263. Private PATRICK CARLIN, 6 April 1858, buried Friar's Bush RC Cemetery, Stanmillis Road, Belfast, Northern Ireland. *VC location: Somerset Light Infantry Museum, Taunton, Somerset.*

264. Captain WILLIAM CAFE, 15 April 1858, buried Brompton Cemetery, Compartment 5 East, 31' x 6'; Old Brompton Road, London. *VC location: National Army Museum, London.*

265. Quartermaster Sergeant JOHN SIMPSON, 15 April 1858, buried Balbeggie Churchyard, St Martin's, Perth, Scotland. *VC location: County Museum of Natural History, Los Angeles, California.*

266. Lance Corporal ALEXANDER THOMPSON, 15 April 1858, buried Wellshill Cemetery, Lair 2348; Jeanfield Road, Perth, Scotland. *VC location: Black Watch Museum, Balhousie Castle, Perth, Scotland.*

267. Private JAMES DAVIS (real name **KELLY**), 15 April 1858, buried North Merchiston Cemetery, Compartment N, Grave 625; Edinburgh, Scotland. *VC location: Ashcroft Collection.*

268. Private SAMUEL MORLEY (sometimes spelt **MORELY**), 15 April 1858, buried General Cemetery, Nottingham. *VC location: Royal HQ RLC Museum, Princess Royal Barracks, Deepcut, Surrey.*

269. Farrier MICHAEL MURPHY, 15 April 1858, buried North Road Municipal Cemetery, North Road, Darlington, Co. Durham. *VC location: Royal HQ RLC Museum, Princess Royal Barracks, Deepcut, Surrey.*

270. Private EDWARD SPENCE, 15 April 1858, buried in unmarked grave, Fort Ruhya Cemetery, Oude, India. *VC location: Black Watch Museum, Balhousie Castle, Perth, Scotland.*

271. Colour Sergeant WILLIAM GARDNER, 5 May 1858, buried Bothwell Park Cemetery, Section A, Lair 1532/3; Lanarkshire, Scotland. *VC location: Ashcroft Collection.*

272. Private VALENTINE BAMBRICK, 6 May 1858, buried in unmarked grave, St Pancras & Islington Cemetery, Plot LL/G, Grave 3731; High Road, East Finchley, London. *VC location: not publicly held.*

273. Lieutenant HARRY LYSTER, 23 May 1858, buried St James the Less Churchyard, Stubbing, near Maidenhead, Berkshire. *VC location: Ashcroft Collection.*

274. Private SAMUEL (often mistakenly called **SAME** or **JOHN**) **SHAW**, 13 June 1858, no known grave, drowned at sea. *VC location: Royal Green Jackets Museum, Winchester, Hampshire.*

275. Private GEORGE RODGERS, 16 June 1858, buried Southern Necropolis, Western Section, A & C Ground – 36/9-4-18-6; Glasgow, Scotland. *VC location: Royal Highland Fusiliers Museum, Glasgow, Scotland.*

276. Captain CLEMENT HENEAGE-WALKER (later known as **WALKER-HENEAGE**), 17 June 1858, buried St Swithun's Parish Church, in vault inside church; Compton Bassett, Wiltshire. *VC location: not publicly held.*

277. Sergeant JOSEPH WARD, 17 June 1858, buried St John's Churchyard, Longford Town, Co. Longford, Ireland. *VC location: not publicly held.*

278. Farrier GEORGE HOLLIS, 17 June 1858, buried Exwick Cemetery, Interment 191, Grave 365; Exwick Road, North Exeter, Devon. *VC location: not publicly held.*

279. Private JOHN PEARSON, 17 June 1858, buried Eastnor Township Cemetery, near Lions Head, Ontario, Canada. *VC location: Ashcroft Collection.*

280. Lieutenant WILLIAM WALLER, 20 June 1858, buried Locksbrook Cemetery, Section HA, Grave 111; Upper Bristol Road, Bath, Avon. *VC location: Ashcroft Collection.*

281. Captain SAMUEL BROWNE, 31 August 1858, ashes interred Town Cemetery, West Street, Ryde, Isle of Wight. *VC location: National Army Museum, London.*

282. Troop Sergeant Major JAMES CHAMPION, 8 September 1858, buried in unmarked grave, Margravine Road Cemetery, Grave 30 E 40; Margravine Road, Hammersmith, London. *VC location: Queen's Royal Hussars Museum, Eastbourne, Sussex.*

283. Lieutenant CHARLES BAKER, 27 September 1858, buried Christchurch Cemetery, Section H, Grave 84; Southbourne, Dorset. *VC location: not publicly held.*

284. Ensign PATRICK RODDY, 27 September 1858, buried Mont a L'Abbe Cemetery, St Helier, Jersey, Channel Islands. *VC location: with recipient's family.*

285. Civilian GEORGE CHICKEN, 27 September 1858, no known grave, drowned at sea, Bay of Bengal, India. *VC location: Ashcroft Collection.*

286. Trumpeter THOMAS MONAGHAN, 8 October 1858, buried Woolwich Cemetery, Section 33, RC Plot 826; Kings Highway, London. *VC location: Queen's Dragoon Guards Museum, Cardiff, Wales.*

287. Private CHARLES ANDERSON, 8 October 1858, buried Princess Road Cemetery, Section A, Grave No. 1271; Princess Road, Seaham Harbour, near Sunderland, Co. Durham. *VC location: Queen's Dragoon Guards Museum, Cardiff, Wales.*

288. Lieutenant HANSON JARRETT, 14 October 1858, buried Saugor New Cemetery, Grave 210, headstone may now be missing; India. *VC location: not publicly held.*

289. Lieutenant EVELYN (christened **HENRY**) **WOOD**, 19 October and 29 December 1858, buried Aldershot Military Cemetery, Section V, Grave 1402; Gallwey Road, Aldershot, Hampshire. *VC location: National Army Museum, London.*

290. Major CHARLES FRASER, 31 December 1858, buried Brompton Cemetery, Compartment 2 East, 59' x 20'. Old Brompton Road, London. *VC location: not publicly held.*

291. Private HENRY ADDISON, 2 January 1859, buried Bardwell Parish Churchyard, Suffolk. *VC location: Royal Green Jackets Museum, Winchester, Hampshire.*

292. Captain HERBERT CLOGSTOUN, 15 January 1859, probably buried Madras Cemetery, India. *VC location: National Army Museum, London.*

293. Private WALTER COOK, 15 January 1859, no known grave, believed to have drowned in the River Ravi, Punjab, India. *VC location: not publicly held.*

294. Private DUNCAN MILLAR (aka **MILLER**), 15 January 1859, buried in unmarked grave, St Kentigern's Cemetery, Glasgow, Scotland. *VC location: National War Museum of Scotland, Edinburgh Castle, Scotland.*

295. Private GEORGE RICHARDSON, 27 April 1859, buried Prospect Cemetery, Veterans Section, Plot 2751; Toronto,

Ontario, Canada. *VC location: lost in a fire.*

296. Lieutenant CHARLES GOODFELLOW, 6 October 1859, buried Royal Leamington Spa Cemetery, Brunswick Street, Royal Leamington Spa, Warwickshire. *VC location: Royal Engineers Museum, Gillingham, Kent.*

297. Leading Seaman WILLIAM ODGERS, 28 March 1860, buried in unmarked grave, St Stephen's Parish Churchyard (headstone removed from original grave); Saltash, Cornwall. *VC location: Sheesh Mahal Museum, Patiala, Punjab, India.*

298. Lieutenant NATHANIEL BURSLEM, 21 August 1860, no known grave, drowned in the Thames River, Auckland, New Zealand. *VC location: Royal Hampshire Regiment Museum, Winchester, Hampshire.*

299. Lieutenant EDMUND LENON, 21 August 1860, buried Kensal Green Cemetery, Square 154/2, Grave 34010; Harrow Road, London. *VC location: Royal Hampshire Regiment Museum, Winchester, Hampshire.*

300. Lieutenant ROBERT ROGERS, 21 August 1860, buried All Saints Churchyard, Maidenhead, Berkshire. *VC location: Ashcroft Collection.*

301. Ensign JOHN CHAPLIN, 21 August 1860, buried Kibworth Harcourt Parish Churchyard, Leicestershire. *VC location: Royal Hampshire Regiment Museum, Winchester, Hampshire.*

302. Private THOMAS LANE, 21 August 1860, buried Gladstone Cemetery, RC Section, Row 4, Grave 23; Kimberley, South Africa. *VC location: Royal Hampshire Regiment Museum, Winchester, Hampshire.*

303. Private JOHN McDOUGALL, 21 August 1860, buried Old Carlton Cemetery, Waterloo Place, Edinburgh, Scotland. *VC location: unknown. The medal was stolen from a house in Scotland in 1960, leaving the suspension bar and ribbon behind; these are now on display at the Essex Regiment Museum, Chelmsford, Essex.*

304. Hospital Apprentice ANDREW FITZGIBBON, 21 August 1860, buried in unmarked grave, Old Delhi Military Cemetery (the Nicholson Cemetery), India. *VC location: believed to have been buried with him.*

305. Colour Sergeant JOHN LUCAS,
18 March 1861, buried in unmarked grave, St James Churchyard, James Street, Dublin, Ireland. *VC location: Queen's Lancashire Regiment Museum, Preston, Lancashire.*

306. Able Seaman GEORGE HINCKLEY,
9 October 1862, buried Ford Park Cemetery, Section P, No. 3/R-16; Ford Park Road, Plymouth, Devon. *VC location: it has been suggested that the original fell into a grave in 1863 when attending a funeral; the replacement is not publicly held.*

307. Colour Sergeant EDWARD McKENNA,
7 September 1863, buried Terrace End Cemetery, Presbyterian Block II, Plot 65; Palmerston North, New Zealand. *VC location: unknown. Original stolen; an official replacement was issued in 1868, which is now in the Auckland War Memorial Museum, Auckland, New Zealand.*

308. Lance Corporal JOHN RYAN,
7 September 1863, buried in unmarked grave, Alexandra Redoubt Commemorative Park Cemetery, near Cameron Town, New Zealand. *VC location: York and Lancaster Regiment Museum, Rotherham, Yorkshire.*

309. Ensign JOHN DOWN, 2 October 1863, buried in unmarked grave, Otahuhu Old Cemetery, Block B, Plot 24; South Auckland, New Zealand. *VC location: not publicly held.*

310. Drummer DUDLEY STAGPOOLE,
2 October 1863, buried Hendon Park Cemetery, Section B-8, Grave 15694; Holders Hill Road, London. *VC location: Princess of Wales's Royal Regiment & Queen's Regiment RHQ, Canterbury, Kent.*

311. Lieutenant GEORGE FOSBERY,
30 October 1863, buried St Mary's Cemetery (aka Bathwick Cemetery), Horseshoe Walk, Bath, Avon. *VC location: Ashcroft Collection.*

312. Lieutenant HENRY PITCHER,
30 October and 16 November 1863, buried Dehra Ismail Khan Cemetery, Kohat, India. *VC location: Jersey Museum, St Helier, Channel Islands.*

313. Assistant Surgeon WILLIAM TEMPLE,
20 November 1863, buried Highland Road Cemetery, Section R; Highland Road, Southsea, Portsmouth, Hampshire. *VC location: with recipient's family.*

314. Lieutenant ARTHUR PICKARD,
20 November 1863, buried Cimetiere Protestant du Grand-Jus, 11th Allee; Cannes, France. *VC location: Ashcroft Collection.*

315. Major CHARLES HEAPHY,
11 February 1864, buried Toowong Cemetery, Portion 1, Section 5, AL/34, 8th Avenue, Grave 252; Brisbane, Queensland, Australia. *VC location: Auckland War Memorial Museum, Auckland, New Zealand.*

316. Lieutenant Colonel JOHN McNEILL,
30 March 1864, buried in family chapel at Oronsay Priory, Isle of Colonsay, Scotland. *VC location: Ashcroft Collection.*

317. Assistant Surgeon WILLIAM MANLEY, 29 April 1864, buried Cheltenham Cemetery, Section Y, Grave 5336; Bouncers Lane, Gloucestershire. *VC location: Not publicly held.*

318. Captain of the Foretop SAMUEL MITCHELL, 29 April 1864, buried on a hillside near Ross, New Zealand. *VC location: West Coast Historical Museum, Hokitika, New Zealand.*

319. Captain FREDERICK SMITH, 21 June 1864, buried in unmarked grave, Duleek Churchyard (family grave); Co. Meath, Ireland. *VC location: Ashcroft Collection.*

320. Sergeant JOHN MURRAY, 21 June 1864, buried in unmarked grave, English Churchyard, near Derrinlough, Co. Offaly, Ireland. *VC location: Durham Light Infantry Museum, Co. Durham.*

321. Midshipman DUNCAN BOYES,
6 September 1864, buried Anderson's Bay Soldiers Cemetery, Anglican Southern Section, Block 6, Plot 24; Dunedin, New Zealand. *VC location: Ashcroft Collection.*

322. Captain of the Afterguard THOMAS PRIDE, 6 September 1864, buried All Saints Churchyard, Branksome Park, Dorset. *VC location: National Maritime Museum, Greenwich, London.*

323. Seaman WILLIAM SEELEY,
6 September 1864, buried in Evergreen Cemetery, Stoughton, Massachusetts, USA.

VC location: not publicly held.

324. Captain HUGH SHAW, 24 January 1865, buried Highland Road Cemetery, Section N, 33-7; Highland Road, Southsea, Portsmouth, Hampshire. *VC location: National Army Museum, London.*

325. Major WILLIAM TREVOR, 30 April 1865, buried Kensal Green Cemetery, Square 179/RS, Grave 31775; Harrow Road, London. *VC location: Royal Engineers Museum, Gillingham, Kent.*

326. Lieutenant JAMES DUNDAS, 30 April 1865, buried Seah Sang Cemetery, near Sherpur, Afghanistan. *VC location: Ashcroft Collection.*

327. Private TIMOTHY O'HEA, 9 June 1866, no known grave, died Noccundra Station, Graham's Creek, Sturt's Desert, Queensland, Australia. *VC location: Royal Green Jackets Museum, Winchester, Hampshire.*

328. Private SAMUEL HODGE, 30 June 1866, buried in unmarked grave, Belize City Military Cemetery, Yarborough, Belize. *VC location: not publicly held.*

329. Assistant Surgeon CAMPBELL DOUGLAS, 7 May 1867, buried Wells Cemetery, Grave M; Weston-super-Mare Road, Wells, Somerset. *VC location: Canadian War Museum, Ottawa, Ontario, Canada.*

330. Private DAVID BELL, 7 May 1867, buried Woodlands Cemetery, Section CH, Grave 782; Woodlands Road, Gillingham, Kent. *VC location: South Wales Borderers Museum, Brecon, Powys, Wales.*

331. Private JAMES COOPER, 7 May 1867, buried Warstone Lane Cemetery, Section P, Grave 1428; Warstone Lane, Hockley, Birmingham. *VC location: Royal Warwickshire (TA) Regiment, Sheldon, Birmingham.*

332. Private WILLIAM GRIFFITHS, 7 May 1867, buried in unmarked mass grave, Isandlwana, Natal, South Africa. *VC location: South Wales Borderers Museum, Brecon, Wales.*

333. Private THOMAS MURPHY, 7 May 1867, buried in unmarked grave, Laurel Hill Cemetery, Plot Q, Family Grave 361; Philadelphia, Pennsylvania, USA. *VC location: not publicly held.*

334. Private JAMES BERGIN (spelt **BERGEN** in cemetery register), 13 April 1868, buried in unmarked grave, St Patrick's Churchyard, Poona, India. *VC location: Duke of Wellington's Regiment Museum, Halifax, Yorkshire.*

335. Drummer MICHAEL MAGNER (aka **BARRY**), 13 April 1868, buried Melbourne General Cemetery, RC Section CC, Grave 300; Victoria, Australia. *VC location: Museum of Victoria, Melbourne, Victoria, Australia.*

336. Major DONALD MacINTYRE, 4 January 1872, buried Rosmarkie Churchyard, in family plot; near Fortrose, Scotland. *VC location: Gurkha Museum, Winchester, Hampshire.*

337. Lieutenant EDRIC GIFFORD, 1873–74, buried Fairfield Road Cemetery, Fairfield Road, Bosham, Sussex. *VC location: not publicly held.*

338. Major REGINALD SARTORIUS, 17 January 1874, buried St Mary's Churchyard, South Baddesley, Hampshire. *VC location: National Army Museum, London.*

339. Lance Sergeant SAMUEL McGAW, 21 January 1874, buried British Cemetery, Kyrenia, Cyprus. *VC location: Ashcroft Collection.*

340. Lieutenant MARK BELL, 4 February 1874, buried All Souls' Churchyard, South Ascot, Berkshire. *VC location: Royal Engineers Museum, Gillingham, Kent.*

341. Captain GEORGE CHANNER, 20 December 1875, buried East-the-Water Cemetery, Section C, Grave 505; Bideford, Devon. *VC location: not publicly held.*

342. Captain ANDREW SCOTT, 26 July 1877, buried Kashmir Cemetery, India. *VC location: not publicly held.*

343. Major HANS MOORE, 29 December 1877, buried Mount Jerome Cemetery, Grave C 25/26-7903; Harold's Cross, Dublin 6, Ireland. *VC location: Museum Africa, Johannesburg, South Africa.*

344. Captain JOHN COOK, 2 December

1878, buried Sherpur Cantonment Cemetery, C of E Section; Sherpur, Afghanistan. *VC location: Ashcroft Collection.*

345. Lieutenant TEIGNMOUTH MELVILL, 22 January 1879, buried with Lieutenant Coghill, Fugitive's Drift, below Itchiane Hill, South Africa. *VC location: South Wales Borderers Museum, Brecon, Wales.*

346. Lieutenant NEVILL COGHILL, 22 January 1879, buried with Lieutenant Melvill, Fugitive's Drift, below Itchiane Hill, South Africa. *VC location: South Wales Borderers Museum, Brecon, Wales.*

347. Private SAMUEL WASSALL, 22 January 1879, buried Barrow-in-Furness Cemetery, Section 3.B, Plot 1952; Devonshire Road, Cumbria. *VC location: Staffordshire Regiment Museum, Lichfield.*

348. Lieutenant JOHN CHARD, 22/23 January 1879, buried St John the Baptist Churchyard, Hatch Beauchamp, Somerset. *VC location: Ashcroft Collection.*

349. Lieutenant GONVILLE BROMHEAD, 22/23 January 1879, buried New Cantonment Cemetery, Plot B-1, Grave 66; Allahabad, India. *VC location: South Wales Borderers Museum, Brecon, Powys, Wales.*

350. Surgeon Major JAMES REYNOLDS, 22/23 January 1879, buried St Mary's RC Cemetery, Grave RC-504; Harrow Road, Kensal Rise, London. *VC location: Army Medical Services Museum, Mytchett, Surrey.*

351. Assistant Commissary JAMES DALTON, 22/23 January 1879, buried Russell Road RC Cemetery, Plot E; Port Elizabeth, South Africa. *VC location: HQ RLC Museum, Princess Royal Barracks, Deepcut, Surrey.*

352. Corporal WILLIAM ALLEN (aka **ALLAN**), 22/23 January 1879, buried Monmouth Cemetery, Section B, Grave 25; Monmouthshire, Wales. *VC location: South Wales Borderers Museum, Brecon, Powys, Wales.*

353. Corporal FERDNAND (commonly known as **FREDERICK) SCHIESS**, 22/23 January 1879, buried at sea, off Angola, South Atlantic. *VC location: National Army Museum, London.*

354. Private ALFRED (commonly known as **HENRY) HOOK**, 22/23 January 1879, buried St Andrew's Parish Churchyard, Churcham, Gloucestershire. *VC location: South Wales Borderers Museum, Brecon, Powys, Wales.*

355. Private WILLIAM JONES, 22/23 January 1879, buried Philips Park Cemetery, C of E Common Ground, Section D-587; Briscoe Lane, Manchester. *VC location: South Wales Borderers Museum, Brecon, Powys, Wales.*

356. Private ROBERT JONES, 22/23 January 1879, buried St Peter's Churchyard, Peterchurch, Hereford. *VC location: Ashcroft Collection.*

357. Private JOHN WILLIAMS (real name **FIELDING**), 22/23 January 1879, buried St Michael's Churchyard, Llanfihangel, Llantarnam, Gwent, Wales. *VC location: South Wales Borderers Museum, Brecon, Powys, Wales.*

358. Private FREDERICK HITCH, 22/23 January 1879, buried St Nicholas' Churchyard, Block P, Grave 17; Church Street, Chiswick, London. *VC location: originally stolen, official replacement with South Borderers Museum, Brecon, Powys, Wales.*

359. Lieutenant REGINALD HART, 31 January 1879, buried Netherbury Churchyard Cemetery, Dorset. *VC location: Ashcroft Collection.*

360. Colour Sergeant ANTHONY BOOTH, 12 March 1879, buried St Michael's RC Churchyard, Brierley Hill, Staffordshire. *VC location: Staffordshire Regiment Museum, Lichfield.*

361. Captain EDWARD LEACH, 17 March 1879, buried Grienze Churchyard, near Cadenabbia, Italy. *VC location: Royal Engineers Museum, Gillingham, Kent.*

362. Brevet Lieutenant Colonel REDVERS BULLER, 28 March 1879, buried Holy Cross Churchyard, family plot; Church Street, Crediton, Devon. *VC location: Royal Green Jackets Museum, Winchester, Hampshire.*

363. Major WILLIAM LEET, 28 March 1879, buried St Mary the Virgin Churchyard, Great Chart, Kent. *VC location: Somerset

Light Infantry Museum, Taunton, Somerset.
364. Lieutenant HENRY LYSONS, 28 March 1879, buried St Peter's Churchyard, Rodmarton, near Cirencester, Gloucestershire. *VC location: Cameronians Museum, Hamilton, Lanarkshire, Scotland.*
365. Private EDMUND FOWLER, 28 March 1879, buried Colchester Cemetery, Section Q, Grave 12-42; Mersea Road, Colchester, Essex. *VC location: Cameronians Museum, Hamilton, Lanarkshire, Scotland.*
366. Lieutenant EDWARD BROWNE, 29 March 1879, buried in unmarked grave, Clarens Cemetery, Protestant Section (grave reused in 1991 and headstone broken up); Chemin de Muraz, Montreux, Switzerland. *VC location: South Wales Borderers Museum, Brecon, Powys, Wales.*
367. Lieutenant WALTER HAMILTON, 2 April 1879, buried in unmarked grave, in a garden near the Residency, Kabul, Afghanistan. *VC location: Ashcroft Collection.*
368. Sergeant ROBERT SCOTT, 8 April 1879, buried Plumstead Cemetery, Allotment EA, Grave 88; Wynberg, South Africa. *VC location: Manchester Regiment Museum, The Town Hall, Ashton-under-Lyne.*
369. Trooper PETER BROWN, 8 April 1879, buried Woltermade Cemetery, Grave 81594A (grave has been reused, and now bears the name Abrahamse); Cape Town, South Africa. *VC location: Amathole Museum, King William's Town, South Africa.*
370. Captain O'MOORE CREAGH, 21 April 1879, buried East Sheen Cemetery, Section B, Grave 193; Kings Ride Gardens, East Sheen, Surrey. *VC location: National Army Museum, London.*
371. Surgeon Major EDMUND HARTLEY, 5 June 1879, buried Brookwood Cemetery, St Judes Avenue, Plot 2, Grave 193293; Cemetery Pales, Woking, Surrey. *VC location: Army Medical Services Museum, Mytchett, Surrey.*
372. Captain WILLIAM 'ULUNDI' BERESFORD, 3 July 1879, buried Clonagem Churchyard, Curraghmore, Co. Waterford, Ireland. *VC location: not publicly held.*

373. Captain HENRY D'ARCY, 3 July 1879, buried King William's Town Cemetery, Section D, Grave 32-33, family plot; Cape Province, South Africa. *VC location: not publicly held.*
374. Sergeant EDMUND O'TOOLE, 3 July 1879, no known grave, died at Harare, Zimbabwe. *VC location: not publicly held.*
375. Major GEORGE WHITE, 6 October 1879, buried Broughshane Presbyterian Churchyard, plot 145; Broughshane, Co. Antrim, Northern Ireland. *VC location: Gordon Highlanders Museum, Aberdeen, Scotland.*
376. Captain EUSTON SARTORIUS, 24 October 1879, buried St Peter & St Paul Churchyard, Ewhurst, Surrey. *VC location: National Army Museum, London.*
377. Captain RICHARD RIDGEWAY, 22 November 1879, cremated Lawnswood Crematorium, ashes scattered in cemetery copse, near Columbarium -- now cleared; Otley Road, Leeds. *VC location: not publicly held.*
378. Private FRANCIS FITZPATRICK, 28 November 1879, buried St Kentigern's Cemetery, Section 9, Lair 1799; Glasgow, Scotland. *VC location: National Army Museum, London.*
379. Private THOMAS FLAWN, 28 November 1879, buried Plumstead Cemetery, Section K, Grave 758; Cemetery Road, London. *VC location: not publicly held.*
380. Reverend JAMES ADAMS, 11 December 1879, buried St Mary's Churchyard, Ashwell, Rutland. *VC location: not publicly held.*
381. Lieutenant WILLIAM DICK-CUNYNGHAM, 13 December 1879, buried Ladysmith Cemetery, Natal, South Africa. *VC location: Gordon Highlanders Museum, Aberdeen, Scotland.*
382. Captain ARTHUR HAMMOND, 14 December 1879, buried St Michael's Churchyard, Camberley, Surrey. *VC location: Ashcroft Collection.*
383. Captain WILLIAM VOUSDEN, 14 December 1879, buried Lahore Cemetery, Pakistan. *VC location: not publicly held.*

384. Lance Corporal GEORGE SELLAR, 14 December 1879, buried Lairg Cemetery, Highland Region, Scotland. *VC location: Highlanders Museum, Fort George, Ardersier, Inverness-shire, Scotland.*

385. Sergeant PATRICK MULLANE, 27 July 1880, buried St Patrick's RC Cemetery, St Matthew's Plot (headstone reads 'Buried nearby'); Langthorne Road, Leytonstone, London. *VC location: not publicly held.*

386. Gunner JAMES COLLIS, 28 July 1880, buried Wandsworth Cemetery, Section F53, Grave 111; Magdalen Road, London. *VC location: Ashcroft Collection.*

387. Lieutenant WILLIAM CHASE, 16 August 1880, buried English Cemetery, Quetta, Pakistan. *VC location: Army Museum of Western Australia, Fremantle, Australia.*

388. Private THOMAS ASHFORD, 16 August 1880, buried Whitwick Cemetery, Church Lane, Leicestershire. *VC location: Royal Fusiliers Museum, Tower of London.*

389. Surgeon JOHN McCREA, 14 January 1881, buried Kokstad Cemetery, Transkei District, Cape Province, South Africa. *VC location: Ashcroft Collection.*

390. Lance Corporal JAMES MURRAY, 16 January 1881, buried Glasnevin Cemetery (not in cemetery register but he does have a headstone); Finglas Road, Dublin, Ireland. *VC location: National Army Museum, London.*

391. Trooper JOHN DANAHER (or **DANAGHER**), 16 January 1881, buried Milton Cemetery, Plot M, Row 1, Grave 6; Milton Road, Portsmouth, Hampshire. *VC location: National Army Museum, London.*

392. Lieutenant ALAN HILL (later **HILL-WALKER**), 28 January 1881, buried St Michael and All Angels Churchyard, Manunby, near Thirsk, Yorkshire. *VC location: not publicly held.*

393. Private JOHN DOOGAN, 28 January 1881, buried Shorncliffe Military Cemetery (aka Garrison Cemetery), Plot V, Grave 1054; near Folkestone, Kent. *VC location: Queen's Dragoon Guards Museum, Cardiff, Wales.*

394. Private JAMES OSBORNE, 22 February 1881, buried St Bartholomew's Churchyard, Wiggington, Hertfordshire. *VC*

location: destroyed in an air raid in April 1941.

395. Corporal JOSEPH FARMER, 27 February 1881, buried Brompton Cemetery, Compartment H, 157' x 4'3"; Old Brompton Road, London. *VC location: Army Medical Services Museum, Mytchett, Surrey.*

396. Gunner ISRAEL HARDING, 11 July 1882, buried Highland Road Cemetery, Section H, Grave 7-59; Highland Road, Southsea, Portsmouth, Hampshire. *VC location: Ashcroft Collection.*

397. Private FREDERICK CORBETT (real name **DAVID EMBLETON**), 5 August 1882, buried London Road Cemetery (aka Maldon Cemetery), Row 4, Grave 27; Maldon, Essex. *VC location: Royal Green Jackets Museum, Winchester, Hampshire.*

398. Lieutenant WILLIAM EDWARDS, 13 September 1882, buried St George's Churchyard, Hardingham, Norfolk. *VC location: King's Own Yorkshire Light Infantry Museum, Doncaster.*

399. Captain ARTHUR WILSON, 29 February 1884, buried St Peter & St Paul Churchyard, Swaffham, Norfolk. *VC location: Royal Naval Museum, Portsmouth.*

400. Quartermaster-Sergeant WILLIAM MARSHALL, 29 February 1884, buried Bennochy Road Cemetery, Lair 23; Bennochy Road, Kirkcaldy, Fife, Scotland. *VC location: 15th/19th Hussars Museum, Newcastle-upon-Tyne.*

401. Lieutenant PERCIVAL MARLING, 13 March 1884, buried in vault in All Saints Church, Selsley, near Stroud, Gloucestershire. *VC location: Ashcroft Collection.*

402. Private THOMAS EDWARDS, 13 March 1884, buried in St Mary's Churchyard (headstone reads 'buried in this churchyard'); Chigwell High Road, Chigwell, Essex. *VC location: Black Watch Museum, Balhousie Castle, Perth, Scotland.*

403. Gunner ALFRED SMITH, 17 January 1885, buried Plumstead Cemetery, Section N, Grave 885; Cemetery Road, Plumstead, Kent. *VC location: Royal Artillery Museum, Woolwich, London.*

404. Surgeon JOHN CRIMMIN, 1 January 1889, buried Wells Cemetery, Section F-D-3,

Grave 274; Portway, Wells, Somerset. *VC location: not publicly held.*

405. Surgeon FERDINAND LE QUESNE, 4 May 1889, buried Canford Cemetery, Section K, Grave 9; Canford Lane, Bristol. *VC location: Jersey Museum, St Helier, Jersey, Channel Islands.*

406. Lieutenant CHARLES GRANT, 21 March–9 April 1891, buried Sidmouth Cemetery, Section O, Grave 40; Temple Street, Sidmouth, Devon. *VC location: not publicly held.*

407. Captain FENTON AYLMER, 2 December 1891, ashes scattered at Golders Green Crematorium; Hoop Lane, London. *VC location: Royal Engineers Museum, Gillingham, Kent.*

408. Lieutenant GUY BOISRAGON, 2 December 1891, buried Kensal Green Cemetery, Square 119, Row 2, Grave 18585; Harrow Road, London. *VC location: not publicly held.*

409. Lieutenant JOHN MANNERS-SMITH, 20 December 1891, buried Kensal Green Cemetery, Square 187, Row 4, Grave 46720; Harrow Road, London. *VC location: Gurkha Museum, Winchester, Hampshire.*

410. Corporal WILLIAM GORDON, 13 March 1892, buried Up Park Camp Military Cemetery, Grave 244; Jamaica. *VC location: unknown. Original stolen in 1892; an official replacement was issued in the same year, which is now in the Jamaica Defence Force Museum, Kingston, Jamaica.*

411. Surgeon Major OWEN LLOYD, 6 January 1893, buried Kensal Green Cemetery, Square 188, Row 3, Grave 44252; Harrow Road, London. *VC location: Army Medical Services Museum, Mytchett, Surrey.*

412. Surgeon Captain HARRY WHITCHURCH, 3 March 1895, buried Dharmsala Churchyard, India. *VC location: Ashcroft Collection.*

413. Trooper HERBERT HENDERSON, 30 March 1896, buried Bulawayo Town Cemetery (aka Centenary Park Cemetery), General Section 2, Grave 887; Harare, Zimbabwe. *VC location: National Army Museum, London.*

414. Trooper FRANK BAXTER, 22 April 1896, buried Bulawayo Town Cemetery (aka Centenary Park Cemetery), General Section 1, Grave 114; Harare, Zimbabwe. *VC location: Ashcroft Collection.*

415. Captain RANDOLPH NESBITT, 19 June 1896, ashes interred in The Cloisters, Anglican Cathedral, Harare, Zimbabwe. *VC location: National Archives of Zimbabwe, Harare, Zimbabwe.*

416. Lieutenant EDMOND COSTELLO, 26 July 1897, buried St Mark's Parish Churchyard, Hadlow Down, Sussex. *VC location: National Army Museum, London.*

417. Brevet Lieutenant Colonel ROBERT ADAMS, 17 August 1897, ashes interred Tomnahurich Cemetery, Inverness, Scotland. *VC location: not publicly held.*

418. Lieutenant HECTOR MacLEAN, 17 August 1897, buried Guides Cemetery, St Alban's Churchyard, Mardan, Pakistan. *VC location: Ashcroft Collection.*

419. Lieutenant ALEXANDER FINCASTLE (cremated under the name **MURRAY**), 17 August 1897, ashes scattered at Golders Green Crematorium, Section 4-C, Garden of Remembrance; Hoop Lane, London. *VC location: not publicly held.*

420. Lieutenant JAMES COLVIN, 16/17 September 1897, ashes scattered at Ipswich Crematorium, December Section, Old Garden of Rest; Cemetery Lane, Ipswich, Suffolk. *VC location: not publicly held.*

421. Lieutenant THOMAS WATSON, 16/17 September 1897, ashes interred in Golders Green Crematorium, Niche 1153, East Columbarium; Hoop Lane, London. *VC location: not publicly held.*

422. Corporal JAMES SMITH, 16/17 September 1897, buried Watling Street Burial Ground, Grave 4134; Dartford, Kent. *VC location: National Army Museum, London.*

423. Lieutenant HENRY PENNELL, 20 October 1897, buried St Gregory's Churchyard, Dawlish, Devon. *VC location: Sherwood Foresters Museum, The Castle, Nottingham.*

424. Piper GEORGE FINDLATER, 20 October 1897, buried Forglen Cemetery,

near Turriff, Grampian, Scotland.
VC location: Gordon Highlanders Museum, Aberdeen, Scotland.

425. Private EDWARD LAWSON,
20 October 1897, buried Heaton Cemetery, Section 2, Grave 56; Benton Road, Newcastle-upon-Tyne, Tyne & Wear.
VC location: Gordon Highlanders Museum, Aberdeen, Scotland.

426. Private SAMUEL VICKERY,
20 October and 16 November 1897, ashes scattered Glyntaff Crematorium, Lawn 4, Plot 4; Cemetery Road, Pontypridd, Mid-Glamorgan, Wales. *VC location: Dorset Regiment Museum, Dorchester, Dorset.*

427. Captain PAUL KENNA, 2 September 1898, buried Lala Baba Cemetery, Plot II, Row A, Grave 1; Gallipoli, Turkey.
VC location: Queen's Royal Lancers Museum, Belvoir Castle, Grantham, Leicestershire.

428. Captain NEVILL SMYTH, 2 September 1898, buried Balmoral Cemetery, Victoria, Australia. *VC location: Queen's Dragoon Guards Museum, Cardiff, Wales.*

429. Lieutenant RAYMOND de MONTMORENCY, 2 September 1898, buried Molteno Cemetery, near Dordrecht, South Africa. *VC location: not publicly held.*

430. Private THOMAS 'PADDY' BYRNE, 2 September 1898, buried Canterbury City Cemetery, RC Section MJ, Grave 22; Westgate Court Avenue, Canterbury, Kent. *VC location: original stolen from his kit while he was in the field. The official replacement is not publicly held.*

431. Surgeon WILLIAM MAILLARD, 6 September 1898, buried Wimborne Road Cemetery, Section V-4, Grave 133 South; Wimborne Road, Landsdowne, Bournemouth, Dorset. *VC location: Ashcroft Collection.*

432. Captain ALEXANDER 'SANDY' HORE-RUTHVEN (later changed to ARKWRIGHT), 22 September 1898, buried St John the Baptist Churchyard, Shipton Moyne, Gloucestershire. *VC location: Ashcroft Collection.*

433. Captain CHARLES 'FITZ' FITZCLARENCE, 14 and 27 October, and 26 December 1899, no known grave, killed at

Polygon Wood, *Belgium. VC location: Ashcroft Collection.*

434. Captain ROBERT JOHNSTON, 21 October 1899, buried St Mary's Churchyard, Inistiogne, Co. Kilkenny, Ireland. *VC location: not publicly held.*

435. Captain MATTHEW MEIKLEJOHN, 21 October 1899, buried Brookwood Cemetery, St Judes Avenue, Plot 3, Grave 172317; Cemetery Pales, Woking, Surrey. *VC location: Gordon Highlanders Museum, Aberdeen, Scotland.*

436. Captain CHARLES MULLINS, 21 October 1899, buried Grahamstown Old Cemetery, South Africa. *VC location: Imperial War Museum, London.*

437. Second Lieutenant JOHN NORWOOD, 30 October 1899, buried Sablonnieres New Communal Cemetery Extension, Plot 4; France. *VC location: on loan to the Imperial War Museum, London.*

438. Sergeant Major WILLIAM ROBERTSON, 21 October 1899, buried Portobello Cemetery (grave number not recorded in register), Edinburgh Road, Musselburgh, Lothian, Scotland. *VC location: National War Museum of Scotland, Edinburgh Castle, Scotland.*

439. Lieutenant HENRY DOUGLAS, 11 December 1899, buried Epsom Cemetery, Section H, Grave 132; Ashley Road, Surrey. *VC location: Army Medical Services Museum, Mytchett, Surrey.*

440. Corporal JOHN SHAUL, 11 December 1899, buried Old Cemetery, Boksburg, South Africa. *VC location: Ashcroft Collection.*

441. Captain ERNEST TOWSE, 11 December 1899 and 30 April 1900, buried St Thomas of Canterbury Churchyard, Goring-on-Thames, Oxfordshire. *VC location: Gordon Highlanders Museum, Aberdeen, Scotland.*

442. Major WILLIAM BABTIE, 15 December 1899, buried Stoke Cemetery, Stoughton Road, Guildford, Surrey. *VC location: Army Medical Services Museum, Mytchett, Surrey.*

443. Captain WALTER 'SQUIBS' CONGREVE, 15 December 1899, buried at sea, off Malta, Mediterranean Sea.

VC location: Royal Green Jackets Museum, Winchester, Hampshire.
444. Captain HAMILTON REED,
15 December 1899, buried East Sheen Cemetery, Section E, Grave 210; Lower Grove Road, Richmond-upon-Thames, Surrey. *VC location: Ashcroft Collection.*
445. Captain HARRY SCHOFIELD,
15 December 1899, buried Putney Vale Cemetery, Block L, Grave 29; Stag Lane, London. *VC location: Ashcroft Collection.*
446. Lieutenant FREDERICK ROBERTS,
15 December 1899, buried Chievely War Cemetery, Plot 136; South Africa. *VC location: National Army Museum, London.*
447. Corporal GEORGE NURSE,
15 December 1899, buried Allerton Cemetery, C of E Section 2-G, Grave 608; Woolton Road, Liverpool. *VC location: Royal Artillery Museum, Woolwich, London.*
448. Private GEORGE RAVENHILL,
15 December 1899, buried in unmarked grave, Witton Cemetery, Section 47, Grave 08654; Moor Lane, Witton, Birmingham. *VC location: Royal Highland Fusiliers Museum, Glasgow, Scotland.*
449. Sergeant HORACE MARTINEAU,
26 December 1899, buried Anderson's Bay Soldiers Cemetery, Returned Servicemen's Area, Block 73, Plot 16; Dunedin, New Zealand. *VC location: Ashcroft Collection.*
450. Trooper HORACE RAMSDEN,
26 December 1899, cremated at The Maitland Crematorium, Woltemade, Cape Town, South Africa. *VC location: Ashcroft Collection.*
451. Lieutenant JOHN MILBANKE,
5 January 1900, no known grave, killed at Gallipoli, Turkey. *VC location: Royal Hussars Museum, Winchester, Hampshire.*
452. Lieutenant ROBERT DIGBY-JONES,
6 January 1900, buried Ladysmith Cemetery, South Africa. *VC location: Royal Engineers Museum, Gillingham, Kent.*
453. Lieutenant JAMES MASTERSON,
6 January 1900, buried Hulbert Road Cemetery, Hulbert Road, Waterlooville, Hampshire. *VC location: Devonshire Regiment Museum, Dorchester, Dorset.*
454. Trooper HERMAN ALBRECHT,

6 January 1900, buried in mass grave, Waggon Hill Cemetery, South Africa. *VC location: Museum of Military History, Johannesburg, South Africa.*
455. Private JAMES PITTS, 6 January 1900, buried Whalley New Road Cemetery, RC Section, Plot D, Grave 2524; Whalley New Road, Blackburn, Lancashire. *VC location: Manchester Regiment Museum, The Town Hall, Ashton-under-Lyne.*
456. Private ROBERT SCOTT, 6 January 1900, buried Christchurch Church of Ireland Cemetery, Newry Street, Kilkeel, Co. Down, Northern Ireland. *VC location: Manchester Regiment Museum, The Town Hall, Ashton-under-Lyne.*
457. Lieutenant FRANCIS PARSONS,
18 February 1900, buried Driefontein Cemetery, an isolated grave on the battlefield; Orange Free State, South Africa. *VC location: Essex Regiment Museum, Chelmsford, Essex.*
458. Sergeant ALFRED ATKINSON,
18 February 1900, buried in unmarked grave, Gruisbank British Cemetery (exact location of grave unknown); Paardeberg, South Africa. *VC location: Green Howards Museum, Richmond, Yorkshire.*
459. Private ALBERT CURTIS, 23 February 1900, buried Bells Hill Cemetery, Plot B5, Grave 435; Spring Close, High Barnet (formerly Chipping Barnet), Hertfordshire. *VC location: Ashcroft Collection.*
460. Lieutenant EDGAR INKSON,
24 February 1900, ashes interred Brookwood Cemetery, Plot 74, Grave 211757, family grave; Cemetery Pales, Woking, Surrey. *VC location: Army Medical Services Museum, Mytchett, Surrey.*
461. Sergeant JAMES FIRTH, 24 February 1900, buried Burngreave Cemetery, Melrose Road, Sheffield, Yorkshire. *VC location: Ashcroft Collection.*
462. Captain CONWYN MANSEL-JONES,
27 February 1900, buried St Nicholas's Churchyard, Brockenhurst, Hampshire. *VC location: not publicly held.*
463. Sergeant HENRY ENGLEHEART,
13 March 1900, ashes scattered at Woking

Crematorium, Byron Garden; Hermitage Road, St John's, Woking, Surrey. *VC location: Royal Hussars Museum, Winchester, Hampshire.*

464. Major EDMUND PHIPPS-HORNBY, 31 March 1900, buried St Andrew's Churchyard, Sonning, Berkshire. *VC location: Royal Artillery Museum, Woolwich, London.*

465. Lieutenant FRANCIS MAXWELL, 31 March 1900, buried Ypres Reservoir Cemetery, Plot I, Row A, Grave 37; North Ypres, Belgium. *VC location: Ashcroft Collection.*

466. Sergeant CHARLES PARKER, 31 March 1900, buried London Road Cemetery, Plot 198, Grave 1; London Road, Coventry. *VC location: Royal Artillery (Battery).*

467. Gunner ISAAC LODGE, 31 March 1900, buried Hendon Park Cemetery, Section D-9, Grave 21820; Holders Hill Road, London. *VC location: National Army Museum, London.*

468. Driver HORACE GLASOCK, 31 March 1900, buried Maitland Road No. 4 Cemetery, Cape Town, South Africa. *VC location: Ashcroft Collection.*

469. Lieutenant WILLIAM NICKERSON, 20 April 1900, buried in private burial ground at his home in Cour, Kintyre, Scotland. *VC location: not publicly held.*

470. Corporal HARRY BEET, 22 April 1900, buried Mountain View Cemetery, Veterans' Section, Abray Section, Grave 3-5-12; Prince Edward Avenue, Vancouver, British Columbia, Canada. *VC location: Sherwood Foresters Museum, The Castle, Nottingham.*

471. Lance Corporal JOHN MacKAY, 20 May 1900, buried Cimetiere de Caucade, Plot 42; Nice, France. *VC location: Gordon Highlanders Museum, Aberdeen, Scotland.*

472. Corporal FRANK KIRBY, 2 June 1900, ashes interred at South London Crematorium (aka Streatham Vale Crematorium), Section Q-69, The Loggia Garden; Rowan Road, Streatham Vale, London. *VC location: Ashcroft Collection.*

473. Sergeant JOHN MacKENZIE, 6 June 1900, buried Guards Cemetery, Plot VIII, Row J, Grave 10; Windy Corner, near Cuinchy, France. *VC location: Highlanders Museum, Fort George, Ardersier, Inverness-shire, Scotland.*

474. Captain LEWIS HALLIDAY, 24 June 1900, buried Medstead Cemetery, South Town Road, Hampshire. *VC location: Royal Marines Museum, Southsea, Portsmouth, Hampshire.*

475. Private CHARLES WARD, 26 June 1900, buried St Mary's Churchyard, Section B, Row 2, Grave 8/4; Whitchurch, Cardiff, Wales. *VC location: not publicly held.*

476. Sergeant ARTHUR RICHARDSON, 5 July 1900, buried in St James's Cemetery (now a park), Plot 57679 (headstone reads 'buried within this cemetery'); St James's Road, Liverpool. *VC location: Canadian War Museum, Ottawa, Ontario, Canada.*

477. Captain WILLIAM GORDON, 11 July 1900, buried St Alban's Churchyard, East Block, Grave 76; Hindhead, Surrey. *VC location: Gordon Highlanders Museum, Aberdeen, Scotland.*

478. Captain DAVID YOUNGER, 11 July 1900, buried Krugersdorp Cemetery, Halgryn Street, Krugersdorp, South Africa. *VC location: not publicly held.*

479. Midshipman BASIL GUY, 13 July 1900, buried St Michael's & All Angels' Churchyard, family grave; Pirbright, Surrey. *VC location: Ashcroft Collection.*

480. Captain NEVILLE HOWSE, 24 July 1900, buried Kensal Green Cemetery, Square 14, Row 4, Grave 49245; Harrow Road, London. *VC location: Australian War Memorial, Canberra, Australia.*

481. Private WILLIAM HOUSE, 2 August 1900, buried St James's Cemetery, Section N, Grave 1-16; Old Charlton Road, Dover, Kent. *VC location: Royal Gloucestershire, Berkshire and Wiltshire Regiment Museum, Salisbury, Wiltshire.*

482. Sergeant BRIAN LAWRENCE, 7 August 1900, cremated Nakuru Crematorium, Kenya. *VC location: Ashcroft Collection.*

483. Sergeant HARRY HAMPTON, 21 August 1900, buried Richmond Cemetery, Old Church Ground, Section X, Grave 62;

Lower Grove Road, Richmond-upon-Thames, Surrey. *VC location: King's (Liverpool) Regiment Museum, Liverpool.*

484. Corporal HENRY KNIGHT, 21 August 1900, ashes scattered at Bournemouth Crematorium, Garden of Remembrance; Strouden Avenue, Bournemouth, Dorset. *VC location: King's (Liverpool) Regiment Museum, Liverpool.*

485. Private WILLIAM HEATON, 23 August 1900, buried Ormskirk Parish Churchyard, Plot 111; Southport, Lancashire. *VC location: King's (Liverpool) Regiment Museum, Liverpool.*

486. Private ALFRED DURRANT, 27 August 1900, buried Tottenham Cemetery, Rosery Section, Grave 221; White Hart Lane, London. *VC location: Royal Green Jackets Museum, Winchester, Hampshire.*

487. Lieutenant GUY GEORGE WYLLY, 1 September 1900, ashes scattered at Woking Crematorium, Tennyson Lake Garden, Garden of Remembrance; Hermitage Road, St John's, Woking, Surrey. *VC location: Tasmanian Museum & Art Gallery, Hobart, Tasmania, Australia.*

488. Trooper JOHN BISDEE, 1 September 1900, buried St James's Churchyard, Jericho to Hobart Road, Tranquillity, Tasmania, Australia. *VC location: Tasmanian Museum & Art Gallery, Hobart, Tasmania, Australia.*

489. Captain CHARLES MELLISS, 30 September 1900, buried St Peter's Churchyard, Frimley, Surrey. *VC location: Wellington College, Crowthorne, Berkshire.*

490. Major EDWARD BROWN (later BROWN-SYNGE-HUTCHINSON), 13 October 1900, ashes scattered at Golders Green Crematorium, Disposal Lawns; Hoop Lane, London. *VC location: 14th/20th Hussars Museum, Preston, Lancashire.*

491. Lieutenant ALEXIS DOXAT, 20 October 1900, buried City Cemetery (aka Newmarket Road Cemetery), Section 15, Grave 8154; Newmarket Road, Cambridge. *VC location: Ashcroft Collection.*

492. Lieutenant HAMPDEN COCKBURN, 7 November 1900, buried St James's Cemetery, Hill A, Section S 1/2, Lot 11; Toronto, Ontario, Canada. *VC location: Canadian War Museum, Ottawa, Ontario, Canada.*

493. Lieutenant RICHARD TURNER, 7 November 1900, buried Mount Hermon Cemetery, Section U, Chemin St Louis; Sillery, Quebec City, Canada. *VC location: Royal Canadian Dragoons, Patawawa, Ontario, Canada.*

494. Sergeant EDWARD HOLLAND, 7 November 1900, ashes scattered on Lake Temagami, Ontario, Canada. *VC location: Royal Canadian Dragoons, Patawawa, Ontario, Canada.*

495. Private CHARLES KENNEDY, 22 November 1900, buried North Merchiston Cemetery, Plot P, Compartment 187; Edinburgh, Scotland. *VC location: Royal Highland Fusiliers Museum, Glasgow, Scotland.*

496. Sergeant DONALD FARMER, 13 December 1900, ashes interred at Anfield Crematorium, Plot 9, Garden of Remembrance; Priory Road, Liverpool. *VC location: Highlanders Museum, Fort George, Ardersier, Inverness-shire, Scotland.*

497. Private JOHN BARRY, 7/8 January 1901, buried Belfast Cemetery, East of Johannesburg, South Africa. *VC location: Ashcroft Collection.*

498. Farrier Major WILLIAM HARDHAM, 28 January 1901, buried Karori Soldiers' Cemetery, Circle O, Plot 20; Wellington, New Zealand. *VC location: National Army Museum, State Highway 1, Waiouru, New Zealand.*

499. Sergeant WILLIAM TRAYNOR, 6 February 1901, buried Charlton Cemetery, Plot XL, Grave 28; Old Charlton Road, Dover, Kent. *VC location: Ashcroft Collection.*

500. Corporal JOHN CLEMENTS, 24 February 1901, buried Town Cemetery, Dutch Reform Section; Newcastle, South Africa. *VC location: Ashcroft Collection.*

501. Lieutenant FREDERIC DUGDALE, 3 March 1901, buried Longborough Churchyard, Gloucestershire. *VC location: Queen's Royal Lancers Museum, Belvoir*

Castle, Grantham, Leicestershire.
502. Lieutenant FREDERICK BELL, 16 May 1901, buried Canford Cemetery, Section O, Colour Pink, Grave 126; Canford Lane, Bristol. *VC location: Western Australia Museum, Perth, Western Australia.*
503. Lieutenant GUSTAVUS COULSON, 18 May 1901, buried Lambrechfontein Farm, near Bothaville, South Africa. *VC location: King's Own Scottish Borderers Museum, Berwick-upon-Tweed, Northumberland.*
504. Sergeant JAMES ROGERS, 15 June 1901, cremated Sprigvale Crematorium, ashes in urn in Columbarium; Melbourne, Victoria, Australia. *VC location: Australian War Memorial, Canberra, Australia.*
505. Lieutenant WILLIAM ENGLISH, 3 July 1901, buried Maala Christian Cemetery, Row I, Grave 21; Yemen. *VC location: Ashcroft Collection.*
506. Private HARRY CRANDON, 4 July 1901, buried Swinton Cemetery, C of E Section A, Grave 3207 (headstone bears the name Henry); Cemetery Road, South Swinton, Manchester. *VC location: not publicly held.*
507. Sergeant Major ALEXANDER YOUNG, 13 August 1901, no known grave, killed at the Somme, France. *VC location: Ashcroft Collection.*
508. Lieutenant LLEWELLYN PRICE-DAVIES, 17 September 1901, buried St Andrew's Churchyard, Sonning, Berkshire. *VC location: Royal Green Jackets Museum, Winchester, Hampshire.*
509. Driver FREDERICK BRADLEY, 26 September 1901, buried Gwelo Cemetery, Grave 971; Gwelo, Zimbabwe. *VC location: not publicly held.*
510. Private WILLIAM BEES, 30 September 1901, buried London Road Cemetery, Grave 3040; London Road, Coalville, Leicestershire. *VC location: Sherwood Foresters Museum, The Castle, Nottingham.*
511. Lieutenant LESLIE MAYGAR, 23 November 1901, buried Beersheba War Cemetery, Row Q, Grave 82; Beersheba, Israel. *VC location: Australian War Memorial, Canberra, Australia.*
512. Surgeon Captain THOMAS CREAN,

18 December 1901, buried St Mary's RC Cemetery, Grave 896; Harrow Road, Kensal Rise, London. *VC location: Army Medical Services Museum, Mytchett, Surrey.*
513. Shoeing Smith ALFRED IND, 20 December 1901, buried St Mary the Virgin Churchyard, Eccleston, Cheshire. *VC location: not publicly held.*
514. Surgeon Captain ARTHUR MARTIN-LEAKE, 8 February 1902, ashes interred at St John the Evangelist Churchyard, High Cross, Ware, Hertfordshire. *VC and Bar location: Army Medical Services Museum, Mytchett, Surrey. (For Bar action, see **551**.)*
515. Captain ALEXANDER COBBE, 6 October 1902, buried St Peter's Churchyard, Sharnbrook, Bedfordshire. *VC location: South Wales Borderers Museum, Brecon, Powys, Wales.*
516. Lieutenant WALLACE WRIGHT, 26 February 1903, buried Brookwood Cemetery, St John's Avenue, Plot 9, Grave 215534; Cemetery Pales, Woking, Surrey. *VC location: Queen's Royal Surrey Regiment Museum, Guildford.*
517. Brevet Major JOHN GOUGH, 22 April 1903, buried Estaires Communal Cemetery, Plot II, Row A, Grave 7; France. *VC location: Royal Green Jackets Museum, Winchester, Hampshire.*
518. Captain GEORGE ROLLAND, 22 April 1903, buried Takli Cemetery, C of E Section, Nagpur, India. *VC location: Ashcroft Collection.*
519. Captain WILLIAM WALKER, 22 April 1903, cremated Woodvale Crematorium, Lewis Road, Brighton, Sussex. *VC location: National Army Museum, London.*
520. Lieutenant HERBERT CARTER, 19 December 1903, buried St Ercus Churchyard, St Erth, Cornwall. *VC location: Duke of Cornwall's Light Infantry Museum, Bodmin, Cornwall.*
521. Lieutenant CLEMENT SMITH, 10 January 1904, buried English Cemetery, Alassio, Italy. *VC location: Duke of Cornwall's Light Infantry Museum, Bodmin, Cornwall.*
522. Lieutenant JOHN GRANT, 6 July 1904,

ashes scattered at Tunbridge Wells Crematorium, Garden of Remembrance; Benhall Mill Road, Tunbridge Wells, Kent. *VC location: not publicly held.*

523. Lieutenant MAURICE DEASE, 23 August 1914, buried St Symphorien Military Cemetery, Plot V, Row B, Grave 2; near Mons, Belgium. *VC location: Royal Fusiliers Museum, The Tower of London.*

524. Private SIDNEY GODLEY (spelt **GODLY** prior to 1909), 23 August 1914 (09:10 hours), buried St John's Churchyard, Section F, Grave 3051; Church Lane, Loughton, Essex. *VC location: private collection in the USA.*

525. Lance Corporal CHARLES JARVIS, 23 August 1914 (16:30 hours), buried St Monance Cemetery, Lair G, Plot 176; near Cupar, Fife, Scotland. *VC location: Birmingham City Museum, Birmingham.*

526. Corporal CHARLES GARFORTH, 23 August and 2/3 September 1914, ashes scattered at Wilford Hill Crematorium (aka Southern Cemetery), headstone in garden of remembrance marks the spot; Nottingham. *VC location: Imperial War Museum, London.*

527. Captain THEODORE WRIGHT, 23 August and 14 September 1914, buried Vailly British Cemetery, Plot II, Row B, Grave 21; France. *VC location: Royal Engineers Museum, Gillingham, Kent.*

528. Major ERNEST ALEXANDER, 24 August 1914, ashes interred Putney Vale Cemetery, Section AB, Grave 149; Stag Lane, London. *VC location: Ashcroft Collection.*

529. Captain FRANCIS GRENFELL, 24 August 1914, buried Vlamertinghe Military Cemetery, Plot II, Row B, Grave 14; near Ypres, Belgium. *VC location: 9th/12th Royal Lancers Regiment Museum, The Strand, Derby.*

530. Lance Corporal GEORGE WYATT, 25/26 August 1914, buried Cadeby Churchyard, near Doncaster, Yorkshire. *VC location: not publicly held.*

531. Major CHARLES YATE, 26 August 1914, buried Berlin South-Western Cemetery, Plot II, Row G, Grave 8; Stahsdorf, Berlin, Germany. *VC location: King's Own Yorkshire Light Infantry Museum, Doncaster.*

532. Lance Corporal FREDERICK HOLMES, 26 August 1914, ashes interred Stirling North Garden Cemetery, Section 2, Row E, Grave 6; Port Augusta, South Australia. *VC location: not publicly held.*

533. Driver JOB DRAIN, 26 August 1914, buried Rippleside Cemetery, Plot U, Grave 158; Ripple Road, Barking, Essex. *VC location: Ashcroft Collection.*

534. Driver FREDERICK LUKE, 26 August 1914, ashes scattered at Linn Crematorium, in garden; Lanshaw Drive, Glasgow, Scotland. *VC location: Ashcroft Collection.*

535. Captain DOUGLAS REYNOLDS, 26 August and 9 September 1914, buried Etaples Military Cemetery, Plot I, Row A, Grave 20; on the D940, Boulogne, France. *VC location: Royal Artillery Museum, Woolwich, London.*

536. Captain EDWARD BRADBURY, 1 September 1914, buried Nery Communal Cemetery, France. *VC location: Imperial War Museum, London.*

537. Battery Sergeant Major GEORGE DORRELL, 1 September 1914, ashes scattered at Randall's Park Crematorium, Plot P-9, K7; Randall's Road, Leatherhead, Surrey. *VC location: on loan to the Imperial War Museum, London.*

538. Sergeant DAVID NELSON, 1 September 1914, buried Lillers Communal Cemetery, Plot V, Row A, Grave 16; France. *VC location: on loan to the Imperial War Museum, London.*

539. Captain WILLIAM JOHNSTON, 14 September 1914, buried Perth Cemetery (China Wall), Plot III, Row C, Grave 12; Zillebeke, near Ypres, Belgium. *VC location: Royal Engineers Museum, Gillingham, Kent.*

540. Lance Corporal WILLIAM FULLER, 14 September 1914, buried Oystermouth Cemetery, Section R, Grave 373; Newton Road, The Mumbles, near Swansea, West Glamorgan, Wales. *VC location: not publicly held.*

541. Private ROSS TOLLERTON, 14 September 1914, buried Knadgerhill Cemetery, Section C, Lair 104; Irvine, Scotland. *VC location: Highlanders Museum,*

Fort George, Ardersier, Inverness-shire, Scotland.

542. Private GEORGE WILSON,
14 September 1914, buried Piershill Cemetery, Section E, Lair 652; Piersfield Terrace, Edinburgh, Scotland. *VC location: Royal Highland Fusiliers Museum, Glasgow, Scotland.*

543. Bombardier ERNEST HORLOCK
(often misspelt **HARLOCK**), 15 September 1914, buried Hadra War Memorial Cemetery, Row F, Grave 171; near Alexandria, Egypt. *VC location: 10 (Assaye) Batt. Royal Artillery.*

544. Captain HARRY RANKEN, 19/20 September 1914, buried Braine Communal Cemetery, Row A, Grave 43; France. *VC location: Army Medical Services Museum, Mytchett, Surrey.*

545. Private FREDERICK DOBSON,
28 September 1914, buried Ryton & Crawcrook Cemetery, Section A, Plot 234; Durham, Co. Durham. *VC location: Coldstream Guards RHQ, Wellington Barracks, London.*

546. Private HENRY MAY, 22 October 1914, buried Riddrie Park Cemetery, Section B, Lair 146 (headstone only shows the names of his children); Cumbernauld Road, Glasgow, Scotland. *VC location: Cameronians Museum, Hamilton, Lanarkshire, Scotland.*

547. Drummer WILLIAM KENNY,
23 October 1914, buried Brookwood Cemetery, Corps of Commissionaires Plot, Grave 199356 (headstone states buried near this spot); Cemetery Pales, Woking, Surrey. *VC location: Gordon Highlanders Museum, Aberdeen, Scotland.*

548. Lieutenant JAMES BROOKE,
29 October 1914, buried Zantvoorde British Cemetery, Plot VI, Row E, Grave 2; Belgium. *VC location: Gordon Highlanders Museum, Aberdeen, Scotland.*

549. Second Lieutenant JAMES LEACH,
29 October 1914, ashes scattered at Mortlake Crematorium, Plot 8, Garden of Remembrance; Mortlake Road, North Sheen, Surrey. *VC location: Ashcroft Collection.*

550. Sergeant JOHN HOGAN, 29 October 1914, buried Chadderton Cemetery, RC

Section, Grave D-9/63; Middleton Road, Oldham, Lancashire. *VC location: Oldham Civic Centre, Lancashire.*

551. Lieutenant ARTHUR MARTIN-LEAKE,
Bar action: 29 October–8 November 1918. (For VC action, see **514.**) Ashes interred at St John the Evangelist Churchyard, High Cross, Ware, Hertfordshire. *VC and Bar location: Army Medical Services Museum, Mytchett, Surrey.*

552. Sepoy KHUDADAD KHAN, 31 October 1914, buried in unmarked grave, Rukham Village Cemetery, near Chakawl, Pakistan. *VC location: Pakistan Army Museum, Rawalpindi, Pakistan.*

553. Drummer SPENCER BENT, 1–3 November 1914, ashes interred at West Norwood Cemetery/Crematorium; a plaque on the wall marks the approximate location; Norwood Road, London. *VC location: Ashcroft Collection.*

554. Captain JOHN VALLENTIN,
7 November 1914, no known grave, killed at Zillebeke, Belgium. *VC location: Wellington College, Berkshire.*

555. Captain WALTER BRODIE,
11 November 1914, buried Beinvillers Military Cemetery, Plot XVIII, Row F, Grave 15; France. *VC location: not publicly held.*

556. Lieutenant JOHN DIMMER,
12 November 1914, buried Vadencourt British Cemetery, Plot II, Row B, Grave 46; France. *VC location: Royal Green Jackets Museum, Winchester, Hampshire.*

557. Lieutenant JOHN BUTLER,
17 November and 27 December 1914, buried Morogoro Cemetery, Plot III, Row C, Grave 43; Tanzania. *VC location: Royal Green Jackets Museum, Winchester, Hampshire.*

558. Bandsman THOMAS RENDLE,
20 November 1914, buried Maitland Road No. 1 Cemetery, family plot No. 24598; Cape Town, South Africa. *VC location: Duke of Cornwall's Light Infantry Museum, Bodmin, Cornwall.*

559. Naik DARWAN SINGH NEGI, 23/24 November 1914, cremated Kafarteer Village, Chamoli Garhwal District, United Provinces, India. *VC location: Garhwal Rifles Museum, Lansdowne, Uttarakhand, India.*

560. Lieutenant FRANK de PASS, 24 November 1914, buried Bethune Town Cemetery, Plot I, Row A, Grave 24; north suburbs of Bethune, France. *VC location: National Army Museum, London.*

561. Commander HENRY RITCHIE, 28 November 1914, cremated Warriston Crematorium, Warriston Road, Edinburgh, Scotland. *VC location: not publicly held.*

562. Lieutenant NORMAN HOLBROOK, 13 December 1914, buried St James's Churchyard, Stedham, near Midhurst, Sussex. *VC location: on loan to the Australian War Memorial, Canberra, Australia.*

563. Private HENRY ROBSON, 14 December 1914, buried York Cemetery, Military/Veterans' Section, Plot B, Grave 302; Toronto, Ontario, Canada. *VC location: Royal Scots Museum, Edinburgh, Scotland.*

564. Lieutenant WILLIAM BRUCE, 19 December 1914, no known grave, killed at Givenchy, France. *VC location: Jersey Museum, St Helier, Jersey, Channel Islands.*

565. Lieutenant PHILIP NEAME, 19 December 1914, buried St Mary the Virgin Churchyard, Selling, Kent. *VC location: on loan to the Imperial War Museum, London.*

566. Private JAMES MacKENZIE, 19 December 1914, no known grave, killed at Rouges Bancs, France. *VC location: Royal Scots Guards RHQ, Wellington Barracks, London.*

567. Private ABRAHAM ACTON, 21 December 1914, no known grave, killed at Festubert, France. *VC location: Beacon Museum, Whitehaven, Cumbria.*

568. Private JAMES SMITH (born **GLENN**), 21 December 1914, ashes scattered at Acklam Crematorium, May Section, Garden of Remembrance; Acklam Road, Middlesbrough. *VC location: Border Regiment Museum, Carlisle, Cumbria.*

569. Captain EUSTACE JOTHAM, 7 January 1915, buried Miranshar Cemetery, Plot 4, Grave 45; North Waziristan, Pakistan. *VC location: Bromsgrove School, Worcestershire.*

570. Lance Corporal MICHAEL O'LEARY, 1 February 1915, buried Mill Hill Cemetery, Section G-3, Grave 1930; Milespit Hill, London. *VC location: Irish Guards RHQ, Wellington Barracks, London.*

571. Lieutenant Commander ERIC ROBINSON, 26 February 1915, buried St John's Churchyard, Langrish, Sussex. *VC location: with recipient's family.*

572. Rifleman GOBAR SING NEGI, 10 March 1915, no known grave, killed at Neuve-Chapelle, France. *VC location: not publicly held.*

573. Private WILLIAM BUCKINGHAM (real name **BILLINGTON**), 10 and 12 March 1915, no known grave, killed at Thiepval, the Somme, France. *VC location: Royal Leicestershire Regiment Museum, Leicester.*

574. Captain CHARLES FOSS, 12 March 1915, buried West Hill Cemetery, Grave 2162/5-8; St James' Lane, Winchester, Hampshire. *VC location: Bedfordshire and Hertfordshire Regiment Museum, Luton.*

575. Lieutenant CYRIL MARTIN, 12 March 1915, ashes scattered at Pew Tor, Devon. *VC location: Royal Engineers Museum, Gillingham, Kent.*

576. Company Sergeant Major HARRY DANIELS, 12 March 1915, ashes scattered at Aldershot Cricket Club, Aldershot, Hampshire. *VC location: Royal Green Jackets Museum, Winchester, Hampshire.*

577. Lance Corporal WILFRED FULLER, 12 March 1915, buried Christchurch Churchyard, Frome, Somerset. *VC location: Grenadier Guards RHQ, Wellington Barracks, London.*

578. Corporal WILLIAM ANDERSON, 12 March 1915, no known grave, killed at Neuve-Chapelle, France. *VC location: Green Howards Museum, Richmond, Yorkshire.*

579. Acting Corporal CECIL NOBLE, 12 March 1915, buried Longuenesse Souvenir Cemetery, Plot I, Row A, Grave 57; near St Omer, France. *VC location: not publicly held.*

580. Private EDWARD BARBER, 12 March 1915, no known grave, killed at Neuve-Chapelle, France. *VC location: Grenadier Guards RHQ, Wellington Barracks, London.*

581. Private ROBERT MORROW, 12 March 1915, buried White House Cemetery, Plot IV,

Row A, Grave 44; St-Jan, near Ypres, Belgium. *VC location: Royal Irish Fusiliers Museum, Co. Armagh, Northern Ireland.*

582. Private JACOB RIVERS, 12 March 1915, no known grave, killed at Neuve-Chapelle, France. *VC location: Sherwood Foresters Museum, The Castle, Nottingham.*

583. Major GEORGE WHEELER, 12/13 April 1915, buried Basra War Cemetery, Plot III, Row C, Grave 22; Basra, Iraq. *VC location: Brighton & Hove Pavilion & Museum, Sussex.*

584. Lieutenant GEORGE ROUPELL, 20 April 1915, ashes scattered at Guildford Crematorium, Garden of Remembrance; New Pond Road, Godalming, Surrey. *VC location: not publicly held.*

585. Private EDWARD DWYER, 20 April 1915, buried Flatiron Copse Military Cemetery, Plot III, Row J, Grave 3; near Albert, France. *VC location: Queen's Royal Surrey Regiment Museum, Guildford.*

586. Second Lieutenant BENJAMIN GEARY, 20/21 April 1915, buried St Mark's Church Cemetery, Niagara-on-the Lake, Ontario, Canada. *VC location: Canadian War Museum, Ottawa, Ontario, Canada.*

587. Second Lieutenant GEOFFREY WOOLLEY, 20/21 April 1915, buried St Mary's Churchyard, left side of churchyard (adjacent to Henry Foote VC); West Chiltington, West Sussex. *VC location: not publicly held.*

588. Lance Corporal FREDERICK FISHER, 23 April 1915, no known grave, killed at St-Julien, Belgium. *VC location: Canadian Black Watch Museum, Montreal, Canada.*

589. Company Sergeant Major FREDERICK HALL, 23/24 April 1915, no known grave, killed at Poelcappelle, Belgium. *VC location: Canadian War Museum, Ottawa, Ontario, Canada.*

590. Lieutenant EDWARD BELLEW, 24 April 1915, buried Hillside Cemetery, Grave 2-5-11; Kamloops, Canada. *VC location: unknown. Stolen from the Royal Canadian Military Institute, Toronto, Ontario, Canada.*

591. Temporary Major CUTHBERT BROMLEY, 25 April 1915, no known grave, drowned at sea, Eastern Mediterranean. *VC location: not publicly held.*

592. Captain FRANCIS SCRIMGER, 25 April 1915, buried Mount Royal Cemetery, Section M, Grave 727; Montreal, Quebec, Canada. *VC location: Canadian War Museum, Ottawa, Ontario, Canada.*

593. Captain EDWARD UNWIN, 25 April 1915, buried St Luke's Churchyard, Grave G-O; Grayshott, Surrey. *VC location: on loan to the Imperial War Museum, London.*

594. Captain RICHARD WILLIS, 25 April 1915, ashes scattered at Cheltenham Crematorium, Garden of Remembrance, No. 4, Plot 84; Bouncers Lane, Gloucestershire. *VC location: Ashcroft Collection*

595. Sub Lieutenant ARTHUR TISDALL, 25 April 1915, no known grave, killed at Krithia, Turkey. *VC location: not publicly held.*

596. Sergeant ALFRED RICHARDS, 25 April 1915, buried Putney Vale Cemetery, Block U-794; Stag Lane, London. *VC location: Ashcroft Collection.*

597. Sergeant FRANK STUBBS, 25 April 1915, no known grave, killed at Gallipoli, Turkey. *VC location: Lancashire Fusiliers Museum, Arts and Craft Centre, Bury, Lancashire.*

598. Corporal JOHN GRIMSHAW, 25 April 1915, ashes scattered at South West Middlesex Crematorium, Lawn 3-C-5, by weeping willow; Hounslow Road, Hanworth. *VC location: Ashcroft Collection.*

599. Midshipman GEORGE DREWRY, 25 April 1915, buried City of London Cemetery, Square 197, Grave 90251; Aldersbrook Road, Manor Park, London. *VC location: on loan to the Imperial War Museum, London.*

600. Midshipman WILFRED MALLESON, 25 April 1915, ashes scattered at sea, off Falmouth, Cornwall. *VC location: Ashcroft Collection.*

601. Private WILLIAM KENEALLY (spelt **KENEALY** on headstone), 25 April 1915, buried Lancashire Landing Cemetery, Row C, Grave 104; Gallipoli, Turkey. *VC location: on loan to Lancashire Fusiliers Museum, Arts and Craft Centre, Bury, Lancashire.*

602. Able Seaman WILLIAM WILLIAMS, 25 April 1915, no known grave, killed at Gallipoli, Turkey. *VC location: Ashcroft Collection.*

603. Seaman GEORGE SAMSON, 25 April 1915, buried St George's Methodist Cemetery, Military Section; Bermuda. *VC location: Ashcroft Collection.*

604. Lieutenant Colonel CHARLES DOUGHTY-WYLIE, 26 April 1915, buried in solitary grave at Sedd-el-Bahr near V Beach Cemetery, Gallipoli, Turkey. *VC location: Royal Welch Fusiliers Museum, Caernarfon Castle, Gwynedd, Wales.*

605. Captain GARTH WALFORD, 26 April 1915, buried V Beach Cemetery, Row O, Grave 1; Gallipoli, Turkey. *VC location: not publicly held.*

606. Second Lieutenant WILLIAM RHODES-MOORHOUSE (born **MOORHOUSE**), 26 April 1915, buried in the grounds of his family home at Parnham House, Dorset. *VC location: Ashcroft Collection.*

607. Jemadar MIR DAST, 26 April 1915, buried in unmarked grave (probably), Warsak Road Cemetery, Shagi Landi Kyan, Tehsil district, Peshawar, Pakistan. *VC location: not publicly held.*

608. Corporal WILLIAM COSGROVE, 26 April 1915, buried Upper Aghada Cemetery, family grave; near Cork, Co. Cork, Ireland. *VC location: Ashcroft Collection.*

609. Acting Corporal ISSY SMITH (born **ISHROULCH SHMEILOWITZ**), 26 April 1915, buried Fawkner Cemetery, Hebrew Section; New Melbourne, Victoria, Australia. *VC location: not publicly held.*

610. Lieutenant Commander EDWARD BOYLE, 27 April–18 May 1915, cremated Woking Crematorium, Hermitage Road, St John's, Woking, Surrey. *VC location: Royal Navy Submarine Museum, Gosport, Hampshire.*

611. Lance Corporal WALTER PARKER, 30 April/1 May 1915, buried Stapleford Cemetery, Cemetery Road, Stapleford, Nottingham. *VC location: Royal Marines Museum, Southsea, Portsmouth, Hampshire.*

612. Private EDWARD WARNER, 1 May 1915, no known grave, killed at Zwarteleen, Belgium. *VC location: Bedfordshire and Hertfordshire Regiment Museum, Luton.*

613. Private JOHN LYNN, 2 May 1915, buried Grooterbreek British Cemetery, near Ypres, Belgium. *VC location: Lancashire Fusiliers Museum, Arts and Craft Centre, Bury, Lancashire.*

614. Corporal JOHN RIPLEY, 9 May 1915, buried Upper Largo Churchyard, near St Andrew's, Fife, Scotland. *VC location: not publicly held.*

615. Corporal JAMES UPTON, 9 May 1915, ashes scattered at Golders Green Crematorium, Garden of Remembrance; Hoop Lane, London. *VC location: Sherwood Foresters Museum, The Castle, Nottingham.*

616. Acting Corporal CHARLES SHARPE, 9 May 1915, buried Newport Cemetery, Plot H, Grave 354; Lincoln, Lincolnshire. *VC location: Museum of Lincolnshire Life, Lincoln.*

617. Lance Corporal DAVID FINLAY, 9 May 1915, no known grave, killed at Karma, Mesopotamia (now Iraq). *VC location: Black Watch Museum, Perth, Scotland.*

618. Lance Sergeant DOUGLAS BELCHER, 13 May 1915, buried Holy Trinity Churchyard, Claygate, Surrey. *VC location: Royal Green Jackets Museum, Winchester, Hampshire.*

619. Company Sergeant Major FREDERICK BARTER, 16 May 1915, ashes scattered Bournemouth Crematorium, Garden of Remembrance, Strouden Avenue, Dorset. *VC location: Royal Welch Fusiliers Museum, Caernarfon Castle, Gwynedd, Wales.*

620. Lance Corporal JOSEPH TOMBS, 16 May 1915, buried Pine Hill Cemetery, War Veterans' Section, Block K, Grave 1056; East Toronto, Ontario, Canada. *VC location: is owned by the Royal Regiment of Canada Foundation and is passed between them and the King's (Liverpool) Regiment Museum, Liverpool, Lancashire..*

621. Lieutenant JOHN SMYTH (sometimes spelt **SMYTHE**), 18 May 1915, cremated Golders Green Crematorium, Hoop Lane, London. *VC location: Imperial War Museum, London.*

622. Lance Corporal ALBERT JACKA, 19/20 May 1915, buried St Kilda Cemetery, Presbyterian Section; near Castleford, Melbourne, Victoria, Australia. *VC location: Australian War Memorial, Canberra, Australia.*

623. Lieutenant Commander MARTIN NASMITH (later **DUNBAR-NASMITH**), 20 May–8 June 1915, buried Holy Trinity Churchyard, family plot, NEE-1073 B; Elgin, Moray, Scotland. *VC location: not publicly held.*

624. Private WILLIAM MARINER (aka **WILLIAM WIGNALL**), 22 May 1915, no known grave, killed at Loos, France. *VC location: not publicly held.*

625. Lance Corporal LEONARD KEYWORTH, 25/26 May 1915, buried Abbeville Communal Cemetery, Plot III, Row C, Grave 2; France. *VC location: Queen's Royal Surrey Regiment Museum, Guildford, Surrey.*

626. Second Lieutenant GEORGE MOOR, 5 June 1915, buried Y Farm Military Cemetery, Row C, Grave 86; Bois-Grenier, France. *VC location: Royal Hampshire Regiment Museum, Winchester, Hampshire.*

627. Flight Sub Lieutenant REGINALD WARNEFORD, 7 June 1915, buried Brompton Cemetery, Compartment 6 East, 34' x 22'; Old Brompton Road, London. *VC location: Fleet Air Arm Museum, Yeovilton, Somerset.*

628. Lance Corporal WILLIAM ANGUS, 12 June 1915, buried Wilton Cemetery, Section O, Lair 36; Wilton Road, Carluke, Lanarkshire, Scotland. *VC location: National War Museum of Scotland, Edinburgh Castle, Scotland.*

629. Lieutenant FREDERICK CAMPBELL, 15 June 1915, buried Boulogne Eastern Cemetery, Plot II, Row A, grave 24; France. *VC location: not publicly held.*

630. Second Lieutenant WALTER JAMES, 28 June and 3 July 1915, ashes scattered at Kensal Green Cemetery, Garden of Remembrance; Harrow Road, London. *VC location: Maryborough Museum, Queensland, Australia.*

631. Captain GERALD O'SULLIVAN, 1/2 July 1915, no known grave, killed at Gallipoli, Turkey. *VC location: Ashcroft Collection.*

632. Sergeant JAMES SOMERS, 1/2 July 1915, buried St Keman's Church of Ireland Churchyard, Modreeny, Co. Tipperary, Ireland. *VC location: not publicly held.*

633. Mercantile Marine Master FREDERICK PARSLOW, 4 July 1915, buried Cobh Old Church Cemetery, Cobh, near Cork, Co. Cork, Ireland. *VC location: not publicly held.*

634. Captain LANOE (sometimes misspelt **LANCE**) **HAWKER**, 25 July 1915, no known grave, killed near Bapaume, France. *VC location: unknown. Original stolen from the family home in France in 1940; an official replacement was issued to his brother in 1960, which is now in the Royal Air Force Museum, Hendon, London.*

635. Second Lieutenant SIDNEY WOODROFFE, 30 July 1915, no known grave, killed at Hooge, Belgium. *VC location: Ashcroft Collection.*

636. Captain JOHN LIDDELL, 31 July 1915, buried Basingstoke Old Cemetery Roman Catholic Section E, Grave 2257-8; Burgess Road, Basingstoke, Hampshire. *VC location: Ashcroft Collection.*

637. Second Lieutenant GEORGE BOYD-ROCHFORT, 3 August 1915, buried Castletown Church of Ireland Old Churchyard, Castletown-Geoghegen, Co. Westmeath, Ireland. *VC location: Royal Scots Guards RHQ, Wellington Barracks, London.*

638. Corporal CYRIL BASSETT, 7 August 1915, ashes interred at Auckland Cemetery, Northern Division, Block A, Row C, Plot 45; Auckland, New Zealand. *VC location: Auckland War Memorial Museum, Auckland, New Zealand.*

639. Private LEONARD KEYSOR (sometimes spelt **KEYZOR**), 7/8 August 1915, ashes in urn at Golders Green Crematorium, Niche 5413 in Hall of Memory; Hoop Lane, London. *VC location: Australian War Memorial, Canberra, Australia.*

640. Lieutenant WILLIAM FORSHAW, 7–9 August 1915, buried in Touchen End

Cemetery, aka Holy Trinity Churchyard (headstone reads 'buried in this churchyard'); near Bray, Berkshire. *VC location: Manchester Regiment Museum, The Town Hall, Ashton-under-Lyne.*

641. Second Lieutenant WILLIAM SYMONS (later **PENN-SYMONS**), 8/9 August 1915, ashes scattered at Golders Green Crematorium, Area D/01361; Hoop Lane, London. *VC location: Australian War Memorial, Canberra, Australia.*

642. Captain PERCY HANSEN, 9 August 1915, buried Garnisons Kirkegaard, Section R, Row K, Grave 3; Dag Hammerskjolds Alle 10, Copenhagen, Denmark. *VC location: on loan to the Imperial War Museum, London.*

643. Captain ALFRED SHOUT, 9 August 1915, buried at sea, Dardanelles, off Gallipoli, Turkey. *VC location: Australian War Memorial, Canberra, Australia.*

644. Lieutenant FREDERICK TUBB, 9 August 1915, buried Lijssenthoek Military Cemetery, Plot XIX, Row C, Grave 5; Belgium. *VC location: Australian War Memorial, Canberra, Australia.*

645. Corporal ALEXANDER BURTON, 9 August 1915, no known grave, killed at Gallipoli, Turkey. *VC location: Australian War Memorial, Canberra, Australia.*

646. Corporal WILLIAM DUNSTAN, 9 August 1915, ashes interred at Springvale Crematorium, Melbourne, Victoria, Australia. *VC location: Australian War Memorial, Canberra, Australia.*

647. Private JOHN HAMILTON, 9 August 1915, buried Woronora Cemetery, C of E Section 8, Grave 518; Sydney, New South Wales, Australia. *VC location: Australian War Memorial, Canberra, Australia.*

648. Private DAVID LAUDER, 13 August 1915, ashes scattered at Daldowie Crematorium, Garden of Remembrance; Hamilton Road, Broomhouse, Glasgow, Scotland. *VC location: not publicly held.*

649. Private FREDERICK POTTS, 21 August 1915, ashes scattered at Reading Crematorium, Garden of Remembrance; All Hallowes Road, Reading, Berkshire. *VC location: Imperial War Museum.*

650. Second Lieutenant HUGO 'JIM' THROSSELL, 29/30 August 1915, buried Karrakatta Cemetery; Anglican Section-2B, Plot 304; Railway Road, Hollywood, Perth, Western Australia. *VC location: Australian War Memorial, Canberra, Australia.*

651. Temporary Lieutenant WILBUR (born **WILLIAM THOMAS**) **DARTNELL**, 3 September 1915, buried Voi Cemetery, Plot V, Row B, Grave 1; Voi, Kenya. *VC location: Australian War Memorial, Canberra, Australia.*

652. Private CHARLES HULL, 5 September 1915, buried Woodhouse Lane Cemetery (now the University of Leeds), Section A, Grave 11804; Woodhouse Lane, Leeds. *VC location: Queen's Royal Lancers Museum, Belvoir Castle, Grantham, Leicestershire.*

653. Captain ARTHUR KILBY, 25 September 1915, buried Arras Road Cemetery, Plot III, Row N, Grave 27; Rodincourt, near Arras, France. *VC location: Ashcroft Collection.*

654. Captain ANKETELL READ, 25 September 1915, buried Dud Corner Cemetery, Plot VII, Row F, Grave 19; Le Rutoire, near Loos, France. *VC location: Northamptonshire Regiment Museum, Northampton.*

655. Lieutenant GEORGE MALING, 25 September 1915, buried Chislehurst Cemetery (aka Town Cemetery), Section A, Grave 2017; Beaverswood Road, Chislehurst, Kent. *VC location: Army Medical Services Museum, Mytchett, Surrey.*

656. Temporary Second Lieutenant FREDERICK JOHNSON, 25 September 1915, no known grave, killed at Cambrai, France. *VC location: it is owned by the widow of Conservative politician Alan Clarke.*

657. Sergeant HARRY WELLS, 25 September 1915, buried Dud Corner Cemetery, Plot V, Row E, Grave 2; Le Rutoire, near Loos, France. *VC location: Royal Sussex Regiment Museum, Eastbourne, Sussex.*

658. Private HENRY (cremated under the name **HARRY**) **KENNY**, 25 September 1915, ashes interred at St Mark's Churchyard, Plot

109; Whiteley Village (private estate), near Hersham, Surrey. *VC location: Ashcroft Collection.*

659. Private GEORGE PEACHMENT, 25 September 1915, no known grave, killed at Puits, France. *VC location: Ashcroft Collection.*

660. Rifleman KULBIR THAPA, 25 September 1915, no known grave, died Niglpani, Palpa District, Nepal. *VC location: Gurkha Museum, Winchester, Hampshire.*

661. Piper DANIEL LAIDLAW, 25 September 1915, buried in unmarked grave (at his own request), Norham Churchyard, Northumberland. *VC location: National War Museum of Scotland, Edinburgh Castle, Scotland.*

662. Private ARTHUR VICKERS, 25 September 1915, buried Witton Cemetery, Section 161, Grave 42776; Moor Lane, Witton, Birmingham. *VC location: Royal Warwickshire Regiment Museum, Warwick.*

663. Temporary Lieutenant Colonel ANGUS DOUGLAS-HAMILTON, 25/26 September 1915, no known grave, killed at Loos, France. *VC location: Highlanders Museum, Fort George, Ardersier, Inverness-shire, Scotland.*

664. Temporary Second Lieutenant RUPERT HALLOWES, 25–30 September 1915, buried Bedford House Cemetery, Enclosure 4, Plot XIV, Row B, Grave 36; Belgium. *VC location: National Army Museum, London.*

665. Sergeant ARTHUR SAUNDERS, 26 September 1915, ashes scattered at Ipswich Crematorium, Garden of Remembrance; Cemetery Lane, Ipswich, Suffolk. *VC location: Suffolk Regiment Museum, Bury St Edmunds, Suffolk.*

666. Private ROBERT DUNSIRE, 26 September 1915, buried Mazingarbe Communal Cemetery, Grave 18; near Bethune, France. *VC location: Royal Scots Museum, Edinburgh Castle, Scotland.*

667. Corporal ALFRED BURT, 27 September 1915, ashes interred at West Hertfordshire Crematorium, Plot AR-48; High Elms Lane, Garston, Watford. *VC location: Hertfordshire Regiment Museum, Hertford.*

668. Corporal JAMES POLLOCK, 27 September 1915, buried Ayr Cemetery,

Wall Section, Lair 103; Holmston Road, Ayr, Scotland. *VC location: Highlanders Museum, Fort George, Ardersier, Inverness-shire, Scotland.*

669. Lieutenant Commander EDGAR COOKSON, 28 September 1915, no known grave, killed at Kut-el-Amara, Mesopotamia. *VC location: not publicly held.*

670. Second Lieutenant ALEXANDER TURNER, 28 September 1915, buried Choques Military Cemetery, Plot I, Row B, Grave 2; near Bethune, France. *VC location: Royal Gloucestershire, Berkshire and Wiltshire Regiment Museum, Salisbury, Wiltshire.*

671. Temporary Second Lieutenant ARTHUR FLEMING-SANDES, 29 September 1915, ashes scattered at Torquay Crematorium, Garden of Remembrance; Hele Road, Devon. *VC location: Queen's Royal Surrey Regiment Museum, Guildford, Surrey.*

672. Private SAMUEL HARVEY, 29 September 1915, buried Ipswich Old Cemetery, Plot X, Division 21, Grave 3; Cemetery Lane, Ipswich, Suffolk. *VC location: unknown. It went missing in the 1920s.*

673. Lance Sergeant OLIVER BROOKS, 8 October 1915, buried Windsor Town Cemetery, Section GN, Grave 352; St Leonard's Road, Windsor, Berkshire. *VC location: Coldstream Guards RHQ, Wellington Barracks, London.*

674. Acting Sergeant JOHN RAYNES, 11 October 1915, buried Harehills Cemetery, Section H, Grave 11; Kimberley Road, Chapeltown, Leeds. *VC location: Royal Artillery Museum, Woolwich, London.*

675. Corporal JAMES DAWSON, 13 October 1915, ashes scattered at Eastbourne Crematorium, Garden of Remembrance; Hide Hollow, Sussex. *VC location: Glasgow University.*

676. Temporary Captain CHARLES VICKERS, 14 October 1915, ashes scattered at Oxford Crematorium, Garden of Remembrance; Bayswater Road, Headington, Oxfordshire. *VC location: Sherwood Foresters Museum, The Castle, Nottingham.*

677. Private HARRY CHRISTIAN, 18 October 1915, buried Egremont Cemetery, SW corner of cemetery; near Whitehaven, Cumbria. *VC location: King's Own Regiment Museum, Lancaster.*

678. Private THOMAS KENNY, 4 November 1915, buried Wheatley Hill Cemetery, Cemetery Road, near Easington, Co. Durham. *VC location: Durham Light Infantry Museum, Co. Durham.*

679. Second Lieutenant GILBERT INSALL, 7 November 1915, ashes interred Nocton Churchyard, School Lane, Nocton Village, Lincolnshire. *VC location: Royal Air Force Museum, Hendon, London.*

680. Private JOHN CAFFREY, 16 November 1915, buried Wilford Hill Cemetery (aka Southern Cemetery), Section R, Grave 23-8, family grave; Loughborough Road, West Bridgford, Nottingham. *VC location: York and Lancaster Regiment Museum, Rotherham, Yorkshire.*

681. Squadron Commander RICHARD BELL-DAVIES, 19 November 1915, ashes scattered at sea, off the Knob Tower. *VC location: Fleet Air Arm Museum, Yeovilton, Somerset.*

682. Corporal SAMUEL MEEKOSHA (name changed to **INGHAM** in 1939), 19 November 1915, cremated Glyntaff Crematorium, Cemetery Road, Pontypridd, Mid-Glamorgan, Wales. *VC location: not publicly held.*

683. Corporal ALFRED DRAKE, 23 November 1915, buried La Brique Military Cemetery, Plot I, Row C, Grave 2; near Ypres, Belgium. *VC location: Ashcroft Collection.*

684. Private WILLIAM YOUNG, 22 December 1915, buried New Hall Cemetery, RC Plot 5, Row C, Grave 10; Preston, Lancashire. *VC location: Museum of Lancashire.*

685. Second Lieutenant ALFRED SMITH, 23 December 1915, buried in Twelve Tree Copse Cemetery (headstone reads 'known to be buried in this cemetery'); Gallipoli, Turkey. *VC location: Towneley Hall Museum, Burnley, Lancashire.*

686. Sepoy CHATTA (sometimes spelt **CHATTAH) SINGH**, 13 January 1916, cremated Tilsara Village, India. *VC location: not publicly held.*

687. Captain JOHN SINTON, 21 January 1916, buried Creggan Presbyterian Churchyard, Co. Tyrone, Northern Ireland. *VC location: Army Medical Services Museum, Mytchett, Surrey.*

688. Lance Naik LALA, 21 January 1916, ashes scattered at Parol Village, Kangra District, India. *VC location: unknown.*

689. Temporary Lieutenant ERIC McNAIR, 14 February 1916, buried Staglieno Commonwealth War Graves Cemetery, Plot I, Row B, Grave 32; Genoa, Liguria Province, Italy. *VC location: Royal Sussex Regiment Museum, Eastbourne, Sussex.*

690. Acting Corporal WILLIAM COTTER, 6 March 1916, buried Lilliers Communal Cemetery, Plot IV, Row E, Grave 45; France. *VC location: National Army Museum, London.*

691. Private GEORGE STRINGER, 8 March 1916, buried Philips Park Cemetery, Section M, Grave 1826; Briscoe Lane, Manchester. *VC location: Manchester Regiment Museum, The Town Hall, Ashton-under-Lyne.*

692. Chaplain EDWARD MELLISH, 27–29 March 1916, ashes scattered at St Mary the Virgin's Churchyard, Church View, Great Dunmow, Essex. *VC location: Royal Fusiliers Museum, Tower of London.*

693. Temporary Captain ANGUS BUCHANAN, 5 April 1916, buried Coleford Cemetery Churchyard, Gloucester. *VC location: South Wales Borderers Museum, Brecon, Powys, Wales.*

694. Corporal SIDNEY WARE, 6 April 1916, buried Amara War Cemetery, grave now destroyed; Iraq. *VC location: Highlanders Museum, Fort George, Ardersier, Inverness-shire, Scotland.*

695. Chaplain WILLIAM ADDISON, 9 April 1916, buried Brookwood Cemetery, Plot 22, Grave 220346; Cemetery Pales, Woking, Surrey. *VC location: with recipient's family.*

696. Lieutenant EDGAR MYLES, 9 April 1916, ashes scattered at Torquay

Crematorium, Garden of Remembrance; Hele Road, Devon. *VC location: Worcestershire Regiment Museum, Worcester.*

697. Private JAMES FYNN (born **FINN**), 9 April 1916, buried Baghdad, Iraq. *VC location: Bodmin Town Council, Bodmin, Cornwall.*

698. Naik SHAHAMAD KHAN, 12/13 April 1916, buried Takhti Village Cemetery, Pakistan. *VC location: original unknown. The official replacement is in the Ashcroft Collection.*

699. Second Lieutenant EDWARD BAXTER, 17/18 April 1916, buried Fillievres British Cemetery, Row A, Grave 10; France. *VC location: Imperial War Museum, London.*

700. Lieutenant Commander CHARLES COWLEY, 24/25 April 1916, no known grave, killed at Kut, Mesopotamia. *VC location: not publicly held.*

701. Lieutenant HUMPHREY FIRMAN, 24/25 April 1916, no known grave, killed near Kut, Mesopotamia. *VC location: not publicly held.*

702. Temporary Lieutenant RICHARD JONES, 21 May 1916, no known grave, killed near Vimy, France. *VC location: Dulwich College, London.*

703. Major FRANCIS HARVEY, 31 May 1916, buried at sea, off Jutland, North Sea. *VC location: Royal Marine Museum, Southsea, Portsmouth, Hampshire.*

704. Commander EDWARD BINGHAM, 31 May 1916, cremated Golders Green Crematorium, Hoop Lane, London. *VC location: North Down Heritage Centre, Bangor, Co. Down, Northern Ireland.*

705. Commander LOFTUS JONES, 31 May 1916, buried Kviberg Cemetery, Engelska Krigsgravar Section, Plot II, Row C, Grave 4; Gothenburg, Sweden. *VC location: Ashcroft Collection.*

706. First Class Boy JOHN (aka **JACK**) **CORNWELL**, 31 May 1916, buried Manor Park Cemetery, Section 55 West, Grave 13; Sebert Road, London. *VC location: Imperial War Museum, London.*

707. Private GEORGE CHAFER, 3/4 June 1916, ashes scattered at Bramley, Yorkshire.

VC location: Prince of Wales's Regiment Museum, York.

708. Private ARTHUR PROCTER, 4 June 1916, ashes interred at All Saints Chapel, Sheffield Cathedral, Church Street, Sheffield. *VC location: King's (Liverpool) Regiment Museum, Liverpool.*

709. Sergeant JOHN ERSKINE, 22 June 1916, no known grave, killed at Arras, France. *VC location: Cameronians Museum, Hamilton, Lanarkshire, Scotland.*

710. Sapper WILLIAM HACKETT, 22/23 June 1916, no known grave, killed near Givenchy, France. *VC location: Royal Engineers Museum, Gillingham, Kent.*

711. Lieutenant ARTHUR BATTEN-POOLL, 25 June 1916, buried St Lawrence's Parish Churchyard, Woolverton, near Bath, Avon. *VC location: National Army Museum, London.*

712. Private WILLIAM (born **JOHN**) **JACKSON**, 25/26 June 1916, ashes interred at Springvale Crematorium, in Boronia Gardens; Melbourne, Victoria, Australia. *VC location: not publicly held.*

713. Private JAMES HUTCHINSON, 28 June 1916, ashes scattered at Torquay Crematorium, Garden of Remembrance; Hele Road, Devon. *VC location: not publicly held.*

714. Company Sergeant Major NELSON CARTER, 30 June 1916, buried Royal Irish Rifles Churchyard, Plot VI, Row C, Grave 17; Laventie, France. *VC location: Royal Sussex Regiment Museum, Eastbourne, Sussex.*

715. Private WILLIAM McFADZEAN, 1 July 1916 (01:00 hours), no known grave, killed at Thiepval, Somme, France. *VC location: Royal Ulster Rifles Museum, Belfast, Northern Ireland.*

716. Temporary Major STEWART LOUDOUN-SHAND, 1 July 1916, buried Norfolk Cemetery, Plot I, Row C, Grave 77; Becourt, near Albert, France. *VC location: Ashcroft Collection.*

717. Temporary Major LIONEL REES, 1 July 1916, buried Nassau War Cemetery for United Nations Airmen, Bahamas.

VC location: Eastbourne College, Eastbourne, East Sussex.

718. Captain JOHN GREEN, 1 July 1916, buried Foncquevillers Military Cemetery, Plot III, Row D, Grave 6; France. *VC location: Army Medical Services Museum, Mytchett, Surrey.*

719. Temporary Captain ERIC BELL, 1 July 1916, no known grave, killed at Thiepval, France. *VC location: Royal Inniskilling Fusiliers Regiment Museum, Enniskillen, Northern Ireland.*

720. Lieutenant GEOFFREY CATHER, 1 July 1916, no known grave, killed at the Somme, France. *VC location: Royal Irish Fusiliers Museum, Co. Armagh, Northern Ireland.*

721. Sergeant JAMES TURNBULL, 1 July 1916, buried Lonsdale Cemetery, Plot IV, Row G, Grave 9; Authuille, near Albert, France. *VC location: not publicly held.*

722. Corporal GEORGE SANDERS, 1 July 1916, ashes scattered at Cottingley Crematorium, Lawn One; Leeds. *VC location: not publicly held.*

723. Private ROBERT QUIGG, 1 July 1916, buried Billy Parish Protestant Cemetery, near Bushmills, Co. Antrim, Northern Ireland. *VC location: Royal Ulster Rifles Museum, Belfast, Northern Ireland.*

724. Drummer WALTER RITCHIE, 1 July 1916, cremated Warriston Crematorium, Warriston Road, Edinburgh, Scotland. *VC location: not publicly held.*

725. Lieutenant Colonel ADRIAN CARTON DE WIART, 2/3 July 1916, buried Killinardrish Church of Ireland Churchyard, family plot; Co. Cork, Ireland. *VC location: National Army Museum, London.*

726. Private THOMAS TURRALL, 3 July 1916, buried Robin Hood Cemetery, Section A-4 North, Grave 193; Olton Road, Solihull, Warwickshire. *VC location: Worcestershire Regiment Museum, Worcester.*

727. Temporary Lieutenant THOMAS WILKINSON, 5 July 1916, no known grave, killed at La Boiselle, Somme, France. *VC location: Imperial War Museum, London.*

728. Temporary Second Lieutenant DONALD BELL, 5 July 1916, buried Gordon Dump Cemetery, Plot IV, Row A, Grave 8; near Albert, France. *VC location: National Football Museum, Manchester.*

729. Major WILLIAM 'BILLY' CONGREVE, 6–20 July 1916, buried Corbie Communal Cemetery Extension, Plot I, Row F, Grave 35; Amiens, France. *VC location: Royal Green Jackets Museum, Winchester, Hampshire.*

730. Sergeant WILLIAM BOULTER, 14 July 1916, ashes scattered at Putney Vale Crematorium, First Lawn, Upper Terrace; Stag Lane, London. *VC location: Northamptonshire Regiment Museum, Northampton.*

731. Private WILLIAM FAULDS, 18 July 1916, buried Pioneer Cemetery, Remembrance Drive, Harare, Zimbabwe. *VC location: unknown. Medal stolen from National Museum of Military History, Johannesburg, South Africa, in 1994.*

732. Corporal JOSEPH DAVIES, 20 July 1916, ashes scattered at Evening Hill, overlooking Poole Harbour, Dorset. *VC location: Royal Welch Fusiliers Museum, Caernarfon Castle, Gwynedd, Wales.*

733. Private ALBERT HILL, 20 July 1916, buried Highland Memorial Park, 'Buttonwood' Division, Section K, Lot 196, Grave 1; Johnston, Rhode Island, USA. *VC location: Royal Welch Fusiliers Museum, Caernarfon Castle, Gwynedd, Wales.*

734. Private THEODORE 'TEDDY' VEALE, 20 July 1916, ashes scattered at Enfield Crematorium, Area M3-D8; Great Cambridge Road, Enfield, Middlesex. *VC location: Devonshire Regiment Museum, Dorchester, Dorset.*

735. Second Lieutenant ARTHUR BLACKBURN, 23 July 1916, buried West Terrace AIF Cemetery, Light Oval Section, Grave 4-C-A North; Adelaide, South Australia. *VC location: Australian War Memorial, Canberra, Australia.*

736. Private JOHN LEAK, 23 July 1916, buried Stirling District Cemetery, Block 14-A; Adelaide, South Australia. *VC location: not publicly held.*

737. Private THOMAS COOKE, 24/25 July

1916, no known grave, killed at Pozieres, Somme, France. *VC location: not publicly held.*
738. Sergeant ALBERT GILL, 27 July 1916, buried Delville Wood Cemetery, Plot IV, Row C, Grave 3; France. *VC location: Ashcroft Collection.*
739. Sergeant CLAUDE CASTLETON, 28/29 July 1916, buried Pozieres Military Cemetery (aka Pozieres British Cemetery), Plot IV, Row L, Grave 43; near Albert, France. *VC location: Australian War Memorial, Canberra, Australia.*
740. Company Sergeant Major WILLIAM EVANS, 30 July 1916, buried Beckenham Cemetery, Row I, T-8, Grave 16239; Elmers End Road, London. *VC location: on loan to the Imperial War Museum, London.*
741. Private JAMES MILLER, 30/31 July 1916, buried Dartmoor Cemetery, Plot I, Row C, Grave 64; near Albert, France. *VC location: King's Own Regiment Museum, Lancaster.*
742. Private WILLIAM SHORT, 6 August 1916, buried Contalmaison Chateau Cemetery, Plot II, Row B, Grave 16; near Albert, France. *VC location: Green Howards Museum, Richmond, Yorkshire.*
743. Second Lieutenant GABRIEL COURY, 8 August 1916, buried St Peter & St Paul Churchyard, family grave; Liverpool Road, Crosby, Merseyside. *VC location: Queen's Lancashire Regiment Museum, Preston, Lancashire.*
744. Captain NOEL CHAVASSE, 9/10 August 1916 (for Bar action see **854**), buried Brandhoek New Military Cemetery, Plot III, Row B, Grave 15; Vlamertinghe, near Ypres, Belgium. *VC and Bar location: Ashcroft Collection*
745. Private MARTIN O'MEARA, 9–12 August 1916, buried Karrakatta Cemetery, RC Section HA, Plot 93; Railway Road, Hollywood, Perth, Western Australia. *VC location: Army Museum of Western Australia, Fremantle, Australia.*
746. Captain WILLIAM BLOOMFIELD (born **BROOMFIELD**), 24 August 1916, buried Ermelo Cemetery, Housthuizen Street, Transvaal, South Africa. *VC location: with recipient's family.*

747. Lieutenant WILLIAM ROBINSON, 2/3 September 1916, buried All Saints Church Cemetery Extension, SE Section; Uxbridge Road, Harrow Weald, Middlesex. *VC location: Ashcroft Collection.*
748. Captain WILLIAM ALLEN, 3 September 1916, buried Earnley Cemetery, Bracklesham Bay, near Chichester, Sussex. *VC location: Army Medical Services Museum, Mytchett, Surrey.*
749. Lieutenant JOHN HOLLAND, 3 September 1916, buried Cornelian Bay Cemetery, RC Section N-D, Lot 63; Hobart, Tasmania, Australia. *VC location: not publicly held.*
750. Sergeant DAVID JONES, 3 September 1916, buried Bancourt British Cemetery, Plot V, Row F, Grave 20; near Bancourt, France. *VC location: Museum of Liverpool, Lancashire.*
751. Private THOMAS HUGHES, 3 September 1916, buried Old Bloomfield Cemetery (aka St Patrick's), between Carrickmacross and Castleblaney, Co. Monaghan, Ireland. *VC location: National Army Museum, London.*
752. Acting Corporal LEO CLARKE, 9 September 1916, buried Etretat Churchyard, Plot II, Row C, Grave 3A; near Bapaume, France. *VC location: Canadian War Museum, Ottawa, Ontario, Canada.*
753. Temporary Lieutenant Colonel JOHN CAMPBELL, 15 September 1916, ashes scattered in River Findhorn, near Drynachan, Highland Region, Scotland. *VC location: Coldstream Guards RHQ, Wellington Barracks, London.*
754. Sergeant DONALD BROWN, 15 September 1916, buried Warlencourt British Cemetery, Plot III, Row F, Grave 11; near Bapaume, France. *VC location: with recipient's family.*
755. Lance Sergeant FREDERICK McNESS, 15 September 1916, ashes scattered at Bournemouth Crematorium, on the Lawns; Strouden Avenue, Dorset. *VC location: Royal Scots Guards RHQ, Wellington Barracks, London.*
756. Private JOHN KERR, 16 September 1916, buried Mountain View Cemetery,

Veterans' Division, Abray Section, Block 5, Lot 12; Prince Edward Avenue, Vancouver, British Columbia, Canada. *VC location: Canadian War Museum, Ottawa, Ontario, Canada.*

757. Private THOMAS 'TODGER' JONES, 25 September 1916, buried Runcorn Cemetery, Greenway Road, Runcorn, Cheshire. *VC location: Cheshire Regiment Museum, Chester.*

758. Private FREDERICK EDWARDS, 26 September 1916, buried Richmond Cemetery, Old Soldiers' Section (Star & Garter Plot), Section 22, Grave 87; Lower Grove Road, Richmond-upon-Thames, Surrey. *VC location: National Army Museum, London.*

759. Private ROBERT RYDER, 26 September 1916, buried St Mary the Virgin Churchyard, Grave 1948; Harefield, Middlesex. *VC location: Imperial War Museum, London.*

760. Temporary Second Lieutenant TOM ADLAM, 27/28 September 1916, buried St Matthew's Churchyard, near Liss, Blackmoor, Hampshire. *VC location: City Guild Hall, Salisbury, Wiltshire.*

761. Temporary Captain ARCHIE WHITE, 27 September–1 October 1916, ashes scattered at Woking Crematorium, Tennyson Lake Garden; Hermitage Road, St John's, Woking, Surrey. *VC location: Green Howards Museum, Richmond, Yorkshire.*

762. Temporary Lieutenant Colonel ROLAND BRADFORD, 1 October 1916, buried Hermies British Cemetery, Row F, Grave 10; France. *VC location: Durham Light Infantry Museum, Co. Durham.*

763. Temporary Second Lieutenant HENRY KELLY, 4 October 1916, buried Southern Cemetery, RC Section, Plot I, Grave 372; Barlow Moor Road, Chorlton-cum-Hardy, Manchester. *VC location: Duke of Wellington's Regiment Museum, Halifax, Yorkshire.*

764. Piper JAMES RICHARDSON, 8/9 October 1916, buried Adanac Military Cemetery, Plot III, Row F, Grave 36; France. *VC location: Canadian War Museum, Ottawa, Ontario, Canada.*

765. Private HUBERT (aka **HERBERT**) **'STOKEY' LEWIS**, 22/23 October 1916, buried St Katherine's Cemetery, Milford Haven, Pembrokeshire, Wales. *VC location: Ashcroft Collection.*

766. Sergeant ROBERT DOWNIE, 23 October 1916, buried St Kentigern's Cemetery, Section 21, Lair 506; Glasgow, Scotland. *VC location: not publicly held.*

767. Lieutenant EUGENE BENNETT, 5 November 1916, ashes at Vicenza Crematorium, Niche 116; Via Trieste, Vicenza, Italy. *VC location: Worcestershire Regiment Museum, Worcester.*

768. Temporary Lieutenant Colonel BERNARD FREYBERG, 13 November 1916, buried St Martha's Churchyard, Chilworth, Surrey. *VC location: not publicly held.*

769. Private JOHN CUNNINGHAM, 13 November 1916, buried in unmarked grave, Western Cemetery, Section 181 (his name is on his mother's grave nearby); Spring Bank West, Hull. *VC location: Prince of Wales's Regiment Museum, York.*

770. Sergeant THOMAS MOTTERSHEAD, 7 January 1917, buried Bailleul Communal Cemetery, Plot III, Row A, Grave 126; France. *VC location: Ashcroft Collection.*

771. Temporary Lieutenant Colonel EDWARD HENDERSON, 25 January 1917, buried Amara War Cemetery, Plot XXIV, Row B, Grave 31; Iraq. *VC location: Ashcroft Collection.*

772. Temporary Lieutenant ROBERT PHILLIPS, 25 January 1917, buried St Veep Parish Churchyard, Cornwall. *VC location: Royal Warwickshire Regiment Museum, Warwick.*

773. Sergeant EDWARD MOTT, 27 January 1917, ashes scattered at Oxford Crematorium, Garden of Remembrance; Bayswater Road, Headington, Oxfordshire. *VC location: both the Border Regiment Museum, Carlisle, and the Fitzwilliam Museum, Cambridge, claim to have his medal. The Border Regiment Museum staff say that the original went missing and an official replacement was issued; they are sure they have the original. The Fitzwilliam*

Museum has all of his campaign medals including a VC. I think it is likely that an official replacement would be with the rest of his medals, and therefore the original is most probably in the Border Regiment Museum.

774. Captain HENRY 'MAD' MURRAY, 4/5 February 1917, cremated Mount Thomson Crematorium, Brisbane, Queensland, Australia. *VC location: not publicly held.*

775. Sergeant FREDERICK BOOTH, 12 February 1917, buried Bear Road Cemetery, Red Cross Plot ZKZ-36; Bear Road, Brighton, Sussex. *VC location: Regimental Depot, British South Africa Police, Salisbury (Harare), South Africa.*

776. Lance Sergeant FREDERICK PALMER, 16/17 February 1917, ashes interred All Saints Churchyard, family grave; Hordle, Hampshire. *VC location: Royal Fusiliers Museum, Tower of London.*

777. Commander GORDON CAMPBELL, 17 February 1917, buried All Saints Churchyard, Crondall, Hampshire. *VC location: Dulwich College, London.*

778. Sergeant THOMAS STEELE, 22 February 1917, ashes interred St Anne's Churchyard, Lydgate, Lancashire. *VC location: Ashcroft Collection.*

779. Major GEORGE WHEELER, 23 February 1917, buried St Mary Magdalene Churchyard, New Milton, Hampshire. *VC location: National Army Museum, London.*

780. Private JOHN READITT, 25 February 1917, buried Gorton Cemetery, Section Z, Grave 223; Thornwood Avenue, Manchester. *VC location: Ashcroft Collection.*

781. Private JACK WHITE, 7/8 March 1917, buried Jewish Cemetery, Section F, Grave 341; Blackley, Manchester. *VC location: not publicly held.*

782. Second Lieutenant GEORGE CATES, 8 March 1917, buried Hem Military Cemetery, Plot I, Row G, Grave 15; Hem-Monacu, France. *VC location: original destroyed in a fire in 1951; official replacement in the Royal Green Jackets Museum, Winchester, Hampshire.*

783. Captain OSWALD REID, 8–10 March 1917, buried Braamfontein Cemetery, Section

EC, Plot 22932; Johannesburg, South Africa. *VC location: Museum of Military History, Johannesburg, South Africa.*

784. Captain ARCHIBALD BISSETT-SMITH, 10 March 1917, no known grave, killed at sea, Atlantic Ocean. *VC location: P & O Heritage Collection, London.*

785. Private CHRISTOPHER COX, 13–17 March 1917, buried Kings Langley Cemetery, Hertfordshire. *VC location: on loan to Imperial War Museum, London.*

786. Lieutenant FRANK McNAMARA, 20 March 1917, buried St Joseph's Priory, Gerrards Cross, Buckinghamshire. *VC location: Royal Air Force Museum, Hendon, London.*

787. Captain PERCY CHERRY, 26 March 1917, buried Queant Road Cemetery, Plot VIII, Row C, Grave 10; Buissy, France. *VC location: Australian War Memorial, Canberra, Australia.*

788. Lieutenant FREDERICK HARVEY, 27 March 1917, buried Union Cemetery, Fort McLeod, Alberta, Canada. *VC location: Lord Strathcona's Horse Museum, Calgary, Alberta, Canada.*

789. Private JOERGAN (sometimes spelt **JORGEN**) **JENSEN**, 2 April 1917, buried West Terrace AIF Cemetery, Light Oval Section-4 West, Grave 3; Adelaide, South Australia. *VC location: Australian War Memorial, Canberra, Australia.*

790. Major FREDERICK LUMSDEN, 3/4 April 1917, buried Berles New Military Cemetery, Plot III, Row D, Grave 1; Berles-au-Bois, France. *VC location: Royal Marines Museum, Southsea, Portsmouth, Hampshire.*

791. Sergeant WILLIAM GOSLING, 5 April 1917, buried St John's & St Helen's Churchyard Cemetery Extension, Wroughton, Wiltshire. *VC location: not publicly held.*

792. Captain JAMES NEWLAND, 7–9 and 15 April 1917, buried East Brighton General Cemetery, Methodist Section, Compartment G, Grave 174A; Melbourne, Victoria, Australia. *VC location: Australian War Memorial, Canberra, Australia.*

793. Captain THAIN MacDOWELL, 9 April

1917, buried Oakland Cemetery, Anglican Section 3, Lot 112; Brockville, Ontario, Canada. *VC location: University of Toronto Memorial Trust, Toronto, Ontario, Canada.*

794. Sergeant HARRY CATOR, 9 April 1917, buried Sprowston Cemetery, Church Lane, Norwich. *VC location: Ashcroft Collection.*

795. Sergeant JOHN WHITTLE, 9 April 1917, buried Rookwood Cemetery, RC Section 15, Grave 63; Sydney, New South Wales, Australia. *VC location: Australian War Memorial, Canberra, Australia.*

796. Lance Sergeant ELLIS SIFTON, 9 April 1917, buried Lichfield Crater Cemetery, Thelus, near Arras, France. *VC location: Elgin County Pioneer Museum, St Thomas, Ontario, Canada.*

797. Lance Corporal THOMAS BRYAN, 9 April 1917, buried Arksey Cemetery, Section J, Grave 237; Station Road, Arksey, Doncaster, Yorkshire. *VC location: Ashcroft Collection.*

798. Private THOMAS KENNY, 9 April 1917, buried Botany Cemetery (aka Eastern Suburbs Cemetery), RC Section 3, Grave 441; Matraville, Sydney, New South Wales, Australia. *VC location: Australian War Memorial, Canberra, Australia.*

799. Private WILLIAM MILNE, 9 April 1917, no known grave, killed at Vimy, France. *VC location: Canadian Museum of Civilization, Hull, Quebec, Canada.*

800. Private JOHN PATTISON, 10 April 1917, buried La Chaudiere Military Cemetery, Plot VI, Row C, Grave 14; France. *VC location: Glenbow Museum, Calgary, Alberta, Canada.*

801. Private HORACE WALLER, 10 April 1917, buried Cojeul British Cemetery, Row C, Grave 55; St-Martin-sur-Cojeul, near Arras, France. *VC location: not publicly held.*

802. Lieutenant DONALD MacKINTOSH, 11 April 1917, buried Brown's Copse Cemetery, Plot II, Row C, grave 49; near Arras, France. *VC location: Highlanders Museum, Fort George, Ardersier, Inverness-shire, Scotland.*

803. Lance Corporal HAROLD MUGFORD,

11 April 1917, ashes scattered at Southend Crematorium, Garden of Remembrance; Sutton Road, Southend, Essex. *VC location: on loan to theImperial War Museum, London.*

804. Corporal JOHN CUNNINGHAM, 12 April 1917, buried Barlin Communal Cemetery, Plot II, Row A, Grave 39; near Bethune, France. *VC location: Imperial War Museum, London.*

805. Sergeant JOHN ORMSBY, 14 April 1917, buried Dewsbury Cemetery, Section R, Grave 718; Ravenshouse Road, Dewsbury, Yorkshire. *VC location: King's Own Yorkshire Light Infantry Museum, Doncaster.*

806. Lieutenant CHARLES POPE, 15 April 1917, buried Moeuvres Communal Cemetery Extension, Plot V, Row D, Grave 22; France. *VC location: Australian War Memorial, Canberra, Australia.*

807. Private ERNEST SYKES, 19 April 1917, buried Lockwood Cemetery, Section F, Grave 227; Meltham Road, Meltham, near Huddersfield, Yorkshire. *VC location: Royal Northumberland Fusiliers Museum, Alnwick Castle, Alnwick, Northumberland.*

808. Private CHARLES MELVIN, 21 April 1917, buried Kirriemuir Cemetery, Brechin Road, Angus, Scotland. *VC location: Black Watch Museum, Balhousie Castle, Perth, Scotland.*

809. Lieutenant JOHN GRAHAM, 22 April 1917, ashes interred at Morton Hall Crematorium, in front of Memorial Cross; Howden Hall Road, Edinburgh, Scotland. *VC location: Argyll and Sutherland Highlanders Museum, Stirling, Scotland.*

810. Acting Captain ARTHUR HENDERSON, 23 April 1917, buried Cojeul British Cemetery, Row B, Grave 61; St-Martin-sur-Cojeul, near Arras, France. *VC location: Ashcroft Collection.*

811. Acting Captain DAVID HIRSCH, 23 April 1917, no known grave, killed near Wancourt, France. *VC location: Green Howards Museum, Richmond, Yorkshire.*

812. Corporal EDWARD 'TINY' FOSTER, 24 April 1917, buried Streatham Cemetery, Block 15, Grave 357; Garratt Lane, London. *VC location: Ashcroft Collection.*

813. Temporary Captain ALBERT 'PILL' BALL, 25 April–6 May 1917, buried Annoeullin Communal Cemetery, German Extension, Grave 643; Annoeullin, France. *VC location: Sherwood Foresters Museum, The Castle, Nottingham.*

814. Company Sergeant Major EDWARD BROOKS, 28 April 1917, buried Rose Hill Cemetery, Plot G-2, Grave 119; Oxford. *VC location: Royal Green Jackets Museum, Winchester, Hampshire.*

815. Second Lieutenant REGINALD HAINE, 28/29 April 1917, ashes scattered at Chichester Crematorium, Garden of Remembrance; Westhampnett Road, Chichester, Sussex. *VC location: on loan to the Imperial War Museum, London.*

816. Second Lieutenant ALFRED POLLARD, 29 April 1917, ashes scattered at Bournemouth Crematorium, Garden of Remembrance; Strouden Avenue, Dorset. *VC location: Honourable Artillery Company, London.*

817. Lance Corporal JAMES WELCH, 29 April 1917, ashes interred North Cemetery, Section 9, Row F, Grave 18; Strouden Avenue, Bournemouth, Dorset. *VC location: Royal Gloucestershire, Berkshire and Wiltshire Regiment Museum, Salisbury, Wiltshire.*

818. Lieutenant WILLIAM SANDERS, 30 April 1917, no known grave, killed at sea, off Southern Ireland, Atlantic Ocean. *VC location: Auckland War Memorial Museum, Auckland, New Zealand.*

819. Lieutenant ROBERT COMBE, 3 May 1917, no known grave, killed south of Acheville, France. *VC location: Saskatchewan Archives, Regina, Saskatchewan, Canada.*

820. Second Lieutenant JOHN HARRISON, 3 May 1917, no known grave, killed at Oppy, France. *VC location: Prince of Wales Yorkshire Regiment Museum, York.*

821. Corporal GEORGE JARRATT, 3 May 1917, no known grave, killed near Pelves, France. *VC location: Royal Fusiliers Museum, Tower of London.*

822. Corporal GEORGE 'SNOWY' HOWELL, 6 May 1917, ashes at Karrakatta Crematorium, Garden of Remembrance; Railway Road, Hollywood, Perth, Western Australia. *VC location: Australian War Memorial, Canberra, Australia.*

823. Private MICHAEL HEAVISIDE, 6 May 1917, buried St Thomas's Churchyard, Craghead, Co. Durham. *VC location: Durham Light Infantry Museum, Co. Durham.*

824. Lieutenant RUPERT 'MICK' MOON, 12 May 1917, buried Mount Duneed Cemetery, C of E Section; Victoria, Australia. *VC location: Australian War Memorial, Canberra, Australia.*

825. Private TOM DRESSER, 12 May 1917, buried Thorntree Cemetery, RC Section, Grave 1901; family grave; Acklam Road, Middlesbrough. *VC location: Green Howards Museum, Richmond, Yorkshire.*

826. Skipper JOSEPH WATT, 15 May 1917, buried Kirktown Cemetery, Fraserburgh, Scotland. *VC location: Ashcroft Collection.*

827. Sergeant ALBERT WHITE, 19 May 1917, no known grave, killed at Monchy-le-Preux, Arras, France. *VC location: not publicly held.*

828. Captain WILLIAM 'BILLY' BISHOP, 2 June 1917, ashes interred Greenwood Cemetery, Owen Sound, Ontario, Canada. *VC location: Canadian War Museum, Ottawa, Ontario, Canada.*

829. Second Lieutenant THOMAS MAUFE, 4 June 1917, buried Ilkley Cemetery, Row A, Grave 768; Yorkshire. *VC location: not publicly held.*

830. Second Lieutenant JOHN CRAIG, 5 June 1917, ashes interred Comrie Cemetery, family plot; near Crieff, Tayside Region, Scotland. *VC location: not publicly held.*

831. Captain ROBERT GRIEVE, 7 June 1917, buried Springvale Cemetery, Presbyterian Section; Melbourne, Victoria, Australia. *VC location: on loan from his family to the Shrine of Remembrance, Melbourne, Victoria, Australia.*

832. Lieutenant RONALD STUART, 7 June 1917, buried Charing Cemetery, Kent. *VC location: on permanent loan to the National Maritime Museum, Greenwich, London.*

833. Lance Corporal SAMUEL FRICKLETON, 7 June 1917, buried Taita Servicemen's Cemetery, Plot 1188; Naena, near Wellington, New Zealand. *VC location: National Army Museum, State Highway 1,Waiouru, New Zealand.*

834. Seaman WILLIAM WILLIAMS, 7 June 1917, buried Amlwch Cemetery, Section 6, Grave 36; Burwen Road, Isle of Anglesey, Wales. *VC location: National Museum of Wales, Cardiff, Wales.*

835 Private JOHN CARROLL, 7–12 June 1917, buried Karrakatta Cemetery, RC Section KA, Plot 658; Railway Road, Hollywood, Perth, Western Australia. *VC location: Australian War Memorial, Canberra, Australia.*

836. Private WILLIAM RATCLIFFE, 14 June 1917, buried Allerton Cemetery, RC Section 19, Grave 274; Woolton Road, Liverpool. *VC location: Imperial War Museum, London.*

837. Second Lieutenant JOHN DUNVILLE, 24/25 June 1917, buried Villers-Faucon Communal Cemetery, Row A, Grave 21; France. *VC location: Household Cavalry Museum, London.*

838. Second Lieutenant FRANK WEARNE, 28 June 1917, no known grave, killed east of Loos, France. *VC location: Ashcroft Collection.*

839. Second Lieutenant FREDERICK YOUENS, 7 July 1917, buried Railway Dugouts Burial Ground, Plot I, Row O, Grave 3; near Ypres, Belgium. *VC location: Durham Light Infantry Museum, Co. Durham.*

840. Private THOMAS BARRATT, 27 July 1917, buried Essex Farm Cemetery, Plot I, Row Z, Grave 8; Boesinghe, Belgium. *VC location: Staffordshire Regiment Museum, Lichfield.*

841. Temporary Brigadier General CLIFFORD COFFIN, 31 July 1917, buried Holy Trinity Churchyard, Colemans Hatch, East Sussex. *VC location: Royal Engineers Museum, Gillingham, Kent.*

842. Temporary Lieutenant Colonel BERTRAM BEST-DUNKLEY, 31 July 1917, buried Mendinghem Military Cemetery, Plot III, Row D, Grave 1; Belgium. *VC location: Lancashire Fusiliers Museum, Arts and Craft Centre, Bury, Lancashire.*

843. Acting Captain THOMAS COLYER-FERGUSSON, 31 July 1917, buried Menin Road South Military Cemetery, Plot II, Row E, Grave 1; near Ypres, Belgium. *VC location: Northamptonshire Regiment Museum, Northampton.*

844. Second Lieutenant DENNIS HEWITT, 31 July 1917, no known grave, killed near St-Julien, Ypres, Belgium. *VC location: not publicly held.*

845. Sergeant ROBERT BYE, 31 July 1917, buried Warsop Cemetery, Grave 2129; Church Warsop, Mansfield, Nottinghamshire. *VC location: Welsh Guards RHQ, Wellington Barracks, London.*

846. Sergeant ALEXANDER EDWARDS, 31 July 1917, no known grave, killed at Bapaume, Somme, France. He has a memorial at Bay 8, Arras Cemetery. *VC location: Highlanders Museum, Fort George, Ardersier, Inverness-shire, Scotland.*

847. Sergeant IVOR REES, 31 July 1917, ashes scattered at Morriston Crematorium, Garden of Remembrance no. 5; Swansea, West Glamorgan, Wales. *VC location: South Wales Borderers Museum, Brecon, Powys, Wales.*

848. Lance Sergeant TOM MAYSON, 31 July 1917, buried St Mary's Churchyard, Whicham, near Silecroft, Cumbria. *VC location: St Mary's Church, Whicham, Cumbria.*

849. Corporal LESLIE ANDREW, 31 July 1917, buried Levin RSA Cemetery, Returned Servicemen's Section, Row 13; Trio Trio Road, Palmerston North, New Zealand. *VC location: National Army Museum, State Highway 1, Waiouru, New Zealand.*

850. Corporal JAMES DAVIES, 31 July 1917, buried Canada Farm Cemetery, Plot II, Row B, Grave 18; near Ypres, Belgium. *VC location: Royal Welch Fusiliers Museum, Caernarfon Castle, Gwynedd, Wales.*

851. Private GEORGE McINTOSH, 31 July 1917, buried New Cemetery, Buckie, Banff, Scotland. *VC location: Ashcroft Collection.*

852. Private THOMAS WHITHAM, 31 July 1917, buried Inghamite Burial Ground, Section 10, Grave 114; Wheatley Lane,

Nelson, Lancashire. *VC location: Townley Hall Museum, Burnley, Lancashire.*

853. Temporary Captain HAROLD ACKROYD, 31 July/1 August 1917, buried in Birr Cross Road Cemetery, headstone reads 'Believed to be buried in this cemetery'; Zillebeke, Belgium. *VC location: Ashcroft Collection.*

854. Captain NOEL CHAVASSE, date of Bar action, 31 July–2 August 1917 (for VC action see **744**), buried Brandhoek New Military Cemetery, Plot III, Row B, Grave 15; Vlamertinghe, near Ypres, Belgium. *VC and Bar location: Ashcroft Collection*

855. Private WILLIAM BUTLER, 6 August 1917, buried Hunslet Cemetery, Section 3, Grave 48; Middleton Road, Leeds. *VC location: Ashcroft Collection.*

856. Lieutenant CHARLES BONNER, 8 August 1917, ashes interred St Mary's Churchyard, Aldridge, near Walsall, Staffordshire. *VC location: not publicly held.*

857. Petty Officer ERNEST PITCHER, 8 August 1917, buried Northbrook Cemetery, Plot F, Grave 122; Northbrook Road, Swanage, Dorset. *VC location: Ashcroft Collection.*

858. Private ARNOLD LOOSEMORE, 11 August 1917, buried Ecclesall Churchyard, in the Johnson family plot; Sheffield, Yorkshire. *VC location: not publicly held.*

859. Skipper THOMAS CRISP, 15 August 1917, no known grave, killed at sea, off Jim Howe Bank, North Sea. *VC location: Waveney District Council, Lowestoft. It can be viewed by request to the Chief Executive. A replica is on display in Lowestoft Town Hall.*

860. Private MICHAEL O'ROURKE, 15–17 August 1917, buried Forest Lawn Cemetery, Abray Section, Grave 6-13-3; Prince Edward Avenue, Vancouver, British Columbia, Canada. *VC location: British Columbia Regiment Museum, Vancouver, British Columbia, Canada.*

861. Acting Company Quartermaster Sergeant WILLIAM GRIMBALDESTON, 16 August 1917, ashes scattered at Pleasington Crematorium, Plot G; Tower Road, Blackburn, Lancashire. *VC location: King's*

Own Scottish Borderers Museum, Berwick-upon-Tweed, Northumberland.*

862. Sergeant EDWARD COOPER, 16 August 1917, ashes scattered at Teesside Crematorium, Garden of Remembrance; Acklam Road, Cleveland, Middlesbrough. *VC location: Preston Hall Museum, Eaglescliffe, Stockton-on Tees.*

863. Acting Lance Corporal FREDERICK ROOM, 16 August 1917, buried Greenbank Cemetery, Section 41-Pink-K; Greenbank Road, Bristol. *VC location: National Army Museum, London.*

864. Private HARRY BROWN, 16 August 1917, buried Noeux-les-Mines Communal Cemetery, Plot 11, Row J, Grave 29; near Lens, France. *VC location: Canadian War Museum, Ottawa, Ontario, Canada.*

865. Private WILFRED EDWARDS, 16 August 1917, buried Upper & Lower Wortley Cemetery, Section M, Grave 42; Green Hill Road, Leeds. *VC location: on loan from the York Castle Museum to The Kings Own Yorkshire Light Infantry Museum, Doncaster.*

866. Acting Major OKILL LEARMONTH, 18 August 1917, buried Noeux-les-Mines Communal Cemetery, Plot 11, Row K, Grave 9; near Lens, France. *VC location: Governor General's Foot Guards Museum, Ottawa, Ontario, Canada.*

867. Company Sergeant Major JOHN SKINNER, 18 August 1917, buried Vlamertinghe New British Cemetery, Plot XVI, Row H, Grave 15; near Ypres, Belgium. *VC location: King's Own Scottish Borderers Museum, Berwick-upon-Tweed, Northumberland.*

868. Sergeant FREDERICK HOBSON, 18 August 1917, no known grave, killed at Lens, France. *VC location: Canadian War Museum, Ottawa, Ontario, Canada.*

869. Second Lieutenant MONTAGUE MOORE, 20 August 1917, ashes scattered in the Serengeti National Park, Tanzania and the Hyaena Dam, Nairobi National Park, Kenya. *VC location: Ashcroft Collection..*

870. Temporary Second Lieutenant HARDY PARSONS, 20/21 August 1917, buried

Villers-Faucon Communal Cemetery, Row A, Grave 16; France. *VC location: Soldiers of Gloucestershire Museum, Gloucester.*

871. Company Sergeant Major ROBERT HANNA, 21 August 1917, buried Masonic Cemetery, Plot 49, Section C, Grave 2; Burnaby, British Columbia, Canada. *VC location: not publicly held.*

872. Acting Corporal FILIP KONOWAL, 22–24 August 1917, buried Notre Dame de Lourdes Cemetery, Section A, Lot 502; Montreal Road, Ottawa, Ontario, Canada. *VC location: stolen in 1973 but recovered in 2004 and now in the Canadian War Museum, Ottawa, Ontario, Canada.*

873. Corporal SIDNEY DAY, 26 August 1917, buried Milton Cemetery, Plot R, Row 11, Grave 6; Milton Road, Portsmouth, Hampshire. *VC location: not publicly held.*

874. Sergeant JOHN CARMICHAEL, 8 September 1917, buried New Monkland (Landward) Cemetery, Condorrat Road, Airdrie, Lanarkshire, Scotland. *VC location: Staffordshire Regiment Museum, Lichfield.*

875. Lance Sergeant JOHN MOYNEY, 12/13 September 1917, buried Roscrea RC Cemetery, Abbey Street, Co. Tipperary, Ireland. *VC location: Irish Guards RHQ, Wellington Barracks, London.*

876. Private THOMAS WOODCOCK, 12/13 September 1917, buried Douchy-les-Ayette British Cemetery, Plot IV, Row F, Grave 3; France. *VC location: Irish Guards RHQ, Wellington Barracks, London.*

877. Private REGINALD INWOOD, 19–22 September 1917, buried West Terrace AIF Cemetery, Light Oval, 5-N 1E; Adelaide, South Australia. *VC location: Adelaide Town Hall, South Australia.*

878. Captain HENRY REYNOLDS, 20 September 1917, buried St Giles' Churchyard, Ashtead, Surrey. *VC location: Royal Scots Regiment Museum, Edinburgh, Scotland.*

879. Second Lieutenant FREDERICK BIRKS, 20 September 1917, buried Perth Cemetery (China Wall), Plot I, Row G, Grave 45; Zillebeke, near Ypres, Belgium. *VC location: Australian War Memorial, Canberra, Australia.*

880. Second Lieutenant HUGH COLVIN, 20 September 1917, buried Carnmoney Cemetery, Prince Charles Way, Newtonabbey, Bangor, Co. Down, Northern Ireland. *VC location: Cheshire Regiment Museum, Chester, Cheshire.*

881. Sergeant WILLIAM BURMAN, 20 September 1917, ashes scattered at Golders Green Crematorium, Garden of Remembrance; Hoop Lane, London. *VC location: Imperial War Museum, London.*

882. Sergeant ALFRED KNIGHT, 20 September 1917, buried Oscott College Road Cemetery, Section 2B, Grave 328A; Oscott College Road, Sutton Coldfield, Birmingham. *VC location: British Post Museum and Archives, London.*

883. Lance Corporal WILLIAM HEWITT, 20 September 1917, ashes scattered at sea, off Hermanus Cliffs, 40 miles east of Cape Town, South Africa. *VC location: on loan to the Imperial War Museum, London.*

884. Lance Corporal WALTER PEELER, 20 September 1917, buried Brighton Cemetery, Lawn Section, Grave 36, Compartment H; Melbourne, Victoria, Australia. *VC location: Australian War Memorial, Canberra, Australia.*

885. Corporal ERNEST EGERTON, 20 September 1917, buried St Peter's Churchyard, Cheadle Road, Blythe Bridge, Staffordshire. *VC location: Sherwood Foresters Museum, The Castle, Nottingham.*

886. Acting Lance Corporal JOHN HAMILTON, 25/26 September 1917, ashes scattered at Daldowie Crematorium, Garden of Remembrance; Hamilton Road, Broomhouse, Glasgow, Scotland. *VC location: National War Museum of Scotland, Edinburgh Castle, Scotland.*

887. Sergeant JOHN DWYER, 26 September 1917, buried Allonah Cemetery, Cornelian Bay, Hobart, Tasmania, Australia. *VC location: Australian War Memorial, Canberra, Australia.*

888. Private PATRICK BUGDEN, 26–28 September 1917, buried Hooge Crater Cemetery, Plot VII, Row C, Grave 5; near Ypres, Belgium. *VC location: Queensland*

Museum, Brisbane, Queensland, Australia.
889. Temporary Lieutenant Colonel PHILIP BENT, 1 October 1917, no known grave, killed at Polygon Wood, Belgium.
VC location: Royal Leicestershire Regiment Museum, Leicester.
890. Acting Lieutenant Colonel LEWIS EVANS, 4 October 1917, buried Llanbadarn Churchyard, Cardiganshire, Wales. His headstone is unusual in that the letters VC do not appear after his name. *VC location: Ashcroft Collection.*
891. Captain CLEMENT ROBERTSON, 4 October 1917, buried Oxford Road Cemetery, Plot III, Row F, Grave 7; near Ypres, Belgium. *VC location: not publicly held.*
892. Sergeant CHARLES COVERDALE, 4 October 1917, buried Edgerton Cemetery, Section 5G, Grave 105; Cemetery Road, Huddersfield, Yorkshire. *VC location: not publicly held.*
893. Sergeant LEWIS McGEE, 4 October 1917, buried Tyne Cot Cemetery, Plot XX, Row D, Grave 1; near Ypres, Belgium. *VC location: Queen Victoria Museum, Launceston, Tasmania, Australia.*
894. Sergeant JAMES OCKENDON (spelt **OCKENDEN** on his VC), 4 October 1917, ashes interred at Portchester Crematorium, North Border Post – Plot 20; Upper Cornaway Lane, Fareham, Portsmouth, Hampshire. *VC location: not publicly held.*
895. Acting Corporal FRED GREAVES, 4 October 1917, ashes scattered at Brimington Crematorium, Garden of Remembrance; Chesterfield Road, Brimington, near Chesterfield, Derbyshire. *VC location: Sherwood Foresters Museum, The Castle, Nottingham.*
896. Private ARTHUR HUTT, 4 October 1917, ashes scattered at Canley Crematorium, Garden of Remembrance; London Road, Coventry. *VC location: not publicly held.*
897. Private THOMAS SAGE, 4 October 1917, buried Tiverton Cemetery, Section - XB; Park Road, Tiverton, Devon.
VC location: not publicly held.
898. Sergeant JOSEPH LISTER, 9 October 1917, buried Willow Grove Cemetery, Section

P, Grave 9931; Reddish, Stockport, Cheshire.
VC location: Ashcroft Collection.
899. Sergeant JOHN MOLYNEUX, 9 October 1917, ashes scattered at St Helens Crematorium, Garden of Remembrance; Rainford Road, St Helens, Lancashire.
VC location: Royal Fusiliers Museum, Tower of London.
900. Lance Sergeant JOHN RHODES, 9 October 1917, buried Rocquigny-Equancourt Road British Cemetery, Plot III, Row E, Grave 1; France. *VC location: Grenadier Guards RHQ, Wellington Barracks, London.*
901. Corporal WILLIAM CLAMP, 9 October 1917, no known grave, killed at Poelcapelle, Belgium. *VC location: Green Howards Museum, Richmond, Yorkshire.*
902. Private FREDERICK 'DANDO' DANCOX, 9 October 1917, no known grave, killed at Masnieres, France. *VC location: Worcestershire Regiment Museum, Worcester.*
903. Captain CLARENCE JEFFRIES, 12 October 1917, buried Tyne Cot Cemetery, Plot XL, Row E, Grave 1; near Ypres, Belgium. *VC location: Warriors' Chapel, Christchurch Cathedral, Newcastle, New South Wales, Australia.*
904. Private ALBERT HALTON, 12 October 1917, ashes interred at Lancaster & Morecambe Crematorium, Plot 38/6; Powderhouse Lane, Lancaster. *VC location: King's Own Regiment Museum, Lancaster.*
905. Acting Captain CHRISTOPHER O'KELLY, 26 October 1917, no known grave, believed to have drowned at Lac Seul, Ontario, Canada. *VC location: Canadian War Museum, Ottawa, Ontario, Canada.*
906. Lieutenant ROBERT SHANKLAND, 26 October 1917, ashes interred at Mountain View Cemetery, Prince Edward Avenue, Vancouver, British Columbia, Canada.
VC location: Canadian War Museum, Ottawa, Ontario, Canada.
907. Private THOMAS HOLMES, 26 October 1917, buried Greenwood Cemetery, Owen Sound, Ontario, Canada.
VC location: unknown. Original stolen from him in 1935; an official replacement issued in

the same year was stolen in 1987 but later recovered.

908. Major ALEXANDER LAFONE, 27 October 1917, buried Beersheba War Cemetery, Row Q, Grave 7; Israel. *VC location: Dulwich College, London.*

909. Lieutenant HUGH McKENZIE, 30 October 1917, no known grave, killed at Meescheele Spur, Belgium. *VC location: original destroyed in a fire in 1955. The official replacement is in the Princess Patricia's Canadian Light Infantry Museum, Calgary, Alberta, Canada.*

910. Sergeant GEORGE MULLIN, 30 October 1917, buried Moosomin South Side Cemetery, Legion Plot; Saskatchewan, Canada. *VC location: Princess Patricia's Canadian Light Infantry Museum, Calgary, Alberta, Canada.*

911. Private CECIL KINROSS, 30 October 1917, buried Lougheed Cemetery, Soldiers' Plot; Alberta, Canada. *VC location: with recipient's family.*

912. Acting Major GEORGE PEARKES, 30/31 October 1917, buried Holy Trinity Cemetery, Section 4 - West; West Saanich, Sydney, Victoria, British Columbia, Canada. *VC location: Canadian War Museum, Ottawa, Ontario, Canada.*

913. Acting Corporal JOHN COLLINS, 31 October 1917, buried Pant Cemetery, Merthyr Tydfil, Mid-Glamorgan, Wales. *VC location: Royal Welch Fusiliers Museum, Caernarfon Castle, Gwynedd, Wales.*

914. Captain JOHN RUSSELL, 6 November 1917, buried Beersheba War Cemetery, Row F, Grave 31; Israel. *VC location: Army Medical Services Museum, Mytchett, Surrey.*

915. Corporal COLIN BARRON, 6 November 1917, buried Prospect Cemetery, Veterans' Section 7, Grave 3562; Toronto, Ontario, Canada. *VC location: not publicly held.*

916. Private JAMES ROBERTSON, 6 November 1917, buried Tyne Cot Cemetery, Plot LVIII, Row D, Grave 26; Ypres, Belgium. *VC location: with recipient's family.*

917. Lieutenant Colonel ARTHUR 'BOSKY' BORTON, 7 November 1917, buried Hunton Churchyard, West Street, Hunton, Kent.

VC location: Queen's Royal Surrey Regiment Museum, Guildford, Surrey.

918. Ordinary Seaman JOHN CARLESS, 17 November 1917, no known grave, killed at sea, off Heligoland, North Sea. *VC location: Walsall City Council, West Midlands.*

919. Acting Lieutenant Colonel JOHN 'BOMB' SHERWOOD-KELLY, 20 November 1917, buried Brookwood Cemetery, Plot 86, Grave 196296; Cemetery Pales, Woking, Surrey. *VC location: National Museum of Military History, Johannesburg, South Africa.*

920. Captain RICHARD WAIN, 20 November 1917, buried in unmarked grave, Marcoing, on the Hindenburg Line, France. *VC location: not publicly held.*

921. Lieutenant HARCUS STRACHAN, 20 November 1917, ashes interred at North Vancouver Crematorium, Rose Garden, Boal Vault; British Columbia, Canada. *VC location: not publicly held.*

922. Sergeant CHARLES SPACKMAN, 20 November 1917, ashes scattered at Swaythling Crematorium, Garden of Remembrance; Bassett Green Road, Southampton, Hampshire. *VC location: not publicly held.*

923. Lance Corporal ROBERT McBEATH (spelt **MacBEATH** on his headstone), 20 November 1917, ashes interred Mountain View Cemetery, Masonic Section 193, Lot 6; Prince Edward Avenue, Vancouver, British Columbia, Canada. *VC location: Highlanders Museum, Fort George, Ardersier, Inverness-shire, Scotland.*

924. Private ALBERT SHEPHERD, 20 November 1917, buried Royston Cemetery, near Barnsley, Yorkshire. *VC location: Royal Green Jackets Museum, Winchester, Hampshire.*

925. Sergeant JOHN McAULAY, 27 November 1917, buried Eastwood New Cemetery, Section L-V11, Lair 139; Thorniebank Road, Glasgow, Scotland. *VC location: Royal Scots Guards RHQ, Wellington Barracks, London.*

926. Private GEORGE CLARE, 28/29 November 1917, no known grave, killed at

Bourlon Wood, France. *VC location: Queen's Royal Lancers Museum, Belvoir Castle, Grantham, Leicestershire.*

927. Temporary Lieutenant Colonel NEVILLE ELLIOTT-COOPER, 30 November 1917, buried Ohlsdorf Cemetery, Plot V, Row A, Grave 16; Hamburg, Germany. *VC location: Royal Fusiliers Museum, Tower of London.*

928. Temporary Captain ROBERT GEE, 30 November 1917, ashes scattered at Karrakatta Crematorium, Rose Garden; Perth, Western Australia. *VC location: Royal Fusiliers Museum, Tower of London.*

929. Acting Captain WALTER STONE, 30 November 1917, no known grave, killed at Moeuvres, near Cambrai, France. *VC location: not publicly held.*

930. Temporary Lieutenant SAMUEL WALLACE, 30 November 1917, buried Moffat Cemetery, right side of main gate; Dumfries & Galloway, Scotland. *VC location: Royal Artillery Museum, Woolwich, London.*

931. Sergeant CYRIL GOURLEY, 30 November 1917, buried Grange Cemetery, Section F, Plot 17; Blackhorse Hill, West Kirby, Wirral, Cheshire. *VC location: Royal Artillery Museum, Woolwich, London.*

932. Lance Corporal JOHN THOMAS, 30 November 1917, buried Stockport Borough Cemetery, Section LB, Grave 550; South Buxton Road, Manchester. *VC location: not publicly held.*

933. Acting Captain ALLASTAIR (spelt **ALASTAIR** on early records) **McREADY-DIARMID** (formerly **DREW**), 30 November/1 December 1917, no known grave, killed at Moeuvres, France. *VC location: National Army Museum, London.*

934. Acting Captain GEORGE PATON, 1 December 1917, buried Metz-en-Couture Cemetery, British Extension, Plot 11, Row E, Grave 24; France. *VC location: Grenadier Guards RHQ, Wellington Barracks, London.*

935. Second Lieutenant STANLEY BOUGHEY, 1 December 1917, buried Gaza War Cemetery, Plot XX, Row A, Grave 1; near Gaza Town, Israel. *VC location: not publicly held.*

936. Lance Dafadar GOBIND (spelt **GOVIND** on later records) **SINGH**, 1 December 1917, cremated Damoe Village, Jodhpur, India. *VC location: not publicly held.*

937. Acting Captain ARTHUR LASCELLES, 3 December 1917, buried Dourlers Communal Cemetery Extension, Plot 11, Row C, Grave 24; France. *VC location: Durham Light Infantry Museum, Co. Durham.*

938. Private HENRY NICHOLAS, 3 December 1917, buried Vertigneul Churchyard, Grave 15; Romieres, France. *VC location: Canterbury Museum, Christchurch, New Zealand.*

939. Temporary Second Lieutenant JAMES EMERSON, 6 December 1917, no known grave, killed near La Vacquerie, France. *VC location: not publicly held.*

940. Corporal CHARLES TRAIN, 8 December 1917, buried Forest Lawn Memorial Park, Field of Honour, Normandy Section, Lot 208, Grave 3; Gilpin Street, Burnaby, British Columbia, Canada. *VC location: London Scottish Regiment Museum, London.*

941. Private WALTER MILLS, 10/11 December 1917, buried Gorre British and Indian Cemetery, Plot V, Row C, Grave 2; near Bethune, France. *VC location: believed to have been buried with his daughter.*

942. Lance Corporal JOHN CHRISTIE, 21/22 December 1917, ashes scattered at Stockport Crematorium, First Garden of Remembrance; South Buxton Road, Manchester. *VC location: not publicly held.*

943. Temporary Captain JAMES McCUDDEN, 23 December 1917–2 February 1918, buried Wavans British Cemetery, Row B, Grave 10; France. *VC location: Royal Engineers Museum, Gillingham, Kent.*

944. Private JAMES DUFFY, 27 December 1917, buried Conwal Cemetery, Letterkenny, Co. Donegal, Ireland. *VC location: Royal Inniskilling Fusiliers Regiment Museum, Enniskillen, Northern Ireland.*

945. Lieutenant Commander GEOFFREY WHITE, 28 January 1918, no known grave, killed at sea, Dardanelles, near Kum Kale, Turkey. *VC location: not publicly held.*

946. Lance Corporal CHARLES ROBERTSON, 8/9 March 1918, buried Dorking Cemetery, Plot 36, Grave 360; Reigate Road, Dorking, Surrey. *VC location: Royal Fusiliers Museum, Tower of London.*

947. Private HAROLD WHITFIELD, 10 March 1918, buried Oswestry Cemetery, Plot W, Grave 26; Victoria Road, Oswestry, Shropshire. *VC location: King's Shropshire Light Infantry Museum, Shrewsbury, Shropshire.*

948. Temporary Lieutenant Colonel WILFRITH ELSTOB, 21 March 1918, no known grave, killed near Quentin, France. *VC location: Manchester Regiment Museum, The Town Hall, Ashton-under-Lyne.*

949. Temporary Captain MANLEY JAMES, 21 March 1918, ashes scattered at Canford Crematorium, on 'the Shrubbery'; Canford Lane, Bristol. *VC location: Ashcroft Collection.*

950. Lieutenant ALLAN KER, 21 March 1918, buried West Hampstead Cemetery, Section Q/4, Grave 7; Fortune Green Road, London. *VC location: Ashcroft Collection.*

951. Second Lieutenant JOHN BUCHAN, 21 March 1918, buried Roisel Communal Cemetery Extension, Plot II, Row I, Grave 6; France. *VC location: not publicly held.*

952. Second Lieutenant EDMUND de WIND, 21 March 1918, no known grave, killed near Groagie, France. *VC location: not publicly held.*

953. Lance Corporal JOHN SAYER, 21 March 1918, buried Le Cateau Military Cemetery, Plot I, Row B, Grave 59; near Le Cateau, France. *VC location: not publicly held.*

954. Gunner CHARLES STONE, 21 March 1918, buried Belper Cemetery, in his mother's grave; Matlock Road, Broadholme, Belper, Derbyshire. *VC location: Royal Artillery Museum, Woolwich, London.*

955. Acting Captain REGINALD HAYWARD, 21/22 March 1918, ashes scattered at Putney Vale Crematorium, Garden of Remembrance; Stag Lane, London. *VC location: Royal Gloucestershire, Berkshire & Wiltshire Regiment Museum, Salisbury, Wiltshire.*

956. Temporary Second Lieutenant ERNEST BEAL, 21/22 March 1918, no known grave, killed at St Leger, France. *VC location: Green Howards Museum, Richmond, Yorkshire.*

957. Temporary Second Lieutenant CECIL KNOX, 22 March 1918, ashes scattered at his home, Fyves Court, Nuneaton, Warwickshire. *VC location: not publicly held.*

958. Sergeant HAROLD JACKSON, 22 March 1918, buried AIF Burial Ground, Plot XV, Row A, Grave 21/30; Glas Lane, Flers, France. *VC location: not publicly held.*

959. Private HERBERT COLUMBINE, 22 March 1918, no known grave, killed at Hervilly Wood, France. *VC location: on loan to the Essex Regiment Museum, Clelmsford, Kent.*

960. Acting Lieutenant Colonel JOHN COLLINGS-WELLS, 22–27 March 1918, buried Bouzincourt Ridge Cemetery, Plot III, Row E, Grave 12; near Albert, France. *VC location: Bedfordshire and Hertfordshire Regiment Museum, Luton.*

961. Acting Lieutenant Colonel FRANK ROBERTS, 22 March–2 April 1918, ashes interred at Bretby Churchyard, family plot; Burton-on-Trent, Staffordshire. *VC location: Worcestershire Regiment Museum, Worcester.*

962. Lieutenant Colonel CHRISTOPHER BUSHELL, 23 March 1918, buried Querrieu British Cemetery, Row E, Grave 6; France. *VC location: Queen's Royal Surrey Regiment Museum, Guildford.*

963. Temporary Captain JULIAN GRIBBLE, 23 March 1918, buried Niederzehren Cemetery, Plot III, Row F, Grave 4; Kessel, Hessen State, Germany. *VC location: destroyed in a fire at his brother's home in 1958. As far as is known, no official replacement has ever been requested by the family.*

964. Temporary Second Lieutenant ALFRED HERRING, 23/24 March 1918, ashes scattered at Woking Crematorium, Garden of Remembrance; Hermitage Road, St John's, Woking, Surrey. *VC location: HQ RLC Museum, Princess Royal Barracks, Deepcut, Surrey.*

965. Corporal JOHN DAVIES, 24 March 1918, buried St Helens Borough Cemetery,

Rainford Road, Lancashire. *VC location: Imperial War Museum, London.*

966. Acting Lieutenant Colonel WILLIAM ANDERSON, 25 March 1918, buried Peronne Road Cemetery, Plot II, Row G, Grave 36; France. *VC location: Imperial War Museum, London.*

967. Acting Captain ALFRED TOYE, 25 March 1918, buried Tiverton Cemetery, Section XF, Grave 36; Park Road, Tiverton, Devon. *VC location: National Army Museum, London.*

968. Lance Corporal ARTHUR CROSS, 25 March 1918, buried Streatham Park Cemetery (aka Streatham Vale Cemetery), Plot E, Square 27, Grave 885; Rowan Road, London. *VC location: not publicly held.*

969. Private THOMAS YOUNG (real name **MORRELL**), 25–31 March 1918, buried St Patrick's Cemetery, High Spen, Co. Durham. *VC location: Durham Light Infantry Museum, Co. Durham.*

970. Sergeant ALBERT MOUNTAIN, 26 March 1918, ashes at Lawnswood Crematorium, Garden of Remembrance, Plot K2-380; Otley Road, Leeds. *VC location: Prince of Wales's Regiment Museum, York.*

971. Second Lieutenant BASIL HORSFALL, 27 March 1918, no known grave, killed near Ablainzeville, France. *VC location: Queen's Lancashire Regiment Museum, Preston, Lancashire.*

972. Second Lieutenant ALAN 'BABE' McLEOD, 27 March 1918, buried Winnipeg Presbyterian Cemetery (aka Old Kildonan Cemetery), Grave 238; Canada. *VC location: Canadian War Museum, Ottawa, Ontario, Canada.*

973. Acting Lieutenant Colonel OLIVER WATSON, 28 March 1918, no known grave, killed at Rossignol Wood, France. *VC location: Green Howards Museum, Richmond, Yorkshire.*

974. Second Lieutenant BERNARD CASSIDY, 28 March 1918, no known grave, killed at Fampoux, Arras, France. *VC location: Ashcroft Collection.*

975. Sergeant STANLEY McDOUGALL, 28 March 1918, ashes interred at Norwood Cemetery, Mitchell, Canberra, Australia. *VC location: Australian War Memorial, Canberra, Australia.*

976. Lieutenant GORDON FLOWERDEW, 30 March 1918, buried Namps-au-Val British Cemetery, Plot I, Row H, Grave 1; France. *VC location: on loan to the Imperial War Museum, London.*

977. Lieutenant ALAN JERRARD, 30 March 1918, ashes interred Uxbridge and Hillingdon Cemetery; Kingston Lane, Middlesex. *VC location: Ashcroft Collection.*

978. Chaplain THEODORE HARDY, 5, 25 and 27 April 1918, buried St Sever Cemetery Extension, Block S, Plot V, Row J, Grave 1; Rouen, France. *VC location: Museum of Army Chaplaincy, Amport, near Andover, Hampshire.*

979. Lieutenant PERCY STORKEY, 7 April 1918, ashes at South-West Middlesex Crematorium, Lawn 3-B3; Hounslow Road, Hanworth. *VC location: National Army Museum, State Highway 1, Waiouru, New Zealand.*

980. Second Lieutenant JOSEPH COLLIN, 9 April 1918, buried Vieille-Chapelle New Military Cemetery, Plot III, Row A, Grave 11; near Bethune, France. *VC location: King's Own Regiment Museum, Lancaster.*

981. Temporary Second Lieutenant JOHN SCHOFIELD, 9 April 1918, buried Vieille-Chapelle New Military Cemetery, Plot III, Row C, Grave 8; near Bethune, France. *VC location: Lancashire Fusiliers Museum, Arts and Craft Centre, Bury, Lancashire.*

982. Private RICHARD MASTERS, 9 April 1918, buried St Cuthbert's Parish Churchyard, Churchtown, Southport, Lancashire. *VC location: HQ RLC Museum, Princess Royal Barracks, Deepcut, Surrey.*

983. Acting Captain ERIC DOUGALL, 10 April 1918, buried in Westoutre British Cemetery (headstone reads 'Known to be buried in this cemetery'); Belgium. *VC location: Pembroke College, Cambridge.*

984. Rifleman KARANBAHADUR RANA, 10 April 1918, buried Bharse Gulmi, Litung, Baghlung District, Nepal. *VC location: Gurkha Museum, Winchester, Hampshire.*

985. Private ARTHUR POULTER, 10 April 1918, buried New Wortley Cemetery, Grave 2500; Tong Road, Leeds. *VC location: Duke of Wellington Regiment Museum, Halifax, Yorkshire.*

986. Acting Captain THOMAS PRYCE, 11 April 1918, no known grave, killed at Vieux Berquin, France. *VC location: Grenadier Guards RHQ, Wellington Barracks, London.*

987. Acting Lieutenant Colonel JAMES FORBES-ROBERTSON, 11/12 April 1918, buried Cheltenham Cemetery, Section E1, Grave 717; Bouncers Lane, Gloucestershire. *VC location: Border Regiment Museum, Carlisle, Cumbria.*

988. Second Lieutenant JOHN CROWE, 14 April 1918, ashes scattered at Downs Crematorium, Garden of Remembrance; Bear Road, Brighton, Sussex. *VC location: Worcestershire Regiment Museum, Worcester.*

989. Private JACK COUNTER, 16 April 1918, ashes interred St Saviour's Churchyard, First Tower, St Helier, Jersey, Channel Islands. *VC location: Jersey Museum, St Helier, Channel Islands.*

990. Lance Sergeant JOSEPH WOODALL, 22 April 1918, buried Dean's Grange Cemetery, St Patrick's Plot, Block H, Grave 173 (grave reused; name on headstone is now Joseph King); Dun Laoghaire, Co. Dublin, Ireland. *VC location: Imperial War Museum, London.*

991. Captain EDWARD BAMFORD, 22/23 April 1918, buried Bubbling Road Cemetery (cemetery levelled and now a shopping centre), Nanjing Road, Shanghai, China. *VC location: Royal Marines Museum, Southsea, Portsmouth, Hampshire.*

992. Captain ALFRED CARPENTER, 22/23 April 1918, ashes scattered at Gloucester Crematorium, Garden of Remembrance; Coney Hill Road, Gloucester. *VC location: on loan to the Imperial War Museum, London.*

993. Lieutenant Commander GEORGE BRADFORD, 22/23 April 1918, buried Blankenberg Town Cemetery, Row A, Grave 5; Belgium. *VC location: Ashcroft Collection.*

994. Lieutenant Commander ARTHUR HARRISON, 22/23 April 1918, no known grave, killed at Zeebrugge, Belgium. *VC location: Britannia Royal Naval College, Dartmouth, Devon.*

995. Lieutenant PERCY DEAN, 22/23 April 1918, ashes scattered at Golders Green Crematorium, Garden of Remembrance; Hoop Lane, London. *VC location: Ashcroft Collection.*

996. Lieutenant RICHARD 'BALDY' SANDFORD, 22/23 April 1918, buried Eston Cemetery, Section J, Plot U, Grave 709; Normanby Road, near Middlesbrough. *VC location: Britannia Royal Naval College, Dartmouth, Devon.*

997. Sergeant NORMAN FINCH, 22/23 April 1918, ashes scattered at South Stoneham Crematorium, Section 3; Mansbridge Road, Swaythling, Hampshire. *VC location: Royal Marine Museum, Southsea, Portsmouth, Hampshire.*

998. Able Seaman ALBERT McKENZIE, 22/23 April 1918, buried Camberwell Old Cemetery, Square 65, Grave 25538; Forest Hill Road, London. *VC location: on loan from his family to the Imperial War Museum, London.*

999. Lieutenant VICTOR CRUTCHLEY, 22/23 April and 9/10 May 1918, buried St Mary's Churchyard, Powerstock, Dorset. *VC location: on loan to the National Museum of the Royal Navy, Portsmouth.*

1000. Lieutenant CLIFFORD SADLIER, 24/25 April 1918, ashes scattered at sea, in the Indian Ocean. *VC location: St George's Cathedral, Perth, Western Australia.*

1001. Lance Corporal JAMES HEWITSON, 26 April 1918, buried Coniston Churchyard, Cumbria. *VC location: not publicly held.*

1002. Lieutenant GEORGE McKEAN, 27/28 April 1918, buried Brighton Extra-Mural Cemetery (aka Lewis Road Cemetery), Lewis Road, Brighton, Sussex. *VC location: Canadian War Museum, Ottawa, Ontario, Canada.*

1003. Private ROBERT CRUICKSHANK, 1 May 1918, ashes interred at Blaby, near Leicester. *VC location: London Scottish Regiment Museum, London.*

1004. Sergeant WILLIAM GREGG, 6 May 1918, ashes scattered at Heanor Crematorium, Garden of Remembrance; Derbyshire. *VC location: Royal Green Jackets Museum, Winchester, Hampshire.*

1005. Private WILLIAM BEESLEY, 8 May 1918, buried St Paul's Cemetery, Harbrook Lane, Coventry. *VC location: Royal Green Jackets Museum, Winchester, Hampshire.*

1006. Lieutenant ROWLAND (sometimes spelt **ROLAND) BOURKE**, 9/10 May 1918, buried Royal Oak Burial Park, Section O, Plot 10, Grave 16; Falaise Drive, Victoria, British Columbia, Canada. *VC location: National Archives of Canada, Ottawa, Ontario, Canada.*

1007. Lieutenant GEOFFREY DRUMMOND, 9/10 May 1918, buried St Peter's Church Cemetery, Row J, Grave 13; Church Lane, Chalfont St Peter, Buckinghamshire. *VC location: Ashcroft Collection.*

1008. Sergeant WILLIAM RUTHVEN, 19 May 1918, ashes interred at Fawkner Crematorium, Garden of Remembrance; Victoria, Australia. *VC location: Australian War Memorial, Canberra, Australia.*

1009. Temporary Brigadier General GEORGE GROGAN, 27 May 1918, ashes scattered at Woking Crematorium, Garden of Remembrance; Woking, Surrey. *VC location: on loan to the Imperial War Museum, London.*

1010. Lance Corporal JOEL HALLIWELL, 27 May 1918, buried Boarshaw New Cemetery (aka Middleton Cemetery), Section 10, Grave 106; Middleton, Lancashire. *VC location: with recipient's family, but may go on loan to the Lancashire Fusiliers Museum, Arts and Craft Centre, Bury, Lancashire.*

1011. Corporal JOSEPH KAEBLE, 8/9 June 1918, buried Wanquentin Communal Cemetery Extension, Plot II, Row A, Grave 8; France. *VC location: Royal 22nd Regiment Museum, Quebec City, Canada.*

1012. Lieutenant Colonel CHARLES HUDSON, 15 June 1918, buried Denbury Churchyard, near Newton Abbot, Devon. *VC location: Sherwood Foresters Museum, The Castle, Nottingham.*

1013. Lieutenant JOHN YOULL, 15 June 1918, buried Giavera British Cemetery, Plot I, Row H, Grave 2; near Treviso, Italy. *VC location: Ashcroft Collection.*

1014. Major EDWARD 'MICK' MANNOCK, 17 June–22 July 1918, possibly buried Laventie British War Cemetery as 'An Unknown British Airman', Plot III, Row F, Grave 12; France. *VC location: Ashcroft Collection.*

1015. Corporal PHILIP DAVEY, 28 June 1918, buried West Terrace AIF Cemetery, Adelaide, South Australia. *VC location: Australian War Memorial, Canberra, Australia.*

1016. Lance Corporal THOMAS AXFORD, 4 July 1918, ashes interred at Karrakatta Crematorium, Portion M, Row C, Niche 1; Railway Road, Hollywood, Perth, Western Australia. *VC location: Australian War Memorial, Canberra, Australia.*

1017. Driver HENRY DALZIEL, 4 July 1918, ashes scattered at Mount Thompson Crematorium, Garden of Remembrance; Brisbane, Queensland, Australia. *VC location: Australian War Memorial, Canberra, Australia.*

1018. Corporal WALTER BROWN, 6 July 1918, no known grave, killed at Singapore, Malaysia. *VC location: Australian War Memorial, Canberra, Australia.*

1019. Lieutenant ALBERT BORELLA (name changed to **CHALMERS-BORELLA** in 1939), 17/18 July 1918, buried Presbyterian Cemetery, North Albury, Victoria, Australia. *VC location: with recipient's family.*

1020. Sergeant JOHN MEIKLE, 20 July 1918, buried Marfaux British Cemetery, Plot VIII, Row C, Grave 1; France. *VC location: Dingwall Museum Trust, Dingwall, Ross-shire, Scotland.*

1021. Sergeant RICHARD TRAVIS (born **DICKSON CORNELIUS SAVAGE**), 24 July 1918, buried Couin New British Cemetery, Row G, Grave 5; France. *VC location: Southland Museum, Invercargill, New Zealand.*

1022. Lieutenant HAROLD AUTEN, 30 July 1918, buried Sandhill Cemetery, in the Steele family plot; Bushkill, Pennsylvania, USA. *VC location: Royal Naval Museum, Portsmouth, Hampshire.*

1023. Lieutenant ALFRED GABY, 8 August 1918, buried Heath Cemetery, Plot V, Row E, Grave 14; Harbonnieres, France. *VC location: Tasmanian Museum and Art Gallery, Hobart, Tasmania, Australia.*

1024. Corporal HERMAN GOOD, 8 August 1918, buried St Alban's Cemetery, Bathurst, New Brunswick, Canada. *VC location: Canadian War Museum, Ottawa, Ontario, Canada.*

1025. Corporal HERBERT MINER, 8 August 1918, buried Crouy British Cemetery, Plot V, Row B, Grave 11; Somme, France. *VC location: Huron County Museum, Goderich, Ontario, Canada.*

1026. Private JOHN CROAK (or CROKE), 8 August 1918, buried Hangard Wood British Cemetery, Plot I, Row A, Grave 9; France. *VC location: Canadian War Museum, Ottawa, Ontario, Canada.*

1027. Lieutenant JEAN BRILLANT, 8/9 August 1918, buried Villers-Bretonneux Military Cemetery, Plot VIa, Row B, Grave 20; Fouilloy, France. *VC location: Royal 22nd Regiment Museum, Quebec City, Canada.*

1028. Lieutenant JAMES TAIT, 8–11 August 1918, possibly buried Fouquescort British Cemetery, Grave 8 (headstone reads 'Believed to be buried in this cemetery'); France. *VC location: Glenbow Museum, Calgary, Alberta, Canada.*

1029. Acting Captain ANDREW BEAUCHAMP-PROCTOR (born PROCTOR), 8 August–8 October 1918, buried Mafeking Cemetery, European Section, Grave 1050-2; South Africa. *VC location: not publicly held.*

1030. Sergeant THOMAS HARRIS, 9 August 1918, buried Dernancourt Communal Cemetery Extension, Plot VIII, Row J, Grave 20; near Albert, France. *VC location: Queen's Own Royal West Kent Regiment Museum, Maidstone, Kent.*

1031. Sergeant RAPHAEL ZENGEL, 9 August 1918, buried Pine Cemetery, Rocky Mountain House, Alberta, Canada. His headstone is unusual in that instead of the letters 'VC' it bears the words 'Victoria Cross' after his name. *VC location: Rocky Mountain House Legion, Alberta, Canada.*

1032. Corporal FREDERICK COPPINS, 9 August 1918, cremated Chapel of the Chimes Crematorium, Oakland, California, USA. *VC location: Royal Winnipeg Rifles, Winnipeg, Canada.*

1033. Acting Corporal ALEXANDER BRERETON, 9 August 1918, buried Elnora Cemetery, Alberta, Canada. His headstone is unusual in that instead of the letters 'VC' it bears the words 'Victoria Cross' after his name. *VC location: Ashcroft Collection.*

1034. Private ROBERT BEATHAM, 9 August 1918, buried Heath Cemetery, Plot VII, Row J, Grave 13; Harbonnieres, France. *VC location: Queensland Museum, Brisbane, Queensland, Australia.*

1035. Captain FERDINAND WEST, 10 August 1918, buried Holy Trinity Churchyard, Sunningdale, Berkshire. His headstone is unusual in that the letters VC do not appear after his name. *VC location: Imperial War Museum, London.*

1036. Sergeant PERCY STATTON, 12 August 1918, ashes interred at Cornelian Bay Crematorium, Garden of Remembrance; Hobart, Tasmania, Australia. *VC location: Australian War Memorial, Canberra, Australia.*

1037. Private THOMAS DINESEN, 12 August 1918, buried Horsholm Cemetery, Ringsted, near Kobenave, Denmark. His headstone is unusual in that the letters VC do not appear after his name. *VC location: not publicly held.*

1038. Sergeant ROBERT SPALL, 13 August 1918, no known grave, killed at Parvillers, France. *VC location: Princess Patricia's Canadian Light Infantry Museum, Calgary, Alberta, Canada.*

1039. Lance Sergeant EDWARD 'NED' SMITH, 21–23 August 1918, buried Beuvry Communal Cemetery Extension, Plot I, Row B, Grave 7; near Bethune, France. *VC location: Ashcroft Collection.*

1040. Acting Lieutenant Colonel RICHARD WEST, 21 August and 2 September 1918, buried Mory Abbey Military Cemetery, Plot III, Row G, Grave 4; near Bapaume, France. *VC location: Ashcroft Collection.*

1041. Temporary Commander DANIEL BEAK, 21–25 August and 4 September 1918, buried in unmarked grave, Brookwood Cemetery, St Gabriel's Avenue, Grave 222960; Cemetery Pales, Woking, Surrey. *VC location: Ashcroft Collection.*

1042. Lance Corporal GEORGE ONIONS, 22 August 1918, buried Quinton Cemetery, Section 6, Grave 7364; Halesowen Road, Birmingham. *VC location: Devonshire Regiment Museum, Dorchester, Dorset.*

1043. Lieutenant WILLIAM JOYNT, 23 August 1918, buried Brighton Lawn Cemetery, Victoria, Australia. *VC location: not publicly held.*

1044. Lieutenant LAWRENCE 'FATS' McCARTHY, 23 August 1918, ashes interred at Springvale Crematorium, Section C, Plot 015; Melbourne, Victoria, Australia. *VC location: Australian War Memorial, Canberra, Australia.*

1045. Private HUGH McIVER, 23 August 1918, buried Vracourt Copse Cemetery, Plot I, Row A, Grave 19; France. *VC location: Royal Scots Museum, Edinburgh Castle, Scotland.*

1046. Sergeant SAMUEL FORSYTH, 24 August 1918, buried Adanac Military Cemetery, Plot I, Row 1, Grave 39; France. *VC location: Ashcroft Collection.*

1047. Temporary Lieutenant DAVID MacINTYRE, 24–27 August 1918, ashes scattered at Warriston Crematorium, Garden of Remembrance; Warriston Road, Edinburgh, Scotland. *VC location: National War Museum of Scotland, Edinburgh Castle, Scotland.*

1048. Acting Sergeant HAROLD COLLEY, 25 August 1918, buried Mailly Wood Cemetery, Plot II, Row Q, Grave 4; near Albert, France. *VC location: Lancashire Fusiliers Museum, Arts and Craft Centre, Bury, Lancashire.*

1049. Lieutenant CHARLES RUTHERFORD, 26 August 1918, buried Union Cemetery, Colbourne, Ontario, Canada. *VC location: not publicly held.*

1050. Sergeant REGINALD JUDSON, 26 August 1918, buried Waikumete Cemetery, Soldiers' Block M, Section 13, Plot 69; Auckland, New Zealand. *VC location: National Army Museum, State Highway 1, Waiouru, New Zealand.*

1051. Lance Corporal HENRY WEALE, 26 August 1918, buried Maeshyfryd Cemetery, Section 10, Grave 4829; Dyserth Road, Denbighshire, Wales. *VC location: Royal Welch Fusiliers Museum, Caernarfon Castle, Gwynedd, Wales.*

1052. Lance Corporal BERNARD GORDON, 26/27 August 1918, ashes interred at Pinaroo Lawn Cemetery, Albany, Queensland, Australia. *VC location: bought at auction by Kerry Stokes in 2006 and donated to the Australian War Memorial, Canberra, Australia.*

1053. Lieutenant Colonel WILLIAM CLARK-KENNEDY, 27/28 August 1918, buried Mount Royal Cemetery, Pine Hill Section, Lot 258; Montreal, Quebec, Canada. *VC location: with recipient's family.*

1054. Lieutenant CECIL SEWELL, 29 August 1918, buried Vaulx Hill Cemetery, Plot I, Row D, Grave 3; near Bapaume, France. *VC location: Royal Tank Regiment Museum, Bovington, Dorset.*

1055. Second Lieutenant JAMES HUFFAM, 31 August 1918, ashes scattered at Golders Green Crematorium, Garden of Remembrance; Hoop Lane, London. *VC location: not publicly held.*

1056. Private GEORGE CARTWRIGHT, 31 August 1918, cremated Northern Suburbs Crematorium, Sydney, New South Wales, Australia. *VC location: Imperial War Museum, London.*

1057. Lieutenant EDGAR TOWNER, 1 September 1918, buried Longreach Town Cemetery, Queensland, Australia. *VC location: not publicly held.*

1058. Sergeant JOHN GRANT, 1 September 1918, buried Golders Cemetery, Block M, Section 9, Plot 95; Waikumete, New Zealand. *VC location: National Army Museum, State Highway 1, Waiouru, New Zealand.*

1059. Sergeant ALBERT LOWERSON, 1 September 1918, buried Myrtleford

Cemetery, Victoria, Australia. *VC location: Australian War Memorial, Canberra, Australia.*

1060. Private WILLIAM CURREY, 1 September 1918, ashes interred at Woronora Crematorium, Columbarium; Sydney, New South Wales, Australia. *VC location: Australian War Memorial, Canberra, Australia.*

1061. Private ROBERT MacTIER, 1 September 1918, buried Hem Farm Cemetery, Plot II, Row J, Grave 3; near Peronne, Hem-Monacu, France. *VC location: Australian War Memorial, Canberra, Australia.*

1062. Corporal ARTHUR HALL, 1/2 September 1918, buried St Matthew's Anglican Churchyard, West Bogan, Coolabahs, New South Wales, Australia. *VC location: Australian War Memorial, Canberra, Australia.*

1063. Temporary Corporal ALEXANDER BUCKLEY, 1/2 September 1918, buried Peronne Communal Cemetery Extension, Plot II, Row C, Grave 32; St Radegonde, France. *VC location: Australian War Memorial, Canberra, Australia.*

1064. Private CLAUDE NUNNEY, 1/2 September 1918, buried Aubigny Communal Cemetery Extension, Plot IV, Row B, Grave 39; France. *VC location: Cornwall Armoury, Cornwall, Ontario, Canada.*

1065. Lieutenant Colonel CYRUS PECK, 2 September 1918, ashes interred at New Westminster Crematorium, Range 23, Block 54, Lot B; Vancouver, British Columbia, Canada. *VC location: Canadian War Museum, Ottawa, Ontario, Canada.*

1066. Captain BELLENDEN HUTCHESON, 2 September 1918, buried Rosehill Cemetery, Section B, Lot 145, Grave C; Mount Carmel, Illinois, USA. His headstone is unusual in that the letters VC do not appear after his name. *VC location: Fort York Armoury, Toronto, Ontario, Canada.*

1067. Chief Petty Officer GEORGE PROWSE, 2 September 1918, no known grave, killed at Arleux, France. *VC location: Ashcroft Collection.*

1068. Company Sergeant Major MARTIN DOYLE, 2 September 1918, buried Grangegorman Cemetery (aka Blackhorse Cemetery), Blackhorse Avenue, near McKee Barracks, Dublin, Ireland. *VC location: Ashcroft Collection.*

1069. Acting Sergeant ARTHUR KNIGHT, 2 September 1918, buried Dominion Cemetery, Plot I, Row F, Grave 15; France. *VC location: Glenbow Museum, Calgary, Alberta, Canada.*

1070. Lance Sergeant ARTHUR EVANS (aka **WALTER SIMPSON**), 2 September 1918, ashes interred Park Cemetery, Regent Avenue, Lytham-St-Annes, Lancashire. *VC location: not publicly held.*

1071. Lance Corporal WILLIAM METCALF, 2 September 1918, buried Bayside Cemetery, Section D, Plot 11-NW; Eastport, Maine, USA. *VC location: Canadian Scottish Regiment Museum, Victoria, British Columbia, Canada.*

1072. Temporary Corporal LAWRENCE WEATHERS, 2 September 1918, buried Unicorn Cemetery, Plot III, Row C, Grave 5; Vendhuille, France. *VC location: not publicly held.*

1073. Private JACK HARVEY, 2 September 1918, buried Redhill Cemetery, Section C, Grave 2359; Redhill, Surrey. *VC location: Ashcroft Collection.*

1074. Private JOHN YOUNG, 2 September 1918, buried Mount Royal Cemetery, Section L/2, Plot 2019; Montreal, Quebec, Canada. *VC location: Canadian War Museum, Ottawa, Ontario, Canada.*

1075. Private WALTER RAYFIELD, 2–4 September 1918, buried Prospect Cemetery, Veterans' Plot, Section 7, Grave 4196; Toronto, Ontario, Canada. *VC location: Canadian War Museum, Ottawa, Ontario, Canada.*

1076. Corporal JOHN McNAMARA, 3 September 1918, buried Romeries Cemetery Extension, Plot IV, Row D, Grave 17; France. *VC location: Royal Surrey Regiment Museum, Guildford, Surrey.*

1077. Private SAMUEL NEEDHAM, 10/11 September 1918, buried Kantara War Memorial Cemetery, Row E, Grave 181; East Kantara, Egypt. *VC location: Bedfordshire and Hertfordshire Regiment Museum, Luton.*

1078. Sergeant LAURENCE CALVERT, 12 September 1918, ashes in South Essex Crematorium, Garden of Remembrance; Ockendon Road, Upminster, Essex. *VC location: Ashcroft Collection.*

1079. Sergeant HARRY LAURENT, 12 September 1918, ashes interred at Servicemen's Cemetery, Memorial Wall; Hawera, Taraniki, New Zealand. *VC location: National Army Museum, State Highway 1, Waiouru, New Zealand.*

1080. Lance Corporal ALFRED WILCOX, 12 September 1918, buried in St Peter & St Paul Parish Churchyard (headstone reads 'Buried near this spot'); High Street, Coleshill, Birmingham. *VC location: Ashcroft Collection.*

1081. Corporal DAVID HUNTER, 16/17 September 1918, buried Dunfermline Cemetery, Division E, Grave 7510; Masterton Road, Fife, Scotland. *VC location: Royal Highland Fusiliers Museum, Glasgow, Scotland.*

1082. Temporary Lieutenant Colonel DANIEL BURGES, 18 September 1918, cremated Arnos Vale Crematorium, Bath Road, Knowle, Bristol. *VC location: Soldiers of Gloucestershire Museum, Gloucester.*

1083. Second Lieutenant FRANK YOUNG, 18 September 1918, buried Hermies Hill British Cemetery, Plot III, Row B, Grave 5; France. *VC location: Bedfordshire and Hertfordshire Regiment Museum, Luton.*

1084. Temporary Second Lieutenant WILLIAM 'CHALKY' WHITE, 18 September 1918, ashes interred St John's Churchyard, Grave 506; Hildenborough, Kent. *VC location: Ashcroft Collection.*

1085. Sergeant MAURICE BUCKLEY (aka **GERALD SEXTON**), 18 September 1918, buried Brighton Cemetery, RC Section, Grave 114; Melbourne, Victoria, Australia. *VC location: Australian War Memorial, Canberra, Australia.*

1086. Lance Sergeant WILLIAM WARING, 18 September 1918, buried Ste Marie Cemetery, Division LXII, Row V-1, Grave 3; Le Havre, France. *VC location: Welshpool Town Council, Powys, Wales.*

1087. Private JAMES WOODS, 18 September 1918, buried Karrakatta Cemetery, Wesleyan Section H-A, Plot 1; Railway Road, Hollywood, Perth, Western Australia. *VC location: Australian War Memorial, Canberra, Australia.*

1088. Lance Corporal LEONARD LEWIS, 18 and 21 September 1918, no known grave, killed near Lempire, France. *VC location: not publicly held.*

1089. Ressaidar BADLU SINGH, 23 September 1918, cremated at Khes Samariveh, Palestine. *VC location: Ashcroft Collection.*

1090. Lieutenant JOHN BARRETT, 24 September 1918, ashes at Gilroes Crematorium, in 'the Glade'; Groby Road, Leicester. *VC location: Royal Leicestershire Regiment Museum, Leicester.*

1091. Temporary Lieutenant DONALD DEAN, 24–26 September 1918, ashes interred in St John the Baptist Churchyard, Tunstall, Kent. *VC location: not publicly held.*

1092. Acting Lieutenant Colonel JOHN GORT, 27 September 1918, buried in family vault at St John the Baptist Church, Penshurst, Kent. *VC location: not publicly held.*

1093. Acting Captain CYRIL FRISBY, 27 September 1918, buried Brookwood Cemetery, St Chad's Avenue, Plot 28, Grave 219662; Cemetery Pales, Woking, Surrey. *VC location: Coldstream Guards RHQ, Wellington Barracks, London.*

1094. Lieutenant SAMUEL HONEY, 27 September 1918, buried Queant Communal Cemetery, British Extension, Row C, Grave 36; France. *VC location: Canadian War Museum, Ottawa, Ontario, Canada.*

1095. Lieutenant GEORGE KERR, 27 September 1918, buried Mount Pleasant Cemetery, Plot 14, Section 36, Lot 6-E-1/2; Inglewood Drive, Toronto, Ontario, Canada. *VC location: Canadian War Museum, Ottawa, Ontario, Canada.*

1096. Corporal THOMAS NEELY, 27 September 1918, buried Masnieres British Cemetery, Plot II, Row B, Grave 21; Marcoing, near Cambrai, France. *VC location: not publicly held.*

1097. Lance Corporal THOMAS JACKSON, 27 September 1918, buried Sanders Keep

Military Cemetery, Plot II, Row D, Grave 4; France. *VC location: Coldstream Guards RHQ, Wellington Barracks, London.*

1098. Lieutenant MILTON GREGG, 27 September–1 October 1918, buried Snider Mountain Baptist Church Cemetery, New Brunswick, Canada. *VC location: unknown. Medal stolen from the Royal Canadian Regiment Museum, London, Ontario, Canada in 1979.*

1099. Lieutenant GRAHAM LYALL, 27 September and 1 October 1918, buried Halfaya Sollum War Cemetery, Plot XIX, Row B, Grave 2; Egypt. *VC location: Royal Electrical & Mechanical Engineers Museum, Arborfield, near Reading.*

1100. Acting Sergeant LOUIS McGUFFIE, 28 September 1918, buried Zantvoorde British Cemetery, Plot I, Row D, Grave 12; Belgium. *VC location: King's Own Scottish Borderers Museum, Berwick-upon-Tweed, Northumberland.*

1101. Private HENRY TANDY (sometimes spelt **TANDEY**), 28 September 1918, ashes scattered at the site of his VC action, Marcoing, France. *VC location: Green Howards Museum, Richmond, Yorkshire.*

1102. Acting Lieutenant Colonel BERNARD VANN, 29 September 1918, buried Bellicourt British Cemetery, Plot II, Row O, Grave 1; France. *VC location: Ashcroft Collection.*

1103. Lance Corporal ERNEST SEAMAN, 29 September 1918, no known grave, killed near Terhand, Belgium. *VC location: HQ RLC Museum, Princess Royal Barracks, Deepcut, Surrey.*

1104. Major BLAIR WARK, 29 September–1 October 1918, ashes interred at Woronga Crematorium, in Columbarium; Sydney, New South Wales, Australia. *VC location: Queensland Museum, Brisbane, Queensland, Australia.*

1105. Temporary Captain JOHN MacGREGOR, 29 September–3 October 1918, buried Cranberry Lake Cemetery, Powell River, British Columbia, Canada. *VC location: Canadian War Museum, Ottawa, Ontario, Canada..*

1106. Private JAMES CRICHTON, 30 September 1918, buried Waikumete Memorial Park Soldiers' Cemetery, Protestant Section, Block L, Section 4, Plot 9; near Auckland, New Zealand. *VC location: Auckland War Memorial Museum, Auckland, New Zealand.*

1107. Private EDWARD (commonly known as **JOHN) RYAN**, 30 September 1918, buried Springvale Cemetery, RC Section; Melbourne, Victoria, Australia. *VC location: Australian War Memorial, Canberra, Australia.*

1108. Temporary Lieutenant ROBERT GORLE, 1 October 1918, buried Stella Wood Cemetery, Section K, Grave 144; Durban, Natal, South Africa. *VC location: Ashcroft Collection.*

1109. Sergeant WILLIAM MERRIFIELD, 1 October 1918, buried West Korah Cemetery, Sault-Ste-Marie, Ontario, Canada. *VC location: Canadian War Museum, Ottawa, Ontario, Canada.*

1110. Sergeant FREDERICK RIGGS, 1 October 1918, no known grave, killed at Epinoy, France. *VC location: York and Lancaster Regiment Museum, Rotherham, Yorkshire.*

1111. Sergeant WILLIAM JOHNSON, 3 October 1918, buried Redhill Cemetery, Section L, Grave 6; Mansfield Road, Nottingham. *VC location: Sherwood Foresters Museum, The Castle, Nottingham.*

1112. Lieutenant JOSEPH MAXWELL, 3 October 1918, ashes scattered at Eastern Suburbs Crematorium, Garden of Remembrance; Botany Bay, Sydney, New South Wales, Australia. *VC location: original lost in a fire around 1936, official replacement is in the Australian War Memorial, Canberra, Australia.*

1113. Lance Corporal WILLIAM COLTMAN, 3/4 October 1918, buried St Mark's Parish Churchyard (aka Winshill Cemetery), Burton-on-Trent, Staffordshire. *VC location: Staffordshire Regiment Museum, Lichfield.*

1114. Lieutenant GEORGE INGRAM, 5 October 1918, buried Frankston Cemetery,

Methodist Section, Grave B-80; Victoria, Australia. *VC location: Australian War Memorial, Canberra, Australia.*

1115. Private JAMES TOWERS, 6 October 1918, ashes scattered at Preston Crematorium, on the Lawns; Longridge Road, Preston, Lancashire. *VC location: not publicly held.*

1116. Company Sergeant Major JOHN WILLIAMS, 7/8 October 1918, buried Ebbw Vale Cemetery, Waun-y-Pound Road, Gwent, Wales. His headstone is unusual in that instead of the letters 'VC' it bears the words 'Victoria Cross' after his name. *VC location: South Wales Borderers Museum, Brecon, Powys, Wales.*

1117. Captain COULSON MITCHELL, 8/9 October 1918, buried Field of Honour Cemetery; Section M, Grave 3051; Pointe Claire, Mount Royal, Quebec, Canada. *VC location: Canadian Military Engineers Museum, Gagetown, New Brunswick, Canada.*

1118. Private WILLIAM HOLMES, 9 October 1918, buried Carnieres Communal Cemetery Extension, Plot I, Row B, Grave 3; near Cambrai, France. *VC location: Grenadier Guards RHQ, Wellington Barracks, London.*

1119. Lieutenant WALLACE ALGIE, 11 October 1918, buried Niagara Cemetery, Row C, Grave 7; Iwuy, near Cambrai, France. *VC location: Ashcroft Collection.*

1120. Corporal FRANK LESTER, 12 October 1918, buried Neuvilly Communal Cemetery Extension, Row B, Grave 15; near Le Cateau, France. *VC location: Ashcroft Collection.*

1121. Corporal HARRY WOOD, 13 October 1918, buried Arnos Vale Cemetery, Soldiers' Corner, Grave 1738; Bath Road, Knowle, Bristol. *VC location: York Castle Museum, Yorkshire.*

1122. Second Lieutenant JAMES JOHNSON, 14 October 1918, ashes scattered at Efford Crematorium, Garden of Remembrance; Efford Road, Plymouth, Devon. *VC location: Royal Northumberland Fusiliers Museum, Alnwick Castle, Alnwick, Northumberland.*

1123. Corporal JAMES McPHIE, 14 October 1918, buried Naves Communal Cemetery Extension, Plot II, Row E, Grave 4; near Cambrai, France. *VC location: Imperial War Museum, London.*

1124. Private MARTIN MOFFAT, 14 October 1918, buried Sligo Town Cemetery, Co. Sligo, Ireland. *VC location: Ashcroft Collection.*

1125. Private THOMAS RICKETTS, 14 October 1918, buried Anglican Cemetery, Forest Road, St John's, Newfoundland, Canada. *VC location: Canadian War Museum, Ottawa, Ontario, Canada.*

1126. Sergeant JOHN O'NEILL (or O'NIELL), 14 and 20 October 1918, buried Holy Trinity Churchyard, Grave 8; Hoylake, Cheshire. *VC location: unknown. In 1962 the medal was stolen from Seaby & Co., London.*

1127. Acting Captain ROLAND ELCOCK, 15 October 1918, buried St Thomas's Churchyard (headstone may still exist); Dehra Dun, India. *VC location: Royal Scots Regiment Museum, Edinburgh, Scotland.*

1128. Sergeant HORACE CURTIS, 18 October 1918, ashes scattered at Penmount Crematorium, Newquay Road, Truro, Cornwall. *VC location: Ashcroft Collection.*

1129. Acting Sergeant JOHN DAYKINS, 20 October 1918, buried Castlewood Cemetery, Grave 1431; Jedburgh, Borders Region, Scotland. *VC location: York and Lancaster Regiment Museum, Rotherham, Yorkshire.*

1130. Private ALFRED WILKINSON, 20 October 1918, buried Leigh Cemetery, Plot 1-U, Grave 99; Manchester Road, Lancashire. *VC location: Ashcroft Collection.*

1131. Lieutenant DAVID McGREGOR, 22 October 1918, buried Stacegham Communal Cemetery, Row A, Grave 1; near Courtrai, Belgium. *VC location: Royal Scots Museum, Edinburgh Castle, Scotland.*

1132. Private FRANCIS MILES, 23 October 1918, buried St Peter's Parish Churchyard, Clearwell, Gloucestershire. *VC location: Ashcroft Collection.*

1133. Lieutenant Colonel HARRY GREENWOOD, 23/24 October 1918, buried Putney Vale Cemetery, Block N, Grave 71-C; Stag Lane, London. *VC location: King's Own*

Yorkshire Light Infantry Regiment Museum, Doncaster, South Yorkshire.

1134. Temporary Lieutenant FREDERICK HEDGES, 24 October 1918, cremated Stonefall Crematorium, Wetherby Road, Harrogate, Yorkshire. *VC location: Bedfordshire and Hertfordshire Regiment Museum, Luton.*

1135. Lieutenant WILLIAM BISSETT, 25 October 1918, ashes interred Aldershot Military Cemetery, Section Z; Gallwey Road, Aldershot, Hampshire. *VC location: Argyll and Sutherland Highlanders Museum, Stirling, Scotland.*

1136. Private NORMAN HARVEY, 25 October 1918, buried Khayat Beach War Cemetery, Plot A, Grave 4; Sharon, Israel. *VC location: Royal Inniskilling Fusiliers Museum, Enniskillen, Northern Ireland.*

1137. Acting Major WILLIAM BARKER, 27 October 1918, buried Mount Pleasant Cemetery, Crypt Room B, Crypt B; Inglewood Drive, Toronto, Ontario, Canada. *VC location: Canadian War Museum, Ottawa, Ontario, Canada.*

1138. Sergeant WILLIAM McNALLY, 27 and 29 October 1918, ashes scattered at Tyne & Wear Crematorium, Garden of Remembrance; Hylton Road, Sunderland, Co. Durham. *VC location: Ashcroft Collection.*

1139. Private WILFRED WOOD, 28 October 1918, ashes scattered at Stockport Crematorium, First Garden of Remembrance; Buxton Road, Cheshire. *VC location: not publicly held.*

1140. Sergeant THOMAS CALDWELL, 31 October 1918, ashes interred at Centennial Park Crematorium, Wall 104, Row E, Niche 12; Adelaide, South Australia. *VC location: Royal Highland Fusiliers Museum, Glasgow, Scotland.*

1141. Sergeant HUGH CAIRNS, 1 November 1918, buried Auberchicourt British Cemetery, Plot I, Row A, Grave 8; France. *VC location: Canadian War Museum, Ottawa, Ontario, Canada.*

1142. Sergeant JAMES CLARKE, 2 November 1918, buried Rochdale Cemetery, Section O/P, Grave 14155; Bury Road, Rochdale, Lancashire. *VC location: Ashcroft Collection.*

1143. Acting Lieutenant Colonel DUDLEY JOHNSON, 4 November 1918, buried Christ Church Churchyard, Church Crookham, Hampshire. *VC location: South Wales Borderers Museum, Brecon, Powys, Wales.*

1144. Acting Lieutenant Colonel JAMES MARSHALL, 4 November 1918, buried Ors Communal Cemetery, near Le Cateau, France. *VC location: Irish Guards RHQ, Wellington Barracks, London.*

1145. Acting Major GEORGE FINDLAY, 4 November 1918, buried Kilmarnock Churchyard, near Gartocham, Helensburgh, Renfrewshire, Scotland. *VC location: Royal Engineers Museum, Gillingham, Kent.*

1146. Acting Major ARNOLD WATERS, 4 November 1918, ashes at All Saints' Church, Garden of Remembrance; Streetly, Warwickshire. *VC location: Royal Engineers Museum, Gillingham, Kent.*

1147. Second Lieutenant JAMES KIRK, 4 November 1918, buried Ors Communal Cemetery, Row A, Grave 22; near Le Cateau, France. *VC location: Military Medal Museum, San Jose, California, USA. (Not on display)*

1148. Lance Corporal WILLIAM AMEY, 4 November 1918, buried Royal Leamington Spa Cemetery, Warwickshire. *VC location: Royal Warwickshire Regiment Museum, Warwick.*

1149. Sapper ADAM ARCHIBALD, 4 November 1918, ashes at Warriston Crematorium, Garden of Remembrance; Warriston Road, Edinburgh, Scotland. *VC location: Royal Engineers Museum, Gillingham, Kent.*

1150. Acting Major BRETT CLOUTMAN, 6 November 1918, ashes at Norfolk Cemetery, Plot I, Row A, Grave 14 (his brother's grave, Lieutenant Wolfred Cloutman), near Albert, Somme, France. *VC location: Royal Engineers Museum, Gillingham, Kent.*

1151. UNKNOWN AMERICAN SOLDIER of WW1, buried Arlington Cemetery, Virginia, USA. *VC location: Arlington National Cemetery, Virginia, USA.*

1152. Lieutenant AUGUSTUS AGAR, 17 June 1919, buried Alton Cemetery, Section R, Grave 238; Old Oldiham Road, Hampshire. *VC location: Imperial War Museum, London.*

1153. Corporal ARTHUR SULLIVAN, 10 August 1919, ashes interred at North Suburbs Crematorium, by a plaque at tree 267A; Sydney, New South Wales, Australia. *VC location: Australian War Memorial, Canberra, Australia.*

1154. Commander CLAUDE DOBSON, 18 August 1919, buried Woodlands Cemetery, Woodlands Road, Gillingham, Kent. *VC location: National Maritime Museum, Greenwich, London.*

1155. Lieutenant GORDON STEELE, 18 August 1919, buried All Saints New Cemetery, Winkleigh, Devon. *VC location: Trinity House, City of London.*

1156. Sergeant SAMUEL PEARSE, 29 August 1919, buried Archangel Allied Cemetery (aka Souset Cemetery), Special Memorial B, Grave 107; Russia. *VC location: not publicly held.*

1157. Temporary Captain HENRY ANDREWS, 22 October 1919, buried Bannu Cemetery, Grave 160 (headstone may still exist); south of Peshawar, North-West Frontier, Pakistan. *VC location: Ashcroft Collection*

1158. Lieutenant WILLIAM KENNY, 2 January 1920, buried Jandola Cemetery, Grave 5 (headstone may still exist); North-West Frontier, Pakistan. *VC location: Ashcroft Collection.*

1159. Captain GEORGE HENDERSON, 24 July 1920, no known grave, killed near Hillah (aka Hillahon), Mesopotamia. *VC location: on loan from the family to the Manchester Regiment Museum, The Town Hall, Ashton-under-Lyne.*

1160. Sepoy ISHAR SINGH, 10 April 1921, cremated Penam Village, Hoshiapur District, Punjab, India. *VC location: Ashcroft Collection.*

1161. Captain GODFREY MEYNELL, 29 September 1935, buried Guides Cemetery, Mardan, North-West Frontier, India. *VC location: not publicly held.*

1162. Commander JOHN 'TUBBY' LINTON, September 1939–March 1943, no known grave, killed in Maddelina Harbour, Sardinia, Italy. *VC location: Ashcroft Collection.*

1163. Lieutenant Commander GERARD 'RAMMER' ROOPE, 8 April 1940, no known grave, drowned in West Fjord, Norway. *VC location: not publicly held.*

1164. Captain BERNARD WARBURTON-LEE, 10 April 1940, buried Ballangen New Cemetery, British Section, Plot IV, Row B, Grave 9; Norway. *VC location: not publicly held.*

1165. Lieutenant RICHARD STANNARD, 28 April–2 May 1940, ashes scattered at Rockwood Crematorium, Garden of Remembrance. Sydney, New South Wales, Australia. *VC location: not publicly held.*

1166. Flying Officer DONALD GARLAND, 12 May 1940, buried Heverlee War Cemetery, Plot VI, Row F, Grave 14-16 (buried with Sergeant Thomas Gray); near Louvain, Belgium. *VC location: Royal Air Force Museum, Hendon, London.*

1167. Sergeant THOMAS GRAY, 12 May 1940, buried Heverlee War Cemetery, Plot VI, Row F, Grave 14-16 (buried with Flying Officer Donald Garland); near Louvain, Belgium. *VC location: not publicly held.*

1168. Second Lieutenant RICHARD 'DICKIE' or 'JAKE' ANNAND, 15/16 May 1940, cremated Durham City Crematorium, South Road, Co. Durham. *VC location: Ashcroft Collection.*

1169. Lieutenant CHRISTOPHER FURNESS, 17–24 May 1940, no known grave, killed near Arras, France. *VC location: Welsh Guards RHQ, Wellington Barracks, London.*

1170. Company Sergeant Major GEORGE GRISTOCK, 21 May 1940, buried Bear Road Cemetery, War Graves Section, Plot ZGL, Grave 28; Bear Road, Brighton, Sussex. *VC location: Royal Norfolk Regiment Museum, Norwich.*

1171. Lance Corporal HARRY NICHOLLS, 21 May 1940, buried Wilford Hill Cemetery (aka Southern Cemetery), Section L, Grave 34; Loughborough Road, West Bridgford,

Nottingham. *VC location: Grenadier Guards RHQ, Wellington Barracks, London.*

1172. Captain HAROLD ERVINE-ANDREWS, 31 May/1 June 1940, ashes scattered on the garden at his home, Trevor Cottage, Gorran, Cornwall. *VC location: Blackburn Museum, Blackburn, Lancashire.*

1173. Squadron Leader GEOFFREY CHESHIRE, June 1940–July 1944, buried Cavendish Churchyard, opposite Cavendish Parish Church, near Sudbury, Suffolk. *VC location: Imperial War Museum, London.*

1174. Acting Leading Seaman JACK MANTLE, 4 July 1940, buried Portland Royal Naval Cemetery, C of E Section, Grave 672; Portland, Dorset. *VC location: on loan to The Royal Naval Museum, Portsmouth, Hampshire.*

1175. Acting Captain ERIC WILSON, 11–15 August 1940, buried St Mary Magdalene Churchyard, Stowell, near Sherbourne, Somerset. *VC location: Ashcroft Collection.*

1176. Flight Lieutenant RODERICK LEAROYD, 12 August 1940, ashes interred at Worthing Crematorium, Garden of Remembrance, Plot 35/34; Horsham Road, Findon, Sussex. *VC location: Ashcroft Collection.*

1177. Flight Lieutenant ERIC 'NICK' NICOLSON, 16 August 1940, no known grave, killed at sea, off Calcutta, India. *VC location: Royal Air Force Museum, Hendon, London.*

1178. Sergeant JOHN HANNAH, 15 September 1940, buried St James's Churchyard, east side of churchyard; Birstall, Leicestershire. *VC location: Royal Air Force Museum, Hendon, London.*

1179. Acting Captain EDWARD FEGEN, 5 November 1940, no known grave, killed at sea, Atlantic Ocean. *VC location: not publicly held.*

1180. Second Lieutenant PREMINDRA SINGH BHAGAT, 31 January–4 February 1941, ashes scattered in various rivers in India. *VC location: Bombay Engineers Museum, Kirkee, Pune, India.*

1181. Subadar RICHHPAL (sometimes spelt **RICHPAL**) **RAM**, 7/8 February 1941, cremated near Keren, Eritrea. *VC location: not publicly held.*

1182. Flying Officer KENNETH CAMPBELL, 6 April 1941, buried Brest (Kerfautras) Cemetery, Plot XL, Row I, Grave 10; Lanbezellec, France. *VC location: 22 Squadron Royal Air Force.*

1183. Corporal JOHN 'JACK' EDMONDSON, 13/14 April 1941, buried Tobruk War Cemetery, Plot III, Row J, Grave 8; Libya. *VC location: Australian War Memorial, Canberra, Australia.*

1184. Sergeant JOHN HINTON, 28/29 April 1941, buried Ruru Lawn Cemetery, Returned Servicemen's League Section; Christchurch, New Zealand. *VC location: National Army Museum, State Highway 1, Waiouru, New Zealand.*

1185. Petty Officer ALFRED SEPHTON, 18 May 1941, buried at sea, off Alexandria, Mediterranean Sea. *VC location: unknown. Medal stolen from Coventry Cathedral in 1990.*

1186. Sergeant NIGEL LEAKEY, 19 May 1941, no known grave, killed near Billate River, Colito, Abyssinia, now Ethiopia. *VC location: with recipient's family.*

1187. Sergeant ALFRED HULME, 20–28 May 1941, buried Dudley Cemetery, Civilian Section; Vercre Drive, Te Puke, New Zealand. *VC location: National Army Museum, State Highway 1, Waiouru, New Zealand.*

1188. Second Lieutenant CHARLES 'PUG' UPHAM, 22–30 May 1941 (for Bar action see **1219**), ashes interred St Paul's Churchyard, Papanui, Christchurch, New Zealand. *VC and Bar location: National Army Museum, State Highway 1, Waiouru, New Zealand.*

1189. Lieutenant Commander MALCOLM 'WANKS' WANKLYN, 24 May 1941, no known grave, killed at sea, Gulf of Tripoli. *VC location: not publicly held.*

1190. Lieutenant ARTHUR CUTLER, 19 June–6 July 1941, buried South Head Cemetery, Vaucluse, Sydney, New South Wales, Australia. *VC location: Australian War Memorial, Canberra, Australia.*

1191. Pilot Officer HUGHIE EDWARDS, 4 July 1941, ashes interred Karrakatta

Cemetery, Welsh Free Church Portion;
Railway Road, Hollywood, Perth, Western
Australia. *VC location: Australian War
Memorial, Canberra, Australia.*
1192. Sergeant JAMES WARD, 7 July 1941,
buried Ohlsdorf Cemetery, Plot A, Row A-1,
Grave 9; Hamburg, Germany. *VC location:
Auckland War Memorial Museum, New
Zealand.*
1193. Private JAMES GORDON, 10/11 July
1941, ashes interred at Karrakatta
Crematorium, Anglican Section; Railway
Road, Hollywood, Perth, Western Australia.
VC location: not publicly held.
**1194. Temporary Lieutenant Colonel
GEOFFREY KEYES**, 17/18 November 1941,
buried Benghazi War Cemetery, Plot VII,
Row D, Grave 5; Libya. *VC location:
Ashcroft Collection.*
1195. Second Lieutenant GEORGE GUNN,
21 November 1941, buried Knightsbridge
War Cemetery, Plot IV, Row F, Grave 1;
Acroma, Libya. *VC location: Royal Artillery
Museum, Woolwich, London.*
1196. Rifleman JOHN BEELEY,
21 November 1941, buried Knightsbridge
War Cemetery, Plot X, Row E, Grave 4;
Acroma, Libya. *VC location: Royal Green
Jackets Museum, Winchester, Hampshire.*
**1197. Acting Brigadier JOHN 'JOCK'
CAMPBELL**, 21/22 November 1941, buried
Cairo War Memorial Cemetery, Row K,
Grave 171; Egypt. *VC location: Royal
Artillery Museum, Woolwich, London.*
1198. Captain PHILIP 'PIP' GARDNER,
23 November 1941, cremated Hove
Crematorium, Old Shoreham Road, East
Sussex. *VC location: on loan to the Imperial
War Museum, London.*
**1199. Temporary Captain JAMES
JACKMAN**, 25 November 1941, buried
Tobruk War Cemetery, Plot VII, Row H,
Grave 9; Libya. *VC location: Stonyhurst
College, near Blackburn, Lancashire. On
permanent loan from his late sister's family.*
1200. Squadron Leader ARTHUR SCARF,
9 December 1941, buried Taiping War
Cemetery (Perkuburan Peperangan
Cemetery), Plot II, Row G, Grave 14;

Malaysia. *VC location: Royal Air Force
Museum, Hendon, London.*
**1201. Company Sergeant Major JOHN
OSBORN**, 19 December 1941, no known
grave, killed at Mount Butler, Hong Kong,
China. *VC location: Canadian War Museum,
Ottawa, Ontario, Canada.*
**1202. Lieutenant Colonel ARTHUR
CUMMING**, 3 January 1942, ashes at
Warriston Crematorium, Garden of
Remembrance; Warriston Road, Edinburgh,
Scotland. *VC location: National Army
Museum, London.*
**1203. Lieutenant Colonel CHARLES
ANDERSON**, 18–22 January 1942, ashes
interred at Norwood Crematorium, Wall 61;
Mitchell, Canberra, Australia. *VC location:
Australian War Memorial, Canberra, Australia.*
**1204. Lieutenant Commander EUGENE
ESMONDE**, 12 February 1942, buried
Woodlands Cemetery, Naval Reservation
Section A, RC Plot, Grave 187; Woodlands
Road, Gillingham, Kent. *VC location:
Imperial War Museum, London.*
**1205. Temporary Lieutenant THOMAS
WILKINSON**, 14 February 1942, no known
grave, killed at sea, Java Sea. *VC location: on
loan to the Imperial War Museum, London.*
1206. Lieutenant PETER ROBERTS,
16 February 1942, ashes interred Holy Cross
Churchyard, Newton Ferrers, Devon.
VC location: Ashcroft Collection.
**1207. Petty Officer THOMAS 'NAT'
GOULD** (born **WILLIAM THOMAS**),
16 February 1942, cremated Peterborough
Crematorium, Mowbray Road,
Cambridgeshire. *VC location: Jewish Military
Museum, London..*
**1208. Commander ANTHONY 'CRAP'
MIERS**, 4 March 1942, buried Tomnahurich
Cemetery, RC Section; Inverness, Scotland.
VC location: Ashcroft Collection.
**1209. Lieutenant Colonel AUGUSTUS 'ACE'
NEWMAN**, 27/28 March 1942, ashes
scattered at Barham Crematorium, Garden of
Remembrance; Canterbury Road, Kent.
VC location: Ashcroft Collection.
**1210. Lieutenant Commander STEPHEN
'SAM' BEATTIE**, 27/28 March 1942, buried

Ruan Minor Churchyard, Helston, Cornwall. *VC location: on loan to the Imperial War Museum, London.*

1211. Commander ROBERT 'RED' RYDER, 27/28 March 1942, ashes interred at Inkpen, Berkshire, and at Headington Crematorium, Flower Bed North-J; Oxford. *VC location: Imperial War Museum, London.*

1212. Sergeant THOMAS DURRANT, 27/28 March 1942, buried Escoublac-La-Baule War Cemetery, Plot I, Row D, Grave 11; near St Nazaire, France. *VC location: Royal Engineers Museum, Gillingham, Kent.*

1213. Able Seaman WILLIAM SAVAGE, 27/28 March 1942, buried Town Cemetery, Section K, Row C, Grave 15; Pennance Road, Falmouth, Cornwall. *VC location: National Maritime Museum, Greenwich, London.*

1214. Squadron Leader JOHN NETTLETON, 17 April 1942, no known grave, shot down and killed, Bay of Biscay, France. *VC location: not publicly held.*

1215. Temporary Lieutenant Colonel HENRY 'FAIRY' FOOTE, 27 May 1942, buried St Mary's Churchyard. left side of churchyard (adjacent to Geoffrey Woolley VC); West Chiltingham, Sussex. *VC location: Royal Tank Museum, Bovington, Dorset.*

1216. Flying Officer LESLIE MANSER, 30/31 May 1942, buried Heverlee War Cemetery, Plot VII, Row G, Grave 1; Belgium. *VC location: Ashcroft Collection.*

1217. Sergeant QUENTIN SMYTHE, 5 June 1942, ashes buried on his farm, Nottingham Road, Natal, South Africa. *VC location: original unknown. The official replacement is in the Ashcroft Collection.*

1218. Private ADAM WAKENSHAW, 27 June 1942, buried El Alamein War Cemetery, Plot XXXII, Row D, Grave 9; Egypt. *VC location: Durham Light Infantry Museum, Co. Durham.*

1219. Captain CHARLES 'PUG' UPHAM, date of Bar action, 14/15 July 1942 (for VC action see **1188**), ashes interred St Paul's Churchyard, Papanui, Christchurch, New Zealand. *VC and Bar location: National Army Museum, State Highway 1, Waiouru, New Zealand.*

1220. Sergeant KEITH ELLIOTT, 15 July 1942, buried Paraparaumu Cemetery, Returned Servicemen's Lawn Section; Lower Hutt, North Island, New Zealand. *VC location: National Army Museum, State Highway 1, Waiouru, New Zealand.*

1221. Private ARTHUR GURNEY, 22 July 1942, buried El Alamein War Cemetery, Plot XVI, Row H, Grave 21; Egypt. *VC location: Australian War Museum, Canberra, Australia.*

1222. Major CHARLES MERRITT, 19 August 1942, buried Ocean View Memorial Park, Burnaby, British Columbia, Canada. His headstone is unusual in that the letters VC do not appear after his name. *VC location: Canadian War Museum, Ottawa, Ontario, Canada.*

1223. Honorary Captain JOHN FOOTE, 19 August 1942, buried St Andrew's Presbyterian Churchyard (Union Cemetery), Coburg, Ontario, Canada. *VC location: Royal Hamilton Light Infantry Museum.*

1224. Temporary Captain PATRICK PORTEOUS, 19 August 1942, buried St Mary's Churchyard, Church Lane, Funtington, Sussex. *VC location: not publicly held.*

1225. Private BRUCE KINGSBURY, 29 August 1942, buried Port Moresby War Cemetery (aka Bomana War Cemetery), Plot C-6, Row E, Grave 1; South Coast, Papua New Guinea. *VC location: Australian War Memorial, Canberra, Australia.*

1226. Corporal JOHN FRENCH, 4 September 1942, buried Port Moresby War Cemetery (aka Bomana War Cemetery), Plot A-2, Row E, Grave 16; South Coast, Papua New Guinea. *VC location: with recipient's family.*

1227. Sergeant WILLIAM KIBBY, 23–31 October 1942, buried El Alamein War Cemetery, Plot XVI, Row A, Grave 18; Egypt. *VC location: Australian War Memorial, Canberra, Australia.*

1228. Private PERCIVAL GRATWICK, 25/26 October 1942, buried El Alamein War Cemetery, Plot XXII, Row A, Grave 6; Egypt. *VC location: Army Museum of Western Australia, Fremantle, Australia.*

1229. Temporary Lieutenant Colonel VICTOR TURNER, 27 October 1942, ashes interred St Mary's Churchyard, Ditchingham, Norfolk. *VC location: Royal Green Jackets Museum, Winchester, Hampshire.*

1230. Acting Captain FREDERICK 'FRITZ' PETERS, 8 November 1942, no known grave, killed in plane crash near Plymouth Harbour. *VC location: Ashcroft Collection.*

1231. Wing Commander HUGH MALCOLM, 17 November–4 December 1942, buried Beja War Cemetery, Plot II, Row E, Grave 6; Tunisia. *VC location: Ashcroft Collection.*

1232. Flight Sergeant RAWDON MIDDLETON, 28/29 November 1942, buried St John's Churchyard, Service Section, Row D, Grave 1; Beck Row, Mildenhall, Suffolk. *VC location: Australian War Memorial, Canberra, Australia.*

1233. Temporary Major HERBERT LE PATOUREL, 3 December 1942, ashes scattered at his home in Chewton Mendip, Somerset. *VC location: Royal Hampshire Regiment Museum, Winchester, Hampshire.*

1234. Captain ROBERT SHERBROOKE, 31 December 1942, buried St Peter & St Paul Churchyard, Oxton, Newark, Nottinghamshire. *VC location: not publicly held.*

1235. Havildar PARKASH SINGH, 6 and 19 January 1943, ashes returned to his home village near Jullundur, Punjab, India. *VC location: on loan to the Imperial War Museum, London.*

1236. Flight Lieutenant WILLIAM 'BILL' NEWTON, 16 and 18 March 1943, buried Lae War Cemetery, Section S, Row A, Grave 4; near Lae Zoo, Papua New Guinea. *VC location: Australian War Memorial, Canberra, Australia.*

1237. Temporary Lieutenant Colonel DEREK SEAGRIM, 20/21 March 1943, buried Sfax War Cemetery, Plot XIV, Row C, Grave 21; Tunisia. *VC location: Imperial War Museum, London..*

1238. Second Lieutenant MOANA-NUI-A-KIWA (spelt **KIWI** on headstone) **NGARIMU**, 26/27 March 1943, buried Sfax War Cemetery, Plot X, Row E, Grave 14; Tunisia. *VC location: Tairawhiti Museum, Gisborne, New Zealand.*

1239. Subadar LALBAHADUR THAPA, 5/6 April 1943, buried in unmarked grave, Paklihawa Camp Cemetery, outside north perimeter fence (accurate location not recorded); Nepal. *VC location: Gurkha Museum, Winchester, Hampshire.*

1240. Temporary Lieutenant Colonel LORNE CAMPBELL, 6 April 1943, buried Warriston Cemetery, Section B-1; Warriston Road, Edinburgh, Scotland. *VC location: Argyll and Sutherland Highlanders Museum, Stirling, Scotland.*

1241. Private ERIC ANDERSON, 6 April 1943, buried Sfax War Cemetery, Plot II, Row C, Grave 14; Tunisia. *VC location: Prince of Wales's Regiment Museum, York.*

1242. Company Havildar Major CHHELU RAM, 19/20 April 1943, buried Sfax War Cemetery, Plot H, Row C, Grave 5; Tunisia. *VC location: not publicly held.*

1243. Captain CHARLES LYELL, 22–27 April 1943, buried Massicault War Cemetery, Plot V, Row H, Grave 5; near Borj-el-Amri, Tunisia. *VC location: not publicly held.*

1244. Acting Major JOHN ANDERSON, 23 April 1943, buried Sangro River War Cemetery, Plot VIII, Row A, Grave 44; Abrizzi Province, Italy. *VC location: Argyll and Sutherland Highlanders Museum, Stirling, Scotland.*

1245. Lieutenant WILWARD SANDYS-CLARKE, 23 April 1943, buried Massicault War Cemetery, Plot V, Row B, Grave 1; near Borj-el-Amri, Tunisia. *VC location: with recipient's family.*

1246. Lance Corporal JOHN KENNEALLY (real name **LESLIE ROBINSON**), 28 and 30 April 1943, buried St Michael's and All Angels Churchyard, Rochford, Worcestershire. *VC location: Irish Guards RHQ, Wellington Barracks, London.*

1247. Squadron Leader LEONARD TRENT, 3 May 1943, cremated North Shore Crematorium, Auckland, New Zealand. *VC location: Royal New Zealand Air Force Museum, Wigram, Christchurch, New Zealand.*

1248. Wing Commander GUY 'GIBBO' GIBSON, 16/17 May 1943, buried Steenbergen-en-Kruisland RC Churchyard, Holland. *VC location: Royal Air Force Museum, Hendon, London.*

1249. Havildar GAJE GHALE, 24–27 May 1943, believed to be buried at Almoda, Dehradun, India. *VC location: not publicly held.*

1250. Flying Officer LLOYD TRIGG, 11 August 1943, no known grave, killed at sea, Atlantic Ocean, off Dakar, Senegal, West Africa. *VC location: Ashcroft Collection.*

1251. Acting Flight Sergeant ARTHUR AARON, 12/13 August 1943, buried Bone War Cemetery, Plot II, Row B, Grave 3; Algeria. *VC location: Leeds City Museum.*

1252. Private RICHARD KELLIHER, 13 September 1943, buried Springvale Lawn Cemetery, Melbourne, Victoria, Australia. *VC location: Australian War Memorial, Canberra, Australia.*

1253. Lieutenant DONALD CAMERON, 22 September 1943, ashes scattered at sea, off the Nub Tower, Hampshire. *VC location: not publicly held.*

1254. Lieutenant BASIL PLACE, 22 September 1943, buried Corton Denham Cemetery, Middle Ridge Lane, Corton Denham, Dorset. *VC location: Imperial War Museum, London.*

1255. Company Sergeant Major PETER WRIGHT, 25 September 1943, buried All Saints Churchyard, Grave 136-5A; Ashbocking, Suffolk. *VC location: not publicly held.*

1256. Acting Flight Lieutenant WILLIAM REID, 3 November 1943, buried St Andrew & St Michael's Churchyard, Crieff, Tayside, Scotland. *VC location: not publicly held.*

1257. Sergeant THOMAS 'DIVER' DERRICK, 24 November 1943, buried Labuan War Cemetery, Plot XXIV, Row A, Grave 9; near Victoria Township, on an island in Brunei Bay, Malaysia. *VC location: Australian War Memorial, Canberra, Australia.*

1258. Captain PAUL TRIQUET, 14 December 1943, ashes interred in the Royal 22nd Regimental Memorial, The Citadel, Quebec, Canada. *VC location: Royal 22nd Regiment Museum, Quebec City, Canada.*

1259. Lieutenant ALEC HORWOOD, 18–20 January 1944, no known grave, killed near Kyauchaw, Burma. *VC location: Ashcroft Collection.*

1260. Private GEORGE MITCHELL, 23/24 January 1944, buried Minturno War Cemetery (aka Sessa Arunca New Military Cemetery), Plot III, Row H, Grave 19; Italy. *VC location: London Scottish Museum, London.*

1261. Temporary Major WILLIAM SIDNEY, 7/8 February 1944, buried in family tomb at St John the Baptist Church, Penshurst, Kent. *VC location: not publicly held.*

1262. Temporary Major CHARLES HOEY, 16 February 1944, buried Taukkyan War Cemetery, Rangoon, Burma. *VC location: Lincolnshire Regiment Museum, Lincoln.*

1263. Acting Naik NAND SINGH, 11/12 March 1944, cremated Uri, Jammu & Kashmir, India. *VC location: Sikh Regiment Centre, Ramgarh, Bihar, India.*

1264. Lieutenant GEORGE CAIRNS, 13 March 1944, buried Taukkyan War Cemetery, Plot VI, Row A, Grave 4; Rangoon, Burma. *VC location: Staffordshire Regiment Museum, Lichfield.*

1265. Pilot Officer CYRIL BARTON, 30/31 March 1944, buried Kingston Cemetery, Class C Consecrated Section, Grave 6700; Bonner Hill Road, Kingston-upon-Thames, Surrey. *VC location: Royal Air Force Museum, Hendon, London.*

1266. Jemadar ABDUL HAFIZ, 6 April 1944, buried Imphal War Cemetery, Plot III, Row Q, Grave 2; Manipur State, India. *VC location: Ashcroft Collection.*

1267. Lance Corporal JOHN HARMAN, 8/9 April 1944, buried Kohima War Cemetery, Plot VIII, Row E, Grave 3; India. *VC location: Queen's Own Royal West Kent Regiment Museum, Maidstone, Kent.*

1268. Sergeant NORMAN JACKSON, 26/27 April 1944, buried Percy Road Cemetery, Section O, Grave 181; Percy Road,

Twickenham, Middlesex. *VC location: Ashcroft Collection.*

1269. Temporary Captain JOHN RANDLE, 4–6 May 1944, buried Kohima War Cemetery, Plot II, Row C, Grave 8; India. *VC location: on loan to the Imperial War Museum, London.*

1270. Sepoy KAMAL RAM, 12 May 1944, cremated Sawai Madhopur, Rajasthan, India. *VC location: Ashcroft Collection.*

1271. Temporary Captain RICHARD WAKEFORD, 13/14 May 1944, ashes scattered at Randall's Park Crematorium, Garden of Remembrance; Randall's Road, Leatherhead, Surrey. *VC location: Haberdashers Company, City of London.*

1272. Fusilier FRANCIS JEFFERSON, 16 May 1944, ashes scattered at Wellington Barracks, Memorial Garden; Bolton Road, Bury. *VC location: unknown. Medal stolen from his mother's house in 1982.*

1273. Major JOHN MAHONY, 24 May 1944, cremated Mount Pleasant Crematorium, London, Ontario, Canada. *VC location: Canadian War Museum, Ottawa, Ontario, Canada.*

1274. Sergeant MAURICE ROGERS, 3 June 1944, buried Beach Head War Cemetery, Plot X, Row D, Grave 8; Anzio, Italy. *VC location: Royal Gloucestershire, Berkshire and Wiltshire Regiment Museum, Salisbury, Wiltshire.*

1275. Company Sergeant Major STANLEY HOLLIS, 6 June 1944, buried Acklam Cemetery, Lawn Section, Grave 260; Acklam Road, Middlesbrough. His headstone is unusual in that instead of the letters 'VC' it bears the words 'Victoria Cross' after his name. *VC location: Green Howards Museum, Richmond, England.*

1276. Acting Sergeant HANSON TURNER, 6/7 June 1944, buried Imphal Indian Army War Cemetery, Plot VI, Row B, Grave 7; Manipur State, India. *VC location: Duke of Wellington Regiment Museum, Halifax, Yorkshire.*

1277. Acting Captain MICHAEL ALLMAND, 11, 13 and 23 June 1944, buried Taukkyan War Cemetery, Rangoon, Burma. *VC location: Gurkha Museum, Winchester,*

Hampshire.

1278. Rifleman GANJU LAMA (real name **GYANTSO SHANGDERPA**), 12 June 1944, burial location unknown, died Rabangla, Sikkim, India. *VC location: Gurkha Museum, Winchester, Hampshire.*

1279. Pilot Officer ANDREW MYNARSKI, 12/13 June 1944, buried Meharicourt Communal Cemetery Extension, British Plot, Grave 20; near Cambrai, France. *VC location: Air Command HQ Heritage Museum, Westwin, Winnipeg, Manitoba, Canada.*

1280. Corporal SEFANAIA SUKANAIVALU, 23 June 1944, buried Rubual War Cemetery, Plot V, Row B, Grave 13; Bita Paka, New Britain, Papua New Guinea. Plans are currently being made to return his remains to Fiji. *VC location: not publicly held.*

1281. Rifleman TULBAHADUR PUN, 23 June 1944, ashes scattered in Gandaki river, Myagdi, Nepal. *VC location: Gurkha Museum, Winchester, Hampshire.*

1282. Flight Lieutenant DAVID HORNELL, 24 June 1944, buried Lerwick New Cemetery, Upper Ground 17, RP Terrace 7B, Grave 17; Knab Road, Shetland Islands, Scotland. *VC location: Air Command HQ Heritage Museum, Westwin, Winnipeg, Manitoba, Canada.*

1283. Acting Subadar NETRABAHADUR THAPA, 25/26 June 1944, no known grave, killed near Bishenpur, Burma. *VC location: not publicly held.*

1284. Naik AGANSING RAI, 26 June 1944, cremated Dharan, Nepal. *VC location: Ashcroft Collection.*

1285. Temporary Major FRANK BLAKER, 9 July 1944, buried Taukkyan War Cemetery, Rangoon, Burma. *VC location: with recipient's family.*

1286. Naik YESHWANT GHADGE, 10 July 1944, no known grave, killed at the Upper Tiber Valley, Italy. *VC location: not publicly held.*

1287. Flying Officer JOHN CRUICKSHANK, 17/18 July 1944, still living. *VC location: with recipient.*

1288. Acting Squadron Leader IAN BAZALGETTE, 4 August 1944, buried Senantes Churchyard, Military Grave 1; France. *VC location: Royal Air Force Museum, Hendon, London.*

1289. Corporal SIDNEY BATES, 6 August 1944, buried Bayeux War Cemetery, Plot XX, Row E, Grave 19; Normandy, France. *VC location: Royal Norfolk Regiment Museum, Norwich.*

1290. Captain DAVID JAMIESON, 7/8 August 1944, buried Burnham Norton Churchyard, Norfolk. *VC location: Royal Norfolk Regiment Museum, Norwich.*

1291. Lieutenant TASKER WATKINS, 16 August 1944, cremated Thornhill Crematorium, Thornhill Road, Cardiff, Wales. *VC location: Ashcroft Collection.*

1292. Major DAVID CURRIE, 18–20 August 1944, buried Greenwood Cemetery, Owen Sound, Ontario, Canada. *VC location: not publicly held.*

1293. Lieutenant GERARD NORTON, 31 August 1944, burial location unknown, died Harare, Zimbabwe. *VC location: not publicly held.*

1294. Lieutenant JOHN GRAYBURN, 17–20 September 1944, buried Arnhem Oosterbeek War Cemetery, Plot XIII, Row C, Grave 11; Holland. *VC location: Airborne Forces Museum, Imperial War Museum, Duxford.*

1295. Rifleman SHERBAHADUR THAPA, 18/19 September 1944, buried Rimini Gurkha War Cemetery, Plot VI, Row E, Grave 7; Italy. *VC location: 9th Gurkha Rifles HQ, Varanasi, India.*

1296. Captain LIONEL QUERIPEL, 19 September 1944, buried Arnhem Oosterbeek Cemetery, Plot V, Row D, Grave 8; Holland. *VC location: Airborne Forces Museum, IWM, Duxford.*

1297. Flight Lieutenant DAVID LORD, 19 September 1944, buried Arnhem Oosterbeek War Cemetery, Plot IV, Row B, Grave 5; Holland. *VC location: Ashcroft Collection.*

1298. Temporary Major ROBERT CAIN, 19–25 September 1944, ashes interred Bradden Cemetery, family grave, name not on headstone; Bradden Road, Douglas, Isle of Man. *VC location: Staffordshire Regiment Museum, Lichfield.*

1299. Lance Sergeant JOHN BASKEYFIELD, 20 September 1944, possibly buried Arnhem Oosterbeek War Cemetery, Plot XXIII, Row C, Grave 12: a body was found in 1981 at the site of his VC action by Dutch workmen and buried as 'unknown'; Holland. *VC location: Staffordshire Regiment Museum, Lichfield.*

1300. Corporal JOHN HARPER, 29 September 1944, buried Leopoldsburg War Cemetery, Plot V, Row B, Grave 15; Belgium. *VC location: York and Lancaster Regiment Museum, Rotherham, Yorkshire.*

1301. Private RICHARD BURTON, 8 October 1944, buried Kirriemuir Cemetery, Section NE, Lair 103; Brechin Road, Angus, Scotland. *VC location: Ashcroft Collection.*

1302. Acting Sergeant GEORGE EARDLEY, 16 October 1944, ashes scattered at Macclesfield Crematorium, Garden of Remembrance; Prestbury Road, Cheshire. *VC location: Ashcroft Collection.*

1303. Private ERNEST 'SMOKEY' SMITH, 21/22 October 1944, burial location unknown despite having a full military funeral; died Vancouver, British Columbia, Canada. *VC location: Museum of the Seaforth Highlanders of Canada, Vancouver, British Columbia, Canada.*

1304. Acting Subadar RAM SARUP SINGH, 25 October 1944, no known grave, killed at Kennedy Peak, Tiddim Area, Burma. *VC location: not publicly held.*

1305. Rifleman THAMAN (spelt **THAMMAN** on headstone) **GURUNG**, 10 November 1944, buried Rimini Gurkha War Cemetery, Plot III, Row B, Grave 5; Italy. *VC location: not publicly held.*

1306. Sepoy BHANDARI (aka **BANDARI**) **RAM**, 22 November 1944, cremated Autur, Himachal Pradesh, India. *VC location: not publicly held.*

1307. Temporary Captain JOHN BRUNT, 9 December 1944, buried Faenza War Cemetery, Plot III, Row A, Grave 8; Italy.

VC location: Royal Lincolnshire Regiment Museum, Lincoln.

1308. Havildar UMRAO SINGH, 15/16 December 1944, cremated Palra Village, Jhajjar District, Punjab, India. *VC location: not publicly held.*

1309. Squadron Leader ROBERT PALMER, 23 December 1944, buried Rheinberg War Cemetery, Plot XIV, Row C, Grave 13-14; Germany. *VC location: not publicly held.*

1310. Flight Sergeant GEORGE THOMPSON, 1 January 1945, buried Brussels Town Cemetery, Plot X, Row 27, Grave 45; Evere-les-Brizelles, Belgium. *VC location: National War Museum of Scotland, Edinburgh Castle, Scotland.*

1311. Fusilier DENNIS DONNINI, 18 January 1945, buried Sittard War Cemetery, Row H, Grave 10; Limburg, Holland. *VC location: Easington Colliery Working Men's Club, Co. Durham.*

1312. Lance Naik SHER SHAH, 19/20 January 1945, no known grave, killed at Kyeyebyin, near Kaladan, Burma. *VC location: not publicly held.*

1313. Lance Corporal HENRY HARDEN, 23 January 1945, buried Nederweert War Cemetery, Plot IV, Row E, Grave 13; Holland. *VC location: Army Medical Services Museum, Mytchett, Surrey.*

1314. Lieutenant GEORGE KNOWLAND, 31 January 1945, buried Taukkyan War Cemetery, Rangoon, Burma. *VC location: unknown. Medal stolen in 1958 from the Spreadeagle Inn, Whitecross Street, London.*

1315. Jemadar PRAKASH SINGH, 16/17 February 1945, no known grave, killed at Kanlan Ywathit, Burma. *VC location: not publicly held.*

1316. Acting Major EDWIN SWALES, 23 February 1945, buried Leopoldsburg War Cemetery, Plot VIII, Row C, Grave 5; Limburg, Belgium. *VC location: National Museum of Military History, Johannesburg, South Africa.*

1317. Sergeant AUBREY COSENS, 25/26 February 1945, buried Groesbeek Canadian War Cemetery, Plot VIII, Row H, Grave 2; Nijmegen, Holland. *VC location: Queen's*

Own Rifles of Canada Museum, Toronto, Ontario, Canada.

1318. Acting Major FREDERICK TILSTON, 1 March 1945, buried Mount Hope Cemetery, RC Section, Plot 23, NW Corner; Erskine Avenue, Toronto, Ontario, Canada. *VC location: Royal Canadian Military Institute, Toronto, Ontario, Canada.*

1319. Private JAMES STOKES, 1 March 1945, buried Reichswald Forest War Cemetery, Plot LXII, Row E, Grave 14; near Kleve, Germany. *VC location: not publicly held.*

1320. Naik GIAN SINGH, 2 March 1945, cremated Jalandhar Cantt, near Jullundur, ashes scattered 'to the rivers'; Northern Punjab, India. *VC location: original stolen in 1960, and an official replacement issued in 1961. The latter is not publicly held.*

1321. Acting Naik FAZAL DIN, 2 March 1945, no known grave, killed near Pakokku, Meiktila, Burma. *VC location: not publicly held.*

1322. Lieutenant WILLIAM WESTON, 3 March 1945, buried Taukkyan War Cemetery, Rangoon, Burma. *VC location: on permanent loan from his nephew, Basil Weston to the Green Howards Museum, Richmond, Yorkshire.*

1323. Rifleman BHANBHAGTA GURUNG, 5 March 1945, cremated Devghal of Chitawan, Nepal. *VC location: Gurkha Museum, Winchester, Hampshire.*

1324. Lieutenant KARAMJEET SINGH JUDGE, 18 March 1945, cremated at unknown location, killed at Myingyan, near Meiktila, Burma. *VC location: not publicly held.*

1325. Lieutenant CLAUD RAYMOND, 21 March 1945, buried Taukkyan War Cemetery, Rangoon, Burma. *VC location: Royal Engineers Museum, Gillingham, Kent.*

1326. Corporal REGINALD RATTEY, 22 March 1945, buried West Wyalong Lawn Cemetery, Shire Street, New South Wales, Australia. *VC location: not publicly held.*

1327. Corporal FREDERICK 'TOPPY' TOPHAM, 24 March 1945, buried Sanctuary Park Cemetery, Etobicke, Ontario, Canada.

VC location: Canadian War Museum, Ottawa, Ontario, Canada.

1328. Lieutenant ALBERT CHOWNE, 25 March 1945, buried Lae War Cemetery, Plot QQ, Row A, Grave 8; near Lae Zoo, Papua New Guinea. *VC location: Australian War Memorial, Canberra, Australia.*

1329. Corporal EDWARD CHAPMAN, 2 April 1945, buried Pantag Cemetery, The Highway, New Inn, Pontypool, Monmouthshire, Wales. *VC location: not publicly held.*

1330. Temporary Corporal THOMAS HUNTER, 3 April 1945, buried Argenta Gap War Cemetery, Plot III, Row G, Grave 20; Ravenna, Italy. *VC location: Royal Marines Museum, Southsea, Portsmouth, Hampshire.*

1331. Temporary Captain IAN LIDDELL, 3 April 1945, buried Becklingen War Cemetery, RC Plot III, Row D, Grave 13; Soltau, Germany. *VC location: Coldstream Guards RHQ, Wellington Barracks, London.*

1332. Temporary Major ANDERS LASSEN, 8/9 April 1945, buried Argenta Gap War Cemetery, Plot II, Row E, Grave 11; Ravenna, Italy. *VC location: Liberation Museum, Copenhagen, Denmark.*

1333. Sepoy ALI HAIDAR, 9 April 1945, buried Shahu Khel Village, Kohat District, Pakistan. *VC location: Ashcroft Collection.*

1334. Sepoy NAMDEO JADHAO, 9 April 1945, cremated Pune, Maharashtra State, India. *VC location: not publicly held.*

1335. Guardsman EDWARD CHARLTON, 21 April 1945, buried Becklingen War Cemetery, Plot VII, Row F, Grave 13; Soltau, Germany. *VC location: Irish Guards RHQ, Wellington Barracks, London.*

1336. Corporal JOHN MACKEY, 12 May 1945, buried Labuan War Cemetery, Plot XXVII, Row C, Grave 9; near Victoria Township, on an island in Brunei Bay, Malaysia. *VC location: Gordon Highlanders Museum, Aberdeen, Scotland.*

1337. Rifleman LACHHIMAN GURUNG, 12/13 May 1945, buried Chiswick New Cemetery, Section V, Grave 59; London. *VC location: 8th Gurkha Rifles, Indian Army.*

1338. Private EDWARD KENNA, 15 May 1945, buried Hamilton Lawn Cemetery, Hamilton, Victoria, Australia. *VC location: not publicly held.*

1339. Private LESLIE STARCEVICH, 25 May 1945, buried Esperance Public Lawn Cemetery, War Graves Section, Grave 1366; Western Australia. *VC location: not publically held.*

1340. Private FRANK PARTRIDGE, 24 July 1945, buried Macksville Cemetery, New South Wales, Australia. *VC location: not publicly held.*

1341. Lieutenant IAN 'TICH' FRASER, 31 July 1945, cremated at Landican Crematorium, Arrowe Park Road, Wirral, Merseyside. *VC location: Ashcroft Collection.*

1342. Acting Leading Seaman JAMES 'MICK' MAGENNIS, 31 July 1945, ashes scattered at Nab Wood Crematorium, Scholemoor Cemetery, Garden of Remembrance; Bingley Road, Shipley, Yorkshire. *VC location: Ashcroft Collection.*

1343. Temporary Lieutenant ROBERT GRAY, 9 August 1945, no known grave, killed when shot down over Onagawa Bay, Honshu, Japan. *VC location: Canadian War Museum, Ottawa, Ontario, Canada.*

1344. Major KENNETH MUIR, 23 September 1950, buried United Nations Memorial Cemetery, Pusan, Korea. *VC location: Argyll and Sutherland Highlanders Museum, Stirling, Scotland.*

1345. Lieutenant Colonel JAMES 'FRED' CARNE, 22/23 April 1951, ashes interred Cranham Churchyard, Gloucestershire. *VC location: Soldiers of Gloucestershire Museum, Gloucester.*

1346. Lieutenant PHILIP CURTIS, 22/23 April 1951, buried United Nations Memorial Cemetery, Pusan, Korea. *VC location: Duke of Cornwall's Light Infantry Museum, Bodmin, Cornwall.*

1347. Private WILLIAM 'BIG BILL' SPEAKMAN (name changed to SPEAKMAN-PITTS), 4 November 1951, still living. *VC location: National War Museum of Scotland, Edinburgh Castle, Scotland.*

1348. Warrant Officer Class II KEVIN 'DASHER' WHEATLEY, 13 November

1965, buried Lawn Cemetery, Pine Grove Memorial Park, Blacktown, New South Wales, Australia. *VC location: Australian War Memorial, Canberra, Australia.*

1349. Lance Corporal RAMBAHADUR LIMBU, 21 November 1965, still living. *VC location: unknown. Original medal stolen from him on a train journey; official replacement with recipient.*

1350. Major PETER BADCOE (spelt **BADCOCK** before 1961), 23 February, 7 March and 7 April 1967, buried Terendak Garrison Camp Cemetery, Malaysia. *VC location: Australian War Memorial, Canberra, Australia.*

1351. Warrant Officer Class II RAYENE SIMPSON, 6 and 11 May 1969, half of his ashes interred at Yokohama War Cemetery, Tokyo, Japan, and half returned to Australia. *VC location: Australian War Memorial, Canberra, Australia.*

1352. Warrant Officer Class II KEITH PAYNE, 24 May 1969, still living. *VC location: Maryborough Military & Colonial Museum, Queensland, Australia.*

1353. Lieutenant Colonel HERBERT (known as **'H'**) **JONES**, 28 May 1982, buried Blue Beach War Cemetery, Port San Carlos, Falkland Islands. *VC location: National Army Museum, London.*

1354. Sergeant IAN McKAY, 12 June 1982, buried Aldershot Military Cemetery, Lower Section, Row A, Grave 101; Gallwey Road, Aldershot, Hampshire. *VC location: Ashcroft Collection.*

1355. Lance Corporal WILLIE 'MUDGUTS' APIATA, between March and October 2004, still living. *VC location: New Zealand SAS Trust, Papakura, Auckland, New Zealand.*

1356. Private JOHNSON 'BEE' BEHARRY, 1 May and 11 June 2004, still living. *VC location: on loan to the Imperial War Museum, London.*

1357. Corporal BRYAN BUDD, 27 July and 20 August 2006, buried Colchester Cemetery, Section 00, Mersea Road, Colchester, Essex. *VC location: on loan to the Airborne Forces Museum, IWM Duxford.*

1358. Trooper MARK DONALDSON, 2 September 2008, still living. *VC location: on loan to the Australian War Memorial, Canberra, Australia.*

1359. Corporal BENJAMIN 'RS' or 'ARSE' ROBERTS-SMITH, 11 June 2010, still living. *VC location: on loan to the Australian War Memorial, Canberra, Australia.*

1360. Corporal DANIEL 'PRINCE HARRY' KEIGHRAN, 24 August 2010, still living. *VC location: on loan to the Australian War Memorial, Canberra, Australia.*

1361. Lance Corporal JAMES ASHWORTH, 13 June 2012, buried Shire Lodge Cemetery, Rockingham Road, Corby. *VC location: with recipient's family.*

1362. Corporal CAMERON 'CAM' BAIRD, 22 June 2013, Reedy Creek Baptist Churchyard, Gemvale Road, Gold Coast, Queensland, Australia. *VC location: Australian War Memorial, Canberra, Australia.*

1363. Lance Corporal JOSHUA LEAKEY, 22 August 2013, still living. *VC location: with recipient.*

Chapter Four

THE CRIMEAN WAR, 1854–56 AND THE PERSIAN WAR, 1856–59

The Crimean War was fought between Tsar Nicholas I's Imperial Russia and the forces of the Ottoman Empire (now Turkey), Britain and France. The war started when Russia invaded Moldavia and Walachia to try to increase her power by expansion south towards the Turkish-owned Dardanelles, which would have given the Russian fleet access to the Mediterranean and a port that was not frozen in winter.

Britain and France declared war on 28 March 1854, and the Allies sent a fleet to the Baltic as well as to the Black Sea. By the time the Allies reached the Black Sea the Turks had already won a victory and the Russians were halted. The British and French, not having much to do, decided to invade the Crimea to knock out the Russian naval base at Sebastopol. A total of 111 Victoria Crosses were awarded for this campaign.

Boatswains Mate CHARLES LUCAS
ALAND ISLANDS, Finland
21 June 1854
He was 20 years old and serving in the Royal Navy when a live shell from an enemy battery landed on the deck of HMS *Hecla*. All hands were ordered to take cover, but Lucas, without a moment's hesitation, coolly picked up the shell and threw it overboard. He was immediately promoted to lieutenant.

Lucas had also served in the Second Burmese War of 1852–3. He died on 7 August 1914. In 2006 Charles Lucas VC featured in a series of Royal Mail postage stamps marking the 150th anniversary of the Victoria Cross.

Lieutenant JOHN BYTHESEA
ALAND ISLANDS, Finland
9–12 August 1854
He was 27 years old and serving in the Royal Navy when he and Stoker William Johnstone from HMS *Arrogant* were landed on the island of Vardo in order to intercept important despatches from the Tsar which were being sent via Vardo to Bomarsund. They spent two nights reconnoitring the island and duly ambushed the five Russians carrying the despatches, despite having just one pistol between them. Two of the carriers dropped their mail bags and ran, but the other three surrendered and were taken to *Arrogant*. Both men were awarded the VC.

Bythesea died on 18 May 1906.

Stoker WILLIAM (enlisted and served as JOHN) JOHNSTONE
ALAND ISLANDS, Finland
9–12 August 1854
He was 31 years old and serving in the Royal Navy when he and Lieutenant Bythesea from HMS *Arrogant* were landed on the island of Vardo in order to intercept important despatches from the Tsar which were being sent via Vardo to Bomarsund. They spent two nights reconnoitring the island and duly ambushed the five Russians carrying the despatches, despite having just one pistol between them. Two of the carriers dropped their mail bags and ran, but the other three surrendered and were taken to *Arrogant*. Both men were awarded the VC.

Johnstone died on 20 August 1857. He cut his own throat after attacking another man with a knife.

Captain EDWARD BELL
ALMA 20 September 1854

He was 30 years old and serving in the 23rd Regiment of Foot, later the Royal Welch Fusiliers, when, without orders, he went to capture a gun that was limbered and being taken from the redoubt. Taking the driver by surprise, he aimed his revolver at his head and the driver ran off. Bell turned the team around and brought the gun back to his regiment, only to be reprimanded for leaving his place without orders. But higher authorities had noticed his action and he was awarded the VC. It was generally felt that if he had not earned it at the Alma, it would have been awarded to him for his action at Inkerman.

He died on 10 November 1879.

Sergeant JAMES McKECHNIE
ALMA 20 September 1854

He was 28 years old and serving in the Scots Fusilier Guards. When the formation of the regiment became disordered, he stood firm alongside Captain Lindsay. Taking out his revolver, he dashed forward, calling out, 'By the centre, Scots, by the centre. Look to the colours and march by them.' He was wounded in this action.

He died on 5 July 1886.

Private WILLIAM REYNOLDS
ALMA 20 September 1854

He was 27 years old and serving in the Scots Fusilier Guards. When the formation of the regiment became disordered, he behaved with conspicuous gallantry in helping to rally the men around the colours.

He died on 20 October 1869.

Senior Subaltern ROBERT LINDSAY (later LOYD-LINDSAY)
ALMA and INKERMAN
20 September and 5 November 1854

He was 22 years old and serving in the Scots Fusilier Guards. When the formation of his regiment's line became disordered, he stood firm with the colours and by his brave conduct and splendid example helped to restore confidence and order. On 5 November he charged a

party of Russians, driving them back and running one through the body with his sword.

Loyd-Lindsay was one of only a few VC holders who became MPs. He was also a founding member of the British Red Cross. He died on 10 June 1901.

Sergeant JOHN PARK
ALMA, INKERMAN and SEBASTOPOL
20 September, 5 November 1854 and
19 April 1855

He was 19 years old and serving in the 77th Regiment of Foot, later the Middlesex Regiment, Duke of Cambridge's Own, when he showed conspicuous bravery at the Alma and at Inkerman. On 19 April 1855 he also distinguished himself highly at the taking of the rifle pits at Sebastopol, during which he was wounded. He also showed great bravery in both attacks on the Redan redoubt.

He died from heat apoplexy on 16 May 1863.

Sergeant JOHN KNOX
ALMA and SEBASTOPOL
20 September 1854 and 18 June 1855

He was 25 years old and serving in the Scots Fusilier Guards when his sterling efforts in reforming the ranks of the guards were noted. On 18 June 1855 Knox volunteered for the ladder party in the attack on the Redan and behaved admirably, remaining on the field until twice wounded. He lost an arm during this action.

He died on 8 January 1897.

Sergeant LUKE O'CONNOR
ALMA
20 September 1854 and 8 September 1855

He was 23 years old and serving in the 23rd Regiment of Foot, later the Royal Welch Fusiliers, when he took the fallen colours from the hands of Lieutenant Anstruther, whose blood drenched them as he fell. Although wounded himself, O'Connor held the Queen's Colour aloft until the end of the action, by which time it had 26 holes through it. O'Connor himself was urged to retire to tend to his wounds but refused. On 8 September

1855 he displayed great gallantry at the storming of the Redan, although shot through both thighs.

He died on 1 February 1915.

Private FRANCIS WHEATLEY
SEBASTOPOL 12 October 1854

He was 33 years old and serving in the 1st Bn the Rifle Brigade (Prince Consort's Own) when a live Russian shell fell into the trench among the men. Without hesitation Wheatley seized it and tried to knock out the fuse with the butt of his rifle. This proved unsuccessful so, with great presence of mind and deliberation, he somehow managed to heave the shell over the parapet. It had scarcely fallen outside when it exploded. Had it not been for his coolness, presence of mind and supreme courage, the shell would have exploded among the men and caused serious casualties, but in the event no one was hurt.

He died from acute myelitis and asphyxia on 21 May 1865.

Lieutenant Colonel COLLINGWOOD DICKSON
SEBASTOPOL 17 October 1854

He was 36 years old and serving in the Royal Regiment of Artillery. When the batteries were running short of ammunition, Dickson carried barrels of powder from the magazine under a hail of shot and shell. He then stood for hours under fire directing the unloading and storing of the ammunition.

He died on 28 November 1904.

Private THOMAS GRADY
SEBASTOPOL
18 October and 22 November 1854

He was 19 years old and serving in the 4th Regiment of Foot, later the King's Own Royal Lancaster Regiment, when he repaired the embrasures of the Sailors' Battery in clear daylight under heavy fire. On 22 November, during the repulse of an enemy attack on the most advanced trenches, Grady refused to leave his post, although he was severely wounded. He kept on encouraging his comrades to 'hold on' and was thus the means of saving the position.

He died from asthma on 18 May 1891.

Captain WILLIAM PEEL
SEBASTOPOL, INKERMAN and the *REDAN* 18 October, 5 November 1854 and 18 June 1855

He was 29 years old and serving in the Royal Navy's Naval Brigade. When a 42-pounder Russian shell with a burning fuse fell among the powder cases, he picked up and carried it until he could throw it over the parapet, where it exploded. On 5 November he led seven charges against the Russians. Later he joined some hard-pressed officers of the Grenadier Guards at the Sandbag Battery and helped them in their retreat. On 18 June 1855 Peel led the first scaling party in the assault on the Redan until he was severely wounded in the arm. He also served in the Indian Mutiny.

He died from smallpox on 21 April 1858. His father was Sir Robert Peel, founder of the Metropolitan Police.

Midshipman EDWARD DANIEL
SEBASTOPOL, INKERMAN and the *REDAN* 18 October, 5 November 1854 and 18 June 1855

He was 17 years old and serving in the Royal Navy's Naval Brigade when a team of horses bringing up ammunition refused to move forward. Daniel took it upon himself to unload the wagon under fire and carry the ammunition into the battery. On 5 November he remained by Captain Peel's side as Peel led seven charges against the Russians. On 18 June 1855 Daniel saved Peel's life by placing a tourniquet around his badly wounded arm before carrying him to safety under a hail of bullets, several of which cut through his uniform and sliced open his pistol case. Daniel also served in the Indian Mutiny.

Daniel was one of eight men to forfeit his VC, for 'taking indecent liberties with four subordinate officers'. He reportedly died from delirium tremens on 20 May 1868. However, Victor Tambling, a Victoria Cross expert, has in his possession a photograph taken in London of a man aged about 40, which was sold to him as a picture of Daniel. Dr Tim Koelmeyer, a forensic pathologist, compared this photo to a known picture of Daniel, and concluded that they show the same man. The later photo was most probably taken after 1875, some considerable time after Daniel's recorded death.

Sergeant WILLIAM McWHEENEY (aka MAWHINNEY)
SEBASTOPOL and INKERMAN
20 October and 5 December 1854

He was 17 years old and serving in the 44th Regiment of Foot, later the Essex Regiment, when he lifted the wounded Private John Keane on to his back and carried him for some time under heavy fire to a place of safety. On 5 December McWheeney went to the assistance of Corporal Courtney, who had been severely wounded in the head, and was under fire. He used his bayonet to dig a pit for cover, and the pair sheltered until dark, when they made good their escape.

He died on 17 May 1866.

Lieutenant ALEXANDER DUNN
BALACLAVA 25 October 1854

He was 21 years old and serving in the 11th Hussars. During the charge of the Light Brigade, he rode at and cut down three Russian lancers who were attacking Sergeant Bentley from the rear; Dunn then dismounted and placed Bentley back on his horse, thus saving his life. He then went to the assistance of Private Levett, cutting down a hussar who was assailing him.

On 25 January 1868 he was found lying dead beside his own gun during a shooting trip. An inquiry found that his death was purely accidental.

Sergeant Major JOHN GRIEVE
BALACLAVA 25 October 1854

He was 32 years old and serving in the 2nd Dragoons (Royal Scots Greys). During the charge of the Heavy Brigade, he went to the rescue of an officer who was surrounded by Russians. Grieve killed one by cutting off his head and drove the others away.

He died on 1 December 1873. His nephew was Captain Robert Grieve VC.

Sergeant JOHN BERRYMAN
BALACLAVA 25 October 1854

He was 29 years old and serving in the 17th Lancers (Duke of Cambridge's Own) when during the charge of the Light Brigade his horse was shot from under him. He stayed on the field with Captain Webb, who was badly wounded. Webb told him to leave him and see to his own safety but Berryman refused to do so, and carried the wounded man to safety with the assistance of Sergeant John Farrell and Sergeant Joseph Malone. He then met the French General Morris, who said to him, 'If you were in the French service I would make you an officer on the spot.' Sadly Captain Webb died of his wounds. All three men were awarded the VC.

Berryman also served in the Indian Mutiny and the Zulu War. He died from an abscess of the liver on 27 June 1896.

Sergeant JOHN FARRELL
BALACLAVA 25 October 1854

He was 28 years old and serving in the 17th Lancers (Duke of Cambridge's Own) when during the charge of the Light Brigade he helped Troop Sergeant Berryman and Sergeant Malone to carry the wounded and dying Captain Webb out of range of the enemy guns; when a stretcher was found, he assisted in carrying him from the field. All three men were awarded the VC.

Farrell died from an abscess of the liver on 31 August 1865.

Lance Sergeant JOSEPH MALONE
BALACLAVA 25 October 1854

He was 21 years old and serving in the 13th Light Dragoons, later the 13th Hussars. While returning on foot from the charge of the Light Brigade, he helped Troop Sergeant Berryman and Sergeant John Farrell to carry the wounded and dying Captain Webb out of range of the enemy guns; when a stretcher was found, he assisted in carrying him from the field. All three men were awarded the VC.

Malone is often referred to as a corporal, but in fact he skipped this rank. He died from bronchitis on 28 June 1883.

Private SAMUEL (aka GEORGE) PARKES
BALACLAVA 25 October 1854

He was 41 years old and serving in the 4th Light Dragoons. During the charge of the Light Brigade he went to the assistance of Trumpeter Crawford, whose horse had been shot from under him, and who had lost his sword. Parkes drove away two Cossacks who were attacking Crawford. Then, while attempting to follow his retreat, he kept six Russians at bay until his sword was shattered by a shot. Both Parkes and Crawford were taken prisoner, making Parkes the first prisoner-of-war VC.

Parkes had also served in the Ghuznee Campaign of 1836. He died from apoplexy on 15 November 1864.

Surgeon JAMES MOUAT
BALACLAVA 26 October 1854

He was 39 years old and serving in the 6th (Inniskilling) Dragoons when, together with Sergeant Charles Wooden, he went out under heavy fire to rescue Lieutenant Colonel William Morris, who was lying in an exposed position, having been wounded during the Light Brigade's charge into the 'valley of death' the day before. They dressed his wounds and succeeded in bringing him back to their own lines. Morris survived, despite a broken arm, broken ribs and three deep head wounds, and died four years later in India. Mouat also served in both Maori Wars.

He died from a stroke on 4 January 1899.

Lieutenant JOHN CONOLLY
SEBASTOPOL 26 October 1854

He was 25 years old and serving in the 49th Regiment of Foot (Princess Charlotte of Wales's). When his company was being attacked by the Russians, Conolly mounted frequent short, sharp charges, and engaged several Russians in hand-to-hand combat. He ultimately fell badly wounded and had to be carried from the field, having lost much blood.

He died on 23 December 1888.

Sergeant Major AMBROSE MADDEN
LITTLE INKERMAN 26 October 1854

He was 34 years old and serving in the 41st Regiment of Foot when he led a party of men from the 41st and captured one Russian officer and fourteen other ranks, three of whom he took prisoner himself.

Madden died from a fever on 1 January 1863.

Sergeant HENRY RAMAGE
BALACLAVA 26 October 1854

He was 27 years old and serving in the 2nd Dragoons (Royal Scots Greys). After the charge of the Light Brigade, he saved the life of the wounded Private McPherson, who was surrounded by seven Russians, whom Ramage dispersed. On the same day he carried Private Gardiner to the rear, after his leg had been broken by round shot.

He died on 29 December 1859.

Sergeant CHARLES WOODEN
BALACLAVA 26 October 1854

He was 27 years old and serving in the 17th Lancers (Duke of Cambridge's Own) when, together with Surgeon James Mouat, he went out under heavy fire to rescue Lieutenant Colonel William Morris, who was lying in an exposed position, having been wounded during the Light Brigade's charge into the 'valley of death' the day before. (Wooden had also taken part in that charge.) They dressed Morris's wounds and succeeded in bringing him back to their own lines. Morris survived, despite a broken arm, broken ribs and three deep head wounds, and died four years later in India. He also served in the Indian Mutiny.

At first Wooden was not put forward for the award, but when Mouat wrote to Horse Guards supporting his claim, it was given to both men.

Wooden killed himself on 24 April 1876, when in a drunken state he tried to 'shoot out' a bad tooth. At his funeral the chaplain spoke of 'a brave soldier who had upheld the honour and fame of England in many battles'.

Private WILLIAM STANLAKE (spelt STANLOCK in the *London Gazette*)

INKERMAN 26 October 1854

He was 23 years old and serving in the Coldstream Guards when he volunteered to reconnoitre an enemy position. Although warned of the risks, Stanlake crawled to within 6 yards of a Russian sentry and brought back such useful information that his officer, Major Goodlake, was able to make a surprise attack.

He died on 24 April 1904.

Lieutenant WILLIAM 'BULLY' HEWETT

SEBASTOPOL and INKERMAN

26 October and 5 November 1854

He was 20 years old and serving in the Royal Navy (Naval Brigade) in charge of the Right Lancaster Battery. Due to a misunderstanding, he was ordered to spike the guns and retire. Shouting 'Retire? Retire be damned!', he swung the guns around and poured into the enemy so steady a fire that their advance was checked. At Inkerman he again acted with great bravery. Hewett also served in the Ashanti War and the First Sudan Campaign.

He died from kidney disease on 13 May 1888.

Brevet Major GERALD GOODLAKE

INKERMAN

28 October and November 1854

He was 22 years old and serving in the Coldstream Guards when, as the only officer present, he commanded the sharpshooters of his battalion, holding the Windmill Ravine against a much larger force of Russians, killing 38 and taking 3 prisoners. In November his men surprised an enemy picquet and seized their knapsacks and rifles.

He died on 5 April 1890.

Corporal JAMES OWENS

SEBASTOPOL 30 October 1854

He was 25 years old and serving in the 49th Regiment of Foot (Princess Charlotte of Wales's), later the Royal Berkshire Regiment, when he greatly distinguished himself in personal encounters with the Russians at Sebastopol, and nobly came to the assistance of Lieutenant Conolly, who had been severely wounded and was surrounded by the enemy.

He died on 20 August 1901.

Colonel HENRY PERCY

INKERMAN 5 November 1854

He was 37 years old and serving in the 3rd Bn, Grenadier Guards when he charged alone into the Sandbag Battery, where he engaged in single combat with a Russian whom he disabled. Later in the battle he mounted the parapet and became a target for a hundred Russian muskets. He was knocked backwards by a stone and fell senseless to the ground, where he lay bleeding, but on hearing the word 'charge' he rose to his feet and joined the advance. Percy soon found himself with a group of men from various regiments, almost surrounded and without ammunition. He led 50 men to safety, where they were able to get more ammunition and rejoin the fight. Percy was one of only a handful of VC holders who became MPs.

He died on 3 December 1877.

Brevet Major CHARLES RUSSELL

INKERMAN 5 November 1854

He was 28 years old and serving in the 3rd Bn, Grenadier Guards when he offered to try to dislodge a party of Russians from the Sandbag Battery, if anyone would follow him. His call was answered by Sergeant Norman, Private Bailey and Private Palmer. The attack was successful, although Russell, as the only man not wearing an overcoat, was a prominent target for the enemy. He was only a slight man, yet he was able to tear a rifle from the hands of a Russian soldier. Private Palmer was also awarded the VC for saving the major's life.

Russell died on 13 April 1883.

Captain HUGH ROWLANDS

INKERMAN 5 November 1854

He was 26 years old and serving in the 41st (Welch) Regiment of Foot when he and Private John McDermond rescued Colonel Hayly of the 47th Regiment, who had been wounded and was surrounded by Russians. (There is a painting depicting this action in the Army HQ at Preston.) Rowlands also acted with great gallantry in holding the ground occupied by his advanced picquet against the enemy at the start of the battle. Both men were awarded the VC. Rowlands was also recommended for a Bar for his actions at the Redan redoubt. This was dropped at a later stage as, according to the fourth clause of the original warrant, he would only have been eligible for a Bar if he had already been awarded the VC.

Rowlands died on 1 August 1909.

Lieutenant HENRY CLIFFORD
INKERMAN 5 November 1854

He was 28 years old and serving in the Rifle Brigade when he led a charge against the Russian lines, cutting off the head of one man and the arm of another. His charge was successful in driving back the Russians. He also saved the life of a wounded soldier during the fight.

Clifford had also served in the Second Frontier War and the Second China War, and later in the Kaffir Wars and Zulu War. He died from cancer on 12 April 1883.

Lieutenant FREDERICK MILLER
INKERMAN 5 November 1854

He was 22 years old and serving in the Royal Regiment of Artillery when he attacked three Russians and led a charge on a battery, thus preventing the guns from coming to any harm.

He died on 17 February 1874.

Lieutenant MARK WALKER
INKERMAN 5 November 1854

He was 26 years old and serving in the 30th Regiment of Foot, later the East Lancashire Regiment, when his battalion was in position behind a wall as two Russian battalions approached. On finding that his battalion's weapons had become damp and thus useless, Walker jumped up on to the wall and called on his men to follow him with the bayonet, leading them straight at the enemy. This caused a panic among the Russians, who in spite of their greater numbers turned and fled.

He died on 18 July 1902.

Sergeant ANDREW HENRY
INKERMAN 5 November 1854

He was 31 years old and serving in the Royal Regiment of Artillery when he defended the guns of his battery against the enemy who charged in with the bayonet, 'howling like mad dogs'. Henry wrested a bayonet from one of the Russians, threw the man down and fought against the other assailants before being stabbed in the chest, arms and back. He was bayoneted twelve times but survived to receive his VC.

He died on 14 October 1870.

Sergeant GEORGE WALTERS
INKERMAN 5 November 1854

He was 23 years old and serving in the 49th Regiment of Foot (Princess Charlotte of Wales's), later the Royal Berkshire Regiment, when he went to the rescue of Brigadier General Adams, who was in great peril, surrounded by Russians. Walters bayoneted one of the assailants and undoubtedly saved Adams's life by his actions.

He died on 3 June 1872.

Corporal JOHN PRETTYJOHNS
(sometimes spelt PRETTYJOHN)
INKERMAN 5 November 1854

He was 31 years old and serving in the Royal Marine Light Infantry. His platoon had used up all its ammunition in clearing enemy snipers from some caves, when Prettyjohns noticed some parties of Russians creeping up the hillside towards him. He ordered his men to collect as many stones as they could carry, and then seized the leading Russian and threw him back down the hill. The other Russians came under a shower of stones and were forced back down the hill.

He died on 20 January 1887. The Royal Marines hold a procession each autumn to honour the memory of Corporal John Prettyjohns.

Able Seaman THOMAS REEVES
INKERMAN 5 November 1854

He was 26 years old and serving in the Royal Navy (Naval Brigade) when the Lancaster

Battery was attacked and many of the men were wounded. Reeves, together with Seaman James Gorman, Seaman Scholefield and two other men, who were killed during the action, mounted the defence work banquette and, under withering attack from the enemy, kept up a rapid fire. The muskets were reloaded for them by the wounded men under the parapet, and eventually the Russians were repulsed. All three men were awarded the VC.

Reeves died from tuberculosis on 4 August 1862.

Private THOMAS BEACH
INKERMAN 5 November 1854
He was 30 years old and serving in the 55th (Westmoreland) Foot. While on picket duty, he attacked several Russians who were robbing Lieutenant Colonel Carpenter as he lay wounded on the ground. Beach killed two of the Russians and protected Carpenter until men from the 41st Regiment came to his aid.

Beach was elected for the award by the privates of the regiment. He died on 24 August 1864.

Private JOHN McDERMOND
INKERMAN 5 November 1854
He was 22 years old and serving in the 47th (Lancashire) Regiment of Foot when he and Captain Hugh Rowlands rescued Colonel Hayly of the 47th Regiment, who had been wounded and was surrounded by Russians. McDermond killed the Russian who had wounded his colonel. Both men were awarded the VC. There is a painting depicting this action in the Army HQ at Preston.

McDermond died on 9 November 1868.

Private ANTHONY PALMER
INKERMAN 5 November 1854
He was 35 years old and serving in the 3rd Bn, Grenadier Guards when he was one of three men to volunteer to help Brevet Major Russell attempt to dislodge a party of Russians from the Sandbag Battery. Palmer saved Russell's life by shooting down a Russian who was about to bayonet him. He was also part of a small group which, by a desperate charge against overwhelming numbers, saved the battalion colours from capture.

He died from heart disease on 12 December 1892.

Seaman MARK SCHOLEFIELD
INKERMAN 5 November 1854
He was 26 years old and serving in the Royal Navy (Naval Brigade). When the Lancaster Battery was attacked and many of the men were wounded, Scholefield, together with Seaman James Gorman, Able Seaman Thomas Reeves and two other men, who were killed during the action, mounted the defence work banquette and, under withering attack from the enemy, kept up a rapid fire. The muskets were reloaded for them by the wounded men under the parapet and eventually the Russians were repulsed. All three men were awarded the VC.

Scholefield died on 15 February 1858 at sea, aboard the sloop *Acorn*.

Seaman JAMES GORMAN
INKERMAN 5 November 1854
He was 20 years old and serving in the Royal Navy (Naval Brigade) when the Lancaster Battery was attacked and many of the men were wounded. Gorman, together with Seaman Mark Scholefield, Able Seaman Thomas Reeves and two other men, who were killed during the action, mounted the defence work banquette and, under withering attack from the enemy, kept up a rapid fire. The muskets were reloaded for them by the wounded men under the parapet and eventually the Russians were repulsed. All three men were awarded the VC.

Gorman died from a stroke on 18 October 1882.

There is another man called James Gorman (who changed his name from Devereaux when he joined the Royal Navy), who also claims to have been awarded the VC. He too served in the Crimea and was present in the action for which Lieutenant William Hewett was awarded his VC, on 6 October 1854, and it is for this action that he made his claim. However, there is no record of him ever being awarded the medal.

Private JOHN BYRNE
INKERMAN and SEBASTOPOL
5 November 1854 and 11 May 1855
He was 22 years old and serving in the 68th Regiment of Foot, later the Durham Light Infantry. When his regiment was ordered to retire, he went back towards the enemy, at the risk of his own life, and picked up and carried back Private Harmon, who had been wounded. On 11 May 1855 Byrne engaged in hand-to-hand combat with an enemy soldier on the part of the parapet he was defending, killing this man and capturing his weapon. He also served in the Second Maori War, where his life was saved by Sergeant John Murray VC.

On 10 July 1879 Byrne accused a man of insulting the Victoria Cross. He shot the man in the shoulder, and when the police arrived he shot himself dead.

Lieutenant CLAUD BOURCHIER
SEBASTOPOL 20 November 1854
He was 23 years old and serving in the 1st Bn, Rifle Brigade (Prince Consort's Own) when he, along with Lieutenant William Cunninghame, was detailed with a party to drive the Russians out of the rifle pits. They launched a surprise attack after dark and drove the enemy out, but in the fighting the officer in charge was killed. The two lieutenants, however, maintained their advantage, withstanding all the enemy's counter-attacks during the night, and held on until relieved the next day. Both men were awarded the VC.

Bourchier died from 'softening of the brain' on 19 November 1877.

Lieutenant WILLIAM CUNNINGHAME
SEBASTOPOL 20 November 1854
He was 20 years old and serving in the 1st Bn, Rifle Brigade (Prince Consort's Own) when he, along with Lieutenant Claud Bourchier, was detailed with a party to drive the Russians out of the rifle pits. They launched a surprise attack after dark and drove the enemy out, but in the fighting the officer in charge was killed. The two lieutenants, however, maintained their advantage, withstanding all the enemy's counter-attacks during the night and held on

until relieved the next day. Both men were awarded the VC.

Cunninghame died on 11 November 1897.

Lieutenant WILBRAHAM LENNOX
SEBASTOPOL 20 November 1854
He was 24 years old and serving in the Corps of Royal Engineers when his working party of 100 men entrenched themselves in the rifle pits taken by Lieutenant Bourchier and Lieutenant Cunninghame. Despite extreme exposure and enemy attacks, they held on to the position all through the night.

Lennox died on 7 February 1897.

Private WILLIAM NORMAN
SEBASTOPOL 19 December 1854
He was 22 years old and serving in the 7th Regiment of Foot, later the Royal Fusiliers, when he was on single sentry duty some distance in front of the advanced sentries of an outlying picquet in the White Horse Ravine. It was a post of much danger, requiring great vigilance, as the Russian picquet was about 300 yards in front of him. When three Russians came reconnoitring under the cover of some brushwood, Norman jumped almost on top of the three men, one of whom ran off. He seized the other two as prisoners.

He died from brain fever on 13 March 1896.

Corporal WILLIAM LENDRIM (aka LENDRUM)
SEBASTOPOL
14 February, 11 and 20 April 1855
He was 25 years old and serving in the Corps of Royal Engineers. When he was in charge of a group of French Chasseurs during the building of a battery, a tremendous fire made a series of small breaches in the parapet. He zealously went from gap to gap and ensured that all the capsized gabions were replaced. On 11 April he extinguished a fire that had broken out among some sandbags on the parapet of a battery, all the time under fire from the enemy. On 20 April he was one of four volunteers to destroy screens that the Russians had put up to conceal their advanced rifle pits.

He died on 28 November 1891.

[91]

Private ALEXANDER WRIGHT
SEBASTOPOL
22 March and 19 April 1855
He was 29 years old and serving in the 77th (East Middlesex) Regiment of Foot, later the Middlesex Regiment (Duke of Cambridge's Own), when he demonstrated particular bravery in repelling a Russian sortie from Sebastopol. On 19 April Wright showed great bravery during the taking of the Russian rifle pits, and was noticed for the encouragement he gave to the other men while holding the pits under very heavy fire, despite being wounded in this action.

He died on 28 July 1858.

Sergeant GEORGE GARDINER
SEBASTOPOL
22 March and 18 June 1855
He was 34 years old and serving in the 57th Regiment of Foot (Duke of Cambridge's Own), later the Middlesex Regiment, when, during a sortie by the Russians, he rallied men who had been pushed out of the trenches, led them on and drove the enemy out, thus regaining the position. On 18 June, during the assault on the Redan, Gardiner jumped into a shell crater, made a parapet from the dead and kept up a steady fire on the enemy. He encouraged others to do the same, and the fire was kept up until all the ammunition was exhausted.

He died on 17 November 1891.

Private WILLIAM COFFEY
SEBASTOPOL 29 March 1855
He was 25 years old and serving in the 34th Regiment of Foot, later the Border Regiment, when he picked up a live shell that had fallen into his trench and threw it over the parapet, thus saving many lives.

Coffey shot himself on 13 July 1875, but an unsubstantiated reference suggests he may have died of diarrhoea.

Brevet Major FREDERICK ELTON
SEBASTOPOL
29 March, 7 June and 4 August 1855
He was 22 years old and serving in the 55th Regiment of Foot when he drove off some Russians who were destroying the works, taking one prisoner. On 7 June he was one of the first to lead his men from the trenches. On 4 August he was with a working party in the trenches, close to the Quarries, when a terrible fire was directed at them, making work there extremely dangerous. Elton took up a pick and shovel and worked fearlessly himself, encouraging the men by his fine example.

He died on 24 March 1888.

Boatswains Mate JOHN SULLIVAN
SEBASTOPOL 10 April 1855
He was 25 years old and serving in the Royal Navy (Naval Brigade) when he volunteered to erect a flagpole to act as an aiming point for no. 5 Greenhill Battery. Sullivan did this with great coolness, taking care to ensure that the pole was in perfect line with the target, even though he was under fire from snipers. His action enabled his battery to open fire on a hitherto concealed enemy battery that was doing great damage to some of the advanced works.

He killed himself on 28 June 1884.

Private SAMUEL EVANS
SEBASTOPOL 13 April 1855
He was 34 years old and serving in the 19th Regiment of Foot, later the Yorkshire Regiment (Alexandra, Princess of Wales's Own). On one occasion, when most of the gunners attached to a battery had been killed or wounded by concentrated Russian fire, Evans entered the embrasure and began to repair the damage. Despite being under heavy fire, he persisted in his work until the breach was repaired and more gunners had arrived.

He died on 4 October 1901.

Captain MATTHEW DIXON
SEBASTOPOL 17 April 1855
He was 34 years old and serving in the Royal Regiment of Artillery when his battery was hit by a shell that blew up the magazine, destroying the parapet, killing or wounding ten men, disabling five guns and covering another with earth. Instead of retiring, Dixon helped his men to keep the one remaining gun in action. He continued to fire his gun for seven

hours, until sunset, working as a gunner himself.

He died on 8 January 1905.

Colour Sergeant HENRY MacDONALD
SEBASTOPOL 19 April 1855

He was 31 years old and serving in the Corps of Royal Engineers when he displayed conspicuous bravery while effecting a lodgement in the enemy's rifle pits, forward of the advance of the attack. Later on the same day, when all the officers were badly wounded, MacDonald took command, and persisted in carrying on the sap, in spite of repeated attacks by the Russians.

He died on 15 February 1893.

Private JOSEPH BRADSHAW
WORONZOFF ROAD 22 April 1855

He was 20 years old and serving in the 2nd Bn, Rifle Brigade (Prince Consort's Own) when a bandsman was killed by a shot from one of the rifle pits that the Russians had constructed among the rocks overlooking the road. This so enraged the men that Bradshaw, accompanied by Private Robert Humpston, attacked and captured one of the pits in broad daylight, holding it until help arrived, when the rest of these 'wasps nests', as they were called, were taken and destroyed. The destruction of these pits was of great importance. Both men were awarded the VC.

Bradshaw died on 29 August 1893.

Private ROBERT HUMPSTON
WORONZOFF ROAD 22 April 1855

He was 23 years old and serving in the 2nd Bn, Rifle Brigade (Prince Consort's Own) when a bandsman was killed by a shot from one of the rifle pits that the Russians had constructed among the rocks overlooking the road. This so enraged the men that Humpston, accompanied by Private Joseph Bradshaw, attacked and captured one of the pits in broad daylight, holding it until help arrived, when the rest of these 'wasps nests', as they were called, were taken and destroyed. The destruction of these pits was of great importance. Both men were awarded the VC.

Humpston died from 'onteritis' on 22 December 1884.

Private RODERICK McGREGOR
SEBASTOPOL 22 April and July 1855

He was 31 years old and serving in the 1st Bn, Rifle Brigade (Prince Consort's Own). When a bandsman was killed as he went to a well in front of the advanced trench, McGregor, along with two others, rushed the position and drove the Russians out. In July, when two Russians in a rifle pit were being most annoying by their continuous sniping, McGregor crossed the open space under a hail of bullets, took shelter under a rock and then dislodged them, occupying the position himself.

He died from bronchitis on 9 August 1888.

Captain THOMAS HAMILTON
SEBASTOPOL 11 May 1855

He was 27 years old and serving in the 68th Regiment of Foot, later the Durham Light Infantry, when, during a most determined sortie with a small force, he boldly charged great numbers of the enemy, driving them from a battery they had just captured. Hamilton was conspicuous for his gallantry on this occasion and his action saved the works from falling into enemy hands.

He died on 3 March 1908.

Lieutenant Hugh BURGOYNE
SEA OF AZOV GENITCHI 29 May 1855

He was 21 years old and serving in the Royal Navy on HMS *Swallow* when, along with Lieutenant Cecil Buckley from HMS *Miranda* and Gunner John Robarts from HMS *Ardent*, he volunteered to land on a beach where the Russians were present in strength. They were beyond the range of covering fire from the ships offshore and met considerable enemy opposition, but managed to set fire to some corn stores and ammunition dumps and to destroy enemy equipment before embarking again. All three men were awarded the VC.

Burgoyne went down with HMS *Captain* on 7 September 1870, and his body was never recovered. His father was Sir John Burgoyne, who served under Wellington throughout the

Peninsular War and was Lord Raglan's adviser in the Crimean War.

Gunner JOHN ROBARTS
SEA OF AZOV GENITCHI 29 May 1855
He was 37 years old and serving in the Royal Navy on HMS *Ardent* when, along with Lieutenant Cecil Buckley from HMS *Miranda* and Lieutenant Hugh Burgoyne from HMS *Swallow*, he volunteered to land at a beach where the Russians were present in strength. They were beyond the range of covering fire from the ships offshore and met considerable enemy opposition, but managed to set fire to some corn stores and ammunition dumps and to destroy enemy equipment before embarking again. All three men were awarded the VC.

Robarts died on 17 October 1888.

Lieutenant CECIL BUCKLEY
SEA OF AZOV GENITCHI and TAGANROG 29 May and 3 June 1855
He was 24 years old and serving in the Royal Navy on HMS *Miranda* when, along with Lieutenant Hugh Burgoyne from HMS *Swallow* and Gunner John Robarts from HMS *Ardent*, he volunteered to land at a beach where the Russians were present in strength. They were beyond the range of covering fire from the ships offshore and met considerable enemy opposition, but managed to set fire to some corn stores and ammunition dumps and to destroy enemy equipment before embarking again. On 3 June Buckley set off for Taganrog with Boatswain Henry Cooper in a four-oared gig, landing while the town was under bombardment. Its garrison numbered 3,000 men, but Buckley and Cooper set fire to various government buildings and stores, and destroyed arms and equipment. All four men were awarded the VC.

Buckley's was the very first VC to be gazetted.

He died from cancer on 7 December 1872.

Boatswain HENRY COOPER
TAGANROG 3 June 1855
He was 30 years old and serving in the Royal Navy on HMS *Miranda* when he set off for Taganrog with Lieutenant Cecil Buckley in a four-oared gig, landing while the town was under bombardment. Its garrison numbered 3,000 men, but Buckley and Cooper set fire to various government buildings and stores, and destroyed arms and equipment. Both men were awarded the VC.

Cooper died on 15 July 1893.

Sergeant GEORGE SYMONS
INKERMAN 6 June 1855
He was 29 years old and serving in the Royal Regiment of Artillery when he volunteered to unmask the embrasures of a five-gun battery on the advanced right flank. This he did under heavy fire from the enemy, which increased with the opening of each embrasure. When Symons came to the last one, he boldly mounted the parapet and threw down the sandbags. As he did so, he was severely wounded by an enemy shell. The original award was for action on 18 October 1854, but this was amended later to the above date.

He died on 18 November 1871.

Captain HENRY JONES
SEBASTOPOL 7 June 1855
He was 24 years old and serving in the 7th Regiment of Foot, later the Royal Fusiliers. After an attack on the 'Quarries', which his party had taken, Jones encouraged the men around him throughout the night to repel repeated counter-attacks by the Russians. Although he had been wounded earlier in the day, he remained at his post until daylight.

He died on 18 December 1916.

Bombardier THOMAS WILKINSON
SEBASTOPOL 7 June 1855
He was 23 years old and serving in the Royal Marine Artillery, Royal Marines. When Russian fire had demolished much of the earthworks in the advanced batteries, Wilkinson went up to the parapet and called for sandbags to be handed up to him. He then proceeded to repair the damage under the most galling fire, cheered on as he worked by the men in the nearby trenches.

He died from diarrhoea on 22 September 1887.

Gunner THOMAS ARTHUR (real name McARTHUR)
SEBASTOPOL 7 and 18 June 1855
He was 20 years old and serving in the Royal Regiment of Artillery when he was suddenly taken ill and left without leave to do so. On his return, he found that his battery had gone. Noticing that the 7th Fusiliers were running short of ammunition, he ran to the magazine and brought as many cartridges as he could to the front under heavy fire. He was, however, marched away in custody for having been absent from his gun, but the colonel of the infantry intervened and his dereliction of duty turned into an act of heroism. On 18 June he volunteered for the party which spiked the guns in the assault on the Redan.
Arthur died on 2 March 1902.

Private MATTHEW HUGHES
SEBASTOPOL 7 and 18 June 1855
He was 33 years old and serving in the Royal Fusiliers (City of London Regiment), later the Royal Regiment of Fusiliers, when he twice went across open ground to fetch ammunition during the attack on the 'Quarries'. Hughes also brought in Private John Hampton, who was lying wounded. On 18 June he volunteered to bring in Lieutenant Hobson of his regiment, who was lying wounded in the open. In the process, Hughes himself was severely wounded. Hughes was only 5 feet tall, so these acts were all the more physically demanding for a man so small.
He died from cirrhosis of the liver on 9 January 1882.

Private JOHN LYONS
SEBASTOPOL 10 June 1855
He was 32 years old and serving in the 19th Regiment of Foot, later the Yorkshire Regiment (Alexandra, Princess of Wales's Own), when he picked up a live shell that had fallen among the guard in the trenches and threw it over the parapet, thus saving many lives.
Lyons died on 20 April 1867.

Private JOSEPH PROSSER
SEBASTOPOL
16 June and 11 August 1855
He was 22 years old and serving in the 2nd Bn, 1st Regiment of Foot, later the Royal Scots, the Lothian Regiment, when he pursued and captured a deserter under heavy cross-fire from the enemy. On 11 August Prosser left the most advanced trench and helped to carry to safety a severely wounded soldier of the 95th Regiment who was unable to move. This was under very heavy fire.
He died on 10 June 1867.

Lieutenant HOWARD ELPHINSTONE
SEBASTOPOL 18 June 1855
He was 25 years old and serving in the Corps of Royal Engineers when, on the night following the unsuccessful attack on the Redan, he volunteered to take a party of men to search for the scaling ladders left behind after the attack. While performing this task, he also conducted a search near the enemy lines for wounded men, 20 of whom he was able to bring back to our trenches.
He died on 8 March 1890, when he slipped, hit his head and fell overboard while on his way to New Zealand.

Lieutenant WILLIAM HOPE
SEBASTOPOL 18 June 1855
He was 21 years old and serving in the 7th Regiment of Foot, later the Royal Fusiliers. After the attack on the Redan, he was informed that Lieutenant Hobson was lying wounded out in the open. Hope went to search for him and found him. He fetched four other men but they found they could not move Hobson without a stretcher. Hope then went to 'Egerton's Pit', where he found a stretcher which he used to bring Hobson in, all the time under continuous fire.
Hope was the inventor of the shrapnel shell for rifled guns.
He died on 17 December 1909.

Lieutenant GERALD GRAHAM
SEBASTOPOL 18 June 1855
He was 23 years old and serving in the Corps

of Royal Engineers when, during the attack on the Redan, and with the help of Sapper John Perie, he showed conspicuous bravery at the head of the ladder party. Graham also rescued a wounded man under very heavy fire and later brought back some of the scaling ladders that had been abandoned. Both Graham and Perie were awarded the VC.

He died on 17 December 1899.

Lieutenant HENRY RABY
SEBASTOPOL 18 June 1855
He was 28 years old and serving in the Royal Navy (Naval Brigade). After the assault on the Redan, he went with Captain of the Forecastle John Taylor, Lieutenant D'Aeth and Boatswains Mate Curtis to the assistance of a wounded soldier from the 57th Regiment, who had been shot through both legs and was sitting up calling for help. They ran 70 yards across open ground under heavy fire and brought him back to safety. Lieutenant D'Aeth was the only one from this group not to be awarded the VC, as he died shortly afterwards and it could not be awarded posthumously at this time.

Although Raby was not the first man to be awarded the VC, he was the first to be officially presented with it. Legend has it that Queen Victoria stabbed him in the chest when pinning the medal on his uniform, while he stood unflinching.

He died on 13 February 1907.

Colour Sergeant PETER LEITCH
SEBASTOPOL 18 June 1855
He was 35 years old and serving in the Corps of Royal Engineers. During the assault on the Redan, he struggled to build a ramp across the ditch of the Redan by tearing down the gabions, filling them with earth and placing them in position in the ditch. He continued in this attempt, under very heavy fire, until he was disabled by his wounds.

He died on 6 December 1892.

Corporal FELIX SMITH
SEBASTOPOL 18 June 1855
He was 30 years old and serving in the 17th Regiment of Foot, later the Leicestershire

Regiment. After the failed attack on the Redan, he went out repeatedly in front of the advanced trenches against the Great Redan, under heavy fire, and brought in wounded comrades who would otherwise almost certainly have died.

He died from bronchitis and pneumonia on 16 January 1906.

Boatswains Mate HENRY CURTIS
SEBASTOPOL 18 June 1855
He was 32 years old and serving in the Royal Navy (Naval Brigade). After the assault on the Redan, he went with Lieutenant Raby, Lieutenant D'Aeth and Captain of the Forecastle Taylor to the assistance of a wounded soldier from the 57th Regiment, who had been shot through both legs and was sitting up calling for help. They ran 70 yards across open ground under heavy fire and brought him back to safety. Lieutenant D'Aeth was the only one from this group not to be awarded the VC, as he died shortly afterwards and it could not he awarded posthumously at this time.

Curtis died from kidney failure on 23 November 1896.

Captain of the Forecastle JOHN TAYLOR
SEBASTOPOL 18 June 1855
He was 33 years old and serving in the Royal Navy (Naval Brigade). After the assault on the Redan, he went with Lieutenant Raby, Lieutenant D'Aeth and Boatswains Mate Curtis to the assistance of a wounded soldier from the 57th Regiment, who had been shot through both legs and was sitting up calling for help. They ran 70 yards across open ground under heavy fire and brought him back to safety. Lieutenant D'Aeth was the only one from this group not to be awarded the VC, as he died shortly afterwards and it could not he awarded posthumously at this time.

Taylor died from bronchitis and pulmonary congestion on 25 February 1857.

Private JOHN SIMS
SEBASTOPOL 18 June 1855
He was 19 years old and serving in the 34th Regiment of Foot, later the Border Regiment,

when after the failed attack on the Redan, he went out into the open under heavy fire and brought back to safety many wounded men who would almost certainly have died.

He died from tuberculosis in the workhouse on 6 December 1881.

Sapper JOHN PERIE
SEBASTOPOL 18 June 1855
He was 24 years old and serving in the Corps of Royal Engineers when he assisted Lieutenant Gerald Graham in leading the sailors with the ladders at the attack on the Redan. He also rescued a wounded man who was lying in the open, despite being wounded in the right side by a rifle bullet. Later he risked his life helping to recover scaling ladders abandoned after the attack. Both men were awarded the VC.

Perie died from liver disease on 17 September 1874.

Captain THOMAS ESMONDE
SEBASTOPOL 18 and 20 June 1855
He was 26 years old and serving in the 18th Regiment of Foot, later the Royal Irish Regiment. After the attack on the Redan, he assisted in rescuing the wounded, at great personal risk to himself, all the time under heavy fire from the enemy. On 20 June, while in command of a covering party, a fireball fell close by. Esmonde called out to his men to take cover and dashed out to extinguish it himself. A hail of fire was directed at him, but he was able to put out the fireball and escape unscathed.

He died on 14 January 1873. His great-nephew was Lieutenant Commander Eugene Esmonde VC.

Private JOHN ALEXANDER
SEBASTOPOL
18 June and 6 September 1855
He was serving in the 90th Perthshire Light Infantry, later the Cameronians (Scottish Rifles). After the attack on the Redan, he went out of the trenches and carried in several wounded men under heavy fire. On 6 September he went out and helped bring in Captain Buckley, who was lying dangerously wounded in an exposed position.

He was killed in action at Alumbagh on 24 September 1857.

Private CHARLES McCORRIE (or McCURRY)
SEBASTOPOL 23 June 1855
He was 25 years old and serving in the 57th Regiment of Foot, later the Middlesex Regiment, when he threw over the parapet a live shell that had been thrown into the trenches from an enemy battery, thus saving many lives.

He died on 8 April 1857.

Seaman JOSEPH TREWAVAS
SEA OF AZOV 3 July 1855
He was 19 years old and serving in the Royal Navy, when he was one of a party of men which set off in a four-oared gig to destroy a pontoon bridge over the Genitchi Strait. They reached the bridge and Trewavas began to cut the hawsers with an axe. He was under heavy fire from the enemy, who were less than 80 yards away. Eventually the strands of the hawser gave way and the two ends of the pontoon drifted apart. As he was getting back into the gig, he was hit in the shoulder; the men escaped, although the gig was riddled with bullet holes.

He died on 20 July 1903, having cut his own throat while suffering from deep depression.

Lieutenant GEORGE DOWELL
FORT OF VIBORG, Finland
13 July 1855
He was 24 years old and serving in the Royal Marine Artillery, Royal Marines when there was an explosion aboard HMS *Arrogant's* second cutter. Under heavy fire, Dowell jumped into a boat, rescued three of the crew from the stricken cutter and took them aboard HMS *Raby*. He then went out again to pick up Captain of the Mast Ingouville and the rest of the cutter's crew, before towing the boat out of range of the Russian guns. Both Dowell and Ingouville were awarded the VC.

Dowell died on 3 August 1910.

Captain of the Mast GEORGE INGOUVILLE
FORT OF VIBORG, Finland 13 July 1855
He was 28 years old and serving in the Royal Navy when the boats of HMS *Arrogant* were engaged by the enemy. Her second cutter was hit in the magazine and drifted inshore under the enemy guns. Ingouville, although wounded, jumped overboard and swam to the boat; taking hold of the painter, he tried to turn the cutter out to sea. Lieutenant Dowell then came to his assistance with three volunteers; they took off the crew from the cutter, rescued Ingouville from the water and then towed the stricken boat out of gun range. Both men were awarded the VC.

Ingouville drowned on 13 January 1869; his body was never found.

Boatswains Mate JOHN SHEPPARD (or SHEPHERD)
SEBASTOPOL
15 July and 16 August 1855
He was 37 years old and serving in the Royal Navy (Naval Brigade) when he went into the harbour at night, in a punt which he had made especially for the purpose, with an explosive device with which he intended to blow up the Russian flagship. He managed to get past the enemy's steamboats at the entrance of Careening Bay, but was prevented from getting further by a long string of boats carrying troops. On 16 August he made a second attempt, which also proved unsuccessful, but he brought back much valuable information. Both actions were carried out in the face of great danger.

Sheppard died on 17 December 1884.

Corporal JOHN ROSS
SEBASTOPOL
21 July, 23 August and 8 September 1855
He was 33 years old and serving in the Corps of Royal Engineers when he displayed great bravery in connecting the 4th Parallel Right Attack with an old Russian rifle pit. All the work was carried out at night, only 40 yards from the lines. On 23 August, while in charge of the advance from the 5th Parallel Right Attack on the Redan, Ross placed and filled 25 gabions under heavy fire from the enemy. On 8 September he crept right up to the Redan during the night and found that the Russians had evacuated it. His information enabled the Redan to be taken. He also brought back a wounded man.

He died on 23 October 1879.

Sergeant JOHN COLEMAN
SEBASTOPOL 30 August 1855
He was 57 years old and serving in the 97th Regiment of Foot, later the Queen's Own Royal West Kent Regiment, when the enemy attacked a new sap and drove the working party in. Coleman remained in the open, exposed to fire from the Russian rifle pits, until all those around him had been killed or wounded. He finally came in, carrying a mortally wounded officer.

He was reportedly killed in action at Lucknow on 21 May 1858. However, some records suggest that he died on 4 June 1882.

Boatswain Third Class JOSEPH KELLAWAY
SEA OF AZOV, MARIONPOL
31 August 1855
He was 30 years old and serving in the Royal Navy when he was one of five men from HMS *Wrangler* put ashore to burn boats, fishing stations and haystacks. They were, however, ambushed by about 50 Russians. In trying to escape, one of the men fell, and Kellaway went back to help him, thinking he was injured. They were surrounded by the enemy and, notwithstanding Kellaway's gallant resistance, they were taken prisoner.

He died on 2 October 1880.

Private ALFRED ABLETT
SEBASTOPOL 2 September 1855
He was 25 years old and serving in the 3rd Bn, Grenadier Guards when a live shell fell into the trench near two cases of ammunition. At once realising the danger, Ablett seized the shell in both hands and threw it over the parapet. It exploded as it touched the ground, but not a man was injured.

He died of a heart attack on 12 March 1897.

Colour Sergeant JAMES CRAIG
SEBASTOPOL 6 September 1855
He was 30 years old and serving in the Scots Fusilier Guards when he went out with a drummer under heavy fire to look for Captain Buckley, who was believed to have been wounded. Craig subsequently brought in Buckley's body, although he was himself badly wounded during this action.

He died on 18 March 1861, when he suddenly cut his own throat and jumped into a river.

Brevet Lieutenant Colonel FREDERICK MAUDE
SEBASTOPOL 8 September 1855
He was 33 years old and serving in the 3rd Regiment of Foot, later the Buffs (East Kent Regiment). In command of the covering party of the 2nd Division, he held a traverse with only nine or ten men until all hope of support was lost, despite being severely wounded. His VC action is often incorrectly dated to the 5th.

He died on 20 June 1897. His cousin was Captain Francis Cornwallis Maude VC.

Assistant Surgeon THOMAS HALE
SEBASTOPOL 8 September 1855
He was 22 years old and serving in the 1st Bn, 7th Regiment of Foot, later the Royal Fusiliers, when during the attack on the Redan he stayed with the severely wounded Lieutenant Hope, when all but one had retreated. On the same day Hale cleared the most advanced sap of wounded, and then went out into the open under heavy fire and carried several wounded men into the sap.

He died on 25 December 1909.

Captain GRONOW DAVIS
SEBASTOPOL 8 September 1855
He was 27 years old and serving in the Royal Regiment of Artillery when he commanded the spiking party in the attack on the Redan, with great coolness and gallantry. Noticing Lieutenant Sanders lying wounded, he jumped over the parapet of a sap and went some distance across open ground under murderous fire, to help carry him back to safety. He also carried several other wounded men back to safety.

He died on 18 October 1891.

Captain CHARLES LUMLEY
SEBASTOPOL 8 September 1855
He was 31 years old and serving in the 97th Regiment of Foot, later the Queen's Own Royal West Kent Regiment, when he was one of the first to enter the works during the attack on the Redan. He attacked three Russian gunners who were reloading a gun, shooting two of them with his revolver. He was then hit by a large stone and stunned but recovered quickly, drew his sword and cheered his men on. He was also wounded in the mouth by a bullet.

He shot himself on 17 October 1858.

Sergeant ANDREW MOYNIHAN
SEBASTOPOL 8 September 1855
He was 24 years old and serving in the 90th Regiment of Foot when he was with the storming party at the assault on the Redan. He personally encountered and killed five Russians. He also, under heavy fire, rescued a wounded officer from near the Redan.

He died from typhoid fever on 18 May 1867.

Corporal ROBERT SHIELDS
SEBASTOPOL 8 September 1855
He was 28 years old and serving in the 23rd Regiment of Foot, later the Royal Welch Fusiliers. After the attack on the Redan, he went with Assistant Surgeon William Sylvester to the aid of Lieutenant Dynely, who was lying mortally wounded. They remained with him, dressing his wounds, in a most dangerous and exposed position. Both were awarded the VC.

Shields died from delirium tremens on 23 December 1864.

Bombardier DANIEL CAMBRIDGE
SEBASTOPOL 8 September 1855
He was 35 years old and serving in the Royal Regiment of Artillery when he volunteered for the spiking party for the assault on the Redan. Despite being severely wounded twice, Cambridge remained with the party, refusing

to leave until the general retirement was ordered, and even then he repeatedly went back into the open to carry wounded men to safety. Later in the day, he sprang forward to bring in another wounded man, and was seen to stagger. Subsequently he was found to have been shot a third time. Finally incapacitated, he took no further action in the campaign.

He died on 12 June 1882, as a result of his wounds, having never fully recovered from them.

Private JOHN CONNERS
SEBASTOPOL 8 September 1855
He was 25 years old and serving in the 3rd Regiment of Foot, later the Buffs (East Kent Regiment), when he showed conspicuous gallantry during the assault on the Redan. Going to the assistance of an officer of the 30th Regiment who was surrounded by Russians, Conners shot one and bayoneted another, and was observed in close combat with the enemy inside the Redan for some time.

He died on 29 January 1857.

Assistant Surgeon WILLIAM SYLVESTER
SEBASTOPOL 8 and 18 September 1855
He was 24 years old and serving in the 23rd Regiment of Foot, later the Royal Welch Fusiliers. After the attack on the Redan, he went with Corporal Robert Shields to the aid of Lieutenant Dynely, who was lying mortally wounded. They remained with him, dressing his wounds, in a most dangerous and exposed position. On 18 September Sylvester performed a similar act under fire. Both men were awarded the VC.

Sylvester died on 13 March 1920.

Lieutenant GEORGE DAY
GENITCHI 17 and 21 September 1855
He was 36 years old and serving in the Royal Navy aboard HMS *Recruit* when he landed behind the Russian lines to reconnoitre the southern shore, where the enemy had four gunboats. He approached to within 200 yards and found that the boats were not strongly manned. On 21 September he returned to the same place, only to find that the boats were now fully manned and ready for action. Day waited for nine hours, fell asleep in the weeds, and was found the next morning more dead than alive.

It was supposedly the sight of George Day wearing his three orders and nine medals across his chest that prompted the Prince of Wales (later Edward VII) to suggest that medals should be collected together and worn neatly on one bar.

Day died on 18 December 1876, after a long illness.

Private GEORGE STRONG
SEBASTOPOL 25–30 September 1855
He was 19 years old and serving in the Coldstream Guards when he picked up a live shell that had fallen into the trench among the men, and threw it over the parapet. Strong was well aware of the extreme danger involved and his action saved many lives. The exact date is not known.

He died on 25 August 1888.

Lieutenant CHRISTOPHER TEESDALE
KARS, Turkey 29 September 1855
He was 22 years old and serving in the Royal Regiment of Artillery when he volunteered to take command of the force engaged in defending the most advanced part of the works. Teesdale threw himself into the midst of the action and encouraged the garrison to make so vigorous an attack that the Russians were driven out. During this action he induced the Turkish artillerymen to return to their post, from which they had been driven out by enemy fire. After the final victorious assault, and at some risk to himself, he saved a considerable number of Russian wounded from the fury of the Turks, an action that was gratefully acknowledged by the Russian Staff.

Teesdale served as equerry to the Prince of Wales until 1890, and then as ADC to the Queen. He died on 1 December 1893.

Commander JOHN COMMERELL
SPIT OF ARABAT 11 October 1855
He was 26 years old and serving in the Royal Navy when he, with Quartermaster William Rickard and Seaman George Milestone,

landed from HMS *Weser* and set fire to 400 tons of corn and forage belonging to the Russians. However, they accidentally alerted the guards and were pursued by about 30 of them as they ran the 2½ miles back to their ship. Milestone became exhausted and begged to be left behind. The others removed his boots and half carried him back, arriving just ahead of the Russians. In spite of heavy fire, they made good their escape. Both men were awarded the VC.

Commerell was one of only a few VC holders who became MPs.

He died on 21 May 1901.

Quartermaster WILLIAM RICKARD

SPIT OF ARABAT 11 October 1855

He was 27 years old and serving in the Royal Navy when he, with Commander John Commerell and Seaman George Milestone, landed from HMS *Weser* and set fire to 400 tons of corn and forage belonging to the Russians. However, they accidentally alerted the guards and were pursued by about 30 of them as they ran the 2½ miles back to their ship. Milestone became exhausted and begged to be left behind. The others removed his boots and half carried him back, arriving just ahead of the Russians. In spite of heavy fire, they made good their escape. Both men were awarded the VC.

Rickard died on 21 February 1905.

Persian War, 1856–57 (3 VCs)

In the days when Britain ruled India, a major influence on British policy was the threat of incursions from Russia into this part of the Empire. It was with the Russian threat in mind that Britain helped to create Afghanistan between India and Persia, as a buffer state. The British supported the city of Herat's incorporation into Afghanistan, but when Persia annexed Herat in October 1856 and diplomatic measures to restore it failed, Britain declared war on 1 November. Three Victoria Crosses were awarded for this campaign.

Captain JOHN WOOD

BUSHIRE 9 December 1856

He was 38 years old and serving in the 20th Bombay Native Infantry, Indian Army when he led the Grenadier Company at the head of the storming party and was the first man on to the parapet of the fort, where he was immediately attacked by a large number of the enemy. A volley was fired at him and his men at very close range. Wood was hit by seven musket balls, but at once threw himself upon the enemy, killing their leader. He was closely followed by the men of the company, who speedily overcame the garrison.

He died from concussion of the brain on 23 January 1878.

Lieutenant JOHN MALCOLMSON

KHOOSH-AB 8 February 1857

He was 21 years old and serving in the 3rd Bombay Light Cavalry, Indian Army when he saw Lieutenant Arthur Moore charge into a square of 500 Persians by jumping his horse over their bayonets; as his stricken horse fell dead, it landed on top of Moore, breaking his sword. Malcolmson, seeing this, fought his way into the square, offered Moore his stirrup and carried him to safety. Had it not been for Malcolmson's help, Moore would almost certainly have been killed. Both men were awarded the VC.

Malcolmson died on 14 August 1902.

Lieutenant ARTHUR MOORE

KHOOSH-AB 8 February 1857

He was 26 years old and serving in the 3rd Bombay Light Cavalry, Indian Army when he charged into a square of 500 Persians by jumping his horse over their bayonets. Moore's horse fell dead and landed on top of him, breaking his sword. Courageously, he tried to fight off the Persians with his broken sword. Had it not been for Lieutenant John Malcolmson's help, he would almost certainly have been killed. Both men were awarded the VC.

Moore died from heart failure brought on by influenza on 25 April 1913.

Chapter Five

THE INDIAN MUTINY, 1857–59

The Indian (or Sepoy) Mutiny began in Meerut on 10 May 1857, and although it was ultimately unsuccessful it tested Britain's military resources to the limit. There had been unrest among the Indian population for several years. The infamous 'greased cartridges' provided the flash-point for the mutiny. Soon the sepoys at the Delhi garrison had joined the Meerut rebels and the mutiny quickly spread across northern India.

British troops were ordered to proceed immediately to India. In all, 182 Victoria Crosses were awarded for this campaign (the same number as for the Second World War), which seems a rather large number. But it must be remembered that the VC was the only bravery award then available, and the feeling at the time was that these men had saved the empire.

Captain DIGHTON PROBYN
AGRA 1857–1858

He was 24 years old and serving in the 2nd Punjab Cavalry, Indian Army when he performed many acts of gallantry. At the battle of Agra he defended himself against five or six rebels, killing two before help arrived. On another occasion he cut down a rebel who had bayoneted him in the wrist, and later that day he killed an enemy standard bearer and captured the colours.

Probyn was Comptroller to Queen Alexandra from 1910 to 1924, and equerry to the Prince of Wales. A regiment in the Indian Army, Probyn's Horse, was named after him. His medal is unusual in that it is undated.

He died on 20 June 1924.

Deputy Assistant Commissary of Ordnance JOHN BUCKLEY
DELHI 11 May 1857

He was 43 years old and serving in the Bengal Veteran Establishment, Indian Army when he was one of nine men, along with Lieutenant George Forrest and Lieutenant William Raynor, who defended the magazine for more than five hours against a large force of mutineers. They barricaded the gates and put two 6-pounder guns loaded with grapeshot at the entrances. When the enemy started scaling the walls with ladders, the entire native garrison went over to join the mutiny. With no hope of help, they fired the magazine to prevent the mutineers capturing the ammunition. Five of the defenders were killed outright and one died of his wounds, but many of the enemy were also killed. Buckley was captured by the enemy and soon learnt that his entire family had been ruthlessly murdered by the rebels. He begged for death from his captors but they refused to kill him on account of his bravery at the magazine. He later escaped and rejoined the British Army, volunteering for all manner of dangerous missions. He also oversaw the execution of 150 rebels who were strapped to the muzzles of cannon and blown to bits. All three men were awarded the VC.

He died on 14 July 1876.

Lieutenant GEORGE FORREST
DELHI 11 May 1857

He was 57 years old and serving in the Bengal Veteran Establishment, Indian Army when he was one of nine men, along with Deputy Assistant Commissary of Ordnance John Buckley and Lieutenant William Raynor, who defended the magazine for more than five

[102]

hours against a large force of mutineers. They barricaded the gates and put two 6-pounder guns loaded with grapeshot at the entrances. When the enemy started scaling the walls with ladders, the entire native garrison went over to join the mutiny. With no hope of help, they fired the magazine to prevent the mutineers capturing the ammunition. Five of the defenders were killed outright and one died of his wounds, but many of the enemy were also killed. All three men were awarded the VC.

He was killed in action at Dehra Dun on 3 November 1859.

Lieutenant WILLIAM RAYNOR
DELHI 11 May 1857
He was 61 years old and serving in the Bengal Veteran Establishment, Indian Army when he was one of nine men, along with Deputy Assistant Commissary of Ordnance John Buckley and Lieutenant George Forrest, who defended the magazine for more than five hours against a large force of mutineers. They barricaded the gates and put two 6-pounder guns loaded with grapeshot at the entrances. When the enemy started scaling the walls with ladders, the entire native garrison went over to join the mutiny. With no hope of help, they fired the magazine to prevent the mutineers capturing the ammunition. Five of the defenders were killed outright and one died of his wounds, but many of the enemy were also killed. All three men were awarded the VC.

Raynor had also served in the Nepal War of 1814–16. At 61 years and 10 months, he was the oldest recipient of the VC.

He died on 13 December 1860.

Ensign EVERARD LISLE-PHILLIPPS
DELHI 30 May–18 September 1857
He was 22 years old and serving in the 11th Bengal Native Infantry when his regiment was one of the first to revolt. When the Queen's proclamation against the insurgents came, he had to read it out as he could speak the native language. Bullets whistled around him as he spoke, but before he had even finished the first sentence his horse was shot from under him, and he fell to the ground, wounded by a stray

bullet. Undeterred, he got to his feet and read through the whole proclamation from beginning to end before taking cover.

After the desertion of the Bengal Infantry, he joined the 60th Rifles. He performed many gallant deeds and was wounded three times. At the assault on the city of Delhi, he captured the Water Bastion with a small party. He was killed in street fighting in the city on 18 September 1857. His VC was awarded 50 years after his death, making him the first posthumous VC.

Lieutenant ALFRED HEATHCOTE
SIEGE OF DELHI June–September 1857
He was 25 years old and serving in the 60th Rifles, later the King's Royal Rifle Corps. Throughout the siege, during which he was wounded, his conduct was most gallant. Heathcote volunteered for services of extreme danger, especially during the six days of the assault against the rebels.

Heathcote was elected for the award by the officers of his regiment.

He died on 21 February 1912.

Sergeant Major PETER GILL
BENARES 4 June 1857
He was 25 years old and serving in the Loodiana Regiment. When the mutineers began burning bungalows and killing the inhabitants, Gill, along with Sergeant Major Matthew Rosamund and Private John Kirk, volunteered to go to the aid of Captain Brown and his family, who were in great danger, and duly brought them back to the safety of the barracks. He also saved the life of a sergeant who had been bayoneted, by cutting off the head of his assailant. On the same evening he faced down a guard of 27 mutineers, despite being armed with only his sword. He is also said to have saved the life of a major who was being attacked by two sepoys. All three men were awarded the VC.

Gill was killed in action at Morar on 24 October 1868.

Sergeant Major MATTHEW ROSAMUND
BENARES 4 June 1857
He was 33 years old and serving in the 37th Bengal Native Infantry. When the mutineers

began burning bungalows and killing the inhabitants, Rosamund, along with Sergeant Major Peter Gill and Private John Kirk, volunteered to go to the aid of Captain Brown and his family, who were in great danger, and duly brought them back to the safety of the barracks. Later he volunteered to go with Lieutenant Colonel Spottiswoode to set fire to the sepoy lines to drive them out. All three men were awarded the VC.

Rosamund died on 14 July 1866.

Private JOHN KIRK
BENARES 4 June 1857

He was 29 years old and serving in the 10th Regiment of Foot, later the Lincolnshire Regiment. When the mutineers began burning bungalows and killing the inhabitants, Kirk, along with Sergeant Major Peter Gill and Sergeant Major Matthew Rosamund, volunteered to go to the aid of Captain Brown and his family, who were in great danger, and duly brought them back to the safety of the barracks. All three men were awarded the VC.

Kirk died from tuberculosis on 31 August 1865.

Colour Sergeant CORNELIUS COUGHLAN (aka COGHLAN)
BADLE-KE-SERAI and DELHI
8 June and 18 July 1857

He was 28 years old and serving in the 75th Regiment of Foot, later the Gordon Highlanders, when he entered a building held by the enemy and rescued Private Corbett, who was severely wounded. On 18 July his party was hesitating before charging down a lane raked with cross-fire. He encouraged and cheered them on. They entered an enclosure filled with rebels and killed every one. Coughlan also returned under cross-fire to collect dhoolies and carry off the wounded. Queen Victoria wrote a personal letter to him on hearing about his brave act.

He died on 14 February 1915.

Lieutenant ALFRED JONES
DELHI 8 June and 10 October 1857

He was 25 years old and serving in the 9th Lancers (The Queen's Royal Regiment), when his squadron charged some rebels with a gun. They rode straight through them, killing the drivers and capturing the gun. Jones then trained the gun on a village held by the mutineers and drove them out. At Agra on 10 October he received 22 wounds, including the loss of an eye and part of his head being cut away.

On the day of his award he was sporting such a shocking bruise above his blind eye that the Queen became nervous and pricked him through his tunic as she pinned on his cross. He died on 29 May 1920.

Pensioned Sergeant HENRY HARTIGAN
BADLE-KE-SERAI and AGRA
8 June and 10 October 1857

He was 31 years old and serving in the 9th Lancers (The Queen's Royal Regiment) when he went to the assistance of Sergeant Helstone, who was wounded and surrounded by the enemy, and at great risk to himself carried the sergeant to safety. On 10 October he ran unarmed to the assistance of Sergeant Crews, who was being attacked by four rebels. He wrenched a tulwar from the first man with one hand and punched him in the mouth with the other. He then attacked the other rebels, killing one and wounding two.

He died on 29 October 1886.

Lieutenant THOMAS CADELL
DELHI 12 June 1857

He was 21 years old and serving in the 2nd European Bengal Fusiliers, later the Royal Munster Fusiliers, when during an attack by the rebels he saw a bugler fall wounded. Under heavy fire, he carried him from the enemy to safety. On the same evening he went with three others towards the advancing mutineers to save the life of a wounded man who had been left behind.

He died on 6 April 1919. His cousin was Lieutenant Samuel Lawrence VC.

Private THOMAS HANCOCK
DELHI 19 June 1857

He was 33 years old and serving in the 9th

Lancers (The Queen's Royal Regiment) when one of the battery's wagons blew up and Brigadier Grant's horse was shot from under him. Private Hancock and Private Purcell, along with Sowar Roopur Khan, stayed with the Brigadier until he could be dragged to safety by the Sowar's horse. He would almost certainly have been killed without their help. Both Hancock and Purcell were awarded VCs, but Sowar Roopur Khan was not, as the award could not be given to members of 'local forces' serving with imperial troops until 1867.

Hancock died on 12 March 1871.

Private JOHN PURCELL
DELHI 19 June 1857
He was 43 years old and serving in the 9th Lancers (The Queen's Royal Regiment) when one of the battery's wagons blew up and Brigadier Grant's horse was shot from under him. Private Purcell and Private Hancock, along with Sowar Roopur Khan, stayed with the Brigadier until he could be dragged to safety by the Sowar's horse. He would almost certainly have been killed without their help. Both Hancock and Purcell were awarded VCs, but Sowar Roopur Khan was not, as the award could not be given to members of 'local forces' serving with imperial troops until 1867.

Purcell was killed in action at Delhi on 19 September 1857.

Private SAMUEL TURNER
DELHI 19 June 1857
He was 31 years old and serving in the 1st Bn, 60th Rifles, later the King's Royal Rifle Corps, when he carried the mortally wounded Lieutenant Humphreys from the midst of the enemy under heavy fire. During this action he was severely wounded by a sword cut to the right arm.

He died on 13 June 1868.

Colour Sergeant STEPHEN GARVIN
DELHI 23 June 1857
He was 31 years old and serving in the 1st Bn, 60th Rifles, later the King's Royal Rifle Corps, when he volunteered to lead a small party in an assault on a well-defended position known as

the 'Sammy House' in order to dislodge a large number of enemy troops who were keeping up a destructive fire on an advanced battery of guns. This action was successful despite heavy fire from the enemy.

He died on 23 November 1874.

Private JOHN McGOVERN (aka McGOWAN)
DELHI 23 June 1857
He was 32 years old and serving in the 1st Bengal Fusiliers, Indian Army (later the Royal Munster Fusiliers), when he carried into camp a wounded man under heavy fire from the enemy's artillery at the risk of his own life.

He died on 22 November 1888.

Lieutenant WILLIAM CUBITT
CHINHUT 30 June 1857
He was 21 years old and serving in the 13th Bengal Native Infantry, Indian Army when he was sent to fight the advancing rebels. He showed great courage in this ill-fated mission, and when the retreat to Lucknow began he saved the lives of three men as the rebels were surging around them.

He died on 25 January 1903. His brother-in-law was Second Lieutenant James Hills VC, and his nephew was Lieutenant Colonel Lewis Evans VC.

Corporal WILLIAM OXENHAM
LUCKNOW 30 June 1857
He was 32 years old and serving in the 32nd Regiment of Foot, later the Duke of Cornwall's Light Infantry, when he saved the life of Mr Capper, a Bengal civil servant, by digging him out from the ruins of a veranda that had fallen on him. Oxenham was exposed to heavy fire while effecting this rescue, which took some considerable time.

He died on 29 December 1875.

Lieutenant ROBERT AITKEN
LUCKNOW 30 June–22 November 1857
He was 29 years old and serving in the 13th Bengal Native Infantry, Indian Army when he prevented a disaster near the Baillie Guard Gate by rushing out and cutting down all the

tents in order to stop a fire spreading to the nearby magazine. On 25 September he and his men attacked and captured two guns and thus prevented them being used against General Havelock's relief column. On 26 September, during an assault on a gateway at the Furreed Buksh Palace, he threw himself against the gate, preventing the enemy from closing it. As a result his men were able to force open the door and capture the position. On 29 September he led a sortie to capture a gun that had been harassing his position. Under heavy fire, he worked his way through lanes and houses until he reached the gun, and then held his ground until help arrived.

Aitken's award is unique in that the ceremony was performed at the Residency at Lucknow, almost on the spot where several of his VC actions took place. He did not, however, receive his medal on this occasion as it had been mislaid.

He died on 18 September 1887.

Corporal JAMES TRAVERS

INDORE 1 July 1857

He was 36 years old and serving in the 2nd Bengal Native Infantry, Indian Army. When the Residency was suddenly attacked by Holkar's men, Travers led a charge against the guns with only five men supporting him. He drove the rebels from the guns and created a diversion that enabled the Bengal Artillery to man their guns, thus saving many lives. During the charge his horse was hit three times and his clothes were riddled with bullets.

He died on 1 April 1884.

Private WILLIAM DOWLING

LUCKNOW

4 and 9 July and 27 September 1857

He was 32 years old and serving in the 32nd Regiment of Foot, later the Duke of Cornwall's Light Infantry, when he went out on a sortie with two other men and spiked the enemy's guns; he also killed a subadar. On 9 July he went out again with three men to spike another of the enemy's guns, but had to abandon the mission as the spike was too small. Nevertheless, he was still exposed to the

same dangers. On 27 September he spiked an 18-pounder gun during yet another sortie, again under heavy fire.

He died from bronchitis on 17 February 1887.

Gunner WILLIAM CONNOLLY

JHELUM 7 July 1857

He was 40 years old and serving in the Bengal Horse Artillery, Indian Army when he received a bullet wound to the left thigh. Nevertheless, he insisted on mounting his horse and staying with his gun as the battery retired to another position. He continued working the gun until he was hit again, this time in the hip. When urged by his officer to retire, he replied, 'I'll not go while I can work here.' Later in the afternoon he was wounded for the third time, in the leg. Still he carried on, until he collapsed into the arms of Lieutenant Cookes, at which point he was carried from the fight.

He died from bronchitis on 31 December 1891.

Lieutenant SAMUEL LAWRENCE

LUCKNOW 7 July and 26 September 1857

He was 26 years old and serving in the 32nd Regiment of Foot, later the Duke of Cornwall's Light Infantry, when he led an attack up a scaling ladder placed against the window of a house where it was believed a mine was being laid. A rebel knocked his pistol from his hand, but the house was captured and all the enemy killed or taken prisoner. On 26 September he charged well ahead of his company and captured a 9-pounder gun.

He had, in fact, been recommended for a VC and Bar for his actions at Lucknow. This was dropped at a later stage as, according to the fourth clause of the original warrant, he would only be eligible for a Bar if he had already been awarded the VC.

He died on 17 June 1868. His cousin was Lieutenant Thomas Cadell VC.

Major HENRY TOMBS

DELHI 9 July 1857

He was 31 years old and serving in the Bengal Horse Artillery, Indian Army. One of his subalterns, Lieutenant James Hills, was on picquet duty when he heard a rumour that a force of rebel cavalry was approaching. As he moved to a better vantage point, the rebels appeared out of nowhere. Hills charged alone at the enemy column. He cut down one and struck a second, but was thrown from his horse. Three men then came at him; he wounded one with his pistol, caught the lance of another in his hand and slashed at him with his sword. The third man took Hills' sword and was about to kill him when Tombs arrived, saw what was happening, and shot the rebel at 30 paces, thus saving Hills' life. Tombs and Hills then went together to attend to the wounded men. Before long they were confronted by a rebel carrying Hills' pistol and brandishing a sword. He ran at Hills, cutting him about the head. Tombs rushed in and put his sword through the man, saving Hills again, but not before he too had been slashed about the head. Both men were awarded the VC.

Tombs was ADC to Queen Victoria.
He died on 2 August 1874.

Second Lieutenant JAMES 'JEMMIE' HILLS (later HILLS-JOHNES)
DELHI 9 July 1857
He was 23 years old and serving in the Bengal Horse Artillery, Indian Army. He was on picket duty when his force was suddenly attacked by rebel cavalry. Without hesitation, he rode straight at the enemy, single handed, in order to cause a delay and allow time for the guns to be loaded. Hills cut down two rebels before being thrown from his horse by two sowars charging together. Now on foot, he fought off two more rebels but was about to be killed by a third when Major Henry Tombs came to his assistance. Tombs and Hills then went together to attend to the wounded men. Before long they were confronted by a rebel carrying Hills' pistol and brandishing a sword. He ran at Hills, cutting him about the head. Tombs rushed in and put his sword through the man, saving Hills again, but not before he too had been slashed about the head. Both men were awarded the VC.

He died from influenza on 3 January 1919.

His brother-in-law was Lieutenant William Cubitt VC, and his nephew was Lieutenant Colonel Lewis Evans VC.

Private JAMES THOMPSON
LUCKNOW 9 July 1857
He was 27 years old and serving in the 1st Bn, 60th Rifles (King's Royal Rifle Corps), later the Royal Green Jackets, when he went to the assistance of his commanding officer, who was surrounded by a party of Ghazis. Thompson killed two of the assailants before further help arrived, and undoubtedly saved the officer's life. He was also commended for his conspicuous gallantry throughout the siege of Lucknow. He was elected for the award by the privates of the regiment.

He is sometimes referred to as 'William Thompson' but this was in fact his younger brother.

James died on 5 December 1891.

Lieutenant WILLIAM KERR
KOLAPORE 10 July 1857
He was 25 years old and serving in the 24th Bombay Native Infantry, Indian Army. When he learned that the rebels had murdered some officers and besieged others, he collected 50 troopers and led them 75 miles to find the mutineers. His men charged the doors and broke them down, and Kerr was the first man into the building. The rebels were forced out and went into another building, which was also taken. Finally they took refuge in a temple, which was razed to the ground, and all the rebels were killed, wounded or captured.

He died on 21 May 1919.

Lance Corporal ABRAHAM BOULGER
LUCKNOW 12 July–25 September 1857
He was 21 years old and serving in the 84th Regiment of Foot, later the 2nd Bn, York and Lancaster Regiment. He distinguished himself in all 25 actions fought by his regiment. He was one of a party which stormed the bridge over the canal at the relief of the Residency, and shot a gunner who was about to fire a 68-pounder into the advancing British. Boulger was also the first man to enter a masked

battery. In the subsequent defence of the Residency he was severely wounded.

He died from influenza on 23 January 1900.

Private PATRICK MYLOTT
LUCKNOW 12 July–25 September 1857

He was 37 years old and serving in the 84th Regiment of Foot, later the 2nd Bn, York and Lancaster Regiment. He distinguished himself in all the actions fought by his regiment, notably for rushing across a road under fierce fire to capture an enclosure. He was elected for the award by the privates of the regiment.

He died in a workhouse from bronchitis on 22 December 1878.

Lieutenant HENRY HAVELOCK (later HAVELOCK-ALLAN)
CAWNPORE 16 July 1857

He was 26 years old and serving in the 10th Regiment of Foot. The 64th had suffered badly from artillery fire. When the rebels were seen rallying their last 24-pounder, Havelock was sent over to give them the order to advance. Seeing they had no mounted officers remaining, he volunteered to lead them. He placed himself at their head, opposite the gun and moved on at a foot pace, in the face of shot and shell. The gun was taken and the rebels retreated.

He was one of only a few VC holders who became MPs.

He was killed in action at Ali-Masjid on 30 December 1897.

Lieutenant RICHARD WADESON
DELHI 18 July 1857

He was 30 years old and serving in the 75th Regiment of Foot, later the Gordon Highlanders. On this day men were collapsing from the effects of the sun, and were then being attacked by prowling horsemen as they fell. Wadeson saved the life of Private Farrell by bayoneting the sowar who was attacking him. Later he also saved Private Barry by cutting down the sowar attacking him.

He was Lieutenant Governor of the Royal Hospital, Chelsea (1881–85).

He died on 24 January 1885.

Lieutenant ANDREW BOGLE
OONAO 29 July 1857

He was 28 years old and serving in the 78th Regiment, later the Seaforth Highlanders Ross-shire Buffs (Duke of Albany's). He got together a few men and stormed a contested passage, then under heavy fire he and his men attacked a fortified house held by rebels; they cleared the building of the enemy, opening the way for the force to advance. Bogle was severely wounded in this action.

He died on 11 December 1890, and was the first VC holder to be cremated.

Sergeant Major GEORGE LAMBERT
OONAO, BITHOOR and LUCKNOW
29 July, 16 August and 25 September 1857

He was 37 years old and serving in the 84th Regiment of Foot, later the 2nd Bn, York and Lancaster Regiment, when he acted with distinguished bravery at Oonao. He also acted with great bravery on 16 August at Bithoor, when the rebels were driven out at the point of the bayonet from a strong position, and on 25 September at the passage through Lucknow to the Residency.

He died on 10 February 1860.

Civilian ROSS MANGLES
ARRAH 30 July 1857

He was 24 years old and serving in the Bengal Civil Service, Indian Army. During the retreat from Arrah, a wounded soldier of the 37th Regiment, Richard Taylor, begged not to be left to the mercy of the rebels. Mangles bound his wounds and carried him for 6 miles through swampy ground. Neither man had eaten for 24 hours nor slept for 48. Mangles finally reached the safety of the river and swam to a boat with his comrade in his arms.

He was one of only four civilians to be awarded the VC, the others being William McDonell, Thomas Kavanagh and George Chicken.

Mangles died on 28 February 1905.

Civilian WILLIAM McDONELL
ARRAH 30 July 1857

He was 27 years old and working for the Bengal

Civil Service. During the retreat from Arrah, he was in a boat with 35 men. It was discovered that the rebels had taken the oars and bound the boat to the bank and fixed the rudder to the right. Exposed to heavy fire, McDonell cut away the rope, then with the help of a breeze he took the boat halfway across the stream, from where he and all but two of the men were able to swim to safety.

He was one of only four civilians to be awarded the VC, the others being Ross Mangles, Thomas Kavanagh and George Chicken.

McDonell died from typhoid fever and pneumonia on 31 July 1894.

Bugler WILLIAM SUTTON
DELHI 2 August and 13 September 1857
He was 27 years old and serving in the 1st Bn, 60th Rifles, later the King's Royal Rifle Corps, when he volunteered to reconnoitre the breach, on the night before the assault. His conduct was conspicuous throughout the operations. During an attack on 2 August he rushed over the trenches and killed one of the enemy's buglers, who was about to sound the alarm. He was elected for the award by the men of the regiment.

He died on 16 February 1888.

Lieutenant JOSEPH CROWE
BUSHERUT-GUNGE 12 August 1857
He was 31 years old and serving in the 78th Regiment of Foot, later the Seaforth Highlanders Ross-shire Buffs (Duke of Albany's), when he led his men in the storming of a strongly held redoubt. Crowe was the first of the Highlanders to enter the redoubt, and within one minute the place was captured, and the rebels killed or taken.

He died from lung congestion and heart disease on 12 April 1876.

Captain JAMES BLAIR
NEEMUCH and JEERUM
12 August and 23 October 1857
He was 29 years old and serving in the 2nd Bombay Light Cavalry, Indian Army when he volunteered to apprehend seven or eight muti-

neers. With sword in hand, he burst into the house they were in and a struggle ensued during which he was badly wounded. The rebels escaped through the roof, and in spite of his wounds Blair pursued them, but was unable to catch them. On 23 October he was surrounded by a group of rebels. He broke his sword on the head of one, who then wounded him in the arm. He escaped to rejoin his men and led them in pursuit of the rebels, who were eventually routed.

He died on 18 January 1905. His cousin was Lieutenant Robert Blair VC.

Private DENIS DEMPSEY
LUCKNOW and ARRAH
12 August and 14 March 1858
He was 31 years old and serving in the 1st Bn, 10th Regiment of Foot, later the Lincolnshire Regiment, when he carried a powder-bag though the burning village of Jugdispore for the purpose of mining a passage in the rear of the enemy's position. During this time Dempsey was exposed to very heavy fire and the greater danger of flying sparks from the burning houses. He was the first man to enter the village on that day, under the most galling fire. On 14 March he helped to carry a mortally wounded ensign for 2 miles.

He died from congestion of the lungs on 10 January 1886.

Major CHARLES GOUGH
DELHI 15 and 18 August 1857, 27 January and 23 February 1858
He was 25 years old and serving in the 5th Bengal European Cavalry when he saved the life of his brother, Lieutenant Hugh Gough, by killing two of his assailants. On 18 August he led a troop of Guide Cavalry in a charge against the rebels, killing two sowars during hand-to-hand combat. On 27 January 1858 he tackled the leader of the enemy cavalry, running him through with his sword. This became lodged in the man's body and Gough was reduced to using his revolver, with which he shot two more men. On 23 February he ran to the aid of Brevet Major Anson and cut down his opponent, killing another immediately

also served in the Second Afghan War.

He died on 6 September 1912. His brother was Lieutenant Hugh Gough VC, and his son was Brevet Major John Gough VC.

Captain HENRY GORE-BROWNE
LUCKNOW 21 August 1857

He was 26 years old and serving in the 32nd Regiment of Foot, later the Duke of Cornwall's Light Infantry, when he led a sortie to spike two heavy guns that were doing much damage to the defences. He was the first man to enter the battery, which was protected by a high palisade and sliding shutters on the embrasures. On entering, he attacked the gunners and spiked the guns. About 100 enemy were killed in this operation.

Gore-Browne later served as a magistrate for Hampshire.

He died on 15 November 1912.

Private JOHN DIVANE (aka DEVINE)
DELHI 10 September 1857

He was 34 years old and serving in the 1st Bn, 60th Rifles, later the King's Royal Rifle Corps, when he was at the head of a charge by the Beloochee and Sikh troops on the enemy trenches. He made straight for the enemy's breastworks but was shot down within a few yards of his goal. He was elected for the award by the privates of the regiment.

He died from senile decay on 1 December 1888.

Private PATRICK GREEN
DELHI 11 September 1857

He was 33 years old and serving in the 75th Regiment of Foot, later the Gordon Highlanders. While on picket duty, he successfully rescued a comrade who had fallen wounded and was surrounded by the enemy.

He died on 19 July 1889.

Lieutenant DUNCAN HOME
DELHI 14 September 1857

He was 29 years old and serving in the Bengal Engineers, Indian Army when he led Lieutenant Philip Salkeld, Sergeant John Smith, Sergeant Carmichael, Corporal Burgess and Bugler Robert Hawthorne, each carrying 25lb bags of gunpowder across the single remaining beam to the Kashmir Gate under heavy fire. As they nailed the bags to the gate, Carmichael fell dead. Having attached his own bag, Sergeant Smith also nailed on Carmichael's, prepared the fuse and called, 'All ready.' As Lieutenant Salkeld stooped down to light the fuse, he was shot through the thigh. He held out the match to Corporal Burgess and fell into the ditch below. Burgess, thinking the match had gone out, reached for a box of lucifers, and as he leant down he was shot. Sergeant Smith then grabbed the match before Burgess fell on to Salkeld. Smith quickly lit the fuse and himself jumped down into the ditch. The gunpowder exploded, destroying the gate, before he reached the bottom. When the smoke cleared, he looked around and saw Burgess lying dead, Salkeld wounded and with two broken arms, and Home uninjured. Hawthorne, as well as assisting the wounded, had to sound the advance three times before it was heard by the waiting men, who were now able to pour into the city. Home, Salkeld, Smith and Hawthorne were awarded the VC. Carmichael and Burgess were not, because it could not be awarded posthumously at this time. Although both Home and Salkeld were dead within weeks, their commanding officer had conferred their awards on the spot.

Home was killed by the accidental detonation of a mine on 1 October 1857.

Lieutenant PHILIP SALKELD
DELHI 14 September 1857

He was 26 years old and serving in the Bengal Engineers, Indian Army when he was in a party with Lieutenant Duncan Home, Sergeant John Smith, Sergeant Carmichael, Corporal Burgess and Bugler Robert Hawthorne, each carrying 25lb bags of gunpowder across the single remaining beam to the Kashmir Gate under heavy fire. As they nailed the bags to the gate, Carmichael fell dead. Having attached his own bag, Sergeant Smith also nailed on Carmichael's, prepared the fuse and called, 'All ready.' As Lieutenant Salkeld stooped down to light the fuse, he was shot through the thigh. He held out the match to Corporal Burgess and fell into the ditch below. Burgess, thinking the match had gone out, reached for a box of lucifers, and as he leant down he was shot. Sergeant Smith grabbed the match before Burgess fell on to Salkeld. Smith quickly lit the fuse and himself jumped into the ditch. The gunpowder exploded, destroying the gate, even before he reached the bottom. When the smoke cleared, he looked around and saw Burgess lying dead, Salkeld wounded and with two broken arms, and Home uninjured. Hawthorne, as well as assisting the wounded, had to sound the advance three times before it was heard by the waiting men, who were now able to pour into the city. Home, Salkeld, Smith and Hawthorne were awarded the VC. Carmichael and Burgess were not, because it could not be awarded posthumously at that time. Although both Home and Salkeld were dead within weeks, their commanding officer had conferred their awards on the spot.

Salkeld died from his wounds on 10 October 1857.

Lieutenant ROBERT SHEBBEARE
DELHI 14 September 1857
He was 30 years old and serving in the 60th Bengal Native Infantry, Indian Army. During the assault he led the Guides and twice charged a loopholed serai but failed to achieve a breach. He was under terrible fire and was wounded in the cheek and the back of the head, but despite this he conducted a most successful withdrawal.

Shebbeare also served in the Third China War. He died from malaria at sea on 16 September 1860. In 2007 his private letters were published under the title *Indian Mutiny and Beyond. The Letters of Robert Shebbeare VC.* His third cousin was Lieutenant Nathaniel Burslem VC.

Sergeant JAMES McGUIRE (sometimes spelt MAGUIRE)
DELHI 14 September 1857
He was 30 years old and serving in the 1st Bengal Fusiliers, Indian Army, later the Royal Munster Fusiliers. When the reserve ammunition was being carried up on to the ramparts to be put into a magazine, five boxes caught fire. Three of them exploded. McGuire and Drummer Miles Ryan dashed for the two remaining boxes and threw them over the parapet. Confused, many men had begun running towards the explosions, so by their actions McGuire and Ryan saved many lives. Both men were awarded the VC.

McGuire was one of eight men to forfeit their VC, for stealing a cow.

He died on 22 December 1862 – or did he? Two petitions were made in 1863 to have his VC and annuity restored under the name 'Maguire'.

Sergeant JOHN SMITH
DELHI 14 September 1857
He was 42 years old and serving in the Bengal Engineers and Miners when he was in a party with Lieutenant Duncan Home, Lieutenant Philip Salkeld, Sergeant Carmichael, Corporal Burgess and Bugler Robert Hawthorne, each carrying 25lb bags of gunpowder across the single remaining beam to the Kashmir Gate under heavy fire. As they nailed the bags to the gate, Carmichael fell dead. Having attached his own bag, Sergeant Smith also nailed on Carmichael's, prepared the fuse and called, 'All ready.' As Lieutenant Salkeld stooped down to light the fuse, he was shot through the thigh. He held out the match to Corporal Burgess and fell into the ditch below. Burgess, thinking the match had gone out, reached for a box of lucifers, and as he leant down he was shot. Sergeant Smith grabbed the match before Burgess fell on to Salkeld. Smith quickly lit the fuse and himself jumped into the ditch. The gunpowder exploded, destroying the gate, even before he reached the bottom. When the smoke cleared, he looked around and saw Burgess lying dead, Salkeld wounded and with two broken arms, and Home uninjured. Hawthorne, as well as assisting the wounded, had to sound the advance three times before it was heard by the waiting men, who were now able to pour into the city. Home, Salkeld, Smith and Hawthorne were awarded the VC.

Carmichael and Burgess were not, because it could not be awarded posthumously at that time. Although both Home and Salkeld were dead within weeks, their commanding officer had conferred their awards on the spot.

Smith died from dysentery on 26 June 1864.

Lance Corporal HENRY SMITH
DELHI 14 September 1857
He was 32 years old and serving in the 52nd Regiment of Foot, later the Oxfordshire and Buckinghamshire Light Infantry, when during the retreat from Chaudney Chouk he carried a wounded comrade to safety under very heavy fire.

He died from cholera on 18 August 1862.

Bugler ROBERT HAWTHORNE
DELHI 14 September 1857
He was 34 years old and serving in the 52nd Regiment of Foot when he was in a party with Lieutenant Duncan Home, Lieutenant Philip Salkeld, Sergeant John Smith, Sergeant Carmichael and Corporal Burgess, each carrying 25lb bags of gunpowder across the single remaining beam to the Kashmir Gate under heavy fire. As they nailed the bags to the gate, Carmichael fell dead. Having attached his own bag, Sergeant Smith also nailed on Carmichael's, prepared the fuse and called, 'All ready.' As Lieutenant Salkeld stooped down to light the fuse, he was shot through the thigh. He held out the match to Corporal Burgess and fell into the ditch below. Burgess, thinking the match had gone out, reached for a box of lucifers, and as he leant down he was shot. Sergeant Smith grabbed the match before Burgess fell on to Salkeld. Smith quickly lit the fuse and himself jumped into the ditch. The gunpowder exploded, destroying the gate, even before he reached the bottom. When the smoke cleared, he looked around and saw Burgess lying dead, Salkeld wounded and with two broken arms, and Home uninjured. Hawthorne, as well as assisting the wounded, had to sound the advance three times before it was heard by the waiting men, who were now able to pour into the city. Home, Salkeld, Smith and Hawthorne were

awarded the VC. Carmichael and Burgess were not, because it could not be awarded posthumously at that time. Although both Home and Salkeld were dead within weeks, their commanding officer had conferred their awards on the spot.

Hawthorne died from rheumatic fever on 2 February 1879.

Drummer MILES RYAN
DELHI 14 September 1857
He was 31 years old and serving in the 1st Bengal Fusiliers, Indian Army, later the Royal Munster Fusiliers. When the reserve ammunition was being carried up on to the ramparts to be put into a magazine, five boxes caught fire. Three of them exploded. Ryan and Sergeant James McGuire dashed for the two remaining boxes and threw them over the parapet. Confused, many men had begun running towards the explosions, so by their actions Ryan and McGuire saved many lives. Both were awarded the VC.

Ryan died in January 1887.

Surgeon HERBERT READE
DELHI 14 and 16 September 1857
He was 28 years old and serving in the 61st Regiment of Foot, later the Gloucestershire Regiment. While he was tending the wounded, a party of rebels suddenly started firing on him from the rooftops of nearby houses. Drawing his sword, Reade gathered a few men and succeeded in dislodging the rebels from their position. Two of his party were killed and six wounded. On 16 September, at the assault on Delhi, he was one of the first men up at the breach of the magazine and he successfully spiked one of the guns.

He died on 23 June 1897.

Lieutenant GEORGE WALLER
DELHI 14 and 18 September 1857
He was 30 years old and serving in the 1st Bn, 60th Rifles, later the King's Royal Rifle Corps, when he charged and captured the enemy's guns near the Kabul Gate. On 18 September he showed conspicuous bravery in repulsing an enemy attack on a gun near the Chaudney

Chouk. He was elected for the award by the officers of the regiment.

He died on 10 January 1877.

Lieutenant GEORGE RENNY
DELHI 16 September 1857

He was 32 years old and serving in the Bengal Horse Artillery, Indian Army. After the capture of the Delhi magazine, vigorous attacks were made on the post by the enemy and shells with lighted fuses were thrown on to the thatched roof. Renny leapt on to the wall above the magazine and flung several of these shells back down on the enemy. Almost at once the attacks became less severe and shortly afterwards ceased entirely.

He died on 5 January 1887.

Second Lieutenant EDWARD THACKERAY
DELHI 16 September 1857

He was 20 years old and serving in the Bengal Engineers, Indian Army when he extinguished a fire in the magazine enclosure, under close and heavy fire from the enemy and at the risk of his own life from large amounts of ammunition exploding in the magazine.

He died on 3 September 1927.

Sergeant PATRICK MAHONEY
MUNGULWAR 21 September 1857

He was 30 years old and serving in the 1st Madras Fusiliers, later the Royal Dublin Fusiliers, when he helped in the capture of the regimental colour of the 1st Regiment Native Infantry, which had mutinied.

He was killed in action at Lucknow on 30 October 1857.

Lieutenant WILLIAM RENNIE
LUCKNOW 21 and 25 September 1857

He was 34 years old and serving in the 90th Regiment, later the Cameronians (Scottish Rifles), when he charged the enemy's guns in advance of the skirmishers of his regiment and prevented them from carrying one of the guns away. On 25 September, while advancing on a battery under grapeshot, Rennie charged ahead of his men and forced the enemy to abandon their guns.

He died on 22 August 1887.

Sergeant ROBERT GRANT
ALUMBAGH 24 September 1857

He was 20 years old and serving in the 1st Bn, 5th Regiment of Foot, later the Northumberland Fusiliers, when under heavy fire he went to the assistance of Private Deveny, whose leg had been shot away. With the help of Lieutenant Brown, he carried him to the safety of the camp.

Later Grant became a constable in the Metropolitan Police. He died from pneumonia on 7 March 1867.

Surgeon JOSEPH JEE
LUCKNOW 25 September 1857

He was 38 years old and serving in the 78th Regiment of Foot, later the Seaforth Highlanders Ross-shire Buffs (Duke of Albany's), when he attended to a large number of wounded men, organising their removal on cots or on the backs of their comrades, until he found the dhooli-bearers, who had fled. Later, when trying to reach the Residency with the casualties, he was besieged and had to remain in the Mote Mehal all night. Next day, under heavy fire, he continued to attend the wounded and eventually succeeded in taking many of them through heavy cross-fire safely into the Residency, although he was repeatedly warned not to make the attempt.

He died on 17 March 1899.

Assistant Surgeon VALENTINE McMASTER
LUCKNOW 25 September 1857

He was 23 years old and serving in the 78th Regiment of Foot, later the Seaforth Highlanders Ross-shire Buffs (Duke of Albany's), when he exposed himself to the heavy fire of the enemy to bring in and attend to the many wounded.

He died from heart disease on 22 January 1872.

Captain FRANCIS MAUDE
LUCKNOW 25 September 1857

He was 28 years old and serving in the Royal

Regiment of Artillery. He was in command of a battery at Char Bagh (Four Gardens), when one-third of his men were shot down at their guns. He replaced them with volunteers from the infantry, and with this force he pushed on and bore down on the enemy. Sir James Outram reported that, 'But for Captain Maude's nerve and coolness on this trying occasion, the army could not have advanced.' Two ballots were held and on both occasions Maude was unanimously nominated by his men for the award. He always considered that his VC was awarded not to him but to the battery.

He died on 19 October 1900. His cousin was Brevet Lieutenant Colonel Frederick Francis Maude VC.

Captain WILLIAM OLPHERTS
LUCKNOW 25 September 1857
He was 35 years old and serving in the Bengal Artillery, Indian Army. When the troops penetrated the city, Olpherts charged on horseback with the 90th Regiment, capturing two guns in the face of very heavy fire. After this he returned under severe fire to bring up limbers and horses to carry off the captured guns. He served continuously for 20 years in the artillery and was known as 'Hell-fire Jack'.

He died on 30 April 1902.

Lieutenant HERBERT MacPHERSON
LUCKNOW 25 September 1857
He was 30 years old and serving in the 78th Regiment of Foot, later the Seaforth Highlanders Ross-shire Buffs (Duke of Albany's), when he led a charge against two 9-pounder guns that the rebels had trained on his regiment along the Cawnpore road. The attack was successful, and the guns were seized and dumped into a canal. It is said that in spite of the danger he faced, MacPherson treated the matter as 'of little importance'.

He died from fever on 20 October 1886.

Private JOEL HOLMES
LUCKNOW 25 September 1857
He was 36 years old and serving in the 84th Regiment of Foot, later the 2nd Bn, York and Lancaster Regiment, when he was the first to volunteer to replace the fallen gunners of Captain Maude's battery, where he worked the gun under heavy fire. His good conduct was also noted while in General Havelock's Field Force. Maude was also awarded the VC.

Holmes died on 27 July 1872.

Private HENRY WARD
LUCKNOW 25/26 September 1857
He was 31 years old and serving in the 78th Regiment of Foot, later the Seaforth Highlanders Ross-shire Buffs (Duke of Albany's), when he was escorting the dhoolie carrying the wounded Lieutenant Havelock. Then Private Pilkington threw himself on to the dhoolie. The bearers were about to drop this double load, but Ward compelled them to remain by his cheerfulness under heavy fire. Both wounded men were taken to the safety of the 'Baillie Guard'.

Ward later became Havelock's servant.

He died on 12 September 1867.

Surgeon ANTHONY HOME
LUCKNOW 26 September 1857
He was 30 years old and serving in the 90th Regiment of Foot, later the Cameronians (Scottish Rifles). When the British were forcing their way into the Residency, he was in charge of the wounded men left behind in the streets. Under heavy fire, and with the help of Assistant Surgeon William Bradshaw, Private James Hollowell, Private Peter McManus and Private John Ryan, Home got the wounded into a house. The three privates kept up a steady fire, shooting rebel after rebel. At one point two privates dashed out into the open to bring back a wounded officer, all the time shouting in chorus to make the enemy think they were more numerous. Meanwhile the two surgeons tended to the wounded, and Home even found time to help in shooting at the rebels. After half an hour the house was set on fire, and they had to flee with the wounded to a nearby shed, which they held for 22 hours. The rebels climbed on to the roof and the defenders had to shoot them through the roof. Soon after dawn, when the group had given up

hope of survival, they were rescued. All five men were awarded the VC.

Home died on 10 August 1914.

Assistant Surgeon WILLIAM BRADSHAW
LUCKNOW 26 September 1857
He was 27 years old and serving in the 90th Regiment of Foot, later the Cameronians (Scottish Rifles). When the British were forcing their way into the Residency, he was with a party of wounded men left behind in the streets. Under heavy fire, and with the help of Surgeon Anthony Home, Private James Hollowell, Private Peter McManus and Private John Ryan, Bradshaw got the wounded into a house. The three privates kept up a steady fire, shooting rebel after rebel, all the time shouting in chorus to make the enemy think they were more numerous. At one point two privates dashed out into the open to bring back a wounded officer. Meanwhile the two surgeons tended to the wounded, and Home even found time to help in shooting at the rebels. After half an hour the house was set on fire, and they had to flee with the wounded to a nearby shed, which they held for 22 hours. The rebels climbed on to the roof and the defenders had to shoot them through the roof. Soon after dawn, when the group had given up hope of survival, they were rescued. All five men were awarded the VC.

He died on 9 March 1861.

Colour Sergeant STEWART McPHERSON
LUCKNOW 26 September 1857
He was 35 years old and serving in the 78th Regiment of Foot, later the Seaforth Highlanders Ross-shire Buffs (Duke of Albany's). Seeing Private James Lowther lying badly wounded in the open, McPherson made his way to him under heavy enemy fire. Despite being exposed to a continuous bombardment, he tended Lowther's wounds and carried him back to safety, although he later died of his wounds.

McPherson died on 7 December 1892.

Private THOMAS DUFFY
LUCKNOW 26 September 1857

He was 52 years old and serving in the 1st Madras Fusiliers, later the Royal Dublin Fusiliers. The enemy kept up such a heavy fire on a 24-pounder gun left in an exposed position that it could not be recovered. Undaunted, Duffy went out and fastened a rope to the gun and retrieved it, preventing it from falling into enemy hands.

He died on 24 December 1868.

Private JAMES HOLLOWELL (aka HOLLIWELL or HULLOWAY)
LUCKNOW 26 September 1857
He was 34 years old and serving in the 78th Regiment of Foot, later the Seaforth Highlanders Ross-shire Buffs (Duke of Albany's). When the British were forcing their way into the Residency, he was with a party of wounded men left behind in the streets. Under heavy fire, he helped Surgeon Anthony Home, Assistant Surgeon William Bradshaw, Private Peter McManus and Private John Ryan to get the wounded into a house. The three privates kept up a steady fire, shooting rebel after rebel, all the time shouting in chorus to make the enemy think they were more numerous. At one point two privates dashed out into the open to bring back a wounded officer. Meanwhile the two surgeons tended to the wounded, and Home even found time to help in shooting at the rebels. After half an hour the house was set on fire, and they had to flee with the wounded to a nearby shed, which they held for 22 hours. The rebels climbed on to the roof and the defenders had to shoot them through the roof. Soon after dawn, when the group had given up hope of survival, they were rescued. All five men were awarded the VC.

He died from heart disease on 4 April 1876.

Private PETER McMANUS
LUCKNOW 26 September 1857
He was 28 years old and serving in the 1st Bn, 5th Regiment of Foot, later the Northumberland Fusiliers. When the British were forcing their way into the Residency, he was with a party of wounded men left behind in the streets. Under heavy fire, he helped Surgeon Anthony Home, Assistant Surgeon

William Bradshaw, Private James Hollowell and Private John Ryan to get the wounded into a house. The three privates kept up a steady fire, shooting rebel after rebel, all the time shouting in chorus to make the enemy think they were more numerous. At one point two privates dashed out into the open to bring back a wounded officer. Meanwhile the two surgeons tended to the wounded, and Home even found time to help in shooting at the rebels. After half an hour the house was set on fire, and they had to flee with the wounded to a nearby shed, which they held for 22 hours. The rebels climbed on to the roof and the defenders had to shoot them through the roof. Soon after dawn, when the group had given up hope of survival, they were rescued. All five men were awarded the VC.

McManus died from smallpox on 27 April 1859.

Private JOHN RYAN
LUCKNOW 26 September 1857
He was 34 years old and serving in the 1st Madras Fusiliers, later the Royal Dublin Fusiliers. When the British were forcing their way into the Residency, he was with a party of wounded men left behind in the streets. Under heavy fire, he helped Surgeon Anthony Home, Assistant Surgeon William Bradshaw, Private James Hollowell and Private Peter McManus to get the wounded into a house. The three privates kept up a steady fire, shooting rebel after rebel, all the time shouting in chorus to make the enemy think they were more numerous. At one point two privates dashed out into the open to bring back a wounded officer. Meanwhile the two surgeons tended to the wounded, and Home even found time to help in shooting at the rebels. After half an hour the house was set on fire, and they had to flee with the wounded to a nearby shed, which they held for 22 hours. The rebels climbed on to the roof and the defenders had to shoot them through the roof. Soon after dawn, when the group had given up hope of survival, they were rescued. All five men were awarded the VC.

He was killed in action at Cawnpore on 4 March 1858.

Bombardier JACOB THOMAS
LUCKNOW 27 September 1857
He was 24 years old and serving in the Bengal Artillery, Indian Army when a soldier of the Madras Fusiliers, who was returning from a sortie, was wounded and in danger of being captured by the enemy. Thomas picked him up and carried him, under heavy fire, back to safety.

He died on 3 March 1911.

Lieutenant ROBERT BLAIR
BOLANDSHAHR 28 September 1857
He was 23 years old and serving in the 2nd Dragoon Guards (Queen's Bays) when he was ordered to bring in a deserted ammunition wagon. As they approached, 50 or 60 horsemen attacked his party of twelve. Blair coolly formed up his men and led them through the rebels, killing four himself. He brought all of his men back to camp safely, despite being seriously wounded by a rebel officer, whom he ran through with his sword.

He died from smallpox on 28 March 1859. His cousin was Captain James Blair VC.

Sergeant BERNARD DIAMOND
BOLANDSHAHR 28 September 1857
He was 30 years old and serving in the Bengal Horse Artillery, Indian Army. He and Gunner Richard Fitzgerald continued to work their gun under very heavy fire after every other man belonging to it had been killed or wounded. Between them, they cleared the enemy from the road. Both men were awarded the VC.

He died on 25 January 1892.

Lance Corporal ROBERT KELLS
BOLANDSHAHR 28 September 1857
He was 25 years old and serving in the 9th Lancers (the Queen's Royal Regiment) when he dashed forward to rescue Captain Drysdale, whose horse was shot from under him, leaving him lying in the street with a broken collar bone. Kells kept the enemy at bay and saved Drysdale from certain death.

Later he was appointed a Yeoman of the Queen's Bodyguard (1881–1905).

He died on 14 April 1905.

Private PATRICK DONOHOE
BOLANDSHAHR 28 September 1857
He was 37 years old and serving in the 9th Lancers (the Queen's Royal Regiment) when he went to the assistance of a severely wounded lieutenant, and brought him back through a large body of enemy cavalry.

He died on 16 August 1876. His brother was awarded the Medal of Honor.

Gunner RICHARD FITZGERALD
BOLANDSHAHR 28 September 1857
He was 26 years old and serving in the Bengal Horse Artillery, Indian Army when he and Sergeant Bernard Diamond continued to work their gun under very heavy fire after every other man belonging to it had been killed or wounded. Between them, they cleared the enemy from the road. Both men were awarded the VC.

He died in 1884.

Private JAMES ROBERTS
BOLANDSHAHR 28 September 1857
He was 31 years old and serving in the 9th Lancers (the Queen's Royal Regiment) when he carried a mortally wounded comrade through the streets under heavy fire. He was seriously wounded while carrying out this act.

He died from an abscess of the liver on 1 August 1859.

Captain AUGUSTUS ANSON
BOLANDSHAHR and *LUCKNOW*
28 September and 16 November 1857
He was 22 years old and serving in the 84th Regiment of Foot, later the 2nd Bn, York and Lancaster Regiment. After the 9th Light Dragoons had charged through the town, the enemy drew carts across the gateway, blocking their path back. Anson rode forward and knocked the rebel drivers off their carts. With his left hand injured, he was unable to control his horse, which plunged into the midst of the rebels. He was fired on but escaped uninjured, although a bullet passed through his coat. On 16 November he showed great gallantry when he entered Lucknow with the storming party. On the gates being burst open, his horse was killed and he was wounded.

Anson is one of only a few VC holders who became MPs.

He died on 17 December 1877.

Corporal DENIS DYNON
CHOTA BEHAR 2 October 1857
He was 35 years old and serving in the 53rd Regiment of Foot, later the King's Shropshire Light Infantry, when he, together with Lieutenant John Daunt, charged the guns of the Ramgurh Battalion. They captured two guns and killed with pistols the gunners who had shot down a third of their detachment, and then turned the guns on the rebels. Both men were awarded the VC.

He died on 16 February 1863.

Lieutenant JOHN DAUNT
CHOTA BEHAR
2 October and 2 November 1857
He was 35 years old and serving in the 53rd Regiment of Foot, later the King's Shropshire Light Infantry, when he, together with Corporal Denis Dynon, charged the guns of the Ramgurh Battalion. They captured two guns and killed with pistols the gunners who had shot down a third of their detachment, and then turned the guns on the rebels. Both men were awarded the VC. On 2 November Daunt chased mutineers across a plain and was seriously wounded while attempting to drive out a large body of these rebels from an enclosure.

Daunt also served in the Third China War.

He died on 15 April 1886.

Private PATRICK McHALE
LUCKNOW and ALUM BAGH
2 October and 22 December 1857
He was 31 years old and serving in the 1st Bn, 5th Regiment of Foot, later the Northumberland Fusiliers, when he was the first man to jump into the embrasure and bayonet the gunners. On 22 December, when the enemy had fled from a village, leaving behind a loaded gun, McHale raced to the gun, turned it around and began firing it into the retreating rebels.

He died from heart failure on 26 October 1866.

Lance Corporal JOHN SINNOTT
LUCKNOW 6 October 1857

He was 28 years old and serving in the 84th Regiment of Foot, later the 2nd Bn, York and Lancaster Regiment, when he went repeatedly with Lieutenant Gibaut to extinguish a fire in the breastworks. When the lieutenant fell mortally wounded, Sinnott carried him, with help from others, into a shelter under heavy fire. He was twice wounded during this action. He was elected for the award by the NCOs of the regiment.

He died on 20 July 1896.

Private JOHN FREEMAN
AGRA 10 October 1857

He was 25 years old and serving in the 9th Lancers (the Queen's Royal Regiment) when he went to the assistance of a severely wounded lieutenant. He killed the leader of the enemy cavalry and kept the rebels at bay.

He died on 1 July 1913.

Conductor JAMES MILLER
FUTTEHPORE 28 October 1857

He was 37 years old and serving in the Bengal Ordnance Depot, Indian Army when he went to the assistance of Lieutenant Glubb, who was severely wounded, and at great personal risk carried him to safety. He was subsequently himself wounded. It took five years for his award to be gazetted.

He died from pneumonia on 12 June 1892.

Civilian THOMAS KAVANAGH
LUCKNOW 9 November 1857

He was 36 years old and working for the Bengal Civil Service when he volunteered to go through the city in disguise to the British camp of the relieving force, so that he could guide them to the beleaguered garrison in the Residency. He went with the spy Kanauji Lal and although they were stopped several times by rebels, they managed to talk their way through each time. Kavanagh received the VC for his daring mission. At a time when native Indians were not eligible for the award, Kanauji Lal did not receive it. Earlier during the siege Kavanagh was involved in mining

operations and was called Burra Surungwalla, 'The Great Miner', by the loyal Sikh soldiers.

He is one of only four civilians to be awarded the VC, the others being Ross Mangles, William McDonell and George Chicken.

Kavanagh died on 13 November 1882.

Lieutenant HUGH GOUGH
ALUM BAGH and JELLALABAD
12 November 1857 and 25 February 1858

He was 23 years old and serving in the 1st Bengal European Light Cavalry when he charged across a swamp with a party of Hodson's Horse and captured two guns. His turban was cut and he was twice wounded in the process. On 25 February 1858 Gough charged enemy guns and engaged in numerous single combats. Two horses were shot from under him and he received bullets through his helmet and scabbard before being shot and disabled in the leg as he was charging two sepoys with fixed bayonets.

He was Keeper of the Crown Jewels at the Tower of London from 1898 until his death on 12 May 1909. His brother was Major Charles Gough VC and his uncle was Brevet Major John Gough VC.

Lieutenant JOHN WATSON
LUCKNOW 14 November 1857

He was 28 years old and serving in the 1st Punjab Cavalry, Indian Army when he came upon a group of rebel cavalry. He was attacked by their leader, who fired at him from only a yard away. It seemed he would be killed but the shot missed, and Watson then ran his opponent through with his sword. He was then set upon by several more rebels, who slashed at him with tulwars. His head, arms and legs were cut and a bullet went through his coat. Nevertheless, he was able to defend himself until his own men joined in the mêlée and utterly routed the enemy.

He died on 23 January 1919.

Lieutenant HASTINGS HARINGTON
LUCKNOW 14–22 November 1857

He was 25 years old and serving in the Bengal Artillery, Indian Army. For nine days during the relief of Lucknow he acted with conspicuous bravery. He was elected for the award by the officers of the regiment.

He died from cholera on 20 July 1861.

Rough Rider EDWARD JENNINGS
LUCKNOW 14–22 November 1857

He was 42 years old and serving as a Rough Rider in the Bengal Artillery, Indian Army. For nine days during the relief of Lucknow he acted with the most conspicuous gallantry. He was elected for the award by the men of the regiment.

He died on 10 May 1889 in dire poverty.

Gunner THOMAS LAUGHNAN
LUCKNOW 14–22 November 1857

He was 33 years old and serving in the Bengal Artillery, Indian Army. For nine days during the relief of Lucknow he acted with conspicuous bravery. He was elected for the award by the men of the regiment.

He died on 23 July 1864.

Gunner HUGH McINNES
LUCKNOW 14–22 November 1857

He was 42 years old and serving in the Bengal Artillery, Indian Army. For nine days during the relief of Lucknow he acted with conspicuous bravery. He was elected for the award by the men of the regiment.

He died from paralysis and debility on 7 December 1879.

Gunner JAMES PARK
LUCKNOW 14–22 November 1857

He was 22 years old and serving in the Bengal Artillery, Indian Army. For nine days during the relief of Lucknow he acted with conspicuous bravery. He was elected for the award by the men of the regiment.

He died from cholera at Lucknow on 14 June 1858.

Captain WILLIAM STEUART (sometimes spelt STEWART)
LUCKNOW 16 November 1857

He was 25 years old and serving in the 93rd Highlanders Regiment, later the Argyll and Sutherland Highlanders (Princess Louise's). During the attack on the Secundra Bagh, he led a brilliant charge on two enemy guns that were commanding the mess house and inflicting severe damage. The guns were taken. He was elected for the award by the officers of the regiment.

He had also taken part in the battle of Balaklava, in 'The Thin Red Line'.

He died on 18 October 1868, when a sword-swallowing trick went fatally wrong. 'Steuart' is the family's preferred spelling.

Lieutenant FRANCIS BROWN
NARNOUL 16 November 1857

He was 20 years old and serving in the 1st European Bengal Fusiliers, later the Royal Munster Fusiliers, when at the risk of his own life he rushed to the assistance of a wounded soldier, whom he carried off under heavy fire from the enemy, whose cavalry were only 40 or 50 yards away at the time.

He died on 21 November 1895.

Lieutenant ALFRED FFRENCH
LUCKNOW 16 November 1857

He was 22 years old and serving in the 53rd Regiment of Foot, later the King's Shropshire Light Infantry, and was commanding the Grenadier Company at the taking of the Secundra Bagh. He was one of the first to enter the building and behaved with conspicuous gallantry. He was elected for the award by the officers of the regiment.

He died on 29 December 1872.

Lieutenant NOWELL SALMON
LUCKNOW 16 November 1857

He was 22 years old and serving in the Royal Navy (Naval Brigade). During the assault on the Shah Nujeff mosque, volunteers were asked to climb a tree to dislodge some rebels who were throwing grenades at the gun crews with great effect. When the first volunteer was killed, his place was taken by Lieutenant Salmon. He shot rebel after rebel while Leading Seaman John Harrison handed loaded rifles to him; when Salmon was wounded, Harrison climbed the tree and continued firing at the rebels. They succeeded in significantly weakening the mutineers' defences and the mosque was taken. Both men were awarded the VC.

He died on 14 February 1912.

Lieutenant THOMAS YOUNG
LUCKNOW 16 November 1857
He was 30 years old and serving in the Royal Navy (Naval Brigade) when some naval guns were brought up close to the Shah Nujeff mosque. The guns were so close to the mosque that each time they fired the crews had to take cover from falling masonry, as well as from rifle fire and grenades thrown by the mutineers. Young moved from gun to gun encouraging his gunners. Before long, the crew of one gun had all been killed and only Young and Able Seaman William Hall remained alive at the other. Young was badly wounded but almost single-handedly Hall kept firing his gun until the wall was breached, allowing the soldiers to rush in and take the building. Both men were awarded the VC for their actions.

Young died on 20 March 1869. His brother-in-law was Midshipman Duncan Boyes VC.

Colour Sergeant JAMES MUNRO
LUCKNOW 16 November 1857
He was 30 years old and serving in the 93rd Highlanders Regiment, later the Argyll and Sutherland Highlanders (Princess Louise's). During the taking of the Secundra Bagh, he rushed forward to rescue Captain Welsh, who was wounded and in danger of being killed. He carried him away to a place of safety, where shortly afterwards he himself was taken, badly wounded. He was elected for the award by the NCOs of the regiment.

He died from 'general paralysis of the insane' on 15 February 1871.

Sergeant JOHN PATON
LUCKNOW 16 November 1857
He was 23 years old and serving in the 93rd Highlanders Regiment, later the Argyll and Sutherland Highlanders (Princess Louise's), when he went alone to reconnoitre the Shah Nujeff Mosque for a means of entry and found a small gap at the rear of the defences. He guided his regiment in and found that the mutineers had gone. He was elected for the award by the NCOs of the regiment.

Paton had also served in the Crimean War. He died on 1 April 1914.

Lance Corporal JOHN DUNLAY (aka DUNLEY or DUNLEA)
LUCKNOW 16 November 1857
He was 26 years old and serving in the 93rd Highlanders Regiment, later the Argyll and Sutherland Highlanders (Princess Louise's). At the taking of the Secundra Bagh, he was the first man of his regiment to enter one of the breaches, gallantly supporting Captain Burroughs against heavy odds. During his action he was shot in the knee. He was elected for the award by the NCOs of the regiment. The musket ball that wounded him is on display with his VC at the Sheesh Mahal Museum, India.

He died on 17 October 1890.

Private PETER GRANT
LUCKNOW 16 November 1857
He was 33 years old and serving in the 93rd Highlanders Regiment, later the Argyll and Sutherland Highlanders (Princess Louise's). At the taking of the Secundra Bagh, he killed five rebels with one of their own swords, while defending a colonel who had captured the enemy's colours. He was elected for the award by the privates of the regiment.

He drowned on 10 January 1868.

Private CHARLES IRWIN
LUCKNOW 16 November 1857
He was 33 years old and serving in the 53rd Regiment of Foot, later the King's Shropshire Light Infantry, when he showed conspicuous bravery at the assault on the Secundra Bagh. Although severely wounded in the right shoulder, he was one of the first to enter the building under heavy fire. He was elected for the award by the privates of the regiment.

He died on 8 April 1873.

Private JAMES KENNY
LUCKNOW 16 November 1857
He was 31 years old and serving in the 53rd Regiment of Foot, later the King's Shropshire Light Infantry. At the taking of the Secundra Bagh, he volunteered to bring up fresh ammunition to his company under heavy cross-fire. He was elected for the award by the privates of the regiment.

He was killed in action at Mooltan on 2 October 1862.

Private DAVID MACKAY
LUCKNOW 16 November 1857
He was 26 years old and serving in the 93rd Highlanders Regiment, later the Argyll and Sutherland Highlanders (Princess Louise's), when at the taking of the Secundra Bagh he captured one of the enemy standards despite their resistance. He was later wounded at the attack on the Shah Nujeff Mosque. He was elected for the award by the privates of the regiment.

MacKay had also served in the Crimea.

He died from valvular heart disease on 18 November 1880.

Private JOHN SMITH
LUCKNOW 16 November 1857
He was 35 years old and serving in the 1st Madras Fusiliers, Indian Army, later the Royal Dublin Fusiliers, when he was one of the first men to enter the north gateway during the attack on the Secundra Bagh. He was instantly surrounded by rebels, but, despite suffering a sword cut to the head and a bayonet wound to the side, he fought his way out and continued to fight all day.

He died from asphyxia on 6 May 1866.

Leading Seaman JOHN HARRISON
LUCKNOW 16 November 1857
He was 25 years old and serving in the Royal Navy (Naval Brigade). During the assault on the Shah Nujeff Mosque, volunteers were asked to climb a tree to dislodge some rebels who were throwing grenades at the gun crews with great effect. The first volunteer was killed and his place was taken by Lieutenant Nowell

Salmon, who shot rebel after rebel while Harrison handed loaded rifles to him. When Salmon was wounded, Harrison climbed the tree and continued firing at the rebels. They succeeded in significantly weakening the mutineers' defences and the mosque was taken. Both men were awarded the VC.

He died on 27 December 1865.

Able Seaman WILLIAM HALL
LUCKNOW 16 November 1857
He was 30 years old and serving in the Royal Navy (Naval Brigade) when he volunteered to man one of two guns that were being used to breach the walls of the Shah Nujeff Mosque. The guns were so close to the mosque that each time they fired, the crews had to take cover from falling masonry, as well as from rifle fire and grenades from the mutineers. Before long, the crew of one gun had all been killed and only Hall and his badly wounded officer, Lieutenant Thomas Young, remained alive at the other. Almost single-handedly, Hall kept firing his gun until the wall was breached, allowing the soldiers to rush in and take the building. Hall's action was described by Sir Colin Campbell as 'almost unexampled in war'. Young also received the VC.

Hall had also served in the Crimean War, and was the first black man to be awarded the VC.

He died from paralysis on 27 August 1904.

Major JOHN GUISE
LUCKNOW 16/17 November 1857
He was 31 years old and serving in the 90th Regiment of Foot, later the Cameronians (Scottish Rifles). At the taking of the Secundra Bagh, he and Sergeant Samuel Hill saved the life of Captain Irby by warding off a tulwar blow aimed at his head by a rebel. They also went out under heavy fire to help two wounded men. They acted most gallantly throughout the relief of Lucknow. Guise was elected for the award by the officers of his regiment.

He died on 5 February 1895.

Sergeant SAMUEL HILL
LUCKNOW 16/17 November 1857
He was 31 years old and serving in the 90th

Regiment of Foot, later the Cameronians (Scottish Rifles). At the taking of the Secundra Bagh he and Major John Guise saved the life of Captain Irby by warding off a tulwar blow aimed at his head by a rebel. They also went out under heavy fire to help two wounded men. They acted most gallantly throughout the relief of Lucknow. Hill was elected for the award by the NCOs of the regiment.

He was killed in action at Meerut on 21 February 1863.

Sergeant Major CHARLES PYE
LUCKNOW 17 November 1857

He was 37 years old and serving in the 53rd Regiment of Foot, later the King's Shropshire Light Infantry, when he showed great courage in bringing up ammunition to the mess house under very heavy fire. He was elected for the award by the NCOs of his regiment.

He died on 12 July 1876.

Private PATRICK GRAHAM
LUCKNOW 17 November 1857

He was 20 years old and serving in the 90th Regiment of Foot, later the Cameronians (Scottish Rifles), when he brought in a wounded comrade under very heavy fire. He was elected for the award by the privates of the regiment.

He died on 3 June 1875.

Lieutenant THOMAS HACKETT
LUCKNOW 18 November 1857

He was 21 years old and serving in the 23rd Regiment of Foot, later the Royal Welch Fusiliers. At Secundra Bagh he and Private Monger rescued a corporal from the 23rd Regiment, who was wounded and exposed to very heavy fire. Hackett also showed conspicuous bravery when, under heavy fire, he jumped on to the roof and cut the thatch away to prevent a fire from spreading. Monger also received the VC.

Hackett died on 5 October 1880, when the trigger of his shotgun caught on a dense thicket, causing the gun to go off.

Private GEORGE MONGER
LUCKNOW 18 November 1857

He was 17 years old and serving in the 23rd Regiment of Foot, later the Royal Welch Fusiliers. At Secundra Bagh he and Lieutenant Thomas Hackett rescued a corporal from the 23rd Regiment, who was wounded and exposed to very heavy fire.

He died from consumption on 9 August 1887. There is a blue plaque on his home in Tower Road, Hastings, Sussex.

Lieutenant HARRY PRENDERGAST
MUNDISORE 21 November 1857

He was 23 years old and serving in the Madras Engineers, Indian Army when he noticed a rebel training his musket on Lieutenant Dew. As he charged at him, the rebel turned and fired a bullet into his left side. The mutineer was then cut down by Major Orr. Prendergast also distinguished himself at Ratgurh and Betwa, where he was severely wounded.

His last field command was the Burma Field Force in 1885–86. He later became an MP, and died on 24 July 1913.

Midshipman ARTHUR MAYO
DACCA 22 November 1857

He was 17 years old and serving in the Indian Naval Brigade when he collected a few men together and charged two 6-pounder guns manned by rebels. He was some 20 yards ahead of the rest of his party and under heavy fire throughout the charge.

He died on 18 May 1920.

Drummer THOMAS FLYNN (incorrectly spelt FLINN on his citation)
CAWNPORE 28 November 1857

He was 15 years old and serving in the 64th Regiment of Foot, later the North Staffordshire Regiment (The Prince of Wales's). During a charge on the enemy's guns, and despite being wounded, Flynn engaged in hand-to-hand fighting with two of the rebel artillery crew.

At just 15 years and 3 months, he is acknowledged as one of the two youngest recipients of the VC. The other is Andrew

Fitzgibbon, also aged 15 years and 3 months.

Flynn died in a workhouse on 10 August 1892.

Lieutenant FREDERICK ROBERTS

KHODAGUNGE 2 January 1858

He was 25 years old and serving in the Bengal Artillery. He was attached to the staff of Sir Colin Campbell when he rode to the aid of a sowar who was being attacked by a rebel. He killed him with one slash of his sword. Later the same day, when he saw two rebels making off with a standard, he rushed them, cut one down and snatched the standard. The other rebel fired point-blank at him but his musket misfired.

In 1880 Roberts took 10,000 men on his celebrated march through Afghanistan to relieve Kandahar. He also superintended the arrangements for Queen Victoria's funeral. His autobiography is called *Forty One Years in India.*

He died on 14 November 1914 while visiting the Western Front. His son was Lieutenant Frederick Hugh Sherston Roberts VC.

Private BERNARD McQUIRT

ROWA 6 January 1858

He was 29 years old and serving in the 95th (Derbyshire) Regiment of Foot, later the Sherwood Foresters (Nottinghamshire and Derbyshire Regiment), when he engaged in hand-to-hand combat with three rebels, killing one and wounding the others. During his action he received a bullet wound and five sabre cuts.

He died from chronic bronchitis on 5 October 1888.

Troop Sergeant Major DAVID SPENCE

SHUNSABAD 17 January 1858

He was 48 years old and serving in the 9th Lancers (The Queen's Royal Lancers), when he went to the defence of Private Kidd, who was wounded and surrounded by rebels. Spence had to cut his way through several of the enemy to reach him.

Later he became a Yeoman of the Guard at the Tower of London.

He died on 17 April 1877.

Lieutenant JOHN TYTLER

CHOORPOORAH 10 February 1858

He was 22 years old and serving in the 66th Bengal Native Infantry, later the 1st Gurkha Rifles. When his men began to waver under grapeshot and musketry, Tytler rushed forward alone on horseback and engaged the rebel gunners in hand-to-hand fighting, during which he was shot through the left arm and speared in the chest. By the time his men caught up with him, the position was taken.

He died from pneumonia on 14 February 1880.

Lieutenant JAMES INNES

SULTANPORE 23 February 1858

He was 28 years old and serving in the Bengal Engineers, Indian Army. Riding far in advance of the leading skirmishers, he was the first to secure a gun which the enemy were abandoning. When the rebels rallied around another gun, the shot from which would have ploughed through the advancing British columns, Innes rode up to them unsupported and shot the gunner. He remained at this gun under heavy fire and kept the enemy at bay until assistance reached him.

He died on 13 December 1907.

Lieutenant FREDERICK AIKMAN

AMETHI 1 March 1858

He was 30 years old and serving in the 4th Bengal Native Infantry, Indian Army, commanding 100 men. When he was informed that the enemy were advancing with 500 men, 200 horse and two guns, Aikman attacked with his force and utterly routed the enemy, killing more than 100 men, capturing both the guns, and driving the survivors over the Goomtee river. He was cut about the face with a sabre during this fight, wounds that ultimately compelled him to retire on half-pay.

He died on 5 October 1888.

Lance Corporal WILLIAM GOATE
(sometimes spelt GOAT)

LUCKNOW 6 March 1858

He was 22 years old and serving in the 9th Lancers (the Queen's Royal Regiment) when he went to the aid of Major Smith, who was lying wounded. He carried him for several hundred yards until surrounded by the enemy, at which he was compelled to put the major down and defend himself. When he was relieved by his comrades, he went back to find the major, but could not locate him. Unfortunately, the major's headless body was found the next morning.

Goate died from gastric cancer on 24 October 1901.

Lieutenant THOMAS BUTLER
LUCKNOW 9 March 1858
He was 22 years old and serving in the 1st European Bengal Fusiliers, later the Royal Munster Fusiliers. When the heavy guns were being placed in position, a message had to be sent to the infantry on the other side of the fast-flowing Goomtee river. Butler swam across under heavy fire and duly contacted the infantry before swimming back. As a result of his information, the infantry took and secured an abandoned enemy battery.

He died on 17 May 1901.

Lieutenant FRANCIS FARQUHARSON
LUCKNOW 9 March 1858
He was 20 years old and serving in the 42nd Regiment of Foot, later the Black Watch (Royal Highlanders), when he led part of his company in the storming of a bastion, spiking the two guns mounted there. This meant that the advanced positions held during the night were rendered safe from artillery fire. Farquharson was severely wounded while holding an advanced position the following day.

He died on 12 September 1875.

Captain HENRY WILMOT
LUCKNOW 11 March 1858
He was 27 years old and serving in the 2nd Bn, Rifle Brigade (Prince Consort's Own) when his company was engaged with a large number of the enemy near the Iron Bridge. At one point Wilmot and three other men found themselves confronting a considerable number of rebels at the end of a street. One of the three men was

shot through both legs and Corporal Nash, together with Private Hawkes, who was himself wounded, lifted the man up and carried him for some considerable distance, while Captain Wilmot covered the retreat of the party using the other men's rifles. All three men were awarded the VC.

Wilmot was one of only a few VC holders who became MPs.

He died on 7 April 1901.

Lieutenant WILLIAM McBEAN
LUCKNOW 11 March 1858
He was 40 years old and serving in the 93rd Highlanders Regiment, later the Argyll and Sutherland Highlanders (Princess Louise's), when he personally killed eleven rebels, one after another, during the assault on the Begum Bagh. When confronted by the next, a havildar, several men came to his aid. He called for them not to interfere, and he and the havildar set to with their swords. McBean feinted a cut but instead gave the point and pierced the heart of his opponent. When presented with his medal and congratulated on a good day's work, he replied, 'Tutts, it didna tak' me twenty minutes.'

He held every rank from private to major general.

He died on 23 June 1878.

Corporal WILLIAM NASH
LUCKNOW 11 March 1858
He was 33 years old and serving in the 2nd Bn, Rifle Brigade (Prince Consort's Own) when his company was engaged with a large number of the enemy near the Iron Bridge. At one point Nash and three other men found themselves confronting a considerable number of rebels at the end of a street. One of these men was shot through both legs and Corporal Nash, together with Private Hawkes, who was himself wounded, lifted the man up and carried him for some considerable distance, with Captain Wilmot covering the retreat of the party using the other men's rifles. All three men were awarded the VC.

Nash died from cystitis on 6 April 1875.

Private DAVID HAWKES
LUCKNOW 11 March 1858

He was 36 years old and serving in the 2nd Bn, Rifle Brigade (Prince Consort's Own) when his company was engaged with a large number of the enemy near the Iron Bridge. At one point Hawkes and three other men found themselves confronting a considerable number of rebels at the end of a street. One of these men was shot through both legs and Private Hawkes, who was himself wounded, together with Corporal Nash, lifted the man up and carried him for some considerable distance, with Captain Wilmot covering the retreat of the party using the other men's rifles. All three men were awarded the VC.

Hawkes died on 14 August 1858.

Able Seaman EDWARD ROBINSON
LUCKNOW 13 March 1858

He was 19 years old and serving in the Royal Navy's Naval Brigade when the sandbags on top of the trenches operated by the naval brigade caught fire. Robinson jumped on top of the trench and extinguished the fire in some of the bags and threw the others clear. As he did so, he was hit in the shoulder by a musket ball and knocked back into the trenches, unconscious.

He died from throat cancer on 2 October 1896.

Major RICHARD KEATINGE
CHUNDAIREE 17 March 1858

He was 32 years old and serving in the Bombay Artillery, Indian Army when on the night before the assault on Chundairee he discovered a small path leading across the ditch towards the fort. During the assault he led his men forward along the path. He was severely wounded but struggled to his feet only to be wounded again as he entered the fort. His discovery of the path and his courageous leadership undoubtedly saved the column from many losses.

He died on 24 May 1904.

Troop Sergeant Major DAVID RUSHE
LUCKNOW 19 March 1858

He was 30 years old and serving in the 9th Lancers (the Queen's Royal Regiment) when he displayed conspicuous bravery by attacking eight rebels posted in a nullah, killing three of them.

He died on 6 November 1886, after a long illness.

Cornet WILLIAM BANKES
LUCKNOW 19 March 1858

He was 21 years old and serving in the 7th Hussars (the Queen's Own) when he led three charges against 50 rebels who had rushed the guns near Moosa Bagh. He shot three of them before he was felled by a young mutineer who hamstrung his horse with a tulwar. He was instantly set upon and hacked almost to pieces, losing a leg and an arm, with his other limbs left barely attached. His wounds became infected and he died from blood poisoning on 6 April 1858.

Bankes had also served in the Second Burma War of 1852.

Private ROBERT NEWELL
LUCKNOW 19 March 1858

He was 23 years old and serving in the 9th Lancers (the Queen's Royal Regiment) when he rescued a comrade whose horse had fallen, and took him to safety under heavy fire from a large number of the enemy.

He died from diarrhoea on 11 July 1858.

Lieutenant AYLMER CAMERON
KOTAH 30 March 1858

He was 24 years old and serving in the 1st Bn, 72nd Regiment of Foot when he led an attack on a strongly defended and loopholed building, killing three rebels single-handedly. The attack was successful but he was severely wounded during his action, losing half of his hand to a blow from a tulwar.

He died on 10 June 1909.

Lieutenant HUGH COCHRANE
JHANSI 1 April 1858

He was 28 years old and serving in the 86th (Royal County Down) Regiment of Foot, Royal Irish Rifles when his company was ordered to take a gun. Cochrane dashed forward alone, hundreds of yards in advance of his men, captured the gun and held it until the rest of his company came up to help. He then had three horses shot from under him as he attacked the enemy's rearguard.

He died on 18 April 1884.

Lieutenant JAMES LEITH
BETWA 1 April 1858
He was 31 years old and serving in the 14th Light Dragoons, later the 14th Hussars (the King's), when he single-handedly charged a party of rebel infantry, rescuing Captain Need, who was surrounded and about to be bayoneted.

He died from liver disease on 13 May 1869.

Corporal MICHAEL SLEAVON
JHANSI 3 April 1858
He was 31 years old and serving in the Corps of Royal Engineers. During the assault on the fort, he worked under heavy fire at the head of a sap, with a cool and steady determination. He maintained his position for hours in the burning sun.

He died from cardiac disease on 15 August 1902.

Bombardier JOSEPH BRENNAN
JHANSI 3 April 1858
He was 39 years old and serving in the Royal Regiment of Artillery. During the assault he brought up two guns manned by natives, laying each of them under very heavy fire from the fort, and directed their fire so accurately that the enemy were compelled to abandon his battery.

He died from pneumonia on 24 September 1872.

Private JAMES BYRNE
JHANSI 3 April 1858
He was 36 years old and serving in the 86th Regiment, later the Royal Irish Rifles. During the assault on the fort, and with the help of Captain Henry Jerome, he rescued Lieutenant Sewell, who was severely wounded and lying in an exposed position. They were under heavy fire throughout.

He died on 6 December 1872.

Private JAMES PEARSON
JHANSI 3 April 1858
He was 35 years old and serving in the 86th Regiment, later the Royal Irish Rifles, when he attacked a number of armed rebels, killing one and bayoneting two others. He was severely wounded during his action. Later he carried the mortally wounded Private Burns out of the line of fire.

He died on 23 January 1900.

Private FREDERICK WHIRLPOOL (born CONKER but later changed to JAMES)
JHANSI and LOHARI
3 April and 6 May 1858
He was 29 years old and serving in the 3rd Bombay European Regiment, later the Prince of Wales's Leinster Regiment, when he twice went out to bring in wounded men to safety under heavy fire from the walls of a fort. On 6 May Whirlpool went to the rescue of Lieutenant Doune, under such heavy fire that he received seventeen wounds, one of which almost severed his head from his body.

Whirlpool's citation states that his second action took place on 2 May, which is incorrect. His was the first public presentation of the VC in Australia, and took place on 20 June 1861.

He died from heart disease on 24 June 1899.

Captain HENRY JEROME
JHANSI and JUMNA
3 April and 28 May 1858
He was 28 years old and serving in the 86th Regiment of Foot, later the Royal Irish Rifles. During the assault on the fort, and with the help of Private Byrne, he rescued Lieutenant Sewell, who was severely wounded and lying in an exposed position. They were under heavy fire throughout. On 28 May his bravery was most conspicuous in action against a rebel force at Jumna, where he was gravely wounded, part of his head being torn off.

He died from heart disease on 25 February 1901.

Sergeant WILLIAM NAPIER
AZAMGARH 6 April 1858
He was 30 years old and serving in the 1st Bn,

13th Regiment of Foot, later the Somerset Light Infantry (Prince Albert's), when at the risk of his own life he defended and finally rescued a private of his regiment who had been severely wounded. Despite being surrounded by rebels, who kept up a steady fire, Napier stayed with the injured man, bandaged his wound and finally carried him to safety.

He died on 2 June 1908.

Private PATRICK CARLIN
AZAMGARH 6 April 1858

He was 26 years old and serving in the 1st Bn, 13th Regiment of Foot, later the Somerset Light Infantry (Prince Albert's). He was carrying a wounded man off the field of battle when he was fired on by a rebel. He took the wounded man's sword and killed the rebel before bringing his comrade to safety.

He died on 11 May 1895.

Captain WILLIAM CAFE
FORT RUHYA 15 April 1858

He was 32 years old and serving in the 56th Bengal Native Infantry, Indian Army. Together with Lance Corporal Alexander Thompson and Private Edward Spence, he went to the assistance of Lieutenant Willoughby (the brother of Captain Willoughby, one of the nine who blew up the Delhi magazine on 11 May 1857). On seeing that he was dead, they removed his body under heavy fire to prevent its mutilation by the enemy. Spence was badly wounded during this action and the two others returned to rescue him also. All three men were awarded the VC.

Cafe died on 6 August 1906.

Quartermaster Sergeant JOHN SIMPSON
FORT RUHYA 15 April 1858

He was 32 years old and serving in the 42nd Regiment of Foot, later the Black Watch (Royal Highlanders), when during the attack he rescued Lieutenant Douglas and a private soldier from an exposed position just 40 yards from the fort under very heavy fire.

He died on 27 October 1884.

Lance Corporal ALEXANDER THOMPSON
FORT RUHYA 15 April 1858

He was 34 years old and serving in the 42nd Regiment of Foot, later the Black Watch (Royal Highlanders). Together with Captain William Cafe and Private Edward Spence, he went to the assistance of Lieutenant Willoughby (brother of Captain Willoughby, one of the nine who blew up the Delhi magazine on 11 May 1857). On seeing that he was dead, they removed his body under heavy fire to prevent its mutilation by the enemy. Spence was badly wounded during this action and the two others returned to rescue him also. All three men were awarded the VC.

He died on 29 March 1880.

Private JAMES DAVIS (real name KELLY)
FORT RUHYA 15 April 1858

He was 23 years old and serving in the 42nd Regiment of Foot, later the Black Watch (Royal Highlanders), when under heavy fire he volunteered to bring the mortally wounded Lieutenant Bramley to safety. He went out with a private and they began to lift him, but then the private was shot and killed; Davis single-handedly carried the lieutenant back to his regiment, and then returned to bring in the private's body.

He died on 2 March 1893.

Private SAMUEL MORLEY (sometimes spelt MORELY)
NATHUPUR 15 April 1858

He was 19 years old and serving in the 2nd Bn, Military Train, later the Royal Army Service Corps, when he went with Farrier Michael Murphy to the assistance of Lieutenant Hamilton, who had been struck from his horse and set upon by rebels. The two men dashed in on foot and fought the rebels hand-to-hand until help arrived, both men being wounded during this action. Hamilton died from his wounds the next day. Although Murphy received his VC promptly, Morley did not. He complained in 1860 and an investigation was held, his medal being gazetted in August 1860.

He died on 16 June 1888.

The Complete Victoria Cross

Farrier MICHAEL MURPHY
NATHUPUR 15 April 1858

He was 21 years old and serving in the 2nd Bn, Military Train, later the Royal Army Service Corps, when he went with Private Samuel Morley to the assistance of Lieutenant Hamilton, who had been struck from his horse and set upon by rebels. The two men dashed in on foot and fought the rebels hand-to-hand until help arrived, both men being wounded during this action. Hamilton died from his wounds the next day.

Murphy is one of eight men to have forfeited their VC after being convicted of theft.

He died from pneumonia on 4 April 1893.

Private EDWARD SPENCE
FORT RUHYA 15 April 1858

He was 28 years old and serving in the 42nd Regiment of Foot, later the Black Watch (Royal Highlanders). Together with Captain William Cafe and Lance Corporal Alexander Thompson, he went to the assistance of Lieutenant Willoughby (brother of Captain Willoughby, one of the nine who blew up the Delhi magazine on 11 May 1857). On seeing that he was dead, they removed his body under heavy fire to prevent its mutilation by the enemy. Spence was badly wounded during this action and the two others returned to rescue him also. All three men were awarded the VC.

Spence died as a result of his wounds on 17 April 1858.

Colour Sergeant WILLIAM GARDNER
BAREILLY 5 May 1858

He was 37 years old and serving in the 42nd Regiment of Foot, later the Black Watch (Royal Highlanders), when his commanding officer was unhorsed and three Ghazis rushed at him. Gardner ran out and bayoneted two of the fanatics, and was in the act of attacking the third when his opponent was shot and killed by another soldier. Without his bravery, his commanding officer would almost certainly have been killed.

He died on 24 October 1897.

Private VALENTINE BAMBRICK
BAREILLY 6 May 1858

He was 21 years old and serving in the 1st Bn, 60th Rifles, later the King's Royal Rifle Corps, when he and Lieutenant Ashburnham were cornered and attacked by three Ghazis, one of whom Bambrick killed. Despite being wounded twice, Bambrick fought furiously to save both their lives.

He was falsely accused and found guilty of stealing another man's medals. For this he became one of eight men to forfeit their VC. Such was his shame at being stripped of his VC that he hanged himself on 1 April 1864 while in Pentonville prison.

Lieutenant HARRY LYSTER
KOONCH 23 May 1858

He was 27 years old and serving in the 72nd Bengal Native Infantry, Indian Army when he was sent with an order for the cavalry to charge the remnants of the rebels. Seeing that some of them had rallied and formed a square, he charged alone into the midst of the square, broke it and killed two or three of the sepoys. He escaped without a wound.

He died on 1 February 1922. His nephew was Captain Hamilton Reed VC.

Private SAMUEL (aka SAME or JOHN) SHAW
LUCKNOW 13 June 1858

He was of unknown age and serving in the 3rd Bn, Rifle Brigade (Prince Consort's Own) when he came upon a Ghazi flourishing his tulwar. Shaw tackled him, armed only with a short sapper's sword. The rebel struck him a heavy blow in the face. Infuriated, he flung himself on to the man and sawed him to death with the serrated edge of his sword.

Shaw had also served in the Kaffir Wars of 1846–7 and 1850–3, and in the Crimean War. His name has caused a problem for many years. On the rolls, the name Samuel is often abbreviated to SamL. In the flowing handwriting of the time, it is easy to mistake the L for a lower case e.

He died on 27 December 1859, when he jumped overboard and drowned. It was said he could not stand the constant gibes from his comrades over the award, but it seems unlikely that a man who fought in four wars and was brave enough to take on a fanatic in single combat would take his own life because of gibes. It probably had more to do with his head injury, which perhaps caused depression, pushing him over the edge.

Private GEORGE RODGERS
MARAR 16 June 1858
He was 29 years old and serving in the 71st Regiment of Foot, later the Highland Light Infantry, when he single-handedly attacked seven well-armed rebels who had taken up a strong position. He killed one of them.

He died on 9 March 1870, after drinking vitriol from an unmarked bottle, thinking it was alcohol.

Captain CLEMENT HENEAGE-WALKER (later WALKER-HENEAGE)
GWALIOR 17 June 1858
He was 27 years old and serving in the 8th Hussars (the King's Royal Irish) when he, along with Sergeant Joseph Ward, Farrier George Hollis and Private John Pearson, formed part of a squadron which routed the rebels and saw the death of the Rani of Jhansi (the rulers of Jhansi led their followers into battle). They charged through the enemy camp and into two batteries, which they captured, bringing back two of the rebel guns. All four men were elected for the award by the regiment.

Heneage-Walker had also served in the Crimea and took part in the Charge of the Light Brigade at Balaklava.

He died on 9 December 1901.

Sergeant JOSEPH WARD
GWALIOR 17 June 1858
He was 24 years old and serving in the 8th Hussars (the King's Royal Irish) when he, along with Captain Clement Heneage-Walker, Farrier George Hollis and Private John Pearson, formed part of a squadron which routed the rebels and saw the death of the Rani of Jhansi (the rulers of Jhansi led their followers into battle). They charged through the enemy camp and into two batteries, which they captured, bringing back two of the rebel guns. All four men were elected for the award by the regiment.

Ward died on 23 November 1872.

Farrier GEORGE HOLLIS
GWALIOR 17 June 1858
He was 24 years old and serving in the 8th Hussars (the King's Royal Irish) when he, with Captain Clement Heneage-Walker, Sergeant Joseph Ward and Private John Pearson, formed part of a squadron which routed the rebels and saw the death of the Rani of Jhansi (the rulers of Jhansi led their followers into battle). They charged through the enemy camp and into two batteries, which they captured, bringing back two of the rebel guns. All four men were elected for the award by the regiment.

Hollis died from 'violent inflammation' on 16 May 1897.

Private JOHN PEARSON
GWALIOR 17 June 1858
He was 33 years old and serving in the 8th Hussars (the King's Royal Irish) when he, along with Captain Clement Heneage-Walker, Sergeant Joseph Ward and Farrier George Hollis, formed part of a squadron which routed the rebels and saw the death of the Rani of Jhansi (the rulers of Jhansi led their followers into battle). They charged through the enemy camp and into two batteries, which they captured, bringing back two of the rebel guns. All four men were elected for the award by the regiment.

Pearson had also served in the Crimea and took part in the Charge of the Light Brigade at Balaklava.

He died on 18 April 1892.

Lieutenant WILLIAM WALLER
GWALIOR 20 June 1858
He was 17 years old and serving in the 25th Bombay Light Infantry, Indian Army when he and another lieutenant (who was killed during the action) attacked and successfully took the

fort at Gwalior with only a handful of men. They climbed on to the roof of a house and shot the gunners opposing them, and then entered the fort killing every rebel inside.

He died on 29 January 1885.

Captain SAMUEL BROWNE
SEERPORAH 31 August 1858
He was 34 years old and commanding the 2nd Punjab Irregular Cavalry, later the 22nd Sam Browne's Cavalry (named in his honour), when during an engagement with rebels he charged a 9-pounder gun to prevent it from firing on the infantry, who were then advancing to the attack. He cut down several of the gunners but received a cut across the left knee and another which severed his left arm at the shoulder.

He also served in the Second Afghan War, and was the inventor of the Sam Browne belt.

He died on 14 March 1901.

Troop Sergeant Major JAMES CHAMPION
BEEJAPORE 8 September 1858
He was 24 years old and serving in the 8th Hussars (the King's Royal Irish). When both his troop officers were wounded early in the day, he took command of the troop. He was shot through the body soon afterwards but remained in the saddle all day, wounding several of the enemy with his revolver.

He died on 4 May 1904.

Lieutenant CHARLES BAKER
SUHEJNEE 27 September 1858
He was 27 years old and serving in the Bengal Police Battalion, Indian Army when he led a mixed force of cavalry and mounted police, including Mr George Chicken, in a charge against 700 rebels, who were utterly routed. The whole operation was brilliantly conceived and most gallantly carried out. Baker and Chicken were awarded the VC.

Baker later took command of the Egyptian police.

He died on 19 February 1906.

Ensign PATRICK RODDY
KUTHIRGA 27 September 1858
He was 31 years old and serving in the Bengal

Army. During an engagement with the enemy, he charged a rebel armed with a musket. The rebel shot his horse from under him and then came at him with his sword. Roddy seized the mutineer and held him until he could get at his own sword, and then ran him through with it.

He was offered a Bar to his VC but chose promotion and higher pay instead. He would have been the first VC and Bar. Roddy also served in the Afghan and the Abyssinian Wars.

He died from bronchitis and cardiac disease on 21 November 1895.

Civilian GEORGE CHICKEN
SUHEJNEE 27 September 1858
He was 25 years old and serving in the Indian Naval Brigade when he joined Lieutenant Charles Baker's fixed force of cavalry and mounted police in a charge against 700 rebels, who were utterly routed. In the pursuit Chicken rode recklessly forward, catching up to 20 armed rebels; he killed five with his sword but was knocked from his horse and was about to be butchered when four troopers came to his rescue. Both Baker and Chicken were awarded the VC.

Chicken is one of only four civilians to win the VC. The others were Ross Mangles, William McDonell and Thomas Kavanagh.

He died in May 1860.

Trumpeter THOMAS MONAGHAN
SUNDEELA 8 October 1858
He was 24 years old and serving in the 2nd Dragoon Guards (the Queen's Bays), when a group of about 35 mutineers opened fire on Colonel Seymour and then rushed at him with swords drawn. In the ensuing fight the Colonel was cut down, and Private Anderson and Trumpeter Monaghan immediately went to his rescue, shooting one of the assailants and driving the others away with their swords, thus allowing the Colonel to rise to his feet and defend himself. Together they routed the entire force. Without their action the Colonel would almost certainly have been killed. Both men were awarded the VC.

He died on 10 November 1895.

Private CHARLES ANDERSON
SUNDEELA 8 October 1858

He was 32 years old and serving in the 2nd Dragoon Guards (the Queen's Bays) when a group of about 35 mutineers opened fire on Colonel Seymour and then rushed at him with swords drawn. In the ensuing fight the Colonel was cut down, and Private Anderson and Trumpeter Monaghan immediately went to his rescue, shooting one of the assailants and driving the others away with their swords, thus allowing the Colonel to rise to his feet and defend himself. Together they routed the entire force. Without their action the Colonel would almost certainly have been killed. Both men were awarded the VC.

Anderson died from a fractured skull on 19 April 1899, after a fall from cliffs near his home.

Lieutenant HANSON JARRETT
BAROUN 14 October 1858

He was 21 years old and serving in the 26th Bengal Native Infantry, Indian Army. Some 70 rebels had fortified themselves in a brick building, and the only way in was from a narrow alley under constant fire. Jarrett called for volunteers to storm the house but only four men responded. Undeterred, he led these men through the alley to the house and forced his way in, fending off the enemy bayonets with his sword. However, being so feebly supported, he was forced to abandon the attack and return under fire to his men.

He died on 11 April 1891.

Lieutenant EVELYN WOOD
SINWAHO and SINDHORA
19 October and 29 December 1858

He was 20 years old and serving in the 17th Lancers (Duke of Cambridge's Own). While in command of a troop of light cavalry, he attacked almost single-handedly a body of rebels, whom he routed. On 29 December he rescued, with the help of a duffadar and a sowar, a potail from a band of robbers who had captured the man and carried him into the jungle where they intended to hang him.

He had also served in the Crimea, where he was recommended for the VC at the age of 16.

(His claim was not supported by the navy, as he had left to join the army by this time.) Wood also served in the Ashanti War, the Ninth Frontier War, the Zulu War and the First Boer War. His autobiography *From Midshipman to Field Marshal* was published in 1906.

He died on 2 December 1919.

Major CHARLES FRASER
RIVER RAPTEE 31 December 1858

He was 29 years old and serving in the 7th Hussars (the Queen's Own) when Captain Sisted and some men got into difficulties and were in danger of drowning, having plunged in while in pursuit of the enemy. Asked if he could swim, Fraser replied 'like a duck', and dived into the river. Despite heavy fire and a severe wound in his thigh, he succeeded in rescuing the officer and his men.

He was one of only a few VC holders who became MPs.

He died on 7 June 1895.

Private HENRY ADDISON
KURREREAH 2 January 1859

He was 37 years old and serving in the 43rd (Monmouthshire) Regiment of Foot, later the Oxfordshire and Buckinghamshire Light Infantry, when he defended a lieutenant from a large force as he fell wounded to the ground. Addison received two wounds and lost his leg in this gallant act.

He died on 18 June 1887.

Captain HERBERT CLOGSTOUN
CHICHUMBAH 15 January 1859

He was 38 years old and serving in the 19th Madras Native Infantry, Indian Army when he charged the rebels, with only eight men, forcing them into the town and causing them to abandon their plunder. During this action he lost seven of the eight men with him and he himself was wounded.

He was killed in action at Hingoli on 6 May 1862.

Private WALTER COOK
MAYLAH GHAT 15 January 1859

He was 25 years old and serving in the 42nd

Regiment of Foot, later the Black Watch (Royal Highlanders), when the fighting was at its fiercest, and the only officer and colour sergeant had been killed. Along with Private Duncan Millar, Cook immediately went to the front and took command, directing the company with courage, coolness and discipline, to the admiration of all who witnessed it. Both men were awarded the VC.

He is believed to have drowned in the Ravi river around 1864.

Private DUNCAN MILLAR (aka MILLER)
MAYLAH GHAT 15 January 1859
He was 34 years old and serving in the 42nd Regiment of Foot, later the Black Watch (Royal Highlanders), when the fighting was at its fiercest, and the only officer and colour sergeant had been killed. Along with Private Walter Cook, Millar immediately went to the front and took command, directing the company with courage, coolness and discipline, to the admiration of all who witnessed it. Both men were awarded the VC.

He died from chronic pleurisy on 15 July 1881.

Private GEORGE RICHARDSON
KEWANE TRANS-GOGRA 27 April 1859
He was 27 years old and serving in the 34th Regiment of Foot, later the Border Regiment, when despite being severely wounded in the arm, he closed with and captured a rebel armed with a loaded revolver.

He died from pneumonia on 28 January 1923.

Lieutenant CHARLES GOODFELLOW
FORT OF BEYT 6 October 1859
He was 22 years old and serving in the Bombay Engineers, Indian Army when during an attack he carried off a mortally wounded man of the 28th Regiment under heavy fire and took him to a place of safety.

He died on 1 September 1915.

Chapter Six

THE MID-VICTORIAN PERIOD, 1860–78

The First Maori (Taranaki) War, New Zealand, 1860–61 (2 VCs)

As more and more immigrants came to New Zealand's North Island in the 1850s, there was an increased demand for land to accommodate them. This land had to be bought from the Maoris by the British government. As a lever, the Governor announced a policy whereby any land could be bought from an individual and anyone obstructing this would be committing treason. This policy was put to the test when a local Te Atiawa chief offered to sell land in North Taranaki. Not surprisingly, the Maoris living there were opposed to this sale, and their chief, Wiremu Kingi, although he did not want war, could not allow the sale to go through. The locals obstructed attempts to survey the area, refused to move out and built a number of forts. The war began on 17 March 1860 when the British attacked the Pah at Te Kohia. Two Victoria Crosses were awarded for this campaign.

Leading Seaman WILLIAM ODGERS
OMATA 28 March 1860

He was 26 years old and serving in the Royal Navy. He was with a party of 48 men from HMS *Niger* who went to the relief of the 65th Regiment. At the storming of a Maori Pah, he was the first man to enter, under heavy fire, and captured the enemy's largest flag. This was the first VC to be awarded in New Zealand.

He died on 20 December 1873.

Colour Sergeant JOHN LUCAS
HUIRANGI BUSH 18 March 1861

He was 34 years old and serving in the 40th (2nd Somersetshire) Regiment of Foot, later the South Lancashire Regiment (Prince of Wales's Volunteers), when he was one of a party of skirmishers ambushed by Maoris. Under heavy fire, he ran to assist a wounded lieutenant and sent a man back with him to the rear. He then collected the arms of the killed and wounded, took post behind a tree and returned fire for 15 minutes until support arrived.

He died on 4 March 1892.

The Third China War, 1860–62 (7 VCs)

Chinese resentment of European traders and diplomats had already resulted in the First China War of 1840–42. The uneasy peace that followed it came to an end when the Chinese executed a French missionary, and five Chinese sailors were removed from a British ship and tried for piracy. This led to the Second China War of 1846–47, which concluded with the Treaty of Tientsin. When the British and French commissioners set sail up the Pei-ho river to ratify the treaty, they were fired on from the three Taku forts, thus starting the Third China War. Seven Victoria Crosses were awarded for this campaign.

Lieutenant NATHANIEL BURSLEM
TAKU FORTS 21 August 1860

He was 24 years old and serving in the 67th

The Complete Victoria Cross

(South Hampshire) Regiment of Foot, later the Royal Hampshire Regiment. During the storming of the forts Burslem and Private Thomas Lane swam across the ditch in front of the North Taku fort and endeavoured to enlarge an opening in the wall before anyone else. They forced their way in and were severely wounded. Both men were awarded the VC.

Burslem drowned on 14 July 1865. His third cousin was Lieutenant Robert Shebbeare VC.

Lieutenant EDMUND LENON
TAKU FORTS 21 August 1860
He was 29 years old and serving in the 67th (South Hampshire) Regiment of Foot, later the Royal Hampshire Regiment. During the storming of the forts, he jumped into the ditch in front of the North Taku fort with Lieutenant Robert Rogers and Private John McDougall, and all three swam to the walls and forced their way in through an opening. Lenon was the third man to gain a footing on the walls. All three men were awarded the VC.

Lenon died from aortic stenosis and dropsy on 15 April 1893.

Lieutenant ROBERT ROGERS
TAKU FORTS 21 August 1860
He was 25 years old and serving in the 44th East Essex Regiment, later the Essex Regiment. During the storming of the forts, he jumped into the ditch in front of the North Taku fort with Lieutenant Edmund Lenon and Private John McDougall, and all three swam to the walls and forced their way in through an opening. Rogers was the first man to gain a footing on the walls. All three men were awarded the VC.

Rogers died on 5 February 1895.

Ensign JOHN CHAPLIN
TAKU FORTS 21 August 1860
He was 20 years old and serving in the 67th (South Hampshire) Regiment of Foot, later the Royal Hampshire Regiment. During the storming of the forts, he planted the regimental colours on the breach made by the storming party. He then planted the colours on the

bastion of the fort, which he was the first to mount. During this action he was severely wounded.

He died on 18 August 1920.

Private THOMAS LANE
TAKU FORTS 21 August 1860
He was 24 years old and serving in the 67th (South Hampshire) Regiment of Foot, later the Royal Hampshire Regiment. During the storming of the forts Lane and Lieutenant Nathaniel Burslem swam across the ditch in front of the North Taku fort, and endeavoured to enlarge an opening in the wall before anyone else. They forced their way in and were severely wounded. Both men were awarded the VC.

Lane also served in the Crimean War, the Indian Mutiny, and later in the Zulu and Mapoch Wars. He was one of eight men to have forfeited their VC, after being convicted of desertion from active service and theft.

He died from inflammation of the lungs on 12 April 1889.

Private JOHN McDOUGALL
TAKU FORTS 21 August 1860
He was 20 years old and serving in the 44th East Essex Regiment, later the Essex Regiment. During the storming of the forts, he jumped into the ditch in front of the North Taku fort with Lieutenant Robert Rogers and Lieutenant Edmund Lenon, and all three swam to the walls and forced their way in through an opening. McDougall was the second man to gain a footing on the walls. All three men were awarded the VC.

McDougall died on 10 March 1869.

Hospital Apprentice ANDREW FITZGIBBON
TAKU FORTS 21 August 1860
He was 15 years old and serving in the Indian Medical Establishment, Indian Army, attached to the 67th Regiment, later the Royal Hampshire Regiment. When the 67th had advanced to within 500 yards of the fort, Fitzgibbon proceeded under heavy fire to attend to a wounded litter-bearer, and while

the regiment was advancing under the enemy's fire he ran across open ground to attend to the wounded Lieutenant Gye. During this act he was severely wounded.

At just 15 years and 3 months he is acknowledged as one of the two youngest recipients of the VC. The other is Thomas Flynn, also 15 years and 3 months.

Fitzgibbon died on 7 March 1883.

The Taiping Rebellion, China, 1851–64
(1 VC)

In 1850 the popular leader Hung Hsiu-ch'an raised an army of T'ai P'ing rebels in Guangxi Province. His aim was to overthrow the weak Manchu Ch'ing emperor and declare a Utopian Christian 'Heavenly Kingdom of Great Peace'. The rebels declared their new republic in 1851. This regime was paralysing trade, so Major Charles Gordon ('Gordon of Khartoum') started a campaign to reduce and retake the rebel strongholds. With an estimated thirty million dead, it was the second bloodiest war ever, only the Second World War causing more deaths. One Victoria Cross was awarded for this campaign.

Able Seaman GEORGE HINCKLEY
FUNG WHA 9 October 1862
He was 43 years old and serving in the Royal Navy's Naval Brigade when he was part of a force attacking a fortified town. They found the main gate blocked and had to retreat under very heavy fire. Hinckley then noticed the assistant master of his ship, HMS *Sphinx*, lying wounded in the open. He ran to him and carried him to the safety of a Joss-house. He then went back to rescue another man and then rejoined the fight.

He died on 31 December 1904.

The Umbeyla Campaign, India, 1863
(2 VCs)

During the late 1850s the Peshawar district of British-held India came under frequent attack by the Hindustani Pathans based in the nearby Mahabun mountains. The war-like Pathans were violently opposed to British rule. An expedition in 1858 drove them from their base, but by 1863 they had regrouped around the mountain outpost of Malka, so an expedition was sent to destroy it. Two Victoria Crosses were awarded for this campaign.

Lieutenant GEORGE FOSBERY
UMBEYLA PASS 30 October 1863
He was 30 years old and serving in the 4th Bengal European Regiment, Indian Army. He led a party of men up one path while Lieutenant Henry Pitcher led a second party up another path to recapture the Crag Piquet after its garrison had been attacked by the enemy. He led his men to the top of the cliff two abreast and was the first man atop the Crag. Afterwards he led his men in pursuit of the fleeing enemy and inflicted many losses on them. Both men were awarded the VC.

Later he brought the machine-gun to the attention of the British government.

He died on 8 May 1907.

Lieutenant HENRY PITCHER
UMBEYLA PASS
30 October and 16 November 1863
He was 22 years old and serving in the 4th Punjab Infantry, Indian Army. He led a party of men up one path while Lieutenant George Fosbery led a second party up another path to recapture the Crag Piquet after its garrison had been attacked by the enemy. He led his men up until he was knocked down and stunned by a large stone thrown from above. On 16 November he led the first charge during the recapture of the same post, it having been taken by the enemy again. Both men were awarded the VC.

Pitcher was killed in action at Dehra Ghazi Khan on 5 July 1875.

The Second Maori (Waikato-Haubau) War, New Zealand, 1863–66 (13 VCs)

The truce that ended the first Maori War of 1861 had dealt only with the immediate territorial problems. By 1863 the increasing flow of settlers to New Zealand's North Island, and the consequent demand for land, was again the cause of fighting. In all, 13 Victoria Crosses were awarded for this campaign.

Colour Sergeant EDWARD McKENNA
CAMERON TOWN 7 September 1863
He was 36 years old and serving in the 65th Regiment of Foot, later the 1st Bn, York and Lancaster Regiment. When both his officers were shot, he took command of a small party and charged a much larger enemy force, causing them to disperse into the bush. His party then held its ground under fire and moved on as darkness fell, spending the night in perfect silence, until support arrived at daybreak.

He died on 8 June 1908.

Lance Corporal JOHN RYAN
CAMERON TOWN 7 September 1863
He was 24 years old and serving in the 65th Regiment of Foot, later the 1st Bn, York and Lancaster Regiment, when he carried the mortally wounded Captain Swift from the field, holding him while he died. He stayed with Swift's body, covering it with leaves to hide it from the surrounding Maoris, until support arrived at daybreak.

He drowned on 29 December 1863, trying to rescue a comrade.

Ensign JOHN DOWN
POUTOKO 2 October 1863
He was 21 years old and serving in the 57th Regiment of Foot, later the Middlesex Regiment (Duke of Cambridge's Own), when he volunteered to go with Drummer Dudley Stagpoole to rescue a wounded man lying in the open. Although the enemy kept up a very heavy fire at short range, they succeeded in bringing back the man, who was lying some 50 yards from the bush which was swarming with Maoris. Both men were awarded the VC.

Down was killed in action at Camp Otahuhu on 27 April 1866.

Drummer DUDLEY STAGPOOLE
POUTOKO 2 October 1863
He was 25 years old and serving in the 57th Regiment of Foot, later the Middlesex Regiment (Duke of Cambridge's Own), when he volunteered to go with Ensign John Down to rescue a wounded man lying in the open. Although the enemy kept up a very heavy fire at short range, they succeeded in bringing back the man, who was lying some 50 yards from the bush which was swarming with Maoris. Both men were awarded the VC.

Stagpoole died on 1 August 1911.

Assistant Surgeon WILLIAM TEMPLE
RANGIRIRI 20 November 1863
He was 30 years old and serving in the Royal Regiment of Artillery. During an assault on the enemy's position, Temple and Lieutenant Arthur Pickard exposed themselves to great danger in crossing the entrance to the Pah at a point where the enemy were concentrating their fire, in order to assist the wounded Captain Mercer. Temple dressed his wounds, while Pickard went back and forth to bring him water. Both men showed great coolness under fire, and both were awarded the VC.

Temple died on 13 February 1919, following a long illness.

Lieutenant ARTHUR PICKARD
RANGIRIRI 20 November 1863
He was 19 years old and serving in the Royal Regiment of Artillery. During an assault on the enemy's position, Pickard and Assistant Surgeon William Temple exposed themselves to great danger in crossing the entrance to the Pah at a point where the enemy were concentrating their fire, in order to assist the wounded Captain Mercer. Temple dressed his wounds, while Pickard went back and forth to bring him water. Both men showed great coolness under fire, and both were awarded the VC.

Pickard died from tuberculosis on 1 March 1880.

Major CHARLES HEAPHY

MANGAPIKO RIVER 11 February 1864

He was 43 years old and serving in the Auckland Militia, New Zealand Military Forces when he went to the assistance of a soldier who had fallen into the river, where the Maoris were concealed in great numbers. A volley was fired at him from close range and he was hit by three bullets. He stayed with the wounded man, assisting him all day. Heaphy was the first colonial soldier to be awarded the VC.

He died from tuberculosis on 3 August 1881. The Heaphy river is named in his honour.

Lieutenant Colonel JOHN McNEILL

OHAUPO 30 March 1864

He was 33 years old and serving in the 107th Regiment (Bengal Infantry), later the Royal Sussex Regiment, when he was riding with his orderly, Private Vosper. They suddenly came upon 50 of the enemy. They turned to gallop back but Vosper's horse went down under a hail of bullets and then ran off. McNeill rode after the horse, caught it and helped Vosper to remount. Although the enemy were very close and firing sharply, by galloping hard they managed to get away.

McNeill was an equerry to Queen Victoria. He died on 25 May 1904.

Assistant Surgeon WILLIAM MANLEY

TE-PAPA 29 April 1864

He was 32 years old and serving in the Royal Regiment of Artillery when, during an attack on the Pah, he accompanied the storming party and attended to the mortally wounded Commander Hay. He then returned to help with the rest of the wounded. He was one of the last to leave the Pah.

During the Franco-Prussian War he was awarded the German Iron Cross for helping the wounded, and he is the only recipient of both awards.

He died on 16 November 1901.

Captain of the Foretop SAMUEL MITCHELL

TE-PAPA 29 April 1864

He was 22 years old and serving in the Royal Navy. During an attack on the Pah, he came across the mortally wounded Commander Hay. Hay ordered Mitchell to leave him and look to his own safety, but he refused to do so and carried him out of the Pah on his back. Hay died from his wounds the next day.

Mitchell drowned on 16 March 1894.

Captain FREDERICK SMITH

TAURANGA 21 June 1864

He was 37 years old and serving in the 43rd Regiment of Foot (Monmouthshire Light Infantry), later the Oxfordshire and Buckinghamshire Light Infantry, when he was wounded while leading his men in an assault on a Maori position. Ignoring his wounds, he jumped into the enemy rifle pits and engaged them in hand-to-hand fighting.

He commanded the 43rd Regiment in the late 1870s.

He died on 22 July 1887.

Sergeant JOHN MURRAY

TAURANGA 21 June 1864

He was 27 years old and serving in the 68th Regiment of Foot, later the Durham Light Infantry, when he was wounded while leading his company in an attack on an enemy position. Ignoring his wounds, he ran up to a rifle pit with about ten Maoris in it and killed or wounded them all. He then carried on up the works, attacking with the bayonet. During this action he also saved the life of Private John Byrne VC.

He died on 8 April 1912.

Captain HUGH SHAW

NUKUMARU 24 January 1865

He was 25 years old and serving in the 18th Regiment of Foot, later the Royal Irish Rifles, when he was ordered to clear the bush of Maoris. Having advanced to within 30 yards of the enemy, his men began to take casualties. He ordered the men to take cover behind a palisade, and then dashed forward with four privates to bring in a wounded man who was lying close to the enemy.

He died on 25 August 1904.

The Shimonoseki Expedition, Japan, 1864 (3 VCs)

The expansion of foreign trade into the Far East was causing mounting resentment in Japan, and in 1863 the Daimyo of the Choshu clan began to expel foreigners from the land around the Straits of Shimonoseki. When his ships attacked European and American ships, they naturally fired back. The European powers formed an international squadron with the intention of wiping out the Choshu ships and forts. Three Victoria Crosses were awarded for this campaign.

Midshipman DUNCAN BOYES
SHIMONOSEKI 6 September 1864

He was 17 years old and serving in the Royal Navy. During the attack on the stockade he carried the Queen's Colour ahead of the storming party under a hail of bullets. The flag was pierced six times by musket balls. Along with Captain of the After Guard Thomas Pride, he was only prevented from advancing further by an order from their superior officer. The stockade was taken and destroyed. Both men were awarded the VC.

Boyes was court-martialled in 1867. The shame was too much to bear and he killed himself by jumping from a window on 26 January 1869. His death certificate shows 'delirium tremens' as the cause of death. His brother-in-law was Lieutenant Thomas Young VC.

Captain of the Afterguard THOMAS PRIDE
SHIMONOSEKI 6 September 1864

He was 29 years old and serving in the Royal Navy. During the attack on the stockade he ran ahead, and then turned to cheer his comrades on, despite being shot in the chest. Along with Midshipman Duncan Boyes, he was only prevented from advancing further by an order from their superior officer. The stockade was taken and destroyed. Both men were awarded the VC.

Pride died on 16 July 1893.

Seaman WILLIAM SEELEY
SHIMONOSEKI 6 September 1864

He was 24 years old and serving in the Royal Navy when he distinguished himself by carrying out a reconnaissance alone to ascertain the enemy's position. Later, although wounded in the arm, he took part in the final assault on the stockade, which was taken and destroyed.

Seeley was the first American citizen to be awarded the VC.

He died on 1 October 1914.

The Bhootan (Bhutan) War, India, 1864–65 (2 VCs)

The Indian state of Bhootan lies to the east of Nepal, and in 1864, following a civil war in the region, the victorious leader of the Punakha people had broken with the central administration and set up a rival government. The legitimate governor was deposed, so Britain, protecting her interests in her Indian Empire, sent a peace mission to restore order. The British tried to mediate, dealing alternately with the supporters of the deposed governor and the new government. But the latter rejected all British attempts to broker peace, so in November Britain declared war on the new regime. Two Victoria Crosses were awarded for this campaign.

Major WILLIAM TREVOR
DEWAN-GIRI 30 April 1865

He was 33 years old and serving in the Bengal Engineers, Indian Army when he led an attack with Lieutenant James Dundas on a blockhouse defended by 200 men. To gain entry, the two men had to climb a 14-foot wall and then crawl through a small hole between the wall and the roof. Inspired by their example, the

Sikh soldiers followed them in. Both officers were wounded but the blockhouse was taken, along with 60 prisoners, the rest being killed, fighting to the last. Both men were awarded the VC.

Trevor died on 2 November 1907.

Lieutenant JAMES DUNDAS
DEWAN-GIRI 30 April 1865
He was 23 years old and serving in the Bengal Engineers, Indian Army when he led an attack with Lieutenant William Trevor on a block-house defended by 200 men. To gain entry, the two men had to climb a 14-foot wall and then enter through a small hole between the wall and the roof. Inspired by their example, the Sikh soldiers followed them in. Both officers were wounded but the blockhouse was taken, along with 60 prisoners, the rest being killed, fighting to the last. Both men were awarded the VC.

Dundas was killed in action at Sherpur Cantonment on 23 December 1879, while trying to blow up a fort. In 2002 the 'Dundas Bridge' built by the Royal Engineers between Kubel and Bagram in Afghanistan was named in his honour.

Canada, 1866 (1 VC)

The Irish-American Fenian Brotherhood, whose principal objective was to free Ireland from British rule, planned to provoke a war between Britain and the US, and decided to carry out attacks on the British dominion of Canada. Two raids were carried out across the border in June 1866, and were repulsed by Canadian volunteers. One Victoria Cross was awarded for this campaign.

Private TIMOTHY O'HEA
DANVILLE 9 June 1866
He was 20 years old and serving in the 1st Bn, Rifle Brigade (Prince Consort's Own) when a railway car containing 2,000 lb (900 kg) of powder and ammunition caught fire. While others took cover, waiting for the inevitable explosion, O'Hea took the keys from the sergeant in charge, rushed to the car, opened the doors, collected some water and suppressed the fire. By his actions the lives of all within reach were saved, along with a good part of the town.

This VC was awarded not for bravery in action against the enemy, but for bravery in which public property might be saved, under the 10 August 1858 Amendment to the Royal Warrant.

O'Hea is said to have died in Queensland's Tirari-Sturt Desert in Australia in 1874 while searching for a lost member of the Leichhardt expedition. Graham Fischer was present at the death but does not describe the specifics of the event. A recent book by Elizabeth Reid, *The Singular Journey of O'Hea's Cross*, suggests the theory that Timothy O'Hea actually died in Ireland shortly after his discharge from the army in 1868. His identity and VC annuity were then assumed by his brother John, and it was this man who actually died in Australia.

The First Gambia War, 1866 (1 VC)

In 1866 British forces were involved in some diffculties with a West African tribe in the Gambia. An expedition was organised by Colonel D'Arcy, in which the tribal land was invaded. One Victoria Cross was awarded for this campaign.

Private SAMUEL HODGE
TUBABECELONG 30 June 1866
He was 26 years old and serving in the 4th West India Regiment when, during the attack on the stockade, he sprang forward and began to cut down the wooden timbers. He then followed his colonel into the town, smashing open two gates with an axe, thus allowing support troops to enter the town. The enemy were routed and Hodge was proclaimed the bravest man in the regiment.

He died on 14 January 1868.

The Andaman Islands Expedition, 1867
(5 VCs)

When Britain needed a new penal settlement to house the prisoners from the Indian Mutiny, they returned to the old penal colony of the Andaman Islands in the Bay of Bengal to establish Fort Blair, despite concerns over the cannibal tendencies of the natives on the islands. The *Assam Valley* put in at the island of Little Andaman and a small party went ashore, never to be seen again. Subsequently an expedition was sent to find out what had happened to them. Five Victoria Crosses were awarded for this campaign.

Assistant Surgeon CAMPBELL DOUGLAS
BAY OF BENGAL 7 May 1867
He was 27 years old and serving in the 2nd Bn, 24th Regiment of Foot, later the South Wales Borderers, when he was one of a party of five (the others being Private David Bell, Private James Cooper, Private William Griffiths and Private Thomas Murphy) who risked their own lives to row a boat through dangerous surf to rescue some of their comrades who had been sent to the island to investigate the fate of the shore party from the *Assam Valley*, feared murdered by the islanders.

This VC was awarded not for bravery in action against the enemy, but for bravery at sea in saving life, under the 10 August 1858 Amendment to the Royal Warrant.

Douglas died on 31 December 1909.

Private DAVID BELL
BAY OF BENGAL 7 May 1867
He was 22 years old and serving in the 2nd Bn, 24th Regiment of Foot, later the South Wales Borderers, when he was one of a party of five (the others being Assistant Surgeon Campbell Douglas, Private James Cooper, Private William Griffiths and Private Thomas Murphy) who risked their own lives to row a boat through dangerous surf to rescue some of their comrades who had been sent to the island to investigate the fate of the shore party from the *Assam Valley*, feared murdered by the islanders.

This VC was awarded not for bravery in action against the enemy, but for bravery at sea in saving life, under the 10 August 1858 Amendment to the Royal Warrant.

Bell died from senile decay on 7 March 1920.

Private JAMES COOPER
BAY OF BENGAL 7 May 1867
He was 27 years old and serving in the 2nd Bn, 24th Regiment of Foot, later the South Wales Borderers, when he was one of a party of five (the others being Assistant Surgeon Campbell Douglas, Private David Bell, Private William Griffiths and Private Thomas Murphy) who risked their own lives to row a boat through dangerous surf to rescue some of their comrades who had been sent to the island to investigate the fate of the shore party from the *Assam Valley*, feared murdered by the islanders.

This VC was awarded not for bravery in action against the enemy, but for bravery at sea in saving life, under the 10 August 1858 Amendment to the Royal Warrant.

Cooper died on 9 August 1889.

Private WILLIAM GRIFFITHS
BAY OF BENGAL 7 May 1867
He was 26 years old and serving in the 2nd Bn, 24th Regiment of Foot, later the South Wales Borderers, when he was one of a party of five (the others being Assistant Surgeon Campbell Douglas, Private David Bell, Private James Cooper and Private Thomas Murphy) who risked their own lives to row a boat through dangerous surf to rescue some of their comrades who had been sent to the island to investigate the fate of the shore party from the *Assam Valley*, feared murdered by the islanders.

This VC was awarded not for bravery in action against the enemy, but for bravery at sea in saving life, under the 10 August 1858 Amendment to the Royal Warrant. Griffiths was killed in action at Isandlwana on 22 January 1879, and his body was recovered five months later, still wearing his VC.

Private THOMAS MURPHY
  BAY OF BENGAL 7 May 1867
He was 28 years old and serving in the 2nd Bn,
24th Regiment of Foot, later the South Wales
Borderers, when he was one of a party of five
(the others being Assistant Surgeon Campbell
Douglas, Private David Bell, Private James
Cooper and Private William Griffiths) who
risked their own lives to row a boat through
dangerous surf to rescue some of their
comrades who had been sent to the island to
investigate the fate of the shore party from the
ship *Assam Valley*, feared murdered by the
islanders.
  This VC was awarded not for bravery in
action against the enemy, but for bravery at sea
in saving life, under the 10 August 1858
Amendment to the Royal Warrant.
  Murphy died on 23 March 1899.

The Abyssinian War, 1867–68 (2 VCs)

Theodor, the Christian Emperor of Abyssinia
(now Ethiopia), had pursued an anti-Muslim
crusade to reform his country. In 1862 a new
British consul arrived, bearing a pair of pistols
as a gift from Queen Victoria, and he suggested
that Theodor approach the Queen directly to
negotiate a treaty of friendship, and a letter was
duly sent. However, it seems the letter was lost
en route, and on getting no response the
volatile Theodor imprisoned the consul (as he
had visited the Muslim Sudan) and some
British missionaries. Diplomatic means having
failed to solve the problem, Britain sent an ultimatum, which was ignored. An expedition was
then sent to attack the mountain capital of
Magdala in 1867. Two Victoria Crosses were
awarded for this campaign.

Private JAMES BERGIN
  MAGDALA 13 April 1868
He was 22 years old and serving in the 33rd
Regiment of Foot, later the Duke of
Wellington's Regiment (West Riding), when
the head of his column was held up by obsta-
cles at the gate. Bergin and Drummer Michael

Magner were part of a group of men who
climbed a cliff and forced their way in through
a strong fence of thorns and fought the enemy
hand-to-hand. Bergin and Magner were the
first two men to enter and both were awarded
the VC. .
  Bergin died from ague and brain fever on
1 December 1880.

**Drummer MICHAEL MAGNER (aka
BARRY)**
  MAGDALA 13 April 1868
He was 27 years old and serving in the 33rd
Regiment of Foot, later the Duke of
Wellington's Regiment (West Riding), when
the head of his column was held up by obstacles at the gate. Magner and Private James
Bergin were part of a group of men who
climbed a cliff and forced their way in through
a strong fence of thorns and fought the enemy
hand-to-hand. Bergin and Magner were the
first two men to enter and both were awarded
the VC.
  Magner died on 6 February 1897.

**The Looshai Expedition, India, 1872
(1 VC)**

Since 1850 the Looshai tribesmen had gradually migrated from the Chin Hills into Assam,
subjugating the local people to their own rule.
They remained untouched by foreign influence
until Britain annexed Assam in 1862. The
Looshai were furious at this foreign intrusion
and started launching raids into British territory, to which Britain responded with punitive
expeditions. In 1872 the Looshai kidnapped a
girl, Mary Winchester, and a field force was
sent out to save her and to punish the kidnap-
pers. One Victoria Cross was awarded for this
campaign.

Major DONALD MacINTYRE
  LALGNOORA 4 January 1872
He was 40 years old and serving in the Bengal
Staff Corps, Indian Army and 2nd Gurkha
Rifles when he was the first man to reach the

9-foot-high stockade. Climbing over it, he ran into the flames of the burning village. He was followed by his men, who stormed the village. MacIntyre was also awarded the CB, making him a rare recipient of military and civilian decorations.

He died on 15 April 1903.

The First Ashanti War, 1873–74 (4 VCs)

In 1872 the coastal fort of Elmina in Ashanti (now Ghana) came into British possession. This was the last outlet for trade to the sea for the native Ashanti people, and their king, Kofi Karikari, was ready to fight to protect it. In 1873 he mustered a 12,000-strong army which crossed the Pre river and invaded the coastal area. The British Governor and Commander-in-Chief Major General Sir Garnet Wolseley issued a warning that he was ready to attack. But he also offered an armistice if the Ashanti would retreat from the coast. Unfortunately the negotiations failed and war became inevitable. Four Victoria Crosses were awarded for this campaign.

Lieutenant EDRIC GIFFORD
BECQUAH 1873–74
He was 23 years old and serving in the 2nd Bn, 24th Regiment of Foot, later the South Wales Borderers, when throughout the campaign his conduct was exceptional. He was placed in command of the native scouts and hung upon the rear of the enemy, dogging their movements, noting their positions and capturing many prisoners single-handed. Before the taking of Becquah, he entered the city and took note of the enemy positions, enabling it to be swiftly captured.

Gifford also served in the Zulu War.

He died on 5 June 1911. His nephew was Captain John Butler VC.

Major REGINALD SARTORIUS
ABOGU 17 January 1874
He was 32 years old and serving in the 6th Bengal Cavalry, Indian Army when during the attack on Abogu, Sartorius went to the assistance of a Houssa NCO, who was lying mortally wounded, and brought him to a place of safety while under heavy fire.

He died on 8 August 1907. His brother was Captain Euston Sartorius VC.

Lance Sergeant SAMUEL McGAW
AMOAFUL 21 January 1874
He was 36 years old and serving in the 42nd Regiment of Foot, later the Black Watch (Royal Highlanders), when McGaw led his section through heavy fighting in the bush all day, despite having been seriously wounded early that morning.

He died from heat apoplexy on 22 July 1878.

Lieutenant MARK BELL
ORDASHU 4 February 1874
He was 30 years old and serving in the Corps of Royal Engineers. He was always out in front, urging on an unarmed working party of Fanti labourers, who were exposed not only to enemy fire but also to the wild and irregular fire of the native troops to their rear. He encouraged them to work under fire without a covering party, and he contributed considerably to the success of the day.

Bell died on 26 June 1906.

The Perak War, Malaya, 1875–76 (1 VC)

Britain, which had occupied Singapore since 1819, had exercised a policy of not getting involved in local upheavals in the Malay states to the north. However, when civil war broke out in nearby Selangor in 1871, Britain intervened, annexing the region. The next year trouble flared up in Perak and threatened to spread to Singapore, so it too was annexed. These areas proved difficult to control, with the British Resident James Birch's measures to keep law and order bringing him into direct conflict with the local Malay leaders.

In July 1875, seeing their power and revenues seriously threatened, the Malay chiefs had Birch murdered. Britain replied with a punitive expedition to find the assassins. One Victoria Cross was awarded for this campaign.

Captain GEORGE CHANNER
PERAK 20 December 1875

He was 32 years old and serving in the Bengal Staff Corps, Indian Army and 1st Gurkha Rifles. In advance of the attack on the enemy stockade, he crept up so close to it that he could hear the people inside talking. Seeing there was no watch, he signalled to his men to attack. He shot the first man dead himself and the stockade was taken. His action undoubtedly saved a great many lives, as it would have been necessary to resort to the bayonet.

Channer died on 13 December 1905.

Baluchistan, India, 1877 (1 VC)

Two treaties were signed in 1859 and 1876, strengthening Baluchistan's ties with the British Indian Empire, and in 1876 British forces set up a strongly garrisoned army station at Quetta in the west of Baluchistan, commanding the Bola n and Khojak passes through the mountains. In July some officers were attacked by a group of coolies. One Victoria Cross was awarded for this campaign.

Captain ANDREW SCOTT
QUETTA 26 July 1877

He was 36 years old and serving in the Bengal Staff Corps, attached to the 4th Sikh Infantry, Indian Army when he heard that British officers were being killed and he immediately went to their assistance. He found one officer cut down and the other wounded and hard-pressed. Scott bayoneted two of the enemy and closed with a third, who fell with him to the ground and was killed by a sepoy.

He died from peritonitis on 5 September 1882.

The Ninth Cape Frontier War, 1877–78 (1 VC)

In 1877 the Ngika and Gaika sections of the Xhosa tribe took arms against the Fingoes, whom they felt to be favoured by the British colonists. But what started as a petty brawl between two tribes near the old mission station at Butterworth suddenly blew up into full-blown tribal conflict. The ensuing war drew in British forces in aid of the colonial police, to support the Fingoes against the Gaikas. It was a war of intermittent raids, ambushes, skirmishes and some small pitched battles around the Cape region, and saw the British using machine-guns for the first time. One Victoria Cross was awarded for this campaign.

Major HANS MOORE
KOMGHA 29 December 1877

He was 43 years old and serving in the 88th Regiment of Foot, later the Connaught Rangers, when he was part of a small force retreating before a large body of Gaikas. Seeing a private surrounded by the enemy and unable to mount his horse, Moore turned back to save him. He killed two Gaikas and was wounded by an assegai in the arm, but was unable to save the private.

He drowned on 7 October 1889 in the Dromineer Bay, Lough Derg, Co. Tipperary, Ireland.

Chapter Seven

THE LATE VICTORIAN PERIOD, 1878–89

The Second Afghan War, 1878–80 (16 VCs)

Britain had been keeping an eye on this important buffer to the north-west of India as part of a 'masterly inactivity' policy. In 1866 the Emir Sher Ali came to power. He was well disposed to Britain and feared Russian intrusion as much as the British. In 1872 Britain and Russia signed an agreement stating that Russia would respect Afghanistan's northern border, and that there would be no need for the British government to give any promises of support to Afghanistan. But alarm bells sounded in 1876, when the Emir reluctantly allowed a Russian mission to Kabul and then refused to admit the British envoy. This intrusion was too close to British-ruled India to go unopposed. Sher Ali had to go, and an ultimatum was sent demanding that a British envoy be admitted. When this was ignored, three columns of British soldiers moved in. Sixteen Victoria Crosses were awarded for this campaign.

Captain JOHN COOK
PEIWAR KOTAL 2 December 1878
He was 35 years old and serving in the Bengal Staff Corps, Indian Army, and 5th Gurkha Rifles when he went to the assistance of Major Galbraith, who was about to be killed by an Afghan warrior. He parried the man's bayonet and they wrestled for some time until the Afghan bit into his sword arm, then hurled him over and charged his bayonet to give the final blow. At this point a Gurkha shot the Afghan in the head.
He was killed in action on 19 December 1879.

Lieutenant REGINALD HART
BAZAR VALLEY 31 January 1879
He was 30 years old and serving in the Corps of Royal Engineers when he ran some 1,200 yards to the assistance of a wounded sowar who was exposed to enemy fire. He reached the man as the enemy were about to cut him to pieces, drove them off and brought him back to safety with the help of others.
He died on 10 October 1931.

Captain EDWARD LEACH
MAIDANAH 17 March 1879
He was 31 years old and serving in the Corps of Royal Engineers when he was covering the retreat of a survey escort. As the enemy began to press from all sides, Leach led a charge of the 45th Sikhs, killing three Afghans single-handedly and receiving a wound to his arm. His actions prevented the annihilation of the whole party.
He died on 27 April 1913.

Lieutenant WALTER HAMILTON
FUTTEHABAD 2 April 1879
He was 22 years old and serving in the Bengal Staff Corps and Corps of Guides when he led a charge of the Guides cavalry against very superior numbers of the enemy. When his commanding officer was killed, Hamilton, the only officer left with the regiment, assumed command and cheered the men on to avenge his death. In this charge, seeing that a sowar was down, entangled with his horse and being attacked by three of the enemy, Hamilton rushed over to him and killed all three of his attackers, thus saving his life.

He was killed in action on 3 September 1879.

Captain O'MOORE CREAGH
KAM DAKKA 21 April 1879

He was 31 years old and serving in the Bombay Staff Corps, Indian Army. Having been ordered to take a detachment of 150 men to protect the village against a threatened incursion by the Mohmands, he had to repel an attack by about 1,500 men. The inhabitants of the village joined with the Mohmands and his force was compelled to retire, so he took up a position in the cemetery and held it resolutely, repulsing repeated attacks with the bayonet, until the 10th Bengal Lancers arrived, charged the enemy and routed them.

Creagh is the author of *The Victoria Cross 1856–1920*.

He died on 9 August 1923.

Major GEORGE WHITE
CHARASIAH 6 October 1879

He was 44 years old and serving in the 92nd Regiment of Foot, later the Gordon Highlanders, when he led an attack on a strongly fortified hill where the enemy outnumbered his party by eight to one. When his men became exhausted, White saw that immediate action was needed. He seized a rifle, ran forward alone and shot the enemy leader. This decided the issue and the enemy fled. Later he led the final charge at Kandahar and personally captured one of the two guns held by the enemy, immediately after which they retired.

White was commander of the garrison at the Siege of Ladysmith during the Second Boer War. He was also Governor of the Chelsea Hospital, where he died on 24 June 1924.

Captain EUSTON SARTORIUS
SHAHJUI 24 October 1879

He was 35 years old and serving in the 59th Regiment of Foot, later the East Lancashire Regiment, when he led a party of four or five men in a surprise attack on an almost inaccessible enemy stronghold on the top of a steep hill. Sartorius and his men crept up on the picket unawares, but were spotted at the last minute, and were then fired on as they reached the top of the steep pathway. Despite this, the position was taken with the loss of only one man. Sartorius suffered sword cuts to both hands.

He died on 19 February 1925. His brother was Major Reginald Sartorius VC.

Reverend JAMES ADAMS
KILLA KAZI 11 December 1879

He was 40 years old and serving in the Bengal Ecclesiastical Department, Indian Army when he spotted two men from the 9th Lancers trapped underneath their horses in a deep ravine and about to drown. Well aware from the shouting and firing that the enemy were nearly upon them, he jumped into the water, pulled the men clear of their horses and then escaped on foot. Adams was known as the 'Fighting Parson'.

He died from an acute neuritis on 24 October 1903. After his death a stained-glass window was dedicated to him at his church in Stow Bardolph, Norfolk.

Lieutenant WILLIAM DICK-CUNYNGHAM
SHERPUR PASS 13 December 1879

He was 28 years old and serving in the 92nd Regiment of Foot, later the Gordon Highlanders. His regiment was beginning to waver under heavy fire, so he rode out, exposing himself to the fire, raised his claymore aloft and called on his men to follow him. With a cheer they charged, and the pass was taken.

He was killed in action at Ladysmith on 7 January 1900.

Captain ARTHUR HAMMOND
ASMAI HEIGHTS 14 December 1879

He was 36 years old and serving in the Bengal Staff Corps and Corps of Guides, Indian Army when he single-handedly defended the top of a hill with only a rifle and fixed bayonet against large numbers of Afghans, allowing the 72nd Highlanders and Guides to retire. On his retreat down the hill, he stopped to help carry a wounded sepoy, although the Afghans were only 60 yards away and firing heavily all the time.

Hammond died on 20 April 1919.

Captain WILLIAM VOUSDEN
ASMAI HEIGHTS 14 December 1879
He was 34 years old and serving in the 5th Punjab Cavalry, Bengal Staff Corps when he charged with a small party into the centre of the retreating Kohistani Force, which greatly outnumbered his own party. After rapidly charging through the enemy backwards and forwards, cutting down at least 30, five of whom he himself killed, Vousden and his party then swept off round the opposite side of a village and joined the rest of the troops.

He died from dysentery on 2 November 1902. His nephew was Lieutenant Colonel Arthur Borton VC.

Lance Corporal GEORGE SELLAR
ASMAI HEIGHTS 14 December 1879
He was 29 years old and serving in the 72nd Regiment of Foot, later the Seaforth Highlanders Ross-shire Buffs (Duke of Albany's), when he dashed up a slope ahead of his party and engaged in hand-to-hand fighting with an Afghan who sprang out to meet him. Sellar defeated the Afghan, despite receiving a knife wound to the arm.

He died on 1 November 1889.

Sergeant PATRICK MULLANE
MAIWAND 27 July 1880
He was 21 years old and serving in the Royal Horse Artillery. During the retreat to Kandahar, he saw a driver lying wounded on the ground. Although the enemy were only 10 yards away, he sprang down from his horse, lifted the mortally wounded man on to the limber of his gun and got him away. Also during the retreat he entered several villages under heavy fire to fetch water for the wounded.

His medal was sold by his family in 1904, when he was abroad and believed dead; on his return, the medal was restored to him.

Mullane died on 20 November 1919.

Gunner JAMES COLLIS
MAIWAND 28 July 1880
He was 24 years old and serving in the Royal Horse Artillery. During the retreat to Kandahar, he behaved splendidly, fetching water, tending to the wounded and maintaining his good humour while many died of fatigue on the road. When he saw twelve enemy cavalrymen approaching, he broke off, lay down in a ravine and opened fire. Thinking that they were facing several men, the enemy halted and returned fire. He killed two of them before he was relieved. His action undoubtedly saved the lives of his comrades.

He is one of eight men to forfeit his medal, after being convicted of bigamy. Collis also served in the First World War.

He died from heart disease on 28 June 1918.

Lieutenant WILLIAM CHASE
DEH KHOJA 16 August 1880
He was 24 years old and serving in the 28th Native Infantry, Indian Army when he and Private Thomas Ashford carried the wounded Private Massey for over 200 yards. Bullets were raising dust all around them and they fell three times but eventually they reached safety. Both men were awarded the VC.

Chase died on 24 June 1908.

Private THOMAS ASHFORD
DEH KHOJA 16 August 1880
He was 21 years old and serving in the Royal Fusiliers when he and Lieutenant William Chase carried the wounded Private Massey for over 200 yards. Bullets were raising dust all around them and they fell three times but eventually they reached safety. Both men were awarded the VC.

Ashford died from bronchitis on 21 February 1913.

The Zulu War, 1879 (23 VCs)

Imperial fever was growing in Britain, and in 1877, to secure the stability of lands in South Africa that were contested by Britain and the Boers, a High Commissioner was sent to create a federal dominion of British colonies and Boer republics. To do this, he needed to control the land bordering Natal and the Transvaal, which belonged to the Zulus. The Zulu King Cetshwayo, however, refused to give up this land. Needing a reason to invade Zululand, the British sent an ultimatum ordering Cetshwayo to disband his army, a course of action they knew he would not take, and when this was ignored, war was inevitable. In all, 23 Victoria Crosses were awarded for this campaign.

Lieutenant TEIGNMOUTH MELVILL
ISANDHLWANA 22 January 1879
He was 36 years old and serving in the 1st Bn, 24th Regiment of Foot, later the South Wales Borderers. During the rout from Isandhlwana, Melvill and Lieutenant Nevill Coghill tried to carry the Queen's Colour of their regiment to safety. Pursued by Zulu warriors, they rode to the swollen Buffalo river. Coghill crossed safely, but Melvill's horse was being carried away by the torrent. As Coghill plunged back into the river to assist his comrade, his horse was shot from under him. Both men struggled to the Natal bank, where they were engulfed by Zulus. When their bodies were discovered, a ring of dead Zulus lay all around them. The colour was found ten days later, downstream. Both men were awarded the VC.

Lieutenant NEVILL COGHILL
ISANDHLWANA 22 January 1879
He was 26 years old and serving in the 1st Bn, 24th Regiment of Foot, later the South Wales Borderers. During the rout from Isandhlwana, Coghill and Lieutenant Teignmouth Melvill tried to carry the Queen's Colour of their regiment to safety. Pursued by Zulu warriors, they rode to the swollen Buffalo river. Coghill crossed safely, but Melvill's horse was being carried away by the torrent. As Coghill plunged back into the river to assist his comrade, his horse was shot from under him. Both men struggled to the Natal bank, where they were engulfed by Zulus. When their bodies were discovered, a ring of dead Zulus

lay all around them. The colour was found ten days later, downstream. Both men were awarded the VC.

Private SAMUEL WASSALL
ISANDHLWANA 22 January 1879
He was 22 years old and serving in the 80th Regiment of Foot, later the South Staffordshire Regiment, when the camp was taken by the Zulus. Wassall was pursued towards the swollen Buffalo river, where he saw Private Westwood being swept away by the water. He dismounted, leaving his horse on the Zulu side of the river. He rescued the private, remounted his horse and dragged him across the river under a heavy shower of bullets.

He died on 31 January 1927. His descendant Genial Wassall is a veteran of the Falklands War and the first Gulf War in Iraq, where he was commended for his bravery by General Norman Schwarzkopf.

Lieutenant JOHN CHARD
RORKE'S DRIFT 22/23 January 1879
He was 31 years old and serving in the Royal Engineers when he and Lieutenant Gonville Bromhead commanded 150 men against an attacking force of 4,000 Zulu warriors. The Zulus arrived only 30 minutes after the first warning was received, but in that time the two men had supervised the building of the barricades. From 4pm until daybreak the next morning they kept up a steady fire and directed the operation, ensuring the successful defence of the post. Had it not been for their example and excellent behaviour, the defence would not have been conducted with the intelligence and tenacity that so eminently characterised it. The success must in great measure be attributable to the two young officers who exercised the chief command on this occasion. Both men were awarded the VC.

Chard died from cancer of the tongue on 1 November 1897.

Lieutenant GONVILLE BROMHEAD
RORKE'S DRIFT 22/23 January 1879
He was 33 years old and serving in the 2nd Bn, 24th Regiment of Foot, later the South Wales

The Complete Victoria Cross

Borderers when he and Lieutenant John Chard commanded 150 men against an attacking force of 4,000 Zulu warriors. The Zulus arrived only 30 minutes after the first warning was received, but in that time the two men had supervised the building of the barricades. From 4pm until daybreak the next morning they kept up a steady fire and directed the operation, ensuring the successful defence of the post. Had it not been for their example and excellent behaviour, the defence would not have been conducted with the intelligence and tenacity that so eminently characterised it. The success must in great measure be attributable to the two young officers who exercised the chief command on this occasion. Both men were awarded the VC.

Bromhead died from enteric fever on 9 February 1891.

Surgeon Major JAMES REYNOLDS
RORKE'S DRIFT 22/23 January 1879
He was 34 years old and serving in the Army Medical Department, later the Royal Army Medical Corps. During the attack by the Zulu warriors, he was constantly moving about and attending the wounded despite the heavy cross-fire from the Zulus on the hill above the post and a constant shower of assegais from those attacking the barricades. He also carried ammunition to the men from the store.

He died on 4 March 1932.

Assistant Commissary JAMES DALTON
RORKE'S DRIFT 22/23 January 1879
He was 46 years old and serving in the Commissariat and Transport Department, later the Royal Army Service Corps. Before the attack by the Zulu warriors, he argued that they should fortify the post and not retreat. When this was agreed, he set about superintending the building of the barricades. When the attack began, he was among those who received the first assault at the corner of the hospital.

He later rushed forward and shot a Zulu as he was about to stab one of the defenders, thus saving the man's life. He was not originally named among the VC recipients, eventually

receiving his VC on 16 January 1880.

He died on 8 January 1887. The 'Dalton VC Centre' in Pembrokeshire is named in his honour.

Corporal WILLIAM ALLEN (aka ALLAN)
RORKE'S DRIFT 22/23 January 1879
He was 35 years old and serving in the 2nd Bn, 24th Regiment of Foot, later the South Wales Borderers, when he was posted as a sharp-shooter on the southern rampart during the attack by the Zulu warriors. The Zulus came within 50 paces of the barricade and were shot down by volley fire. However, they still held the hills to the south and could fire at the post at will, causing serious casualties. Allen was determined to eliminate this threat and laid himself open to great danger as he positioned himself over the top of the barricade to fire at the enemy.

Inside the compound Allen and Private Frederick Hitch between them kept communications open with the main building as the patients were rescued from the hospital. Together they helped the wounded out through a high window, and held a perilously exposed post in the middle of the compound in order to keep back the Zulus who were climbing over the barricades. Most of the men from the hospital were safely withdrawn behind the inner defences.

Allen, like Hitch, was shot in the shoulder and their wounds were dressed by Surgeon Major Reynolds, but Allen was quickly back in action. Although too badly wounded to fight on, he distributed ammunition as the fighting continued.

Allen also served in the Cape Frontier War.

He died from influenza on 12 March 1890.

Corporal FERDINAND (commonly known as FREDERICK) SCHIESS
RORKE'S DRIFT 22/23 January 1879
He was 22 years old and serving in the Natal Native Contingent, South African Forces. During the attack by the Zulu warriors, he left his hospital bed in spite of a wounded foot. When the garrison had retired to the inner defences and the Zulus had moved up to the

wall of mealie bags, which had been abandoned, Schiess jumped on to the barricade and bayoneted a Zulu, jumped back down and shot another and then leapt on to the wall again to bayonet a third. He then returned to the inner defences.

He died at sea on 14 December 1884. It is said that there are no known portraits of Schiess, and in Lady Butler's painting of 'Rorke's Drift' he is shown from the back. In fact, the Imperial War Museum has a photograph of him, but it is a group picture and of poor quality.

Private ALFRED (commonly known as HENRY) HOOK
RORKE'S DRIFT 22/23 January 1879
He was 28 years old and serving in the 2nd Bn, 24th Regiment of Foot, later the South Wales Borderers. During the attack by the Zulu warriors, he shot several Zulus through a loophole in the hospital building. As the Zulus burst into the building and set the roof ablaze, he bayoneted countless attackers. Then Private John Williams broke down a wall and passed two patients from the hospital through to Hook. Williams pickaxed one partition wall after another as Hook bayoneted countless attackers, until they had moved eight patients through four rooms and into the inner defences. At that moment the burning roof collapsed, killing the pursuing Zulus.

Hook died from tuberculosis on 12 March 1905. Contrary to his portrayal in the film *Zulu*, Hook was in fact a model soldier.

Private WILLIAM JONES
RORKE'S DRIFT 22/23 January 1879
He was 39 years old and serving in the 2nd Bn, 24th Regiment of Foot, later the South Wales Borderers. During the attack by the Zulu warriors, he and Private Robert Jones kept up a steady fire against enormous odds. While one man worked to cut a hole through to the next room, the other shot Zulu after Zulu through the loopholed walls, using his own and then his comrade's rifle as the barrels became too hot to hold. They hurried six patients through to the next room, then out of the window and into the

inner defences. The last man, Sergeant Maxwell, was delirious with fever and refused to move; when they came back for him, they found him being stabbed to death in his bed. Both men were awarded the VC.

William Jones died on 15 April 1913.

Private ROBERT JONES
RORKE'S DRIFT 22/23 January 1879
He was 21 years old and serving in the 2nd Bn, 24th Regiment of Foot, later the South Wales Borderers. During the attack by the Zulu warriors, he and Private William Jones kept up a steady fire against enormous odds. While one man worked to cut a hole through to the next room, the other shot Zulu after Zulu through the loopholed walls, using his own and then his comrade's rifle as the barrels became too hot to hold. They hurried six patients through to the next room, then out of the window and into the inner defences. The last man, Sergeant Maxwell, was delirious with fever and refused to move; when they came back for him, they found him being stabbed to death in his bed. Both men were awarded the VC.

Robert Jones was plagued with nightmares for years following his desperate hand-to-hand combat with the Zulus, and he shot himself on 6 September 1898.

Private JOHN WILLIAMS (real name FIELDING)
RORKE'S DRIFT 22/23 January 1879
He was 21 years old and serving in the 2nd Bn, 24th Regiment of Foot, later the South Wales Borderers. With two other men (William Horrigan and Joseph Williams), he was posted in a distant room in the hospital. They held out for an hour, until they had no ammunition left. The Zulus then burst in and stabbed to death Joseph Williams, William Horrigan and two of the patients. John Williams grabbed a pickaxe and broke down a wall, through which he passed the two remaining patients to Private Henry Hook. He pickaxed one partition wall after another as Hook bayoneted countless attackers, until they had moved eight patients through four rooms and into the inner

defences. At that moment the burning roof collapsed, killing the pursuing Zulus.

Fielding enlisted under the name Williams to prevent his parents from discovering that he had joined the army. The last survivor of the Rorke's Drift VCs, he died from heart failure on 25 November 1932.

Private FREDERICK HITCH
RORKE'S DRIFT 22/23 January 1879
He was 22 years old and serving in the 2nd Bn, 24th Regiment of Foot, later the South Wales Borderers. During the attack by the Zulu warriors, Hitch and Corporal William Allen between them kept communications open with the main building as the patients were rescued from the hospital. Together they helped the wounded out through a high window, and held a perilously exposed post in the middle of the compound in order to keep back the Zulus who were climbing over the barricades. Most of the men from the hospital were safely withdrawn to the inner defences.

Hitch, like Allen, was shot in the shoulder and their wounds were dressed by Surgeon Major Reynolds, but he was quickly back in action. Although too badly wounded to fight on, he distributed ammunition as the fighting continued.

Hitch became a London taxi driver. When he died from pneumonia on 6 January 1913, the hundreds of cabbies who turned out for his funeral were astonished to see the South Wales Borderers parading in full force, as his friends had no inkling he was a VC holder. Today there is the Fred Hitch gallantry award for taxi drivers.

Colour Sergeant ANTHONY BOOTH
INTOMBI RIVER 12 March 1879
He was 32 years old and serving in the 80th Regiment of Foot, later the South Staffordshire Regiment. When 4,000 Zulus had attacked a laager of 20 wagons, killing the officers, Booth took command of the few surviving men and led them to safety, despite being pursed by the enemy for 3 miles.

He died from jaundice on 8 December 1899.

Brevet Lieutenant Colonel REDVERS BULLER
HLOBANE 28 March 1879
He was 39 years old and serving in the 60th Rifles, later the King's Royal Rifle Corps. During the retreat from Hlobane he saved the lives of Captain Henry D'Arcy, Lieutenant Everitt and a trooper of the Frontier Light Horse when their horses had been shot or speared from under them. Rallying his men, he rode time and time again at the Zulus, under heavy fire from shot and spear.

Buller served in many campaigns but is best remembered for his poor performance in the Second Boer War, which earned him the nickname 'Reverse Buller'.

He died from carcinoma of the gall bladder and liver on 2 June 1908. Buller is related to the brothers Lieutenant Colonel Victor Turner VC and Second Lieutenant Alexander Turner VC.

Major WILLIAM LEET
HLOBANE 28 March 1879
He was 45 years old and serving in the 1st Bn, 13th Regiment of Foot, later the Somerset Light Infantry (Prince Albert's), when during the retreat Lieutenant Smith's horse was killed from under him. Leet rode to Smith, picked him up and carried him on his horse to a place of safety under a shower of assegais and bullets.

He died on 29 June 1898.

Lieutenant HENRY LYSONS
HLOBANE 28 March 1879
He was 20 years old and serving in the 2nd Bn, Cameronians (Scottish Rifles). Together with Captain Campbell and Private Edmund Fowler, he advanced between the rocks to a cave commanded by the enemy. Advancing in single file to the mouth of the cave, they opened fire, driving the Zulus away in disarray. Campbell was killed during this action.

Lysons died on 24 July 1907.

Private EDMUND FOWLER
HLOBANE 28 March 1879
He was 18 years old and serving in the 2nd Bn, Cameronians (Scottish Rifles). Together with

Captain Campbell and Lieutenant Henry Lysons, he advanced between the rocks to a cave commanded by the enemy. Advancing in single file to the mouth of the cave, they opened fire, driving the Zulus away in disarray. Campbell was killed during this action.

The Secretary of State for War asked to have Fowler's name removed from the register after he was convicted of embezzlement in 1887, but the Queen would not do so; since his sole punishment was to be reduced to the ranks, it appeared to her that his offence was not too serious.

He died on 26 March 1926.

Lieutenant EDWARD BROWNE
KHAMBULA 29 March 1879
He was 26 years old and serving in the 1st Bn, 24th Regiment of Foot, later the South Wales Borderers, when he saved the life of Colonel Russell, who had become unseated from his horse. Due to a clerical error, his VC action is often stated as being on 28 March, at Hlobane, but this is incorrect.

He died from heart disease on 16 July 1907.

Captain WILLIAM 'ULUNDI' BERESFORD
ULUNDI 3 July 1879
He was 31 years old and serving in the 9th Queen's Lancers, later the 9th/12th Royal Lancers. During the retirement of a recon-noitring party Beresford and Sergeant Edmund O'Toole went to the assistance of Sergeant Fitzmaurice, whose horse had fallen and rolled on top of him, only a few yards from the pursuing Zulus. Fitzmaurice urged him to ride on and save himself, but Beresford told him, 'If you don't get up, I'll punch your head in!' As he helped him into his saddle, they were joined by Sergeant O'Toole, who rode along-side, shooting Zulu after Zulu, as well as holding the wounded man up in his saddle until they all reached safety.

Beresford was the first man into the Zulu royal kraal at Ulundi, and was known as 'Ulundi' Beresford for the rest of his life. When awarded the medal by Queen Victoria, he told her that he could not in honour receive it unless it was shared with O'Toole. He had also served in the Persian War and the Second Afghan War.

He died from dysentery and peritonitis on 28 December 1900.

Captain HENRY D'ARCY
ULUNDI 3 July 1879
He was 28 years old and serving in the Cape Frontier Light Horse, South African Forces. During the retirement of a reconnoitring party he saw Trooper Raubenheim fall from his horse. He stopped and picked him up, but his horse kicked them both off. Raubenheim was stunned and D'Arcy made several vain attempts to lift him back into the saddle as the Zulus closed in. Eventually he was forced to ride on alone. His own life had been saved by Lieutenant Colonel Redvers Buller VC three months earlier. D'Arcy also served in the Basuto War.

He died in August 1881 after going missing for some time. Or did he? A note discovered in the Killie Campbell Africana Library suggested that he may have changed clothes with a dead man. He was said to have been recognised from a photograph 56 years later in Natal. When confronted, he begged the man not to make his identity known, wishing 'to remain dead to the world'.

Sergeant EDMUND O'TOOLE
ULUNDI 3 July 1879
He was of unknown age and serving in the Cape Frontier Light Horse, South African Forces. During the retirement of a recon-noitring party he rode alongside Captain Beresford, keeping the pursuing Zulus back with steady fire, and holding the wounded Sergeant Fitzmaurice in his saddle until they all reached safety. He was only awarded the VC after Beresford told Queen Victoria that he could not in honour receive his unless it was shared by O'Toole.

He died in 1891.

The Second Naga Hills Expedition, India, 1879–80 (1 VC)

Although Britain controlled most of India, the tribal Naga people in the north were turbulent and resisted British rule. In 1879 they murdered a British commissioner and besieged the garrison at Kohima. A punitive expedition under Brigadier General J. Nation was sent to restore order. One Victoria Cross was awarded for this campaign.

Captain RICHARD RIDGEWAY
KONOMA 22 November 1879
He was 31 years old and serving in the Bengal Staff Corps and 44th Gurkha Rifles, later the 1/8th Gurkha Rifles, Indian Army. During the attack he charged up to a barricade and attempted to tear down the planking surrounding it under very heavy fire. During this action he was severely wounded in the shoulder.
He died from pneumonia on 11 October 1924.

The Basuto War, South Africa, 1879–82 (6 VCs)

Basutoland, on the border with Natal, had been a British Protectorate since 1868, but in 1871 Britain officially annexed it, interfering with the chiefs' authority and the tribes' traditional laws. Resentment grew and in 1879 troops from the Cape were sent to suppress the unrest. Then in 1880 the Cape authorities prepared to enforce the Cape Peace Preservation Act of 1878, which would disarm the natives. This gave rise to the 'Gun War'. Six Victoria Crosses were awarded for this campaign.

Sergeant ROBERT SCOTT
MOROSI'S MOUNTAIN 8 April 1879
He was 21 years old and serving in the Cape Mounted Riflemen, South African Forces when he volunteered to throw time-fused shells as hand-grenades. Having made his men take cover in case the shells exploded prematurely, he crept up to the enemy's position and threw the first bomb over a wall. As he released the second bomb it exploded, blowing his right hand off and wounding him severely in the leg.
Scott also served in the Boer War and the First World War.
He died from natural causes on 3 October 1918.

Trooper PETER BROWN
MOROSI'S MOUNTAIN 8 April 1879
He was 42 years old and serving in the Cape Mounted Riflemen, South African Forces. Hearing three wounded men repeatedly crying out for water, he said, 'I can't stand this any longer, has anyone any water?' Someone gave him a tin and he walked across open ground to the men and began pouring water into their mouths. As he did this, he was hit by a bullet that shattered his arm. Another struck his leg but he did not stop until the tin was shot through and useless.
He died from Bright's disease on 11 September 1894.

Surgeon Major EDMUND HARTLEY
MOROSI'S MOUNTAIN 5 June 1879
He was 32 years old and serving in the Cape Mounted Riflemen, South African Forces when he crossed open ground under heavy fire and carried Corporal Johns to safety. He then returned under fire in order to dress the wounds of the other wounded men. This work he did throughout the day.
He died on 20 March 1919.

Private FRANCIS FITZPATRICK
SEKUKUNI'S TOWN 28 November 1879
He was 20 years old and serving in the 94th Regiment of Foot, later the Connaught Rangers, when he and Private Thomas Flawn, assisted by six men from the Native Contingent, were carrying a wounded lieutenant. Suddenly 30 enemy appeared in pursuit. The six natives fled, while the two privates alternated between carrying the officer and firing at the pursuers. The wounded man was eventually brought to safety, and both men were awarded the VC.
Fitzpatrick died on 10 July 1933.

Private THOMAS FLAWN
SEKUKUNI'S TOWN 28 November 1879
He was 22 years old and serving in the 94th Regiment of Foot, later the Connaught Rangers, when he and Private Francis Fitzpatrick, assisted by six men from the Native Contingent, were carrying a wounded lieutenant. Suddenly 30 enemy appeared in pursuit. The six natives fled, while the two privates alternated between carrying the officer and firing at the pursuers. The wounded man was eventually brought to safety. Both men were awarded the VC.
Flawn died on 19 January 1925.

Surgeon JOHN McCREA
TWEEFONTEIN 14 January 1881
He was 26 years old and serving in the 1st Cape Mounted Yeomanry, South African Forces. After an enemy charge, which resulted in 37 casualties, McCrea, as the only doctor present, and despite a serious chest wound, which he dressed himself, attended to the wounded under fire throughout the day. Had it not been for his devotion to duty, there would undoubtedly have been much higher losses.
He died from influenza on 16 July 1894.

The Transvaal War (First Boer War), 1880–81 (6 VCs)

After the end of the Zulu War in 1879, Britain failed to deliver the desired federal dominion of British colonies and Boer republics. There was growing tension between the British and the Boers. Britain was not prepared to give back territory of the Transvaal which had been annexed, and the Boer resentment was escalated by the revenue collecting activities of the Administrator of the Transvaal. This, with allegations of undisciplined behaviour by British troops, drove the Boers to boiling point, and on 16 December 1880 they declared a republic. Six Victoria Crosses were awarded for this campaign.

Lance Corporal JAMES MURRAY
ELANDSFONTEIN 16 January 1881

He was 21 years old and serving in the 2nd Bn, Connaught Rangers when he went with Trooper John Danaher to the assistance of a wounded man lying in the open near the Boer lines. They advanced under fire and on reaching the man, Murray was wounded by a bullet that entered his right side and exited near his spine. Murray ordered Danaher to take his carbine and escape with the wounded man. Murray himself was taken prisoner but released the next day. Both men were awarded the VC.
Murray died on 19 July 1942.

Trooper JOHN DANAHER (or DANAGHER)
ELANDSFONTEIN 16 January 1881
He was 20 years old and serving in Nourse's (Transvaal) Horse, South African Forces when he went with Lance Corporal James Murray to the assistance of a wounded man lying in the open near the Boer lines. They advanced under fire and on reaching the man, Murray was wounded by a bullet that entered his right side and exited near his spine. Murray ordered Danaher to take his carbine and escape with the wounded man. Murray himself was taken prisoner but released the next day. Both men were awarded the VC.
Danaher died on 9 January 1919.

Lieutenant ALAN HILL (later HILL-WALKER)
LAING'S NEK 28 January 1881
He was 21 years old and serving in the 2nd Bn, Northamptonshire Regiment. When the retreat was ordered, he remained behind and tried to carry Lieutenant Baillie to safety, but Baillie was shot and killed as he was being carried. Twice more Hill braved the open ground, each time bringing back a wounded man.
He died on 21 April 1944.

Private JOHN DOOGAN
LAING'S NEK 28 January 1881
He was 27 years old and serving in the 1st Dragoon Guards (the King's) when he rode to assist Major Brownlow, who had been

surrounded by the Boers during a charge. Although wounded himself, Doogan dismounted and persuaded the major to take his horse. He was wounded again at this time. Both men managed to escape.

He died on 24 January 1940.

Private JAMES OSBORNE
WESSELSTROOM 22 February 1881

He was 23 years old and serving in the 2nd Bn, Northamptonshire Regiment when he galloped out in the direction of a large force of Boers. He picked up Private Mayes, who was lying wounded, and brought him back to camp under heavy fire.

He died on 1 February 1928.

Corporal JOSEPH FARMER
MAJUBA MOUNTAIN
27 February 1881

He was 23 years old and serving in the 1st Bn, Queen's Own Cameron Highlanders when he was with a party of men who went to the assistance of a picquet which was heavily engaged, most of the men having been killed or wounded. The enemy immediately opened fire on the relief party, killing two and wounding five, including the officer. Farmer at once went to this officer, who was quite helpless, and carried him under heavy fire to a place of comparative safety, after which he returned to the firing line and was eventually taken prisoner.

He died on 30 June 1930.

The Occupation of Egypt, 1882 (3 VCs)

Egypt at this time was under the control of the Ottoman Empire. The Sultan forbade the Khedive to impose any taxes, a policy that spelled financial disaster. But with the opening of the Suez Canal in 1869, influence in Egypt took on a new significance, and Disraeli's government was quick to buy up the Khedive's shares in the canal in 1875. By 1878 the country was virtually bankrupt, and to protect their interests in the canal, England and France took joint control of Egypt's finances, effectively running the country.

With Nationalist feelings running high against the Khedive for allowing this, the Egyptian Minister of War Ahmed Arabi led a revolt against European interference in May 1882. The Khedive tried to dismiss Arabi and rioting broke out in Alexandria, with 50 Europeans being killed. British protests about Arabi's fortifying of the forts came to nothing, so British ships started bombarding the city and harbour. Three Victoria Crosses were awarded for this campaign.

Gunner ISRAEL HARDING
ALEXANDRIA 11 July 1882

He was 48 years old and serving in the Royal Navy when his ship HMS *Alexandra* was bombarding the forts. A 10-inch shell penetrated the ship's side armour and rolled along the deck near the magazine. Hearing the screams, he dashed up from below, seized the hot shell and plunged it into a vat of water. His action undoubtedly saved many lives.

He also served in the First World War, although by then he was over 80 years old.

Harding died on 11 May 1917.

Private FREDERICK CORBETT (real name DAVID EMBLETON)
KAFR DOWAR 5 August 1882

He was 28 years old and serving in the 3rd Bn, King's Royal Rifle Corps. During a reconnaissance sortie Lieutenant Howard-Vyse was mortally wounded. There being no time to move him, Corbett asked to remain with him and was given permission to do so, and although under constant fire, he at once tried to stop the bleeding. When ordered to retreat, he helped carry the officer from the field.

He is one of eight men to forfeit his VC, after being convicted of embezzlement and theft from an officer.

He died from cancer of the brain in a workhouse on 25 September 1912.

Lieutenant WILLIAM EDWARDS
TEL-EL-KEBIR 13 September 1882

He was 27 years old and serving in the 2nd Bn, Highland Light Infantry. Leading an attack on a redoubt, he charged ahead of his men and dashed alone into the enemy battery, killing the officer in charge. He was knocked down by an enemy gunner and was about to be killed when his men arrived, saving him.

He died on 17 September 1912.

The First Sudan Campaign, 1881–85
(5 VCs)

In 1881 the political situation in the Sudan was descending into chaos. General Gordon had resigned as Governor-General, and as his successor was receiving no direction from the government in Cairo, he soon lost control. The slave trade returned and the army was woefully under-resourced. Taxes were getting higher and higher. It was in this atmosphere that the self-styled Mahdi, or 'Guide', gathered the support of Islamic fanatics. A full-scale revolt led to the Mahdi's forces taking over most of the country. When Britain had occupied Egypt, it had also taken on responsibility for the Sudan, and it became evident that military action would be necessary to suppress the revolt here. Five Victoria Crosses were awarded for this campaign.

Captain ARTHUR WILSON
EL TEB 29 February 1884
He was 41 years old and serving in the Royal Navy (Naval Brigade) when he attached himself to the Right Half battery, in place of a lieutenant who was mortally wounded. (He later remarked that he had had nothing else to do that day.) As the troops closed on the enemy's Krupp battery, the Arabs charged the gunners before they could deploy the guns. Wilson sprang to the front and attacked an Arab, but his sword stuck in the man's ribs and snapped in two. He fought on with his fists and was slashed across the head before being relieved by men from the York and Lancaster Regiment. His action protected the gunners so they were able to deploy their guns.

Wilson had also served in the Third China War. He was an early advocate of the torpedo but a committed opponent of the submarine,

describing it as 'a damned un-English weapon'.
He died on 25 May 1921.

Quartermaster Sergeant WILLIAM MARSHALL
EL TEB 29 February 1884
He was 29 years old and serving in the 19th Hussars when the regiment's Commanding Officer, Lieutenant Colonel Barrow, was severely wounded during a charge. His horse was killed and he was left lying on the ground surrounded by the enemy. Marshall rode to his assistance, seized his hand and dragged him through the midst of the enemy and back to the regiment, saving him from certain death.

He died on 11 September 1920.

Lieutenant PERCIVAL MARLING
TAMAI 13 March 1884
He was 23 years old and serving in the 3rd Bn, King's Royal Rifle Corps. He lifted the wounded Private Morley on to the saddle in front of him, but when Morley immediately fell off again, he dismounted even as the enemy were closing in and carried him for 800 yards under fire to safety.

He died on 29 May 1936.

Private THOMAS EDWARDS
TAMAI 13 March 1884
He was 20 years old and serving in the 1st Bn, Black Watch (Royal Highlanders) when No. 4 gun was attacked by a large enemy force, and all the crew were killed, leaving him in charge of the gun and two mules loaded with Gatling ammunition. He bayoneted two Arabs and shot another who had just cut through the arm of an officer. He defended his gun throughout the action.

He died from bronchitis on 27 March 1952.

Gunner ALFRED SMITH
ABU KLEA 17 January 1885
He was 24 years old and serving in the Royal Regiment of Artillery when Lieutenant Guthrie, who had no weapon in his hand, was attacked by a native with a spear. Smith warded off the spearman with a handspike, giving Guthrie time to draw his sword and

bring the assailant to his knees. In the ensuing struggle, the assailant managed to stab the lieutenant in the leg with a long knife, but Smith killed him with the handspike before he could strike again. Guthrie died of his wounds a few days later.

Smith died in his sleep on 6 January 1932.

The Karen-Ni Expedition and the Chin Field Force, Burma, 1888–89 (2 VCs)

Despite the British victory in the Third Anglo-Burmese War, many of the natives refused to accept the authority of the occupying British Army and resorted to guerrilla action. They were led mainly by former officers of the disbanded Burmese Royal Army, village headmen and even some royal princes. Two punitive expeditions were sent to crush the rebels. One Victoria Cross was awarded for each of these campaigns.

Surgeon JOHN CRIMMIN
LWEKAW 1 January 1889
He was 29 years old and serving in the Bombay Medical Service, Indian Army as part of the Karen-Ni expedition when he attended to a wounded man in the midst of a skirmish with bullets flying all around him. Then he was attacked by several bandits. He jumped to his feet and ran his sword through one of the assailants and engaged boldly with another, causing them to flee into the bush.

He died on 20 February 1945.

Surgeon FERDINAND LE QUESNE
TARTAN 4 May 1889
He was 25 years old and serving in the Medical Staff, later the Royal Army Medical Corps, as part of the Chin Field Force. During the attack on a stockade he dressed the wounds of a mortally wounded officer for 10 minutes only 5 yards from the enemy position and under steady fire. He was later wounded while dressing the wounds of another officer.

He died on 14 April 1950.

The Manipur Expedition, India, 1891 (1 VC)

Manipur was a small hill state lying between Assam and Burma on India's north-east border. In September 1890 the Raja of Manipur was ousted in a palace coup and the British government in India saw this as an act of rebellion. In March 1891 an expedition was sent to crush it. One Victoria Cross was awarded for this campaign.

Lieutenant CHARLES GRANT
THOBAL 21 March–9 April 1891
He was 29 years old and serving in the Indian Staff Corps, Indian Army. After the disaster at Manipur, he volunteered to attempt the relief of the British captives with just 80 native troops. Inspiring his men by his fine example of personal daring and resourcefulness, he captured Thobal and held it against a large force for ten days. During this action he was wounded by a bullet that pulled part of his shirt and collar through his neck and out the other side.

He died on 23 November 1932.

The Hunza-Naga Campaign, India, 1891 (3 VCs)

In 1891, following tribal unrest in the Hunza-Naga district, an expedition was sent to this mountainous region to storm the fort at Nilt. Three Victoria Crosses were awarded for this campaign.

Captain FENTON AYLMER
NILT FORT 2 December 1891
He was 29 years old and serving in the Corps of Royal Engineers. During the assault on the fort, he forced the Inner Gate open with gun cotton. He was shot in the leg and hit on the hand by a rock dropped from above. However, he dashed through and engaged the enemy hand-to-hand, killing several with his revolver, until he collapsed from loss of blood.

Aylmer also served in the First World War. He died on 3 September 1935.

Lieutenant GUY BOISRAGON
NILT FORT 2 December 1891
He was 27 years old and serving in the Indian Staff Corps and 5th Gurkha Rifles, Indian Army when he led the assault on the Outer Gate. Finding his forces insufficient for the task, he went back under heavy cross-fire to get more men to relieve the first party. His actions ensured the fort's capture.
He died on 14 July 1931.

Lieutenant JOHN MANNERS-SMITH
NILT FORT 20 December 1891
He was 27 years old and serving in the Indian Staff Corps and 5th Gurkha Rifles, Indian Army when he led a small party of men up a steep cliff in an attack on a strong enemy position that had barred any advance for seventeen days. Avoiding the rocks that were being dropped from above, he was the first man to reach the summit, and then charged his men at the enemy, shooting the first tribesman himself. The position was duly taken.
He died from a wasting disease on 6 January 1920.

The Second Gambia War, 1891–92 (1 VC)

In 1891 a party from the Anglo-French Boundary Commission was attacked by tribesmen led by Fodeh Cabbah, and several members of the group were wounded. Then HMS *Alecto* arrived and a landing party was sent ashore. The situation was defused when a local chief, hearing of the expedition, came to meet them and apologised for the attack. The men returned to the ship, but Cabbah continued to cause trouble and a punitive expedition was sent to capture him. One Victoria Cross was awarded for this campaign.

Corporal WILLIAM GORDON
TONIATABA 13 March 1892
He was 27 years old and serving in the West India Regiment when he was one of a party of men under Major Madden attempting to break down the south gate of the town with a battering ram. Suddenly several musket barrels

appeared through loopholes in the walls, and were aimed at the major while his back was turned. Shouting 'Look out!', Gordon flung himself between the major and the muskets as they fired. He was shot through the lungs, but Madden was unhurt.
He died from natural causes on 15 August 1922.

The Kachin Hills Expedition, Burma, 1892–93 (1 VC)

During the 1880s British and Indian troops were deployed throughout the operational zones of Burma to control the border 'dacoits', who rose up against the British presence in their region. By 1891 the British-held northern area of Burma was under control, but the Kachin tribe continued plundering caravans and preying on travellers. In December 1885 a British force moved in to occupy the Bhamo region of the Kachin hills. The tribesmen resisted annexation fiercely, and when they attacked a military police column an expedition was sent in to restore order. One Victoria Cross was awarded for this campaign.

Surgeon Major OWEN LLOYD
FORT SIMA 6 January 1893
He was 39 years old and serving in the Army Medical Service, later the Royal Army Medical Corps, when he went to the assistance of the mortally wounded Captain Morton and treated his wounds although the enemy were only about 15 paces away and firing heavily. He was wounded while returning to the fort.
Lloyd died on 5 July 1941.

The North-West Frontier, India, 1895 (1 VC)

In 1889 the British entered the Chitral district of India (now Pakistan) and established an agency, to which the local tribesmen were very hostile. In 1895 the Chitral chief was murdered. This signalled the start of fighting among local tribes. When Umrah Khan, ruler of the Narai

The Complete Victoria Cross

district, invaded Chitral, Britain sent in 400 men to restore order. One Victoria Cross was awarded for this campaign.

Surgeon Captain HARRY WHITCHURCH
CHITRAL FORT 3 March 1895
He was 28 years old and serving in the Indian Medical Service, Indian Army when he went out to the assistance of a wounded captain who was lying 1½ miles from the fort. The wounded man was placed in a dhooli, but on the return journey three of the bearers were killed and the fourth wounded, so Whitchurch took the wounded man on his back and carried him for some distance. They were fired on incessantly the whole way, but he eventually succeeded in getting them back to the fort, although they were nearly all wounded and the captain died.

Whitchurch died from enteric fever on 16 August 1907.

The Matabeleland Rebellion, Rhodesia, 1896 (2 VCs)

In 1895 all territories subject to the British South Africa Company were drawn together under the name of Rhodesia. By the end of March 1896 conditions among the Matabele tribesmen were so bad that they rose up in rebellion. Two Victoria Crosses were awarded for this campaign.

Trooper HERBERT HENDERSON
BULAWAYO 30 March 1896
He was 26 years old and serving in the Bulawayo Field Force, South African Forces when his patrol was ambushed and he and Trooper Celliers were cut off from the rest of the men. Celliers was shot in the knee and his horse was killed. Henderson put the wounded man on his own horse, and led him back the 35 miles to Bulawayo, travelling by night and hiding during the day. They arrived three days later, having had almost nothing to eat. Celliers died two months later from his wounds.

Henderson died from duodenal ulcer complications on 10 August 1942.

Trooper FRANK BAXTER
UMGUZA RIVER 22 April 1896
He was 26 years old and serving in the Bulawayo Field Force, South African Forces when he selflessly gave his horse to the wounded Trooper Wise, who was then able to gallop away to safety. As the enemy approached Baxter, three of his comrades rode past and tried to lift him to safety, but they all failed and Baxter was killed moments later.

The Mashona Rebellion, Rhodesia, 1896–97 (1 VC)

Anti-colonial feelings among the tribal people of Rhodesia had been running high for a long time, and in June 1896 the Mashona tribe revolted, fired up by their spirit mediums who convinced them they would be impervious to bullets. One Victoria Cross was awarded for this campaign.

Captain RANDOLPH NESBITT
ALICE MINE, MAZOE VALLEY 19 June 1896
He was 28 years old and serving in the Mashonaland Mounted Police when he led a patrol of only 13 men to the rescue of some miners who were surrounded by hordes of rebels. Nesbitt and his men fought their way through the enemy and succeeded in getting the beleaguered miners and three women back to Salisbury, in spite of heavy fighting in which three of the small party were killed and five wounded.

Nesbitt was always very embarrassed at having been singled out for the award, as he felt the whole party had behaved heroically. He also served in the Second Boer War.

He died on 23 July 1956, following a short illness.

The Malakand Frontier War, India, 1897–98 (1 VC)

In 1894 the new frontier between India and Afghanistan was finalised by Colonel Sir

Mortimer Durand's commission, bringing many tribes under Britain's influence. These tribes were extremely hostile to this annexation and widespread unrest followed. In 1897 the Amir of Afghanistan published a fiercely anti-Christian work in his assumed capacity as the King of Islam. This incited uprisings against the British garrisons all along the frontier. One Victoria Cross was awarded for this campaign.

Lieutenant EDMOND COSTELLO
MALAKAND 26 July 1897
He was 23 years old and serving in the 22nd Punjab Infantry, Indian Army when he saved the life of a wounded lance havildar lying some 60 yards away on a football field. With the help of two sepoys, Costello brought the wounded man back to safety. The field was overrun with the enemy's swordsmen and raked with rifle fire.

Costello also served in the First World War. He died on 7 June 1949.

The Mohmand Campaign, India, 1897–98 (3 VCs)

On 8 August 1897 Mohmand tribesmen raided Shabkadar near Peshawar, but the means to crush this uprising were already in the region. Two divisions of Sir Bindon Blood's expedition had advanced from Malakand and these men would do the work. Three Victoria Crosses were awarded for this campaign.

Lieutenant JAMES COLVIN
MOHMAND VALLEY
16/17 September 1897
He was 27 years old and serving in the Corps of Royal Engineers when he was in a party of volunteers (including Lieutenant Thomas Watson and Corporal James Smith) who made a bayonet charge on the burning village of Bilot, to try to dislodge the enemy who were inflicting losses on British troops. Watson was wounded in the hand, but made two more attempts to take the village. He did not desist in his efforts until he was severely wounded and

had to be carried back. Colvin then led a further two attempts on the village, while Corporal Smith, although injured, assisted in removing the wounded to shelter. All three men were awarded the VC.

Colvin died on 7 December 1945.

Lieutenant THOMAS WATSON
MOHMAND VALLEY
16/17 September 1897
He was 30 years old and serving in the Corps of Royal Engineers when he led a party of volunteers (including Lieutenant James Colvin and Corporal James Smith) who made a bayonet charge on the burning village of Bilot, to try to dislodge the enemy who were inflicting losses on British troops. After being wounded in the hand, he made two more attempts to take the village. He did not desist in his efforts until he was severely wounded and had to be carried back. Colvin then led a further two attempts on the village, while Corporal Smith, although injured, assisted in removing the wounded to shelter. All three men were awarded the VC.

Watson died on 15 June 1917.

Corporal JAMES SMITH
MOHMAND VALLEY
16/17 September 1897
He was 26 years old and serving in the East Kent Regiment (The Buffs) when he was in a party of volunteers (with Lieutenant James Colvin and Lieutenant Thomas Watson) who made a bayonet charge on the burning village of Bilot, to try to dislodge the enemy who were inflicting losses on British troops. Although wounded himself, he assisted in removing the wounded to a place of safety. When Colvin left to get help, Smith was placed in charge. He held the position until Colvin's return, exposing himself to great danger and directing the fire of his men.

Smith's VC was not granted until seventeen months later, and only then after the matter was raised in Parliament.

He died on 18 March 1946.

The Tirah Campaign, India, 1897–98
(7 VCs)

In a spate of various uprisings by Afghanis against the British, fighting broke out in the Tirah region. This was put down by Lockhart's punitive expedition. Seven Victoria Crosses were awarded for this campaign.

Brevet Lieutenant Colonel ROBERT ADAMS
NAWA KILI 17 August 1897
He was 41 years old and serving in the Staff Corps and Corps of Guides, Indian Army when, together with Lieutenant Alexander Fincastle, Lieutenant Hector MacLean and five guides, he went to the assistance of Lieutenant Greaves (the correspondent for the *Times of India*), who had fallen from his pony and been set upon by the enemy with tulwars and knives. The enemy were driven away and Adams held them off while Fincastle and MacLean attempted to move Greaves, but he was shot and killed before they could get him away. MacLean was also mortally wounded during this action. All three men were awarded the VC.

Adams died on 13 February 1928. Lieutenant Edward Bellew VC was his second cousin.

Lieutenant HECTOR MacLEAN
NAWA KILI 17 August 1897
He was 26 years old and serving in the Staff Corps and Corps of Guides, Indian Army when, together with Brevet Lieutenant Colonel Robert Adams, Lieutenant Alexander Fincastle and five guides, he went to the assistance of Lieutenant Greaves (the correspondent for the *Times of India*), who had fallen from his pony and been set upon by the enemy with tulwars and knives. The enemy were driven away and Adams held them off while Fincastle and MacLean attempted to move Greaves, but he was shot and killed before they could get him away. MacLean was also mortally wounded during this action. All three men were awarded the VC.

Lieutenant ALEXANDER FINCASTLE
NAWA KILI 17 August 1897
He was 26 years old and serving in the 16th Lancers, as well as acting as a war correspondent. Together with Brevet Lieutenant Colonel Robert Adams, Lieutenant Hector MacLean and five guides, he went to the assistance of Lieutenant Greaves (the correspondent for the *Times of India*), who had fallen from his pony and been set upon by the enemy with tulwars and knives. The enemy were driven away and Adams held them off while Fincastle and MacLean attempted to move Greaves, but he was shot and killed before they could get him away. MacLean was also mortally wounded. All three men were awarded the VC.

He also served in the Second Boer War and the First World War.

He died on 29 January 1962.

Lieutenant HENRY PENNELL
DARGAI HEIGHTS 20 October 1897
He was 23 years old and serving in the 2nd Bn, Derbyshire Regiment, later the Sherwood Foresters (Nottinghamshire and Derbyshire Regiment), when he ran to the assistance of the wounded Captain Smith, twice trying to carry him to cover under very heavy fire. He only gave up the attempt when Smith died.

Pennell also served in the Second Boer War.

He died on 19 January 1907, while tobogganing on the Cresta Run.

Piper GEORGE FINDLATER
DARGAI HEIGHTS 20 October 1897
He was 25 years old and serving in the 1st Bn, Gordon Highlanders. During the attack he was hit in the foot, but carried on playing. He was then hit in the ankle; finding he could not stand, he propped himself up against a boulder and went on playing the pipes under heavy fire, to encourage the advance. Officially it is said he played 'Cock o' the North' but he later said that he played 'Haughs of Cromdale'.

Finding that he had become something of a celebrity, Findlater soon found he could earn good money by appearing in music halls, re-enacting his actions nightly on stage.

He died on 4 March 1942.

Private EDWARD LAWSON
DARGAI HEIGHTS 20 October 1897
He was 24 years old and serving in the 1st Bn, Gordon Highlanders. During the attack he carried the wounded Lieutenant Dingwall out of danger, and then went back to pick up Private MacMillan. He was under heavy fire for the whole time and was twice wounded himself.

Lawson died on 2 July 1955.

Private SAMUEL VICKERY
DARGAI HEIGHTS
20 October and 16 November 1897
He was 24 years old and serving in the 1st Bn, Dorsetshire Regiment when he ran down the slope and rescued a wounded man under heavy fire, bringing him back to cover. On 16 November he distinguished himself again in the Waran Valley, killing three of the enemy who attacked him when he was separated from his company.

Vickery died on 20 June 1952.

The Second Sudan Campaign, 1896–1900 (5 VCs)

The defeat of General Gordon in 1885 was seen as a major British humiliation, but nothing was done about it until Lord Salisbury came to power in 1895. By then the government was concerned with the Khalifa's regime in the Sudan, which bordered British-held Egypt. In March 1896 the Egyptian army under Kitchener was ordered into the Sudan. Five Victoria Crosses were awarded for this campaign.

Captain PAUL KENNA
OMDURMAN 2 September 1898
He was 36 years old and serving in the 21st Lancers (Empress of India's). Seeing that Major Crole Wyndham's horse had been killed, he rode up to him and took him on to his own horse and rode away to safety. He then, together with Corporal Swarbrick, rode to the assistance of Lieutenant de Montmorency, who was dismounted amidst

the enemy. He kept the enemy at bay with his revolver while Swarbrick caught the lieutenant's horse, which had bolted. They were then able to return to their regiment.

Kenna also served in the Second Boer War and the 3rd and 4th Somaliland Expeditions. In 1906 he was ADC to King Edward VII. He was also a member of the 1912 Olympics team with Brian Lawrence VC, and in 1913 he won the King's Cup for riding.

He was killed in action at Gallipoli on 30 August 1915.

Captain NEVILL SMYTH
OMDURMAN 2 September 1898
He was 30 years old and serving in the 2nd Dragoon Guards (Queen's Bays) when he galloped forward and attacked an Arab who had run amok among some war correspondents. He received the charge and killed him, being wounded in the arm while doing so. He saved the life of at least one war correspondent.

Smyth also served in the Second Boer War and the First World War.

He died on 21 July 1941.

Lieutenant RAYMOND de MONTMORENCY
OMDURMAN 2 September 1898
He was 31 years old and serving in the 21st Lancers (Empress of India's) when after the charge he went to the assistance of Lieutenant Grenfell, who was lying surrounded by a great many Dervishes. He drove off the enemy, only to find that the lieutenant was dead; he put the body on his horse, which then bolted. Captain Paul Kenna and Corporal Swarbrick then came to his assistance and they were able to return to their regiment.

He was killed in action on 23 February 1900.

Private THOMAS 'PADDY' BYRNE
OMDURMAN 2 September 1898
He was 17 years old and serving in the 21st Lancers (Empress of India's) when, despite having been wounded in the right arm, he went to the assistance of Lieutenant Molyneux, who was wounded, unhorsed and surrounded by Dervishes. He attacked these men, receiving a

severe wound, but his gallant action enabled the lieutenant to escape. It was Winston Churchill (the *Morning Post*'s correspondent) who identified Byrne as Molyneux's saviour.

He died on 17 February 1944.

Captain ALEXANDER 'SANDY' HORE-RUTHVEN (later changed to ARKWRIGHT)
GEDARIF 22 September 1898

He was 26 years old and serving in the 3rd Bn, Highland Light Infantry when he saw an Egyptian officer lying wounded within 50 yards of the attacking Dervishes, who were firing as they advanced. He picked up the wounded man and carried him to safety, but had to put him down several times in order to fire upon the enemy to check their advance.

Hore-Ruthven also served in the First World War.

He died on 2 May 1955.

The Crete Rebellion, 1897–98 (1 VC)

For many years the Turkish Muslim regime had oppressed the Christian people of Crete. In 1897, with the support of the Greek military, the Christians rose up in revolt. Britain, France, Russia, Italy, Germany and Austria sent warships to restore the peace. However, no lasting solution was reached. By 1898 the British garrison in Candia was down to a single regiment. When, in September, the colonel attempted to install a new collector of taxes, a Muslim mob protested and killed nearly a hundred British soldiers and a thousand Christian civilians. British ships bombarded the town and sent two parties of 50 men ashore to restore order. One Victoria Cross was awarded for this campaign.

Surgeon WILLIAM MAILLARD
CANDIA 6 September 1898

He was 35 years old and serving in the Royal Navy when his party was attacked while being brought ashore from HMS *Hazard*. Although he had already reached cover, he ran back to help a wounded seaman. He tried to lift him but could not as the boat was drifting. When he returned to his post his clothes were found to be riddled with bullet holes. He remains the only naval medical officer to be awarded the VC.

He died on 10 September 1903.

Chapter Eight

VICTORIA'S FINAL WARS, 1899–1901

The Second Boer War, 1899–1902
(78 VCs)

Having subjugated the southern African tribes to create the colonies of Natal and Cape Colony, Britain now wanted to bring together her colonies and Boer republics, the Orange Free State and the Transvaal into one British-dominated South African Federation. The Dutch-speaking Boers, whose population was now in the majority, had already suffered incursions from other nations, mostly Britain. After gold was discovered in the Transvaal in 1886, the Boers were unwilling to lose their independence. The resulting war cost Britain 52,156 casualties. In all, 78 Victoria Crosses were awarded for this campaign.

Captain CHARLES 'FITZ' FITZCLARENCE
MAFEKING
14 and 27 October, 26 December 1899
He was 34 years old and serving in the Royal Fusiliers, attached to the Bechuanaland Protectorate Regiment, when he went to the assistance of an armoured train with a partially trained squadron. The enemy were present in greatly superior numbers and his party was for a time surrounded. But he so inspired his men that not only was the train relieved, but they inflicted 50 casualties on the Boers. On 27 October he led a night charge with 60 men against the Boer positions. He was the first man to reach the enemy and killed four of them personally. The Boers retreated and in their panic fired on their own men. In all, 150 Boers were killed or wounded for the loss of just 15

of Fitzclarence's force. On 26 December he led an attack on a Boer stronghold known as Game Tree Fort. The enemy fired constantly through loopholes. According to one report, 'Fitzclarence alone got inside and stabbed two or three. They shot him once, but he proceeded to bayonet another when they shot him a second time and he dropped down . . . though not dead.' He had in fact been shot in both legs. Baden-Powell called him 'The Demon'.

He was killed in action at Polygon Wood on 12 November 1914. His body was never found.

Captain ROBERT JOHNSTON
ELANDSLAAGTE 21 October 1899
He was 27 years old and serving in the Imperial Light Horse, South African Forces when the advance was met with such a terrific fire the men wavered for an instant. Johnston and Captain Mullins rushed forward through a hail of bullets and rallied the men. The operation was a success from that moment on. Both men were awarded the VC.

Johnston died on 24 March 1950.

Captain MATTHEW MEIKLEJOHN
ELANDSLAAGTE 21 October 1899
He was 28 years old and serving in the 2nd Bn, Gordon Highlanders. After the main Boer position was taken, the Gordons started to waver under heavy fire as they were about to charge a kopje. Seeing the danger, Meiklejohn sprang forward, calling on the men to follow him. The position was captured, but he was severely wounded, losing an arm.

He died on 4 July 1913, following a fall from his horse.

Captain CHARLES MULLINS
ELANDSLAAGTE 21 October 1899
He was 30 years old and serving in the Imperial Light Horse, South African Forces when the advance was met with such a terrific fire the men wavered for an instant. Mullins and Captain Johnston rushed forward through a hail of bullets and rallied the men. The operation was a success from that moment on. Both men were awarded the VC.

Mullins died on 24 May 1916, as a result of wounds received during the Boer War.

Second Lieutenant JOHN NORWOOD
LADYSMITH 30 October 1899
He was 23 years old and serving in the 5th Dragoon Guards (Princess Charlotte of Wales's) when he went out in charge of a small patrol. They came under such heavy fire that when they had got to within about 600 yards of the enemy, the patrol had to retire at full speed. One man dropped and Norwood galloped back through heavy fire, dismounted, picked up the fallen trooper and carried him to safety on his back, at the same time leading his horse with one hand. All the time the enemy kept up an incessant fire on them.

He was killed in action at Sablonnieres on 8 September 1914, the first VC to die during the First World War.

Sergeant Major WILLIAM ROBERTSON
ELANDSLAAGTE 21 October 1899
He was 34 years old and serving in the 2nd Bn, Gordon Highlanders. During the final advance on the enemy's position, he led each successive rush. Once the main position had been taken, he led a party of men to seize the Boer camp. He then held this position under heavy fire, even after he was severely wounded.

He died on 6 December 1949.

Lieutenant HENRY DOUGLAS
MAGERSFONTEIN 11 December 1899
He was 24 years old and serving in the Royal Army Medical Corps when he attended to the wounded Captain Gordon and Major Robinson under very heavy fire. He performed many similar acts of gallantry on the same day.

Douglas also served in the First World War. He died on 14 February 1939.

Corporal JOHN SHAUL
MAGERSFONTEIN 11 December 1899
He was 26 years old and serving in the 1st Bn, Highland Light Infantry when he was in charge of the stretcher-bearers. He went from one man to another, dressing their wounds, under terrific fire. At one point he was seen encouraging the men to advance across open ground.

He died on 14 September 1953.

Captain ERNEST TOWSE
MAGERSFONTEIN and MOUNT THADA
11 December 1899 and 30 April 1900
He was 35 years old and serving in the 1st Bn, Gordon Highlanders when he tried to carry on his back the mortally wounded Colonel Dowman. Finding it impossible to lift him, Towse remained with him in the firing line until assistance arrived. On 30 April 1900, in one of the most dramatic episodes of the war, he and a small party of twelve men from the Gordons and Kitchener's Horse confronted 150 Boers. Called on to surrender, Towse ordered his men to open fire and remained firing himself until the Boers were driven back in utter confusion. He was wounded in both eyes, leaving him blind for the rest of his life.

He had previously distinguished himself with the Chitral Relief Force in 1895 and in the campaign on the North-West Frontier of India in 1898. It is said that Queen Victoria shed tears when pinning on his VC. Probably at her insistence the War Office awarded Towse a special wounds pension of £300 a year.

He died on 21 June 1948.

Major WILLIAM BABTIE
COLENSO 15 December 1899
He was 40 years old and serving in the Royal Army Medical Corps when he rode up under heavy fire to attend to the wounded who were lying in a donga close to the guns. He was exposed to heavy fire while dressing their wounds. Later the same day he went out to bring in, under heavy fire, the mortally

wounded Lieutenant Frederick Roberts, with the help of Captain Walter Congreve. All three men were awarded the VC.

Babtie died on 11 September 1920.

Captain WALTER 'SQUIBS' CONGREVE
COLENSO 15 December 1899

He was 37 years old and serving in the Rifle Brigade (Prince Consort's Own) when he, with Captain Harry Schofield, Lieutenant Frederick Roberts, Corporal George Nurse and Private George Ravenhill, tried to save the guns of the 14th and 66th Batteries, when the men serving these guns had all either become casualties or been driven back from the guns. Some of the horses and drivers were sheltering in a donga about 500 yards behind the guns, and the ground between them was swept with rifle and shell fire. Under heavy fire Congreve, Schofield, Roberts, Nurse and Ravenhill helped to hook up a team of horses and then to limber up a gun. Then Nurse managed on his own to limber up a second gun. Congreve also helped bring back the mortally wounded Lieutenant Roberts with Major William Babtie. All six men were awarded the VC.

Congreve also served in the 3rd Burma War and the Karen Field Force, in the First World War, where he lost a hand, and in Palestine.

He died from heart disease on 26 February 1927. His son was Major William Congreve VC.

Captain HAMILTON REED
COLENSO 15 December 1899

He was 30 years old and serving in the 7th Battery, RFA. After two guns had been recovered by others, he brought three teams of horses from his own battery in an attempt to save the remaining guns of the 14th and 66th Batteries. The rifle and shell fire was intense and Reed was wounded almost at once, as were five of the thirteen men who went with him. Another was killed, along with thirteen of the horses, before they got half-way to the guns and they were forced to retire.

Reed also served in the First World War.

He died on 7 March 1931. His uncle was Lieutenant Harry Lyster VC.

Captain HARRY SCHOFIELD
COLENSO 15 December 1899

He was 34 years old and serving in the Royal Artillery (Royal Field Artillery) when he, with Captain Walter Congreve, Lieutenant Frederick Roberts, Corporal George Nurse and Private George Ravenhill, tried to save the guns of the 14th and 66th Batteries, when the men serving these guns had all either become casualties or been driven back from the guns. Some of the horses and drivers were sheltering in a donga about 500 yards behind the guns, and the ground between them was swept with rifle and shell fire. Under heavy fire Congreve, Schofield, Roberts, Nurse and Ravenhill helped to hook up a team of horses and then to limber up a gun. Then Nurse managed on his own to limber up a second gun. Congreve also helped bring back the mortally wounded Lieutenant Roberts with Major William Babtie. All six men were awarded the VC.

Schofield also served in the First World War.

He died on 10 October 1931, following a long illness.

Lieutenant FREDERICK ROBERTS
COLENSO 15 December 1899

He was 27 years old and serving in the King's Royal Rifle Corps when he, Captain Harry Schofield, Captain Walter Congreve, Corporal George Nurse and Private George Ravenhill, tried to save the guns of the 14th and 66th Batteries, when the men serving these guns had all either become casualties or been driven back from the guns. Some of the horses and drivers were sheltering in a donga about 500 yards behind the guns, and the ground between them was swept with rifle and shell fire. Under heavy fire Congreve, Schofield, Roberts, Nurse and Ravenhill helped to hook up a team of horses and then to limber up a gun. Then Nurse managed on his own to limber up a second gun. Roberts was mortally wounded during this action and was helped back by Captain Walter Congreve and Major William Babtie.

He died two days later. All six men were awarded the VC.

His father was Lieutenant Frederick Sleigh Roberts VC.

Corporal GEORGE NURSE
COLENSO 15 December 1899
He was 26 years old and serving in the 66th Battery, RFA when he, with Captain Harry Schofield, Captain Walter Congreve, Lieutenant Frederick Roberts and Private George Ravenhill, tried to save the guns of the 14th and 66th Batteries, when the men serving these guns had all either become casualties or been driven back from the guns. Some of the horses and drivers were sheltering in a donga about 500 yards behind the guns, and the ground between them was swept with rifle and shell fire. Under heavy fire Congreve, Schofield, Roberts, Nurse and Ravenhill helped to hook up a team of horses and then to limber up a gun. Then Nurse managed on his own to limber up a second gun. Roberts was mortally wounded during this action and was helped back by Captain Walter Congreve and Major William Babtie. All six men were awarded the VC.

Nurse died on 25 November 1945.

Private GEORGE RAVENHILL
COLENSO 15 December 1899
He was 27 years old and serving in the Royal Scots Fusiliers when he, with Captain Harry Schofield, Captain Walter Congreve, Lieutenant Frederick Roberts and Corporal George Nurse, tried to save the guns of the 14th and 66th Batteries, when the men serving these guns had all either become casualties or been driven back from the guns. Some of the horses and drivers were sheltering in a donga about 500 yards behind the guns, and the ground between them was swept with rifle and shell fire. Under heavy fire Congreve, Schofield, Roberts, Nurse and Ravenhill helped to hook up a team of horses and then to limber up a gun. Then Nurse managed on his own to limber up a second gun. Roberts was mortally wounded during this action and was helped back by Captain Walter Congreve and Major William Babtie. All six men were awarded the VC.

Ravenhill is one of eight men to forfeit his VC, when he was convicted of stealing iron.

He died on 14 April 1921.

Sergeant HORACE MARTINEAU
GAME TREE FORT 26 December 1899
He was 25 years old and serving in the Protectorate Regiment (North-West Cape Colony), South African Forces when he remained behind after the retreat had been sounded to assist Corporal Le Clamp, who was lying wounded just 10 yards from the Boer trenches. Half dragging and half carrying him, Martineau got Le Clamp to cover under a bush, where he attended to his wounds. He was wounded twice himself and forced to give up. As a result of his wounds his left arm was amputated.

Martineau also served in the First World War.

He died from fever on 7 April 1916.

Trooper HORACE RAMSDEN
GAME TREE FORT 26 December 1899
He was 21 years old and serving in the Protectorate Regiment (North-West Cape Colony), South African Forces when he remained behind after the retreat had been sounded to assist his brother, who had been shot through both legs and was lying just 10 yards from the Boer trenches. He carried him 800 yards under heavy fire, putting him down from time to time to rest, until help arrived and he was taken to a place of safety.

He died on 3 August 1948.

Lieutenant JOHN MILBANKE
COLESBERG 5 January 1900
He was 27 years old and serving in the 10th Hussars. On a reconnaissance sortie, the horse of one of his men was unable to keep up. Milbanke rode back under heavy fire and despite being wounded himself took the man on to his own horse and carried him back to camp.

He was killed in action at Gallipoli on 21 August 1915.

Lieutenant ROBERT DIGBY-JONES
LADYSMITH 6 January 1900
He was 23 years old and serving in the Corps of Royal Engineers when he led the attack on Waggon Hill with Trooper Herman Albrecht.

They scrambled to the gun pits before the enemy could reach them. Once there, Digby-Jones shot the Boer leader 'De Villiers' and killed three more with successive shots; he then killed another with the butt of his revolver before he was mortally wounded by a bullet to the throat. Meanwhile Albrecht also killed at least two Boers before he too was shot dead. Their action prevented the Boers from capturing this critical position. Both men were awarded the VC.

The *South African Review* of 24 February declared that they 'saved Ladysmith and the British Army from defeat'.

Lieutenant JAMES MASTERSON
LADYSMITH 6 January 1900
He was 37 years old and serving in the 1st Bn, Devonshire Regiment when he led his company in a successful charge at Waggon Hill. His men were then exposed to very heavy fire from the flanks, so he crossed an open plain under fire to request support. Despite being shot through both thighs, he crawled on and delivered the message before collapsing with exhaustion.

He died on 24 December 1935.

Trooper HERMAN ALBRECHT
LADYSMITH 6 January 1900
He was 24 years old and serving in the Imperial Light Horse (Natal), South African Forces when he, with Lieutenant Robert Digby-Jones, led the attack on Waggon Hill. They scrambled to the gun pits before the enemy could reach them. Once there, Digby-Jones shot the Boer leader 'De Villiers' and killed three more with successive shots; he then killed another with the butt of his revolver before he was killed by a bullet to the throat. Meanwhile Albrecht also killed at least two Boers before he too was shot dead. Their action prevented the Boers from capturing this critical position. Both men were awarded the VC.

Private JAMES PITTS
CAESAR'S CAMP 6 January 1900
He was 22 years old and serving in the 1st Bn, Manchester Regiment when sixteen men from D Company were defending a sangar on the hillside. The men were under heavy fire all day, the majority being killed and their positions occupied by the enemy. At last only Pitts and Private Scott remained. They held their post for 15 hours without food or water, all the time exchanging fire with the enemy, until relief troops had retaken the lost ground and pushed the Boers off the hill. Both men were awarded the VC.

Pitts died on 18 February 1955.

Private ROBERT SCOTT
CAESAR'S CAMP 6 January 1900
He was 25 years old and serving in the 1st Bn, Manchester Regiment when sixteen men from D Company were defending a sangar on the hillside. The men were under heavy fire all day, the majority being killed and their positions occupied by the enemy. At last only Scott and Private James Pitts remained. They held their post for 15 hours without food or water, all the time exchanging fire with the enemy, until relief troops had retaken the lost ground and pushed the Boers off the hill. Both men were awarded the VC.

Scott died on 21 February 1961.

Lieutenant FRANCIS PARSONS
PAARDEBERG 18 February 1900
He was 24 years old and serving in the 1st Bn, Essex Regiment when he went to the assistance of Private Ferguson, who was lying wounded. He dressed his wounds and twice fetched water before carrying him to safety. He was under heavy fire for the whole time.

He was killed in action at Driefontein on 10 March 1900.

Sergeant ALFRED ATKINSON
PAARDEBERG 18 February 1900
He was 26 years old and serving in the 1st Bn, Yorkshire Regiment when he carried water for the wounded. Seven times he went back and forth. On the last trip he was shot in the head.

He died on 21 February 1900, as a result of his wounds.

Private ALBERT CURTIS
ONDERBANK SPRUIT
23 February 1900
He was 34 years old and serving in the 2nd Bn, East Surrey Regiment when he saw the wounded Colonel Harris lying in the open. The Boers were firing at anyone who moved, and Harris was shot eight or nine times. After several efforts, Curtis succeeded in reaching the colonel; he tended his wounds, gave him a drink and then carried him to safety with the help of Private Morton.
He died on 18 March 1940.

Lieutenant EDGAR INKSON
COLENSO 24 February 1900
He was 27 years old and serving in the Royal Army Medical Corps when he carried Lieutenant Devenish, who was severely wounded and unable to walk, 300–400 yards under heavy fire, until he brought him to a place of safety.
He died on 19 February 1947.

Sergeant JAMES FIRTH
PLEWMAN'S FARM 24 February 1900
He was 26 years old and serving in the 1st Bn, Duke of Wellington's (West Riding) Regiment when he carried in Lance Corporal Blackman, who was wounded and exposed to enemy fire. Later when the Boers had advanced to within a short distance of the firing line, he rescued the wounded Second Lieutenant Wilson and carried him over the crest of a ridge to safety. He was shot through the nose and eye during this act.
He died from tuberculosis on 29 May 1921.

Captain CONWYN MANSEL-JONES
TUGELA 27 February 1900
He was 28 years old and serving in the West Yorkshire Regiment (Prince of Wales's Own) when his regiment was met with heavy shell and rifle fire and their advance was checked. He rallied his men and, although he fell severely wounded, the ridge was taken.
He died on 29 May 1942.

Sergeant HENRY ENGLEHEART
BLOEMFONTEIN 13 March 1900
He was 36 years old and serving in the 10th Royal Hussars (Prince of Wales's Own). When returning from blowing up the railway line, his party found a Boer picquet and four deep spruits in their path. He led the way into the first spruit, causing the enemy to flee. At the last spruit he went back under very heavy fire to pull Sapper Webb and his horse, who had been left in a dangerous position, to safety.
He died on 9 August 1939, following a long illness.

Major EDMUND PHIPPS-HORNBY
KORN SPRUIT 31 March 1900
He was 42 years old and serving in the Royal Horse Artillery. When Q and U Batteries ware ambushed by the Boers, he retired his battery 800 yards and began firing at the enemy. The Boers returned such a heavy fire that bullets were rattling on the guns like hail. As the enemy fire was too fierce for his horses to face, he ordered the guns to be retired by hand. All but one gun were saved. He was elected for the award by the officers of the regiment.
Phipps-Hornby also served in the First World War.
He died on 13 December 1947.

Lieutenant FRANCIS MAXWELL
KORN SPRUIT 31 March 1900
He was 28 years old and serving in the Indian Staff Corps, Indian Army attached to Robert's Light Horse. When Q and U Batteries were ambushed by the Boers, he helped the men to save the guns. Five times he went out under a hail of bullets, bringing in two guns and three limbers, one of which was dragged back by hand. He was one of those trying to bring in the last gun when the attempt had to be abandoned.
Maxwell had also served in the Chitral Expedition of 1895, during which he recovered the body of a lieutenant colonel under fire.
He was killed in action at Ypres on 21 September 1917.

Sergeant CHARLES PARKER
KORN SPRUIT 31 March 1900
He was 30 years old and serving in the Royal Horse Artillery when Q and U Batteries were ambushed by the Boers, and Major Phipps-Hornby ordered the guns to retire. Parker, with Gunner Isaac Lodge and Driver Horace Glasock, helped bring the guns to safety by hand, the fire being too heavy for the horses to face. He was elected for the award by the NCOs of the regiment. All four men were awarded the VC.

Parker also served in the First World War.

He died from heart disease on 5 December 1918.

Gunner ISAAC LODGE
KORN SPRUIT 31 March 1900
He was 33 years old and serving in the Royal Horse Artillery when Q and U Batteries were ambushed by the Boers, and Major Phipps-Hornby ordered the guns to retire. Lodge, with Sergeant Charles Parker and Driver Horace Glasock, helped bring the guns to safety by hand, the fire being too heavy for the horses to face. He was elected for the award by the privates of the regiment. All four men were awarded the VC.

He died on 18 June 1923 following an operation.

Driver HORACE GLASOCK
KORN SPRUIT 31 March 1900
He was 19 years old and serving in the Royal Horse Artillery when Q and U Batteries were ambushed by the Boers, and Major Phipps-Hornby ordered the guns to retire. Glasock, with Sergeant Charles Parker and Gunner Isaac Lodge, helped bring the guns to safety by hand, the fire being too heavy for the horses to face. He was elected for the award by the privates of the regiment. All four men were awarded the VC.

He died on 20 October 1916.

Lieutenant WILLIAM NICKERSON
WAKKERSTROOM 20 April 1900
He was 25 years old and serving in the Royal Army Medical Corps when he went out under rifle and shell fire to stitch up the stomach of a man whose entrails were protruding. He then stayed with him until the fire slackened and the stretcher-bearers arrived.

Nickerson also served in an Atlantic convoy during the First World War.

He died on 10 April 1954.

Corporal HARRY BEET
WAKKERSTROOM 22 April 1900
He was 27 years old and serving in the 1st Bn, Derbyshire Regiment when during the retreat he dragged the wounded Corporal Burnett to cover, dressed his wounds and kept up such a heavy fire that the Boers were prevented from approaching until dark. He was under very heavy fire the whole time.

Beet also served in the First World War.

He died on 10 January 1946.

Lance Corporal JOHN MacKAY
CROW'S NEST HILL 20 May 1900
He was 26 years old and serving in the 1st Bn, Gordon Highlanders when he repeatedly went forward under heavy fire to attend to wounded comrades, far from any cover. He carried one man from open ground to shelter under heavy fire.

He died on 9 January 1930.

Corporal FRANK KIRBY
DELAGOA BAY RAILWAY 2 June 1900
He was 28 years old and serving in the Royal Engineers when he was in a party sent to cut the railway. While retreating, they were attacked by the Boers. When one man had his horse shot from under him, Kirby went back towards the enemy under heavy fire, picked him up and rode back to rejoin his troop. His action undoubtedly saved the man's life.

Kirby also served in the First World War.

He died on 8 July 1956.

Private CHARLES WARD
LINDLEY 26 June 1900
He was 22 years old and serving in the 2nd Bn, King's Own Yorkshire Light Infantry when a picquet of his regiment was attacked by 500 Boers from three sides. Reinforcements were

desperately needed and Ward volunteered to deliver a message to that effect. His offer was at first refused but he insisted. Crossing 150 yards of open ground, he delivered the message and then returned to his comrades. The reinforcements duly arrived and the post was saved. He was, however, severely wounded during his action. Ward's VC was the last to be presented by Queen Victoria.

Ward died on 30 December 1921.

A silent film interview with Private Ward following the award of his VC was made by the Lancashire cinematographers Sager Mitchell and James Kenyon. It was sealed in a steel barrel with many other spools of film when their company went out of business in the 1920s, but was discovered during demolition work in 1994 and has been restored by the British Film Institute.

Sergeant ARTHUR RICHARDSON
WOLWESPRUIT 5 July 1900
He was 27 years old and serving in Lord Strathcona's Horse, Canadian Forces. While retreating from a large enemy force, he spotted a badly wounded comrade who had been thrown from his horse. He rode back towards the Boers, picked the man up and carried him to safety. He was under heavy fire the whole time, and his own horse was wounded.

He died on 15 December 1932.

Captain WILLIAM GORDON
KRUGERSDORP 11 July 1900
He was 34 years old and serving in the 1st Bn, Gordon Highlanders when he and Captain David Younger took out a party of men and successfully dragged an artillery wagon into cover behind a small kopje, although exposed to very heavy and accurate fire. They then tried to pull in a gun but Younger was mortally wounded. Both men were awarded the VC.

Gordon died on 10 March 1941.

Captain DAVID YOUNGER
KRUGERSDORP 11 July 1900
He was 29 years old and serving in the 1st Bn, Gordon Highlanders when he and Captain William Gordon took out a party of men and

successfully dragged an artillery wagon into cover behind a small kopje, although exposed to very heavy and accurate fire. They then tried to pull in a gun but Younger was mortally wounded. Both men were awarded the VC.

Captain NEVILLE HOWSE
VREDEFORT 24 July 1900
He was 36 years old and serving in the New South Wales Medical Staff Corps, Australian Forces when he saw a trooper fall wounded and went through very heavy cross-fire to rescue the man. His horse was soon shot from under him, so he continued on foot. Reaching the casualty, he dressed his wound and then carried him to safety. Howse was the first Australian to be awarded the VC. Years later he dismissed his VC action as 'nothing more than a fit of insanity'.

Howse also served in the First World War.

He died from cancer on 19 September 1930. In 2000 a postage stamp commemorating Howse's action was issued by the Australia Post.

Private WILLIAM HOUSE
MOSILIKATSE NEK 2 August 1900
He was 20 years old and serving in the 2nd Bn, Royal Berkshire Regiment (Princess Charlotte of Wales's) when he went out into the open to assist a wounded sergeant under heavy fire, although he had been warned not to do so. On reaching the wounded man, he was himself wounded. In spite of his pain, he called to his comrades not to risk their lives coming to his aid.

He died on 28 February 1912.

Sergeant BRIAN (sometimes spelt BRYAN) LAWRENCE
ESSENBOSCH FARM 7 August 1900
He was 26 years old and serving in the 17th Lancers (Duke of Cambridge's Own). He was on patrol with Private Hayman when they were attacked by fourteen Boers. Seeing Hayman thrown from his horse, Lawrence dismounted, lifted him on to his own horse and told him to ride back to their piquet line. He then walked for 2 miles, keeping the enemy at bay with two carbines until help arrived.

Lawrence was a member of the 1912 Olympics team with Paul Kenna VC.

He died on 7 June 1949.

Sergeant HARRY HAMPTON

VAN WYK'S VLEI 21 August 1900

He was 29 years old and serving in the 2nd Bn, King's (Liverpool) Regiment. When in command of a small party of mounted infantry, he held an important position for some time against heavy odds, and when forced to retire saw all of his men safely into cover. Then, although he had been wounded in the head, he helped a lance corporal who was unable to walk, until the man was hit again and killed. Hampton was wounded a second time.

He died on 2 November 1922, after being hit by a train.

Corporal HENRY KNIGHT

VAN WYK'S VLEI 21 August 1900

He was 21 years old and serving in the 1st Bn, King's (Liverpool) Regiment. While he and four others were covering the rear of his detachment, they were attacked by 50 Boers. He ordered his small party to retire one by one to better cover while he maintained his position for nearly an hour. He lost two men killed, and when he retired he carried a wounded man for 2 miles, under fire the whole time.

He died on 24 November 1955.

Private WILLIAM HEATON

GELUK 23 August 1900

He was 25 years old and serving in the 1st Bn, King's (Liverpool) Regiment when his company was surrounded by the Boers and suffering severely. He volunteered to take a message back asking for relief. Under heavy fire, he accomplished his mission at imminent risk to his life. Had he not done so, his company would have suffered very heavily.

He died on 5 June 1941.

Private ALFRED DURRANT

BERGENDAL 27 August 1900

He was 35 years old and serving in the 2nd Bn, Rifle Brigade (Prince Consort's Own) when Acting Corporal Weller became confused and

began running towards the enemy. Durrant raced after him, caught up with him and pulled him down, and then carried him 200 yards back to a place of safety, under heavy fire. Then he returned to his place in the firing line.

He died on 29 March 1933.

Lieutenant GUY GEORGE WYLLY

WARM BATHS 1 September 1900

He was 20 years old and serving in the Tasmanian Imperial Bushmen, Australian Imperial Forces when he was one of an advanced scouting party passing through a narrow gorge. When the Boers opened fire at close range, six out of eight men were hit, including Wylly; despite his own wounds, he went back for one of his men who was badly wounded. As the man's own horse had been shot, Wylly made the wounded man take his horse while he opened fire from behind a rock on the advancing Boers, to cover the retreat of the others, at the imminent risk of being cut off himself.

In 1909 Wylly was appointed aide-de-camp to the Commander-in-Chief, India. He also served in the First World War and was aide-de-camp to the King from 1926 to 1933.

He died on 9 January 1962.

Trooper JOHN BISDEE

WARM BATHS 1 September 1900

He was 30 years old and serving in the Tasmanian Imperial Bushmen, Australian Imperial Forces when he was one of an advanced scouting party passing through a narrow gorge. When the Boers opened fire at close range, six out of eight men were hit, including two officers. Bisdee dismounted, placed one of the wounded officers on his horse, mounted behind him and rode out of range of the enemy.

Bisdee also served in the First World War.

He died from chronic nephritis on 14 January 1930.

Major EDWARD BROWN (later BROWN-SYNGE-HUTCHINSON)

GELUK 13 October 1900

He was 39 years old and serving in the 14th

The Complete Victoria Cross

Hussars when, seeing a dismounted sergeant, he helped him on to his own horse and rode him to safety. Shortly afterwards he held a lieutenant's horse steady so he could mount, and finally he carried a wounded lance corporal out of the action. All these acts were carried out under heavy fire.

He died on 3 March 1940.

Lieutenant ALEXIS DOXAT
ZEERUST 20 October 1900
He was 33 years old and serving in the 3rd Bn, Imperial Yeomanry. He was with a party of men reconnoitring an enemy position when his men came under heavy fire. Seeing one man thrown from his wounded horse, he galloped back, took the man on his own horse and rode him out of range of the enemy.

Doxat also served in the First World War. He died on 29 November 1942.

Lieutenant HAMPDEN COCKBURN
KOMATI RIVER 7 November 1900
He was 32 years old and serving in the Royal Canadian Dragoons, Canadian Army when he, with Lieutenant Richard Turner and Sergeant Edward Holland, tried to stop 200 mounted Boers from capturing two 12-pounder guns. Cockburn and a few men held them off long enough to enable the guns to be got away to safety, although Cockburn was wounded at this time. When the Boers again threatened to capture the guns, Sergeant Holland used his Colt revolver to deadly effect, until the Boers were almost on top of him. Lieutenant Turner, although twice wounded, then dismounted and deployed some men at close quarters to drive off the Boers. All three men were awarded the VC.

Cockburn died on 12 July 1913 as the result of a riding accident.

Lieutenant RICHARD TURNER
KOMATI RIVER 7 November 1900
He was 29 years old and serving in the Royal Canadian Dragoons, Canadian Army when he, with Lieutenant Hampden Cockburn and Sergeant Edward Holland, tried to stop 200 mounted Boers from capturing two

12-pounder guns. Cockburn and a few men held them off long enough to enable the guns to be got away to safety, although Cockburn was wounded at this time. When the Boers again threatened to capture the guns, Sergeant Holland used his Colt revolver to deadly effect, until the Boers were almost on top of him. Lieutenant Turner, although twice wounded, then dismounted and deployed some men at close quarters to drive off the Boers. All three men were awarded the VC.

Turner died on 19 June 1961.

Sergeant EDWARD HOLLAND
KOMATI RIVER 7 November 1900
He was 22 years old and serving in the Royal Canadian Dragoons, Canadian Army when he, with Lieutenant Hampden Cockburn and Lieutenant Richard Turner, tried to stop 200 mounted Boers from capturing two 12-pounder guns. Cockburn and a few men held them off long enough to enable the guns to be got away to safety, although Cockburn was wounded at this time. When the Boers again threatened to capture the guns, Sergeant Holland used his Colt revolver to deadly effect, until the Boers were almost on top of him. Lieutenant Turner, although twice wounded, then dismounted and deployed some men at close quarters to drive off the Boers. All three men were awarded the VC.

Holland died from a heart attack on 18 June 1948.

Private CHARLES KENNEDY
DEWETSDORP 22 November 1900
He was 24 years old and serving in the 2nd Bn, Highland Light Infantry. When one of his comrades, Private McGregor, was mortally wounded, he carried him for nearly a mile under heavy fire to the hospital. The following day he volunteered to take a message to the commanding officer across an area under enemy fire. He was severely wounded after just 20 yards and had to give up.

He died on 24 April 1907 from injuries received when he tried to stop a runaway horse and cart.

Sergeant DONALD FARMER

NOOITGEDACHT 13 December 1900

He was 23 years old and serving in the 1st Bn, Queen's Own Cameron Highlanders when he was part of a small force that went to the assistance of a picquet that had lost most of its men. The enemy opened fire on his party from close range. Seeing his officer wounded, he carried him to safety under heavy fire and then returned to the firing line. He was eventually taken prisoner.

He died on 23 December 1956.

Private JOHN BARRY

MONUMENT HILL 7/8 January 1901

He was 27 years old and serving in the 1st Bn, Royal Irish Regiment when his party was surrounded by the enemy. Despite being wounded, he smashed the breech of their Maxim gun, rendering it useless and preventing it from falling into Boer hands. It was during this action that he was killed.

Farrier Major WILLIAM HARDHAM

NAAUWPOORT 28 January 1901

He was 24 years old and serving in the 4th New Zealand Contingent, New Zealand Military Forces when he saw Trooper McCrae wounded and on the ground. He rode over to him under heavy fire, dismounted and helped him on to his own horse and then ran alongside until they were out of range.

Hardham also served in the First World War.

He died on 13 April 1928.

Sergeant WILLIAM TRAYNOR

BOTHWELL CAMP 6 February 1901

He was 30 years old and serving in the 2nd Bn, West Yorkshire Regiment when, during a night attack, he dashed out of his trench to help a wounded man but was himself wounded. Unable to continue alone, he called for help. Corporal Lintott ran to him and they carried the man to safety. He remained in command of his section until the attack was repulsed.

He died on 20 October 1954.

Corporal JOHN CLEMENTS

STRIJDENBURG 24 February 1901

He was 28 years old and serving in Rimington's Guides, South African Forces when he was badly wounded in the lungs. But when five Boers came towards him, calling on him to surrender, he jumped up, shot and wounded three of them and forced all of them to surrender to him.

He died on 18 June 1937.

Lieutenant FREDERIC DUGDALE

DERBY 3 March 1901

He was 23 years old and serving in the 5th Lancers (Royal Irish) when, retiring from an outpost, his party came under heavy fire from the enemy. He dismounted and placed a wounded man on his own horse. Catching and mounting a riderless horse, he rode over to another casualty, took him up behind him and then brought both men safely out of action.

He died on 13 November 1902 as a result of injuries sustained after falling from his horse.

Lieutenant FREDERICK BELL

BRAKPAN 16 May 1901

He was 26 years old and serving in the West Australian Mounted Infantry, Australian Forces when he saw a dismounted trooper retreating under heavy fire. He took the man behind him on his horse but the weight was too much for the animal and it fell. He then ordered the trooper to save himself and remained behind to fire on the pursuing Boers until his comrade was out of danger.

He died on 28 April 1954.

Lieutenant GUSTAVUS COULSON

LAMBRECHTFONTEIN 18 May 1901

He was 22 years old and serving in the King's Own Scottish Borderers. During a rearguard action he saw Corporal Cranmer's horse had fallen. Coulson took the corporal on to his own horse but it was shot and both men fell. With the enemy rapidly approaching, he ordered Cranmer to ride the wounded horse away as best he could. Another corporal came to his aid, taking him upon his horse, but almost at once both men were shot dead.

The Complete Victoria Cross

Sergeant JAMES ROGERS
THABA 'NCHU 15 June 1901
He was 26 years old and serving in the South African Constabulary, South African Forces. During a rearguard action, under attack by 60 Boers, he lifted an officer on to his own horse and rode with him for half a mile to cover. He then went back to within 400 yards of the enemy to rescue two more men who had lost their horses. Finally he captured two riderless horses and helped their riders to mount and escape.

Rogers also served in the First World War. He died on 28 October 1961.

Lieutenant WILLIAM ENGLISH
VLAKFONTEIN 3 July 1901
He was 18 years old and serving in the 2nd Scottish Horse (a South African unit) when he and five men were holding a position under attack by the Boers. As ammunition ran short, he crossed 15 yards of open ground to get a fresh supply, all the time under fire from the enemy who were only 30 yards away. The position was held.

English also served in both world wars. He died from natural causes on 4 July 1941.

Private HARRY CRANDON
SPRINGBOK LAAGTE 4 July 1901
He was 27 years old and serving in the 18th Hussars (Queen Mary's Own) when he dismounted and gave his horse to the wounded Private Berry, whose own horse had been killed. He then ran, leading his comrade's horse, for over 1,000 yards under fire, until they reached cover.

He died on 2 January 1953.

Sergeant Major ALEXANDER YOUNG
RUITER'S KRAAL 13 August 1901
He was 28 years old and serving in the Cape Police, South African Forces when towards the close of the action, he and a handful of men rushed some kopjes which were being held by about 20 Boers. On reaching the objective, the Boers galloped back to another kopje. Young then galloped on for 50 yards ahead of his men and closed with the enemy; he shot one of them and captured their commandant, the latter

firing three times at him at point-blank range before being taken prisoner.

He was killed in action on the Somme on 19 October 1916.

Lieutenant LLEWLLYN PRICE-DAVIES
BLOOD RIVER POORT
17 September 1901
He was 23 years old and serving in the Royal Rifle Corps when the Boers overwhelmed the right of the British column and 400 of them charged the gun drivers, calling on them to surrender. He at once drew his revolver and charged, firing into them in an effort to rescue the guns. He was immediately shot and knocked from his horse.

He died on 26 December 1965.

Driver FREDERICK BRADLEY
ITALA 26 September 1901
He was 24 years old and serving in the 69th Battery, RFA when a driver who had volunteered to carry ammunition 150 yards up a hill under fire was hit by a bullet. Bradley rushed out and brought him to safety, and then took the ammunition up the hill himself.

He died on 10 March 1943, following an operation.

Private WILLIAM BEES
MOEDWIL 30 September 1901
He was 29 years old and serving in the 1st Bn, Derbyshire Regiment, later the Sherwood Foresters (Nottinghamshire and Derbyshire Regiment), when six out of nine men deploying a Maxim gun were wounded. Unable to bear the cries of the wounded any longer, he dashed forward under heavy fire to a spruit 500 yards away, filled his camp kettle and returned to quench the men's thirsts. The kettle was hit by several bullets during his dash, but he was unharmed.

He died on 20 June 1938.

Lieutenant LESLIE MAYGAR
GEELHOUTBOOM 23 November 1901
He was 29 years old and serving in the 5th Victorian Mounted Rifles, Australian Forces when, seeing a man's horse shot from under

him, he lifted him on to his own horse. The animal, not up to carrying two men, bolted into a swamp. Maygar ordered the man to ride to safety while he made his way back on foot. He was under heavy fire the whole time.

He was killed in action at Beersheba on 17 November 1917.

Surgeon Captain THOMAS CREAN
TYGERKLOOF SPRUIT
18 December 1901
He was 28 years old and serving in the 1st Imperial Light Horse, South African Forces. Despite being himself wounded, he tended the wounded under heavy fire only 150 yards from the enemy. He only stopped when he was wounded for a second time. His wounds were so serious that he was not at first expected to live.

He died from natural causes on 25 March 1923.

Shoeing Smith ALFRED IND
TAFELKOP 20 December 1901
He was 29 years old and serving in the Royal Horse Artillery when he stuck to his pom-pom gun under very heavy fire after all the remainder of the team had been shot down. Ind continued to fire into the advancing Boers until the last possible moment. A captain, who was mortally wounded in this action, requested that Ind's gallant conduct on this and in every other action since he joined the pom-pom service be brought to notice.

He died on 29 November 1916.

Surgeon Captain ARTHUR MARTIN-LEAKE (VC action)
VLAKFONTEIN 8 February 1902
He was 27 years old and serving in the South African Constabulary when he risked his life to tend to a wounded man, going 100 yards into open ground under fire from 40 Boers. Later, while dressing an officer's wounds, he was himself wounded, but gave up his efforts only when completely exhausted, and then he refused water until all the other wounded had been attended to.

For his Bar action, see 29 October–8 November 1914.

The Boxer Rebellion, 1898–1900 (2 VCs)

In the late 1800s a society was formed in China with the objective of ridding China of foreigners and Christians. Its members were known as 'Boxers' in the west. With the appointment of one of its founder members, Yu Hsien, as governor of Shantung province in March 1899, the way was clear for them to start their campaign. Two Victoria Crosses were awarded for this campaign.

Captain LEWIS HALLIDAY
PEKING 24 June 1900
He was 30 years old and serving in the Royal Marine Light Infantry when an attack was made on the British Legation by the Boxers, who set fire to the stables and occupied some adjoining buildings. It being imperative to drive them out, a hole was made in the legation wall and 20 men of the RMLI went in. Halliday, leading a party of six men, was involved in desperate fighting and was severely wounded, but despite his injuries he killed four of the enemy. Finally, unable to carry on, he ordered his men to go on without him. He then walked 3 miles unaided to the hospital, although shot through his shoulder and with a punctured lung.

He also served in the First World War. He was one of 74 VC holders who formed the honour guard at the interment of the Unknown Soldier at Westminster Abbey on 11 November 1920. He died on 9 March 1966.

Midshipman BASIL GUY
TIENTSIN 13 July 1900
He was 18 years old and serving in the Royal Navy (Naval Brigade) when he went to the assistance of Able Seaman McCarthy, who was wounded 50 yards from cover. While he treated his wounds, the enemy concentrated all their fire on them. Guy ran to fetch some stretcher-bearers, but McCarthy was hit again and killed before he could be carried to safety.

He died on 28 December 1956.

The Complete Victoria Cross

The Third Ashanti War, 1900–01 (2 VCs)

First suppressed in 1874, the Ashanti people of Gambia had risen again in 1895. This rising was likewise crushed and a resentful peace followed until 1900, when the British decided to capture the symbolic 'Golden Stool' regarded by the Ashanti as a sign of authority. Two Victoria Crosses were awarded for this campaign.

Sergeant JOHN MacKENZIE
DOMPOASSI 6 June 1900
He was 29 years old and serving in the 2nd Bn, Seaforth Highlanders Ross-shire Buffs (Duke of Albany's) when he worked two Maxim guns under heavy fire and was wounded. He nevertheless volunteered to clear the enemy from a strongly held stockade. His own company was ordered up and he led them into the charge. The enemy fled in confusion.

He was killed in action at Loos on 17 May 1915.

Captain CHARLES MELLISS
OBASSA 30 September 1900
He was 38 years old and serving in the Indian Staff Corps, Indian Army when he collected as many men as he could and led a charge through the bush. Although wounded, he fought the enemy hand-to-hand, during which he grappled with one of the enemy before running him through with his sword. As the enemy fled in panic, they were pursued by the Sikhs.

In 1903 he was attacked by a lion while hunting, almost losing an arm.

He died on 6 June 1936.

Chapter Nine

THE EDWARDIAN PERIOD, 1902–04

The Second Somaliland Expedition, 1902 (1 VC)

Since the mid-nineteenth century Britain had been securing territory in Somaliland and defining its borders with France, Italy and Abyssinia. The majority of local tribal chiefs accepted Britain's protection, but the most belligerent chief was Mahommed bin Abdullah, dubbed the 'Mad Mullah'. He mustered an army of 15,000 Dervishes. In 1899 bin Abdullah declared himself Mahdi and launched attacks on pro-British tribes. These tribes asked for British protection and Colonel E.J. Swayne was sent to help with an army of Somali levies. One Victoria Cross was awarded for this campaign.

Captain ALEXANDER COBBE
EREGO 6 October 1902
He was 32 years old and serving in the Indian Army, attached to the King's African Rifles, when the retirement of some companies left him alone in front of the line with a Maxim gun. Without any assistance he brought in the gun and used it most effectively at a critical time. He then went out under heavy fire and carried back a wounded orderly who was lying 20 yards from the enemy.

Cobbe also served in the Third Ashanti War, the Fourth Somaliland Expedition and the First World War.

He died on 29 June 1931.

The Kano-Sokoto Expedition, Nigeria, 1903 (1 VC)

When Sir Frederick Lugard arrived in Nigeria as High Commissioner in 1900, the British government declared a protectorate over the region. In 1902 Lugard ordered a series of raids against the Fulani emirates of Sokoto, Kano, Gando and Katsina, all of which were resisting his rule. One Victoria Cross was awarded for this campaign.

Lieutenant WALLACE WRIGHT
NIGERIA 26 February 1903
He was 27 years old and serving in the 1st Bn, Queen's West Surrey Regiment when, with just 45 men, he repulsed the most determined attacks by 1,000 cavalry and 2,000 infantry for two hours. When the enemy, after heavy losses, fell back in good order, Wright continued to pursue them until they were in full retreat. The personal example of this officer, as well as his skilful leadership, contributed largely to the brilliant success of the operation.

He also served in both world wars, and was mentioned in dispatches five times. Wright is one of only a few VC holders who became MPs.

He died on 25 March 1953.

The Third Somaliland Expedition, 1903–04 (3 VCs)

As the Mullah retreated, it became apparent that the Somali levies were not seasoned enough to deal with the threat he posed, so a much bigger force was sent to the region. Three Victoria Crosses were awarded for this campaign.

Brevet Major JOHN GOUGH
DARATOLEH 22 April 1903
He was 32 years old and serving in the Rifle Brigade, Indian Army. When Captain Rolland came to report that the rear guard was under attack and that Captain Bruce had been wounded, Gough returned with Rolland to find Captain Walker maintaining a desperate fire to keep the enemy at bay. Gough and Rolland lifted Bruce on to a camel. The enemy remained in close pursuit for a further three hours, during which time Bruce died from his wounds. All three men were awarded the VC.

Gough was killed in action at Estaires on 22 February 1915. His father was Major Charles Gough VC, and Lieutenant Hugh Gough VC was his uncle.

Captain GEORGE ROLLAND
DARATOLEH 22 April 1903
He was 34 years old and serving in the 1st Bombay Grenadiers, Indian Army. Along with Captain Walker and four others, he was in the rear guard under heavy fire from the pursuing enemy. When Captain Bruce was shot through the body, Rolland ran 500 yards to fetch help, while Walker maintained a desperate fire to keep the enemy at bay. When Rolland returned with Major Gough, the column commander, he helped lift Bruce on to a camel. The enemy remained in close pursuit for a further three hours, during which time Bruce died. All three men were awarded the VC.

Rolland died on 8 July 1910 from a fractured skull following a fall.

Captain WILLIAM WALKER
DARATOLEH 22 April 1903
He was 39 years old and serving in the 4th Gurkha Rifles, Indian Army when he, with Captain Rolland and four others, was in the rear guard under heavy fire from the pursuing enemy. When Captain Bruce was shot through the body, Rolland ran 500 yards to fetch help, while Walker maintained a desperate fire to

keep the enemy at bay. When Rolland returned with Major Gough, the column commander, he helped lift Bruce on to a camel. The enemy remained in close pursuit for a further three hours, during which time Bruce died. All three men were awarded the VC.

Walker died on 16 February 1936.

Armed Mission to Tibet, 1903–04 (1 VC)

Although notionally under Chinese rule, Tibet had never subscribed to the trade regulations and border demarcations agreed by China and Britain. This led to considerable unrest. Word had reached the British government that China was engaged in secret talks with the Russians about giving up her interest in Tibet to them. This would provide Russia with a base that would threaten India's north-eastern frontiers. Britain sent a mission to talk with the Chinese and Tibetans, but the Tibetans refused to negotiate. One Victoria Cross was awarded for this campaign.

Lieutenant JOHN GRANT
GYANTSE JONG 6 July 1904
He was 26 years old and serving in the 8th Gurkha Rifles, Indian Army when he led a storming party up a precipitous rock face in single file, crawling on hands and knees under heavy fire. He and a havildar attempted to scale the final defence, but on reaching the top they were both wounded and hurled back. They made another attempt and this time they were successful, Grant being the first man into the fort. Once inside the Gurkhas quickly routed the enemy.

He died on 20 February 1967.

The Fourth Somaliland Expedition, 1903–04 (2 VCs)

In an effort to destroy the Mullah's power once and for all, some 8,000 British troops under Major General C. Egerton were sent to the region. Two Victoria Crosses were awarded for this campaign.

Lieutenant HERBERT CARTER

JIDBALLI 19 December 1903

He was 29 years old and serving in the Mounted Infantry, Indian Army when during a reconnaissance he rode back 400 yards towards a large force of Dervishes in order to assist Private Jai Singh, who had lost his horse. He was so badly wounded it took three attempts to lift him on to his horse. Singh would almost certainly have been killed without Carter's help.

Carter was killed in action at Mwelo Mdogo on 13 January 1916.

Lieutenant CLEMENT SMITH

JIDBALLI 10 January 1904

He was 25 years old and serving in the 2nd Bn, Duke of Cornwall's Light Infantry, attached to the 5th Somaliland Light Infantry, when they were ambushed by the enemy. During the ensuing fight, Smith and Lieutenant Welland tried to rescue a wounded hospital assistant by placing him on a horse; when the horse was killed, they put him on a mule. The enemy surrounded them, killing the hospital assistant and wounding Welland with their spears. Smith stayed with the lieutenant, trying to keep the enemy at bay with his revolver.

He died on 14 December 1927.

Chapter Ten

THE FIRST WORLD WAR, 1914–18

The causes of the First World War are well known. When the Austro-Hungarian Archduke Franz Ferdinand was assassinated in Serbia on 28 June 1914, Austria-Hungary turned for support to Germany, which on 6 July confirmed that it would back Austria-Hungary in reprisals against the Serbs. The war might have remained a local Balkan war were it not for a series of complex treaties that locked countries together.

On 30 July Austria-Hungary declared war on Serbia. Russia and France, linked by treaty, began to mobilise on Serbia's behalf. Germany then presented ultimatums to Russia and France, threatening war if they did not demobilise. On 1 August Germany declared war on Russia and the next day entered Luxembourg. On 3 August Germany declared war on France and a day later German troops entered neutral Belgium. Britain, which had promised to protect Belgium's neutrality, then declared war on Germany. Austria-Hungary declared war on Russia the same day. Five days later France declared war on Austria-Hungary.

In all, 629 Victoria Crosses were awarded for the campaigns of the First World War, of which over 500 were awarded for actions on the Western Front. This illustrates the ferocity of the fighting there.

1914

Lieutenant MAURICE DEASE
NIMY BRIDGE, MONS, Belgium
23 August 1914
He was 24 years old and serving in the 4th Bn,

Royal Fusiliers. When the two machine-guns under his command came under heavy attack at about 09:10, Dease kept the guns firing despite heavy casualties. He was wounded in the leg when he went forward to check on one of the guns. He refused to go back to the aid post, and was wounded again. Lieutenant Steele could not persuade him to rest; he returned to his guns and was hit again but kept on firing. After being wounded twice more he was carried back to a place of safety where he died. His place was taken by Private Sidney Godley.

This action took place on the first day British soldiers were engaged with the enemy in the First World War. It was also the first VC of the First World War to be 'gazetted'. The sheets of paper on which Lieutenant Steele made his notes for the Dease and Godley VC recommendations are in the Regimental Museum of the Royal Fusiliers in the Tower of London. The note reads:

On 23rd August 1914, Dease was in command of the machine-guns with No. 9 platoon who were defending the bridge at Nimy. On the attack developing on the bridge, he was one of the first to be hit – somewhere about the knee. He continued to direct the fire of his guns, although obviously in great pain, until he was hit again, this time somewhere in the body, after which he remained, for a short time, under cover.

Shortly afterwards, the gunners having been shot, Dease asked me why the gun was not firing and insisted on crawling to the gun emplacement in order to control the fire, another man having taken the place of the man who was shot. He then received a third wound, which incapacitated him, and I am of the opinion that he received other wounds but on this point I cannot speak definitely.

23-8-1914 F.W.A. Steele, C Coy

Private SIDNEY 'MUG' GODLEY
(sometimes spelt GODLY prior to 1909)
NIMY BRIDGE, MONS, Belgium
23 August 1914

He was 25 years old and serving in the 4th Bn, Royal Fusiliers when he was stationed on the bridge, helping to supply ammunition to the guns. The German attack began at about 09:10. Godley, despite his own serious wounds, volunteered to cover the retreat from the bridge, after Lieutenant Dease had been mortally wounded. Godley kept the Germans off the bridge single-handedly for two hours under very heavy fire. His gallant action covered the retreat of the Royal Fusiliers, who withdrew in good order. When he finally ran out of ammunition he was able to dismantle the machine-gun and throw it into the canal. He was taken prisoner, and was treated for no fewer than 27 wounds. While in captivity he learned of his VC award.

This action took place on the first day British soldiers were engaged with the enemy in the First World War, making him the first private to earn the VC in that war. The sheets of paper on which Lieutenant Steele made his notes for the Dease and Godley VC recommendations are in the Regimental Museum of the Royal Fusiliers in the Tower of London. The note reads:

In defence of the railway bridge near Nimy 23rd Aug. 1914. This afternoon Private Godley of 'B' Coy showed particular heroism in his management of the machine-gun. Lt Dease having been severely wounded and each machine gunner in turn shot, I called Private Godley to me in the firing line on the bridge and under an extremely heavy fire

he had to move three dead bodies and go to a machine-gun on the right under a most deadly fire:

This he did & not a shot did he fire except as I directed & with the utmost coolness until it was irreparably damaged & he was shot in the head. He then left the firing line under orders to go to the rear.

23-8-1914 F.W.A. Steele, C Coy

Godley was evidently an unassuming man. His grandson Colin remarked: 'When he took part in a parade, he would wait till the last moment to put on his medals, then when it was all over he would pocket his medals and catch the bus home.'

Sidney, also sometimes called 'Old Bill' due to his likeness to the cartoon character created by Bruce Bairnsfather, died of pneumonia on 29 June 1957. In 1992 Sidney Godley VC House, in Digby Street, Bethnal Green, London, was named in his honour.

Lance Corporal CHARLES JARVIS
JEMAPPES, MONS CANAL, Belgium
23 August 1914

He was 33 years old and serving in the 57th Field Company, Royal Corps of Engineers when he worked for 1½ hours under continuous fire from the enemy and fixed 22 slabs of gun cotton on to the bridge's three girders. Finding he had no exploder or leads, he commandeered a bicycle from a Belgian to search for them. Having found what he needed, he returned, connected the leads and destroyed the bridge.

He died on 19 November 1948.

Corporal CHARLES GARFORTH
HARMINGNIES, France
23 August and 2/3 September 1914

He was 22 years old and serving in the 15th Hussars (The King's). While fighting a rearguard action at 16:30, he cut through wire under heavy fire and thus enabled his squadron to escape. Later he pulled Sergeant Scatterfield from under his wounded horse and carried him to safety. When another sergeant lost his horse in a similar way, Garforth opened a heavy fire on an enemy machine-gun and thus drew its fire on to himself, allowing the sergeant to escape.

He died from natural causes on 1 July 1973.

Captain THEODORE WRIGHT
JEMAPPES, MONS, Belgium
23 August and 14 September 1914
He was 31 years old and serving in the 57th Field Company, Corps of Royal Engineers when he attempted to connect up a lead to demolish a bridge under heavy fire. Despite being wounded in the head, he refused assistance and made a second attempt. On 14 September he helped the 5th Cavalry Brigade to cross a pontoon bridge over the Aisne river by repairing its shattered sections. The bridge was under fire and he was mortally wounded just after the last men crossed over.

Major ERNEST ALEXANDER
AUDREGNIES, Belgium 24 August 1914
He was 43 years old and serving in the 119th Battery, RFA. When under attack by a German corps, he handled his battery with great success, saving all the guns even though all the horses and most of his men were killed. With the help of Captain Francis Grenfell, who was severely wounded, and men from the 9th Lancers the guns were withdrawn by hand. Later in the day Alexander also rescued a wounded man under heavy fire. Both men were awarded the VC.

He died on 25 August 1934, following an operation.

Captain FRANCIS GRENFELL
AUDREGNIES, Belgium 24 August 1914
He was 33 years old and serving in the 9th Lancers when he took part in a charge against massed German infantry. Casualties were heavy and Grenfell soon found himself the senior officer. Despite being wounded in the hand and thigh, he assisted Major Ernest Alexander in saving the guns of the 119th Battery. This was done by turning the guns, lifting them over the dead gunners and withdrawing them by hand. An enemy shell landed under one of the guns he was lifting but it did not explode. Both men were awarded the VC.

Grenfell had also served in the Second Boer War.

He was killed in action at Hooge on 24 May 1915.

Lance Corporal GEORGE WYATT
LANDRECIES, France
25/26 August 1914
He was 27 years old and serving in the 3rd Bn, Coldstream Guards when his unit was hotly engaged close to some farm buildings, the enemy fire setting light to some straw sacks in the farmyard. Wyatt twice dashed out under very heavy fire from the enemy, who were only 25 yards away, and extinguished the fire, making it possible to hold on to the position. Later, although wounded in the head, he continued firing until he could no longer see owing to the blood pouring down his face. The medical officer bound up his wound and ordered him to the rear, but he refused to go and returned to the firing line and went on fighting.

He died on 22 January 1964.

Major CHARLES YATE
LE CATEAU, France 26 August 1914
He was 42 years old and serving in the 2nd Bn, King's Own Yorkshire Light Infantry when his company was subjected to a heavy bombardment, leaving just nineteen survivors. Rather than surrender, Yate led the remaining men in a charge against the Germans, during which he was severely wounded. When the charge was over, only three of the men were able to be formed up. Yate was taken prisoner.

He was shot and killed during an escape attempt on 20 September 1914.

Lance Corporal FREDERICK HOLMES
LE CATEAU, France 26 August 1914
He was 24 years old and serving in the 2nd Bn, King's Own Yorkshire Light Infantry when he carried a wounded man out of the trenches under heavy fire, and later helped to drive a gun out of action by taking the place of its wounded driver. (This may have been one of the guns of the 37th Battery – see next entry.)

He died on 22 October 1969.

Driver JOB DRAIN

LE CATEAU, France 26 August 1914

He was 18 years old and serving in the 37th Battery, RFA when the Germans swept towards his guns. He was in one of two teams of volunteers to save them, including Captain Douglas Reynolds and Driver Frederick Luke. Two guns were limbered up but one was lost when all the horses were shot down. The other was brought safely out of action. Reynolds was forced to ride alongside the unguided pair of horses after their driver had been killed. They were under very heavy fire all the time. All three men were awarded the VC.

Drain was one of 74 VC holders who formed the honour guard at the interment of the Unknown Soldier at Westminster Abbey on 11 November 1920.

He died on 26 July 1975.

Driver FREDERICK LUKE

LE CATEAU, France 26 August 1914

He was 18 years old and serving in the 37th Battery, RFA when the Germans swept towards his guns. He was in one of two teams of volunteers to save them, including Captain Douglas Reynolds and Driver Job Drain. Two guns were limbered up but one was lost when all the horses were shot down. The other was brought safely out of action. Reynolds was forced to ride alongside the unguided pair of horses after their driver had been killed. They were under very heavy fire all the time. All three men were awarded the VC.

Luke also served in the Second World War. He was one of 74 VC holders to form the honour guard at the interment of the Unknown Soldier at Westminster Abbey on 11 November 1920.

He died on 12 March 1983.

Captain DOUGLAS REYNOLDS

LE CATEAU and PYSLOUP, France 26 August and 9 September 1914

He was 31 years old and serving in the 37th Battery, RFA when the Germans swept towards his guns. He got together two teams of volunteers to save them, including Drivers Job Drain and Frederick Luke. Two guns were limbered up but one was lost when all the horses were shot down. The other was brought safely out of action. Reynolds was forced to ride alongside the unguided pair of horses after their driver had been killed. They were under very heavy fire all the time. All three men were awarded the VC. On 9 September, while reconnoitring between the lines, he discovered an enemy battery and silenced it.

He died on 23 February 1916 as a result of a gas bomb explosion.

Captain EDWARD BRADBURY

NERY, France 1 September 1914

He was 33 years old and commanding L Battery, RHA when the enemy launched a fierce attack. All the officers and most of the men were either killed or wounded, including Bradbury, whose leg was taken off by a shell. However, he kept on directing the fire until he died. Battery Sergeant Major George Dorrell then took over command and with the help of Sergeant David Nelson continued to fire one of the guns until all the ammunition was used up. All three men were awarded the VC.

Battery Sergeant Major GEORGE DORRELL

NERY, France 1 September 1914

He was 34 years old and serving in L Battery, RHA when the enemy launched a fierce attack. All the officers and most of the men were either killed or wounded, including the commanding officer, Captain Edward Bradbury, whose leg was taken off by a shell; despite this, he kept on directing the fire until he died. Dorrell then took over command and with the help of Sergeant David Nelson continued to fire one of the guns until all the ammunition was used up. All three men were awarded the VC.

Dorrell died on 7 January 1971, following a long period of poor health.

Sergeant DAVID NELSON

NERY, France 1 September 1914

He was 28 years old and serving in L Battery, RHA when the enemy launched a fierce attack. All the officers and most of the men were either killed or wounded, including the commanding officer, Captain Edward Bradbury, whose leg was taken off by a shell; despite this, he kept on directing the fire until he died. Dorrell then took over command and with the help of Sergeant Nelson continued to fire one of the guns until all the ammunition was used up. All three men were awarded the VC.

Nelson was killed in action at Lillers on 8 April 1918.

Captain WILLIAM JOHNSTON
MISSY, France 14 September 1914
He was 34 years old and serving in the 59th Field Company, Corps of Royal Engineers when with his own hands he worked two rafts on the Aisne river. He took ammunition across and returned with wounded. He continued to do this under heavy fire all day, thus enabling an advanced brigade to maintain its position across the river.

He was killed in action at Ypres on 8 June 1915.

Lance Corporal WILLIAM FULLER
CHIVY-SUR-AISNE, France
14 September 1914
He was 30 years old and serving in the 2nd Bn, Welch Regiment when he went forward under fire and carried the mortally wounded Captain Haggard 100 yards to the cover of a ridge, where he dressed his wounds. At the captain's request, Fuller ran back to retrieve the captain's rifle, to prevent it falling into enemy hands.

He died on 29 December 1974.

Private ROSS TOLLERTON
AISNE, France 14 September 1914
He was 24 years old and serving in the 1st Bn, Queen's Own Cameron Highlanders when he carried the wounded Lieutenant J. Matheson under heavy fire as far as he could, to a place of greater safety. Then, although wounded in the head and hand, he went back to the firing line, where he remained until his battalion had to retire. He then returned to the wounded man and stayed with him for three days until the Germans pulled back and they were both rescued.

He died from cancer on 7 May 1931, and Lieutenant Matheson sent a wreath.

Private GEORGE WILSON
VERNEUIL, France 14 September 1914
He was 28 years old and serving in the 2nd Bn, Highland Light Infantry when he located the position of an enemy machine-gun which was holding up the advance. Alone, he dashed towards it, and jumped into a hollow where he found a group of eight Germans with two British prisoners. He shouted: 'Come on, men, charge!' as if his regiment were with him. The Germans instantly surrendered. Once they were secured, he continued his attack on the machine-gun, shooting six of the enemy, bayoneting the officer and capturing the gun.

He died from tuberculosis on 26 April 1926.

Bombardier ERNEST HORLOCK (often misspelt HARLOCK)
VENDRESSE, France 15 September 1914
He was 28 years old and serving in the 113th Battery, RFA when his battery came under fire and he was wounded in the thigh. The doctor ordered him to go to the hospital, but he returned to the battery. Five minutes later he was wounded again, this time in the back. The doctor again ordered him to hospital, but again he returned to the battery. A few minutes later he was wounded in the arm. Not wanting to explain to the doctor why he wasn't yet in the hospital, he stayed with the battery. He was later reprimanded for disobeying orders.

He drowned on 30 December 1917, when HMS *Aragon* was torpedoed.

Captain HARRY RANKEN
HAUTE-AVESNES, France
19/20 September 1914
He was 31 years old and serving in the Royal Army Medical Corps. While he was attending to the wounded, a shell blew his leg to bits. He arrested the bleeding himself, bound up his leg and immediately returned to dressing the wounds of his men. When he could no longer continue, he was carried to the rear and died shortly afterwards.

The administration block of the Queen

Boatswain's Mate Charles Lucas (1), Crimean War. He was the very first VC. (*Victoria Cross Society*)

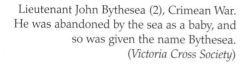

Lieutenant John Bythesea (2), Crimean War. He was abandoned by the sea as a baby, and so was given the name Bythesea. (*Victoria Cross Society*)

Lieutenant George Day (107), Crimean War. It was supposedly the sight of Day wearing his three orders and nine medals across his chest that prompted the Prince of Wales (later Edward VII) to suggest that medals should be collected together and worn neatly on one bar. (*Victoria Cross Society*)

Able Seaman William Hall (225), Indian Mutiny. He was the first black man to be awarded the VC. (*Victoria Cross Society*)

Drummer Thomas Flynn (234), Indian Mutiny. He shared the distinction of being one of the two youngest VC recipients, at 15 years and 3 months. (*Victoria Cross Society*)

Lieutenant Frederick Roberts (235), Indian Mutiny. Roberts was Queen Victoria's favourite soldier. (*Imperial War Museum: Q82615*)

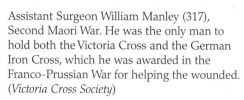

Assistant Surgeon William Manley (317), Second Maori War. He was the only man to hold both the Victoria Cross and the German Iron Cross, which he was awarded in the Franco-Prussian War for helping the wounded. (*Victoria Cross Society*)

Lieutenant Evelyn Wood (289), Indian Mutiny. In fact, he was first recommended for the VC in the Crimea at the age of 16. (*Imperial War Museum: Q82618*)

Private Alfred Hook (354), Zulu War. Unlike his portrayal in the film *Zulu*, he was in fact a model soldier. (*Victoria Cross Society*)

Brevet Lieutenant Colonel Redvers Buller (362), Zulu War. He later became known as 'Reverse Buller' due to his poor performance during the Second Boer War. (*Imperial War Museum: Q80478*)

Captain William Beresford (372), Zulu War. When presented with his medal, he told Queen Victoria that he could not receive the honour unless it was shared with Sergeant Edmund O'Toole. (*Victoria Cross Society*)

(*Left*) Captain Henry D'Arcy (373) with Sergeant Edmund O'Toole (374), Zulu War. (*Victoria Cross Society*)

(Below right) Sergeant Harry Hampton (483), Second Boer War. Although wounded himself, he helped another wounded man. (*Victoria Cross Society*)

Corporal Henry Knight (484), Second Boer War. He carried a wounded man for 2 miles. (*Victoria Cross Society*)

Surgeon Captain later Lieutenant Arthur Martin-Leake VC and Bar (514 and 551), Second Boer War and First World War. He was the first man to win a Bar to his VC, and the only VC and Bar holder whose awards were made for different wars. (*Trustees of the Army Medical Corps Museum*)

Private Sidney Godley (524), First World War. He was the first private to be awarded the VC in the First World War. (*Victoria Cross Society*)

(*Right*) Lance Corporal Wilfred Fuller (577) and Company Sergeant Major Frederick Barter (619), First World War. Between them they captured over 150 Germans. (*Imperial War Museum: Q79801*)

Captain Edward Unwin (593), First World War. Witnessing Unwin's action, General Julian Byng remarked, 'We want several little Unwins'. (*Victoria Cross Society*)

Lance Corporal Albert Jacka (622), First World War. Many believe Jacka should also have been awarded a Bar to his VC. (*Victoria Cross Society*)

Captain Lanoe Hawker (634), First World War. He was shot down and killed by Manfred von Richthofen, the 'Red Baron'. (*Victoria Cross Society*)

Captain Noel Chavasse VC and Bar (744 and 854), First World War. He was the only man to be awarded the VC and Bar in the First World War. (*Victoria Cross Society*)

First Class Boy John Cornwell (706), First World War. His 5.5-inch gun is on display at the Imperial War Museum. (*Victoria Cross Society*)

Private Martin O'Meara (745), First World War. He was wounded three times during the war. (*Victoria Cross Society*)

Major Edward Mannock (1014), First World War. He was the highest-scoring Allied ace of the war. (*Victoria Cross Society*)

Lieutenant Augustus Agar (1152), North Russia Relief Force. He torpedoed the cruiser *Olig*. (*Imperial War Museum: Q68014*)

Second Lieutenant later Captain Charles Upham VC and Bar (1188 and 1219), Second World War. He was the only combat VC and Bar, and the only man to be awarded the VC and Bar in the Second World War. (*Victoria Cross Society*)

Flying Officer Lloyd Trigg (1250), Second World War. He was the only man to be awarded the VC solely on the evidence of the enemy. (*Victoria Cross Society*)

Jemadar Abdul Hafiz (1266), Second World War. He led an attack against 40 Japanese. (*Victoria Cross Society*)

Rifleman Ganju Lama (1278), Second World War. He knocked out two tanks at close range with a PIAT. (*Victoria Cross Society*)

Lieutenant Tasker Watkins (1291), Second World War. He won his VC in his very first combat action. (*Victoria Cross Society*)

Temporary Major Robert Cain (1298), Second World War. His son-in-law is the television presenter Jeremy Clarkson. (*Victoria Cross Society*)

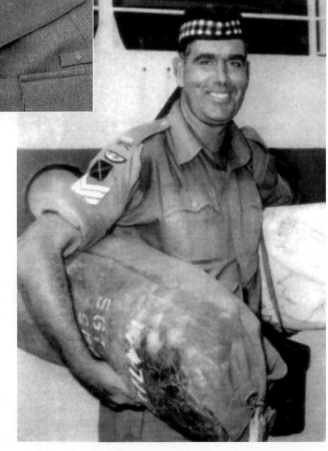

Private Bill Speakman (1347), Korea. He was known as the 'Beer Bottle VC'. (*Victoria Cross Society*)

Warrant Officer Class II Kevin 'Dasher' Wheatley (1348), Vietnam. He refused to leave a dying comrade. (*Victoria Cross Society*)

Lance Corporal Rambahadur Limbu (1349), Malaysia/Indonesia Conflict. (*Victoria Cross Society*)

Warrant Officer Class II Keith Payne (1352), Vietnam. He saved 40 men who were trapped behind enemy lines. (*Keith Payne*)

Lieutenant Colonel H. Jones (1353), Falkland Islands. He was killed storming an enemy machine-gun position. (*Victoria Cross Society*)

Private Johnson Beharry (1356), Iraq. He saved the lives of his entire platoon. (*Victoria Cross Society*)

Elizabeth Hospital in Woolwich, London, is named Ranken House in his honour.

Private FREDERICK DOBSON
CHAVANNE, AISNE, France
28 September 1914
He was 27 years old and serving in the 2nd Bn, Coldstream Guards when he crawled out to assist some wounded men. Finding only one alive, he dressed his wounds and then crawled back to find a stretcher. He then crawled out again with Corporal Brown, and together they dragged the man back to safety.
Dobson died on 13 November 1935.

Private HENRY MAY
LA BOUTILLERIE, France
22 October 1914
He was 29 years old and serving in the 1st Bn, Cameronians (Scottish Rifles) when he tried to rescue a wounded man under heavy fire, but as he made his way back the man was shot dead in his arms. Then he went to the aid of the wounded Lieutenant Graham and carried him back 300 yards to safety.
He died on 26 July 1941.

Drummer WILLIAM KENNY
YPRES, Belgium 23 October 1914
He was 34 years old and serving in the 2nd Bn, Gordon Highlanders. He rescued wounded men on five occasions under heavy fire. Twice previously he had saved machine-guns by carrying them out of action, and he conveyed many urgent messages under very heavy fire.
He was one of 74 VC holders who formed the honour guard at the interment of the Unknown Soldier at Westminster Abbey on 11 November 1920.
Kenny died on 10 January 1936.

Lieutenant JAMES BROOKE
GHELUVELT, Belgium 29 October 1914
He was 30 years old and serving in the 2nd Bn, Gordon Highlanders when he led two attacks on German-held trenches under heavy rifle and machine-gun fire, regaining a lost trench at a most critical time. By his marked coolness on this occasion, he prevented the enemy from

breaking through the lines at a time when a general counter-attack could not have been organised. Having established control of the trench, he returned to bring up reinforcements but was killed while doing so.

Second Lieutenant JAMES LEACH
FESTUBERT, France 29 October 1914
He was 22 years old and serving in the 2nd Bn, Manchester Regiment when he, together with Sergeant John Hogan and ten men, launched a counter-attack on a lost trench. As the Germans were pushed back into the next traverse and then the next, Leach and Hogan advanced further into the trench, shooting around corners with their revolvers until they gradually succeeded in regaining possession of the whole trench, killing 8, wounding 2 and capturing 16 Germans. Both men were awarded the VC.
Leach died on 15 August 1958.

Sergeant JOHN HOGAN
FESTUBERT, France 29 October 1914
He was 22 years old and serving in the 2nd Bn, Manchester Regiment when he, with Second Lieutenant James Leach and ten men, launched a counter-attack on a lost trench. As the Germans were pushed back into the next traverse and then the next, Leach and Hogan advanced further into the trench, shooting around corners with their revolvers until they gradually succeeded in regaining possession of the whole trench, killing 8, wounding 2 and capturing 16 Germans. Both men were awarded the VC.
Hogan was one of 74 VC holders who formed the honour guard at the interment of the Unknown Soldier at Westminster Abbey on 11 November 1920.
He died from cancer on 6 October 1943.

Lieutenant ARTHUR MARTIN-LEAKE VC (Bar action)
ZONNEBEKE, Belgium
29 October–8 November 1914
He was 40 years old and serving in the Royal Army Medical Corps when he showed conspicuous bravery and devotion to duty in

rescuing, while exposed to heavy fire, a large number of wounded men who were lying close to the enemy trenches.

For his VC action, see the Second Boer War section, 8 February 1902. The other two men to be awarded the VC and Bar are Noel Chavasse and Charles Upham. There are further links between these men: Martin-Leake was serving with the 46th Field Ambulance, RAMC which brought Chavasse back to Brandhoeck, and Upham was distantly related to Chavasse by marriage.

Arthur Martin-Leake died from lung cancer on 22 June 1953.

Sepoy KHUDADAD KHAN
HOLLEBEKE, Belgium 31 October 1914
He was 26 years old and serving in the 129th Duke of Connaught's Own Baluchis, Indian Army when he was part of a machine-gun section. After all but one of the guns had been destroyed by a shell, he kept on firing his gun until all the other men were killed. Badly wounded himself, he was left for dead by the Germans but managed to crawl back to his unit. He was the first Indian to be awarded the VC.

He died on 8 March 1971.

Drummer SPENCER BENT
LE GHEER, YPRES, Belgium
1–3 November 1914
He was 23 years old and serving in the 1st Bn, East Lancashire Regiment when he was sent to bring back some men of his platoon. The men assembled but were attacked by the enemy, who believed the trench to be empty. All the officers and the platoon sergeant were killed or wounded. Bent took command, and with great valour and coolness succeeded in holding the position until relieved. On 3 November he was about to lift the wounded Private McNulty on to his back when he slipped and fell. Realising that bullets were flying overhead, he remained on the ground, hooked his feet under McNulty's armpits and pulled himself backwards with his hands, dragging the wounded man to the safety of his trench.

Bent was one of 74 VC holders who formed the honour guard at the interment of the Unknown Soldier at Westminster Abbey on 11 November 1920.

He died in his sleep on 3 May 1977.

Captain JOHN VALLENTIN
ZILLEBEKE, Belgium 7 November 1914
He was 32 years old and serving in the 1st Bn, South Staffordshire Regiment. While leading an attack against German trenches he was struck down, and on rising to continue the attack he was hit again and killed. He had instilled such confidence in his men that the enemy trenches were captured.

Captain WALTER BRODIE
BECELAERE, Belgium
11 November 1914
He was 29 years old and serving in the 2nd Bn, Highland Light Infantry when he led a gallant bayonet charge and cleared the enemy out of the trenches they had occupied during a thick mist. He bayoneted several Germans himself and 80 of the enemy were killed and 51 prisoners taken.

He was killed in action near Behagnies on 23 August 1918.

Lieutenant JOHN DIMMER
KLEIN ZILLEBEKE, Belgium
12 November 1914
He was 31 years old and serving in the 2nd Bn, King's Royal Rifle Corps when he fired his machine-gun into the advancing Germans, mowing them down. He was shot in the jaw while clearing a jam caused by the ammunition belt becoming wet. He got his gun working again but was struck in the shoulder by another bullet. Then a shell burst above him, wounding him for the third time. With blood pouring from his wounds, he continued to fire until his gun was destroyed by a hail of shrapnel.

He was killed in action at Marteville on 21 March 1918.

Lieutenant JOHN BUTLER
CAMEROONS, Nigeria
17 November and 27 December 1914
He was 25 years old and serving in the King's Royal Rifle Corps, attached to the Pioneer

Company of the Gold Coast Regiment, West African Frontier Force when with a party of only thirteen men he went into thick bush and attacked and defeated a force of about 100 of the enemy, capturing a machine-gun and much ammunition. On 27 December, while on patrol with a few men, he swam the Ekam river under heavy fire, carried out his reconnaissance on the far bank and swam back to safety.

He was killed in action at Motomba on 5 September 1916. His uncle was Lieutenant Edric Gifford VC.

Bandsman THOMAS RENDLE
WULVERGHEM, Belgium
20 November 1914
He was 29 years old and serving in the 1st Bn, Duke of Cornwall's Light Infantry when he carried the wounded Lieutenant Colebrook on his back and worked his way back across an open gap, being narrowly missed by two or three bullets. He also rescued several men from the trenches who had been buried by the enemy's heavy artillery.

He died from coronary thrombosis on 1 June 1946.

Naik DARWAN SINGH NEGI
FESTUBERT, France
23/24 November 1914
He was 33 years old and serving in the 1st Bn, 39th Garhwal Rifles, Indian Army when his regiment was engaged in retaking some trenches and clearing out the enemy. In this risky operation he was always either first or among the first to push around every traverse. He did not even report that he had been wounded in the head and arm until the fighting had ceased, by which time over 30 Germans had been killed and more than 100 captured.

He died on 24 June 1950.

Lieutenant FRANK de PASS
FESTUBERT, France 24 November 1914
He was 27 years old and serving in the 34th Prince Albert Victor's Own Poona Horse, Indian Army when he entered an enemy sap and crawled along it until he reached a traverse from which the enemy had been lobbing bombs

into the British trench. He placed a charge into the loophole and fired it, destroying the traverse. Later he carried a wounded sepoy to safety under heavy fire. He was the first Jewish VC of the war.

He was killed in action the next day.

Commander HENRY RITCHIE
DAR-ES-SALAAM, German East Africa
28 November 1914
He was 38 years old and serving in the Royal Navy when he took the small steam gun-boat *Helmuth* into the harbour to lay demolition charges on any German ships he could find. The harbour was almost deserted and he scented a trap, so he lashed two steel lighters to his boat as protection. Suddenly an immense fire opened up on him from all sides. Taking over at the wheel, he guided the boat towards the mouth of the harbour. He was hit eight times in the next 20 minutes, fainting from loss of blood just before the boat reached safety. In fact, he had been hit in the forehead, his left thumb, his left arm (twice), his right arm and his right hip. He also had a broken right leg after being hit by two large-calibre bullets. He never fully recovered from his injuries, and he never commanded at sea again.

He died on 9 December 1958.

Lieutenant NORMAN HOLBROOK
DARDANELLES, Turkey
13 December 1914
He was 26 years old and serving in the Royal Navy aboard HM Submarine *B11* when he dived under five rows of mines, sighted the 10,000-ton Turkish battleship *Messudiyeh*, fired his starboard torpedo and sank her. He then dived back under the rows of mines to escape being shelled as he went. By the time he got back to the Mediterranean, he had been submerged for nine hours. This was the first time a battleship had been sunk by a submarine.

In 1915 the town of Holbrook in New South Wales was renamed in his honour. He was one of 74 VC holders who formed the honour guard at the interment of the Unknown Soldier at Westminster Abbey on 11 November 1920.

He died on 3 July 1976.

Private HENRY ROBSON
KEMMEL, Belgium 14 December 1914
He was 20 years old and serving in the 2nd Bn,
Royal Scots (Lothian Regiment) when during
an attack he left his trench under heavy fire and
carried back a wounded NCO. Later, during
another attack, he tried to rescue another
wounded man. He was himself wounded but
kept trying to reach the man until he was
wounded again and was forced to give up.
He died from cancer on 4 March 1964.

Lieutenant WILLIAM BRUCE
GIVENCHY, France 19 December 1914
He was 24 years old and serving in the 59th
Scinde Rifles, Indian Army. During a night
attack his men captured an enemy trench.
Ignoring a severe neck wound, he paced up and
down for several hours urging his men to hold
the trench against repeated German counter-
attacks. It was largely due to his example and
encouragement that the position was held until
dusk, when it was finally retaken by the enemy
and he was killed.

Lieutenant PHILIP NEAME
NEUVE CHAPELLE, France
19 December 1914
He was 26 years old and serving in the 15th
Field Company, Royal Corps of Engineers
when he was in a captured trench that the
Germans were counter-attacking with bombs.
He trimmed the damp fuses on the home-made
'jam tin' bombs, then lit them with matches
and started hurling them over the traverse of
the trench. Huge explosions were followed by
the screams of wounded Germans. A machine-
gun opened up on him every time he stood up
to throw another bomb, but was unable to hit
him. For almost an hour he single-handedly
held up the German advance. He was told later
that from a distance it looked like they were
throwing coconuts at each other.
Neame was one of 74 VC holders who
formed the honour guard at the interment of
the Unknown Soldier at Westminster Abbey
on 11 November 1920. He won a gold medal in
the 1924 Paris Olympics and is the only VC
recipient to have done so. He also served in the

Second World War. Captured in North Africa
in 1941, he made a number of escape attempts
with colleagues, including Major General
Richard O'Connor and Lieutenant General
Adrian Carton de Wiart VC.
He died on 28 April 1978.

Private JAMES MacKENZIE
ROUGES BANCS, France
19 December 1914
He was 25 years old and serving in the 2nd Bn,
Scots Guards when under heavy fire he rescued
a wounded man from in front of the German
trenches, after a stretcher party had been
forced to give up.
He was killed later the same day trying to
rescue another wounded man.

Private ABRAHAM ACTON
ROUGES BANCS, France
21 December 1914
He was 22 years old and serving in the 2nd Bn,
Border Regiment when he and Private James
Smith voluntarily left their trench and went to
the aid of a wounded man, who had lain out in
the open near the German lines for some hours.
Together they dragged him to safety. Later
that day they went out again and brought in
another wounded man. They were under fire
for an hour while carrying him to safety. Both
men were awarded the VC.
Acton was killed in action at Festubert on
16 May 1915.

Private JAMES SMITH (born GLENN)
ROUGES BANCS, France
21 December 1914
He was 33 years old and serving in the 3rd Bn,
Border Regiment, attached to the 2nd Bn,
when he and Private Abraham Acton voluntarily left their trench and went to the aid of a
wounded man who had lain out in the open
near the German lines for some hours.
Together they dragged him to safety. Later
that day they went out again and brought in
another wounded man. They were under fire
for an hour while carrying him to safety. Both
men were awarded the VC.
Smith died on 21 May 1968.

1915

Captain EUSTACE JOTHAM
SPINA KHAISORA, India 7 January 1915
He was 31 years old and serving in the 51st Sikhs (Frontier Force), Indian Army. While commanding a small force, he was attacked in a nullah and almost surrounded by 1,500 tribesmen. He gave the order to retire, and could have escaped himself but he turned back to save one of the sowars, who had been knocked off his horse. He killed seven of the enemy before he was killed.

In 1913 while on leave and returning home from Scotland, his train was involved in a collision. Jotham was seen to rescue at least four people from the burning wreckage.

Lance Corporal MICHAEL O'LEARY
CUINCHY, France 1 February 1915
He was 26 years old and serving in the 1st Bn, Irish Guards when he was part of a storming force which was advancing towards the enemy barricades. He rushed to the front and killed five Germans who were holding the first barricade, after which he attacked a second barricade some 60 yards further on. This he captured after killing three men and capturing another two. O'Leary thus practically took the position by himself and prevented the rest of the attacking party from being fired on.

'O'Leary VC' was featured on a recruiting poster. He also served in the Second World War, and died on 1 August 1961.

Lieutenant Commander ERIC ROBINSON
DARDANELLES, KUM KALE, Turkey 26 February 1915
He was 33 years old and serving in the Royal Navy when he led an attack on the Turkish gun battery known as 'Achilles Tomb'. His small force landed without being noticed and destroyed two small artillery pieces, and then made for the main battery. Their white naval uniforms made them easy targets for the Turks and casualties mounted. Robinson moved his men through some gulleys and came out close to a small rise behind the main battery. Here he

delegated command of the party to a junior officer and advanced alone into the battery, where he destroyed two 4-inch guns.

On 18 April he led a raid to destroy the grounded and captured submarine HMS *E15*, it being considered vital for morale that it not be allowed to remain in Turkish hands. The submarine was torpedoed and rendered useless to the enemy. This action did not form part of his citation.

Robinson had a long career, serving in four wars: the Boxer Rebellion, the First World War, the Russian Civil War and the Second World War.

He died on 20 August 1965.

Rifleman GOBAR SING NEGI
NEUVE CHAPELLE, France
10 March 1915
He was 21 years old and serving in the 2/39th Garhwal Rifles, Indian Army when he was accompanying a bombing party into the German trenches. Resistance was heavy but he was the first man to go round each traverse. He killed several Germans and forced the remainder back until they surrendered. He was killed during this action.

Private WILLIAM BUCKINGHAM (real name BILLINGTON)
NEUVE CHAPELLE, France
10 and 12 March 1915
He was 29 years old and serving in the 2nd Bn, Leicestershire Regiment when he carried several wounded men to safety under heavy fire. Among those he rescued was a German soldier whose leg had been blown off. He became known as the 'Leicester VC', and he said of his actions 'Of course I did what I could, but really it's not worth talking about.'

He was killed in action at Thiepval on 15 September 1916.

Captain CHARLES FOSS
NEUVE CHAPELLE, France
12 March 1915
He was 30 years old and serving in the 2nd Bn, Bedfordshire Regiment. After the Germans had captured part of a trench and a counter-

attack had failed to retake it, he dashed forward with just eight men under heavy fire and attacked the enemy with bombs. The trench was duly retaken, along with 52 prisoners.

Foss was one of 74 VC holders who formed the honour guard at the interment of the Unknown Soldier at Westminster Abbey on 11 November 1920.

He died on 9 April 1953.

Lieutenant CYRIL MARTIN
SPANBROEKMOLEN, Belgium
12 March 1915
He was 30 years old and serving in the 56th Field Company, Corps of Royal Engineers when he volunteered to lead a small bombing party against a section of the enemy's trenches that was holding up the attack. Before he even started he was wounded, but taking no notice he carried on with the attack, which was completely successful. The Germans counter-attacked, but Martin's men held them off for 2½ hours until ordered to abandon the position.

Martin also served in the Second World War and was ADC to King George VI.

He died on 14 August 1980.

Company Sergeant Major HARRY DANIELS
NEUVE CHAPELLE, France
12 March 1915
He was 30 years old and serving in the 2nd Bn, Rifle Brigade (Prince Consort's Own) when the advance of the battalion was held up by wire entanglements and heavy machine-gun fire. Daniels and Acting Corporal Cecil Noble rushed forward and under very heavy fire succeeded in cutting the wire, allowing the attack to go forward and take the trench. Both men were awarded the VC.

Daniels died from pneumonia on 13 December 1953.

Lance Corporal WILFRED FULLER
NEUVE CHAPELLE, France
12 March 1915
He was 21 years old and serving in the 1st Bn, Grenadier Guards when during an attack he saw a party of Germans trying to escape along a communication trench. He ran forward alone and killed the first man with a bomb; the remainder, nearly 50 of them, seeing no means of evading his bombs, surrendered to him.

After the war he joined the Somerset Constabulary.

He died on 22 November 1947.

Corporal WILLIAM ANDERSON
NEUVE CHAPELLE, France
12 March 1915
He was 29 years old and serving in the 2nd Bn, Yorkshire Regiment (Alexandra, Princess of Wales's Own) when he led three men with bombs against a large group of Germans who had captured part of the British trenches. He first threw his own bombs and then those of his comrades, all of whom had been wounded. Now on his own, he opened rapid fire on the enemy with great effect. He was killed in action the following day.

Acting Corporal CECIL NOBLE
NEUVE CHAPELLE, France
12 March 1915
He was 23 years old and serving in the 2nd Bn, Rifle Brigade (Prince Consort's Own) when the advance of the battalion was held up by wire entanglements and heavy machine-gun fire. Noble and Company Sergeant Major Harry Daniels rushed forward and under very heavy fire succeeded in cutting the wire, allowing the attack to go forward and take the trench. Both men were awarded the VC.

Noble died from his wounds the following day.

Private EDWARD BARBER
NEUVE CHAPELLE, France
12 March 1915
He was 21 years old and serving in the 1st Bn, Grenadier Guards when he ran ahead of his grenade company and began throwing bombs at the enemy to such effect that a great number of them surrendered at once. When his company reached him they found him alone and with the enemy surrendering all around him. He was killed soon afterwards.

Private ROBERT MORROW
MESSINES, Belgium 12 March 1915
He was 23 years old and serving in the 1st Bn, Royal Irish Fusiliers when under heavy fire and on his own initiative he carried to a place of comparative safety several men who had been buried in the trenches by shell fire.

He was killed in action at St Jean in the Ypres Salient on 26 April 1915.

Private JACOB RIVERS
NEUVE CHAPELLE, France
12 March 1915
He was 34 years old and serving in the 1st Bn, Sherwood Foresters (Nottinghamshire and Derbyshire Regiment) when he crept to within a few yards of a large number of Germans who were massed on the flank of an advanced company of his battalion, and threw several bombs into them. His action caused the enemy to retire in confusion. He repeated this act later the same day, but was killed.

Major GEORGE WHEELER
SHAIBAH, Mesopotamia
12/13 April 1915
He was 42 years old and serving in the 7th Hariana Lancers, Indian Army when he led his squadron in an attempt to capture a flag which was the centre point of a group of the enemy who were firing on one of his troop's picquets. He advanced, attacking the enemy line with the lance, but had to retire when the enemy swarmed out of hidden ground. The next day Wheeler led his squadron to attack the North Mound. He was seen far ahead of his men and galloping straight for the enemy's standard when he was killed.

Lieutenant GEORGE ROUPELL
HILL 60, ZWARTELEEN, Belgium
20 April 1915
He was 23 years old and serving in the 1st Bn, East Surrey Regiment when he was commanding a company which was under heavy bombardment. Although wounded, he refused to leave his men, helping to repel a German assault. During a lull he had his wounds dressed, but then returned to his post which was again under heavy bombardment. Later that evening, faint from loss of blood, he made his way across open ground under fire to the reserve trench to bring up reinforcements. With these men he held on until 2am, when his company was relieved.

Roupell was one of 74 VC holders who formed the honour guard at the interment of the Unknown Soldier at Westminster Abbey on 11 November 1920. Roupell also served in the Second World War.

He died on 4 March 1974.

Private EDWARD DWYER
HILL 60, ZWARTELEEN, Belgium
20 April 1915
He was 19 years old and serving in the 1st Bn, East Surrey Regiment when he went out into the open under heavy shell fire to attend to the wounded. Later he found himself alone in his trench, his comrades having been driven out by a German bombing party. He collected all the grenades he could find and climbed on to the parapet, from where he threw the grenades at the advancing enemy. He came under immediate fire but managed to keep the enemy at bay until reinforcements arrived and the trench was saved.

He was killed in action at Guillemont on 3 September 1916.

Second Lieutenant BENJAMIN GEARY
HILL 60, ZWARTELEEN, Belgium
20/21 April 1915
He was 23 years old and serving in the 4th Bn, East Surrey Regiment, attached to the 1st Bn, when he led his men across open ground swept by fierce fire to join the survivors of the Bedfordshire Regiment in a crater at the top of Hill 60. His men were first subjected to artillery fire and then repeated bomb attacks throughout the night. Geary was in the forefront of the defence, using a rifle and grenades to great effect. He often exposed himself to fire in order to see the enemy's whereabouts by the light of flares. He also arranged for ammunition and reinforcements.

He died on 26 May 1976.

Second Lieutenant GEOFFREY WOOLLEY
HILL 60, ZWARTELEEN, Belgium
20/21 April 1915
He was 22 years old and serving in the 9th (City of London) Bn, London Regiment (Queen Victoria's Rifles) when he was the only officer left on Hill 60. With only 30 men left he successfully repelled several attacks, throwing bombs and encouraging the men until relief arrived several hours later.

Woolley was the first Territorial Army officer to be awarded the VC. He was also one of 74 VC holders who formed the honour guard at the interment of the Unknown Soldier at Westminster Abbey on 11 November 1920. Later he was ordained and served as a chaplain in the Second World War. Woolley was Vice-Chairman of the VC & GC Association from 1956 to 1968.

He died on 10 December 1968.

Lance Corporal FREDERICK FISHER
ST JULIEN, Belgium 23 April 1915
He was 20 years old and serving in the 13th Bn (Royal Highlanders of Canada), CEF when the Germans used gas for the first time, before making an attack on the Canadians. Setting up his machine-gun in an exposed position, Fisher opened fire in defence of an 18-pounder battery, falling back when several of his men were killed or wounded. Later he went forward again with four more men to set up his gun at another position, firing into the advancing Germans until he was killed.

He was the first Canadian to be awarded the VC in the First World War.

Company Sergeant Major FREDERICK HALL
YPRES, Belgium 23/24 April 1915
He was 30 years old and serving in the 8th Bn (Winnipeg Rifles), CEF when he discovered a number of his men were missing. He could also hear the moans of wounded men. Under cover of darkness he went out on two separate occasions and each time returned with a wounded man. By 9am the next day there were still more men to bring in. In full daylight and under a hail of enemy fire, Hall crawled out with Corporal Payne and Private Rogerson towards the wounded men. Payne and Rogerson were both wounded and had to return, but Hall went on to a man lying some 15 yards from the trench. He was unable to reach him owing to enemy fire. He then made a second most gallant attempt, and was in the act of lifting the wounded man when he was mortally wounded. The soldier he was helping was also shot and killed.

Hall is one of three men to come from Pine Street, Winnipeg to be awarded the VC, the others being Corporal Leo Clarke and Lieutenant Robert Shankland. The street was renamed Valour Road in their honour.

Lieutenant EDWARD BELLEW
KERSELAERE, YPRES, Belgium
24 April 1915
He was 32 years old and serving in the 7th Bn (1st British Columbia Regiment), CEF when during an attack he sited his machine-guns on high ground and fired at the Germans. The reinforcements sent forward were destroyed, and with the enemy less than 100 yards away he and Sergeant Peerless decided to fight it out. Despite being wounded and the sergeant being killed, Bellew continued to fire until his ammunition ran out. He then smashed his machine-gun and used a rifle. Fighting to the last, he was eventually taken prisoner. The Germans sentenced him to death for continuing to fire after part of his unit had surrendered, and he was brought before a firing squad. He protested vehemently and at the last moment his sentence was commuted.

He died from a stroke on 1 February 1961. His second cousin was Brevet Lieutenant Colonel Robert Adams VC.

Temporary Major CUTHBERT BROMLEY
CAPE HELLES, GALLIPOLI, Turkey
25 April 1915
He was 37 years old and serving in the 1st Bn, Lancashire Fusiliers. As the Fusiliers were being rowed ashore to W Beach, it became clear that the barbed wire entanglements had not been cut by the bombardment, and a hail

of bullets swept across them from hidden Turkish machine-guns. Sailors were shot dead at their oars. The relentless fire continued as the Fusiliers hurled themselves ashore and cut their way through. Although most of the men were killed or wounded, the beach was taken.

Bromley was one of six men elected by the regiment for the VC, the others being John Grimshaw, William Keneally, Edward Stubbs, Alfred Richards and Richard Willis. They are known as 'the six VCs before breakfast'. Bromley drowned on 13 August 1915, while returning from Gallipoli to recuperate.

Captain FRANCIS SCRIMGER
ST JULIEN, YPRES, Belgium
25 April 1915
He was 35 years old and serving in the Canadian Army Medical Corps, attached to 14th Bn, Royal Montreal Regiment when he was in charge of an advanced dressing station in a farmhouse. The advancing enemy were bombarding the area with intense shelling. German infantry were within sight. Scrimger directed the removal of the wounded under heavy fire. He was the last to leave and carried Captain MacDonald, who had been left behind as a hopeless case. The shelling forced him to stop and place MacDonald on the road. He then lay on top of him to protect him with his body. During a lull he again carried the wounded officer towards help, but when unable to carry him any further, he remained with him until help could be obtained.

He died on 13 February 1937.

Captain EDWARD UNWIN
GALLIPOLI, Turkey 25 April 1915
He was 51 years old and serving in the Royal Navy aboard the SS *River Clyde* when he observed that the lighters which were to form a bridge to V Beach had broken away. Unwin jumped into the water with William Williams, George Drewry, Wilfred Malleson and George Samson, and under a murderous fire attempted to get the lighters back into position. Williams was mortally wounded and Unwin went to his aid, but the lighters were then swept away.

Now suffering from the effects of cold, Unwin was obliged to return to the ship, where he was wrapped in blankets. When he had recovered to some degree, he went back against doctor's orders to finish the work. He was wounded and collapsed. Once the attempts to land had ceased, he went out a third time to recover wounded men from the beach, and according to one account he retrieved seven men. All of these men received the VC.

Unwin was back at V beach in December for the evacuation, and he was aboard the last boat to leave. When a man fell overboard, he dived in to rescue him. Seeing his action, General Julian Byng, the new IX Corps commander, remarked to Commodore Roger Keyes: 'You really must do something about Unwin. You should send him home; we want several little Unwins.'

Unwin was one of 74 VC holders who formed the honour guard at the interment of the Unknown Soldier at Westminster Abbey on 11 November 1920. He died on 19 April 1950.

Captain RICHARD WILLIS
CAPE HELLES, GALLIPOLI, Turkey
25 April 1915
He was 38 years old and serving in the 1st Bn, Lancashire Fusiliers. While the Fusiliers were being rowed ashore to W beach, it became clear that the barbed wire entanglements had not been cut by the bombardment, and then a hail of bullets swept across them from hidden Turkish machine-guns. Sailors were shot dead at their oars. The relentless fire continued as the Fusiliers hurled themselves ashore and cut their way through. Although most of the men were killed or wounded, the beach was taken.

Willis was one of six men elected by the regiment for the VC, the others being Cuthbert Bromley, John Grimshaw, William Keneally, Alfred Richards and Frank Stubbs. They are known as 'the six VCs before breakfast'.

Willis had also served in the Sudan. He became known as 'Walking Stick Willis' and died on 9 February 1966.

Sub Lieutenant ARTHUR TISDALL
GALLIPOLI, Turkey 25 April 1915
He was 24 years old and serving in the Royal Naval Volunteer Reserve (Anson Battalion, Royal Naval Division) aboard the SS *River Clyde*. While he was waiting his turn to land on V beach, he was unable to bear the cries of the wounded, who were being cut down by Turkish machine-gun fire. Tisdall jumped into the water and called for assistance. Four men came to his aid, and the rescuers made four or five boat trips, each time bringing back wounded men to the SS *River Clyde*.

He was killed in action at Krithia on 6 May 1915.

Sergeant ALFRED RICHARDS
CAPE HELLES, GALLIPOLI, Turkey 25 April 1915
He was 36 years old and serving in the 1st Bn, Lancashire Fusiliers. While the Fusiliers were being rowed ashore to W beach, it became clear that the barbed wire entanglements had not been cut by the bombardment, and then a hail of bullets swept across them from hidden Turkish machine-guns. Sailors were shot dead at their oars. The relentless fire continued as the Fusiliers hurled themselves ashore and cut their way through. Although most of the men were killed or wounded, the beach was taken.

Richards was one of six men elected by the regiment for the VC, the others being Cuthbert Bromley, John Grimshaw, William Keneally, Edward Stubbs and Richard Willis. They are known as 'the six VCs before breakfast'.

Richards was one of 74 VC holders who formed the honour guard at the interment of the Unknown Soldier at Westminster Abbey on 11 November 1920.

He died on 21 May 1953 after a short illness.

Sergeant FRANK STUBBS
CAPE HELLES, GALLIPOLI, Turkey 25 April 1915
He was 27 years old and serving in the 1st Bn, Lancashire Fusiliers. While the Fusiliers were being rowed ashore to W beach, it became clear that the barbed wire entanglements had not been cut by the bombardment, and then a hail of bullets swept across them from hidden Turkish machine-guns. Sailors were shot dead at their oars. The relentless fire continued as the Fusiliers hurled themselves ashore and cut their way through. Although most of the men were killed or wounded, the beach was taken. Stubbs was killed during this action.

He was one of six men elected by the regiment for the VC, the others being Cuthbert Bromley, John Grimshaw, William Keneally, Alfred Richards and Richard Willis. They are known as 'the six VCs before breakfast'.

Corporal JOHN GRIMSHAW
CAPE HELLES, GALLIPOLI, Turkey 25 April 1915
He was 22 years old and serving in the 1st Bn, Lancashire Fusiliers. While the Fusiliers were being rowed ashore to W beach, it became clear that the barbed wire entanglements had not been cut by the bombardment, and then a hail of bullets swept across them from hidden Turkish machine-guns. Sailors were shot dead at their oars. The relentless fire continued as the Fusiliers hurled themselves ashore and cut their way through. Although most of the men were killed or wounded, the beach was taken. He was one of six men elected by the regiment for the VC, the others being Cuthbert Bromley, William Keneally, Alfred Richards, Frank Stubbs and Richard Willis. They are known as 'the six VCs before breakfast'.

Grimshaw died on 20 July 1980.

Midshipman GEORGE DREWRY
GALLIPOLI, Turkey 25 April 1915
He was 20 years old and serving in the Royal Naval Reserve aboard the SS *River Clyde* when with three other men (William Williams, Wilfred Malleson and George Samson) he assisted Edward Unwin in trying to secure the lighters forming the bridge to V beach. Despite being wounded in the head, he continued his work and twice attempted to swim from lighter to lighter with a line, but became too exhausted to continue. All five men were awarded the VC.

Drewry died at Scapa Flow on 3 August 1918 when a 'block' fell and fractured his skull. Drewry's medal is on display at the Imperial

War Museum. Interestingly, it has a blue naval ribbon, which should have been changed for the crimson ribbon issued when the RAF was formed in April 1918. This should have been done for all naval recipients still living at the time.

Midshipman WILFRED MALLESON
GALLIPOLI, Turkey 25 April 1915
He was 18 years old and serving in the Royal Navy aboard the SS *River Clyde* when with three other men (William Williams, George Drewry and George Samson), he assisted Edward Unwin in trying to secure the lighters forming the bridge to V beach. When Drewry was no longer able to carry the line from lighter to lighter through exhaustion, Malleson swam with it himself and succeeded. The line subsequently broke and he made two further unsuccessful attempts at his self-imposed task. All five men were awarded the VC.

He died on 21 July 1975.

Private WILLIAM KENEALLY (spelt KENEALY on headstone)
CAPE HELLES, GALLIPOLI, Turkey
25 April 1915
He was 29 years old and serving in the 1st Bn, Lancashire Fusiliers. While the Fusiliers were being rowed ashore, it became clear that the barbed wire entanglements had not been cut by the bombardment, and then a hail of bullets swept across them from hidden Turkish machine-guns. Sailors were shot dead at their oars. The relentless fire continued as the Fusiliers hurled themselves ashore and cut their way through. Although most of the men were killed or wounded, the beach was taken.

Keneally was one of six men elected by the regiment for the VC, the others being Cuthbert Bromley, John Grimshaw, Alfred Richards, Frank Stubbs and Richard Willis. They are known as 'the six VCs before breakfast'.

He was killed in action at Gully Ravine, Gallipoli on 29 June 1915.

Able Seaman WILLIAM WILLIAMS
GALLIPOLI, Turkey 25 April 1915
He was 34 years old and serving in the Royal Navy aboard the SS *River Clyde* when with three other men (George Drewry, Wilfred Malleson and George Samson) he assisted Edward Unwin in trying to secure the lighters forming the bridge to V beach. He held on to a rope for over an hour, standing in chest-deep water, under continuous fire. He was eventually mortally wounded by a shell, as Unwin tried to rescue him. Unwin described him as 'the bravest sailor he had ever met'. All five men were awarded the VC.

Seaman GEORGE SAMSON
GALLIPOLI, Turkey 25 April 1915
He was 26 years old and serving in the Royal Navy Reserve aboard the SS *River Clyde* when with three other men (George Drewry, Wilfred Malleson and William Williams) he assisted Edward Unwin in trying to secure the lighters forming the bridge to V beach. Under heavy machine-gun fire, he busied himself among the wounded and offered assistance to those repairing the bridge. Samson was hit over and over again. When he returned to England, he still had a dozen pieces of shrapnel in his body. All five men were awarded the VC.

Samson was one of 74 VC holders who formed the honour guard at the interment of the Unknown Soldier at Westminster Abbey on 11 November 1920. While on his way, in civilian dress, to a public reception in honour of his VC, he was presented with a white feather by a stranger – a sign of cowardice.

He died from pneumonia on 23 February 1923.

Lieutenant Colonel CHARLES DOUGHTY-WYLIE
SEDD-EL-BAHR, GALLIPOLI, Turkey
26 April 1915
He was 46 years old and serving in the Royal Welch Fusiliers (but attached to General Sir Ian Hamilton's Headquarters Staff owing to his knowledge of all things 'Turkish') when, following the landings at Cape Helles, during which the brigadier general and the brigade major had been killed, Lieutenant Colonel Doughty-Wylie and Captain Garth Walford organised and made an attack through and on

both flanks of the village, and on to the old fort at the top of the hill. The enemy's position was very strong and well defended but, mainly due to the initiative, skill and great gallantry of both officers, the attack was a complete success. Both men were killed at the moment of their victory. Walford was also awarded the VC.

Doughty-Wylie was buried close to the spot where he fell, the solitary British or Commonwealth war grave on the Gallipoli peninsula.

Captain GARTH WALFORD
SEDD-EL-BAHR, GALLIPOLI, Turkey
26 April 1915
He was 32 years old and serving in the Royal Regiment of Artillery when, following the landings at Cape Helles, during which the brigadier general and the brigade major had been killed, Lieutenant Colonel Doughty-Wylie and Captain Garth Walford organised and made an attack through and on both flanks of the village, and on to the old fort at the top of the hill. The enemy's position was very strong and well defended but, mainly due to the initiative, skill and great gallantry of both officers, the attack was a complete success. Both men were killed at the moment of their victory. Doughty-Wylie was also awarded the VC.

Second Lieutenant WILLIAM RHODES-MOORHOUSE (born MOORHOUSE)
COURTRAI, Belgium 26 April 1915
He was 27 years old and serving in 2 Squadron RFC. After dropping a 100lb bomb on the railway junction he had been ordered to attack, he immediately came under machine-gun and small arms fire from the ground and the belfry of Kortrijk Church. He was severely wounded by a bullet to the thigh and his plane was also badly damaged. Returning to the Allied lines, he again came under heavy fire from the ground and was wounded twice more. He was still able to fly his plane back to his airfield, and insisted on making his report before being taken to the aid post where he died the next day.

His last words were: 'It's strange dying, Blake old boy – unlike anything one has ever done before, like one's first solo flight.' His was the first RFC VC.

Jemadar MIR DAST
WIELTJE, Belgium 26 April 1915
He was 40 years old and serving in the 55th Coke's Rifles (Frontier Force), attached to the 57th Wilde's Rifles (Frontier Force), Indian Army when he led his platoon with great gallantry during an attack. Later when no British officers were left, he collected various groups of men together and kept them under his command until the order to retreat was given. He subsequently helped to carry eight wounded officers to safety while exposed to heavy fire.

He died on 19 January 1945.

Corporal WILLIAM COSGROVE
CAPE HELLES, GALLIPOLI, Turkey
26 April 1915
He was 26 years old and serving in the 1st Bn, Royal Munster Fusiliers when his company was trying to take the village behind the Sedd-el-Bahr fort overlooking the bay. Cosgrove single-handedly set about clearing a way through the Turkish wire entanglements. He managed to pull several posts out of the ground under heavy fire from the front and flanks. He contributed greatly to the successful clearing of the wire, enabling the attack to continue. He was affectionately known as the 'East Cork Giant'.

He died on 14 July 1936, having never fully recovered from his wounds.

Acting Corporal ISSY SMITH (born ISHROULCH SHMEILOWITZ)
ST JULIEN, Belgium 26 April 1915
He was 25 years old and serving in the 1st Bn, Manchester Regiment when on his own initiative and under heavy machine-gun fire he carried a wounded man some 250 yards to safety. He then brought in many other wounded men throughout the day, and attended to them with the greatest devotion to duty regardless of personal risk. The *Daily*

Mail correspondent Sergeant Rooke said of him: 'He behaved with wonderful coolness and presence of mind the whole time, and no man deserved a Victoria Cross more thoroughly than he did.'

Smith was one of 74 VC holders who formed the honour guard at the interment of the Unknown Soldier at Westminster Abbey on 11 November 1920. He died from coronary thrombosis on 10 September 1940.

Lieutenant Commander EDWARD BOYLE
DARDANELLES, Turkey
27 April–18 May 1915
He was 32 years old and serving in the Royal Navy aboard HM Submarine *E14*. In the Dardanelles he sank a 700-ton Turkish gunboat and then, avoiding minefields, sunken ships and enemy patrols, entered the Sea of Marmara. This was the first submarine patrol of the Sea of Marmara. He sank a transport, a 200-ton gun boat and a 5,000-ton liner carrying 6,000 troops. For weeks he disrupted Turkish troop movements and went undetected in an area only 75 miles long by 50 miles wide.

He died on 16 December 1967, after being hit by a lorry.

Lance Corporal WALTER PARKER
GABA TEPE, GALLIPOLI, Turkey
30 April/1 May 1915
He was 33 years old and serving in the Royal Marine Light Infantry when he volunteered to go to the assistance of a party of men in an isolated trench, even though several men had already been killed attempting to reach them. He joined a group of men and they crossed 400 yards of open ground under fire, carrying vital supplies. Parker was the only man to make it across, the rest of his party being killed or wounded. He tended to the wounded despite being wounded twice himself. When the trench was evacuated, he was wounded again.

He died from 'brain fever' on 28 November 1931, having never fully recovered from his wounds.

Private EDWARD WARNER
HILL 60, ZWARTELEEN, Belgium
1 May 1915
He was 31 years old and serving in the 1st Bn, Bedfordshire Regiment when a gas attack forced the evacuation of a trench. Acting alone, he re-entered the trench in order to prevent the enemy from taking possession of it. Reinforcements were sent to him, but could not reach him due to the gas. He then left the trench and brought up more men, by which time he was completely exhausted. The trench defences held due to his actions, but he died the next day from gas poisoning.

Private JOHN LYNN
YPRES, Belgium 2 May 1915
He was 28 years old and serving in the 2nd Bn, Lancashire Fusiliers. During a German attack on 'Suicide Corner', a cloud of gas was seen rolling forward from the enemy lines. Lynn rushed to his machine-gun without fixing his gas mask, and began firing into the advancing Germans behind the gas cloud. To get a better field of fire he moved his machine-gun on to the parapet. Once he had single-handedly stopped the enemy attack, he collapsed, gasping for breath, his face turning black. His last words were, 'This is the last carry, Flash,' uttered to a friend as he died.

Corporal JOHN RIPLEY
RUE DU BOIS, France 9 May 1915
He was 47 years old and serving in the 1st Bn, Black Watch (Royal Highlanders). Leading his men in an assault, he was the first man from his battalion to reach the enemy's parapet. He directed the men to the gaps in the wire and led them through a breach to the second line of trenches. With seven or eight others, he held this position until all his men had been killed or wounded, and he was badly wounded in the head.

He died from a spinal injury on 14 August 1933, after falling from a ladder.

Corporal JAMES UPTON
ROUGES BANCS, France 9 May 1915
He was 27 years old and serving in the 1st Bn,

Sherwood Foresters (Nottinghamshire and Derbyshire Regiment) when he crawled out to a man lying in the open. He bandaged the man's broken leg with a flag and carried him in. He then returned to help another wounded man, but this one was too heavy to carry so he put him on his groundsheet and dragged him back. Even when a shell exploded near him while carrying a man, he continued his work, bringing another ten wounded men back to the trench. When not actually carrying in wounded men he was engaged in dressing the serious cases out in the open.

He died on 10 August 1949.

Acting Corporal CHARLES SHARPE
ROUGES BANCS, France 9 May 1915
He was 26 years old and serving in the 2nd Bn, Lincolnshire Regiment when he was in charge of a blocking party sent forward to take a part of the German trench. He was the first man to reach the enemy's position, and began using bombs to great effect, but by the time he had cleared the Germans from 50 yards of trench, every member of his party had became casualties. Sharpe was then joined by four other men, with whom he successfully captured a further 150 yards of enemy trench.

He died from cerebral thrombosis on 17 February 1963.

Lance Corporal DAVID FINLAY
RUE DU BOIS, France 9 May 1915
He was 22 years old and serving in the 2nd Bn, Black Watch (Royal Highlanders) when he led a twelve-man bombing party, until ten of them had fallen. He then ordered the remaining two back, while he went to the assistance of a wounded man, carrying him back under heavy fire for 100 yards, regardless of his own safety.

He was killed in action at Kama on 21 January 1916.

Lance Sergeant DOUGLAS BELCHER
WIELTJE-ST JULIEN ROAD, Belgium 13 May 1915
He was 25 years old and serving in the 1/5th (City of London) Bn, London Regiment. Placed in charge of an advanced breastwork during a German bombardment, he decided to stay and defend the position with just a handful of men, even though he could see the troops near him had withdrawn. Throughout the day he fired at the enemy, who were 150–200 yards away, whenever he saw them massing for an attack. His bold stand prevented the enemy from breaking through. He was the first Territorial from the ranks to be awarded the VC.

He died on 3 June 1953.

Company Sergeant Major FREDERICK BARTER
FESTUBERT, France 16 May 1915
He was 24 years old and serving in the 1st Bn, Royal Welch Fusiliers. While in the first line of German trenches, he called for volunteers to extend the line. Just eight men responded. They attacked the German position with bombs, capturing two officers and over a hundred men. Later they cut eleven of the enemy's mine leads, enabling another battalion to advance.

He died on 15 May 1952.

Lance Corporal JOSEPH TOMBS
RUE DU BOIS, France 16 May 1915
He was 26 years old and serving in the 1st Bn, King's (Liverpool Regiment) when on his own initiative he crawled out repeatedly under very heavy machine-gun and shell fire to bring in four wounded men, who were lying 100 yards from our trenches. Tombs dragged back one man by means of a rifle sling placed around his neck and the wounded man's body.

He died on 28 June 1966. His citation incorrectly states his VC action took place in June.

Lieutenant JOHN SMYTH (sometimes spelt SMYTHE)
RICHEBOURG L'AOUVE, France 18 May 1915
He was 21 years old and serving in the 15th Ludhiana Sikhs, Indian Army. After three failed attempts to advance in support of two companies holding a captured German trench, he took a volunteer party of ten men with two boxes of bombs. They worked their way forward 300 yards from the British lines, and crossed a stream through most heavy machine-

gun and rifle fire. Only Smyth and two of his party reached the trench.

He was vice-president of the VC and GC Association, and author of *The Story of the Victoria Cross*. He was also one of the very few VC holders who became MPs.

Smyth died on 26 April 1983.

Lance Corporal ALBERT JACKA
COURTNEY'S POST, GALLIPOLI, Turkey 19/20 May 1915

He was 22 years old and serving in the 14th (Victoria) Bn, AIF when Jacka and three others moved to outflank a Turkish position. He was the only one to make it (the rest were wounded and pinned down); charging the position over open ground and jumping into the Turkish-held trench behind the Turks, he shot five and bayoneted another two. He took up a position and held the trench alone for the rest of the night. When his platoon commander Lieutenant Crabbe found him, Jacka told him: 'I got the beggars, Sir.'

By 1916 he had been promoted to second lieutenant and was at the Somme on the Western Front. On the morning of 7 August 1916, following a night of shelling, it became apparent to Jacka that his platoon had been bypassed and was now behind enemy lines. Upon emerging from the dug-out, he found they were in the middle of the second line of a successful German assault. A nearby group of Germans were escorting 42 prisoners from the 48th Battalion to the rear. Jacka made the cold-blooded decision to launch his seven men in an attack on the 60 Germans in the vicinity. Two men were killed instantly and all the others were hit, but they charged on and attacked the enemy with rifle and bayonet. Jacka was wounded seven times. However, he kept getting up and fighting on. After emptying his revolver, he picked up a rifle and bayonet and accounted personally for at least twelve of the enemy. Two more of his men were killed before the engagement was over, but the captured men of the 48th Battalion turned on their captors, with the result that the Germans surrendered the ridge, which had been lost but was now retaken.

Jacka was awarded the Military Cross for this action. Many present at the time, as well as many historians since, have voiced the opinion that he deserved a Bar to his VC. He died from kidney failure on 17 January 1932, as a result of being gassed. His last words to his father were: 'I'm still fighting, dad.' He had eight VC holders as his pallbearers, and an estimated 50,000 people lined the route to the cemetery.

Lieutenant Commander MARTIN NASMITH (later DUNBAR-NASMITH)
DARDANELLES, Turkey 20 May–8 June 1915

He was 32 years old and serving in the Royal Navy aboard HM Submarine *E11* when he sank one large Turkish gunboat, two transports, one ammunition ship, three store ships and four other vessels in the Sea of Marmara. When he was safely past the most dangerous part of his homeward journey, he received information that a cargo of coal was heading towards Istanbul from the Black Sea. Realising that coal was essential for the morale of the besieged city, Nasmith turned back. As the coal-carrying ship came into sight of the docks, a welcoming committee of municipal officials soon formed, along with a happy crowd. Water, electricity and rail transport had all suffered from the lack of coal. But hardly had the ship berthed than it blew up before the eyes of the astounded crowd. Nasmith successfully slipped out again.

He died on 29 June 1965.

Private WILLIAM MARINER (aka WILLIAM WIGNALL)
CAMBRIN, France 22 May 1915

He was 32 years old and serving in the 2nd Bn, King's Royal Rifle Corps when he crept up to a German gun emplacement and threw a bomb in under the roof. He heard the enemy running away and later, when they returned, he threw another bomb into the position. He then had to lie still while the Germans opened fire. After fifteen minutes he was able to return to his own lines. He had been out for 1½ hours.

He was killed in action at Loos, the Somme, on 1 July 1916.

Lance Corporal LEONARD KEYWORTH
GIVENCHY, France 25/26 May 1915
He was 21 years old and serving in the 24th (County of London) Bn, London Regiment (the Queen's) when, after a successful assault on the German positions, a bombing party was launched during which 58 out of 75 men became casualties. For two hours Keyworth stood exposed to the enemy, who were only a few yards away, and threw around 150 bombs.

He died on 10 October 1915, as a result of wounds received in action at Noux-les-Mines.

Second Lieutenant GEORGE MOOR
KRITHIA, GALLIPOLI, Turkey
5 June 1915
He was 18 years old and serving in the 2nd Bn, Hampshire Regiment when a detachment of the battalion, which had lost all its officers, was rapidly retiring before a heavy Turkish attack. Moor, realising the threat to the rest of the line, took the decision to shoot the four men at the front of the retreat. His action stopped the rout, and he was able to lead the battalion forward again. As a result the lost trench was retaken. This action may actually have taken place on 6 June.

He died from influenza on 3 November 1918.

Flight Sub Lieutenant REGINALD WARNEFORD
GHENT, Belgium 7 June 1915
He was 23 years old and serving in 1 Squadron, Royal Naval Air Service when he attacked the German airship *LZ37*. He chased the airship from the coast and despite its defensive machine-gun fire, succeeded in dropping several bombs on to it, the last one setting the airship on fire. The explosion overturned his plane and the engine stopped. Having no alternative, he landed in enemy territory, but after a short time spent on repairs he was able to return to his base.

He died on 17 June 1915, as a result of a flying accident.

Lance Corporal WILLIAM ANGUS
GIVENCHY, France 12 June 1915
He was 27 years old and serving in the 8th Bn, Highland Light Infantry when he volunteered to bring in Lieutenant Martin, who was lying wounded near the German lines. When warned that he was going to certain death, he replied, 'It does not matter much, sir, whether sooner or later.' He crawled to the wounded man and brought him back under heavy bomb and rifle fire, and received 40 wounds. Angus was also a professional football player for Celtic FC, although he never made a first team appearance.

He died on 14 June 1959.

Lieutenant FREDERICK CAMPBELL
GIVENCHY, France 15 June 1915
He was 48 years old and serving in the 1st Bn (WO), CEF when he led two machine-gun detachments forward and in the face of heavy fire reached the German front line with one gun, which he kept in action after nearly all of his men had been killed or wounded. When the enemy counter-attacked he moved the gun still further forward and fired 1,000 rounds, repulsing the attack. Sadly he was mortally wounded and died four days later.

Second Lieutenant WALTER JAMES
GALLIPOLI, Turkey
28 June and 3 July 1915
He was 26 years old and serving in the 4th Bn, Worcestershire Regiment. When the advance of his regiment had been checked, he went to a neighbouring unit and gathered together a body of men and led them forward under heavy fire. He then returned, organised a second party and again led them forward, putting fresh life into the attack. On 3 July he headed a party of bomb-throwers up a Turkish communication trench and when all of his party were either killed or wounded, remained alone under murderous fire and kept the enemy back until the trench could be secured.

James was one of 74 VC holders who formed the honour guard at the interment of the Unknown Soldier at Westminster Abbey on 11 November 1920.

He died from uraemia on 15 August 1958.

Captain GERALD O'SULLIVAN
KRITHIA, GALLIPOLI, Turkey
1/2 July 1915
He was 26 years old and serving in the 1st Bn, Royal Inniskilling Fusiliers when he volunteered to lead a bombing party to recapture a vital trench. He advanced in the open under heavy fire and in order to throw his bombs with greater effect, he got up on to the parapet, completely exposed to enemy fire. He was finally wounded but his example led his men on to capture the trench.

He was killed in action at Hill 70, Suvla, Gallipoli on 21 August 1915.

Sergeant JAMES SOMERS
GALLIPOLI, Turkey 1/2 July 1915
He was 31 years old and serving in the 1st Bn, Royal Inniskilling Fusiliers. Left alone in a sap after his comrades had retired, Somers remained until a party brought up some bombs. He then climbed over the Turkish trench and bombed them to great effect. Later, he advanced into the open under heavy fire and held back the enemy by throwing bombs into their flank until a barricade had been established. During this time he frequently ran to and from our trenches to get more bombs.

He died from the effects of gas poisoning on 7 May 1918.

Mercantile Marine Master FREDERICK PARSLOW
ATLANTIC 4 July 1915
He was 59 years old and serving in the Royal Naval Reserve when his unarmed ship, HM Horse Transport *Anglo-Californian* came under attack from a U-boat. For 90 minutes Parslow constantly altered course, keeping the submarine astern of him, and was on the point of abandoning ship when he received orders to hold on as long as possible. He did so, and remained on the bridge without protection until it was wrecked and he was killed.

Captain LANOE (sometimes misspelt LANCE) HAWKER
PASSCHENDAELE, Belgium
25 July 1915

He was 25 years old and serving in 6 Squadron RFC. While on patrol he engaged three enemy aircraft in combat. The first he sent spinning down, the second was damaged and driven to the ground, and the third went down in flames. This was the first time anyone had shot down three aircraft in one mission.

He was killed in action at Bapaume on 23 November 1916, by Manfred von Richthofen, the 'Red Baron'. Hawker's cousin was Sub-Lieutenant Arthur Bagot GC.

Second Lieutenant SIDNEY WOODROFFE
HOOGE, Belgium 30 July 1915
He was 19 years old and serving in the 8th Bn, Rifle Brigade (Prince Consort's Own). When the enemy broke through the centre of our front trenches, Woodroffe's position was heavily attacked with bombs from the flank and subsequently from the rear, but he managed to defend his post until all his bombs were used. He then skilfully withdrew his remaining men and immediately led them forward in a counter-attack under intense rifle and machine-gun fire. He was killed in the act of cutting the wire obstacles while in the open.

Captain JOHN LIDDELL
OSTEND, Belgium 31 July 1915
He was 26 years old and serving in the 3rd Bn, Argyll and Sutherland Highlanders and later the Royal Flying Corps when his aircraft was attacked from above and he was badly wounded in the right thigh. Despite becoming unconscious and being fired on again, he recovered partial control of his plane and brought it in to land behind Allied lines, thus saving his observer's life. He was taken to hospital, where his right leg was amputated.

He died from septic poisoning on 31 August 1915.

Second Lieutenant GEORGE BOYD-ROCHFORT
CAMBRIN, France 3 August 1915
He was 35 years old and serving in the 1st Bn, Scots Guards (Special Reserve) when a German trench-mortar bomb landed on the parapet of the communication trench in which

he was standing, close to a small working party of his battalion. Instead of taking cover, he shouted to his men to look out, rushed at the bomb and threw it over the parapet where it at once exploded. His presence of mind and courage saved the lives of many of the working party.

He died on 7 August 1940, following an operation.

Corporal CYRIL BASSETT
GALLIPOLI, Turkey 7 August 1915
He was 23 years old and serving in the New Zealand Divisional Signal Company, NZEF. After his brigade had established itself on Chunuk Bair Ridge, he succeeded in laying a telephone line from the old position to the new one on the ridge in full daylight and under continuous fire. He did further gallant work repairing telephone lines by day and night. He said of his action: 'I was so short that the bullets just passed over me.'

He died on 9 January 1983.

Private LEONARD KEYSOR (sometimes spelt KEYZOR)
'LONE PINE', GALLIPOLI, Turkey 7/8 August 1915
He was 29 years old and serving in the 1st Bn (New South Wales) Bn, AIF when his trench was being heavily bombed by the enemy. He picked up two live bombs and threw them back at the enemy at great personal risk. He continued to throw bombs until wounded. On 8 August he successfully bombed the Turks out of a trench they had captured, again being wounded. He refused to go to the aid post and volunteered to throw bombs for another company which had lost all its bomb-throwers. He continued bombing until the situation was relieved.

He died from cancer on 12 October 1951.

Lieutenant WILLIAM FORSHAW
'THE VINEYARD', GALLIPOLI, Turkey 7–9 August 1915
He was 25 years old and serving in the 1/9th Bn, Manchester Regiment when he held the north-west corner of the Vineyard against sustained attacks by the Turks. While directing operations, he also threw bombs continuously for over 40 hours. When his detachment was relieved, he volunteered to continue to direct the defence. Later, when the enemy captured part of the trench, he shot three of them and recaptured it. It was due to his fine example and courage that this important position was held. He became known as the 'Cigarette VC' because he threw bombs made from jam tins ignited with cigarettes.

He died from a heart attack on 26 May 1943.

Second Lieutenant WILLIAM SYMONS (later PENN-SYMONS)
'LONE PINE', GALLIPOLI, Turkey 8/9 August 1915
He was 26 years old and serving in the 7th (Victoria) Bn, AIF. While his unit was defending a section of newly captured trench, the Turks made an attack on an isolated sap in the morning, resulting in six officers becoming casualties and part of the sap being lost. Symons retook it, shooting two Turks with his revolver, and built up a barricade. When the enemy set fire to it, he extinguished the flames and rebuilt it. His coolness and determination compelled the enemy to abandon their attack.

He died from a brain tumour on 24 June 1948.

Captain PERCY HANSEN
HILL 70, YILGHIN BUMU, GALLIPOLI, Turkey 9 August 1915
He was 24 years old and serving in the 6th Bn, Lincolnshire Regiment when his battalion was forced to retire in the face of intense heat from the burning scrub, which had been set on fire by shell bursts. He called for volunteers and with three or four men he dashed forward 300–400 yards while under heavy fire from the Turks and rescued six wounded men who would otherwise have burnt to death.

Hansen also served in the Second World War.

He died from pneumonia on 12 February 1951.

Captain ALFRED SHOUT
'LONE PINE', GALLIPOLI, Turkey
9 August 1915

He was 34 years old and serving in the 1st (New South Wales) Bn, AIF when he led a small party down trenches strongly held by the Turks and personally threw four bombs among them, killing eight and routing the remainder. In the afternoon of the same day, from the position gained in the morning, he captured a further length of trench under similar conditions and continued personally to bomb the enemy at close range, laughing and joking all the time. Then a bomb blew up in his right hand, shattering it and destroying his left eye. Still encouraging his men by shouting, 'Good old First Brigade, well done', he was carried out of action. He remained conscious, talking cheerfully and drinking tea.

Shout had also served in the Second Boer War.

He died two days later as a result of his wounds.

Lieutenant FREDERICK TUBB
'LONE PINE', GALLIPOLI, Turkey
9 August 1915

He was 33 years old and serving in the 7th (Victoria) Bn, AIF. While he was holding a newly captured trench with Corporal Alexander Burton and Corporal William Dunstan, the enemy counter-attacked along a sap and blew in a sandbag barricade, leaving only a foot of it still standing. Tubb, Burton and Dunstan repulsed this and two more enemy attacks and rebuilt the barricade on each occasion. Although Tubb was wounded in the head and arm, he held his ground. Burton was killed by a hail of bullets while helping to rebuild the barricade. The position was held under very heavy fire. All three men were awarded the VC.

Tubb was killed in action near Polygon Wood on 20 September 1917.

Corporal ALEXANDER BURTON
'LONE PINE', GALLIPOLI, Turkey
9 August 1915

He was 20 years old and serving in the 7th (Victoria) Bn, AIF. While he was holding a newly captured trench with Lieutenant Frederick Tubb and Corporal William Dunstan, the enemy counter-attacked along a sap and blew in a sandbag barricade, leaving only a foot of it still standing. Tubb, Burton and Dunstan repulsed this and two more enemy attacks and rebuilt the barricade on each occasion. Although Tubb was wounded in the head and arm, he held his ground. Burton was killed by a hail of bullets while helping to rebuild the barricade. The position was held under very heavy fire. All three men were awarded the VC.

Corporal WILLIAM DUNSTAN
'LONE PINE', GALLIPOLI, Turkey
9 August 1915

He was 22 years old and serving in the 7th (Victoria) Bn, AIF. While he was holding a newly captured trench with Lieutenant Frederick Tubb and Corporal Alexander Burton, the enemy counter-attacked along a sap and blew in a sandbag barricade, leaving only a foot of it still standing. Tubb, Burton and Dunstan repulsed this and two more enemy attacks and rebuilt the barricade on each occasion. Although Tubb was wounded in the head and arm, he held his ground. Burton was killed by a hail of bullets while helping to rebuild the barricade. The position was held under very heavy fire. All three men were awarded the VC.

Dunstan died from coronary vascular disease on 2 March 1957.

Private JOHN HAMILTON
'LONE PINE', GALLIPOLI, Turkey
9 August 1915

He was 19 years old and serving in the 3rd (New South Wales) Bn, AIF when during a heavy bomb attack by the enemy on a newly captured position, Hamilton, with utter disregard for his personal safety, climbed on to the parapet and exposed himself to heavy fire to get a better firing position against the enemy's bomb-throwers. His daring example had an immediate effect. The defenders were encouraged and the enemy were driven off with heavy losses.

He died from a cerebro-vascular disease on 27 February 1961.

Private DAVID LAUDER
CAPE HELLES, GALLIPOLI, Turkey
13 August 1915

He was 21 years old and serving in the 1/4th Bn, Royal Scots Fusiliers when he threw a bomb which failed to clear the parapet and landed among his comrades. Having no time to smother the bomb, he put his foot on it to minimise the explosion. His foot was blown off but the rest of his party were unhurt.

He died on 4 June 1972.

Private FREDERICK POTTS
HILL 70, GALLIPOLI, Turkey
21 August 1915

He was 22 years old and serving in the 1/1st Bn, Berkshire Yeomanry when he was wounded in the thigh during an attack. Although he could have retired, he remained for over 48 hours in the open with a severely wounded comrade, who was unable to move. Finally he fixed his shovel to the man's equipment and used it as a sledge, dragging him back 600 yards to safety, being under fire the whole time.

Potts was one of 74 VC holders who formed the honour guard at the interment of the Unknown Soldier at Westminster Abbey on 11 November 1920.

He died on 3 November 1943.

Second Lieutenant HUGO 'JIM' THROSSELL
HILL 60, KAIAKIJ AGHALA, GALLIPOLI, Turkey 29/30 August 1915

He was 31 years old and serving in the 10th Light Horse Regiment, AIF when his men were ordered to take part in an attack on Turkish positions at the Nek, as part of the fourth wave. The first and second waves were cut down instantly by machine-gun fire. At this point a major of the 10th Light Horse pleaded with HQ to halt the attack. The plea was ignored because someone reported seeing a flag of the 8th Horse within yards of the Turkish lines. The third wave charged but was also cut down. The Commanding Officer of the 10th echoed the major's plea, but he was ignored. The fourth wave went over the top and was shot to pieces. Throssell and his men on the left flank were lucky to find a hollow in which they could take cover. No part of the Turkish line was reached in the attack. These events are depicted in the 1981 film *Gallipoli*.

Almost immediately Throssell and his men were sent to Hill 60, an important tactical feature which the Allies wanted to capture. During the attack he led the second wave, which took part of the enemy trench. He, with the few remaining men, held the trench in the face of a fierce counter-attack, during which Throssell was shot through the right shoulder, the bullet exiting through the back of his neck. A piece of shrapnel laid his left shoulder open to the bone, but he was so intent on resisting the attack he barely felt the wounds. He recalled: 'When the first Turks got within 10 yards we cheered and shouted and started firing as fast as we could. There was no thought of cover, we blazed away until the rifles grew red-hot and the chocks jammed and then picked up the rifles the killed men had left. When we were wondering how long we could stand against such numbers the Turks turned and fled.' The Turks mounted two further attacks, the final one from all sides as day was breaking, but Throssell and his men stood firm and repulsed them both. His wounds were so bad that he was twice ordered from the firing line, but refused to go. On several occasions he picked up Turkish bombs which landed in the trench and threw them back. All the time he kept up the morale of his men.

In the years following the war he became an outspoken opponent of war, and his stance on the futility of conflict outraged many people, especially as he was a national hero. His publicly-held political opinions damaged his job prospects, and he fell into deep financial debt.

He shot himself on 13 November 1933, but was still buried with full military honours.

Temporary Lieutenant WILBUR (born WILLIAM THOMAS) DARTNELL
MAKTAU, Kenya 3 September 1915

He was 30 years old and serving in the 25th

(Frontiersmen) Bn, Royal Fusiliers. During a mounted infantry engagement, the enemy were so close that it was impossible to get the more severely wounded men away to safety. While he was being carried away wounded in the leg, Dartnell, knowing full well that the enemy's black soldiers murdered the wounded, insisted on being left behind, so that other wounded men could be saved. He gave his life in a gallant attempt to save others.

Private CHARLES HULL
HAFIZ KOR, India 5 September 1915

He was 25 years old and serving in the 21st Lancers (Empress of India's) when he rescued Captain Learoyd, whose horse had been shot from under him. Hull took him on to his own horse and they both rode away to safety, all the while under fire from the enemy, who were only a few yards away.

Hull was one of 74 VC holders who formed the honour guard at the interment of the Unknown Soldier at Westminster Abbey on 11 November 1920.

He died on 13 February 1953.

Captain ARTHUR KILBY
CUINCHY, France 25 September 1915

He was 30 years old and serving in the 2nd Bn, South Staffordshire Regiment when he was, at his own request, selected to attack a strong enemy redoubt with his company. Despite being wounded at the outset, he led his men along a narrow path up to the enemy wire under very heavy fire. His foot was blown off, but he continued to use his rifle and cheer his men on. His body was not found until 1929.

Captain ANKETELL READ
HULLUCH, France 25 September 1915

He was 30 years old and serving in the 1st Bn, Northamptonshire Regiment when, although gassed, he went out several times in order to rally parties of different units which were disorganised and retiring. He led them back into the trenches and, regardless of the danger to himself, moved about under fire, encouraging them. He was mortally wounded while carrying out this work. He had previously shown great courage when he carried a dying officer out of action under heavy fire.

Lieutenant GEORGE MALING
FAUQUISSART, France
25 September 1915

He was 26 years old and serving in the Royal Army Medical Corps, attached to the 12th Bn, Rifle Brigade when he worked with untiring energy for 24 hours, collecting and treating 300 wounded men in the open under heavy fire. He was temporarily stunned by the bursting of a shell which wounded his only assistant and killed several of his patients. A second shell covered him in debris, but he continued to do his work single-handed.

He died on 9 July 1929.

Temporary Second Lieutenant FREDERICK JOHNSON
HILL 70, LOOS, France
25 September 1915

He was 25 years old and serving in the 73rd Field Company, Royal Corps of Engineers. He led one section of his company in several charges on a German redoubt, and although wounded in the leg, he stuck to his duty throughout the attack. At a very critical moment, under heavy fire, he repeatedly rallied his men. By his splendid example and cool courage he was largely instrumental in saving the situation and in establishing firmly his part of the captured position. He remained at his post until relieved.

He was killed in action near Cambrai on 26 November 1917.

Sergeant HARRY WELLS
LE RUTOIRE, LOOS, France
25 September 1915

He was 27 years old and serving in the 2nd Bn, Royal Sussex Regiment. When his platoon officer was killed, he took command and led the men forward to within 15 yards of the German wire. Nearly half the men were killed or wounded, but he rallied the survivors and led them on. Finally, when only a few were left, he stood up and urged them forward once again, and while doing so he was killed.

The Complete Victoria Cross

Private HENRY KENNY
LOOS, France 25 September 1915
He was 27 years old and serving in the 1st Bn, Loyal North Lancashire Regiment when he went out six times under heavy fire and each time carried back a wounded man from open ground to safety. He was himself wounded in the neck as he brought the last man in.

Kenny was one of 74 VC holders who formed the honour guard at the interment of the Unknown Soldier at Westminster Abbey on 11 November 1920.

He died on 6 May 1979.

Private GEORGE PEACHMENT
LOOS, France 25 September 1915
He was 18 years old and serving in the 2nd Bn, King's Royal Rifle Corps when he saw his company commander lying wounded and crawled to help him, despite intense enemy fire. Although there was a shell-hole close by, he never thought of saving himself. He knelt in the open and tried to help the wounded officer, but while doing so was first injured by a bomb and a minute later mortally wounded by a bullet.

Rifleman KULBIR THAPA
FAUQUISSART, France
25 September 1915
He was 26 years old and serving in the 2nd Bn, 3rd Gurkha Rifles, Indian Army. Despite being wounded, when he came across a badly wounded man of the Leicestershire Regiment behind the front-line German trench, he stayed with him all day and night, although urged by the soldier to save himself. The next morning he brought him through the German wire and placed him in a shell-hole. Then he returned to the German wire and brought back two wounded Gurkhas to the British lines. He then went back and carried the first wounded man in, under fire most of the way.

He died on 3 October 1956.

Piper DANIEL LAIDLAW
HILL 70, LOOS, France
25 September 1915
He was 40 years old and serving in the 7th Bn, King's Own Scottish Borderers. Prior to an assault, and during the worst of the bombardment, he could see that his company was shaken by the effects of gas. With complete disregard for danger, he mounted the parapet and marched up and down, playing his company out of the trench. The effect of his splendid example was immediate and the men dashed to the assault. Even after he was wounded, Laidlaw continued playing until the position was taken.

He was one of 74 VC holders who formed the honour guard at the interment of the Unknown Soldier at Westminster Abbey on 11 November 1920.

He died on 2 June 1950.

Private ARTHUR VICKERS
HULLOCH, France 25 September 1915
He was 33 years old and serving in the 2nd Bn, Royal Warwickshire Regiment. During an attack by his battalion on the first line of German trenches, he went forward on his own initiative ahead of his company, under very heavy shell, rifle and machine-gun fire, to cut the wire that was holding up the greater part of the battalion. Although it was broad daylight at the time, he carried out his work standing up and his gallant action contributed largely to the success of the assault.

He was one of 74 VC holders who formed the honour guard at the interment of the Unknown Soldier at Westminster Abbey on 11 November 1920.

He died on 27 July 1944.

Temporary Lieutenant Colonel ANGUS DOUGLAS-HAMILTON
HILL 70, LOOS, France
25/26 September 1915
He was 52 years old and commanding the 6th Bn, Queen's Own Cameron Highlanders when the battalions on both his flanks were forced to retire. He rallied his own battalion and led his men forward four times, the last time with just 50 men remaining. He did this in a most gallant manner, but was killed at their head. It was due to his bravery and splendid leadership that the line at this point held, checking the enemy's advance.

Temporary Second Lieutenant RUPERT HALLOWES

HOOGE, Belgium 25–30 September 1915

He was 34 years old and serving in the 4th Bn, Middlesex Regiment (Duke of Cambridge's Own) when he set a magnificent example to his men during four days of heavy and prolonged bombardments. More than once he climbed on to the parapet, utterly regardless of the danger to himself, in order to put fresh heart into his men. He made daring reconnaissances of the German positions, and when the supply of bombs was running short he went back under very heavy fire to bring up fresh supplies. Even when mortally wounded by a bomb which was accidentally dropped into the trench, Hallowes continued to cheer those round him to inspire them with fresh courage.

Sergeant ARTHUR SAUNDERS

LOOS, France 26 September 1915

He was 36 years old and serving in the 9th (Service) Bn, Suffolk Regiment when he took charge of two machine-guns and a few men. Although severely wounded in the thigh, Saunders closely followed the last four charges made by another battalion, giving them all possible supporting fire. Later, when the remains of that battalion were forced to retire, he stuck to one of his guns and in spite of his wound continued to give clear orders and by continuous firing did his best to cover the retreat. It is often said that his leg was amputated; in fact, it was saved, but he was left with one leg shorter than the other.

Saunders served in the Home Guard during the Second World War. He died on 30 July 1947, having never fully recovered from wounds received during his VC action.

Private ROBERT DUNSIRE

HILL 70, LOOS, France
26 September 1915

He was 23 years old and serving in the 13th Bn, Royal Scots (Lothian Regiment) when he went out under very heavy fire and rescued a wounded man from between the lines. Hearing another man calling for help, he then crawled out again and with complete dis-

regard for the enemy went very close to the German lines to bring him to safety.

He was killed in action at Mazingarbe on 30 January 1916.

Corporal ALFRED BURT

CUINCHY, France 27 September 1915

He was 20 years old and serving in the 1st Bn, Hertfordshire Regiment. When his company was getting ready to attack, a large Minenwerfer bomb fell into the trench. Knowing well the destructive power of this type of bomb, Burt, who could have taken cover, went forward, put his foot on the fuse, pulled it out of the bomb and threw it over the parapet, so saving the lives of many of his comrades.

Burt was one of 74 VC holders who formed the honour guard at the interment of the Unknown Soldier at Westminster Abbey on 11 November 1920.

He died on 9 June 1962, following a serious illness.

Corporal JAMES POLLOCK

'LITTLE WILLIE TRENCH', HOHEN-ZOLLERN REDOUBT, France
27 September 1915

He was 25 years old and serving in the 5th Bn, Queen's Own Cameron Highlanders. When an enemy bombing party was advancing along the trench towards his position, he got out of the trench alone and walked along the top under heavy fire. He then began bombing the enemy from above, forcing them to retreat. At length he was wounded, but not before he had held up the German advance for an hour.

His second cousin Corporal James Dawson was awarded the VC for an action in the same trench just over two weeks later.

Pollock died on 10 May 1958.

Lieutenant Commander EDGAR COOKSON

KUT-EL-AMARA, Mesopotamia
28 September 1915

He was 31 years old and serving in the Royal Navy when his ship, HMS *Comet,* was ordered to destroy an obstruction that had been placed across the river by the Turks. As they approached, very heavy machine-gun and rifle fire was opened on them. An attempt to sink the centre dhow by gunfire having failed, Cookson ran the *Comet* alongside the dhow and jumped on to it with an axe. He tried to cut the lines connecting it to the other dhows forming the obstruction, but was shot several times and was dragged back on to the *Comet*, where he died. His last words were: 'I'm done. It's a failure. Get back at full speed.'

Second Lieutenant ALEXANDER TURNER
'FOSSE 8', VERMELLES, France
28 September 1915
He was 22 years old and serving in the 3rd Bn, Royal Berkshire Regiment, attached to the 1st Bn, when he volunteered to lead a bombing attack. He made his way down the communication trench practically alone, throwing bombs with such dash that he drove the Germans back about 150 yards without check. His action enabled the reserves to advance with very few losses and he subsequently covered the flank of his regiment as it retired, thus probably avoiding the loss of some hundreds of men.

He died on 1 October 1915 from wounds received during his VC action. His brother was Lieutenant Colonel Victor Turner VC, and he was also related to Brevet Lieutenant Colonel Redvers Buller VC.

Temporary Second Lieutenant ARTHUR FLEMING-SANDES
HOHENZOLLERN REDOUBT, France
29 September 1915
He was 21 years old and serving in the 2nd Bn, East Surrey Regiment. When some men from his company were beginning to retire, he collected together a few bombs and jumped up on to the parapet in full view of the Germans, and threw them. He was wounded almost at once, but struggled to his feet and continued to advance, throwing bombs, until he was wounded again. His action put new heart into his men and saved the situation.

He died from natural causes on 24 May 1961.

Private SAMUEL HARVEY
'BIG WILLIE TRENCH', HOHEN-ZOLLERN REDOUBT, France
29 September 1915
He was 34 years old and serving in the 1st Bn, York and Lancaster Regiment when he volunteered to bring up urgently needed bombs. The communication trench was full of wounded men and reinforcements, so he went back and forth under heavy fire across the open, bringing up 30 boxes of bombs before eventually being wounded in the head. It was mainly due to his actions that the enemy were driven back.

He died on 23 September 1960.

Lance Sergeant OLIVER BROOKS
HAISNES, LOOS, France 8 October 1915
He was 26 years old and serving in the 3rd Bn, Coldstream Guards when he gathered together a bombing party and led them forward in an attempt to recapture 200 yards of trench that had fallen to the enemy. His bravery in the midst of a hail of bullets ensured the complete success of the operation.

Brooks was one of 74 VC holders who formed the honour guard at the interment of the Unknown Soldier at Westminster Abbey on 11 November 1920.

He died on 25 October 1940, following a long illness.

Acting Sergeant JOHN RAYNES
FOSSE 7 DE BETHUNE, France
11 October 1915
He was 28 years old and serving in A Battery, 71 Brigade, RFA when he went to the assistance of a wounded sergeant. He bandaged his wounds and went back to his gun, but when the battery stopped firing he returned and carried the sergeant to a dug-out. When gas shells started falling, he put his own gas mask on the wounded man, and in consequence was badly gassed himself. Later he was buried under a house that had been shelled; although he was the first man rescued, he insisted on helping to dig out the others. Then, having had his wounds dressed, he reported for duty.

After the war he joined the Police and rose to the rank of sergeant.

He died on 12 November 1929, having never fully recovered from being gassed.

Corporal JAMES DAWSON
HOHENZOLLERN REDOUBT, France
13 October 1915
He was 23 years old and serving in the 187th Company, Corps of Royal Engineers when during a gas attack he walked up and down under heavy fire, clearing men out of gas-filled sections of trench. Finding three leaking cylinders, he rolled them away from the trench and fired on them, allowing the gas to escape.

His second cousin Corporal James Pollock was awarded the VC for an action in the same trench just over two weeks earlier.

Dawson died on 15 February 1967.

Temporary Captain CHARLES VICKERS
HOHENZOLLERN REDOUBT, France
14 October 1915
He was 21 years old and serving in the 1/7th (Robin Hood) Bn, Sherwood Foresters (Nottinghamshire and Derbyshire Regiment). On the day after his 21st birthday, with only two men left to hand him bombs, he held a barrier across a trench for some hours against heavy German bombing attacks. Regardless of the fact that his retreat would be cut off, Vickers ordered another barrier to be built behind him in order to secure the safety of the trench. Eventually he was severely wounded, but not before his courage and determination had enabled the second barrier to be completed.

He died on 16 March 1982.

Private HARRY CHRISTIAN
CUINCHY, France 18 October 1915
He was 23 years old and serving in the 2nd Bn, King's Own (Royal Lancaster) Regiment. He and several others were holding a crater which came under such a heavy bombardment he was forced to retire. When he found three men were missing, he went back alone and dug out all three of them, and then carried them back to safety one at a time. His action undoubtedly saved their lives. Later he placed himself in a position from where he could see the bombs coming, and directed his comrades where to seek cover.

He died on 2 September 1974.

Private THOMAS KENNY
LA HOUSSOIE, France
4 November 1915
He was 33 years old and serving in the 13th Bn, Durham Light Infantry. During a patrol in thick fog, his lieutenant was shot through both thighs. Kenny put the officer on his back and crawled for more than an hour, under fire, trying to find the British lines. The officer urged him to go on alone but he refused. At last he came to a familiar ditch, where he placed the lieutenant, and went for help. He returned with a rescue party and guided them to the wounded man, who was brought to safety.

He was killed in a mining accident on 29 November 1958.

Second Lieutenant GILBERT INSALL
near ACHIET, France 7 November 1915
He was 21 years old and serving in 11 Squadron, RFC. During a patrol in a Vickers FB5 Gunbus, he engaged an enemy machine, forcing it to make a rough landing in a field. Seeing the Germans scramble out and preparing to fire, Insall dived down to 100 feet and his gunner opened fire, whereupon the Germans fled. After dropping an incendiary bomb on the downed aircraft, he came under renewed attack, so he fired on the enemy trenches. The Vickers' petrol tank was hit, but he managed to make an emergency landing 500 feet inside the Allied lines. He and his gunner repaired the machine overnight, and then Insall flew back to base at dawn. He was shot down and taken prisoner a week later. In August 1917 he escaped from his prison camp at Strohen near Hanover and walked 150 miles, travelling by night, until he reached the safety of the Dutch border.

He was one of 74 VC holders who formed the honour guard at the interment of the Unknown Soldier at Westminster Abbey on 11 November 1920. After the war he stayed in the RAF and in 1925 spotted a strange formation of pits on the ground below him. He took a photograph, and expert analysis found he had discovered the Bronze Age site now known as Woodhenge, 2 miles from Stonehenge. In 1929 he discovered Arminghall Henge in a similar way.

He died from a heart attack on 17 February 1972.

Private JOHN CAFFREY
LA BRIQUE, France
16 November 1915
He was 24 years old and serving in the 2nd Bn, York and Lancaster Regiment when he went out with a corporal from the Royal Army Medical Corps to rescue a wounded man lying in the open. As they reached him, the corporal was shot in the head. Caffrey dressed his wound and carried him to safety, then went back for the other man, and carried him in also.

Caffrey was one of 74 VC holders who formed the honour guard at the interment of the Unknown Soldier at Westminster Abbey on 11 November 1920.

He died on 26 February 1953.

Squadron Commander RICHARD BELL-DAVIES
FERRIJIK JUNCTION, Bulgaria
19 November 1915
He was 29 years old and serving in 3 Squadron, RFC when a member of his squadron was shot down, the pilot making a safe landing. Seeing that Bulgarian troops were approaching, Bell-Davies landed nearby to pick up the stranded pilot just as the enemy came into rifle range. Then he took off under a hail of bullets.

He died on 26 February 1966.

Corporal SAMUEL MEEKOSHA (name changed to INGHAM in 1939)
YSER, France 19 November 1915
He was 22 years old and serving in the 1/6th Bn, West Yorkshire Regiment (Prince of Wales's Own) when his trench was hit by heavy artillery fire, killing or wounding the senior NCOs. He took command and sent a runner for help. He dug out the buried and wounded men in full view of the enemy, and even though more large shells were falling within 20 yards of him, he

worked on. His actions saved at least four lives.

Meekosha also served in the Second World War, under the name Ingham.

He died on 8 December 1950.

Corporal ALFRED DRAKE
LA BRIQUE, France 23 November 1915
He was 21 years old and serving in the 8th Bn, Rifle Brigade (Prince Consort's Own). While on patrol with an officer, they came under heavy fire, the officer being wounded. Drake stayed with him and bandaged his wounds. Some time later a rescue party found the officer lying unconscious but alive; beside him was Drake's bullet-riddled body.

Private WILLIAM YOUNG
FONQUEVILLERS, France
22 December 1915
He was 39 years old and serving in the 8th Bn, East Lancashire Regiment when he was told that one of the company's NCOs was lying wounded in front of the wire. Acting without orders and exposing himself to enemy fire, he climbed over the parapet and went to the rescue of his sergeant. He was hit twice, one bullet shattering his jaw and the other entering his chest. Undeterred, he went on and, with another man who came to assist, brought the wounded sergeant back to safety. Later Young walked back to the dressing station to have his wounds seen to.

He died on 27 August 1916, during an operation on his jaw.

Second Lieutenant ALFRED SMITH
HELLES, GALLIPOLI, Turkey
23 December 1915
He was 24 years old and serving in the 1/5th Bn, East Lancashire Regiment. He was about to throw a grenade when it slipped from his hand and fell to the bottom of the crowded trench. Smith shouted a warning and jumped clear. Realising that the others were not taking cover, he ran back and threw himself on top of the grenade. It exploded, killing him instantly, but his action saved many lives.

1916

Sepoy CHATTA (sometimes spelt CHATTAH) SINGH

RIVER WADI, Mesopotamia
13 January 1916
He was 29 years old and serving in the 9th Bn, Bhopal Infantry, Indian Army when he went out into the open to the assistance of his commanding officer, who was lying wounded. He dug cover for him with his entrenching tool, and remained with him under heavy fire until dark. Then he went back to get help and brought him to safety.

He died on 28 March 1961.

Captain JOHN SINTON

ORAH RUINS, Mesopotamia
21 January 1916
He was 31 years old and serving in the Indian Medical Service, Indian Army when he showed the most conspicuous bravery and devotion to duty. Although shot through both arms and the side, he refused to go to the hospital, and remained as long as daylight lasted, attending to his duties under very heavy fire. In three previous actions Sinton also displayed the utmost bravery.

Sinton re-enlisted in the IMS during the Second World War.

He died on 25 March 1956.

Lance Naik LALA

EL ORAH, Mesopotamia
21 January 1916
He was 33 years old and serving in the 41st Dogras, Indian Army when he dragged a wounded British officer to a temporary shelter and bandaged his wounds. Then, hearing the cries of his adjutant, who was also lying wounded only 100 yards from the enemy, he crawled to him; staying with him until nightfall, he used his own clothes to keep him warm. After dark he carried first one man then the other to safety.

He died from polio on 23 March 1927. His last words were, 'We fought true.'

Temporary Lieutenant ERIC McNAIR

HOOGE, Belgium 14 February 1916
He was 21 years old and serving in the 9th Bn, Royal Sussex Regiment when the enemy exploded a mine and many men were buried. Although shaken by the blast, he immediately organised a machine-gun party and opened fire on the advancing Germans. He then ran back to bring up reinforcements, but as the communication trench was blocked, he went across open ground under heavy fire, bringing the reinforcements back the same way. His prompt action saved the situation.

He died from chronic dysentery on 12 August 1918.

Acting Corporal WILLIAM COTTER

HOHENZOLLERN REDOUBT, France
6 March 1916
He was 33 years old and serving in the 6th Bn, The Buffs (East Kent Regiment) when his leg was blown off at the knee and he was wounded in both arms. He somehow made his way unaided 50 yards to a crater, steadied the men who were holding it, controlled their fire, issued orders and altered dispositions to meet a fresh attack. For two hours he held this position and only allowed his wounds to be dressed when the attack had died down. He could not be moved back for 14 hours and during all this time he had a cheery word for everyone.

He died on 14 March 1916, from wounds received during his VC action.

Private GEORGE STRINGER

ES SINN, Mesopotamia 8 March 1916
He was 26 years old and serving in the 1st Bn, Manchester Regiment when, after the capture of an enemy position, he was posted on the extreme right of his battalion to guard against any flank attack. His battalion was subsequently forced back by a counter-attack, but Stringer held his ground single-handedly and kept the enemy back with grenades until his supply ran out. His gallant action saved the flank of his battalion and made a steady withdrawal possible.

He died on 10 November 1957.

The Complete Victoria Cross

Chaplain EDWARD MELLISH
ST ELOI, Belgium 27–29 March 1916
He was 35 years old and serving in the Army
Chaplains Department when he went out
repeatedly under heavy fire to attend to the
wounded. He brought in ten badly wounded
men on the 27th and twelve more on the 28th;
on the night of the 29th he took a party of
volunteers and once more returned to the
trenches with wounded men.

He had also served in the Second Boer War.
He died on 8 July 1962.

Temporary Captain ANGUS BUCHANAN
FALAUYAH LINES, Mesopotamia
5 April 1916
He was 21 years old and serving in the 4th Bn,
South Wales Borderers when two men went
out under heavy machine-gun fire to bring in a
wounded officer who was lying 150 yards from
cover. One of them was hit almost at once.
Buchanan immediately went out and with the
help of the other man carried the first casualty
to cover under machine-gun fire. He then went
out again to bring in the other wounded man,
still under fire.

He died on 1 March 1944, having never fully
recovered from being shot in the head and
blinded in 1917.

Corporal SIDNEY WARE
SANNA-I-YAT, Mesopotamia
6 April 1916
He was 23 years old and serving in the 1st Bn,
Seaforth Highlanders Ross-shire Buffs (Duke
of Albany's). When the order to retire was
given, Ware was one of the few remaining
unwounded men. He picked up a wounded
man and carried him some 200 yards to cover
and then returned to help the other wounded.
He moved to and fro under very heavy fire for
more than two hours until he had brought in
all of the wounded.

He died on 16 April 1916, from wounds
received on 10 April.

Chaplain WILLIAM ADDISON
SANNA-I-YAT, Mesopotamia 9 April 1916
He was 32 years old and serving in the Army

Chaplains Department when he carried a
wounded man to cover and assisted several
others to the same cover, after binding their
wounds. This was carried out under heavy fire.
By his splendid example he encouraged the
stretcher-bearers to go forward under fire and
collect the wounded.

He was one of 74 VC holders who formed
the honour guard at the interment of the
Unknown Soldier at Westminster Abbey on 11
November 1920.

He died on 7 January 1962.

Lieutenant EDGAR MYLES
SANNA-I-YAT, Mesopotamia
9 April 1916
He was 21 years old and serving in the 8th Bn,
Welch Regiment, attached to the 9th Bn,
Worcestershire Regiment, when he went out
alone several times in front of the advanced
trenches and assisted wounded men lying in the
open. On one occasion he carried a badly
wounded officer to safety. Throughout he was
under heavy fire.

He died on 31 January 1977.

Private JAMES FYNN (born FINN)
SANNA-I-YAT, Mesopotamia
9 April 1916
He was 22 years old and serving in the 4th Bn,
South Wales Borderers. When he was in a
forward trench, 300 yards from the Turkish
lines, he went out and bandaged several
wounded men lying in the open. Unable to find
a stretcher, he carried one of the men to safety
on his back. He then returned to carry in
another man. He was constantly under fire.

He died on 30 March 1917 as a result of
wounds received in action. In 1966, following
the redevelopment of Bodmin, the 'Finn VC
Estate' was named in his honour; it included
Finn's former home in Downing Street.

Naik SHAHAMAD KHAN
BEIT AYEESA, Mesopotamia
12/13 April 1916
He was 36 years old and serving in the 89th
Punjab Regiment, Indian Army when he was in
charge of a machine-gun covering a gap in our

line, within 150 yards of the enemy. He beat off three counter-attacks and worked his gun single-handed after all except two belt-feeders had become casualties. For three hours he held the gap under very heavy fire, and when his gun was finally knocked out of action he and his two belt-feeders held on with rifles until ordered to withdraw. With some help, Shahamad Khan then brought back his gun, one severely wounded man, and finally all remaining arms and equipment.

He died on 28 July 1947.

Second Lieutenant EDWARD BAXTER
BLAIRVILLE, France 17/18 April 1916
He was 30 years old and serving in the 1/8th Bn, King's (Liverpool) Regiment when on the two nights prior to an attack, he was out cutting wire close to the enemy trenches. At one point he dropped a grenade with the pin removed. Instantly he picked it up, unscrewed the base and smothered the detonator in the ground. This prevented the alarm being given, and saved many lives. Later he led one of the storming parties and was the first man into the enemy trenches, but was never seen alive again.

Lieutenant Commander CHARLES COWLEY
MAGASIS, Mesopotamia 24/25 April 1916
He was 44 years old and serving in the Royal Naval Volunteer Reserve aboard the SS *Julnar* on the Tigris river when he volunteered to take supplies to the garrison at Kut, along with Lieutenant Humphrey Firman and twelve ratings. The task was so dangerous that no married man was allowed to volunteer. The steamer came under heavy fire from Turkish guns on both sides of the river, but passed safely through one steel cable that had been placed across the river. She was then fired on by guns brought down to the river's edge. One shell hit the bridge, killing Lieutenant Firman. The boat then fouled another cable and the remaining crew had no option but to surrender. They were almost certainly executed by the Turks.

Lieutenant HUMPHREY FIRMAN
MAGASIS, Mesopotamia 24/25 April 1916

He was 29 years old and serving in the Royal Naval Volunteer Reserve aboard the SS *Julnar* on the Tigris river when he volunteered to take supplies to the garrison at Kut, along with Lieutenant Commander Charles Cowley and twelve ratings. The task was so dangerous that no married man was allowed to volunteer. The steamer came under heavy fire from Turkish guns on both sides of the river, but passed safely through one steel cable that had been placed across the river. She was then fired on by guns brought down to the river's edge. One shell hit the bridge, killing Lieutenant Firman. The boat then fouled another cable and the remaining crew had no option but to surrender. They were almost certainly executed by the Turks.

Temporary Lieutenant RICHARD JONES
'BROADMARSH CRATER', VIMY, France 21 May 1916
He was 19 years old and serving in the 8th Bn, Royal North Lancashire Regiment when his platoon was holding a position recently captured from the enemy. Just 40 yards away the enemy exploded a mine and isolated the platoon by a heavy barrage. Attacked by over-whelming numbers, the platoon was in great danger of being overrun, but Jones organised his men and set a fine example by shooting fifteen Germans as they advanced. When all his ammunition had been used, he picked up a bomb and was about to throw it when he was shot through the head and killed.

Major FRANCIS HARVEY
JUTLAND, Denmark 31 May 1916
He was 29 years old and serving in the Royal Marine Light Infantry aboard HMS *Lion* when, despite being mortally wounded by a shell which exploded in the gunhouse, he displayed sufficient presence of mind to order the magazine to be flooded. His action saved the ship and over a thousand lives. Winston Churchill said of his actions: 'In the long, glorious history of the Royal Marines there is no name and deed which in its character and consequences ranks above this.'

Commander EDWARD BINGHAM

JUTLAND, Denmark 31 May 1916

He was 34 years old and serving in the Royal Navy aboard HMS *Nestor*, commanding a destroyer division, when he engaged a flotilla of enemy destroyers, sinking two of them. He then led his ships towards the German battle-cruisers. Later he sighted the enemy fleet and closed to within 3,000 yards to bring his torpe-does to bear. His ships were under concentrated fire throughout this attack and *Nestor* was subsequently sunk. Bingham was picked up by the Germans and spent the rest of the war as a prisoner.

Bingham was one of 74 VC holders who formed the honour guard at the interment of the Unknown Soldier at Westminster Abbey on 11 November 1920.

He died on 24 September 1939.

Commander LOFTUS JONES

JUTLAND, Denmark 31 May 1916

He was 36 years old and serving in the Royal Navy aboard HMS *Shark* when he was in command of a division of destroyers attacking an enemy battlecruiser squadron. In the course of this attack *Shark* became disabled by shell fire and was lying helpless between the two enemy fleets. Jones was wounded in the leg, but with help from the three surviving seaman he kept the midship gun in action until he was hit by a shell that took off his leg. However, he continued to give orders to his gun crew until *Shark* was hit by a torpedo and sunk. Commander Jones went down with his ship. His body was washed ashore in southern Sweden some days later.

First Class Boy JOHN (aka JACK) CORNWELL

JUTLAND, Denmark 31 May 1916

He was 16 years old and serving in the Royal Navy when his ship, HMS *Chester*, which was scouting ahead of the 3rd Battlecruiser Squadron, came under intense fire from four Kaiserliche Marine cruisers that emerged out of the haze. The 5.5-inch gun mounting which Cornwell was serving as a sight-setter was affected by at least four hits. *Chester's* gun mountings were open backed and did not reach down to the deck. When shells exploded nearby, splinters were thus able to pass under or enter the open back. Although severely wounded, Cornwell remained at his post until *Chester* retired from action with only one main gun still working. The situation on deck was a bloody shambles. Many of the gun crews had lost lower limbs owing to splinters passing under the gun shields. Crews on British ships reported passing *Chester* to cheers from limb-less gun crews laid out on the deck, smoking cigarettes, only to hear that many of them died a few hours later. After the action Cornwell was found to be the sole survivor at his gun. Despite several shards of steel penetrating his chest, he was looking at the gun-sights and still waiting for orders. He died at Grimsby General Hospital before his mother arrived to see him. He was buried in a pauper's grave, but when the story of his actions caught the public imag-ination, his body was exhumed and he was reburied with full military honours.

Sir Robert Baden-Powell, leader of the Scout Movement, created a Cornwell Badge, which is awarded by Scouting organisations throughout the Commonwealth to youth members for fortitude in the face of severe adversity. Jack Cornwell Street in Manor Park, London was named in his honour. The 5.5-inch gun which he served is on display at the Imperial War Museum. In 2006 Jack Cornwell VC was featured in a series of Royal Mail postage stamps marking the 150th anniversary of the Victoria Cross. The epitaph on his grave reads: 'It is not wealth or ancestry but honourable conduct and a noble disposition that maketh men great.'

Private GEORGE CHAFER

MEAULTE, France 3/4 June 1916

He was 22 years old and serving in the 1st Bn, East Yorkshire Regiment when during a heavy bombardment he saw a messenger disabled by a shell blast. Although wounded, blinded and choking from gas, he picked up the message and ran along the parapet under heavy fire. He succeeded in delivering the message before collapsing from his wounds.

Chafer was one of 74 VC holders who formed the honour guard at the interment of the Unknown Soldier at Westminster Abbey on 11 November 1920.

He died on 1 March 1966.

Private ARTHUR PROCTER
FICHEUX, France 4 June 1916
He was 25 years old and serving in the 1/5th Bn, King's (Liverpool) Regiment when he noticed two men lying wounded in the open in full view of the Germans. He jumped out of his trench and under heavy fire crawled to them. He dragged them to the cover of a small bank, dressed their wounds, left them some warm clothes and promised they would be rescued after dark, then he returned to his trench still under heavy fire. The two men were rescued that night. Procter was later ordained, and served in the Second World War as a chaplain.

He died on 26 January 1973.

Sergeant JOHN ERSKINE
GIVENCHY, France 22 June 1916
He was 22 years old and serving in the 5th Bn, Cameronians (Scottish Rifles) when he rushed out, under continuous fire, to rescue a sergeant and private who were wounded. Later, seeing his officer, who was believed to be dead, showing signs of movement, Erskine ran over to him, bandaged his head and stayed with him for fully an hour under fire before bringing him in, shielding him with his own body to lessen the chance of him being hit again.

He was killed in action at Arras on 14 April 1917.

Sapper WILLIAM HACKETT
'SHAFTESBURY AVENUE MINE',
GIVENCHY, France 22/23 June 1916
He was 43 years old and serving in the 254th Tunnelling Company, Corps of Royal Engineers when he was entombed with four others in a gallery after an enemy mine exploded. After working for 24 hours a hole was made and the rescue party outside was contacted. Hackett helped three of the men through the hole and could easily have followed, but he refused to leave the last man,

who had been seriously injured. The hole gradually got smaller, but still he refused to leave his injured comrade. Finally the gallery collapsed and although the rescue party worked desperately for four days, they were unable to reach the two men. His body was never recovered.

Lieutenant ARTHUR BATTEN-POOLL
COLONNE, France 25 June 1916
He was 24 years old and serving in the 3rd Bn, Royal Munster Fusiliers when he led a raiding party and was wounded by a bomb which mutilated all the fingers of his right hand. In spite of this he refused to retire and continued to direct operations. He was wounded twice more while assisting in the rescue of other wounded men. He collapsed within yards of our lines and was carried in by the covering party.

He died on 21 January 1971.

Private WILLIAM (born JOHN) JACKSON
ARMENTIERES, France
25/26 June 1916
He was 18 years old and serving in the 17th Bn, 5th Infantry Brigade, AIF when during a night raid he captured an enemy soldier and returned with him through no-man's-land. On learning that some of his party had been wounded in the intense shelling, Jackson returned to no-man's-land. He helped to bring in a wounded man, and had gone out again to help Sergeant Camden bring in the seriously wounded Private Robinson when a shell exploded nearby. The blast rendered Camden unconscious, inflicted more wounds on Robinson and blew Jackson's right arm off above the elbow. Despite this, he returned to his trenches, claiming he only felt 'a numbing sensation'. An officer applied a tourniquet to his arm, using a piece of string and a stick, and he then went back out to find Robinson and Camden. He only came in when he was satisfied there were no more wounded men left on the battlefield. Private Robinson died of his wounds.

Sergeant Camden was awarded the Distinguished Conduct Medal for his part in the rescue of wounded men that night. He later said of Jackson: 'Bill was not looking for a VC that night, he was looking for a cobber.'

Jackson died from heart disease on 5 August 1959.

Private JAMES HUTCHINSON

FICHEUX, France 28 June 1916

He was 20 years old and serving in the 2/5th Bn, Lancashire Fusiliers. During a raid on the enemy trenches, he was the first man into the trench, shooting two sentries and clearing two traverses. Afterwards, when the objective had been taken and the retirement ordered, on his own initiative he covered the retreat under heavy machine-gun fire, thus allowing the wounded to be evacuated.

He died from chronic bronchitis on 21 January 1972.

Company Sergeant Major NELSON CARTER

'BEAR'S HEAD', RICHEBOURG L'AVOUE, France
30 June 1916

He was 29 years old and serving in the 12th Bn, Royal Sussex Regiment. He was in command of the fourth wave of an assault on the German lines when he and a few men, under very heavy shell and machine-gun fire, penetrated into the second line of defence, inflicting heavy casualties with bombs. When forced to retire back into the first line, he shot a gunner with his revolver and captured his machine-gun. Finally, after carrying several wounded men to safety, he was mortally wounded and died in just a few minutes.

Private WILLIAM McFADZEAN

THIEPVAL WOOD, SOMME, France
1 July 1916

He was 20 years old and serving in the 14th Bn, Royal Irish Rifles when at 01:00 hours a box of six bombs being opened for distribution slipped into the trench, which was full of men, and two of the pins fell out. McFadzean, instantly realising the danger, threw himself with heroic courage on top of the bombs. He was blown to pieces, but only one other man was wounded. He well knew the danger, being a bomber himself, but without hesitation he gave his life to save his comrades.

Temporary Major STEWART LOUDOUN-SHAND

FRICOURT, SOMME, France 1 July 1916

He was 36 years old and serving in the 10th Bn, Yorkshire Regiment (Alexandra, Princess of Wales's Own). When his company climbed over the parapet to attack the enemy, they were met by very heavy machine-gun fire and stopped in their tracks. He immediately leapt on to the parapet and began helping men over it and encouraging them until he was mortally wounded. Even then, he insisted on being propped up in the trench and continued encouraging the men until he died.

He had also served in the Second Boer War.

Temporary Major LIONEL REES

DOUBLE CRASSIEURS, France
1 July 1916

He was 31 years old and serving in 32 Squadron RFC and the Royal Regiment of Artillery when during an air patrol he sighted ten aircraft, and went up to escort them. As he neared them, however, he realised they were enemy aircraft; one of them attacked him, but he damaged it and it disappeared. Five others then came at him but he dispersed them and chased two before receiving a wound to the thigh and losing control of his machine. Having regained control, he closed with the enemy, used up all his ammunition and then returned home.

Rees was one of 74 VC holders who formed the honour guard at the interment of the Unknown Soldier at Westminster Abbey on 11 November 1920.

He died from leukaemia on 28 September 1955.

Captain JOHN GREEN

FONCQUEVILLERS, SOMME, France
1 July 1916

He was 27 years old and serving in the Royal Army Medical Corps, attached to 1/5th Bn, Sherwood Foresters (Nottinghamshire and Derbyshire Regiment), when, although wounded himself, he rescued a wounded officer who was caught up on the enemy's barbed wire entanglements. He dragged him into a shell-hole where he dressed his wounds despite a bombing attack. He then tried to carry the officer to safety and had nearly succeeded when he was himself killed.

Temporary Captain ERIC BELL
THIEPVAL, SOMME, France
1 July 1916

He was 20 years old and serving in the 9th Bn, Royal Inniskilling Fusiliers. When an attack was halted by enfilading machine-gun fire, he crept forward and shot the gunner. On three subsequent occasions, when bombing parties were unable to advance, he went forward alone and threw bombs among the enemy. When he had no bombs left, he stood on the parapet under heavy fire and used a rifle with great effect against the advancing Germans.

He was killed while rallying and reorganising groups of infantry that had lost their officers.

Lieutenant GEOFFREY CATHER
HAMEL, SOMME, France 1 July 1916

He was 25 years old and serving in the 9th Bn, Royal Irish Fusiliers when he searched no-man's-land and brought in three wounded. The next morning he continued to search, bringing in another wounded man. He also took water to others, arranging for their rescue later.

He was killed on 2 July 1916 while taking water to wounded men.

Sergeant JAMES TURNBULL
'LEIPZIG SALIENT', AUTHVILLE, SOMME, France 1 July 1916

He was 32 years old and serving in the 17th (Glasgow Commercials) Bn, Highland Light Infantry when his party captured a post of apparent importance to the enemy, who immediately counter-attacked, and continued to do so throughout the day. Although his party was wiped out and replaced several times, Turnbull never wavered in his determination to hold the post, the loss of which would have been very serious. Almost single-handedly he maintained his position, displaying the highest degree of valour and skill in the performance of his duty.

He was killed in action several hours later.

Corporal GEORGE SANDERS
THIEPVAL, SOMME, France
1 July 1916

He was 21 years old and serving in the 1/7th Bn, West Yorkshire Regiment (Prince of Wales's Own) when he became isolated in enemy trenches with a party of 30 men. He organised defences, detailed a bombing party and impressed upon the men that their duty was to hold the position at all costs. His party was eventually relieved some 36 hours later, having seen off three attacks and bombing raids. Throughout this period they had been without food and water, having given the water to the wounded during the night.

He died on 4 April 1950, following a long illness.

Private ROBERT QUIGG
HAMEL, SOMME, France
1 July 1916

He was 21 years old and serving in the 12th Bn, Royal Irish Rifles when his platoon advanced three times towards the heavily defended German lines. They were beaten back each time. The final assault left many hundreds of dead and wounded in no-man's-land. When it was reported that Lieutenant Harry Macnaughten, the platoon commander, was missing, Quigg volunteered to go out and look for him. He went out seven times to search for the missing officer, but without success. On each occasion he came under machine-gun fire, but managed to return with a wounded colleague. It was reported that on one of his forays he crawled within yards of the German wire in order to rescue a wounded man, whom he dragged back on a ground sheet. After 7 hours exhaustion got the better of him and he had to rest from his efforts. The body of Lieutenant Macnaughten was never recovered.

Quigg died on 14 May 1955.

Drummer WALTER RITCHIE
BEAUMONT-HAMEL, SOMME, France
1 July 1916

He was 24 years old and serving in the 2nd Bn, Seaforth Highlanders Ross-shire Buffs (Duke of Albany's) when he stood on the parapet of an enemy trench, under heavy machine-gun fire, and repeatedly sounded the 'Charge', thereby rallying men from various units who, having lost their officers, were wavering and beginning to retire. Throughout the remainder of the day he carried messages over fire-swept ground.

Ritchie was one of 74 VC holders who formed the honour guard at the interment of the Unknown Soldier at Westminster Abbey on 11 November 1920.

He died on 17 March 1965.

Lieutenant Colonel ADRIAN CARTON de WIART

LA BOISELLE, SOMME, France
2/3 July 1916

He was 36 years old and serving in the 4th Dragoon Guards (Royal Irish). After three other battalion commanders had become casualties, he took over their commands and ensured that the ground won was held at all costs. Under very heavy fire, he organised the positions to be held and arranged for supplies to be brought up. It was due to his courage and example that a serious reverse was averted.

He had served in the Second Boer War and in Somaliland, where he was shot in the face, which resulted in him having to wear an eye-patch for the rest of his life. Despite his many war wounds, which included losing his left hand, he said of the First World War: 'Frankly I had enjoyed the war'. He also served in the Second World War, being captured and making an escape attempt with Lieutenant Philip Neame VC.

He died on 5 June 1963.

Private THOMAS TURRALL

LA BOISELLE, SOMME, France
3 July 1916

He was 33 years old and serving in the 10th Bn, Worcestershire Regiment when he was part of a bombing party and the officer in charge was badly wounded. The rest of the group was compelled to retire, but Turrall remained with the wounded officer for 3 hours under continuous fire from bombs and machine-guns. Even when completely cut off from our troops, he held his ground with determination and finally carried the wounded man back to our lines, after a counter-attack made this possible.

He died on 21 February 1964.

Temporary Lieutenant THOMAS WILKINSON

LA BOISELLE, SOMME, France
5 July 1916

He was 22 years old and serving in the 7th Bn, Royal North Lancashire Regiment. When a party of men were retiring without their machine-gun, he rushed forward and with two others got the gun into action and held off the Germans until the men were relieved. Later, when he spotted a group of men from different units trapped behind a block of earth over which the enemy were throwing bombs, he at once mounted the machine-gun on the parapet and dispersed the bombers. He then attempted to bring in a wounded man but was killed. He body was never recovered.

Temporary Second Lieutenant DONALD BELL

HORSESHOE TRENCH, SOMME, France 5 July 1916

He was 25 years old and serving in the 9th Bn, Yorkshire Regiment (Alexandra, Princess of Wales's Own) when his company came under very heavy enfilade fire from a machine-gun. On his own initiative he crept along a communication trench, followed by Corporal Colwill and Private Batey. They rushed across the open under very heavy fire and attacked the gun, shooting the gunner and destroying the gun and crew with bombs.

In a letter to his mother he said: 'I did nothing. I only chucked the bomb and it did the trick.' Bell was killed in action near Contalmaison on 10 July 1916. He was best friends with Temporary Captain Archie White, and both were awarded the VC in the same battle. Before the war Bell had been a professional football player for Bradford Park Avenue.

Major WILLIAM 'BILLY' CONGREVE
LONGUEVAL, DELVILLE WOOD,
MONTAUBAN and BAZENTIN RIDGE,
SOMME, France 6–20 July 1916
He was 25 years old and serving in the Rifle Brigade (Prince Consort's Own) when he constantly inspired those around him by numerous acts of gallantry. As brigade major, he led his battalions in the attack, but also went out with the medical officer to bring the wounded to safety, although he himself was suffering from the effects of gas. He subsequently tended to the wounded on many occasions under fire.

He was killed in action at Longueval on 20 July 1916. His father was Captain Walter Congreve VC.

Sergeant WILLIAM BOULTER
TRONES WOOD, SOMME, France
14 July 1916
He was 23 years old and serving in the 6th Bn, Northamptonshire Regiment when his company was held up by machine-gun fire which was causing heavy casualties. He advanced alone towards the gun and bombed it. This act not only saved many casualties, but materially helped in clearing the enemy from the woods.

He died on 1 June 1955 following a long illness.

Private WILLIAM FAULDS
DELVILLE WOOD, SOMME, France
18 July 1916
He was 21 years old and serving in the 1st Bn, South African Infantry, SAF when a bombing party came under heavy rifle and machine-gun fire, the majority of men being killed or wounded, including the lieutenant in charge who lay unable to move. In full daylight Faulds, accompanied by two other men, climbed over the parapet, ran out and picked up the officer and carried him back to safety. Later he went out alone, under intense artillery fire, and brought in a wounded man.

Faulds was the first South African-born man serving with the South African Forces to be awarded the VC.

He died on 16 August 1950.

Corporal JOSEPH DAVIES
DELVILLE WOOD, SOMME, France
20 July 1916
He was 27 years old and serving in the 10th Bn, Royal Welch Fusiliers. Prior to an attack on the enemy he, along with eight other men, became separated from the rest of his company. The enemy surrounded them, but Davies got his men into a shell-hole, threw bombs and opened fire, succeeding in routing the Germans. Then he followed their retreat and bayoneted several of them.

He died on 16 February 1976.

Private ALBERT HILL
DELVILLE WOOD, SOMME, France
20 July 1916
He was 21 years old and serving in the 10th Bn, Royal Welch Fusiliers when during an attack he dashed forward and bayoneted two enemy soldiers. Then, finding himself surrounded by 20 Germans, he attacked them with bombs, killing and wounding almost all of them. He then fought his way back to his own lines, accompanied by a sergeant. Hearing that his company officer Captain Scales was wounded, he went out and assisted in bringing him back, although Scales later died of his wounds. His last act on this day was to bring in two German prisoners.

He died from a cerebral haemorrhage on 17 February 1971.

Private THEODORE 'TEDDY' VEALE
HIGH WOOD, SOMME, France
20 July 1916
He was 23 years old and serving in the 8th Bn, Devonshire Regiment. Hearing that Lieutenant Savill was lying in the open just 50 yards from the enemy, he went out and dragged him into a shell-hole and then took him water. As Veale could not carry the officer by himself, he fetched some volunteers, one of whom was killed almost at once. Due to heavy fire, they had to leave the wounded officer in the shell-hole until dusk, when Veale went out again with volunteers. When an enemy patrol

The Complete Victoria Cross

approached, he went back for a Lewis gun and covered the party while the officer was carried to safety.

He died on 6 November 1980.

Second Lieutenant ARTHUR BLACKBURN
POZIERES, SOMME, France
23 July 1916

He was 21 years old and serving in the 10th (South Australia) Bn, AIF when he led four separate bombing parties and captured 150 yards of enemy trench. He then crawled forward with a sergeant to reconnoitre. On his return he led another attack which captured a further 120 yards of trench, enabling communications to be established with the battalion on his left.

Blackburn also served in the Second World War.

He died from an aneurism on 24 November 1960.

Private JOHN LEAK
POZIERES, SOMME, France
23 July 1916

He was 20 years old and serving in the 9th (Queensland) Bn, AIF when he ran forward into heavy fire and threw bombs into the enemy's bombing post, before jumping in and bayoneting three Germans. Later, as his party had to withdraw, he was the last man to pull back at each stage and he continued to throw bombs. His courage had such an effect as to inspire the reinforcements to retake the whole trench.

He died from a heart attack on 20 October 1972.

Private THOMAS COOKE
POZIERES, SOMME, France
24/25 July 1916

He was 35 years old and serving in the 8th (Victoria) Bn, AIF. When a Lewis gun was disabled, he was ordered to take his gun team to a dangerous part of the line. He did fine work but came under very heavy fire, until he was the only man left. He stuck to his post and continued firing. When assistance came, he was found dead beside his gun.

Sergeant ALBERT GILL
DELVILLE WOOD, SOMME, France
27 July 1916

He was 36 years old and serving in the 1st Bn, King's Royal Rifle Corps. When the enemy had rushed a bombing post and killed all the bombers, he rallied the remnants of his platoon, although none of them were skilled bombers, and reorganised the defences. When they were nearly surrounded, the enemy started sniping at them from only 20 yards away. Gill stood up to direct his men's fire, fully aware of the danger, and was killed almost instantly.

Sergeant CLAUDE CASTLETON
POZIERES, SOMME, France
28/29 July 1916

He was 23 years old and serving in the 5th Machine Gun Corps, AIF when after an attack many wounded men were left lying in shell-holes. He went out into the open twice under heavy fire and both times carried in a wounded man. He went out for a third time and was carrying a wounded man back when he was shot and killed.

Company Sergeant Major WILLIAM EVANS
GUILLEMONT, SOMME, France
30 July 1916

He was 40 years old and serving in the 18th Bn, Manchester Regiment (3rd Manchester Pals) when he volunteered to take an important message, after five runners had already been killed while attempting it. He had to cover 700 yards of open ground in both directions under machine-gun fire. He succeeded in delivering the message in spite of being wounded, and rejoined his company although advised to go to the dressing station.

He died on 28 September 1937.

Private JAMES MILLER
BAZENTIN-LE-PETIT, France
30/31 July 1916

He was 26 years old and serving in the 7th Bn, King's Own (Royal Lancaster) Regiment when he was ordered to take an important message through heavy shell and rifle fire, and to return with an answer at all costs. He was almost immediately wounded, being shot in the back with the bullet exiting from his abdomen. Undaunted, he compressed the wound with his hand, delivered the message and staggered back with the reply. He died at the feet of the officer to whom he delivered it.

While on leave for the last time, he told his sister that he had had a premonition that the end was near, and said that he would like to die a hero.

Private WILLIAM SHORT
MUNSTER ALLEY, SOMME, France
6 August 1916

He was 29 years old and serving in the 8th Bn, Yorkshire Regiment (Alexandra, Princess of Wales's Own), later the Green Howards, when he was foremost in the attack, bombing the enemy with great gallantry. When he was wounded in the foot, he was urged to go back, but he refused and continued to throw bombs. Later his leg was shattered by a shell and he was unable to stand. So he lay in the trench, adjusting detonators and straightening the pins of bombs for other men to throw. He died from his wounds the next day.

Second Lieutenant GABRIEL COURY
ARROW HEAD COPSE, France
8 August 1916

He was 20 years old and serving in the 3rd Bn, South Lancashire Regiment (Prince of Wales's Volunteers), attached to 1/4th Bn, when he was in command of two platoons ordered to dig a communication trench from the old firing line to a newly won position. By his fine example and utter contempt for danger, he kept up the spirits of his men and completed the task under intense fire. Later he went out into the open under fire to find his commanding officer, who had been wounded. He then carried him back to safety.

Coury also served in the Second World War. He died from cancer on 23 February 1956.

Captain NOEL CHAVASSE (VC action)
GUILLEMONT, SOMME, France
9/10 August 1916

He was 32 years old and serving in the Royal Army Medical Corps, attached to the 1/10th (Scottish) Bn, King's (Liverpool) Regiment, when he attended to the wounded all day under heavy fire, frequently in full view of the enemy. During the night he continued searching for wounded men in front of the enemy's lines. One soldier witnessed him using a torch at night to look for wounded men close to the German lines. The next day, under heavy shell fire, he and a stretcher-bearer carried an urgent case 500 yards to safety, Chavasse being wounded on the way. Then, together with some volunteers, he rescued three wounded men from a shell-hole just 35 yards from the enemy trenches, buried two dead officers and collected many identity discs. Altogether he saved the lives of some 20 wounded men.

Committed and caring, Chavasse was openly critical of some areas of the RAMC and had great sympathy for men suffering from shell-shock. This is probably why he was never promoted above the rank of captain. He had also taken part in the 1908 London Olympics. (For his Bar action, see 31 July–2 August 1917.)

Private MARTIN O'MEARA
POZIERES, SOMME, France
9–12 August 1916

He was 24 years old and serving in the 16th (South Australia & Western Australia) Bn, AIF when during four days of very heavy fighting, he repeatedly went out and brought in wounded men from no-man's-land under intense artillery and machine-gun fire. He also volunteered to carry ammunition and bombs through a heavy barrage to a part of the trenches that was being heavily shelled. Throughout this time he showed utter contempt for danger and undoubtedly saved many lives. He was wounded three times during the war.

He died from chronic mania on 20 December 1935.

Captain WILLIAM BLOOMFIELD (born BROOMFIELD)

MLALI, German East Africa
24 August 1916

He was 43 years old and serving in the Scout Corps, 2nd South African Mounted Brigade, SAF when under attack he withdrew to a new position with the wounded. However, realising that a corporal was missing, he went back 400 yards across open ground under heavy machine-gun fire. Finding the wounded man unable to walk, Bloomfield carried him back over the same fire-swept ground to safety.

He died from heart failure on 12 May 1954.

Lieutenant WILLIAM ROBINSON

CUFFLEY, England 2/3 September 1916

He was 21 years old and serving in 39 Squadron, RFC. Flying a BE2c fighter at night, he sighted a German airship (actually the wooden-framed Schutte-Lanz *SL11*, not, as is often assumed, a Zeppelin), one of sixteen engaged on a mass raid on London. He made his attack at a height of 11,500ft, approaching from below; closing to within 500ft, he raked the airship with gunfire. As he was preparing for another attack, it burst into flames and crashed in a field behind the Plough Inn in Cuffley, killing all the crew. His is the only VC to be awarded for action on (or in fact above) British soil.

He was shot down in April 1917 by a group of five Albatros aircraft led by Manfred von Richthofen (the 'Red Baron'), but not by the Baron himself. When he was taken prisoner, the Germans quickly realised who he was and made his life all the more difficult because of it. His health suffered during this time. He was returned from captivity on 14 December 1918 and died from influenza on 31 December 1918.

Captain WILLIAM ALLEN

MESNIL, France 3 September 1916

He was 24 years old and serving in the Royal Army Medical Corps, attached to 246th (West Riding) Brigade, RFA when the enemy started shelling men who were unloading high explosive ammunition. The first shell landed on one of the ammunition wagons, killing and wounding many men. Allen immediately ran across the open and began treating the wounded, saving many from bleeding to death. He was hit four times by shell fragments, one of which fractured his ribs, but he continued to help the others and only reported his injuries when the other men had all been seen to.

He died from opium poisoning on 27 August 1933.

Lieutenant JOHN HOLLAND

GUILLEMONT, France 3 September 1916

He was 27 years old and serving in the 3rd Bn, Prince of Wales's Leinster Regiment when he not only led his bombing party of 26 men against the enemy dug-outs within the objective, but then went through our own barrage and cleared a great part of the village. With only five men left, he returned to the British lines with 50 prisoners. By this gallant action he undoubtedly broke the spirit of the enemy and saved many lives.

He died on 27 February 1975.

Sergeant DAVID JONES

GUILLEMONT, France 3 September 1916

He was 25 years old and serving in the 12th Bn, King's (Liverpool) Regiment when his platoon advanced on a forward position and came under machine-gun fire, killing the officer in charge. Jones ran forward, took command and led the advance on, taking the position under intense shell fire. Despite having no food or water, he and his men drove off two fierce German counter-attacks, holding the position for two days until relief arrived. A fellow NCO described Jones as: 'The right man in the right place at the right moment.'

He was killed in action at Guedecourt on 7 October 1916.

Private THOMAS HUGHES

GUILLEMONT, France 3 September 1916

He was 31 years old and serving in the 6th Bn, Connaught Rangers when he returned to the firing line having had his four wounds from an earlier attack dressed. Spotting a machine-gun, he dashed ahead of his company, shot the gunner and single-handedly captured the gun. Although wounded again, he also brought back four prisoners.

He died on 8 January 1942.

Acting Corporal LEO CLARKE
POZIERES, SOMME, France
9 September 1916
He was 24 years old and serving in the 2nd Bn (EO) Regiment, CEF. When the first three companies went over the top, Clarke was assigned to take a section to clear the enemy on the flank to allow his company to build a fortified dug-out that would secure the position once the salient was overrun. When his men reached the trench, they found it heavily defended and had to battle their way through with grenades, bayonets and clubs. At the end Clarke was the only man standing, the rest having been killed or wounded. At this time the Germans counter-attacked. Clarke advanced, emptying his revolver into them. He then picked up two enemy rifles and fired those too. An enemy officer attacked him with a bayonet, wounding him in the leg but Clarke shot him dead. The Germans retreated but Clarke pursued them, shooting four more and capturing one. In total, he killed 19 men and captured another.

Shortly before his death on 19 October 1916, from wounds received during his VC action, he wrote to his parents, saying: 'I don't care so much for the VC as getting home for a couple of months.' He is one of three men from Pine Street, Winnipeg, Manitoba to be awarded the VC. The others are Company Sergeant Major Frederick Hall and Lieutenant Robert Shankland. The street was renamed Valour Road in their honour.

Temporary Lieutenant Colonel JOHN CAMPBELL
GINCHY, France 15 September 1916
He was 39 years old and serving in the 3rd Bn, Coldstream Guards when he took personal command of the third line after the first two waves of his battalion had been slaughtered by enemy machine-gun fire. He rallied his men

and led them against the enemy machine-guns, capturing them and killing the crews. Later in the same day he again rallied the survivors of his battalion and led them through very heavy fire. His personal gallantry and initiative at a very critical moment enabled the division to press on and capture objectives of high tactical importance.

He was ADC to the King from 1919 to 1933. He died on 21 May 1944.

Sergeant DONALD BROWN
HIGH WOOD, SOMME, France
15 September 1916
He was 26 years old and serving in the 2nd Bn, Otago Infantry Regiment, NZEF when his company was held up by a machine-gun. He, together with another man, rushed the machine-gun, killed four of the crew and captured the gun. They went on to rush another machine-gun and killed its crew also. On a third occasion he attacked a gun single-handedly, killing the crew and capturing it.

He was killed in action near Eaucourt L'Abbaye on 1 October 1916.

Lance Sergeant FREDERICK McNESS
GINCHY, France 15 September 1916
He was 24 years old and serving in the 1st Bn, Scots Guards when his company had gained the front line of German trenches. The left flank was exposed and the enemy were bombing their way down the trench. He organised and led a counter-attack, and although wounded in the neck and jaw did not give up. Finally he established a 'block' and continued to encourage his men and throw bombs until exhausted from loss of blood.

He killed himself on 4 May 1958 while 'the balance of his mind was disturbed'.

Private JOHN KERR
COURCELETTE, France
16 September 1916
He was 29 years old and serving in the 49th Bn, Edmonton Regiment, CEF. Shortly after the fingers of his right hand were blown away during an attack, he noticed that bombs were running short, so he ran along the top of the

trench under heavy fire until he closed with the enemy. He then opened fire at point-blank range, inflicting heavy casualties. Thinking they were surrounded, 62 Germans surrendered and 250 yards of trench was taken. Kerr's wounds were dressed only after he had escorted his prisoners back.

He died on 19 February 1963.

Private THOMAS 'TODGER' JONES
MORVAL, France 25 September 1916
He was 35 years old and serving in the 1st Bn, Cheshire Regiment. When his company was covering the advance in front of a village, he noticed an enemy sniper 200 yards away. He went out after him, and although one bullet went through his helmet and another through his coat, he returned the sniper's fire and killed him. He then saw two more Germans firing on him, although they were displaying a white flag. He shot both of them. On reaching the enemy trench, Jones found several occupied dug-outs and single-handedly disarmed over 100 Germans, including several officers, and took them prisoner.

He died from a heart attack on 30 January 1956.

Private FREDERICK EDWARDS
THIEPVAL, SOMME, France
26 September 1916
He was 21 years old and serving in the 12th Bn, Middlesex Regiment (Duke of Cambridge's Own) when the advance was held up by machine-gun fire and all the officers had become casualties. There was confusion and the possibility of a retreat. Grasping the situation, and on his own initiative, Edwards dashed towards the gun and destroyed it with bombs. This gallant act, coupled with his presence of mind and disregard of personal danger, made further advances possible. Edwards' action took place during the same attack in which Private Robert Ryder was also awarded the VC.

Edwards died from acute coronary thrombosis on 9 March 1964.

Private ROBERT RYDER
THIEPVAL, SOMME, France
26 September 1916
He was 20 years old and serving in the 12th Bn, Middlesex Regiment (Duke of Cambridge's Own) when his company was held up by rifle and machine-gun fire and all the officers had become casualties. He dashed forward alone and by skilful use of his Lewis gun, cleared the enemy trench. This turned what could have been failure into success and made further advances possible. Ryder's action took place during the same attack in which Private Frederick Edwards was also awarded the VC.

Ryder died on 1 December 1978, following a long illness.

Temporary Second Lieutenant TOM ADLAM
THIEPVAL, SOMME, France 27/28 September 1916
He was 22 years old and serving in the 7th Bn, Bedfordshire Regiment when a portion of a village had to be taken. He went from shell-hole to shell-hole under heavy fire, collecting men for a sudden rush. At this point he was wounded in the leg but despite this he led the attack, captured the position and killed the occupants.

He also served in the Second World War. He died on 28 May 1975.

Temporary Captain ARCHIE WHITE
'STUFF REDOUBT', THIEPVAL, SOMME, France
27 September–1 October 1916
He was 25 years old and serving in the 6th Bn, York Regiment (Alexandra, Princess of Wales's Own) when he was in command of troops holding the southern and western faces of the 'Stuff Redoubt'. For four days and nights by skilful disposition he held the position under heavy fire of all kinds and against several attacks. Although short of supplies and ammunition, his determination never wavered and when the enemy attacked in greatly superior numbers and had almost ejected our men from the redoubt, he personally led a counter-attack that cleared the enemy out of the redoubt.

He was best friends with Temporary Second

Lieutenant Donald Bell, and they were both awarded the VC. White also served in the Second World War.

He died on 20 May 1971.

Temporary Lieutenant Colonel ROLAND BRADFORD

EAUCOURT L'ABBAYE, France
1 October 1916

He was 24 years old and serving in the 9th Bn, Durham Light Infantry when the leading battalion had suffered very heavy casualties and its commander was wounded. The flank was also dangerously exposed to the enemy. At the request of the wounded commander, Bradford took command of the battalion as well as his own. By fearless energy and skilful leadership, he rallied the men, secured the flank and captured the objective.

He was killed in action near Graincourt on 30 November 1917. His brothers were Lieutenant Commander George Bradford VC, Captain Thomas Bradford DSO and Second Lieutenant James Bradford MC. They were known as 'The Bradford Boys'.

Temporary Second Lieutenant HENRY KELLY

LE SARS, France 4 October 1916

He was 29 years old and serving in the 10th Bn, Duke of Wellington's (West Riding) Regiment when he twice rallied his company under heavy fire and then led the only three available men into the German trenches, remaining there until two of his men were hit and enemy reinforcements arrived. He then carried his wounded sergeant major back 70 yards to safety, after which he brought in three more wounded men.

Kelly also served in the Spanish Civil War.

He died on 18 July 1960, after a long illness.

Piper JAMES RICHARDSON

'REGINA TRENCH', SOMME, France
8/9 October 1916

He was 20 years old and serving in the 16th (Canadian Scottish) Bn, CEF when his company was held up by barbed wire and intense fire. He strode up and down in front of

the wire, coolly playing his pipes. Inspired by his bravery, the company rushed the wire with such ferocity that the position was taken. Having taken some wounded men and prisoners back, he returned to find his pipes but he was never seen again.

Private HUBERT (aka HERBERT) 'STOKEY' LEWIS

MACAKOVO, Greece 22/23 October 1916

He was 20 years old and serving in the 11th Bn, Welch Regiment when during a raid he was twice wounded, but refused aid. While searching enemy dug-outs he was wounded again, but still he refused medical attention. At this point three enemy soldiers approached. He immediately attacked them single-handedly, capturing all three. Later, during the retirement, he went to the assistance of a wounded man and brought him back to safety under heavy fire, after which he collapsed.

He also served in the Second World War.

He died on 22 February 1977.

Sergeant ROBERT DOWNIE

LESBOEUFS, France 23 October 1916

He was 22 years old and serving in the 2nd Bn, Royal Dublin Fusiliers. During an attack most of the officers had become casualties, temporarily halting the advance. Downie, utterly regardless of personal danger and under very heavy fire, reorganised the men and at the critical moment he rushed forward shouting 'Come on the Dubs!' This had an immediate response and the line rushed forward at his call. He accounted for several of the enemy himself and in addition captured a machine-gun, killing the crew. Although wounded early on in the fight, he remained with his company, giving valuable assistance while the position was consolidated.

He died on 18 April 1968.

Lieutenant EUGENE BENNETT

LE TRANSLOY, France
5 November 1916

He was 24 years old and serving in the 2nd Bn, Worcestershire Regiment when he was in command of the second wave of an attack.

Finding that the first wave had suffered heavy casualties, including its commander, and the line was wavering, he advanced at the head of the second wave and reached the objective with only 60 men. Isolated with his small force, he took steps to consolidate his position under heavy machine-gun and rifle fire from both flanks, and although wounded he remained in command. But for his fine example of courage the attack would have been checked at the outset.

Bennett was one of 74 VC holders who formed the honour guard at the interment of the Unknown Soldier at Westminster Abbey on 11 November 1920. He also served in the Second World War.

He died on 6 April 1970.

Temporary Lieutenant Colonel BERNARD FREYBERG

BEAUCOURT, SOMME, France
13 November 1916
He was 27 years old and serving in the Queen's Royal West Surrey Regiment, commanding the Hood Bn, when his battalion became disordered after leading the attack through the enemy's front line. He rallied his men, leading them to a successful assault on the second objective, during which he was wounded. His unsupported battalion then held the ground throughout the following day and night. When reinforced, he led an attack in which a village and 500 German prisoners were taken. Despite two further wounds, he refused to leave the line until he had issued his final instructions. On arrival at the casualty station, he was put with those who were expected to die and was only given pain-killers. Fortunately he was later removed.

He had been in Mexico in 1914 and may have taken part in the civil war there. Freyberg was one of 74 VC holders who formed the honour guard at the interment of the Unknown Soldier at Westminster Abbey on 11 November 1920. He also served in the Second World War. As well as the VC, he was awarded the DSO and three Bars.

He died on 4 July 1963, after one of his war wounds ruptured.

Private JOHN CUNNINGHAM

ANCRE, HEBUTERNE SECTOR, France
13 November 1916
He was 19 years old and serving in the 12th (Hull Sportsmen's Pals) Bn, East Yorkshire Regiment when he went up a communication trench with a bombing party. There was much opposition and all of the rest of his party were killed or wounded. Collecting all the bombs from the casualties, he continued alone, and when he ran out of bombs he returned for more. Again he went alone and ran into a party of ten Germans. He killed them all, and cleared the trench up to the new line.

He died from tuberculosis on 21 February 1941.

1917

Sergeant THOMAS MOTTERSHEAD

PLOEGSTEERT WOOD, Belgium
7 January 1917
He was 24 years old and serving in 20 Squadron, RFC when he came under attack at 9,000ft. Bullets pierced his petrol tank, setting the aircraft on fire. His observer, Lieutenant Gower, was unable to subdue the flames. Mottershead managed to fly back to his own lines with the aircraft still burning, and made a successful landing. However, the undercarriage collapsed on landing and he was pinned under the burning wreckage. He suffered severe burns and died on 12 January, but his remarkable endurance undoubtedly saved his observer's life.

Temporary Lieutenant Colonel EDWARD HENDERSON

RIVER HAI KUT, Mesopotamia
25 January 1917
He was 38 years old and serving in the North Staffordshire Regiment, attached to the Royal Warwickshire Regiment, commanding the 9th Bn. When he was leading his battalion in an assault, the enemy counter-attacked and penetrated his line in several places. Although wounded in the arm, he leapt on to the parapet,

ran ahead of his men and cheered them on over 500 yards of open ground as they advanced. Despite another two wounds, he led a bayonet charge which captured the position, during which he was wounded again and fell to the ground. Temporary Lieutenant Robert Phillips saw him lying in the open and went to his aid with a corporal. They carried him back under very heavy fire, but Henderson died shortly afterwards. Phillips also received the VC.

Temporary Lieutenant ROBERT PHILLIPS
RIVER HAI KUT, Mesopotamia
25 January 1917
He was 21 years old and serving in the 13th Bn, Royal Warwickshire Regiment when he noticed Lieutenant Colonel Henderson lying wounded in the open. Assisted by a corporal, he went out under very heavy fire. They carried their commanding officer back to the British lines, but he died shortly afterwards.
He died on 23 September 1968.

Sergeant EDWARD MOTT
LE TRANSLOY, France 27 January 1917
He was 23 years old and serving in the 1st Bn, Border Regiment when during an attack his company was held up by machine-gun fire. Although he was severely wounded in the eye, he rushed forward, capturing the gun and gunner. As a result the attack was successful.
He was one of 74 VC holders who formed the honour guard at the interment of the Unknown Soldier at Westminster Abbey on 11 November 1920.
He died on 20 October 1967.

Captain HENRY 'MAD' MURRAY
'STORMY TRENCH', GUEUDE-COURT, France 4/5 February 1917
He was 36 years old and serving in the 13th (New South Wales) Bn, AIF when he successfully led his company in an assault, quickly capturing an enemy position, and so inspiring his men that they resisted three fierce counter-attacks. Throughout the night his men suffered heavy casualties from shell fire. He saved the situation by leading several bayonet charges.

Murray also carried wounded men to safety.
He died on 7 January 1966. His biography, *Mad Murray,* was published in 2003.

Sergeant FREDERICK BOOTH
JOHANNESBRUCK, German East Africa
12 February 1917
He was 26 years old and serving in the British South African Police, attached to the Rhodesian Native Infantry, when during an attack in thick bush he went forward alone under fire and brought back a wounded man. He then rallied the native troops and brought them to the firing line.
He died on 14 September 1960.

Lance Sergeant FREDERICK PALMER
COURCELETTE, France
16/17 February 1917
He was 25 years old and serving in the 22nd Bn, Royal Fusiliers. After all the officers had been killed or wounded, he took command of the company, then went out alone to cut his way through the wire entanglements under machine-gun fire, before rushing the enemy trenches with just six men. He then dislodged a machine-gun and established a 'block'. He collected some more men and held on for 3 hours against seven determined counter-attacks. While he was fetching more bombs another attack was delivered, threatening the flank. At this critical moment, despite suffering from exhaustion, he rallied his men, drove back the enemy and maintained his position. When his battalion was disbanded, he joined the RFC as an observer.
Palmer also served in the Second World War.
He died on 10 September 1955.

Commander GORDON CAMPBELL
NORTH ATLANTIC, Ireland
17 February 1917
He was 31 years old and serving in the Royal Navy aboard the Q-ship *Q-5*, or HMS *Farnborough*, when the ship was torpedoed by *U-83*, causing great damage. The 'panic party' got away in the boats as the gun crews waited. They did not have to wait long as *U-83* surfaced

just 10 yards from the *Q-5*. She opened a hail of fire with her 6-pounder gun and several machine-guns, the first shot killing the U-boat commander Captain Bruno Hoppe, while the U-boat was rapidly reduced to a battered wreck. The Q-ship too was sinking and Commander Campbell radioed for help. His message read: 'Q-5 slowly sinking respectfully wishes you goodbye.' Two ships arrived to help and *Q-5* was taken under tow, with a small crew remaining on board, including a man called Stuart and Campbell. During the night a depth-charge accidentally exploded and the tow was dropped. Campbell ordered the remaining men into a lifeboat, but stayed behind to make a final survey of his ship, only to be driven back by another explosion. On returning to the lifeboat, he discovered that Stuart had disobeyed his order and had remained on board to make sure his captain disembarked safely. The tow was reattached and the battered ship finally beached at Mill Cove.

Campbell was one of 74 VC holders who formed the honour guard at the interment of the Unknown Soldier at Westminster Abbey on 11 November 1920. Campbell wrote several books, including *My Mystery Ships*.

He died on 3 July 1953. His nephew was Temporary Lieutenant Colonel Lorne Campbell VC.

Sergeant THOMAS STEELE
SANNA-I-YAT, Mesopotamia
22 February 1917
He was 26 years old and serving in the 1st Bn, Seaforth Highlanders Ross-shire Buffs (Duke of Albany's) when during a Turkish counter-attack he rushed forward, brought a machine-gun into position and kept it in action until he was relieved, thus keeping our lines intact. Several hours later, during another Turkish attack, he rallied the wavering men and led a number forward, again helping to re-establish the line. However, on this occasion he was badly wounded.

He died on 11 July 1978.

Major GEORGE WHEELER
SHUMRAN, Mesopotamia
23 February 1917
He was 36 years old and serving in the 2nd Bn, 9th Gurkha Rifles, Indian Army when he crossed the Tigris river with one Gurkha officer and eight men and rushed the enemy's trench in the face of very heavy fire. Having got a footing on this bank, they were almost immediately counter-attacked by enemy bomb-throwers. He at once led a charge, receiving in the process a severe bayonet wound to the head. In spite of this, he managed to disperse the enemy and consolidate the position.

He died on 26 August 1938.

Private JOHN READITT
ALQAYAT-AL-GAHARBIGAH BEND, Mesopotamia 25 February 1917
He was 20 years old and serving in the 6th Bn, South Lancashire Regiment (Prince of Wales's Volunteers) when he advanced five times along a watercourse in the face of heavy machine-gun fire, being the sole survivor on each occasion. These advances drove the Turks back and about 300 yards of watercourse was made good in an hour. After his officer was killed, Readitt, on his own initiative, made several more advances. When the enemy barricade was reached, he was forced to retire, but gave ground slowly and continued to throw bombs. When support reached him, he held a forward bend by bombing until the position was consolidated.

Readitt was one of 74 VC holders who formed the honour guard at the interment of the Unknown Soldier at Westminster Abbey on 11 November 1920.

He died on 9 June 1964.

Private JACK WHITE
DIALAH RIVER, Mesopotamia
7/8 March 1917
He was 20 years old and serving in the 6th Bn, King's Own (Royal Lancaster) Regiment when he watched the pontoons ahead of him being raked by machine-gun fire. When his own pontoon was hit and every man except him was killed or wounded, he tied a length of telephone

wire to the pontoon, dived into the river and towed it to shore, thereby saving the lives of all the wounded, and also their rifles and equipment.

He died on 27 November 1949.

Second Lieutenant GEORGE CATES
BOUCHAVESNES, France 8 March 1917
He was 24 years old and serving in the 2nd Bn, Rifle Brigade (Prince Consort's Own) when he was engaged with others in deepening a captured trench. When his spade struck a buried bomb, which immediately started to burn, Cates without hesitation put his foot on it and it exploded. This act cost him his life but saved many of those with him.

Captain OSWALD REID
DIALAH RIVER, Mesopotamia
8–10 March 1917
He was 23 years old and serving in the 1st Bn, King's (Liverpool) Regiment, attached to the 6th Bn, Loyal North Lancashire Regiment, when he consolidated a small post on the river after his lines of communication had been cut by the sinking of pontoons. He maintained this position for 36 hours against continuous attacks by bombs, machine-guns and shells. Knowing that repeated attempts at relief had failed and that his ammunition was running low, he effected a crossing of the river the next night and was wounded during that operation.

He died from pneumonia on 27 October 1920.

Temporary Lieutenant ARCHIBALD BISSETT-SMITH
NORTH ATLANTIC 10 March 1917
He was 38 years old and serving in the Royal Naval Reserve aboard the SS *Otaki* when his ship was called on to stop by the German raider *Moewe*, armed with four 5.9in guns, one 4.1in gun, two 22-pounders and two torpedo tubes. *Otaki* had only one 4.7in gun. Bissett-Smith refused to comply and a duel ensued at a range of 2,000 yards. *Otaki* scored several hits on the *Moewe*, starting a fire which burned for three days. Perhaps inevitably, *Otaki* was seriously

damaged herself and Bissett-Smith ordered the boats to be lowered. He himself remained on board and went down with his ship, still flying the British colours. An enemy account described it as 'a duel as gallant as naval history can relate'.

Private CHRISTOPHER COX
ACHIET-LE-GRAND, France
13–17 March 1917
He was 27 years old and serving in the 7th Bn, Bedfordshire Regiment when during an attack the battalion's first wave was checked by heavy artillery and machine-gun fire, and the whole line had to take cover in shell-holes to avoid annihilation. Cox, a stretcher-bearer, went out into the open and single-handedly rescued four wounded men. Having finished helping the men from his own battalion, he went to the aid of the wounded from the adjoining battalion. On two subsequent days he carried out similar work with complete disregard for his own safety.

He died on 28 April 1959.

Lieutenant FRANK McNAMARA
TEL-EL-HESI, Egypt 20 March 1917
He was 22 years old and serving in 1 Squadron RFC when during a sortie a fellow pilot was forced down behind enemy lines. Seeing enemy cavalry approaching, McNamara landed nearby under heavy fire and picked up the airman but was wounded in the thigh and his airplane overturned. Both men crawled from the wreckage, set it on fire and made it to the damaged aircraft. McNamara was able to start it and flew back 70 miles to his own airfield.

McNamara also served in the Second World War.

He died on 2 November 1961 as a result of a fall.

Captain PERCY CHERRY
LAGNICOURT, France 26 March 1917
He was 21 years old and serving in the 26th (Queensland & Tasmania) Bn, AIF. When his company was storming a village and all the other officers had became casualties, he carried on in the face of fierce opposition and took the

objective. Having done this, he then beat off many counter-attacks. He was wounded early the next morning, but refused to leave his post, encouraging his men to hold on, until he was killed by an enemy shell.

Lieutenant FREDERICK HARVEY
GUYENCOURT, France 27 March 1917
He was 28 years old and serving in Lord Strathcona's Horse (Royal Canadians), CEF when during a mounted attack his troop suffered heavy casualties from close-range rapid fire. On seeing a wired trench, he galloped ahead of his men, leapt from his horse into the trench, shot the machine-gunner and captured the gun.

He died on 24 August 1980, following a long illness.

Private JOERGAN (sometimes spelt JORGEN) JENSEN
NOREUIL, France 2 April 1917
He was 26 years old and serving in the 50th Bn, AIF when with five comrades he attacked a barricade behind which were about 45 of the enemy and a machine-gun. One of the party shot the gunner and Private Jensen rushed the post and threw in a bomb. Then, with a bomb in each hand, he threatened the rest and made them surrender. He sent one of his prisoners to another group of the enemy, ordering them to surrender, which they did, but our troops began firing on them. Jensen, regardless of the danger, stood on top of the barricade waving his helmet, and the firing stopped. He then sent his prisoners back to his lines.

He died on 31 May 1922, having never fully recovered from his war wounds.

Major FREDERICK LUMSDEN
FRANCILLY, France 3/4 April 1917
He was 44 years old and serving in the Royal Marine Artillery when he undertook to bring in six captured field guns which had been left in dug-in positions 300 yards in front of British lines. The enemy kept these guns under heavy artillery fire. Lumsden led four horse teams and a party of men through the barrage, and despite casualties they retrieved all six

guns. He personally made three trips to the guns and then stayed with them until the last gun was removed. As well as the VC, he was also awarded the CB, DSO and three Bars, making him one of the most decorated men in the British Army.

He was killed in action at Blairvill on 4 June 1918.

Sergeant WILLIAM GOSLING
ARRAS, France 5 April 1917
He was 24 years old and serving in the 3rd Wessex Brigade, RFA when a bomb from his battery fell just 10 yards away because of a faulty cartridge. He immediately sprang from the trench and lifted the nose off the bomb, which had sunk into the ground; unscrewing the fuse, he threw it on the ground, where it exploded. His prompt action undoubtedly saved the lives of the whole detachment. He also served in the Second World War.

He died on 12 February 1945, following a long illness.

Captain JAMES NEWLAND
BAPAUME and LANGNICOURT, France 7–9 and 15 April 1917
He was 37 years old and serving in the 12th (South Australia, Western Australia & Tasmania) Bn, AIF when his company was attacking an important objective. He personally led a bombing party under heavy fire, rallying his men who had suffered many casualties, and taking the position. The following night his company, holding the captured position, was heavily attacked, but Newland succeeded in holding on to it. On 15 April, when one company was overpowered and his own attacked from the rear, he drove off several attacks and it was his tenacity and his disregard for his own safety that encouraged his men to hold out.

He died on 19 March 1949.

Captain THAIN MacDOWELL
VIMY RIDGE, France 9 April 1917
He was 26 years old and serving in the 38th (Ottawa) Bn, CEF when he advanced towards the enemy position with two company runners.

As he went, he bombed a machine-gun and killed the crew of another. He then saw a German going into a tunnel, and was able to bluff the enemy into thinking he was part of a larger force and over 75 men surrendered to him. He sent the prisoners out of the tunnel in groups of 12 so his runners could take them back to the Canadian lines. Although wounded in the hand, he continued to hold the position for five days, until relieved by his battalion.

He died on 27 March 1960, although some references say 29 March.

Sergeant HARRY CATOR
ARRAS, France 9 April 1917
He was 23 years old and serving in the 7th Bn, East Surrey Regiment when his platoon had suffered heavy casualties from a machine-gun. Under heavy fire he and another man advanced across open ground, and when his companion was killed Cator went on alone. Picking up a Lewis gun and some ammunition drums on his way, he succeeded in reaching the enemy trench. Once there he set up the Lewis gun and killed the entire machine-gun crew, including the officer. He held this trench to such good effect that a bombing party was able to capture 100 prisoners and five machine-guns.

He was one of 74 VC holders who formed the honour guard at the interment of the Unknown Soldier at Westminster Abbey on 11 November 1920.

He died from pneumonia on 7 April 1966.

Sergeant JOHN WHITTLE
BOURSIES, France 9 April 1917
He was 33 years old and serving in the 12th (South Australia, Western Australia & Tasmania) Bn, AIF. He was in command of a platoon, when the enemy, under cover of an intense artillery barrage, attacked the small trench he was holding, and owing to their great numbers succeeded in entering it. Whittle collected his men, charged the enemy and regained the position. On another occasion, when the enemy broke through our line and tried to bring up a machine-gun to enfilade the position, he rushed across the fire-swept ground and attacked the enemy with bombs, killing all of them and capturing the gun.

After the war Whittle saved a small boy from drowning in an ornamental pool in University Park, the act becoming well known despite the fact he did not give his name at the time of the incident.

He died on 2 March 1946.

Lance Sergeant ELLIS SIFTON
NEUVILLE-ST-VAAST, VIMY RIDGE, France 9 April 1917
He was 25 years old and serving in the 18th (WO) Bn, CEF when during an attack in enemy trenches his company was held up by machine-gun fire that was inflicting many casualties. Having located the gun, he leapt into the trench and bayoneted all of the crew. A small enemy party advanced down the trench, but Sifton succeeded in keeping them off with bayonet and club until his comrades had gained the position. When it seemed the danger had passed, a German lying wounded picked up a rifle and shot him dead. His conspicuous valour undoubtedly saved many lives and contributed largely to the success of the operation.

Lance Corporal THOMAS BRYAN
ARRAS, France 9 April 1917
He was 35 years old and serving in the 25th Bn, Northumberland Fusiliers. Although wounded during an attack, he went forward alone to silence a machine-gun which had inflicted many casualties. Working his way along a communication trench, he got behind it, killed two of the crew and disabled the gun. This allowed the advance to continue.

Bryan had played Rugby League for Castleford in the 1906/07 season.

He died on 13 October 1945.

Private THOMAS KENNY
HERMIES, France 9 April 1917
He was 20 years old and serving in the 2nd (New South Wales) Bn, AIF when his platoon was held up by a strongpoint and severe casualties prevented progress. Kenny dashed forward alone under heavy fire, killed a

German who tried vainly to stop him, and bombed the position, capturing a gun crew, killing an officer who fought back and seizing the gun. His action enabled his platoon to occupy the position, which was of great local importance.

He died from a 'combination of illnesses' on 15 April 1953.

Private WILLIAM MILNE
THELUS, VIMY RIDGE, France
9 April 1917
He was 24 years old and serving in the 16th (Canadian Scottish) Bn, CEF when he saw a machine-gun firing on his comrades. He crawled to it, killed the crew with bombs and captured the gun. Seeing another machine-gun, he made his way to it and put its crew out of action, capturing that gun too.

He was killed shortly afterwards.

Private JOHN PATTISON
VIMY RIDGE, France 10 April 1917
He was 41 years old and serving in the 50th (Calgary) Bn, CEF. When the advance was held up by machine-gun fire, he sprang forward, jumping from shell-hole to shell-hole until he was only 30 yards away. He then threw bombs which killed some of the gun crew. He then ran forward and bayoneted the remainder. His initiative and valour undoubtedly saved the situation, allowing the advance to continue.

He was killed in action near Lens on 3 June 1917.

Private HORACE WALLER
HENINEL, France 10 April 1917
He was 18 years old and serving in the 10th Bn, King's Own Yorkshire Light Infantry. He was part of a bombing party forming a 'block' in the enemy line, when the Germans made an attack on his position. Five of his comrades were killed. One officer described the scene as 'the most violent hand-to-hand fighting I ever witnessed'. Waller continued for more than an hour to throw bombs and finally the attack was repulsed. In the evening the enemy attacked again and all were killed except Waller, who, although wounded, continued to throw bombs

for another half hour until he too was killed.

Lieutenant DONALD MacKINTOSH
FAMPOUX, France 11 April 1917
He was 21 years old and serving in the 3rd Bn, Seaforth Highlanders Ross-shire Buffs (Duke of Albany's). During the initial advance on an enemy trench, he was shot through the right leg, but continued to lead his men, capturing the trench. He then collected men from another company who had lost their officer and drove back a counter-attack, during which he was again wounded in the leg and left unable to stand. Nevertheless he continued to control the situation and with only 15 men left he ordered them to be ready to advance to the final objective. With great difficulty he hauled himself out of the trench, encouraging the men to advance, but then was mortally wounded. His dying words were 'Carry on.'

Lance Corporal HAROLD MUGFORD
MONCHY-LE-PREUX, France
11 April 1917
He was 22 years old and serving in the 8th Squadron, Machine Gun Corps when he got his machine-gun into an exposed forward position, from which he dealt effectively with the enemy. Almost immediately his no. 2 was killed and he himself was badly wounded. He was ordered to a new position and although told to get his wounds dressed, he refused to go, staying to inflict severe casualties on the enemy. Soon afterwards a shell broke both his legs, but he still remained with his gun. When he was at last removed to the dressing station, he was wounded again.

Mugford was left paralysed and used a wheelchair for 40 years.

He died on 16 June 1958.

Corporal JOHN CUNNINGHAM
BOIS-EN-HACHE, France 12 April 1917
He was 26 years old and serving in the 2nd Bn, Leinster Regiment (Prince of Wales's) when he was in command of a Lewis gun section that came under very heavy enfilade fire. Although wounded, he almost alone succeeded in reaching the objective with his gun, which he

got into action. When counter-attacked by 20 Germans, he exhausted his ammunition against them and then threw bombs. He was wounded again but picked himself up and continued to throw bombs until they ran out. He then made his way back to the British lines with a fractured arm, among other injuries. There is little doubt that his superb courage cleared up a most critical situation.

He died on 16 April 1917, from wounds received during his VC action.

Sergeant JOHN ORMSBY
FAVET, France 14 April 1917
He was 36 years old and serving in the 2nd Bn, King's Own Yorkshire Light Infantry when his company cleared a village under heavy machine-gun and rifle fire. He was acting as company sergeant major. After clearing the village, he pushed on and drove out many snipers from localities further forward. When the only officer left was wounded, Ormsby took command of the company and led them forward under heavy fire for 400 yards to a new position, skilfully organising its defence until relieved.

He died on 29 July 1952.

Lieutenant CHARLES POPE
LOUVERAL, France 15 April 1917
He was 34 years old and serving in the 11th (Western Australia) Bn, AIF when he was in command of a very important picquet post, with orders to hold it at all costs. The enemy attacked in greatly superior numbers and surrounded the position. With ammunition running short and no hope of any more getting through, in a desperate bid to save the position Pope was seen to charge with his men into the superior force, by whom his men were over-whelmed, although heavy casualties were inflicted. This officer had obeyed his orders to hold out to the last man, and his body and those of his men were found in proximity to 80 dead Germans.

Private ERNEST SYKES
ARRAS, France 19 April 1917
He was 32 years old and serving in the 27th Bn, Northumberland Fusiliers when his battalion was held up by intense fire from front and flank, and was suffering heavy casualties. Sykes went forward four times despite this heavy fire and brought back a wounded man each time. He made another journey and remained out under conditions that seemed to invite certain death, until he had bandaged all those men too badly wounded to move.

He died on 3 August 1949.

Private CHARLES MELVIN
ISTABULAT, Mesopotamia
21 April 1917
He was 31 years old and serving in the 2nd Bn, Black Watch. His company had advanced to within 50 yards of the Turkish trenches, where, owing to the very heavy fire, the men had to lie down and wait for reinforcements. Melvin rushed forward alone over fire-swept ground, and on reaching the enemy trench fired two or three shots into it, killing some of the enemy. But as the others in the trench continued to fire, he jumped into it, and attacked them with his bayonet as his rifle was now damaged. On being attacked in this manner, most of the enemy fled to their second line, but not before he killed two more and captured nine prisoners, one of whom was wounded. He then tended to the wounded man and marched his prisoners back to his own lines, where he collected a load of ammunition and returned to the firing line to report to his sergeant. All this was done under heavy rifle and machine-gun fire.

He died on 17 July 1941.

Lieutenant JOHN GRAHAM
ISTABULAT, Mesopotamia
22 April 1917
He was 24 years old and serving in the 9th Bn, Argyll and Sutherland Highlanders (Princess Louise's), attached to the 136th Company, Machine Gun Corps, and was in command of a machine-gun section. When most of his men had become casualties, he carried ammunition until wounded. Then he opened accurate fire on the enemy until his gun was put out of action and he was again wounded, forcing him to retire. He then brought a Lewis gun into

action to excellent effect until he was wounded again and again forced to retire.

Graham also served in the Second World War.

He died on 6 December 1980.

Acting Captain ARTHUR HENDERSON
FONTAINE-LES-CROISILLES, France 23 April 1917

He was 23 years old and serving in the 4th Bn, Argyll and Sutherland Highlanders (Princess Louise's) when, despite being wounded in the left arm, he led his company through the enemy front line until he gained his objective. He then proceeded to consolidate his position, despite heavy machine-gun fire and bombing attacks. By his cheerful courage and coolness he was able to maintain the spirit of his men under the most trying circumstances. He was killed in action the next day.

Acting Captain DAVID HIRSCH
WANCOURT, France 23 April 1917

He was 20 years old and serving in the 4th Bn, Yorkshire Regiment (Alexandra, Princess of Wales's Own) when, despite being wounded during an attack, he went back over open and fire-swept ground to ensure that the flank position was being established. He continuously exposed himself to intense machine-gun fire in order to encourage and steady his men, until during a German counter-attack he was killed while standing on the parapet.

Corporal EDWARD 'TINY' FOSTER
VILLERS PLOUICH, France 24 April 1917

He was 31 years old and serving in the 13th Bn, East Surrey Regiment when he was in charge of two Lewis guns during an advance, which was held up by two entrenched enemy machine-guns. He succeeded in entering the trench and engaged the enemy guns. When one Lewis gun was lost, he rushed forward and recovered it, then opened fire on a German gun team, killing the crew and capturing their gun, thus enabling the advance to continue.

Foster was one of 74 VC holders who formed the honour guard at the interment of the Unknown Soldier at Westminster Abbey on 11 November 1920.

He died from bronchial pneumonia on 22 January 1946.

Temporary Captain ALBERT 'PILL' BALL
France 25 April–6 May 1917

He was 20 years old and serving in 56 Squadron, RFC when during a 12-day period he took part in 26 air combats, destroyed 11 enemy aeroplanes, drove down two more out of control and forced several others to land. In these combats he flew alone and on one occasion took on six enemy machines. Twice he fought five and once four. When leading two other aeroplanes, he attacked an enemy formation of eight. On each of these occasions he brought down at least one of the enemy. Several times his aeroplane was badly damaged, once so seriously that but for the most delicate handling his machine would have collapsed, as nearly all the control wires had been shot away. On returning with a damaged machine, he always had to be restrained from immediately going out in another. In all, Ball is credited with 43 'destroyed' German aeroplanes and a balloon. It must be remembered that 'drove down' and 'forced to land' did not necessarily mean destroyed, and pilots often used such manoeuvres as a ploy to escape, but they were credited as victories by the British.

On 7 May 1917 he took off with ten other aircraft and encountered German fighters from Jasta 11. The running battle that followed was fought in deteriorating visibility. Both Ball and Lothar von Richthofen (the Red Baron's brother) came down behind the German lines. Ball was killed, but Richthofen survived and was credited by the Germans with shooting Ball down. There is, however, some doubt as to exactly what happened, as Richthofen's claim was for a Sopwith triplane and Ball was flying an SE5 (types that are very different). German propaganda of the time made great play of air aces, and Richthofen may well have been ordered to take the credit. Ball was also awarded the MC, DSO and two Bars.

Company Sergeant Major EDWARD BROOKS
FAYET ST-QUENTIN, France
28 April 1917
He was 30 years old and serving in the 2/4th Bn, Oxfordshire and Buckinghamshire Light Infantry when during a raid he rushed forward from the second wave as the first wave was pinned down by a machine-gun. He shot the gunner and bayoneted another of the gun's crew. The rest ran off, so he turned the gun on the retreating Germans before carrying it back to his own lines.

He died from thrombosis on 26 June 1944.

Second Lieutenant REGINALD HAINE
GAVRELLE, France 28/29 April 1917
He was 20 years old and serving in the 1st Bn, Honourable Artillery Company, holding a salient that was under repeated counter-attack by the Germans. Haine organised and led six bombing attacks against a strongpoint and captured the position, together with 50 prisoners and 2 machine-guns. The enemy at once counter-attacked and regained the lost ground, but Haine formed a blocking line in his trench and for the whole of the night maintained his position. The next morning he again attacked and recaptured the position. His splendid example inspired his men during more than 30 hours of continuous fighting.

He died on 12 June 1982.

Second Lieutenant ALFRED POLLARD
GAVRELLE, France 29 April 1917
He was 23 years old and serving in the 1st Bn, Honourable Artillery Company when he saw that men from various units had become disorganised owing to heavy casualties from shell fire and an attack which forced a retirement. Realising the seriousness of the situation, with just four men he led a counter-attack with bombs, pressing home until he had broken the enemy and regained all the lost ground. His splendid example gave courage to all who saw him.

Pollard was one of 74 VC holders who formed the honour guard at the interment of the Unknown Soldier at Westminster Abbey on 11 November 1920. Pollard wrote some 50 books, including his autobiography, *Fire-Eater: The Memoirs of a VC*.

He died from a heart attack on 5 December 1960.

Lance Corporal JAMES WELCH
OPPY, France 29 April 1917
He was 27 years old and serving in the 1st Bn, Royal Berkshire Regiment (Princess Charlotte of Wales's) when he entered an enemy trench and killed a man after a severe hand-to-hand struggle. Then, armed only with an empty revolver, he chased four of the enemy across open ground and captured them. Then he handled his machine-gun with the utmost fearlessness, and often went into the open while exposed to heavy fire to search for and collect ammunition and spare parts to keep his gun in working order, which he succeeded in doing for over 5 hours, until wounded by a shell.

He died on 28 June 1978.

Lieutenant WILLIAM SANDERS
NORTH ATLANTIC, Ireland
30 April 1917
He was 34 years old and serving in the Royal Naval Reserve when his Q-ship HMS *Prize* was attacked by *U-93* and badly damaged by shell fire. After the 'panic party' had taken to the boats and the *Prize* appeared to be sinking, the U-boat approached to within 80 yards of the port quarter, whereupon the white ensign was hoisted and *Prize* opened fire. Within a few minutes the submarine was on fire and her bows rose in the air, while the *Prize* was further damaged. The submarine disappeared from sight and was believed sunk. Several of the German crew, including the captain, were taken aboard *Prize*, but in fact the U-boat limped back to her base. *Prize* was towed back in flames to Kinsale.

Sanders was killed in action on 14 August 1917 when HMS *Prize* was torpedoed by *U-43*, whose crew had been warned about the Q-ship by the survivors of *U-93*. The Sanders Cup for inter-provincial competition Centreboard X-class yachts, named in his honour, is still contested to this day.

Lieutenant ROBERT COMBE
ACHEVILLE, France 3 May 1917

He was 36 years old and serving in the 27th (City of Winnipeg) Bn, CEF when he steadied his company under intense fire and led the men through the enemy barrage, reaching his objective with only five men. He proceeded to bomb the enemy, inflicting heavy casualties, and then, after collecting several small groups of men, he succeeded in capturing the objective together with 80 prisoners. Combe repeatedly charged the enemy, driving them before him. He was killed by a sniper later the same day while leading a bombing party.

Second Lieutenant JOHN HARRISON
OPPY, France 3 May 1917

He was 26 years old and serving in the 11th Bn, East Yorkshire Regiment when he led his men against a well-defended wood which was considered vital for the British to take. His platoon was heavily involved in the attack and became pinned down by heavy machine-gun fire. Armed only with his revolver and a Mills bomb, Harrison set about eliminating the enemy position. His men looked on as he dodged between shell-holes and weaved his way in and out of the barbed wire towards the enemy machine-gun post. He fell in the act of throwing a bomb at one of the machine-gun posts. The gun fell silent, but he was never seen again.

Before the war he had been a professional Rugby League player and in the 1913/14 season he scored a still unbeaten 52 tries.

Corporal GEORGE JARRATT
PELVES, France 3 May 1917

He was 25 years old and serving in the 8th Bn, Royal Fusiliers. He had been taken prisoner and placed under guard in a dug-out with some wounded men. The same evening the enemy were driven back by British troops and the leading infantry started to bomb the dug-outs. A grenade fell into the dug-out and without hesitation Jarratt put both feet on it to muffle the blast. The subsequent explosion blew off both his legs. The rest of the wounded were later safely removed to the Allied lines, but

Jarratt died before he could be moved. His action undoubtedly saved the lives of many of the wounded men around him.

Corporal GEORGE 'SNOWY' HOWELL
BULLECOURT, France 6 May 1917

He was 23 years old and serving in the 1st (New South Wales) Bn, AIF when, seeing that his battalion was about to be outflanked, he climbed to the top of the parapet on his own initiative and under heavy fire bombed the enemy, pressing them back along the trench. When his stock of bombs was used up, he continued the attack with his bayonet, until he was severely wounded. This prompt and gallant action was seen by the rest of his battalion and inspired them in the subsequent successful counter-attack.

He died on 23 December 1964.

Private MICHAEL HEAVISIDE
FONTAINE-LES-CROISILLES, France 6 May 1917

He was 36 years old and serving in the 15th Bn, Durham Light Infantry when he saw a wounded man holding up a water bottle in a shell-hole close to the enemy lines. Under very heavy rifle and machine-gun fire, he made his way to the man with water. When he reached the soldier, he found him demented with thirst for he had been lying in the shell-hole for three days. Heaviside dressed his wounds and promised to return with help. That night he led two men out across no-man's-land and they carried the wounded man back to safety. Without doubt, Heaviside saved this man's life. He had also served in the Second Boer War as a stretcher-bearer.

Heaviside died on 26 April 1939, following a long illness.

Lieutenant RUPERT 'MICK' MOON
BULLECOURT, France 12 May 1917

He was 24 years old and serving in the 58th (Victoria) Bn, AIF when he led his men against a position in advance of the enemy trench, being wounded at this time. Then he led his men on to the trench itself, and was wounded again. While consolidating the position he was wounded for a third time, but he continued to inspire and encourage his men. Only when wounded for the fourth time did he agree to retire from the fight.

He died on 28 February 1986.

Private TOM DRESSER
ROEUX, France 12 May 1917
He was 24 years old and serving in the 7th Bn, Yorkshire Regiment (Alexandra, Princess of Wales's Own) when he carried a crucial message from battalion headquarters to the front line despite being wounded twice en route, arriving exhausted and in great pain. His fearlessness and determination to deliver his message at all costs proved of the greatest value to his battalion.

He died on 9 April 1982.

Skipper JOSEPH WATT
STRAITS OF OTRANTO, Italy
15 May 1917
He was 30 years old and serving as skipper of the *Gowan Lea,* which was one of several drifters forming a blocking line known as the 'Otranto Barrage'. During an attack, 3 Austrian cruisers, 2 destroyers and 3 submarines attacked and sank 14 helpless trawlers and drifters. Watt was confronted by the cruiser SMS *Novara,* which demanded the surrender of the tiny ship and ordered the crew off so they could sink her. Instead, Watt ordered full speed ahead and called on the crew to give three cheers and fight to the finish. He then opened fire with their 6-pounder gun. But the *Gowan Lea* was hit by four heavy shells and seriously damaged. The Austrian fleet headed for home but was engaged by British, Italian and French units in the inconclusive Battle of the Otranto Barrage.

For Watt and the other survivors on their battered boats and in the water, the fight was now with the sea. The *Gowan Lea,* despite suffering damage and casualties, moved among the wreckage, rescuing wounded men and providing medical attention. In particular, her crew saved the lives of the men from the sinking drifter *Floandi* who would otherwise have drowned.

There was some dispute at the time as to whether the award of the VC was appropriate given the nature of the defeat inflicted on the barrage, despite Watt's courageous fight against overwhelming odds. Watt was characteristically uncomfortable with his award, commenting after the war, 'There has been too much said already and it should get a rest . . . I'm ashamed to read the exaggerations which have been printed.' He served on drifters again in the Second World War with his son.

He died of cancer on 13 February 1955.

Sergeant ALBERT WHITE
MONCHY-LE-PREUX, France
19 May 1917
He was 21 years old and serving in the 2nd Bn, South Wales Borderers. During an attack, realising that an enemy machine-gun would hold up the advance of his company, he dashed forward alone to capture the gun. Within a few yards of it he fell riddled with bullets, having sacrificed his life in an attempt to secure the success of the operation.

Captain WILLIAM 'BILLY' BISHOP
CAMBRAI, France 2 June 1917
He was 23 years old and serving in 60 Squadron, RFC when he flew to attack an enemy airfield. Finding no machines there, he flew on to another airfield 12 miles behind enemy lines, where he saw seven machines on the ground, some with their engines running. He attacked them from about 50 feet, and as one took off he fired 15 rounds into it at very close range, and it crashed. A second machine got off the ground and he fired 30 rounds into it at 150 yards range and it fell into a tree. Two more machines then rose from the airfield. One of these he engaged at a height of 1,000 feet, emptying the rest of his drum of ammunition. This machine crashed 300 yards from the airfield, after which Bishop emptied a whole drum into a fourth enemy machine, and then flew back to his own lines.

This VC was awarded solely on the evidence of Bishop himself, and is the only one ever awarded in violation of the warrant requiring witnesses. Since the German records have been

The Complete Victoria Cross

lost, along with the archived papers of his VC, there is no way of ever knowing if there were any witnesses or not. However, it is highly unlikely that Bishop made it up, or even thought about the possibility of being awarded the VC for it.

Bishop is credited with 72 victories, including 16 'out of control'. He is the author of *Winged Warfare* and *Winged Peace*. In 1942 he appeared as himself in the film *Captains of the Clouds*. His decorations include the VC, DSO and Bar, MC, DFC, CB, Legion d'Honneur and the Croix de Guerre with palm.

He died in his sleep on 11 September 1956.

Second Lieutenant THOMAS MAUFE
FEUCHY, France 4 June 1917
He was 19 years old and serving in the 124th Siege Battery, Royal Garrison Artillery when under intense artillery fire he repaired on his own initiative the telephone wire between the forward and rear positions, enabling his battery to open fire on the enemy. Then he extinguished a fire in an advanced ammunition dump, knowing the risk from gas shells stored at the dump.

Maufe also served in the Second World War.

He died on 28 March 1942 when a trench mortar exploded during training.

Second Lieutenant JOHN CRAIG
SUEZ CANAL, Egypt 5 June 1917
He was 21 years old and serving in the 1/4th Bn, Royal Scots Fusiliers. When an advanced post was rushed by the Turks, he organised a counter-attack to drive them back. Then he organised a rescue party to remove the dead and wounded under heavy fire. He rescued an NCO and a medical officer, but was himself wounded while bringing the latter to safety.

He died on 19 February 1970.

Captain ROBERT GRIEVE
MESSINES, Belgium 7 June 1917
He was 27 years old and serving in the 37th (Victoria) Bn, AIF. When his company was suffering heavy casualties, he located two enemy machine-guns that were holding up the advance. Under continuous fire from the two guns, he succeeded in bombing and killing the crews of both guns. Then he reorganised the remnants of his own company and gained his original objective. Grieve set a splendid example and when he finally fell wounded, the position had been secured.

He died from cardiac failure on 4 October 1957. His uncle was Sergeant Major John Grieve VC.

Lieutenant RONALD STUART
NORTH ATLANTIC, Ireland 7 June 1917
He was 30 years old and serving in the Royal Naval Reserve when his Q-ship HMS *Pargust* was hit by a torpedo from *U-29* and the engine room damaged. The explosion loosened the gun covers, but Seaman William Williams with great presence of mind took the whole weight of the covers on himself, physically preventing them from falling and thus betraying the ship to the enemy. The 'panic party' took to the boats. However, the U-boat's commander, Captain Ernst Rosenow, was well aware of the Q-ships and took no risks, remaining 400 yards away and watching the staged evacuation of the ship. Lieutenant Hereford, commanding the panic party in the life-boats, realised that the submarine would follow his movements, assuming him to be the ship's captain, and therefore he ordered his men to row back towards the ship. This persuaded Rosenow to think they were trying to regain the ship and he closed to just 50 yards, surfaced and began angrily semaphoring to the 'survivors'. The gun crew on the *Pargust* now opened fire, and numerous hits were made on the conning tower. *U-29* attempted to flee on the surface before slowing down and heeling over, trailing oil. The gun crews stopped firing, only to see the submarine start to move off again, trying to escape. In a final barrage of shells the submarine was blown apart. Her captain and 22 crewmen were killed, while two survivors were rescued by the panic party. The wrecked *Pargust* was taken in tow and reached port two days later. Stuart and Williams were elected for the award by the officers of HMS *Pargust*.

Stuart died on 8 February 1954.

Lance Corporal SAMUEL FRICKLETON
MESSINES, Belgium 7 June 1917
He was 26 years old and serving in the 3rd Bn,
New Zealand Rifle Brigade when, although
wounded, he dashed forward into our barrage
and personally destroyed with bombs an
enemy machine-gun that was causing heavy
casualties. He then attacked a second gun,
killing all of the crew. By his actions he
undoubtedly saved his and other units from
very severe losses. During the consolidation of
this position he was severely wounded.

He died on 6 August 1971, following a long
illness.

Seaman WILLIAM WILLIAMS
NORTH ATLANTIC, Ireland 7 June 1917
He was 26 years old and serving in the Royal
Naval Reserve when his Q-ship *HMS Pargust*
was hit by a torpedo from *U-29* and the engine
room damaged. The explosion loosened the
gun covers and Williams, with great presence of
mind, took the whole weight of the covers on
himself and physically prevented them from
falling and thus betraying the ship to the enemy.
The U-boat was eventually sunk by gunfire.
He was elected for the award by the men of
HMS *Pargust*.

He died on 22 October 1965.

Private JOHN CARROLL
ST YVES, Belgium 7–12 June 1917
He was 26 years old and serving in the 33rd
(New South Wales) Bn, AIF when he rushed an
enemy trench and bayoneted four of the occupants. He then went to the assistance of a
comrade, killing another of the enemy. Next he
single-handedly attacked a machine-gun,
killing three of the crew and capturing the gun.
Later, when two of his comrades were buried
by a shell, he rescued them both in spite of
heavy shelling and machine-gun fire.

The story goes that Carroll failed on three
occasions to appear at Buckingham Palace for
his award ceremony. On the fourth occasion,
he is supposed to have called out the Palace
Guard, one of the entitlements of VC recipients, but he may have just made it up.

He died on 4 October 1971.

Private WILLIAM RATCLIFFE
MESSINES, Belgium 14 June 1917
He was 35 years old and serving in the 2nd Bn,
South Lancashire Regiment (Prince of Wales's
Volunteers). After an enemy trench had been
captured, he spotted an enemy machine-gun
firing on his comrades from the rear, and on his
own initiative immediately rushed it, bayoneting the crew. He then brought the gun back
into action against the enemy.

He died on 26 March 1963.

Second Lieutenant JOHN DUNVILLE
EPEHY, France 24/25 June 1917
He was 21 years old and serving in the 1st
Royal Dragoons when, in order to ensure the
successful demolition of the enemy's wire, he
placed himself between an NCO of the Royal
Engineers and the enemy's fire, thus enabling
the NCO to complete his vital work. Although
severely wounded, Dunville continued to direct
his men in the wire cutting and in general
operations until the raid was successfully
completed. He subsequently died of his
wounds.

Second Lieutenant FRANK WEARNE
LOOS SALIENT, France 28 June 1917
He was 23 years old and serving in the 3rd Bn,
Essex Regiment, attached to the 11th Bn. In
command of a small party on a trench raid, he
took the trench and held it against repeated
counter-attacks. Aware of the danger to his left
flank, Wearne leapt on to the parapet and ran
along the top of the trench, firing and throwing
bombs as he went. He was badly wounded but
remained in command, directing operations
until he was mortally wounded.

Second Lieutenant FREDERICK YOUENS
HILL 60, ZWARTELEEN, Belgium
7 July 1917
He was 21 years old and serving in the 13th Bn,
Durham Light Infantry when it was reported
that the enemy were preparing to raid the
trenches. Youens, who had already been
wounded, set out to rally a Lewis gun team that
had become disorganised. As he did so, an
enemy bomb fell into the Lewis gun position

without exploding. Youens picked it up and threw it over the parapet. Soon afterwards another bomb fell near him and again he picked it up, but this one exploded in his hand, severely wounding him and some of the other men. He subsequently died of his wounds.

Private THOMAS BARRATT
YPRES, Belgium 27 July 1917
He was 22 years old and serving in the 7th Bn, South Staffordshire Regiment. While working as a scout with a patrol, he stalked and killed two snipers. When he saw an enemy party trying to outflank his patrol as it pulled back, he volunteered to cover the withdrawal and his accurate shooting caused many casualties, thus preventing an enemy advance. After safely returning to our own lines, he was killed by a shell.

Temporary Brigadier General CLIFFORD COFFIN
WESTHOEK, Belgium 31 July 1917
He was 47 years old and serving in the Corps of Royal Engineers but commanding the 25th Infantry Brigade when his command was held up by heavy rifle and machine-gun fire. Coffin went forward to make an inspection of his front line. Although he was under the heaviest fire and in full view of the enemy, he showed an utter disregard for danger, walking quietly from shell-hole to shell-hole, giving advice and cheering his men by his presence. His gallant conduct had the greatest effect on all ranks and it was largely due to his personal courage and example that the line was held.
He died on 4 February 1959.

Temporary Lieutenant Colonel BERTRAM BEST-DUNKLEY
WIELTJE, Belgium 31 July 1917
He was 26 years old and serving in the 2/5th Bn, Lancashire Fusiliers. When the leading waves of an attack had become disorganised by heavy fire from positions that were believed to be in British hands, Best-Dunkley dashed forward, rallied the men and personally led them to attack these positions, which were taken despite heavy casualties. He continued to lead

his men until all their objectives were gained. Later an enemy advance threatened the line, so he gathered up his battalion HQ and successfully counter-attacked, during which he was mortally wounded.

Acting Captain THOMAS COLYER-FERGUSSON
BELLEWAARDE, Belgium 31 July 1917
He was 21 years old and serving in the 2nd Bn, Northamptonshire Regiment when, despite finding himself with only a sergeant and five men, he carried out the planned attack and succeeded in capturing an enemy trench. During a counter-attack, this time assisted only by his orderly, he attacked and captured a machine-gun, turning it on the enemy. Later, helped only by his sergeant, he again attacked and captured a machine-gun, but shortly afterwards was killed by a sniper.

Second Lieutenant DENNIS HEWITT
YPRES Belgium 31 July 1917
He was 19 years old and serving in the 14th Bn, Hampshire Regiment when he was hit by a shell, which ignited the signal lights in his haversack, setting fire to his equipment and clothes. He put out the flames and then, in spite of his wounds and the severe pain, he led the remnants of the company forward under very heavy machine-gun fire and captured the objective. Then he consolidated the position but was subsequently killed by a sniper while inspecting the position and encouraging his men.

Sergeant ROBERT BYE
YSER CANAL, Belgium 31 July 1917
He was 27 years old and serving in the 1st Bn, Welsh Guards when he saw the leading waves of an attack coming under fire from two blockhouses. He rushed one of them, putting it out of action, then he rejoined his company and went forward to the second objective. Later he volunteered to take charge of a party detailed to clear a line of blockhouses that had been passed by. Having accomplished this, taking many prisoners, he then advanced to the third objective, again taking

a number of prisoners. In all, he captured over 70 prisoners.

He was one of 74 VC holders who formed the honour guard at the interment of the Unknown Soldier at Westminster Abbey on 11 November 1920.

Bye died on 23 August 1962.

Sergeant ALEXANDER EDWARDS
PILCKEM RIDGE, YPRES, Belgium
31 July 1917

He was 22 years old and serving in the 1/6th (Morayshire) Bn, Seaforth Highlanders when, with great dash and courage, he led some men against a machine-gun, killing all the crew and capturing the gun. Later, when a sniper was causing some casualties, he crawled out to stalk him and, although badly wounded in the arm, went on to kill him. Only one officer now remained with the company, and realising that the success of the operation depended on the capture of the objective, Edwards, regardless of his wound, led his men on until it was taken. He subsequently showed great skill in consolidating the position, and very great daring in personal reconnaissance. Although wounded twice more on the following day, he maintained a complete disregard for his personal safety, which set a fine example to his men.

He was killed in action near Loupart Woods on 24 March 1918.

Sergeant IVOR REES
PILCKEM, YPRES, Belgium
31 July 1917

He was 19 years old and serving in the 11th Bn, South Wales Borderers when his platoon came under machine-gun fire at close range, suffering many casualties. Rees led his men forward and worked his way in short rushes to the rear of the enemy position. From a distance of 20 yards he rushed the gun, shooting one of the crew and bayoneting the other. Then he bombed a large concrete emplacement, killing five men and taking 30 prisoners, including two officers, and seizing an undamaged machine-gun.

Rees also served in the Second World War. He died on 11 March 1967.

Lance Sergeant TOM MAYSON
WIELTJE, Belgium 31 July 1917

He was 23 years old and serving in the 1/4th Bn, King's Own (Royal Lancaster) Regiment when his platoon was held up by a machine-gun. Without waiting for orders, he rushed the gun and put it out of action with bombs, wounding four of the crew. He pursued the remaining three crewmen as they fled and killed them. Later he again attacked a machine-gun single-handedly, killing six of the crew. Finally, during an enemy attack he held an isolated post until his ammunition was used up and he was ordered to withdraw.

Mayson wrote to his mother saying, 'I have been recommended for a great honour, but I leave you to guess what it is.'

He died on 21 February 1958.

Corporal LESLIE ANDREW
LA BASSEE VILLE, France
31 July 1917

He was 20 years old and serving in the 2nd Bn, Wellington Infantry Regiment, NZEF. While he was leading his men against a machine-gun located in an isolated building, he encountered another machine-gun that was holding up another company. He immediately attacked it, killing several of the crew before taking his original objective.

Andrew also served in the Second World War.

He died on 8 January 1969, following a short illness.

Corporal JAMES DAVIES
POLYGON WOOD, PILCKEM, Belgium
31 July 1917

He was 31 years old and serving in the 13th Bn, Royal Welch Fusiliers when during an attack on the enemy line, he single-handedly attacked a machine-gun emplacement after several other men had been killed attempting to take it. He bayoneted one of the crew and captured another, along with the machine-gun. Then, although wounded, he led a bombing party to assault a defended house, and killed a sniper who was harassing his platoon.

He died of his wounds later the same day.

Private GEORGE McINTOSH
PILCKEM RIDGE, YPRES, Belgium
31 July 1917
He was 20 years old and serving in the 1/6th Bn, Gordon Highlanders. When his unit was consolidating a new position, his company came under machine-gun fire from close range. He immediately rushed forward under heavy fire. On reaching the emplacement, he threw a bomb into it, killing two crew and wounding another. He captured two machine-guns and carried them back with him. His quick grasp of the situation and the speed with which he acted undoubtedly saved many of his comrades and enabled the consolidation of the position to proceed unhindered.

He also served in the Second World War.

He died from heart disease on 20 June 1968.

Private THOMAS WHITHAM
PILCKEM, YPRES, Belgium
31 July 1917
He was 29 years old and serving in the 1st Bn, Coldstream Guards when during an attack an enemy machine-gun was seen to be enfilading the battalion on the right. On his own initiative, Whitham immediately worked his way from shell-hole to shell-hole, through our own barrage, reached the gun and although under very heavy fire captured it, together with an officer and two men. His bold action was of great assistance to the battalion and undoubtedly saved many lives.

After the war he fell on hard times and he was rejected for many jobs by Burnley Council even though he had served king and country. He was forced to sell his VC and a gold watch that had been presented to him by the council in recognition of his bravery. Both ended up in a pawn shop, but were bought by the council and remain in the Townley Hall Art Gallery & Museum in Burnley.

He died, in poverty, from peritonitis on 22 October 1924, aged just 36 years.

Temporary Captain HAROLD ACKROYD
YPRES, Belgium 31 July/1 August 1917
He was 40 years old and serving in the Royal Army Medical Corps, attached to the 6th Bn, Royal Berkshire Regiment. Regardless of the danger, he worked continuously, tending the wounded and saving the lives of officers and men in the front line. In doing so, he had to move across open ground under machine-gun, rifle and shell fire. On one occasion he carried a wounded officer to a place of safety under heavy fire, and on another went some way in front of the advanced line and brought in a wounded man under continuous sniping.

He was killed in action at Glencourse Wood, on 11 August 1917.

Captain NOEL CHAVASSE (Bar action)
WIELTJE, Belgium
31 July–2 August 1917
He was 33 years old and serving in the Royal Army Medical Corps, attached to the 1/10th (Scottish) Bn, King's (Liverpool) Regiment when, although severely wounded while carrying a wounded officer to the dressing station, he refused to leave his post. As well as his normal duties, he went out repeatedly under heavy fire to attend to the wounded. A stretcher-bearer was sent to bring him back, but reported back that 'the Doc refused to go and told us to take another man instead'. During this time, exhausted and faint from his wounds, he helped to carry in several wounded men, being instrumental in saving many who would otherwise have died.

He died of his wounds on 4 August 1917. Perhaps his best epitaph comes from his last message to his fiancée, when he wrote: 'Duty called, and duty must be obeyed.' Chavasse Park in Liverpool is named in his honour. The other two men to be awarded the VC and Bar are Arthur Martin-Leake and Charles Upham. There are further links between these men: Martin-Leake was serving with the 46th Field Ambulance, RAMC which brought Chavasse back to Brandhoeck, and Upham was a distant relation to Chavasse by marriage.

Private WILLIAM BUTLER
LEMPIRE, France 6 August 1917
He was 22 years old and serving in the 17th Bn, West Yorkshire Regiment (Prince of Wales's Own), attached to the 106th Trench Mortar

Battery, when he was in charge of a Stokes gun in trenches that were being shelled. Suddenly one of the fly-off levers of a Stokes shell came off, firing the shell into the emplacement. Butler picked up the shell and shouted a warning to a group of men nearby. He then turned and put himself between the men and the shell, holding it until they took cover, then he threw the shell on to the parapet and took cover. The shell exploded, damaging the trench but killing no one.

He was one of 74 VC holders who formed the honour guard at the interment of the Unknown Soldier at Westminster Abbey on 11 November 1920.

He died on 25 March 1972.

Lieutenant CHARLES BONNER
BAY OF BISCAY, France
8 August 1917

He was 32 years old and serving in the Royal Naval Reserve when his Q-ship HMS *Dunraven* was shelled by an enemy submarine. He was in the thick of the fighting and throughout the whole action his pluck and determination had a considerable influence on the crew.

His biography is entitled *Bonner VC. The Biography of Gus Bonner, VC and Master Mariner.*

He died on 7 February 1951.

Petty Officer ERNEST PITCHER
BAY OF BISCAY, France 8 August 1917

He was 28 years old and serving in the Royal Navy when his Q-ship HMS *Dunraven* was shelled by an enemy submarine. He and his gun crew waited while the battle went on overhead. When the magazine below them caught fire, they took the shells and held them on their knees to prevent the heat igniting them. When the magazine finally exploded, they were all blown into the air. Pitcher was elected for the award by the gun crew.

He was one of 74 VC holders who formed the honour guard at the interment of the Unknown Soldier at Westminster Abbey on 11 November 1920. Pitcher also served in the Second World War.

He died on 10 February 1946.

Private ARNOLD LOOSEMORE
LANGEMARCK, Belgium
11 August 1917

He was 21 years old and serving in the 8th Bn, Duke of Wellington's (West Riding) Regiment when during an attack his platoon was held up by machine-gun fire. He crawled through partially cut wire with his Lewis gun and opened fire, killing about 20 Germans. Immediately afterwards his Lewis gun was destroyed and the enemy rushed him, but he shot them with his revolver. Later he shot several enemy snipers, and on returning to the original post he brought back a wounded man under heavy fire.

He died from tuberculosis on 10 April 1924.

Skipper THOMAS CRISP
NORTH SEA 15 August 1917

He was 41 years old and serving in the Royal Naval Reserve aboard the armed smack HMS *Nelson* when the German submarine *UC-41* was spotted some 6,000 yards away. An exchange of fire began, but the large disparity in firepower between the smack's 3-pounder and the submarine's 88mm deck gun meant the engagement was short-lived. The *UC-41* fired eight shots before *Nelson* (formerly *I'll Try*) was in range. The fourth shot from the submarine holed the smack, and the seventh took off both of Crisp's legs. Calling for the confidential papers to be thrown overboard, he also dictated a message to be sent by the boat's carrier pigeons. It read: '*Nelson* being attacked by submarine. Skipper killed. Jim Howe Bank. Send assistance at once.'

The sinking smack was abandoned by the unwounded crew. They tried to take Crisp off, but he ordered them to throw him overboard as he didn't want to slow them down. This the crew refused to do, but finding they were unable to move him, they had to leave without him. He died in his son's arms, as Tom Crisp Jr knelt beside him to say goodbye. It is said that he was smiling as the ship sank beneath him.

Meanwhile another vessel, *Ethel & Millie* (formerly *Boy Alfred*), arrived on the scene as *Nelson* sank, and her skipper Charles Manning called for the lifeboat to come alongside.

Realising that this would greatly overcrowd the little boat, *Nelson*'s survivors refused, so Manning sailed on towards the U-boat, coming under lethal fire as he did so, causing his ship to take on water and begin sinking. The crew of *Ethel & Millie* abandoned their battered ship and were taken aboard *UC-41*, where the survivors from *Nelson* last saw them standing in line being addressed by a German officer. They were never seen again, and much controversy surrounds their disappearance. The prevailing opinion at the time was that they had been murdered by the Germans. But it is more probable that they were killed when *UC-41* was sunk on 21 August 1917.

Thomas Crisp's self-sacrifice in the face of this 'unequal struggle' was used by the government to bolster morale during some of the toughest days of the First World War for Britain. His exploits were read aloud by David Lloyd George in the Houses of Parliament and made headline news for nearly a week.

Private MICHAEL O'ROURKE
HILL 70, LENS, France
15–17 August 1917
He was 39 years old and serving in the 7th (1st British Columbia) Bn, CEF when he worked unceasingly for three days and nights bringing in wounded men, dressing their wounds and fetching them food and water. During the whole time the area in which he was working was swept by heavy machine-gun and rifle fire, and on several occasions O'Rourke was knocked down and partially buried by enemy shells. His courage and devotion in carrying out his rescue work in spite of exhaustion and heavy enemy fire inspired all ranks and undoubtedly saved many lives.

He died on 6 December 1957.

Acting Company Quartermaster Sergeant WILLIAM GRIMBALDESTON
WIJDENDRIFT, Belgium 16 August 1917
He was 27 years old and serving in the 1st Bn, King's Own Scottish Borderers when he noticed that the unit to his left was held up by machine-gun fire from a blockhouse. Arming himself with a rifle and bombs, he started

crawling towards it, and when he had gone about 100 yards another man came forward to give him covering fire. Although wounded, he pushed on to the blockhouse, threatened the machine-gun teams inside with a bomb and forced 36 men to surrender; he also captured six machine-guns and a trench mortar.

He died on 13 August 1959.

Sergeant EDWARD COOPER
LANGEMARCK, Belgium
16 August 1917
He was 21 years old and serving in the 12th Bn, King's Royal Rifle Corps when heavy machine-gun fire from a concrete blockhouse was causing heavy casualties and holding up the advance of the battalion. With four men, Cooper rushed towards the blockhouse and ordered the men with him to fire on it, but the machine-guns were not silenced. He then ran forward alone, firing his revolver through an opening. The guns ceased firing and the garrison surrendered. In all, 7 machine-guns and 45 prisoners were taken.

He died from a heart attack on 19 August 1985.

Acting Lance Corporal FREDERICK ROOM
FREZENBERG, Belgium 16 August 1917
He was 22 years old and serving in the 2nd Bn, Royal Irish Regiment when his company was holding a line of shell-holes and short trenches, and had suffered many casualties. He was in charge of the stretcher-bearers and he worked continuously under heavy fire, dressing wounds and helping to evacuate the wounded. With complete disregard for his own safety, he showed unremitting devotion to duty.

He died of pneumonia on 19 January 1932.

Private HARRY BROWN
HILL 70, LOOS, France 16 August 1917
He was 19 years old and serving in the 10th (Quebec) Bn, CEF when the Germans had massed in force and were counter-attacking. The situation was becoming critical. Artillery support was needed but all the signal wires had been cut. Brown and another soldier were given an important message to be delivered at

all costs. The other messenger was killed almost immediately and Brown's arm was shattered, but he struggled on to complete his mission before collapsing. He died shortly afterwards from his wounds.

Private WILFRED EDWARDS
LANGEMARCK, Belgium
16 August 1917
He was 24 years old and serving in the 7th Bn, King's Own Yorkshire Light Infantry when all of the company officers had been killed or wounded. Without hesitation, and under heavy machine-gun and rifle fire from a concrete fort, he rushed forward at great personal risk and threw bombs into the bunker. He then climbed on top of it and waved to the rest of his company to advance. In all, 3 officers and 30 men surrendered to him. Later Edwards did most valuable work as a runner and guided most of the battalion out through difficult ground. Throughout he set a splendid example despite the danger.

He died on 2 January 1972.

Acting Major OKILL LEARMONTH
LOOS, France 18 August 1917
He was 23 years old and serving in the 2nd (EO) Bn, CEF when during an enemy counter-attack on his position, he instantly charged and personally disposed of the attackers. Later, although mortally wounded and under heavy shell fire, he stood on the parapet bombing the enemy, catching their bombs and throwing them back. He refused to be evacuated and continued giving instructions and advice before being removed to a hospital, where he died the following day.

Company Sergeant Major JOHN SKINNER
WIJDENDRIFT, PASSCHENDAELE, Belgium 18 August 1917
He was 34 years old and serving in the 1st Bn, King's Own Scottish Borderers when his company was held up by machine-gun fire from three blockhouses. Although wounded in the head, Skinner collected six men and with great courage and determination worked around the left flank of the blockhouses and

succeeded in bombing and taking the first blockhouse single-handedly. Then leading his men towards the other two, he cleared them, taking 60 prisoners and capturing 3 machine-guns and 2 trench mortars.

Skinner was killed in action near Vlamertinghe on 17 March 1918. He had six VC holders as his pall bearers.

Sergeant FREDERICK HOBSON
LENS, France 18 August 1917
He was 43 years old and serving in the 20th Bn, 1st (CO) Regiment, CEF when during a strong enemy counter-attack a Lewis gun in a forward position was buried by a shell and all but one of the crew killed. Although not a gunner himself, Hobson dashed forward from his trench, dug out the gun and got it back into action. When the gun jammed, he rushed at the advancing enemy with his bayonet and clubbed rifle, holding them back until he was killed.

Second Lieutenant MONTAGUE MOORE
'TOWER HAMLETS', YPRES, Belgium
20 August 1917
He was 20 years old and serving in the 15th Bn, Hampshire Regiment when he volunteered to make a fresh attack on a final objective. He went forward with 70 men, but the opposition was so strong that only six men made it to the objective. Undaunted, Moore at once bombed a large dug-out, taking 28 prisoners and capturing 2 machine-guns and a light field gun. When reinforced with 60 men, he held out for 36 hours, beating off a number of counter-attacks, until his party was reduced to ten men. He eventually got away his wounded and withdrew under cover of thick mist.

He died on 12 September 1966.

Temporary Second Lieutenant HARDY PARSONS
EPEHY, France 20/21 August 1917
He was 20 years old and serving in the 14th Bn, Gloucestershire Regiment. During a night attack on his post, all the bombers were forced back, but Parsons, who had been badly burned by liquid fire, remained and single-handedly held on. He continued to hold up the enemy

with bombs until he was again severely wounded. His gallant action held the enemy at bay long enough for the defence of the post to be consolidated, but he died later the same day.

Company Sergeant Major ROBERT HANNA
HILL 70, LENS, France 21 August 1917
He was 30 years old and serving in the 29th Bn (British Columbia Regiment), CEF when his company met with severe enemy resistance at a heavily defended strongpoint, which had already beaten off three assaults. When all the officers had become casualties, Hanna, under heavy machine-gun and rifle fire, coolly collected and led a party of men against the strongpoint; he rushed through the wire and personally killed four of the enemy, capturing the position and silencing the machine-guns. His courageous action was responsible for the capture of this most important tactical point.
He died on 15 June 1967.

Acting Corporal FILIP KONOWAL
HILL 70, LENS, France
22–24 August 1917
He was 28 years old and serving in the 47th Bn (British Columbia, later WO, Regiment), CEF when he led his section as it mopped up cellars, craters and gun emplacements after the main attack had moved on. In one cellar he bayoneted three of the enemy, while later in a crater he killed seven more Germans single-handedly. The next day he rushed alone into a machine-gun emplacement, killing all the crew and capturing the gun, and the day after that he killed another gun crew, destroying the gun and post with explosives before being severely wounded. He killed at least 16 of the enemy.
He died on 3 June 1959.

Corporal SIDNEY DAY
HARGICOURT, France 26 August 1917
He was 26 years old and serving in the 11th Bn, Suffolk Regiment when he was in command of a bombing party detailed to clear a maze of trenches still held by the enemy; this he did, killing two machine-gunners and capturing four others before returning to his section. When a grenade fell into a trench occupied by five men, one of them badly wounded, Day picked it up and threw it out of the trench where it immediately exploded. He afterwards completed the trench clearing and established himself in an advanced position, remaining for 66 hours at his post despite coming under intense fire.

He was one of 74 VC holders who formed the honour guard at the interment of the Unknown Soldier at Westminster Abbey on 11 November 1920.

He died on 17 July 1959.

Sergeant JOHN CARMICHAEL
HILL 60, ZWARTELEEN, Belgium
8 September 1917
He was 24 years old and serving in the 9th Bn, North Staffordshire Regiment (Prince of Wales's). While excavating a trench, Carmichael saw that a shell had been unearthed and was starting to burn. Shouting to his men to take cover, he rushed to the shell and put his steel helmet over it and then stood on the helmet. When the shell exploded, the blast blew him out of the trench. He was seriously injured. He could have thrown the bomb out of the trench but by doing so would have endangered the lives of the men working on top. He said of his action: 'They tell me it blew me right out of the trench, but all I remember is being carried away. That's how I got this thing [the VC].'
He died on 20 December 1977.

Lance Sergeant JOHN MOYNEY
NEY COPSE, BROEMBEEK, Belgium
12/13 September 1917
He was 22 years old and serving in the 2nd Bn, Irish Guards when his advanced post had held out for 96 hours. Then, on the fifth day, as a large enemy force advanced, his men attacked the enemy with bombs while he opened fire with a Lewis gun from the flank. He then led a charge through the enemy and reached a stream, which he ordered his men to cross while he and Private Woodcock covered them. He was thus able to bring his entire force safely out of action. Both men were awarded the VC.
He died on 10 November 1980.

Private THOMAS WOODCOCK
NEY COPSE, BROEMBEEK, Belgium
12/13 September 1917

He was 29 years old and serving in the 2nd Bn, Irish Guards. His advanced post had held out for 96 hours before it was finally forced to retire, with Woodcock and Lance Sergeant John Moyney covering the retreat. After crossing a stream, Woodcock heard cries for help behind him. He returned and waded into the stream amid a shower of bombs to rescue a wounded member of the party, whom he carried across open ground in daylight towards our lines, regardless of the machine-gun fire. Both men were awarded the VC.

Woodcock was killed in action at Bullecourt on 27 March 1918.

Private REGINALD INWOOD
POLYGON WOOD, ZONNEBEKE, Belgium 19–22 September 1917

He was 27 years old and serving in the 10th (South Australia) Bn, AIF when he moved forward alone through the Allied barrage and captured an enemy strongpoint, killing several Germans and taking nine prisoners. During the evening he volunteered for a special all-night patrol that went out 600 yards in front of the Allied trenches and succeeded in bringing back valuable information. In the early morning of 21 September he again went out in company with another man and located a machine-gun that was causing much trouble. They bombed it so effectively that only one gunner survived, and he was brought back as a prisoner, along with the gun.

He died on 23 October 1971.

Captain HENRY REYNOLDS
FREZENBERG, Belgium
20 September 1917

He was 38 years old and serving in the 12th Bn, Royal Scots (Lothian Regiment) when his company was suffering heavy casualties from a machine-gun in a pillbox. He advanced alone, going from shell-hole to shell-hole under heavy fire. When he got near the pillbox he threw a grenade, but when this failed to enter it, he crawled up to the entrance and forced in a phosphorus grenade. This set the place on fire, killing three men and forcing the rest to surrender with their two machine-guns. Despite being wounded, Reynolds then captured another objective, this time taking 70 prisoners and two more machine-guns.

He died on 26 March 1948.

Second Lieutenant FREDERICK BIRKS
GLENCORSE WOOD, YPRES, Belgium
20 September 1917

He was 23 years old and serving in the 6th (Victoria) Bn, AIF when he rushed a strongpoint accompanied only by a corporal. When the corporal was wounded, Birks went on alone, killing the rest of the enemy holding the position and capturing a machine-gun. He then attacked another strongpoint, capturing an officer and 15 men.

He was killed in action on 21 September 1917, trying to rescue some of his men who had been buried by a shell.

Second Lieutenant HUGH COLVIN
HESSIAN WOOD, YPRES, Belgium
20 September 1917

He was 30 years old and serving in the 9th Bn, Cheshire Regiment when all the officers in his company and all but one in the leading company had become casualties. He took command of both companies and led them forward under heavy fire with great success. He went with only two other men to a dug-out, entered it alone and brought out 14 prisoners. Then he stormed another dug-out, capturing two machine-guns and many prisoners.

He died on 16 September 1962.

Sergeant WILLIAM BURMAN
BULGAR WOOD, YPRES, Belgium
20 September 1917

He was 20 years old and serving in the 16th Bn, Rifle Brigade (Prince Consort's Own) when his company was held up by machine-gun fire at close range. He shouted to his men to wait and went forward alone to what seemed certain death. However, he killed the gunner and carried the machine-gun to the company's objective, where he used it to great effect.

Within minutes, about 40 Germans were seen enfilading the battalion from the right. Burman and two others got behind them, killing six and capturing two officers and 29 men.

He was one of 74 VC holders who formed the honour guard at the interment of the Unknown Soldier at Westminster Abbey on 11 November 1920.

He died on 23 October 1974.

Sergeant ALFRED KNIGHT
HUBNER FARM, YPRES, Belgium
20 September 1917

He was 29 years old and serving in the 2/8th (City of London) Bn, London Regiment (Post Office Rifles) when his platoon came under heavy machine-gun fire. He rushed through our own barrage and captured the enemy gun single-handed. He performed several other acts of conspicuous bravery, all under heavy machine-gun and rifle fire and without regard to personal safety. When all the platoon officers had become casualties, he took command not only of his own platoon but of all the other platoons without officers. His energy in consolidating and reorganising was untiring.

He died on 4 December 1960.

Lance Corporal WILLIAM HEWITT
YPRES, Belgium 20 September 1917

He was 19 years old and serving in the 14th Bn, Hampshire Regiment when his section made an attack on a pillbox. The defenders proved to be very stubborn, and Hewitt was wounded severely in the arm. Undaunted, he made his way to the loophole and tried to insert a bomb through it, but was again wounded in the arm. He finally forced the bomb in and dislodged the defenders, who were dealt with by his men.

He died from Parkinson's disease on 7 December 1966.

Lance Corporal WALTER PEELER
LEVI COTTAGES, YPRES, Belgium
20 September 1917

He was 30 years old and serving in the 3rd Bn, AIF when during the first wave of an attack he encountered an enemy party sniping at the advancing troops. He immediately rushed their position and accounted for nine of them, clearing the way for the advance. He repeated this action on two subsequent occasions, and each time accounted for a number of the enemy. Later he was directed to an enemy machine-gun that was causing casualties among our men. He located and killed the gunner and then bombed the remainder of the crew from a dug-out where they had taken cover.

He died on 23 May 1968.

Corporal ERNEST EGERTON
BULGAR WOOD, YPRES, Belgium
20 September 1917

He was 19 years old and serving in the 16th Bn, Sherwood Foresters (Nottinghamshire and Derbyshire Regiment) when during an attack in poor visibility, due to thick fog and smoke, the two leading waves passed over some enemy dug-outs without clearing them, and machine-gun and rifle fire from these positions were causing casualties. Egerton at once volunteered to help clear them and dashed at the dug-outs under heavy fire from close range. He shot three men, by which time support had arrived and 29 prisoners were taken.

A few days before his VC action he received a letter informing him that his brother had been killed on 17 August. He said later: 'I was longing to get into action and pay back a debt.' Egerton also served in the Second World War.

He died on 14 February 1966.

Acting Lance Corporal JOHN HAMILTON
YPRES–MENIN ROAD, PASSCHEN-DAELE, Belgium 25/26 September 1917

He was 21 years old and serving in the 1/9th Bn, Highland Light Infantry. At this time great difficulty was experienced in keeping the front lines supplied with small arms ammunition, owing to the intense artillery fire. When supplies reached a seriously low level, Hamilton on several occasions and on his own initiative brought up bandoliers of ammunition through the enemy's fire and then, in full view of their snipers and machine-guns, distributed it to the men.

He died on 18 July 1973.

Sergeant JOHN DWYER
ZONNEBEKE, Belgium
26 September 1917

He was 27 years old and serving in the 4th Company, Machine Gun Corps, AIF when he rushed his Vickers gun to within 30 yards of an enemy machine-gun and opened fire, killing the crew. He then seized their gun and carried it back across shell-swept ground to our lines. Later, when his Vickers gun was blown up, he took his team through the enemy barrage to fetch a reserve gun which was put into use instantly.

He was Speaker of the Tasmanian House of Assembly (1941–48) and Deputy Premier (1958–61).

He died from dermatitis, a legacy of mustard gas poisoning, on 17 January 1962.

Private PATRICK BUGDEN
*POLYGON WOOD, ZONNEBEKE,
Belgium* 26–28 September 1917

He was 20 years old and serving in the 31st (Queensland & Victoria) Bn, AIF when an advance was held up by strongly defended pill-boxes. Bugden twice led small parties of men against these strongpoints despite heavy machine-gun fire, successfully silencing the guns and capturing the crews at the point of the bayonet. On another occasion he rescued a corporal from capture, when single-handedly he rushed at the enemy, shooting one and bayoneting two others. On five occasions he rescued wounded men under intense machine-gun and shell fire, showing contempt and disregard for danger. He was killed on the last of these missions.

Temporary Lieutenant Colonel PHILIP BENT
*POLYGON WOOD, ZONNEBEKE,
Belgium* 1 October 1917

He was 26 years old and serving in the 9th Bn, Leicestershire Regiment when during an enemy attack, the situation had become critical. Bent collected a reserve platoon and led it forward in a counter-attack, which was successful, the Germans being checked. The coolness and magnificent example of this officer resulted in the securing of a portion of the line that was essential to subsequent operations. He was killed soon afterwards leading another charge. His body was never found.

Acting Lieutenant Colonel LEWIS EVANS
ZONNEBEKE, Belgium 4 October 1917

He was 36 years old and serving in the Black Watch (Royal Highlanders), but commanding the 1st Bn, Lincolnshire Regiment, when he took his battalion though a heavy enemy barrage. While his men were trying to outflank a machine-gun emplacement, he rushed it himself, firing his revolver through the loop-hole and forcing the garrison to surrender. Although severely wounded in the shoulder, he refused to be bandaged and again led his battalion forward, being wounded again. Nevertheless he carried on until the next objective was taken, and then he collapsed. As there were numerous casualties, he again refused assistance, making his own way back to the dressing station.

He died on 30 November 1962. His uncles were Lieutenant William Cubitt VC and Second Lieutenant James Hills VC.

Captain CLEMENT ROBERTSON
ZONNEBEKE, Belgium 4 October 1917

He was 26 years old and serving in the Queen's Royal West Surrey Regiment, Special Reserve, Tank Corps when he led his tanks into an attack under heavy shell and machine-gun fire over ground ploughed up by artillery. He and his batman had spent the three previous nights going back and forth, reconnoitring and taping routes for the tanks. Knowing the risk of the tanks missing the way, he now led them on foot, guiding them carefully towards their objective, although he must have known that his action would almost certainly cost him his life. He was killed after the objective had been reached, but his skilful leadership had already ensured success.

Sergeant CHARLES COVERDALE

POELCAPELLE, Belgium 4 October 1917

He was 29 years old and serving in the 11th Bn, Manchester Regiment when he disposed of three snipers close to his unit's objective. He then rushed two machine-guns, killing or wounding the crews. Subsequently he reorganised his platoon in order to capture another position, but after getting to within 100 yards of it was held up by our own barrage and had to return. Later he went out again with just five men to capture the position, but was forced to retire when a considerable number of the enemy advanced on him.

He died on 20 November 1955.

Sergeant LEWIS McGEE

HAMBURG REDOUBT, PASSCHEN-DAELE, Belgium 4 October 1917

He was 29 years old and serving in the 40th (Tasmania) Bn, AIF when his company was held up by machine-gun fire from a pillbox. He rushed the position armed only with his revolver, shooting some of the crew and capturing the rest, and thus enabled the advance to continue. He then reorganised the remnants of his platoon and did splendid work during the consolidation of the position. His coolness and bravery contributed largely to the success of the company's operation.

He was killed in action at Augustus Wood on 13 October 1917.

Sergeant JAMES OCKENDON (spelt OCKENDEN on his VC)

LANGEMARCK, Belgium 4 October 1917

He was 26 years old and serving in the 1st Bn, Royal Dublin Fusiliers. Seeing that the platoon on his right was being held up by a machine-gun, he immediately rushed it, regardless of his own safety, and captured the gun, killing the crew. He then led an attack on a farm with a section of men, where under heavy fire Ockendon rushed forward and called on the garrison to surrender. When the enemy continued to fire on him, he opened fire in return, killing 4 and forcing 16 to surrender.

He died on 29 August 1966.

Acting Corporal FRED GREAVES

POELCAPELLE, YPRES, Belgium
4 October 1917

He was 27 years old and serving in the 9th Bn, Sherwood Foresters (Nottinghamshire and Derbyshire Regiment) when his platoon was held up by machine-gun fire from a concrete strongpoint. He rushed forward with another NCO and bombed the occupants, killing or capturing the garrison and a machine-gun. Later, at a most critical moment during a heavy counter-attack, when all the officers had become casualties, he took command, threw out an extra post on the threatened flank and opened fire to enfilade the enemy, repulsing them in disorder.

He died on 11 June 1973.

Private ARTHUR HUTT

'TERRIER FARM', POELCAPELLE, Belgium 4 October 1917

He was 28 years old and serving in the 1/7th Bn, Royal Warwickshire Regiment when during an advance he took command of his platoon when all the officers and NCOs had become casualties. He led the platoon forward but was held up by a strongpoint which he immediately rushed, killing an officer and three men. Some 40 to 50 more men then surrendered. Later, having pushed too far forward, he withdrew his men, covering them by sniping at the enemy, and then carried back a wounded man. After he had consolidated his position, he went out and carried in four more wounded men under heavy fire.

He died from a brain tumour on 14 April 1954.

Private THOMAS SAGE

'TOWER HAMLETS SPUR', YPRES, Belgium 4 October 1917

He was 34 years old and serving in the 8th Bn, Somerset Light Infantry. He was sharing a shell-hole with eight other men when one of them was shot while throwing a bomb, which dropped into their position. With great presence of mind, Sage immediately threw himself on top of it. He was severely wounded when it exploded, but his action saved the lives of those around him.

He died on 20 July 1945, following a long illness.

Sergeant JOSEPH LISTER
OLGA HOUSE, YPRES, Belgium
9 October 1917

He was 30 years old and serving in the 1st Bn, Lancashire Fusiliers. When the advance of his company was held up by machine-gun fire, he dashed ahead and shot two of the crew, at which the remainder surrendered. He then went on to a pillbox and shouted to the occupants to surrender, which they did with the exception of one man, whom he shot. Then almost a hundred Germans surrendered as they emerged from nearby shell-holes.

He died on 19 January 1963.

Sergeant JOHN MOLYNEUX
LANGEMARCK, Belgium
9 October 1917

He was 26 years old and serving in the 2nd Bn, Royal Fusiliers. When an attack was held up by heavy machine-gun fire, which was causing many casualties, he organised a bombing party to clear a trench in front of a house. He captured the gun and killed the crew. He then called for volunteers to follow him and rushed to the house, but by the time help arrived he was in the thick of a hand-to-hand fight which had only lasted for a short while when 20 to 30 of the enemy surrendered.

He died on 25 March 1972.

Lance Sergeant JOHN RHODES
HOUTHULST FOREST, YPRES,
Belgium 9 October 1917

He was 26 years old and serving in the 3rd Bn, Grenadier Guards. While in charge of a Lewis gun section covering the consolidation of the right front company, he accounted for several of the enemy. When he saw three Germans leave a pillbox, he went alone through our barrage and enemy machine-gun fire and entered the pillbox, capturing nine Germans, including a forward observation officer. He brought these prisoners back, along with valuable information.

He was killed in action at Fontaine Notre Dame on 27 November 1917.

Corporal WILLIAM CLAMP
POELCAPELLE, Belgium
9 October 1917

He was 25 years old and serving in the 6th Bn, Yorkshire Regiment (Alexandra, Princess of Wales's Own) when the advance was checked by heavy machine-gun fire from concrete blockhouses and snipers. Clamp attempted to rush the largest blockhouse but failed, and the two men with him became casualties. Collecting more bombs and two more men, he dashed forward again, being the first to reach the blockhouse. He then hurled his bombs, killing many of the occupants. Entering the blockhouse, he captured about 20 men and a machine-gun, bringing them back under heavy fire. He went forward again encouraging his men and displaying the greatest heroism until killed by a sniper.

Private FREDERICK 'DANDO' DANCOX
BOESINGHE SECTOR, Belgium
9 October 1917

He was 38 years old and serving in the 4th Bn, Worcestershire Regiment when after the first objective had been taken, work was hampered by an enemy machine-gun firing from a pill-box. Dancox, who was part of a mopping-up team, managed to work his way to the pill-box and entered it from the rear, threatening the garrison with a bomb. Shortly afterwards, he reappeared with a machine-gun and about 40 prisoners. He returned to his position and kept the gun in action throughout the day.

Someone wrote to tell him that a civic reception was being organised for his return. But he volunteered to stay at the front as he was shy, and did not believe in any sort of celebration when so many of his comrades had been killed.

He was killed in action at Masnieres on 30 November 1917.

Captain CLARENCE JEFFRIES
PASSCHENDAELE, Belgium
12 October 1917

He was 22 years old and serving in the 34th

(New South Wales) Bn, AIF when he organised a party of men and rushed a machine-gun emplacement, capturing 4 machine-guns and 35 prisoners. He then led his company forward under extremely heavy artillery and enfilading machine-gun fire to the next objective. Later, he again organised a successful attack on a machine-gun position, capturing 2 machine-guns and 30 more prisoners, but was killed during the attack.

Private ALBERT HALTON
POELCAPELLE, Belgium 12 October 1917
He was 24 years old and serving in the 1st Bn, King's Own (Royal Lancaster) Regiment when after the objective had been taken, he rushed forward for 300 yards under very heavy fire and captured the crew of a machine-gun that had caused heavy losses. He then went out again and came back with 12 prisoners, showing the greatest disregard for his own safety and setting a fine example to those around him.

He died on 24 July 1971.

Acting Captain CHRISTOPHER O'KELLY
PASSCHENDAELE, Belgium
26 October 1917
He was 21 years old and serving in the 52nd Bn (96th Lake Superior Regiment), CEF when he led his company with extraordinary skill and determination, capturing 6 pillboxes, 100 prisoners and 10 machine-guns. Later his company repelled a strong counter-attack, taking more prisoners, and subsequently during the night captured a hostile raiding party, consisting of an officer, 10 men and a machine-gun.

He died in a boating accident on 15 November 1922. His body was never recovered.

Lieutenant ROBERT SHANKLAND
PASSCHENDAELE, Belgium
26 October 1917
He was 30 years old and serving in the 43rd Bn (Cameron Highlanders of Canada), CEF when he led his company to a position on the crest of a hill. He then held this line for 4 hours in the face of relentless enemy shelling that threw up so much mud that weapons became clogged. In spite of this, he repulsed a counter-attack,

which enabled supporting troops to come up unmolested. He personally communicated to his headquarters an accurate report of the situation. Shankland then rejoined his command and carried on until relieved.

He is one of three men from Pine Street, Winnipeg, Manitoba, Canada to be awarded the VC. The others are Corporal Leo Clarke and Lieutenant Frederick Hall. The street was renamed Valour Road in their honour.

He died on 20 January 1968.

Private THOMAS HOLMES
PASSCHENDAELE, Belgium
26 October 1917
He was 19 years old and serving in the 2nd Bn, 4th Canadian Mounted Rifles, CEF when the right flank of an attack was held up by heavy machine-gun fire from a pillbox, causing severe casualties and making the situation critical. Single-handedly, and on his own initiative, he ran forward and threw two bombs, killing and wounding the crew. He then fetched another bomb which he threw into the pillbox, causing 19 men to surrender.

The youngest Canadian to be awarded the VC, he died from cancer on 4 January 1950.

Major ALEXANDER LAFONE
BEERSHEBA, Palestine 27 October 1917
He was 47 years old and serving in the 1/1st County of London Yeomanry when he held his position for over 7 hours against vastly superior forces. Several enemy cavalry charges were beaten off with heavy losses, and when all but three of his men had become casualties he ordered those still able to walk to move to a trench in the rear, while he maintained a most heroic resistance. When finally surrounded, Lafone stepped into the open and continued to fight until he was mortally wounded.

Lieutenant HUGH McKENZIE
MEESCHEELE SPUR, PASSCHENDAELE, Belgium 30 October 1917
He was 31 years old and serving in the 7th Company, Canadian Machine Gun Corps, CEF when he was in charge of a machine-gun section accompanying an attack. Seeing that

all the officers and most of the NCOs had become casualties, and that the men were faltering, he handed over command of his section and rallied the men, organised an attack and captured the strongpoint. He then led a successful frontal attack on the pillbox that was causing the casualties, but was killed in the attempt. His body was never found.

Sergeant GEORGE MULLIN
PASSCHENDAELE, Belgium
30 October 1917
He was 25 years old and serving in the Princess Patricia's Canadian Light Infantry, CEF when an enemy pillbox was causing heavy casualties and holding up the attack. He single-handedly rushed a post beside the pillbox and killed the occupants before climbing on top of the pillbox. He then shot two gunners and compelled the remaining ten members of the garrison to surrender. The whole time rapid fire was directed at him and his clothes were riddled with bullet holes, but he never faltered in his purpose and helped to save not only the situation, but many lives as well.

He also served in the Second World War. He died from natural causes on 5 April 1963.

Private CECIL KINROSS
FURST FARM, PASSCHENDAELE, Belgium 30 October 1917
He was 21 years old and serving in the 49th (Edmonton) Bn, CEF when shortly after the attack was launched, his company came under intense artillery fire and further advance was held up by very heavy machine-gun fire. Kinross dumped all his equipment save his rifle and bandolier, and advanced alone over open ground. Charging at the enemy machine-gun, he killed the crew of six and destroyed the gun. His superb example and courage instilled the greatest confidence in his men and enabled a further advance of 300 yards to be made.

Shortly after the award of his Cross, Kinross was stopped by two Military Policemen and accused of wearing a VC ribbon to which he was not entitled. He had to produce his VC and show them his name on it to avoid arrest.

He died on 21 June 1957.

Acting Major GEORGE PEARKES
VAPOUR FARM, PASSCHENDAELE, Belgium 30/31 October 1917
He was 29 years old and serving in the 5th Bn, Canadian Mounted Rifles, CEF when he was wounded in the leg just before an attack but insisted on leading his men. Their advance was held up by a strongpoint which another battalion had failed to take, so he led an attack which carried the position. He then managed to hold his post with his few remaining men against repeated counter-attacks, until support arrived.

Pearkes also served in the Second World War. He was Minister of National Defence (1957–60) and Lieutenant-Governor of British Columbia (1960–68).

He died following a stroke on 30 May 1984.

Acting Corporal JOHN COLLINS
WADI SABA, Palestine 31 October 1917
He was 29 years old and serving in the 25th Bn, Royal Welch Fusiliers when his battalion was forced to lie in the open under heavy shell and machine-gun fire. He went out alone to bring back many wounded men and then led the final assault with great skill, despite heavy fire at close range and uncut wire, killing 15 of the enemy. With a Lewis gun section, he later covered the reorganisation and consolidation of the men under heavy fire.

He died on 3 September 1951.

Captain JOHN RUSSELL
TEL-EL-KHUWEILFEH, Palestine 6 November 1917
He was 20 years old and serving in the Royal Army Medical Corps, attached to the 1/6th Bn, Royal Welch Fusiliers, when he repeatedly went out to attend the wounded under murderous fire from machine-guns and snipers. Although exhausted, he carried many wounded men back to safety until he was mortally wounded.

Corporal COLIN BARRON
VINE COTTAGE, PASSCHENDAELE, Belgium 6 November 1917
He was 24 years old and serving in the 3rd

(Toronto) Bn, CEF when his unit was held up by three machine-guns. He opened fire on them before rushing the guns, killing four of the crew and capturing the rest. He then turned one of the guns on the retiring enemy, causing heavy casualties.

He died on 15 August 1959.

Private JAMES ROBERTSON
PASSCHENDAELE, Belgium
6 November 1917
He was 34 years old and serving in the 27th (City of Winnipeg) Bn, CEF when his platoon was held up by a machine-gun. He rushed the gun, killed four of the crew and turned the gun on the remainder as they retreated. He then led the platoon to the final objective and again used the gun on the retreating enemy. Later, he went out under heavy fire to bring back two wounded men, but was killed while carrying the second man back.

Lieutenant Colonel ARTHUR 'BOSKY' BORTON
SHERIA, Palestine 7 November 1917
He was 30 years old and serving in the 2/22nd (County of London) Bn, London Regiment when he deployed his battalion for attack under the most difficult conditions. As the first waves were checked by withering fire, he moved along the line under heavy fire before leading them forward and taking the objective. Later, he led a party of volunteers against a battery of field guns, capturing both the guns and the detachments.

Borton had also served in the Second Boer War and with the North Russia Relief Force.

He died from a drink-related illness on 5 January 1933. His uncle was Captain William Vousden VC.

Ordinary Seaman JOHN CARLESS
HELIGOLAND, North Sea
17 November 1917
He was 21 years old and serving in the Royal Navy aboard HMS *Caledon*. Although mortally wounded, he still went on serving his gun and helping to clear away the casualties. He collapsed once but struggled up again and

cheered on the new gun crew. He then fell dead. He not only set a very inspiring example to the men, but continued to do effective work against the enemy while mortally wounded.

Acting Lieutenant Colonel JOHN 'BOMB' SHERWOOD-KELLY
MARCOING, CAMBRAI, France
20 November 1917
He was 37 years old and commanding the 1st Bn, Norfolk Regiment (Royal Inniskilling Fusiliers). When heavy fire prevented another battalion from crossing the canal, he personally led the leading company of his battalion across, and then under heavy fire reconnoitred the high ground held by the enemy. The left flank of his battalion became held up by wire, so he crossed to that flank and with a Lewis gun team covered the advance. He later led a successful charge against some rifle pits, during which he captured 5 machine-guns and 46 prisoners.

Sherwood-Kelly had also served in the Matabele Revolt of 1896, the Second Boer War, the Zululand Rebellion of 1906 and with the North Russia Relief Force, but was court-martialled for publicly criticising the handling of the BEF. He died from malaria on 18 August 1931. His grandfather Private James Kelly took part in the 'Charge of the Light Brigade'.

Captain RICHARD WAIN
MARCOING, CAMBRAI, France
20 November 1917
He was 20 years old and serving in A Bn, Tank Corps when his tank was disabled by a direct hit from an enemy strongpoint. Despite being wounded, he refused medical aid and captured the strongpoint using a Lewis gun, taking half the garrison prisoner. He was wounded again but picked up a rifle and continued firing until mortally wounded.

Lieutenant HARCUS STRACHAN
MASNIERES, CAMBRAI, France
20 November 1917
He was 33 years old and serving in the Fort Garry Horse, CEF. When his squadron leader was killed, he took command and led the men

through a line of machine-gun posts, and then charged on to an enemy battery, killing seven gunners with his sword. With the battery silenced, Strachan rallied his men and fought his way back at night on foot through the enemy lines, bringing fifteen prisoners with him.

He also served during the Second World War. He died on 1 May 1982.

Sergeant CHARLES SPACKMAN
MARCOING, CAMBRAI, France
20 November 1917

He was 26 years old and serving in the 1st Bn, Border Regiment when the leading company was checked by heavy fire from a machine-gun in a commanding position. Spackman went forward alone through the fire to attack the gun, killing all but one of the crew and capturing the gun. The advance was then able to continue.

He died on 6 May 1969.

Lance Corporal ROBERT McBEATH (spelt MacBEATH on his headstone)
CAMBRAI, France 20 November 1917

He was 19 years old and serving in the 1/5th Bn, Seaforth Highlanders Ross-shire Buffs (Duke of Albany's). When an advance was held up by machine-gun fire, he volunteered to go forward alone, armed with a Lewis gun and a revolver. Finding that several other enemy machine-guns were also in action, he attacked them, and with help from a tank he drove the gunners to ground in a dug-out. Then he rushed in after them, shot the first man and captured 3 officers and 30 men.

He was shot dead on 9 October 1922 while serving in the Canadian Police.

Private ALBERT SHEPHERD
VILLERS PLOUICH, France
20 November 1917

He was 20 years old and serving in the 12th (Service) Bn, King's Royal Rifle Corps when he volunteered to rush a machine-gun that was holding up the advance of his company. He was ordered not to, but ran forward anyway and threw a Mills bomb, killing two of the gunners. He then captured the rest of the crew.

The company continued its advance but came under heavy enfilade fire. When the last officer and NCO became casualties, Shepherd took command, ordering the men to lie down while he went back 70 yards to get the help of a tank. He then led them to their final objective.

He died on 23 October 1966.

Sergeant JOHN McAULAY
FONTAINE NOTRE DAME, France
27 November 1917

He was 28 years old and serving in the 1st Bn, Scots Guards. When all his officers had become casualties, he assumed command of the company and under shell and machine-gun fire successfully held and consolidated the objectives gained. He then reorganised the company and repulsed a counter-attack by the skilful use of his machine-guns, causing heavy losses among the enemy. Later he carried his mortally wounded company commander to a place of safety.

After the war he resumed his career in the Police, rising to the rank of inspector.

He died on 14 January 1956.

Private GEORGE CLARE
BOURLON WOOD, France
28/29 November 1917

He was 28 years old and serving in the 5th Lancers (Royal Irish). Acting as a stretcher-bearer, he dressed the wounded under heavy fire and then crossed open ground to a detached post where all the occupants had become casualties. Having dressed all their wounds, he manned the post single-handedly until relief could be sent. Then, after carrying a seriously wounded man through intense fire to a dressing station, he went to every company post under heavy fire to warn them that the enemy were using gas shells.

He was killed in action on 29 November 1917. His body was never found.

Temporary Lieutenant Colonel NEVILLE ELLIOTT-COOPER
LA VACQUERIE, CAMBRAI, France
30 November 1917

He was 28 years old and commanding the 8th

Bn, Royal Fusiliers when the enemy broke through our outpost line. On seeing this, he mounted the parapet, calling upon the reserve company and men from the battalion head-quarters to follow. Unarmed, he made his way straight for the advancing Germans and under his direction his men forced them back 600 yards. While still some way ahead of his own men, he was severely wounded. Realising that his force was greatly outnumbered, he signalled to them to withdraw, knowing that he would be captured.

He died of his wounds on 11 February 1918 in Hannover.

Temporary Captain ROBERT GEE
MASNIERES, France 30 November 1917
He was 41 years old and serving in the 2nd Bn, Royal Fusiliers when his brigade HQ and ammunition dump were captured, he being taken prisoner. Gee managed to escape and organised a party of the brigade HQ staff with which he attacked the enemy, closely followed by two companies of infantry. He cleared the HQ area and established a defensive flank. Although wounded, when he found an enemy machine-gun still in action, he rushed it with a revolver in each hand, killing eight of the crew. He refused to have his wound dressed until the defence was organised.

Gee was one of 74 VC holders who formed the honour guard at the interment of the Unknown Soldier at Westminster Abbey on 11 November 1920. Gee is one of the few VC holders to become an MP.

He died on 2 August 1960.

Acting Captain WALTER STONE
CAMBRAI, France 30 November 1917
He was 25 years old and serving in the 3rd Bn, Royal Fusiliers. While in command of an isolated company some 1,000 yards in front of the main line, he observed the enemy massing for an attack and sent this information to battalion HQ. He was ordered to withdraw but the attack developed too quickly, so he sent back three platoons and remained with the rearguard. He stood on the parapet passing information by telephone under terrific

bombardment until the wire was cut. The rear-guard was surrounded and cut to pieces. Stone was seen fighting until he was shot dead. His body was never found. The accuracy of his information enabled the line to be held.

Temporary Lieutenant SAMUEL WALLACE
GONNELIEU, France 30 November 1917
He was 25 years old and serving in C Battery, 63rd Brigade, Royal Field Artillery when his battery was reduced to five men, having lost their commander and five sergeants, and was surrounded by the enemy. He maintained fire by swinging the trails of the guns close together and having the men running from gun to gun to keep up the shooting. He was in action for 8 hours, firing the whole time and inflicting heavy losses on the enemy. Then, owing to the exhausted state of his men, he withdrew when infantry support arrived, taking with him all the essential gun parts and all of his wounded men.

He died on 2 February 1968.

Sergeant CYRIL GOURLEY
LITTLE PRIEL FARM, EPEHY, France 30 November 1917
He was 24 years old and serving in D Battery, 276th (West Lancashire) Brigade, Royal Field Artillery when he was commanding a section of howitzers. The enemy advanced to within 400 yards of his front and 300–400 yards of his flank. He managed to keep one gun firing, although his men were plagued by snipers. At one point he pulled the gun out of the pit and engaged a machine-gun at 500 yards, knocking it out. All day he held the Germans in check, firing over open sights, thus saving the guns, which were withdrawn at nightfall.

He died in his sleep on 31 January 1982.

Lance Corporal JOHN THOMAS
FONTAINE, France 30 November 1917
He was 31 years old and serving in the 2/5th Bn, Staffordshire Regiment (Prince of Wales's) when he saw the enemy making preparations for a counter-attack. He crawled out into the open and fooled the snipers by pretending to be hit and lying still. In this way he was able to

shoot three snipers. He then crawled to a building from which he could see the enemy congregating. He worked his way back to his own lines and as a result of his information, the counter-attack was swiftly broken up.

He died on 28 February 1954.

Acting Captain ALLASTAIR (spelt ALASTAIR on early records) McREADY-DIARMID (formerly DREW)
MOEUVRES SECTOR, France
30 November/1 December 1917
He was 29 years old and serving in the 17th Bn, Middlesex Regiment (Duke of Cambridge's Own). When the enemy penetrated into our position, the situation became critical. He led his company forward through a heavy barrage and engaged the enemy and drove them back 300 yards. The next day the enemy again attacked and drove back another company. This time he called for volunteers and led the attack, again driving the enemy back. It was largely due to his bomb-throwing that the ground was retaken, but he was killed by a bomb. His body was never found.

Acting Captain GEORGE PATON
GONNELIEU, France 1 December 1917
He was 22 years old and serving in the 4th Bn, Grenadier Guards. When the company on his left was driven back, practically surrounding him, he walked up and down, adjusting the line, within 50 yards of the enemy's withering fire. He personally removed several wounded men and was the last to leave the village. He again adjusted his line under fire. The enemy counter-attacked four times, and each time he jumped on to the parapet to encourage his men, until he was mortally wounded.

Second Lieutenant STANLEY BOUGHEY
EL BURF, Palestine 1 December 1917
He was 21 years old and serving in the 1/4th Bn, Royal Scots Fusiliers. When Turkish soldiers in large numbers had managed to get within 30 yards of the British firing line, and were pinning down our men with bombs and automatic fire, Boughey rushed forward alone right up to the Turks and killed many with bombs,

causing the surrender of 30 men. As he turned to go back for more bombs, he was mortally wounded at the very moment the Turks were surrendering.

His commanding officer wrote of him: '[His] was quite one of the pluckiest acts of the war.'

Lance Dafadar GOBIND (spelt GOVIND on later records) SINGH
PEIZIERES, France 1 December 1917
He was 29 years old and serving in the 28th Light Cavalry, attached to the 2nd Lancers, when he volunteered to carry messages from his regiment to brigade HQ, a distance of 3 miles. Three times he did this under heavy fire, and each time his horse was shot from under him, compelling him to continue on foot.

He died on 9 December 1943.

Acting Captain ARTHUR LASCELLES
MASNIERES, France 3 December 1917
He was 37 years old and serving in the 3rd Bn, Durham Light Infantry. During a heavy bombardment, he continued to encourage his men and organise his defences until the attack was driven off, although wounded. Shortly afterwards the enemy attacked again, this time capturing part of the trench. He at once jumped on to the parapet and followed by twelve men rushed across the fire-swept ground and drove 60 of the enemy back. During the next attack his trench was captured and he was taken prisoner, but he managed to escape despite two further wounds.

He was killed in action at Limont on 8 November 1918.

Private HENRY NICHOLAS
POLDERHOEK, Belgium
3 December 1917
He was 26 years old and serving in the 1st Bn, Canterbury Infantry Regiment, NZEF when his section was checked by heavy machine-gun and rifle fire from an enemy strongpoint. He went forward with the rest of the section some 25 yards behind him, shot the officer in command and overcame the garrison of sixteen men with bombs and the bayonet, capturing four wounded prisoners and a machine-gun.

He did this practically single-handedly and thereby saved many casualties. Later he went out and collected ammunition under heavy machine-gun fire.

He was killed in action near Le Quesnoy on 23 October 1918, just 19 days before the armistice.

Temporary Second Lieutenant JAMES EMERSON

LA VACQUERIE, CAMBRAI, France
6 December 1917

He was 22 years old and serving in the 9th Bn, Royal Inniskilling Fusiliers. While leading his company in an attack on the Hindenberg line, he cleared 400 yards of trench. Although he was wounded, when the enemy attacked in superior numbers he met their attack with just eight men, killing many of the enemy and taking six prisoners. He held on for 3 hours afterwards, all the other officers having been killed or wounded, remaining with his company and refusing to go to the dressing station. He repeatedly repelled bombing attacks. Later, while helping to repel another, he was mortally wounded. His heroism inspired his men to hold on until reinforcements arrived.

Corporal CHARLES TRAIN

EIN KARIM, Palestine 8 December 1917

He was 27 years old and serving in the 2/14th (County of London) Bn, London Regiment (London Scottish). When his company's assault was halted by Turkish machine-gun fire, he dashed forward for 20 yards, then crept up to the end of the enemy barricade and began firing and throwing bombs. He shot an officer, at which point the remaining men ran to the other end of the barricade, where they were engaged by his comrades. Train then shot a Turk who was attempting to escape with one of the machine-guns. His action allowed his battalion to advance to their objective at a time when the situation was critical. He was twice offered a commission but turned it down to stay in the ranks.

He died on 28 March 1965.

Private WALTER MILLS

'RED DRAGON CRATER', GIVENCHY, France 10/11 December 1917

He was 23 years old and serving in the 1/10th Bn, Manchester Regiment when following an intense gas attack a strong enemy patrol tried to rush our posts, the garrisons of which had been overcome by the gas. Although badly gassed, Mills met the attack single-handedly, throwing bombs until the arrival of reinforcements. He remained at his post until the enemy had been driven off. It was entirely due to his action that the enemy were defeated and the line remained intact. He died soon afterwards from the effects of gas poisoning.

Lance Corporal JOHN CHRISTIE

FEJJA, Palestine 21/22 December 1917

He was 22 years old and serving in the 1/11th (County of London) Bn, London Regiment (Finsbury Rifles) when the enemy captured our position and were making forays along the communication trenches. Seeing what was happening, Christie took a supply of bombs, went out alone and started bombing the enemy in spite of heavy opposition, until a block was established. His prompt action cleared a difficult position at a most critical time.

He died on 10 September 1967.

Temporary Captain JAMES McCUDDEN

France
23 December 1917–2 February 1918

He was 22 years old and serving in 56 Squadron, RFC. During this period he accounted for 57 enemy aeroplanes, of which 42 were destroyed. Only 12 of them were driven down 'out of control'. On two occasions he destroyed four two-seater planes in a day, the last time in the space of just 1½ hours. On 23 September 1917 he was involved in the epic dog-fight which saw the death of Werner Voss (Germany's fourth highest scoring ace of the war). On 23 December 1917 he was leading a patrol when eight enemy aeroplanes were attacked, two of which were shot down by McCudden over our lines. On the same day he also encountered four enemy aeroplanes, two of which he shot down. On 30 January 1918 he single-handedly attacked five enemy scouts, shooting down two of them. On this occasion he only returned to his base when the enemy had been driven east, his Lewis gun ammunition was used up and his Vickers gun-belt had broken. As a patrol leader he had at all times shown the utmost gallantry, not only in the manner in which he attacked the enemy, but in the way he protected newer members of his flight, thus keeping casualties to a minimum.

He died on 9 July 1918, when his plane crashed on take-off. The most highly decorated British airman of the war, his awards include the VC, DSO and Bar, MC and Bar, MM and the Croix de Guerre. He is the author of *Flying Fury – Five Years in the RFC*.

Author's Note: the date for his VC action is often shown as August 1917 to March 1918, but I wrote to the Royal Engineers Museum and staff there confirmed that the actual date on the medal is 23 December 1917 to 2 February 1918.

Private JAMES DUFFY
KEREINA PEAK, Palestine
27 December 1917
He was 28 years old and serving in the 6th Bn, Royal Inniskilling Fusiliers when his company was holding a very exposed position. Duffy and another man went out to bring in a wounded comrade. When the other man was wounded, Duffy returned to get another stretcher-bearer, who was killed almost immediately. So he went forward alone and, under very heavy fire, succeeded in getting both men under cover, where he attended to their wounds. His gallantry undoubtedly saved both men's lives.

He died on 8 April 1969.

1918

Lieutenant Commander GEOFFREY WHITE
DARDANELLES, Turkey
28 January 1918
He was 31 years old and serving in the Royal Navy aboard HM Submarine *E14*. He was hunting for the German battlecruiser *Goeben*, but when he could not find it he fired a torpedo at another ship. There was an explosion and the submarine was badly damaged. As the air began to run out, White gave the order to surface and the submarine immediately came under fire from all sides. Indeed, it received so much damage that White turned towards the shore in order to save the crew. He remained on deck until he was killed by a shell.

Lance Corporal CHARLES ROBERTSON
POLDERHOEK CHATEAU, Belgium
8/9 March 1918
He was 38 years old and serving in the 10th Bn, Royal Fusiliers when he repelled a strong attack with his Lewis gun, but was almost cut off in the process. He sent for reinforcements and manned his post with just one other man, killing large numbers of the enemy. When help did not arrive, he withdrew to a defended post where he got on to the parapet and continued firing until severely wounded. Despite this, he managed to crawl back with his gun, having used all his ammunition.

Robertson died on 10 May 1954.

Private HAROLD WHITFIELD
BURJ EL LISANEH, Egypt
10 March 1918
He was 31 years old and serving in the 10th Bn, King's Shropshire Light Infantry. During the third counter-attack by the enemy on the position that had just been captured by his battalion, Whitfield single-handedly charged and captured a machine-gun, killing the whole crew; turning the gun on the Turks, he drove them back with heavy casualties. Later he organised and led a bombing attack on the enemy, again inflicting many casualties. He then established his party in their position and assisted in the defeat of another counter-attack. His actions this day saved many lives.

He died on 19 December 1956.

Temporary Lieutenant Colonel WILFRITH ELSTOB
MANCHESTER REDOUBT, ST QUENTIN, France 21 March 1918
He was 29 years old and commanding the

16th Bn, Manchester Regiment. While encouraging his men during the preliminary bombardment of the Manchester Redoubt, giving personal support with revolver, rifle and bombs, he single-handedly repulsed one bombing assault, and later, when ammunition was running out, he made several journeys under heavy fire to replenish the supply. He sent his brigade commander the message: 'The Manchester Regiment will defend Manchester hill to the last.' Although wounded twice, he continued to inspire his men to hold on, but the post was overrun and he was killed.

Temporary Captain MANLEY JAMES
VELU WOOD, France 21 March 1918
He was 26 years old and serving in the 8th Bn, Gloucestershire Regiment when he led his company forward, capturing 27 prisoners and 2 machine-guns. Although wounded, he refused to leave his company and repulsed three enemy assaults, despite being wounded again. Two days later, the enemy having broken through, James made a determined stand, inflicting heavy losses and gaining time for the withdrawal of some guns. He was wounded again during a local counter-attack before being taken prisoner.

He also served in the Second World War.
He died on 23 September 1973.

Lieutenant ALLAN KER
ST QUENTIN, France 21 March 1918
He was 35 years old and serving in the 3rd Bn, Gordon Highlanders. When the enemy had broken through our lines, he succeeded in stopping their attack by manning a Vickers gun, with which he inflicted heavy casualties on the enemy. He stayed at his post with several wounded men, fighting with revolvers, but was finally forced to surrender when he was totally exhausted, suffering the effects of gas poisoning, and out of food and ammunition. He had held up 500 Germans for 3 hours.

Ker was one of 74 VC holders who formed the honour guard at the interment of the Unknown Soldier at Westminster Abbey on 11 November 1920.

He died from an aneurism on 12 September 1958.

Second Lieutenant JOHN BUCHAN
MARTEVILLE, France 21 March 1918
He was 25 years old and serving in the 7th Bn, Argyll and Sutherland Highlanders (Princess Louise's). Although wounded earlier in the day, he insisted on remaining with his platoon, which was under severe attack and suffering heavy casualties. He continually visited all his posts, encouraging his men under heavy machine-gun fire. When called on to surrender, he fought his way back to the support line, where he held out until dusk, still refusing to accept any medical aid. Totally cut off, he was last seen fighting against overwhelming odds.

He died from his wounds on 22 March 1918, while a prisoner-of-war.

Second Lieutenant EDMUND de WIND
*'RACECOURSE REDOUBT',
GROAGIE, France* 21 March 1918
He was 34 years old and serving in the 15th Bn, Royal Irish Rifles when for 7 hours he held this important post; although wounded twice, he almost single-handedly maintained his position until another section could be sent to help. On two occasions, with only two NCOs to support him, he got out on top of the trench under heavy fire, and cleared the enemy from the trench, killing many of them. He continued to repel attack after attack until he was mortally wounded.

Mount de Wind in Alberta, Canada is named in his honour.

Lance Corporal JOHN SAYER
LE VERGUIER, France 21 March 1918
He was 38 years old and serving in the 8th Bn, Queen's (Royal Surrey) Regiment when he held the left flank of a small isolated post for 2 hours. Owing to mist, the enemy approached from both sides of his position to within 30 yards before being discovered, but Sayer, on his own initiative, beat off a succession of attacks, inflicting heavy losses on the enemy. During the whole time he was exposed to heavy fire but his contempt for danger and skill in the

use of his firearms enabled the post to hold out until nearly all the men had been killed and he was wounded and captured. His leg had to be amputated.

He died as a result of his wounds on 18 April 1918. His VC action is sometimes incorrectly dated to 31 March.

Gunner CHARLES STONE
CAPONNE FARM, France
21 March 1918

He was 29 years old and serving in C Battery, 83rd Brigade, Royal Artillery when, after working at his gun for 6 hours, he was sent to the rear. However, he returned voluntarily with a rifle and lay in the open under heavy fire, shooting at the Germans. Later, he captured four Germans who had worked their way around the rear of the gun position armed with a machine-gun.

Stone was one of 74 VC holders who formed the honour guard at the interment of the Unknown Soldier at Westminster Abbey on 11 November 1920.

He died on 29 August 1952.

Acting Captain REGINALD HAYWARD
FREMICOURT, France
21/22 March 1918

He was 26 years old and serving in the 1st Bn, Wiltshire Regiment. When his company came under heavy enemy attack, he displayed supreme powers of endurance. In spite of being buried by a shell, wounded in the head and left deaf and having his arm shattered on the first day of operations, he refused to leave his men, even after receiving another wound to his head. Throughout this time the enemy were attacking the company's front without cessation, but he continued to move across the open, going from trench to trench with absolute disregard for his own safety, until he collapsed from exhaustion.

He died from natural causes on 17 January 1970.

Temporary Second Lieutenant ERNEST BEAL
ST LEGER, France 21/22 March 1918

He was 33 years old and serving in the 13th Bn, Yorkshire Regiment (Alexandra, Princess of Wales's Own) when he led a small party of men up a communication trench to clear a 400-yard gap held by the Germans. During this action he captured four machine-guns and inflicted heavy casualties on the enemy. Later in the evening he carried back to safety a wounded man who was lying near the enemy lines, but was killed shortly afterwards. His body was never recovered.

Temporary Second Lieutenant CECIL KNOX
TUGNY, AISNE, France 22 March 1918

He was 29 years old and serving in the 150th Field Company, Corps of Royal Engineers when he was entrusted with the demolition of 12 bridges over the Somme Canal. All were destroyed except for one, where the time fuse failed. Without hesitation, he ran to the intact bridge under heavy fire, and even as the Germans were starting to cross it he lit the instantaneous fuse. As a trained engineer, he undoubtedly realised the grave risk he was taking in doing this.

He also served in the Second World War.

He died on 4 February 1943 from a fractured skull, following a motorcycle accident.

Sergeant HAROLD JACKSON
HERMIES, France 22 March 1918

He was 25 years old and serving in the 7th Bn, East Yorkshire Regiment when he went through an enemy barrage and brought back valuable information regarding the enemy's movements. When the enemy had established themselves in the British line, Jackson single-handedly bombed them out into the open. Again single-handedly, he stalked an enemy machine-gun and threw Mills bombs that put the gun out of action. On a subsequent occasion, when all his officers had become casualties, he led the company to the attack, withdrawing successfully when ordered to do so. He repeatedly went out under fire and carried in wounded men.

He was killed in action near Thiepval on 24 August 1918.

Private HERBERT COLUMBINE
HERVILLY WOOD, France
22 March 1918
He was 24 years old and serving in the 9th Squadron, Machine Gun Corps when he kept his machine-gun firing from 9am for 4 hours in an isolated position with no wire. Wave after wave of Germans failed to take the position, until he came under attack from a low-flying aircraft. He was then bombed from both flanks, but kept on firing until killed by a bomb. His body was never found.

Acting Lieutenant Colonel JOHN COLLINGS-WELLS
MARCOING to ALBERT, France
22–27 March 1918
He was 37 years old and commanding the 4th Bn, Bedfordshire Regiment. When his rear-guard was almost surrounded, he called for volunteers to stay behind with him so the remainder of the rearguard could withdraw. He held the enemy up for 1½ hours. Later, when ordered to counter-attack, and knowing how exhausted his men were, he personally led them forward and even when twice wounded continued to lead and encourage them. He was killed as the objective was taken.

Acting Lieutenant Colonel FRANK ROBERTS
PARGNY, France 22 March–2 April 1918
He was 26 years old and commanding the 1st Bn, Worcestershire Regiment when over a twelve-day period he displayed exceptional skill in dealing with many difficult situations during the German offensive. On one occasion the enemy attacked and cleared a village. Roberts led a counter-attack which temporarily drove the enemy out, thus covering the retreat of the men on both flanks. The success of this action was due entirely to his personal courage and skill.
He died on 12 January 1982.

Lieutenant Colonel CHRISTOPHER BUSHELL
TERGNIER, France 23 March 1918
He was 29 years old and commanding the 7th

Bn, Queen's Royal West Surrey Regiment when he led C Company of his battalion, in cooperation with another Allied regiment, in a counter-attack, in the course of which he was severely wounded in the head. Refusing aid, he carried on, walking in front of the men, encouraging them and visiting every part of the line under heavy rifle and machine-gun fire. He was finally removed from the line after fainting.
He was killed in action near Morlencourt on 8 August 1918.

Temporary Captain JULIAN GRIBBLE
HERMIES RIDGE, BEAUMETZ, France
23 March 1918
He was 21 years old and serving in the 10th Bn, Royal Warwickshire Regiment when he was ordered to hold on at all costs. He could have withdrawn when the battalion on his left was driven back, but he obeyed his orders to the letter, and when his company was completely surrounded, he was seen fighting to the last.
He died from his wounds, complicated by pneumonia, on 25 November 1918, while a prisoner-of-war.

Temporary Second Lieutenant ALFRED HERRING
MONTAGNE BRIDGE, France
23/24 March 1918
He was 29 years old and serving in the Royal Army Service Corps, attached to the 6th Bn, Northamptonshire Regiment when the enemy gained a position on the south bank of the canal and he was surrounded. He immediately counter-attacked, recapturing the position and taking 20 prisoners and 6 machine-guns. During the night his post was continually attacked, but all such attacks were beaten off, largely due to his bravery and his skilful handling of his men. The enemy advance was held up for 11 hours.
Herring was one of 74 VC holders who formed the honour guard at the interment of the Unknown Soldier at Westminster Abbey on 11 November 1920.
He died on 10 August 1966.

Corporal JOHN DAVIES
EPPEVILLE, France 24 March 1918
He was 22 years old and serving in the 11th Bn, South Lancashire Regiment (Prince of Wales's Volunteers). When almost surrounded and forced to withdraw, he knew the only line of retreat was through a stream blocked by barbed wire. To hold the enemy up as long as possible, he mounted the parapet in full view of the enemy and kept his Lewis gun in action, causing heavy casualties and allowing the company to get away. He was taken prisoner shortly afterwards.

Davies also served in the Second World War.

He died on 28 October 1955.

Acting Lieutenant Colonel WILLIAM ANDERSON
BOIS FAVIERES, MARICOURT, France 25 March 1918
He was 36 years old and commanding the 12th Bn, Highland Light Infantry when the enemy penetrated the line to his right. Fearing that his flank would be turned, he led a counter-attack and drove the Germans out, capturing 70 prisoners and 12 machine-guns. Later the same day he led another counter-attack which resulted in the enemy being driven from his position, but he was killed during this action.

In 2007 his great-grandson Robin Scott-Elliot published the story of Anderson and his three brothers, all of whom were killed in the war, as *The Way Home*.

Acting Captain ALFRED TOYE
ETERPIGNY RIDGE, France 25 March 1918
He was 25 years old and serving in the 2nd Bn, Middlesex Regiment (Duke of Cambridge's Own) when he recaptured a post three times, before fighting his way through the enemy together with an officer and six men of his company. Toye gathered 70 men and mounted an attack, which then took up a defensive line that held until reinforcements arrived. He later covered the battalion's retreat on two occasions and re-established a line that had been abandoned before his arrival. He was

wounded twice but remained with his men.

He died from cancer on 6 September 1955.

Lance Corporal ARTHUR CROSS
ERVILLERS, France 25 March 1918
He was 33 years old and serving in the 40th Bn, Machine Gun Corps when he volunteered to make a reconnaissance of a machine-gun position captured by the enemy. He crept back to the trench alone with only a revolver and surprised seven Germans who threw down their weapons and surrendered. He then marched them back, carrying two machine-guns complete with tripods and ammunition, to the British lines. After handing over his prisoners, he collected teams for the guns, which he brought back into action immediately, annihilating a very heavy attack by the enemy.

He died on 26 November 1965. His medal was used as a prop for the film *Carrington VC* starring David Niven.

Private THOMAS YOUNG (real name MORRELL)
BUCQUOY, France 25–31 March 1918
He was 23 years old and serving in the 9th Bn, Durham Light Infantry. Working as a stretcher-bearer, he unceasingly evacuated the wounded from seemingly impossible places. On nine occasions he went out in front of the lines in full daylight, under heavy rifle, machine-gun and shell fire, to bring wounded men back to safety. Those too badly wounded to be moved before dressing, he tended to under fire, and then carried them back unaided. In this manner he saved nine lives.

He died on 15 October 1966.

Sergeant ALBERT MOUNTAIN
HAMELINCOURT, France 26 March 1918
He was 22 years old and serving in the 15/17th Bn, West Yorkshire Regiment (Prince of Wales's Own). When his company fell back, the enemy advanced in strength. He immediately led a counter-attack with ten men, killing half of the advanced guard of 200 men with a Lewis gun. Then with just four men he held back the main attack of 600 men for 30

minutes. Later he took command of his battalion's flank, holding on for 27 hours before rejoining his company.

He died on 7 January 1967.

Second Lieutenant BASIL HORSFALL
near ABLAINZEVELLE, France
27 March 1918
He was 30 years old and serving in the 1st Bn, East Yorkshire Regiment, attached to the 11th Bn, when during an attack his centre platoon was driven back and he was wounded in the head. He immediately reorganised his men and counter-attacked, retaking the position. He refused any medical aid and made another successful counter-attack. When ordered to retire, he stayed to cover the withdrawal, and was killed. His body was never found.

Second Lieutenant ALAN 'BABE' McLEOD
ALBERT, France 27 March 1918
He was 18 years old and serving in 2 Squadron, RFC when he and his observer Arthur Hammond destroyed an enemy triplane, but were then attacked by eight more, two of which they brought down, but not before their petrol tank was hit and the machine burst into flames. Both men were badly burned, although McLeod tried to keep the flames away from Hammond. When the machine crashed in no-man's-land, he dragged Hammond from the burning wreckage and under heavy fire carried him to safety before collapsing. Hammond survived but lost a leg.

McLeod died from Spanish influenza on 6 November 1918.

Acting Lieutenant Colonel OLIVER WATSON
ROSSIGNOL WOOD, HEBUTERNE, France 28 March 1918
He was 41 years old and serving in the 1st City of London Yeomanry, but commanding the 5th Bn, King's Yorkshire Light Infantry. After a counter-attack had been made against the enemy, which achieved its object but was left holding two improvised strongpoints, Watson saw that immediate action was needed and led his reserve to the attack, organising bombing

parties and leading more attacks under intense fire. The assault took place at a critical moment and without doubt saved the line. Outnumbered, he finally ordered his men to retire, but he remained in a communication trench to cover the retreat with his revolver until he was killed.

Second Lieutenant BERNARD CASSIDY
ARRAS, France 28 March 1918
He was 25 years old and serving in the 2nd Bn, Lancashire Fusiliers. When the flank of the 26th Division was threatened, he was ordered to hold on at all costs and he carried out his instructions to the letter. Although the enemy attacked in overwhelming numbers, he continued to rally and encourage his men under very heavy bombardment until the company was eventually surrounded and he was killed. His body was never found.

Sergeant STANLEY McDOUGALL
DERNANCOURT, France 28 March 1918
He was 27 years old and serving in the 47th (Queensland) Bn, AIF. When the first wave of an enemy attack succeeded in breaking into the line, he charged the second wave single-handed, killing seven men and capturing a machine-gun, which he turned on the attackers, causing many casualties and routing them. He continued firing until his ammunition ran out, then he seized a bayonet and charged again, killing four more before using a Lewis gun to kill many more of the enemy. By his prompt action 33 prisoners were taken and the line was held.

Eight days later he repelled another attack at the same spot, for which he was awarded the MM.

He died on 7 July 1968.

Lieutenant GORDON FLOWERDEW
BOIS DE MOREUIL France
30 March 1918
He was 33 years old and serving in Lord Strathcona's Horse (Royal Canadians), CEF when he led a cavalry charge with three squadrons in a suicidal attack on two advancing lines of Germans, each about 60

men strong and armed with machine-guns. The charge successfully reached its objective, passing through the enemy and wheeling about, then charging them again from the rear. Flowerdew was wounded through both thighs and his men suffered 70 per cent casualties, but the enemy were routed. It became known as 'The Last Great Cavalry Charge'.

He died the following day.

Lieutenant ALAN JERRARD
MANSUE, Italy 30 March 1918
He was 20 years old and serving in 66 Squadron, RFC. During an offensive patrol in his Sopwith Camel, he shot down an enemy plane. He then attacked an enemy aerodrome from a height of 50 feet, destroying one of at least 20 aeroplanes that were either landing or taking off. Seeing another pilot in difficulties, Jerrard went to his assistance and shot down a third enemy machine. He only withdrew when ordered to by his patrol leader. Even then, he repeatedly turned to beat off the pursuing enemy until finally he was forced down and captured. His Camel had 163 bullet holes in it.

He died on 14 May 1968.

Chaplain THEODORE HARDY
BUCQUOY, France
5, 25 and 27 April 1918
He was 56 years old and serving in the Army Chaplains Department, attached to the 8th Bn, Lincolnshire Regiment when he showed conspicuous bravery in tending the wounded under heavy fire, regardless of his personal safety. He helped to bring in a wounded officer from 400 yards in front of our lines. Then, when an enemy shell buried several men, he went out under fire and managed to dig out two of them. On another occasion he went out with a sergeant and brought back a wounded man who was lying just 10 yards from a German pillbox.

Ignoring pleas from his superiors, both in the military and the Church, and indeed despite an offer of a post in England from the King himself, Hardy would not leave the front. He was wounded at Briastres while tending the injured and died on 18 October 1918.

Lieutenant PERCY STORKEY
HANGARD WOOD, France 7 April 1918
He was 24 years old and serving in the 19th (New South Wales) Bn, AIF when with another officer and ten men he charged an enemy position defended by 80–100 men. His small force drove out the enemy, killing and wounding 30 men and capturing 3 officers and 50 men, and also a machine-gun. Storkey's courage and initiative, together with his skilful method of attack against such odds, removed a dangerous obstacle and inspired the remainder of his men.

He later became a judge on the District Court Northern Circuit.

He died on 3 October 1969.

Second Lieutenant JOSEPH COLLIN
'ORCHARD KEEP', GIVENCHY, France 9 April 1918
He was 24 years old and serving in the 1/4th Bn, Royal Lancaster Regiment (King's Own). When his platoon had been reduced to five men by overwhelming numbers, he began to withdraw. Single-handedly he attacked a machine-gun with his revolver and a Mills bomb, killing or wounding the crew, before spotting another machine-gun. Taking a Lewis gun, he mounted it on the parapet and kept them at bay until he was mortally wounded.

Temporary Second Lieutenant JOHN SCHOFIELD
GIVENCHY, France 9 April 1918
He was 26 years old and serving in the 2/5th Bn, Lancashire Fusiliers when he led a party of nine men against an enemy strongpoint. They were attacked by about 100 Germans. His men returned fire with a Lewis gun and 20 men were captured. Schofield then led his men on towards the enemy lines where they met another large German force in a communication trench. His men opened fire once again and the enemy surrendered. As a result 123 prisoners were taken. He was killed a few minutes later.

Private RICHARD MASTERS
BETHUNE, France 9 April 1918
He was 41 years old and serving in the Royal Army Service Corps, attached to the 141st Field Ambulance, when an enemy attack cut off communications and the wounded could not be evacuated. The road was reported to be impassable, but he volunteered to try to drive the wounded to safety. He set off and had to clear the road of all sorts of debris. He made many journeys throughout the day, under constant machine-gun and shell fire. The vast majority of the wounded were evacuated by him, as his was the only vehicle to get through.

He died on 4 April 1963.

Acting Captain ERIC DOUGALL
MESSINES, Belgium 10 April 1918
He was 31 years old and serving in the Special Reserve, Royal Field Artillery, attached to A Battery, 88th Brigade, when during a withdrawal he moved his guns to the top of a ridge to fire over open sights. By now the infantry had been pushed back in line with his guns, so he organised a supply of Lewis guns for them and told them: 'So long as you stick to your trenches, I will keep my guns here.' As a result of this, the enemy were held up for 12 hours. When his battery was ordered at last to withdraw, the guns were manhandled over 800 yards of shell-cratered ground under very heavy fire.

He was killed in action at Kemmel on 14 April 1918.

Rifleman KARANBAHADUR RANA
EL KEFR Egypt 10 April 1918
He was 19 years old and serving in the 2nd Bn, 3rd Gurkha Rifles (Queen Alexandra's Own), Indian Army when he and a few others crept forward with a Lewis gun under intense fire to engage an enemy machine-gun. When the leader of the gun team was killed, he took over and quickly knocked out the enemy gun, then silenced the enemy bombers and infantry to his front. Later, he assisted with covering fire in the withdrawal, waiting until the enemy were almost upon him before retiring.

He died on 25 July 1973.

Private ARTHUR POULTER
ERQUINGHEM LYS, France
10 April 1918
He was 24 years old and serving in the 1/4th Bn, Duke of Wellington's West Riding Regiment. Acting as a stretcher-bearer, he carried ten wounded men on his back one after the other through heavy shell and machine-gun fire. Two of the wounded were hit a second time while he was carrying them. During the withdrawal over the River Lys, he ran back under fire to bring in a wounded man who had been left behind. He also bandaged 40 men under fire and was seriously wounded when attempting to rescue another man.

Poulter was one of 74 VC holders who formed the honour guard at the interment of the Unknown Soldier at Westminster Abbey on 11 November 1920. After the war his young son swapped his VC for a bag of marbles. However, it was returned when the transaction was discovered.

He died on 29 August 1956.

Acting Captain THOMAS PRYCE
VIEUX BERQUIN, France 11 April 1918
He was 32 years old and serving in the 4th Bn, Grenadier Guards when he led two platoons in a successful attack on a village. Early the next morning he occupied the position with just 40 men. He beat off four counter-attacks during the day, but by evening the enemy were within 60 yards of his position. He led a bayonet charge that drove the enemy back some 100 yards, but he was left with only 17 men and no ammunition when yet another counter-attack came. He again led a bayonet charge and was last seen engaged in fierce hand-to-hand fighting against overwhelming odds. His body was never found.

Acting Lieutenant Colonel JAMES FORBES-ROBERTSON
VIEUX BERQUIN, France
11/12 April 1918
He was 33 years old and serving in the 1st Bn, Border Regiment when he saved the line from breaking four times, first by making a reconnaissance on horseback under fire, and then by

leading a counter-attack which re-established our line. After the loss of his horse, he continued on foot, steadying the men and inspiring confidence in them by his disregard for personal safety. The next day he rode to all of his positions encouraging his men, until his horse was killed. Then, on foot, he organised effective defences to which his men could withdraw.

He died on 5 August 1955.

Second Lieutenant JOHN CROWE
NEUVE EGLISE, Belgium 14 April 1918
He was 41 years old and serving in the 2nd Bn, Worcestershire Regiment when the enemy attacked and took a position on high ground, and established a machine-gun and snipers. He led nine men to engage the German position, forcing them to retire. Later, with just two men, he attacked two machine-guns, killing the crews and capturing the guns.

He died on 27 February 1965.

Private JACK COUNTER
BOISIEUX ST MARC, France
16 April 1918
He was 19 years old and serving in the 1st Bn, King's (Liverpool) Regiment. His battalion HQ was in desperate need of information about the front line, but the only way to get it was by moving over open ground. A small party tried without success, followed by six men who went singly, but each was killed. Counter then volunteered and managed to get through under very heavy fire and return with vital information. He repeated this task on five more occasions.

He died on 16 September 1970.

Lance Sergeant JOSEPH WOODALL
LA PANNERIE, France 22 April 1918
He was 21 years old and serving in the 1st Bn, Rifle Brigade (Prince Consort's Own) when his platoon was held up by a machine-gun during an advance. On his own initiative, he rushed forward and single-handedly captured the gun and eight men. He then collected ten men together and rushed a farmhouse from which heavy fire was coming, taking another 30 pris-

oners. Shortly afterwards, when the officer in charge was killed, he took over command. He reorganised and repositioned his two platoons most skilfully. Throughout the day this NCO was constantly encouraging the men and finding and sending back invaluable information.

He died on 2 January 1962.

Captain EDWARD BAMFORD
ZEEBRUGGE, Belgium 22/23 April 1918
He was 30 years old and serving in the Royal Marine Light Infantry when he landed with three platoons of marines from HMS *Vindictive*. Under heavy fire and with a complete disregard for his personal safety, he first established a strongpoint on the right of the disembarkation area, and then led his men in an assault on the battery to the left. He was elected for the award.

He was awarded the DSO at the battle of Jutland in 1916 when serving on HMS *Chester*, in the same action in which John Cornwell was awarded his VC.

Bamford died on 30 September 1928.

Captain ALFRED CARPENTER
ZEEBRUGGE, Belgium 22/23 April 1918
He was 36 years old and serving in the Royal Navy. In command of HMS *Vindictive,* he navigated the mined waters and brought the ship alongside in darkness. When the ship was within a few yards of the mole the enemy opened a very heavy fire from batteries, machine-guns and rifles. He supervised the landings, walking the deck and encouraging the men. His power of command, personal bearing and encouragement greatly contributed to the success of the operation. He was elected for the award.

He had also served in the Crete and Boxer Rebellions. Carpenter was one of 74 VC holders who formed the honour guard at the interment of the Unknown Soldier at Westminster Abbey on 11 November 1920.

He died on 27 December 1955.

Lieutenant Commander GEORGE BRADFORD
ZEEBRUGGE, Belgium 22/23 April 1918

He was 30 years old and serving in the Royal Navy aboard HMS *Iris II* when his craft was encountering difficulties in placing parapet anchors on the mole. Although it was not part of his duties, he climbed a derrick projecting out over the mole, waited for his moment as the ship was under heavy fire and being violently tossed about, and jumped with the anchor, which he placed in position. He was killed shortly afterwards.

His brothers were Lieutenant Colonel Roland Bradford VC, MC, Captain Thomas Bradford DSO and Second Lieutenant James Bradford MC. They were known as 'The Bradford Boys'.

Lieutenant Commander ARTHUR HARRISON

ZEEBRUGGE, Belgium 22/23 April 1918
He was 32 years old and serving in the Royal Navy. He was commanding the naval storming parties, but as his ship came alongside the mole he was hit by shrapnel which broke his jaw and knocked him senseless. Regaining consciousness, he resumed command and although in great pain pressed home his attack, knowing that any delay would jeopardise the entire operation. He was killed almost immediately leading his men in the attack on the seaward batteries.

Lieutenant PERCY DEAN

ZEEBRUGGE, Belgium
22/23 April 1918
He was 40 years old and serving in the Royal Navy Volunteer Reserve aboard *ML282*. After *Intrepid* and *Iphigenia* had been scuttled to block the canal, Dean took on board over 100 of their crews under heavy fire. He was about to clear the canal when the steering gear broke down and he was informed that an officer was in the water, so he turned back to rescue him before heading for the open sea.

Dean was one of 74 VC holders who formed the honour guard at the interment of the Unknown Soldier at Westminster Abbey on 11 November 1920, and one of the very few VC holders who became MPs.

He died on 20 March 1939.

Lieutenant RICHARD 'BALDY' SANDFORD

ZEEBRUGGE, Belgium 22/23 April 1918
He was 26 years old and serving in the Royal Navy in command of HM Submarine *C3*. He skilfully placed his submarine between the piles of the viaduct connecting the mole to the shore before lighting the fuses and abandoning her. He was aware that if the planned means of rescue failed, he and his crew were certain to be killed, yet he refused to use the gyro steering that would have enabled him and the crew to abandon *C3* at a safe distance, such was his determination to complete his mission successfully.

Sandford was remembered as a man of exceptionally good humour. It was said that if a submarine was the 'most cheery and most piratical of her flotilla, one may be sure that Baldy's laugh and joy in life had something to do with it'.

He died from typhoid fever on 23 November 1918, just 12 days after the Armistice.

Sergeant NORMAN FINCH

ZEEBRUGGE, Belgium 22/23 April 1918
He was 27 years old and serving in the Royal Marine Artillery aboard HMS *Vindictive*. He was second-in-command of the pom-pom and Lewis guns, and he and his commander kept up a continuous fire until a direct hit killed or wounded most of the crews. Finch himself was severely wounded. Nevertheless he remained at his post harassing the enemy on the mole until another hit put the gun out of action. He was elected for the award.

Finch was one of 74 VC holders who formed the honour guard at the interment of the Unknown Soldier at Westminster Abbey on 11 November 1920. Finch also served in the Second World War.

He died on 15 March 1966.

Able Seaman ALBERT McKENZIE

ZEEBRUGGE, Belgium 22/23 April 1918
He was 19 years old and serving in the Royal Navy. As part of the storming party, he landed with his Lewis gun under intense fire, most of his party being killed. As he

advanced along the mole towards the seaward batteries, he killed several Germans, but was severely wounded while working his gun in an exposed position. He was elected for the award.

He died from influenza on 3 November 1918.

Lieutenant VICTOR CRUTCHLEY
ZEEBRUGGE and OSTEND, Belgium
22/23 April and 9/10 May 1918

He was 24 years old and serving in the Royal Navy when he took command of HMS *Vindictive* after all her officers had become casualties, displaying great bravery. On 9/10 May he and Lieutenant Geoffrey Drummond, commanding *ML254*, rescued 40 of *Vindictive*'s crew under heavy fire, after she was sunk to block the harbour. Drummond was badly wounded when a shell hit *ML254*. Crutchley then fought to keep the sinking motor launch full of wounded afloat until HMS *Warwick* came to the rescue. Both men were awarded the VC.

Crutchley also served in the Second World War.

He died on 24 January 1986.

Lieutenant CLIFFORD SADLIER
VILLERS-BRETONNEUX, France
24/25 April 1918

He was 26 years old and serving in the 51st Bn, AIF. When his platoon was held up by a German machine-gun position, he led a bombing party against it. Two machine-guns were captured but all his men were either killed or wounded in the attack, so he rushed a third gun alone, armed only with his revolver. He killed the crew of four and took the gun, although he was seriously wounded.

He died on 28 April 1964.

Lance Corporal JAMES HEWITSON
GIVENCHY, France 26 April 1918

He was 25 years old and serving in the 1/4th Bn, King's Own (Royal Lancaster) Regiment when during an attack on a series of craters held by the enemy, he led his men to their objective, clearing both trenches and dug-outs and killing six men who would not surrender. After capturing the final objective, he saw an enemy machine-gun team coming into action, so he worked his way around the edge of the crater and killed four of the crew and captured another. Shortly afterwards, he routed a bombing party which was attacking a Lewis gun, killing six of them.

Hewitson was a true victim of the war, spending more than 16 years in mental institutions.

He died on 2 March 1963.

Lieutenant GEORGE McKEAN
GAVRELLE SECTOR, France
27/28 April 1918

He was 29 years old and serving in the 14th Bn, Royal Montreal Regiment, CEF. When his party was held up at a block in the trench by intense fire, he ran into the open and leapt over the barricade head first and landed on top of two Germans, whom he killed. He then sent for more bombs and held the position single-handedly until they arrived. Then he rushed the next block, killing two Germans, capturing four and destroying their dug-out.

He died on 28 November 1926, following an accident with a chainsaw.

Private ROBERT CRUICKSHANK
JORDAN, Palestine 1 May 1918

He was 29 years old and serving in the 2/14th (County of London) Bn, London Regiment (London Scottish) when he volunteered to take an urgent message from his platoon, in the bottom of a wadi, to the company HQ. He rushed up the slope but was wounded; he tried again but was wounded again. After having his wounds dressed, he tried yet again, but this time was so badly wounded that he could not stand. He lay all day in a dangerous position, being sniped at and repeatedly wounded where he lay, but he displayed great endurance and was cheerful and uncomplaining throughout.

Cruickshank also served in the Second World War.

He died on 30 August 1961.

Sergeant WILLIAM GREGG
BUCQUOY, France 6 May 1918
He was 28 years old and serving in the 13th Bn, Rifle Brigade (Prince Consort's Own). When all of his company officers were wounded, he took command, rushing two enemy machine-gun posts, killing some of the crew and capturing a machine-gun. He started to consolidate his position but was driven back by a counter-attack. Reinforced, he led a charge and personally put a gun out of action. Driven back a second time, he again counter-attacked, this time successfully holding the position until ordered to withdraw.

He died on 10 August 1969.

Private WILLIAM BEESLEY
BUCQUOY, France 8 May 1918
He was 22 years old and serving in the 13th Bn, Rifle Brigade (Prince Consort's Own). When all the section commanders were killed, he took command. Single-handedly he rushed an enemy post, shooting four of the enemy and taking six prisoners. He and another man then brought a Lewis gun into action and kept it firing for 4 hours, inflicting many casualties, until his comrade was wounded. Beesley then held his position until nightfall, when he brought back to our lines both the wounded man and his Lewis gun.

He died on 23 September 1966.

Lieutenant ROWLAND (sometimes spelt ROLAND) BOURKE
OSTEND, Belgium 9/10 May 1918
He was 32 years old and serving in the Royal Navy Volunteer Reserve. Commanding *ML276*, he went into the harbour to ensure that all of HMS *Vindictive*'s crew had got away after she was scuttled to block the harbour. Hearing cries from the water, he found three men clinging to an upturned boat and rescued them. During this time he was under very heavy fire, the motor launch being hit 55 times, once by a 6-inch shell that killed two of her crew. He managed to get her into the open sea and was taken in tow.

He died on 29 August 1958.

Lieutenant GEOFFREY DRUMMOND
OSTEND, Belgium 9/10 May 1918
He was 32 years old and serving in the Royal Navy Volunteer Reserve commanding *ML 254*. He and Lieutenant Victor Crutchley rescued 40 of *Vindictive*'s crew under heavy fire, after she was sunk to block the harbour, but Drummond was badly wounded when a shell hit the launch. Lieutenant Crutchley then managed to keep the sinking *ML254*, which was full of wounded, afloat until HMS *Warwick* came to the rescue. Both men were awarded the VC.

Drummond also served in the Second World War.

He died on 21 April 1941, after slipping on some coal and banging his head.

Sergeant WILLIAM RUTHVEN
VILLE-SUR-ANCRE, France
19 May 1918
He was 24 years old and serving in the 22nd (Victoria) Bn, AIF when during an attack his company commander was wounded. He took over command of the company HQ, rallied the men and captured a machine-gun, wounding two of the crew and taking six prisoners. Later, he rushed a position armed only with his revolver, shooting two men and taking 32 prisoners. Throughout this time he showed magnificent courage and determination, inspiring everyone by his fine fighting spirit.

He died on 12 January 1970.

Temporary Brigadier General GEORGE GROGAN
RIVER AISNE, France 27 May 1918
He was 40 years old and serving in the Worcestershire Regiment, commanding the 23rd Infantry Brigade. When the remnants of the infantry were wavering, he rode up and down the line encouraging his men under very heavy fire, showing utter disregard for his personal safety. When his horse was shot from under him, he continued encouraging the men on foot until another horse was brought to him. As a result of his action the line was held.

He died on 3 January 1962.

Lance Corporal JOEL HALLIWELL
MUSCOURT, France 27 May 1918

He was 44 years old and serving in the 11th Bn, Lancashire Fusiliers when the remnants of his battalion were withdrawing, being closely engaged by the enemy. Halliwell, having captured a loose horse, rode out under heavy fire and rescued a wounded man from no-man's-land. He repeated this feat several times and succeeded in rescuing an officer and nine other ranks. He made a last effort to reach a wounded man but was driven back by the very close advance of the enemy.

He died on 14 June 1958.

Corporal JOSEPH KAEBLE
NEUVILLE-VITASSE, France
8/9 June 1918

He was 25 years old and serving in the 22nd Bn, Quebec Regiment (Canadien Francais), CEF when during an enemy attack all but one of his section became casualties. As soon as the barrage lifted, he jumped over the parapet with his Lewis gun and emptied one magazine after another into the advancing enemy. Although hit several times, he continued to fire and held up the enemy advance, until he fell mortally wounded. Even then, while lying in the trench, he fired his last remaining rounds into the enemy.

Lieutenant Colonel CHARLES HUDSON
ASIAGO Italy 15 June 1918

He was 26 years old and commanding the 11th Bn, Sherwood Foresters (Nottinghamshire and Derbyshire Regiment) when the enemy penetrated the front line. He collected various HQ personnel, orderlies, servants, runners and the like, and as they advanced under his leadership he shouted to the enemy to surrender, and some of them did. Hudson was then badly wounded by a bomb which exploded at his feet. In great pain, he gave directions for a successful counter-attack that captured 100 prisoners and 6 machine-guns.

He was one of 74 VC holders who formed the honour guard at the interment of the Unknown Soldier at Westminster Abbey on 11 November 1920. Hudson also served in the

Second World War, and was ADC to the King (1944–46). He died on 4 April 1959.

Temporary Lieutenant JOHN YOULL
ASIAGO, Italy 15 June 1918

He was 21 years old and serving in the 1st Bn, Northumberland Fusiliers, attached to the 11th (Service) Bn. He was leading a patrol when he came under heavy enemy fire. Sending his men back to safety, he remained to watch the situation and then, finding himself unable to rejoin his company, he reported to a neighbouring unit, where he took command of a party of men from different units, holding his position against enemy attack. When an enemy machine-gun opened fire behind him, Youll rushed out and captured the gun, killing most of the crew. He used this gun to inflict heavy casualties on the enemy. He also carried out three separate counter-attacks, driving the enemy back each time.

He was killed in action at the Piave river on 27 October 1918, just two weeks before the Armistice. His last words to his adjutant were: 'It's all right, Cowling, we got them stone cold.'

Major EDWARD 'MICK' MANNOCK
France and Flanders 17 June–22 July 1918

He was 31 years old and serving in 85 Squadron, RAF. In flying operations, he was officially credited with 73 combat victories. In May 1918 he scored no fewer than 24 victories and on one occasion in July, while leading an attack on a formation of Fokker aircraft, he shot down two and was the cause of another pair colliding. The whole of his career was an outstanding example of fearless courage, remarkable skill, devotion to duty and self-sacrifice. He grieved for every pilot loss and was inconsolable when he saw one of his best students, Lieutenant Dolan, shot down in flames. After this, he always carried a pistol with him in the cockpit, telling Lieutenant MacLanachan, 'They'll never burn me.'

Mannock was killed in action at Lillers on 26 July 1918. His plane was hit by anti-aircraft fire and crashed in flames. It is thought that he may have jumped out as his body was found some distance from the crash site. He was buried by the Germans with full military honours, but his grave was later lost.

After the war there was much lobbying by those who had served under him, and a year after his death he was awarded the VC.

Corporal PHILIP DAVEY
MERRIS, France 28 June 1918

He was 21 years old and serving in the 10th (South Australia) Bn, AIF. When an enemy machine-gun was causing heavy casualties, Davey moved forward in the face of point-blank fire and attacked the gun with grenades, putting half of its crew out of action. Having run out of grenades, he fetched a further supply and again attacked the gun, the crew of which had been reinforced. This time he killed all eight crewmen and captured the gun, which he then used to repel a determined counter-attack. During this action he was severely wounded.

He died on 21 December 1953.

Lance Corporal THOMAS AXFORD
HAMEL WOOD, France 4 July 1918

He was 23 years old and serving in the 16th (South Australia and Western Australia) Bn, AIF. His commanding officer had already become a casualty when Axford noticed the adjoining platoon was being held up by wire and machine-gun fire. Single-handedly he charged the enemy gun crews, throwing bombs at them. He then jumped into the trench, killed ten men and took six prisoners. He threw the machine-guns over the parapet, allowing the delayed platoon to advance.

He also served in the Second World War.

He died on 11 October 1983, while returning home from a VC celebration.

Driver HENRY DALZIEL
HAMEL WOOD, France 4 July 1918

He was 25 years old and serving in the 15th (Queensland & Tasmania) Bn, AIF. Meeting determined resistance from an enemy strong-point protected by wire entanglements, Dalziel, armed only with a revolver, attacked an enemy machine-gun. He killed or captured the crew and gun. He was badly wounded in the hand but carried on until the final objective

was captured. He twice went over open ground under heavy artillery and machine-gun fire to bring up ammunition, and continued to fill magazines and serve his gun until he was wounded in the head. His dash and unselfish actions turned what could have been a serious setback into a splendid success.

He died from a stroke on 24 July 1965.

Corporal WALTER BROWN
VILLERS-BRETONNEUX, France
6 July 1918

He was 33 years old and serving in the 20th (New South Wales) Bn, AIF when on his own initiative he rushed a machine-gun post that had been causing many casualties. Despite being fired on by another machine-gun, he reached his objective and with a bomb in his hand ordered the garrison to surrender. After a short scuffle during which he knocked down a man with his fist, an officer and eleven men surrendered to him, and he brought them all back under heavy machine-gun fire.

He re-enlisted at the outbreak of the Second World War, giving his age as 39 instead of 54. When the Japanese entered Singapore on 28 February 1942, he walked towards them with a grenade in each hand, shouting 'No surrender for me.' His body was never found.

Lieutenant ALBERT BORELLA (name changed to CHALMERS-BORELLA in 1939)
VILLERS-BRETONNEUX France
17/18 July 1918

He was 37 years old and serving in the 26th (Queensland & Tasmania) Bn, AIF. Leading his platoon, he charged and captured a machine-gun. Then he led his party, by now reduced to ten men and two Lewis guns, against a strongly held trench, using his revolver and later a rifle to great effect, causing many casualties. Two large dug-outs were bombed and 30 prisoners taken. Later, although outnumbered 10 to 1, he and his men repulsed an enemy attack, inflicting great losses on them.

As Chalmers-Borella, he also served in the Second World War.

He died on 7 February 1968.

Sergeant JOHN MEIKLE
MARFAUX, France 20 July 1918
He was 19 years old and serving in the 4th Bn, Seaforth Highlanders Ross-shire Buffs (Duke of Albany's). Armed only with his revolver and a stick, he single-handedly rushed a machine-gun that was delaying his company and put it out of action. Later, he charged another machine-gun post, but was killed when almost on the gun position. His actions enabled the two men following him to put the gun out of action.

Sergeant RICHARD TRAVIS (born DICKSON CORNELIUS SAVAGE)
ROSSIGNOL WOOD, HEBUTERNE, France 24 July 1918
He was 34 years old and serving in the 2nd Bn, Otago Infantry Regiment, NZEF when he crawled out into the open and bombed a wire block, enabling the attacking parties to pass through it. Later, when a bombing party was held up by two machine-guns, he rushed them, killed the crews and captured the guns. He then killed a German officer and three men who rushed at him in an attempt to retake the position.
He was killed in action at Rossignol Wood on 25 July 1918.

Lieutenant HAROLD AUTEN
ENGLISH CHANNEL 30 July 1918
He was 26 years old and serving in the Royal Naval Reserve. He was commanding the Q-ship HMS *Stock Force* when she was torpedoed by a U-boat and badly damaged. The 'panic party' took to the boats and the U-boat surfaced half a mile away. After 15 minutes the panic party started to row back to the ship, followed by the submarine. When it was 300 yards away *Stock Force* opened fire, severely damaging the submarine, which sank almost immediately. The Q-ship sank about 4 hours later, and her crew was taken off by a torpedo boat.
Auten was one of 74 VC holders who formed the honour guard at the interment of the Unknown Soldier at Westminster Abbey on 11 November 1920. He also served in the

Second World War.
He died on 3 October 1964.

Lieutenant ALFRED GABY
VILLERS-BRETONNEUX, France
8 August 1918
He was 26 years old and serving in the 28th (Western Australia) Bn, AIF. He was leading his company when the advance was checked by a strongpoint. Finding a gap in the wire, Gaby approached the enemy under heavy machine-gun fire. He emptied his revolver into the enemy, drove the crews from their guns and captured 50 men and 4 machine-guns.
He was killed in action at Villers-Bretonneux on 11 August 1918.

Corporal HERMAN GOOD
HANGARD WOOD, France
8 August 1918
He was 30 years old and serving in the 13th Bn (Royal Highlanders of Canada), CEF when his company was held up by fire from three machine-guns. He dashed forward alone and killed several of their crews and captured the rest. Later, he collected three men and charged a battery of 5.9-inch guns under point-blank fire, capturing the guns and their crews.
He died on 18 April 1969.

Corporal HERBERT MINER
DEMUIN, France 8 August 1918
He was 27 years old and serving in the 58th (CO) Bn, CEF when he rushed an enemy machine-gun post single-handed, killing the crew and turning the gun on the enemy. Later, with two others he attacked another machine-gun post, putting the gun out of action. Then he single-handedly rushed an enemy bombing post, bayoneting two of the garrison and putting the remainder to flight. He was mortally wounded by a grenade in this action.

Private JOHN CROAK (or CROKE)
AMIENS, France 8 August 1918
He was 26 years old and serving in the 13th Bn (Royal Highlanders of Canada), CEF when he became separated from his section. Encountering a machine-gun, he proceeded to

bomb it, taking the crew prisoner and capturing the gun. Soon afterwards he was severely wounded, but managed to rejoin his platoon. When several more machine-guns were encountered, he rushed forward and was first into the enemy trench, bayoneting or capturing the entire garrison. He was again wounded and died shortly afterwards.

Lieutenant JEAN BRILLANT
MEHARICOURT, France
8/9 August 1918
He was 28 years old and serving in the 22nd (CO) Bn (Canadien Francais), CEF. He was wounded while capturing a machine-gun that had been holding up his company, but he refused to leave his command. Later, when his company was again held up by machine-gun fire, he rushed forward with two platoons, capturing 150 prisoners and 15 machine-guns, but was wounded for a second time. Subsequently he led a rushing party towards a field gun and was seriously wounded, but continued to advance until he collapsed.

He died on 10 August 1918, as a result of his wounds.

Lieutenant JAMES TAIT
AMIENS, France 8–11 August 1918
He was 32 years old and serving in the 78th (Winnipeg Grenadiers) Bn, CEF. When their advance was checked by intense machine-gun fire, Tait rallied his men and led them forward with skill and dash under a hail of bullets. Taking a rifle, he then went forward alone and killed the machine-gunner who was causing so many casualties. His action so inspired his men that they rushed the position and captured 12 machine-guns and 20 prisoners. Later, when the enemy counter-attacked under intense artillery bombardment, he displayed outstanding courage and, although mortally wounded, continued to direct his men's fire until he died.

Acting Captain ANDREW BEAUCHAMP-PROCTOR (born PROCTOR)
France 8 August–8 October 1918
He was 24 years old and serving in 84

Squadron, RAF when during this period he was victorious in 26 air combats. During the entire war he claimed 54 victories. He destroyed 22 aircraft, 16 kite balloons and drove down 'out of control' a further 16 enemy machines. In addition, his work from 8 August in attacking enemy troops on the ground and carrying out reconnaissance for the advancing Allied armies was almost unsurpassed in its brilliance.

He was killed during an RAF display on 21 June 1921.

Sergeant THOMAS HARRIS
MORLANCOURT, France
9 August 1918
He was 26 years old and serving in the 6th Bn, Queen's Own Royal West Kent Regiment when the advance was held up by machine-gun fire from concealed positions in some crops. Harris led his section against one of them, capturing it and killing seven Germans. Later, on two occasions he attacked two other machine-guns that were inflicting heavy casualties, capturing the first and killing the crew, but he was killed while attacking the second. Through his courage and initiative, his battalion was able to continue the advance.

Sergeant RAPHAEL ZENGEL
WARVILLERS, France 9 August 1918
He was 23 years old and serving in the 5th (Western Cavalry) Bn, CEF. While leading his platoon, he realised that an enemy machine-gun was firing into the advancing cavalry. He rushed forward to the gun emplacement, killed the officer and gunner and dispersed the rest of the crew. Later in the day he was rendered unconscious by a shell but on recovering he continued to direct harassing fire on the enemy. His utter disregard for his personal safety and the confidence he inspired greatly assisted in the successful outcome of the attack.

He died on 27 February 1977.

Corporal FREDERICK COPPINS
HACKETT WOODS, AMIENS, France
9 August 1918
He was 28 years old and serving in the 8th Bn

(Winnipeg Rifles), CEF when his platoon was in an exposed position and unexpectedly came under fire from several machine-guns. He called for volunteers and rushed forward with four men. They were all killed and Coppins was wounded, but he went on alone and killed the gunner and three of the crew; he also took four prisoners. Despite being wounded, he led his platoon on to the final objective.

He died on 20 March 1963.

Acting Corporal ALEXANDER BRERETON
AUBRECOURT, AMIENS, France
9 August 1918
He was 25 years old and serving in the 8th Bn (Winnipeg Rifles), CEF when during an attack his platoon came under fire in an exposed position from five machine-guns. Realising his platoon would be wiped out unless something was done, he at once charged forward alone, shot a machine-gunner and bayoneted another man, whereupon nine others surrendered. His action inspired the platoon to charge and capture the remaining posts.

He died on 11 June 1976.

Private ROBERT BEATHAM
ROSIERE, France 9 August 1918
He was 24 years old and serving in the 8th (Victoria) Bn, AIF. When the advance was held up by machine-gun fire, he and another man bombed the crews of four enemy machine-guns, killing 10 men and capturing 10 others. When the final objective was reached, Beatham, although wounded, again dashed forward and bombed a machine-gun, but was killed.

Captain FERDINAND WEST
ROYE, France 10 August 1918
He was 22 years old and serving in 8 Squadron, RAF when he located a huge concentration of enemy troops and transports. He had just made notes about their strength when he was attacked by several German scouts. Three exploding bullets partially severed his leg, which fell powerless on to the controls. Lifting it off, he twisted his underwear into an improvised tourniquet. He then managed to get in

some bursts of fire at his attackers, seeing them off. He landed in a field near some Canadian troops. He fainted, but regained consciousness for long enough to make his report. He was taken to hospital and his leg was amputated.

West was one of 74 VC holders who formed the honour guard at the interment of the Unknown Soldier at Westminster Abbey on 11 November 1920. Years later he said of his VC action: 'I was very young and strong and healthy and had a bit of luck.' West was fitted with an artificial leg and continued to fly in the RAF.

He died on 7 July 1988.

Sergeant PERCY STATTON
PROYART, France 12 August 1918
He was 27 years old and serving in the 40th (Tasmania) Bn, AIF when he engaged two machine-gun posts with his Lewis gun, thus enabling his battalion to advance. Then, armed only with a revolver, he rushed four enemy machine-gun posts in succession, putting two out of action and killing five Germans. The remaining two posts were evacuated. Later, Statton went out under heavy fire and brought back two badly wounded men.

He died on 7 December 1959.

Private THOMAS DINESEN
PARVILLERS, France 12 August 1918
He was 26 years old and serving in the 42nd Bn (Royal Highlanders of Canada), CEF when he displayed conspicuous bravery over a 10-hour period of hand-to-hand fighting, which resulted in the capture of over a mile of strongly defended enemy trenches. Five times in succession he rushed forward alone and put enemy guns out of action, accounting for twelve of the enemy with bomb and bayonet. His sustained valour inspired his comrades at a very critical stage of the action.

After the war he wrote a book about his life called, *Merry Hell: A Dane with the Canadians;* he also wrote *No Man's Land* and *Twilight on the Betz*. His sister was Karen Blixen, author of *Out of Africa*.

Dinesen died on 10 March 1979.

Sergeant ROBERT SPALL
PARVILLERS, France 13 August 1918
He was 28 years old and serving in the Princess Patricia's Canadian Light Infantry when during an enemy counter-attack his platoon became isolated, whereupon Spall took a Lewis gun and climbed on to the parapet, firing into the advancing enemy and inflicting many casualties. He then directed his men to a sap 75 yards away, after which he picked up another Lewis gun, again climbed on to the parapet and kept the enemy back with his fire. This time, however, he was killed. He gave his life to save his platoon.

Lance Sergeant EDWARD 'NED' SMITH
SERRE, France 21–23 August 1918
He was 19 years old and serving in the 1/5th Bn, Lancashire Fusiliers when he charged alone a machine-gun post, armed only with a rifle and bayonet. The enemy threw grenades at him, but heedless of the danger and almost without stopping, he shot at least six of them. Later, seeing another platoon in need of assistance, he led his men to them, took command and captured the objective.

He had been awarded the DCM just 11 days earlier. At 19 years and 9 months he was the youngest VC in the Army at that time. At the outbreak of the Second World War he re-enlisted into the Lancashire Fusiliers and by a strange twist of fate found himself virtually at the same spot where he had fought 22 years earlier. It was reported that he was killed in action near Bucquoy on 12 January 1940. But in fact he shot himself, leaving a note saying that he could not live through the horrors of another war.

Acting Lieutenant Colonel RICHARD WEST
COURCELLES and VAULX - VRACOURT, France
21 August and 2 September 1918
He was 39 years old and serving in the North Irish Horse (SR) but seconded to the 6th Bn, Tank Corps. During an attack the infantry lost their bearings in dense fog and West collected any men he could find and led them to their objective, in the face of heavy machine-gun fire. On 2 September he arrived at the front line as the enemy were counter-attacking. Aware the infantry might give way, and despite the enemy being almost upon them, he rode up and down in front of the men under heavy machine-gun and rifle fire, encouraging them and calling: 'Stick it, men. Show them fight and for God's sake put up a good fight!' He fell riddled with bullets. His magnificent bravery at a critical moment so inspired the men that the enemy attack was defeated.

Temporary Commander DANIEL BEAK
LOGEAST WOOD, France
21–25 August and 4 September 1918
He was 27 years old and serving in the Royal Navy Volunteer Reserve when he led his men to capture four enemy positions under heavy fire. Four days later, although dazed by a shell fragment, he reorganised the whole brigade under heavy fire, and led the men towards their objective. When the attack was held up, he and another man rushed forward and broke up a nest of machine-gun posts, personally bringing back ten prisoners.

He died on 3 May 1967, following a long illness.

Lance Corporal GEORGE ONIONS
ACHIET-LE-PETIT, France
22 August 1918
He was 35 years old and serving in the 1st Bn, Devonshire Regiment. Having been sent with another man to get in touch with the battalion on the right flank, he saw the enemy advancing in large numbers. Seizing his opportunity, he placed himself and his comrade on the enemy's flank and opened fire on them. When the Germans were about 100 yards from him they wavered and some hands were thrown up, whereupon Onions rushed forward and, helped by his comrade, took some 200 prisoners, whom he marched back to his own company commander.

He died on 2 April 1944.

Lieutenant WILLIAM JOYNT
HERLEVILLE WOOD SOMME, France
23 August 1918

He was 29 years old and serving in the 8th (Victoria) Bn, AIF. When his company commander had been killed, he took command. Seeing that the lead battalion had been demoralised by heavy casualties, he rushed forward and reorganised the remnants. When heavy fire on the flanks was causing delay and casualties, he led a frontal bayonet charge into the woods, thus saving a critical situation. Later, at Plateau Wood, after some severe hand-to-hand fighting, he turned a stubborn defence into an enemy surrender. He was subsequently badly wounded by a shell.

He died on 5 May 1986.

Lieutenant LAWRENCE 'FATS' McCARTHY
MADAME WOOD, France
23 August 1918

He was 26 years old and serving in the 16th (South Australia and Western Australia) Bn, AIF when his battalion was opposed by two enemy machine-guns. He dashed across open ground with two other men to the nearest post; arriving first, having outpaced the others, he put the gun out of action, and then continued fighting his way down the trench until he made contact with the British. During this action he killed 22 men, took 50 prisoners and captured 5 machine-guns.

He died on 25 May 1975.

Private HUGH McIVER
COURCELLE-LE COMPRIVATE, France 23 August 1918

He was 28 years old and serving in the 2nd Bn, Royal Scots (Lothian Regiment). He was employed as a company runner, and under heavy machine-gun and artillery fire carried messages regardless of his personal safety. Single-handedly he pursued an enemy scout into a machine-gun post and having killed six of the garrison, captured a further 20 men and two machine-guns. Later he succeeded at great personal risk in stopping a British tank firing on our own men in error.

He was killed in action near Courcelles on 2 September 1918.

Sergeant SAMUEL FORSYTH
GREVILLERS, France 24 August 1918

He was 27 years old and serving in the New Zealand Engineers, attached to the 2nd Bn, Auckland Infantry Regiment, NZEF. When his company was under heavy machine-gun fire, he led attacks on three machine-gun positions and took the crews prisoner before they could inflict many casualties. Subsequently, when trying to get support from a tank to deal with other machine-guns, he was wounded and the tank put out of action. He then led the tank crew and his own men in an attack which forced the remaining enemy machine-guns to retire, enabling the advance to continue.

He was killed by a sniper shortly afterwards.

Temporary Lieutenant DAVID MacINTYRE
HENIN-SUR-COJEUL and
FRONTAINE, France 24–27 August 1918

He was 23 years old and serving in the Argyll and Sutherland Highlanders (Princess Louise's), attached to the 1/6th Bn, Highland Light Infantry. Acting as adjutant of his battalion, he was constantly in the firing line, and by his coolness under heavy shell and machine-gun fire inspired his men. Later, when extra strong wire entanglements were encountered during an attack, he organised and led a party of men under machine-gun fire and supervised the cutting of gaps in the wire. When the battalion's advance was held up, he rallied a small party of men and led them forward in pursuit of an enemy machine-gun, killing three men and capturing an officer, ten men and the gun. After he had been relieved of his command in the front line, an enemy machine-gun opened fire close to him, which he rushed single-handed, putting the crew to flight and capturing the gun.

He was one of 74 VC holders who formed the honour guard at the interment of the Unknown Soldier at Westminster Abbey on 11 November 1920.

He died on 31 July 1967.

Acting Sergeant HAROLD COLLEY
MARTINPUICH, France 25 August 1918
He was 24 years old and serving in the 10th Bn,

Lancashire Fusiliers. During an enemy counter-attack, his company was holding a position in front of the main line, with two platoons in advance and two in support. Ordered to hold on at all costs, he went out on his own initiative to assist the forward platoons, rallying them and forming a defensive flank when threatened. The position was held with just three men surviving. Colley was mortally wounded. It was entirely due to his action that the Germans did not break through.

Lieutenant CHARLES RUTHERFORD
MONCHY, France 26 August 1918
He was 26 years old and serving in the 5th Bn, Canadian Mounted Rifles, CEF. When leading an assault party, he found himself a considerable distance ahead of his men and at the same time noticed a fully armed enemy party outside a pillbox. He went over to them and by a masterly piece of bluff managed to persuade them that they were surrounded; in all, 45 men, including two officers and three machine-guns, surrendered to him. Joined by the rest of his men, he then attacked a nearby pillbox with a Lewis gun section, capturing another 35 prisoners and their guns.

Rutherford also served in the Second World War.

He died on 11 June 1989.

Sergeant REGINALD JUDSON
BAPAUME, France 26 August 1918
He was 36 years old and serving in the 1st Bn, Auckland Regiment, NZEF when during an attack he led a bombing party under heavy fire and captured an enemy machine-gun. He then proceeded up the sap alone, bombing three machine-gun crews. Jumping out of the trench, he ran ahead of the enemy and, standing on the parapet, ordered a group of twelve men to surrender. They opened fire on him, so he threw a bomb in and then jumped for cover.

He died on 26 August 1972.

Lance Corporal HENRY WEALE
BAZENTIN-LE-GRAND, France
26 August 1918
He was 20 years old and serving in the 14th Bn,

Royal Welch Fusiliers. When the advance of the adjacent battalion was held up by enemy machine-guns, Weale was ordered to deal with the hostile machine-gun post. When his Lewis gun failed him, on his own initiative he rushed the nearest post and killed the crew, then he went for the others but the crews fled on his approach. His dashing action cleared the way for the advance, inspired his comrades and resulted in the capture of several machine-guns.

The Henry Weale VC TA Centre in Queensferry, North Wales is named in his honour.

He died on 13 January 1959.

Lance Corporal BERNARD GORDON
FARGNY WOOD, BRAY, France
26/27 August 1918
He was 27 years old and serving in the 41st (Queensland) Bn, AIF when he single-handedly attacked an enemy machine-gun that was persistently enfilading his company's position, killing the gunner and capturing an officer and ten men. Entering the wood, he cleared more trenches, capturing 51 prisoners and 6 machine-guns. His action allowed the company to take over 1,000 yards of ground.

He died on 19 October 1963.

Lieutenant Colonel WILLIAM CLARK-KENNEDY
FRESNES-ROUVROY LINE, France
27/28 August 1918
He was 39 years old and commanding the 24th Bn (Victoria Rifles), CEF when he led the centre battalion in an attack. His unit became the focal point for the enemy fire, incurring heavy casualties. As his own and neighbouring men began to waver, he reorganised and inspired them, leading from the front and enabling the brigade to take its objectives. The next day he was severely wounded, but despite the pain he refused to be evacuated until he had gained a position from which the advance could be resumed.

He died on 25 October 1961.

Lieutenant CECIL SEWELL
FREMICOURT, France 29 August 1918
He was 23 years old and serving in the Queen's Own Royal West Kent Regiment, attached to the 3rd (Light) Bn, Tank Corps. He was in command of a section of Whippet light tanks when one of his tanks slipped into a shell-hole, overturned and caught fire. Sewell got out of his tank and crossed open ground under heavy machine-gun fire. The door of the stricken tank had become jammed against the side of the shell-hole, but unaided he dug away the earth and released the crew. As he did so, he was killed.

Second Lieutenant JAMES HUFFAM
ST SERVIN'S FARM, France
31 August 1918
He was 21 years old and serving in the 5th Bn, Duke of Wellington's (West Riding) Regiment, attached to the 2nd Bn, when with three men he rushed an enemy machine-gun post and put it out of action. When his position was counter-attacked he withdrew, carrying a wounded man on his back. Later that night, with just two men, he rushed another machine-gun and captured eight prisoners, allowing the advance to continue.

Huffam also served in the Second World War.
He died on 16 February 1968.

Private GEORGE CARTWRIGHT
ROAD WOOD, BOUCHAVESNES,
France 31 August 1918
He was 23 years old and serving in the 33rd (New South Wales) Bn, AIF. When two companies were held up by machine-gun fire, he attacked the gun single-handed, bombed it and shot three of the crew, capturing the gun and nine prisoners. His action so inspired his battalion that they stood up and cheered him before renewing their attack with vigour.

Cartwright also served in the Second World War.
He died on 2 February 1978.

Lieutenant EDGAR TOWNER
MONT ST QUENTIN, France
1 September 1918

He was 28 years old and serving in the 2nd Bn, Australian Machine Gun Corps, AIF when he located and single-handedly captured 25 prisoners and an enemy machine-gun, which he turned on the enemy, inflicting heavy losses. Later, he gave valuable support to the infantry advance by fearless reconnaissance under heavy fire. Although by now wounded, he secured another enemy machine-gun which he fired in full view of the enemy, making them retreat. He was finally evacuated 30 hours after being wounded.

Towner also served in the Second World War.
He died on 18 August 1972.

Sergeant JOHN GRANT
BANCOURT, France 1 September 1918
He was 29 years old and serving in the 1st Bn, Wellington Infantry Regiment, NZEF when during an attack his battalion was met by five enemy machine-gun posts lining a crest. He led his company towards these posts under point-blank fire, and from about 20 yards away rushed ahead and entered the centre post, demoralising the garrison so that his men were able to mop up the position. In the same manner he rushed another machine-gun post, and the remaining posts were then quickly occupied and cleared by his company.

He died on 25 November 1970.

Sergeant ALBERT LOWERSON
MONT ST QUENTIN, PERONNE,
France
1 September 1918
He was 22 years old and serving in the 21st (Victoria) Bn, AIF when his company was held up by a strongpoint. Taking seven men with him, he attacked the flanks of the strongpoint, rushed it and took the position, together with 12 machine-guns and at least 30 prisoners. He was severely wounded in the right thigh, but refused to leave until the position was consolidated.

He died from leukaemia on 15 December 1945.

The Complete Victoria Cross

Private WILLIAM CURREY
PERONNE, France 1 September 1918
He was 22 years old and serving in the 53rd (New South Wales) Bn, AIF when his company was held up by a 77mm field gun, which was inflicting heavy casualties. Currey rushed the position, killed the crew and captured the field gun. Later, he rushed a strongpoint single-handedly, causing many casualties with his Lewis gun. Subsequently he volunteered to carry orders for withdrawal to an isolated company, which he did under heavy fire.

He died from a coronary vascular disease on 30 April 1948.

Private ROBERT MacTIER
MONT ST QUENTIN, PERONNE, France 1 September 1918
He was 28 years old and serving in the 23rd (Victoria) Bn, AIF. Following the failure of the bombing parties to clear enemy strongpoints, preventing the battalion from advancing, he rushed out of the trench and killed the eight-man crew of a machine-gun, then threw the gun over the parapet. Attacking another strongpoint, he captured six men. He dealt with a third machine-gun, but as he attacked another he was killed. His action allowed the battalion to continue its advance.

Corporal ARTHUR HALL
PERONNE, France 1/2 September 1918
He was 22 years old and serving in the 54th (New South Wales) Bn, AIF when he rushed a machine-gun post, shooting four of the enemy and capturing nine more and two machine-guns. Continuously in advance of the main party, he personally led assault parties, capturing many of the enemy and more machine-guns. The next day, during a heavy barrage, he carried to safety a wounded man who was in need of urgent medical attention.

He died on 25 February 1978.

Temporary Corporal ALEXANDER BUCKLEY
PERONNE, France 1/2 September 1918
He was 27 years old and serving in the 54th (New South Wales) Bn, AIF when he and another man rushed an enemy machine-gun post, shooting four Germans and taking 22 prisoners. Later, on reaching a footbridge covered by a machine-gun, he tried to rush across to attack the position but was killed.

Private CLAUDE NUNNEY
DROCOURT-QUEANT LINE, ARRAS, France 1/2 September 1918
He was 25 years old and serving in the 38th (Ottawa) Bn, CEF. As his battalion was preparing to advance, the enemy laid down a heavy barrage and launched a counter-attack. Nunney on his own initiative went forward through the barrage to the company outpost lines and went from post to post, encouraging the men by his own fearless example. The enemy attack was repulsed and a critical situation saved. The next day during another attack his leadership undoubtedly helped to carry his company forward to its objective and he again displayed the highest degree of valour until severely wounded.

He died as a result of his wounds on 18 September 1918.

Lieutenant Colonel CYRUS PECK
CAGNICOURT, DROCOURT-QUEANT LINE, ARRAS, France 2 September 1918
He was 47 years old and commanding the 16th Bn, Manitoba Regiment (Canadian Scottish), CEF when his battalion, having taken its first objective, was held up by machine-gun fire. He went forward alone to reconnoitre the situation under heavy fire. He then reorganised his battalion and pushed them forward until he sighted our tanks. From his personal knowledge of the German positions, he directed them to new targets, thus paving the way for the infantry to push ahead.

Peck was a member of the Canadian House of Commons from 1917 to 1921.

He died on 27 September 1956.

Captain BELLENDEN HUTCHESON
DROCOURT-QUEANT LINE, ARRAS, France 2 September 1918
He was 35 years old and serving in the

Canadian Army Medical Corps, CEF, attached to the 75th Bn (CO). He remained on the field under very heavy fire until every wounded man had been attended to. He himself dressed the wounds of an officer and succeeded in evacuating him to safety with the help of some prisoners and his own men. He then went out again in full view of the enemy to attend to a wounded sergeant, whose wounds he dressed after carrying him to a shell-hole.

He died on 9 April 1954.

Chief Petty Officer GEORGE PROWSE
PRONVILLE, France 2 September 1918
He was 32 years old and serving in the Drake Bn, Royal Navy Volunteer Reserve. When his company became disorganised by heavy fire, he led a small party of men against a strong-point and captured it alone, taking 23 prisoners and 5 machine-guns. On three other occasions he displayed great heroism in action. At one point he dashed forward, attacked and captured two machine-gun posts, killing six men, taking 13 prisoners and two machine-guns. He was the only survivor of his party, but his action enabled the battalion to push forward.

He was killed in action near Arleux on 27 September 1918.

Company Sergeant Major MARTIN DOYLE
RIENCOURT, France 2 September 1918
He was 26 years old and serving in the 1st Bn, Royal Munster Fusiliers, 16th (Irish) Division when command of the company fell to him after all the officers had become casualties. He extricated a party of men who were surrounded, and carried back a wounded officer under heavy fire. Later, he went forward under intense fire to the assistance of a tank, and when an enemy machine-gun opened fire on it, making it impossible for the tank crew to get away, he single-handedly captured the machine-gun and took three prisoners. Subsequently, when the enemy counter-attacked, he drove them back, taking many more prisoners.

He was one of 74 VC holders who formed the honour guard at the interment of the Unknown Soldier at Westminster Abbey on 11 November 1920.

He died on 20 November 1940.

Acting Sergeant ARTHUR KNIGHT
VILLERS-LES-CAGNICOURT, France
2 September 1918
He was 22 years old and serving in the 10th (Alberta) Bn, CEF. When his bombing section was held up, he went forward alone, bayo-neting several machine-gunners and mortar crews and forcing the remainder to retire. Then, bringing forward a Lewis gun, he directed fire on the retreating enemy as his men went in pursuit. Seeing about 30 Germans going into a tunnel, Knight again went forward alone, killing an officer and two NCOs and taking 20 prisoners. Later, he single-handedly routed another enemy party before being mortally wounded.

Lance Sergeant ARTHUR EVANS (aka WALTER SIMPSON)
ETAING, France 2 September 1918
He was 27 years old and serving in the 6th Bn, Lincolnshire Regiment when during a patrol he spotted a machine-gun on the opposite bank of a river. He swam across, crept up to the rear of the post and shot two sentries; four more immediately surrendered. He was soon joined by the rest of the patrol, but another machine-gun then opened fire on them. His officer was wounded and Evans covered the withdrawal under very heavy fire.

His VC was originally awarded under the name Walter Simpson.

He died on 1 November 1936.

Lance Corporal WILLIAM METCALF
ARRAS, France 2 September 1918
He was 33 years old and serving in the 16th Bn, Manitoba Regiment (Canadian Scottish), CEF when the right flank of his battalion was held up by machine-gun fire from a strongpoint. The decision was taken to wait for a tank before the advance continued. On arrival, however, the tank lost its bearings. When it was within 100 yards of the German wire, Metcalf rushed

forward under a hail of bullets and used flags to direct it towards the enemy trench. He led it along the line until the strongpoint had been overcome. Many casualties were inflicted and 17 machine-guns taken. Later, although wounded, he continued to advance until ordered into a shell-hole to have his wounds dressed.

He died on 8 August 1968.

Temporary Corporal LAWRENCE WEATHERS
ALLAINES, France 2 September 1918
He was 28 years old and serving in the 43rd (South Australia) Bn, AIF when the attack was held up by a strongly held enemy trench. Weathers went forward alone and attacked the enemy with bombs. He returned for more bombs, and again went forward with three comrades and attacked under heavy fire. Regardless of personal danger, he mounted the parapet and bombed the trench, and 180 prisoners and three machine-guns were taken.

He was killed in action at Peronne on 29 September 1918.

Private JACK HARVEY
CLERY, PERONNE, France
2 September 1918
He was 27 years old and serving in the 1/22nd (County of London) Bn, London Regiment (Queen's) when his company was held up by machine-gun fire. He dashed forward alone for some 50 yards, through our barrage and in the face of heavy enemy fire, shooting two members of the gun crew and bayoneting another. He then destroyed the gun and worked his way along the trench, single-handedly rushing a dug-out, taking about 40 prisoners. His two acts of bravery saved his company heavy casualties and materially assisted in the success of the operation.

He died on 15 August 1940.

Private JOHN YOUNG
DURY-ARRAS SECTOR, France
2 September 1918
He was 25 years old and serving in the 87th Bn, Canadian Grenadier Guards, CEF. Working as a stretcher-bearer, he went forward to dress the wounded in open ground swept by machine-gun fire. He did this for over an hour, displaying absolute fearlessness, and on more then one occasion, having used up all his dressings, returned to his own lines to get more and went out again. Later in the same day he organised and led stretcher-bearers to bring in the wounded men he had dressed. He spent a full hour rescuing well over a dozen men. One of his lungs was damaged by mustard gas.

He died from tuberculosis on 7 November 1929. The Canadian Grenadier Guards Junior Ranks Mess was named the 'John Francis Young Club' in his honour.

Private WALTER RAYFIELD
DROCOURT-QUEANT LINE, ARRAS, France 2–4 September 1918
He was 37 years old and serving in the 7th Bn, 1st British Columbia Regiment, CEF when he moved ahead of his company and rushed a trench, bayoneting two men and taking ten prisoners. Later, after engaging a sniper, he rushed his position and so demoralised the enemy that 30 men surrendered to him. Subsequently he went out into the open under machine-gun fire and carried in a badly wounded man.

He died on 19 February 1949.

Corporal JOHN McNAMARA
LENS, France 3 September 1918
He was 31 years old and serving in the 9th Bn, East Surrey Regiment. When operating a telephone in a captured trench, he realised that a heavy counter-attack was gaining ground. Rushing to the nearest post, he made good use of a revolver taken from a wounded officer, and then seized a Lewis gun which he fired until it jammed. By this time he was alone in the post. Having destroyed the telephone, he joined the nearest post and manned a Lewis gun until reinforcements arrived.

He was killed in action at Solesmes on 16 October 1918.

Private SAMUEL NEEDHAM
KEFR KASIM, Palestine
10/11 September 1918

He was 33 years old and serving in the 1/5th Bn, Bedfordshire Regiment when his patrol was attacked by Turks in considerable force, supported by artillery and machine-gun fire. At a critical moment Needham turned to face the enemy as they approached to within 30 yards, fired rapidly into them and checked their advance, giving the patrol commander time to get his men together again. Half of the party had become casualties but they managed to get back with all of the wounded. His action in standing up to the enemy alone did much to inspire the men and undoubtedly saved the situation.

He died on 4 November 1918.

Sergeant LAURENCE CALVERT
'BOGGART'S HOLE', HAVRINCOURT, France 12 September 1918

He was 26 years old and serving in the 5th Bn, King's Own Yorkshire Light Infantry when his company was held up by enfilading machine-gun fire. He went forward alone and rushed the position, bayoneting three of the gun crew and shooting four more. His valour and determination in capturing two machine-guns single-handed ensured the success of the operation.

He was one of 74 VC holders who formed the honour guard at the interment of the Unknown Soldier at Westminster Abbey on 11 November 1920.

He died on 7 July 1964.

Sergeant HARRY LAURENT
GOUZEAUCOURT WOOD France 12 September 1918

He was 23 years old and serving in the 2nd Bn, NZ (Rifle) Brigade, NZEF when during an attack he was detailed to exploit an initial success and keep in touch with enemy movements. With a party of 12 men, he located a very strong enemy support line. He at once charged the position, completely disorganising the enemy by the suddenness of his attack. In the hand-to-hand fighting that followed, 30 enemy were killed and 112 men surrendered.

Laurent also served in the Second World War.

He died on 9 December 1987.

Lance Corporal ALFRED WILCOX
LAVENTIE, France 12 September 1918

He was 33 years old and serving in the 2/4th Bn, Oxfordshire and Buckinghamshire Light Infantry when his company was held up by enemy machine-guns, firing at close range. Wilcox rushed the nearest gun, bombing it and killing the gunner. He was then attacked by an enemy bombing party. After hand-to-hand fighting, he picked up some German 'stick grenades' because his rifle was clogged with mud, and led his men against the next gun, finally capturing and destroying it. Then, with just one man left, he continued bombing and captured a third gun. Going up the trench, bombing as he went, he captured a fourth gun, and then returned to his platoon, having killed at least 12 Germans.

During an informal occasion in 1920 he said of his deed: 'I saw a lot of square-heads, as I like to call 'em, in front of me, and I was after 'em. If I hadn't been after 'em they'd been after me, and I used more language than the British army ever learnt.' He died on 30 March 1954. In 2006 his nephew John Wilcox, who had attended his uncle's funeral, helped historian Chris Sutton in locating his grave. A service was held and a memorial unveiled on 12 September 2006, 88 years to the day after he was awarded his VC.

Corporal DAVID HUNTER
MOEUVRES, France 16/17 September 1918

He was 26 years old and serving in the 1/5th Bn, Highland Light Infantry when he was detailed to take and hold an advanced post which was established in shell-holes near the enemy. The following day he found that the enemy had established posts all around him, isolating his command. Determined to hold out, and despite being short of food and water, he managed to maintain his position for over 48 hours, repelling many attacks, until he was relieved.

He died on 14 February 1965.

Temporary Lieutenant Colonel DANIEL BURGES
JUMEAUX, Balkans 18 September 1918

He was 45 years old and serving in the Gloucestershire Regiment, commanding the 7th Bn, South Wales Borderers, when his reconnaissance of the enemy front line enabled his battalion to reach its assembly point without casualties. Later, while still at some distance from the objective, his men came under very heavy machine-gun fire. Although Burges was wounded, he continued to lead his men with skill and courage until he was wounded again and fell unconscious. He was taken prisoner but abandoned in a dug-out with his left leg shattered. He was recovered on 22 September and his leg was amputated.

Burges was one of 74 VC holders who formed the honour guard at the interment of the Unknown Soldier at Westminster Abbey on 11 November 1920.

He died on 24 October 1946.

Second Lieutenant FRANK YOUNG
HAVRINCOURT, France
18 September 1918

He was 22 years old and serving in the 1st Bn, Hertfordshire Regiment. During an enemy counter-attack, and throughout intense enemy fire, Young visited all the posts, warning the garrisons and encouraging the men. In the early stages of the attack he rescued two men who had been captured, and silenced a machine-gun with bombs. Then he fought his way back to the main position and drove out a party of Germans assembling there. Through 4 hours of heavy fighting he set a fine example, and was last seen fighting hand-to-hand against a considerable number of the enemy. He was killed in action the same day.

Temporary Second Lieutenant WILLIAM 'CHALKY' WHITE
GOUZEAUCOURT, France
18 September 1918

He was 23 years old and serving in the 38th Bn, Machine Gun Corps. When the advance was held up by enemy machine-guns, White rushed a gun position single-handedly, shot the three-man crew and captured the gun. Later, accompanied by two other men, both of whom were shot down, he attacked a gun position. He went on alone, killed the gunners and captured the gun. On a third occasion, when the advance was again held up, he collected a small party of men and rushed the position, inflicting heavy losses on the garrison. Subsequently he consolidated this position by the skilful use of his own and captured enemy machine-guns.

White also served with the North Russia Relief Force and was captured but made good his escape.

He died on 13 September 1974.

Sergeant MAURICE BUCKLEY (aka GERALD SEXTON)
LE VERGUIER, ST QUENTIN, France
18 September 1918

He was 27 years old and serving in the 13th (New South Wales) Bn, AIF when his company was held up by a field gun. He rushed the gun and killed the crew, then he rushed across open ground under machine-gun fire and fired into some dug-outs, forcing 30 Germans to surrender. When the advance was held up again by machine-gun fire, he put these guns out of action. Later, he again showed conspicuous bravery in capturing several enemy posts.

Having been declared a deserter in January 1916 when he went missing from a containment camp in Australia, he re-enlisted in May 1916 under the name Gerald Sexton.

He died on 27 January 1927, from injuries received in a fall from a horse.

Lance Sergeant WILLIAM WARING
ROSSNOY, LEMPIRE, France
18 September 1918

He was 32 years old and serving in the 25th Bn, Royal Welch Fusiliers when he led an attack on machine-guns under devastating fire, single-handedly rushing a strongpoint, bayoneting four Germans and capturing two more, with their guns. He then reorganised his men, inspiring them in another attack until he fell severely wounded.

He died on 18 October 1918, as a result of wounds received during his VC action.

Private JAMES WOODS
LE VERGUIER, ST QUENTIN, France
18 September 1918
He was 27 years old and serving in the 48th (South Australia) Bn, AIF. He was out with a weak patrol when they attacked and captured a formidable enemy post, which with two comrades he held against heavy counter-attacks. Jumping on to the parapet under heavy fire, he fired and kept on firing, inflicting severe casualties and holding up the enemy until help arrived.

He died on 18 January 1963.

Lance Corporal LEONARD LEWIS
RONSSOY, LEMPIRE, France
18 and 21 September 1918
He was 23 years old and serving in the 6th Bn, Northamptonshire Regiment when his company was held up by enfilading machine-gun fire. He crawled forward alone, successfully bombed the guns, and with rifle fire forced the crews to surrender. On 21 September he rushed his company through the enemy barrage, but was killed while getting his men under cover from heavy machine-gun fire. He was buried by the Australians, but his grave was later lost.

Ressaidar BADLU SINGH
RIVER JORDAN, Palestine
23 September 1918
He was 42 years old and serving in the 14th Murray's Jat Lancers, Indian Army, attached to the 29th Lancers (Deccan Horse). When his squadron was charging a strong enemy position, he realised that heavy casualties were being inflicted on his unit from a small hill, occupied by some 200 men. Without hesitation, he collected six men and with utter disregard of the danger he charged and captured the position. He was mortally wounded on the very top of the hill when capturing one of the machine-guns single-handedly, but all the guns and men had surrendered to him before he died.

Lieutenant JOHN BARRETT
PONTRUET, France 24 September 1918
He was 21 years old and serving in the 1/5th Bn,

Leicestershire Regiment when during an attack he collected all the available men and charged a trench containing numerous machine-guns. In spite of being wounded, he gained the trench and personally disposed of two machine-guns, inflicting many casualties. He was wounded a second time but climbed out of the trench to fix his position and locate the enemy, then ordered his men to fight their way to the battalion, which they did. He was again wounded, so seriously that he had to be carried away.

He died on 7 March 1977.

Temporary Lieutenant DONALD DEAN
LENS, France 24–26 September 1918
He was 21 years old and serving in the 8th Bn, Queen's Royal West Kent Regiment when he and his platoon held an advanced post established in a newly captured trench. The position was ill prepared for defence and he worked unceasingly with his men to consolidate the position, under heavy fire. Five times he was attacked and five times the attackers were beaten off. Throughout the whole time he inspired his men with his contempt for danger and set the highest example of valour, leadership and devotion to duty.

Dean also served in the Second World War. He died on 9 December 1985.

Acting Lieutenant Colonel JOHN GORT
CANAL DU NORD, FLESQUIERES, France 27 September 1918
He was 22 years old and commanding the 1st Bn, Grenadier Guards when he led his battalion under very heavy fire and despite being wounded. When the battalion was held up, he went across open ground to obtain assistance from a tank, which he personally led to the best advantage. He was wounded again, but after lying down on a stretcher for a while insisted on getting up and directing a further attack, which resulted in the capture of over 200 prisoners, two batteries of guns and many machine-guns. He refused to leave the field until the signal had gone up to say the final objective had been taken. His batman, Ransome, was killed while helping Gort to safety.

At the outbreak of the Second World War he

The Complete Victoria Cross

was given command of the British Expedi-
tionary Force (BEF). When the Germans broke
through in the Ardennes, splitting the Allied
forces, communications between the BEF and
the French effectively broke down, and on 25
May Gort took the unilateral decision to ignore
his orders for a southward attack. His decision
to withdraw the BEF and avoid likely capture
surely helped Britain to remain in the war and
prevented national morale from collapsing after
the defeats of 1940.

He served in many positions during the war.
As Governor of Malta (1942–44) his courage
and leadership during the siege was recognised
by the Maltese people, who awarded him the
Sword of Honour. The King gave Gort his
Field Marshal's baton in 1943 while in Malta.
Together with Generals Eisenhower and
Alexander, he witnessed Marshal Badoglio
sign the Italian surrender document in Valletta
Harbour in 1943.

He died from cancer on 31 March 1946. His
son-in-law was Major William Sidney VC.

Acting Captain CYRIL FRISBY
CANAL DU NORD, GRAINCOURT,
France 27 September 1918
He was 33 years old and serving in the 1st Bn,
Coldstream Guards when his company had to
capture a canal crossing. Together with Lance
Corporal Thomas Jackson, he rushed an
enemy machine-gun post, capturing two
machine-guns and 12 prisoners, and so enabled
the company to advance. Then, having consolidated his position, Frisby gave timely support
to a company which had lost all its officers and
NCOs, organising the defences and beating off
a heavy counter-attack. Both men were
awarded the VC.

Frisby was one of 74 VC holders who
formed the honour guard at the interment of
the Unknown Soldier at Westminster Abbey
on 11 November 1920.

He died on 10 September 1961.

Lieutenant SAMUEL HONEY
BOURLON WOOD, France
27 September 1918
He was 24 years old and serving in the 78th Bn

(Winnipeg Grenadiers), CEF. When all the
other officers of his company had become
casualties, he took command, continuing the
advance and taking the objective. Then,
finding his men suffering from enfilading
machine-gun fire, he located the post and
rushed it single-handedly, capturing the guns
and ten prisoners. He then repelled four
counter-attacks and later captured another
machine-gun post.

He died from his wounds three days later.

Lieutenant GEORGE KERR
BOURLON WOOD, France
27 September 1918
He was 23 years old and serving in the 3rd Bn
(CO), CEF when he acted with conspicuous
bravery and leadership during operations,
giving support by outflanking a machine-gun
post which was holding up the advance. Later,
when the advance was again held up by a
strongpoint, and being far in advance of his
company, he rushed the post single-handed,
capturing four machine-guns and 31 prisoners.

He died from carbon monoxide poisoning
on 8 December 1929, while running his car in
the garage at his home.

Corporal THOMAS NEELY
FLESQUIERES, France
27 September 1918
He was 21 years old and serving in the 8th Bn,
King's Own (Royal Lancaster) Regiment when
his company was held up by heavy machine-
gun fire. Realising the seriousness of the
situation, Neely at once dashed forward with
two other men and stormed the gun positions,
disposing of the garrisons and capturing three
machine-guns. Subsequently on two occasions
he rushed concrete strongpoints, killing or
capturing the occupants. His actions allowed
his company to advance 3,000 yards along the
Hindenberg support line.

He was killed in action at Romilly on
1 October 1918.

Lance Corporal THOMAS JACKSON
CANAL DU NORD, GRAINCOURT,
France 27 September 1918

He was 21 years old and serving in the 1st Bn, Coldstream Guards when he volunteered to cross the canal with Captain Frisby. They rushed an enemy machine-gun post, capturing two machine-guns and 12 prisoners, and so enabled the company to advance. Later that morning Jackson was the first man to jump into a German trench which had to be cleared, calling 'Come on, boys'. He killed two Germans before being killed. Both men were awarded the VC.

Lieutenant MILTON GREGG

CAMBRAI, France
27 September–1 October 1918
He was 26 years old and serving in the Royal Canadian Regiment, CEF when, although wounded twice, he led his men against enemy trenches in which he personally killed or wounded 11 Germans, and captured 25 prisoners and 12 machine-guns. In spite of his wounds, he stayed with his men and was again wounded leading his company in the attack. He showed most conspicuous bravery and initiative.

Gregg also served in the Second World War. He died on 13 March 1978.

Lieutenant GRAHAM LYALL

BOURLON WOOD and BLECOURT,
France 27 September and 1 October 1918
He was 26 years old and serving in the 102nd Bn (CO), CEF when he led his platoon in the capture of a strongpoint, taking 13 prisoners as well as four machine-guns and a field gun. Later, when leading his men against another strongpoint, he rushed forward alone and captured the post single-handed, taking 45 prisoners and five machine-guns. When the final objective was captured, it resulted in a further 47 prisoners being taken. On 1 October he captured a strongly defended position, taking 60 prisoners and 17 machine-guns. On both occasions he also tended the wounded under fire.

He died from heart failure on 28 November 1941, according to his medical records, and not 'in action' as some reports claim.

Acting Sergeant LOUIS McGUFFIE

WYTSCHAETE, Belgium
28 September 1918
He was 25 years old and serving in the 1/5th Bn, King's Own Scottish Borderers when during an advance he entered dug-out after dug-out, forcing an officer and 25 men to surrender. During the consolidation of the first objective, he pursued and brought back several Germans who were trying to slip away, and was also responsible for rescuing a group of British soldiers who were being led off as prisoners. Later the same day, while commanding a platoon, he took many more prisoners.

He was killed in action at Wytschaete on 4 October 1918.

Private HENRY TANDY (sometimes spelt TANDEY)

MARCOING, France 28 September 1918
He was 27 years old and serving in the 5th Bn, Duke of Wellington's (West Riding) Regiment. When his platoon was held up by machine-gun fire, he crawled forward, located the gun and knocked it out with a Lewis gun team. Arriving at a vital crossing in the village, he repaired the plank bridge under a hail of bullets. Later that evening, during another attack, he and his party of eight men were surrounded by an overwhelming force. Although the position seemed hopeless, he led a bayonet charge, fighting so fiercely that 37 Germans were driven into the hands of the remainder of his company.

Tandy was the most highly decorated private soldier in the First World War, being awarded the VC, the DCM and the MM. He also served in the Second World War. Tandy was one of 74 VC holders who formed the honour guard at the interment of the Unknown Soldier at Westminster Abbey on 11 November 1920. He died on 20 December 1977.

When Chamberlain visited Hitler in 1938, Hitler pointed to a picture of Tandy at the Menin Crossroads in 1914. He told Chamberlain that this man 'came so close to killing me that I thought I should never see Germany again'. Tandy had been about to shoot Hitler but when he saw that he was wounded and unarmed he changed his mind. Hitler asked Chamberlain to contact Tandy and offer his thanks, which Chamberlain did. Tandy believed the incident took place at Marcoing in 1918, as Hitler told Chamberlain, but this does not seem possible as Hitler's unit was not in the area at the time. However, Tandy was well known for not shooting wounded soldiers and as both men were at the Battle of Ypres in 1914, it is just possible that the dates have been confused.

Acting Lieutenant Colonel BERNARD VANN
BELLENGLISE and LEHAUCOURT, France 29 September 1918

He was 31 years old and serving in the 1/8th Bn, Sherwood Foresters (Nottinghamshire and Derbyshire Regiment) when he led his battalion with great skill across the Canal du Nord through very thick fog and under heavy fire. When the attack was held up by fire from the front and flank, Vann, realising the importance of keeping the advance going with the barrage, rushed forward and led the line himself. Later, he rushed a field gun single-handedly and knocked out three of its crew, enabling the advance to continue.

He was killed in action at Rammicourt on 3 October 1918. He was ordained in 1911, and tried to join the army as a chaplain but was unwilling to wait for a position to become available, so he enlisted in 1914 as an infantryman.

Lance Corporal ERNEST SEAMAN
TERHAND, Belgium 29 September 1918

He was 25 years old and serving in the 2nd Bn, Royal Inniskilling Fusiliers. When the right flank of his company was held up by enemy machine-guns, Seaman went forward under heavy fire with his Lewis gun and engaged the enemy single-handedly, killing one officer and two men and capturing 12 more men and two machine-guns. Later the same day he again rushed an enemy machine-gun post, capturing the gun under very heavy fire. He was killed immediately afterwards, but it was due to his gallant conduct that his company was able to push forward to its objective.

Major BLAIR WARK
BELLICOURT and JONCOURT, France 29 September–1 October 1918

He was 24 years old and serving in the 32nd (South Australia & Western Australia) Bn, AIF. He moved fearlessly at the head of, and sometimes far in advance of, his men, cheering them on and showing great gallantry in attack. At one point, while leading his assaulting companies, he rushed a battery of field guns, capturing four guns and ten prisoners. Then, with only two NCOs, he surprised and captured 50 Germans. Subsequently he again silenced machine-guns at great personal risk.

Wark also served in the Second World War. He died on 13 June 1941.

Temporary Captain JOHN MacGREGOR
CAMBRAI, France 29 September–3 October 1918

He was 29 years old and serving in the 2nd Bn, Canadian Mounted Rifles, CEF when he led his company forward under intense machine-gun fire and, although wounded, located and put out of action several enemy machine-guns that were holding up progress, killing four of the crew and taking eight prisoners. He then reorganised his men under heavy fire, and led them in the face of stubborn resistance. Later, after making a daylight reconnaissance under fire, he established his company in a new position, thereby greatly assisting the advance.

He died on 9 June 1952, following a long illness.

Private JAMES CRICHTON
CREVECOEUR, France 30 September 1918

He was 39 years old and serving in the 2nd Bn, Auckland Infantry Regiment, NZEF. Despite being wounded in the foot, he stayed with his platoon during its advance over rivers and a canal. When his men were forced back, he volunteered to take a message to his HQ, which involved swimming a river and crossing open ground swept by machine-gun fire. Later, under fire, he single-handedly removed five charges from beneath a bridge.

He died on 22 September 1961.

Private EDWARD (commonly known as JOHN) RYAN
HINDENBURG LINE, France
30 September 1918
He was 28 years old and serving in the 55th (New South Wales) Bn, AIF when the enemy succeeded in establishing a bombing party in the rear of his battalion's recently won position. On his own initiative, he organised and led a party of men with bombs and bayonets against the enemy. Ryan reached the position with only three men left but they succeeded in driving the Germans back. He cleared the last of them himself, despite a severe shoulder wound.

He died from pneumonia on 3 June 1941.

Temporary Lieutenant ROBERT GORLE
LEDEGHEM, Belgium 1 October 1918
He was 22 years old and serving in A Battery, 50th Brigade, Royal Field Artillery when he brought his gun into action in the most exposed position on four occasions and disposed of enemy machine-guns by firing over open sights. Later, when the infantry were driven back, he galloped his gun forward of the leading men and twice knocked out enemy machine-guns which were causing casualties. His disregard for personal safety was a magnificent example to the men in the wavering line, who rallied and retook their objective.

He died from pneumonia on 11 January 1937.

Sergeant WILLIAM MERRIFIELD
ABANCOURT, France 1 October 1918
He was 28 years old and serving in the 4th Bn (CO), CEF when the advance was held up by machine-gun fire. He dashed out alone, making his way from shell-hole to shell-hole. He killed the crew of the first post and, although wounded, he went on to the next and killed the crew with a bomb. He refused to be evacuated and led his platoon until he was severely wounded.

He died from a stroke on 8 August 1943.

Sergeant FREDERICK RIGGS
EPINOY, France 1 October 1918

He was 30 years old and serving in the 6th Bn, York and Lancaster Regiment when he led his platoon through uncut wire under heavy fire. He continued on and, although incurring numerous casualties from flanking fire, succeeded in reaching his objective, where he captured a machine-gun. Later, he used two captured machine-guns to such good effect that 50 Germans surrendered. When the enemy began to advance in force, he cheerfully encouraged his men to resist to the last, and while doing so was killed.

Sergeant WILLIAM JOHNSON
RAMICOURT, France 3 October 1918
He was 27 years old and serving in the 1/5th Bn, Sherwood Foresters (Nottinghamshire and Derbyshire Regiment). When his platoon was held up by a nest of machine-guns, firing at very close range, Johnson worked his way forward under heavy fire and single-handedly charged the post, bayoneting several men and capturing two machine-guns. During the charge he was severely wounded by a bomb, but continued to lead his men forward. Shortly afterwards the line was again held up by machine-gun fire, and again he single-handedly attacked the post, bombing the garrison, putting the guns out of action and capturing the crew.

He died on 25 April 1945.

Lieutenant JOSEPH MAXWELL
BEAUREVOIR-FONSOMME LINE ESTREES, France 3 October 1918
He was 22 years old and serving in the 18th (New South Wales) Bn, AIF when his company commander was severely wounded and he took over command. On two occasions he advanced alone through heavy wire entanglements, killing and capturing a number of prisoners and a machine-gun. Later, he skilfully extricated his men from an encounter with a large enemy force. Throughout the whole day he set a fine example of personal bravery.

In 1932 he and Hugh Buggy wrote *Hell's Bells and Mademoiselles*, a book about his wartime exploits.

He died from a heart attack on 6 July 1967.

The Complete Victoria Cross

Lance Corporal WILLIAM COLTMAN
MANNEQUIN HILL, SEQUEHART,
France 3/4 October 1918
He was 26 years old and serving in the 1/6th Bn, North Staffordshire Regiment (Prince of Wales's) as a stretcher-bearer. When he heard that some wounded men had been left behind, he went forward alone in the face of heavy enfilading fire, found the men, dressed their wounds and made three successive journeys carrying them on his back to safety. He tended the wounded unceasingly for 48 hours.

Coltman was the most highly decorated NCO of the war, being awarded the VC, the DCM and Bar, and the MM and Bar. He was one of 74 VC holders who formed the honour guard at the interment of the Unknown Soldier at Westminster Abbey on 11 November 1920.

He died on 29 June 1974.

Lieutenant GEORGE INGRAM
MONTBREHAIN, France 5 October 1918
He was 29 years old and serving in the 24th (Victoria) Bn, AIF. At the head of his men, he rushed forward and captured nine enemy machine-guns, and killed 42 of the enemy after overcoming stubborn resistance. Later, when his company had suffered severe casualties, including many of the officers, he again rushed a machine-gun post, shooting six Germans and capturing the gun. He displayed great dash and resource in the capture of two further posts, during which 62 prisoners were taken.

He died on 30 June 1961.

Private JAMES TOWERS
MERICOURT, France 6 October 1918
He was 21 years old and serving in the 2nd Bn, Cameronians. After five runners had been killed or wounded while attempting to deliver a message, Towers volunteered to try himself, in the full knowledge of the fate of the others. In spite of the heavy fire opened on him as soon as he moved, he dashed from cover to cover and eventually got the message through. His determination and disregard for danger proved an inspiring example to all. He said of his action: 'We were young men, old before our time... I had been in worse situations than that

before and no medals were awarded, but that's how it was.'

Towers was one of 74 VC holders who formed the honour guard at the interment of the Unknown Soldier at Westminster Abbey on 11 November 1920.

He died on 24 January 1977.

Company Sergeant Major JOHN WILLIAMS
VILLERS OUTREAUX, France
7/8 October 1918
He was 32 years old and serving in the 10th Bn, South Wales Borderers. His company was suffering heavy casualties from an enemy machine-gun, so he ordered a Lewis gun to open fire on it and rushed the gun single-handed. He engaged fifteen Germans, one of whom grabbed his rifle. He managed to break free and bayoneted five of the enemy, whereupon the rest surrendered. His action enabled his company and those on the flanks to advance.

Williams was one of 74 VC holders who formed the honour guard at the interment of the Unknown Soldier at Westminster Abbey on 11 November 1920.

He died on 7 March 1953.

Captain COULSON MITCHELL
CANAL DE L'ESCAUT CAMBRAI,
France 8/9 October 1918
He was 28 years old and serving in the 1st Tunnelling Company, 4th Canadian Engineers, CEF when he led a small party to examine the bridges over the canal and if possible prevent their demolition. He managed to cut a number of wires on one bridge, and then in total darkness he dashed across the main bridge, which was heavily charged for demolition. While Mitchell and an NCO were cutting wires, the enemy attacked. He killed three of them and captured another twelve. Under heavy fire he then continued to cut the wires and remove the charges.

He died on 17 November 1978.

Private WILLIAM HOLMES
CATTENIERES, France 9 October 1918
He was 23 years old and serving in the 2nd Bn,

Grenadier Guards when he carried in two wounded men under heavy fire, and was severely wounded while attending to a third. In spite of this he continued to carry in the wounded, but was shortly afterwards mortally wounded. By his self-sacrifice he saved the lives of many men.

Lieutenant WALLACE ALGIE
CAMBRAI, France 11 October 1918
He was 27 years old and serving in the 20th Bn (CO), CEF when his men came under enfilading machine-gun fire. Rushing forward with nine volunteers, he shot the crew of an enemy machine-gun and then turned the gun on the enemy, enabling his party to advance. He then rushed another machine-gun, killing the crew and capturing an officer and ten men. Then he went back for reinforcements but was killed while bringing them forward.

Corporal FRANK LESTER
NEUVILLY, France 12 October 1918
He was 22 years old and serving in the 10th Bn, Lancashire Fusiliers when he was taking part in the clearing of the village with a party of seven men and an officer. He was the first to enter a house and shot two Germans who were inside. As his party was leaving, they found the street was being swept by fire and a sniper was targeting the door. Lester volunteered to tackle the sniper, which he did, but in killing him he was himself mortally wounded.

Corporal HARRY WOOD
ST PYTHON, France 13 October 1918
He was 37 years old and serving in the 2nd Bn, Scots Guards when the advance was desperately opposed and the streets of the village were raked by fire. Wood's platoon sergeant was killed and he took over command of the leading platoon. The River Selle had to be crossed and the ruined bridge was the only way over. The area was swept with sniper fire, so he went forward and, using a large brick as cover, started firing on the snipers. He fired continuously on them, covering his men while they worked their way across. Later in the day he repeatedly drove off enemy counter-attacks.

Wood was one of 74 VC holders who formed the honour guard at the interment of the Unknown Soldier at Westminster Abbey on 11 November 1920. His nerves were badly affected by his wartime experiences. While on holiday, he was walking along the street with his wife when a car mounted the pavement and hurtled towards them. His wife pushed him out of the way, but was herself pinned against a wall. Although she suffered only minor injuries, Wood was so shocked that he collapsed and fell into a deep coma, from which he died on 15 August 1924.

Second Lieutenant JAMES JOHNSON
WEZ MACQUART, France
14 October 1918
He was 28 years old and serving in the 2nd Bn, Northumberland Fusiliers, attached to the 36th Bn, when during operations by strong patrols he repelled frequent counter-attacks, and for 6 hours held back the enemy. When at length he was ordered to retire, he was the last man to leave the advanced position and was carrying a wounded man. Three times Johnson returned and brought in wounded men under intense enemy machine-gun fire.
He died on 23 March 1943.

Corporal JAMES McPHIE
CANAL DA SENSEE NORD, France
14 October 1918
He was 23 years old and serving in the 416th (Edinburgh) Field Company, Corps of Royal Engineers when he was working on a cork-float bridge, which our infantry were crossing. Just before dawn the bridge began to break up and sink. He jumped into the water and tried to hold the timbers together but could not, so he swam back and collected materials for a repair. Although it was now full daylight and the bridge was under fire, he led the way to the bridge with his axe in his hand, but was shot dead almost at once.

Private MARTIN MOFFAT
LEDEGHEM, Belgium 14 October 1918
He was 36 years old and serving in the 2nd Bn, Leinster Regiment. He was with a party of five

others advancing across the open when they suddenly came under heavy fire at close range from a house. Rushing forward alone through a hail of bullets, he bombed it and then rushed the door, killing two and capturing 30 men.

Moffat drowned on 5 January 1946. He had seven VC holders as his pallbearers.

Private THOMAS RICKETTS

LEDEGHEM, Belgium 14 October 1918
He was 17 years old and serving in the Newfoundland Regiment (but not as part of the CEF, as Newfoundland did not become a province of Canada until 1949), when he volunteered to go with his NCO and a Lewis gun in an attempt to outflank an enemy battery that was causing casualties. As they approached the battery, their ammunition ran out. Ricketts doubled back 100 yards under heavy machine-gun fire to collect more ammunition and bring it back to the Lewis gun. They then drove the enemy gun teams into a farm and the platoon was able to advance. They captured four field guns, four machine-guns and eight men.

The King said at his investiture: 'This is the youngest VC in my army.'

He died on 10 February 1967.

Sergeant JOHN O'NEILL (or O'NIELL)

MOORSEELE, Belgium
14 and 20 October 1918
He was 21 years old and serving in the 2nd Bn, Leinster Regiment (Prince of Wales's) when the advance was checked by two machine-guns and a battery of field guns firing over open sights. O'Neill, with only eleven men in support, charged the battery and captured four field guns, two machine-guns and sixteen prisoners. On 20 October, with one man, he rushed an enemy machine-gun position, routing about 100 men and causing many casualties.

O'Neill was one of 74 VC holders who formed the honour guard at the interment of the Unknown Soldier at Westminster Abbey on 11 November 1920.

He died on 16 October 1942.

Acting Corporal ROLAND ELCOCK

CAPELLE ST CATHERINE, France
15 October 1918
He was 19 years old and serving in the 11th Bn, Royal Scots (Lothian Regiment). He was in charge of a Lewis gun team when he rushed his gun to within 10 yards of two enemy machine-guns that were causing heavy casualties and holding up the attack. He put both guns out of action, capturing five prisoners, enabling the advance to continue. Later, he again attacked an enemy machine-gun and captured the crew.

He was one of 74 VC holders who formed the honour guard at the interment of the Unknown Soldier at Westminster Abbey on 11 November 1920.

Elcock died from cirrhosis of the liver on 6 October 1944.

Sergeant HORACE CURTIS

LE CATEAU, France 18 October 1918
He was 27 years old and serving in the 2nd Bn, Royal Dublin Fusiliers. When his platoon was advancing and came unexpectedly under heavy machine-gun fire, he went forward through our own barrage and under enemy fire. He killed the crews of two machine-guns, whereupon the remaining four guns surrendered. He then succeeded in capturing 100 men from a train loaded with reinforcements before his platoon joined him.

He died on 1 July 1968.

Acting Sergeant JOHN DAYKINS

SOLESMES, France 20 October 1918
He was 35 years old and serving in the 2/4th Bn, York and Lancaster Regiment. With the twelve remaining men of his platoon, he rushed a machine-gun post, and during the subsequent severe hand-to-hand fighting he disposed of many of the enemy himself and secured the objective. Then he located another enemy machine-gun, which was holding up an operation by his company. Under heavy fire he worked his way along to the post and shortly afterwards came back with 25 prisoners and a machine-gun, which he mounted at his position. His magnificent fighting spirit and splendid example inspired his men, saved many

casualties and contributed to the success of the attack.

He died on 24 January 1933, when he left his house with a gun to investigate a noise and was found dead with a bullet wound to the head.

Private ALFRED WILKINSON
MAROU, France 20 October 1918

He was 21 years old and serving in the 1/5th Bn, Manchester Regiment. During an attack four runners had been killed in attempting to deliver a message to the supporting company. Wilkinson volunteered to go next, and he succeeded in delivering the message although the journey involved exposure to extremely heavy machine-gun and shell fire for a distance of 600 yards. He showed magnificent courage and complete indifference to the danger. Later the same day he donated blood to save the life of a wounded Australian dispatch rider, despite having been wounded in the face by shrapnel.

When he took time off work in 1929 to attend a VC reunion dinner at the Royal Gallery in the House of Lords, his employers docked his pay. A newspaper-led public outcry followed, ensuring that he got the money back.

He died from carbon monoxide poisoning on 18 October 1940, and an inquest found that a dead bird had blocked one of the ventilation pipes at the colliery where he was working.

Lieutenant DAVID McGREGOR
HOOGEMOLEN, Belgium
22 October 1918

He was 23 years old and serving in the 6th Bn, Royal Scots (Lothian Regiment) and 29th Bn, Machine Gun Corps. While in command of a section of machine-guns attached to an assaulting battalion, he concealed his guns in a sunken road. During the advance they came under heavy fire and he ordered the teams to take a safer route. He then lay flat on a limber as the driver galloped forward under heavy fire, and the guns were immediately put into action. He was killed while directing the fire of his guns shortly afterwards.

Private FRANCIS MILES
BOIS DE L'EVEQUE, LANDRECIES, France 23 October 1918

He was 22 years old and serving in the 1/5th Bn, Gloucestershire Regiment when his company was held up by a line of enemy machine-guns in a sunken road. On his own initiative Miles went forward under very heavy fire, located a machine-gun, shot the gunner and put the gun out of action. Then, on seeing another machine-gun nearby, he again went forward alone, shot the gunner and captured eight men. Finally he stood up and beckoned to the men of his company, who, acting on his signals, were able to capture 16 machine-guns, an officer and 50 men.

In 1917 Miles had been the sole survivor when 50 men were buried alive by an exploding shell.

He died on 8 November 1961.

Lieutenant Colonel HARRY GREENWOOD
OVILLERS, France 23/24 October 1918

He was 36 years old and commanding the 9th Bn, King's Own Yorkshire Light Infantry when the advance of his battalion was checked by machine-gun fire. Greenwood single-handedly rushed the position and killed the crew. Subsequently, accompanied by two runners he took another machine-gun post, but found that his battalion was almost surrounded by an enemy counter-attack. Repulsing this attack, he led his men forward again, capturing 150 prisoners, eight machine-guns and a field gun. Later he again inspired his men to such a degree that their final objective was captured.

Greenwood was one of 74 VC holders who formed the honour guard at the interment of the Unknown Soldier at Westminster Abbey on 11 November 1920. Greenwood also served in the Second Boer War and the Second World War.

He died on 5 May 1948.

Temporary Lieutenant FREDERICK HEDGES
North-east of BOURSIES, France
24 October 1918

He was 32 years old and serving in the Bedfordshire Regiment, attached to the 6th

Bn, Northamptonshire Regiment, when he led his company with great skill to the final objective, maintaining direction under the most difficult conditions. When a line of machine-guns held up the advance, he went forward accompanied by an NCO, with a Lewis gun following some distance behind, and captured six machine-guns and 14 prisoners. His gallantry and initiative enabled the whole line to advance and contributed largely to the success of subsequent operations.

Hedges also served in the Second World War. He hanged himself on 29 May 1954, while suffering from depression. Most records give his date of birth as 1896, but his death certificate and cremation records state that he died aged 67, making his date of birth 1886, not 1896.

Lieutenant WILLIAM BISSETT

MAING, France 25 October 1918
He was 25 years old and serving in the 1/6th Bn, Argyll and Sutherland Highlanders (Princess Louise's) when due to officer casualties he was commanding the company when an enemy counter-attack turned his left flank. Realising the danger, he withdrew, but the enemy continued to advance. When his ammunition ran out, he led a bayonet charge under heavy fire, driving the enemy back with heavy losses. Again he drove forward, establishing a line and saving a critical situation.

Bissett also served in the Second World War. He died on 12 May 1971.

Private NORMAN HARVEY

INGOYGHEM, Belgium 25 October 1918
He was 19 years old and serving in the 1st Bn, Royal Inniskilling Fusiliers when his battalion was held up by machine-gun fire and was suffering heavy casualties. On his own initiative he rushed forward and engaged the enemy single-handed, killing 20 of them and capturing their guns. Later, when the advance was again checked by a strongpoint, he rushed forward and put the enemy to flight. Subsequently after dark he voluntarily went out on reconnaissance and gained valuable information.

Harvey had enlisted in November 1914 at the age of 15.

He was killed in action at Haifa, Palestine on 16 February 1942.

Acting Major WILLIAM BARKER

FORET DE MORMAL, France
27 October 1918
He was 26 years old and serving in 201 Squadron, RAF when he attacked a two-seater which broke up, its crew escaping by parachute. By his own admission, he was careless and was bounced by 15 Fokker DVIIs. In a running dog-fight, Barker was wounded three times in the legs, then his left elbow was blown off, yet he managed to control his plane and shoot or drive down three more enemy planes.

Barker was the most highly decorated Canadian of the First World War, being awarded the VC, the DSO and Bar and the MC and two Bars.

He died on 12 March 1930, while demonstrating a new two-seater aeroplane.

Sergeant WILLIAM McNALLY

PIAVE RIVER and VAZZOLA, Italy
27 and 29 October 1918
He was 23 years old and serving in the 8th Bn, Yorkshire Regiment. When his company was seriously hindered by machine-gun fire, he rushed the post regardless of personal safety, killing the crew and capturing the gun. On 29 October he crept up to the rear of an enemy position and put the garrison to flight, capturing their machine-guns. On the same day, when holding a newly captured position, he beat off a strong counter-attack from both flanks, by coolly controlling the fire of his men and inflicting heavy casualties.

McNally was one of 74 VC holders who formed the honour guard at the interment of the Unknown Soldier at Westminster Abbey on 11 November 1920.

He died on 5 January 1976.

Private WILFRED WOOD

CASA VANA, Italy 28 October 1918
He was 21 years old and serving in the 10th Bn, Northumberland Fusiliers when the advance was being held up by enemy machine-guns and snipers. On his own initiative Wood worked his

way forward and with his Lewis gun enfiladed the enemy machine-gun posts and forced the surrender of 140 men. Later, when a hidden machine-gun opened fire at point-blank range, he charged the gun, firing his Lewis gun from the hip at the same time. He killed the gun crew and, without orders, pushed further on and enfiladed a ditch from which three officers and 160 men surrendered.

Wood was one of 74 VC holders who formed the honour guard at the interment of the Unknown Soldier at Westminster Abbey on 11 November 1920.

He died on 3 January 1982.

Sergeant THOMAS CALDWELL

AUDENARDE, Belgium 31 October 1918
He was 24 years old and serving in the 12th Bn, Royal Scots Fusiliers. He was in command of a Lewis gun section engaged in clearing a farmhouse when his men came under heavy fire at close range. He rushed the farm, captured the position single-handed and took 18 prisoners. This gallant and determined exploit removed a serious obstacle from the line of advance and led to the capture by his men of about 70 prisoners, eight machine-guns and a trench mortar.

He died on 6 June 1969.

Sergeant HUGH CAIRNS

VALENCIENNES, France
1 November 1918
He was 21 years old and serving in the 46th (South Saskatchewan) Bn, CEF when a machine-gun fired on his platoon. Cairns seized a Lewis gun and single-handedly rushed the enemy position, killing the crew of five and capturing the gun. Later, after killing 12 of the enemy and capturing a further 18 men, including two guns, he went forward with a small party and, although wounded, outflanked more field guns and machine-guns, killing many and capturing the guns. After consolidation, he went with a patrol to exploit Marly and forced 60 men to surrender, but he was severely wounded. He collapsed and died the following day.

Sergeant JAMES CLARKE

HAPPEGARBES SPUR, France
2 November 1918
He was 24 years old and serving in the 15th Bn, Lancashire Fusiliers when his platoon was held up by heavy machine-gun fire. He rushed forward through a strongly held position, capturing in succession four machine-guns and killing the crews. Later, with the remains of his platoon, he captured three more machine-guns and many prisoners, and when his platoon was again held up by fire he led a tank against the enemy guns. Throughout the whole of these operations he acted with great bravery and total disregard for personal safety.

He died from pneumonia on 16 June 1947.

Acting Lieutenant Colonel DUDLEY JOHNSON

SAMBRE-OISE CANAL, CATILLON, France 4 November 1918
He was 34 years old and commanding the 2nd Bn, Royal Sussex Regiment when his battalion was ordered to assault the canal. The enemy position was strong and the assaulting and bridging parties were halted 100 yards from the canal by a heavy barrage. At this point Johnson arrived and personally led an assault, but heavy fire again broke up the attack. He reorganised the assaulting and bridging parties and this time effected a crossing. He was untouched throughout this action, even though the troops were decimated. The success of this dangerous operation was entirely due to his splendid leadership.

Johnson was one of 74 VC holders who formed the honour guard at the interment of the Unknown Soldier at Westminster Abbey on 11 November 1920, and he was ADC to King George VI from 1936 to 1939. He also served in the Second World War.

He died on 21 December 1975.

Acting Lieutenant Colonel JAMES MARSHALL

SAMBRE-OISE CANAL, CATILLON, France 4 November 1918
He was 31 years old and serving in the Irish Guards (Special Reserve), attached to the 16th

The Complete Victoria Cross

Bn, Lancashire Fusiliers, when repairs were needed to a badly damaged bridge so it could be crossed. All the members of the first repair party he organised were killed or wounded, but his personal example was such that more volunteers were forthcoming for another attempt. Under heavy fire, and with complete disregard for his own safety, he stood in the open on the bank encouraging his men and helping them with the work. When the bridge was repaired, he led his men across, but he was killed as he did so.

Acting Major GEORGE FINDLAY
SAMBRE-OISE CANAL, CATILLON, France 4 November 1918
He was 29 years old and serving in the 409th (Low) Field Company, Corps of Royal Engineers. He was with the leading bridging and assault parties when they came under heavy fire, stopping their advance. Nevertheless he collected what men he could and repaired the bridge, under very heavy fire. Although wounded, he continued with his work and after two unsuccessful attempts managed to place the bridge in position across the lock. He was the first man to cross, remaining at this dangerous post until the work was completed.
Findlay also served in the Second World War.
He died on 26 June 1967.

Acting Major ARNOLD WATERS
SAMBRE-OISE CANAL, ORS, France
4 November 1918
He was 32 years old and serving in the 218th Field Company, Corps of Royal Engineers when his building party at a damaged bridge was taking severe casualties from artillery and close-range machine-gun fire. When all his officers had been killed or wounded, he at once went forward and personally supervised the completion of the bridge, working on cork-floats while under such intense fire that it seemed impossible he could survive. The success of the operation was due entirely to his valour.
Waters was one of 74 VC holders who formed the honour guard at the interment of

the Unknown Soldier at Westminster Abbey on 11 November 1920.
He died on 22 January 1981.

Second Lieutenant JAMES KIRK
SAMBRE-OISE CANAL, ORS, France
4 November 1918
He was 21 years old and serving in the 10th Bn, Manchester Regiment, attached to the 2nd Bn, when his battalion was attempting to cross the canal. In order to cover them, he took a Lewis gun, paddled across the canal and opened fire. Further ammunition was paddled over to him and he continued to fire until he was killed. His courage and self-sacrifice enabled two platoons to cross and prevented many casualties.

Lance Corporal WILLIAM AMEY
LANDRECIES, France
4 November 1918
He was 27 years old and serving in the 1/8th Bn, Royal Warwickshire Regiment when many enemy machine-guns were overlooked because of thick fog during an advance. Amey returned and led his section against a machine-gun nest under heavy fire, and drove the garrison into a farm, finally capturing 50 men and several machine-guns. Later, he single-handedly and under fire attacked a machine-gun post, killed two of the garrison and drove the remainder into a cellar until assistance arrived. Subsequently he rushed a strongly held post, capturing 20 more prisoners.
He died on 28 May 1940.

Sapper ADAM ARCHIBALD
SAMBRE-OISE CANAL, ORS, France
4 November 1918
He was 40 years old and serving in the 218th Field Company, Royal Corps of Engineers when he was with a party of men building a bridge across the canal. He was foremost in the work under very heavy artillery and machine-gun fire. The latter was directed at him from close range while he was working on the cork-floats. Nevertheless he persevered in his work and his example was such that the bridge – which was essential to the success of the

operation – was very quickly completed. Immediately afterwards he collapsed from the effects of gas poisoning.

Archibald was one of 74 VC holders who formed the honour guard at the interment of the Unknown Soldier at Westminster Abbey on 11 November 1920.

He died on 10 March 1957.

Acting Major BRETT CLOUTMAN
PONT-SUR-SAMBRE, France
6 November 1918

He was 27 years old and serving in the 59th Field Company, Royal Corps of Engineers. While reconnoitring a river crossing, he found the bridge almost intact but prepared for demolition. Leaving his men under cover, he went forward alone, swam across the river and cut the wires under heavy shell and machine-gun fire. He returned the same way. Although the bridge was blown later by other means, the abutments remained intact.

Cloutman also served in the Second World War. He died on 15 August 1971. The 'Cloutman Award' is still presented annually to the most promising Lance Corporal of the RE Squadron on 6 November each year.

UNKNOWN AMERICAN SOLDIER of WWI

The United States awarded the Medal of Honor to the 'unknown British soldier' by an Act of Congress approved on 4 March 1921, and in the same spirit of comradeship a Cabinet meeting of 26 October 1921 approved the award of the Victoria Cross to the unknown soldier of the United States. It arrived by diplomatic bag on board HMS *Eurydice* on 31 October, and was presented on behalf of King George V by Admiral of the Fleet Lord Beatty on 11 November 1921 at Arlington National Cemetery. The medal is inscribed 'The Unknown Warrior of the United States of America'.

Chapter Eleven

THE INTER-WAR YEARS, 1919–35

North Russia Relief Force, 1919 (5 VCs)

Following the overthrow of the Tsar and Russia's withdrawal from the First World War, Germany was allowed to occupy large areas of Russia under the terms of the Treaty of Brest-Litovsk. The Allies had large stocks of supplies in this area and to prevent them from falling into German hands, an Allied force was sent to Russia. These men were subsequently drawn into action against the Bolsheviks. Trapped and iced in by the winter, there was a real threat of mutiny. The British then raised the North Russia Relief Force to oversee their withdrawal. Five Victoria Crosses were awarded for this campaign.

Lieutenant AUGUSTUS AGAR
COASTAL MOTOR BOAT 4, KRON-STADT 17 June 1919
He was 29 years old and serving in the Royal Navy. He had penetrated a destroyer screen to engage a larger warship further inshore when his boat finally broke down, its hull having been damaged by gunfire. It had to be taken alongside a breakwater for repairs, and for 20 minutes was in full view of the enemy. Once it was repaired, Agar again went into action, this time attacking and sinking the cruiser *Olig*, after which he retired to the safety of the open bay under heavy fire. But he had drawn the attention of the Russians, who put a bounty of £5,000 on his head. Undeterred, he took part in a second raid on Kronstadt on 18 August.

Agar also served in both world wars, and is the author of *Showing the Flag, Baltic Episode*

and his autobiography *Footprints in the Sea*. He died on 30 December 1968.

Corporal ARTHUR SULLIVAN
SHEIKA RIVER 10 August 1919
He was 22 years old and serving in the 45th Bn, Royal Fusiliers when his platoon was fighting a rearguard action and had to cross a river over a narrow plank. When four men fell in, Sullivan immediately jumped in after them, under heavy fire, pulling them out one at a time. But for his action they would undoubtedly have drowned, as all the men were exhausted and the enemy were only 100 yards away.

He died on 9 April 1937, when he was struck by a bicycle and banged his head on the pavement.

Commander CLAUDE DOBSON
COASTAL MOTOR BOAT 31, KRON-STADT 18 August 1919
He was 34 years old and serving in the Royal Navy in command of the CMB Flotilla, which he led through the chain of forts to the entrance of the harbour. He directed operations and then under heavy fire he torpedoed the battleship *Andrei Pervozanni*, then he returned through heavy fire to the open bay.

He died on 26 June 1940.

Lieutenant GORDON STEELE
COASTAL MOTOR BOAT 88, KRON-STADT 18 August 1919
He was 26 years old and serving in the Royal Navy when his boat was illuminated by an enemy searchlight after entering the harbour.

Very heavy fire followed, the captain being killed and the boat thrown off course. A British aircraft saw the incident, dived in on the searchlight and put it out of action with machine-gun fire. Steele then took the wheel and steadied the boat, lifting his dead captain away from the steering and firing position. He then torpedoed the battleship *Andrei Pervozanni* from 100 yards. Then he manoeuvred the CMB in a very confined space to get a clear shot at the other battleship, *Petropavlosk,* before making for the safety of the bay.

He was one of 74 VC holders who formed the honour guard at the interment of the Unknown Soldier at Westminster Abbey on 11 November 1920. Steele also served in the Second World War. In 1940 he met by chance the pilot of the aircraft who had attacked the searchlight. He is also the author of *The Waziristan Campaign, 1919–1921*.

He died on 4 January 1981.

Sergeant SAMUEL PEARSE
EMTSA 29 August 1919
He was 22 years old and serving in the 45th Bn, Royal Fusiliers when he cut his way through the wire under heavy rifle and machine-gun fire, clearing a way for the men to enter an enemy battery position. He then single-handedly charged a blockhouse which was causing casualties and killed the garrison with bombs. He was killed a few moments later, but it was due to his action that the position was taken with so few casualties.

The Waziristan Campaign, India, 1919–21 (3 VCs)

British-occupied towns and military posts on India's north-west frontier had come under continual attack by Mahsud tribesmen. A force of 63,000 men was mustered to put down the growing insurrection. Three Victoria Crosses were awarded for this campaign.

Temporary Captain HENRY ANDREWS
KHAJURI 22 October 1919
He was 48 years old and serving in the Indian Medical Service, Indian Army when he heard that a convoy had been attacked nearby, and he went out to tend the wounded. He set up an aid post which offered some protection to the wounded, but none for him. Although compelled to move the aid post, he continued to attend to the wounded. Finally, when a van became available, he collected the wounded and under fire loaded them into it. He was killed while stepping into the van, having completed his task.

Lieutenant WILLIAM KENNY
KOT KAI 2 January 1920
He was 20 years old and serving in the 4/39th Garhwal Rifles, Indian Army when he was in command of a company holding an advanced position which was attacked three times by the Mahsuds in greatly superior numbers. He held them off for 4 hours, being foremost in the hand-to-hand fighting which took place. In the subsequent withdrawal, he led a counter-attack with a small party to allow the wounded to be got away. His party was overcome, but he was seen fighting to the last.

Sepoy ISHAR SINGH
HAIDARI KACH 10 April 1921
He was 25 years old and serving in the 28th Punjab Regiment, Indian Army when he received a very severe wound to the chest and fell beside his Lewis gun. Hand-to-hand fighting having commenced, all the officers and NCOs were either killed or wounded, and Singh's Lewis gun was taken by the enemy. Calling to two other men, he got up and charged the enemy, recovering the gun; although bleeding profusely, he again got the gun into action. When his Jemadar arrived, he took the Lewis gun from Singh and ordered him to go and have his wound dressed. Instead, he went to the medical officer and was of great assistance in pointing out where the wounded were lying, and in carrying water to them. He made many trips to the river for this purpose. On one occasion, when the enemy fire was very heavy, he took a rifle and helped keep the fire down. On another occasion he stood in front of the medical officer who was dressing a

wounded man, thus shielding him with his body. It was over 3 hours before he finally submitted to being evacuated, by now too weak from loss of blood to object.

He died on 2 December 1963.

Arab Revolt, Mesopotamia, 1920 (1 VC)

After the end of the First World War the German and Ottoman empires were shared among the victors under the Sykes-Picot Agreement. Under this agreement, Britain received Mesopotamia and Palestine, which would remain under British guidance until they were considered able to rule themselves. In Mesopotamia, however, Sunni and Shia Muslim clerics cooperated to incite revolt. Already crippled by the war, Britain was obliged to draft in men from India to deal with the rebellion. One Victoria Cross was awarded for this campaign.

Captain GEORGE HENDERSON
near HILLAH 24 July 1920
He was 26 years old and serving in the 2nd Bn, Manchester Regiment when he led his company in three charges against the enemy, who had opened fire on his flank. At one point, when the situation was critical, he steadied his men by sheer pluck and coolness, preventing his company from being cut up. During the second charge he fell wounded but refused to leave his command and just as the company reached the enemy trench he was again wounded, this time mortally. His last words were: 'I'm done now, don't let them beat you.'

The Second Mohmand Campaign, India, 1935 (1 VC)

After years of unrest, the tribes of India's north-west frontier battled against British colonial expansion, and continued political pressure eventually achieved the same rights for the people of the north-west frontier as were enjoyed in British India. However, the hill tribes remained fiercely anti-British and embarked on a two-year rampage of robbery and murder which the Indian Army struggled to contain. Eventually the Nowshera Brigade had to be sent to deal with the Mohmands. One Victoria Cross was awarded for this campaign.

Captain GODFREY MEYNELL
MAMUND VALLEY
29 September 1935
He was 31 years old and serving in the 5th Bn (Corps of Guides), 12 Frontier Force Regiment, Indian Army when in the final phase of an attack he went to the most forward troops, finding them involved in a struggle against vastly superior numbers. He at once took command and with two Lewis guns and about 30 men maintained a heavy and accurate fire on the advancing enemy, but their numbers nevertheless succeeded in reaching the position and putting the Lewis guns out of action. In the hand-to-hand fighting that followed, Meynell was mortally wounded, but the heavy losses inflicted on the enemy prevented them from exploiting their success.

Chapter Twelve

THE SECOND WORLD WAR, 1939–45

The causes of the Second World War are well known, and their roots lie in Hitler's rise to power in 1933. After his reoccupation of the Rhineland, he annexed Austria and took over the Sudetenland of Czechoslovakia. Next came his demand to Poland to allow him access to Danzig. When this was refused, Germany attacked Poland. Britain and France had guaranteed Poland's sovereignty and declared war on 3 September 1939. The conflict became truly a world war when Japan attacked the USA on 7 December 1941. The Second World War was the most destructive conflict the world had ever known, resulting in the deaths of 60 million people worldwide. In all, 182 Victoria Crosses were awarded for the campaigns of the Second World War.

1939

Commander JOHN 'TUBBY' LINTON
MEDITERRANEAN SEA
September 1939–March 1943
He was 34 years old and serving in the Royal Navy, commanding HM Submarine *Turbulent*. From the outbreak of war until 1943, he was responsible for sinking one cruiser, one destroyer, one U-boat and 28 supply ships, some 100,000 tons in all, and he destroyed three trains with gunfire. In his last year he spent 254 days at sea, submerged for almost half of that time. His submarine was hunted 13 times and had 250 depth-charges fired at her. His many brilliant successes were due to his constant skill and daring, which never failed him when there was an enemy to

be attacked. On one such occasion he sighted a convoy of two merchant ships and two destroyers. He worked his way to the head of the convoy and dived to attack it as it passed through the moonlight. As he brought his sights to bear, he found himself ahead of a destroyer. Yet he held his course until it was almost on top of him, and when his sights came on the convoy he fired. He sank one merchant ship and one destroyer, while the other merchant ship caught fire and blew up.

He was killed in action at Maddelina Harbour on 23 March 1943, when his submarine hit a mine.

1940

Lieutenant Commander GERARD 'RAMMER' ROOPE
WEST FJORD, Norway 8 April 1940
He was 35 years old and serving in the Royal Navy, commanding HMS *Glowworm*, when he met and engaged two enemy destroyers, scoring at least one hit. The enemy broke off the action and headed north to lead *Glowworm* on to their supporting forces. Roope correctly guessed the enemy's intentions and gave chase. The German heavy cruiser *Admiral Hipper* was sighted closing on *Glowworm* at high speed. Undaunted, Roope attacked her with torpedoes but without success. *Glowworm* was badly damaged by *Admiral Hipper*, one gun being put out of action and her speed much reduced. Nevertheless, with her three remaining guns still firing, she closed and rammed the German cruiser. As she drew away, she fired again and

scored another hit. By now *Glowworm*'s bow was badly damaged and she was riddled with hits. Roope gave the order to 'abandon ship' as she heeled over to starboard, and he and some of the survivors managed to get on to the upturned hull. Roope turned to Lieutenant Ramsey and said: 'I don't think we'll be playing cricket for a long time yet.' The German cruiser stopped to pick up survivors, but due to the heavy seas only 31 men were saved. Roope was not among them. His body was never recovered.

Captain BERNARD WARBURTON-LEE
OFOT FJORD, NARVIK, Norway
10 April 1940
He was 44 years old and serving in the Royal Navy, commanding HMS *Hardy,* when he led his flotilla of five destroyers against six enemy destroyers, one submarine and two coastal defence ships. He took the enemy completely by surprise and made three successful attacks on the warships and merchant ships in the harbour. On withdrawing, five more enemy destroyers were engaged. Warburton-Lee was mortally wounded by a shell which hit *Hardy*'s bridge. His last signal was: 'Continue to engage the enemy.'

Lieutenant RICHARD STANNARD
NAMSOS, Norway 28 April–2 May 1940
He was 37 years old and serving in the Royal Naval Reserve, commanding HMS *Arab,* when enemy bombing attacks set fire to many tons of grenades on the wharf at Namsos. With no shore water supply, Stannard ran *Arab*'s bow against the wharf and held her there. Sending all but two men aft, he then worked for 2 hours to extinguish the fire with hoses from the forecastle. He persisted in this work until he had to give it up as hopeless. After helping other ships against air attacks, he placed his own damaged ship under the shelter of a cliff, landed his crew and those of two other trawlers, and established an armed camp. Here, off-duty men could rest while he attacked enemy aircraft which approached by day, and kept up an anti-submarine watch by night. When another trawler nearby was hit and set on fire, he, with two other men, boarded HMS *Arab* and moved her 100 yards before the other ship blew up. Finally, when leaving the fjord, he was attacked by a German bomber which then ordered him to steer east into captivity or be sunk. He maintained his course and held his fire until the enemy was within 800 yards, and then he brought her down with gunfire. Throughout a period of five days HMS *Arab* was subjected to 31 bombing attacks and the camp and gun positions ashore were repeatedly machine-gunned and bombed. Yet the defensive position was so well planned that only one man was wounded. Stannard eventually brought his ship back to a British port.

He died on 22 July 1977. There is a blue plaque on his house in The Avenue, Loughton, Essex.

Flying Officer DONALD GARLAND
ALBERT CANAL, Belgium 12 May 1940
Donald Garland was 21 years old and serving in 12 Squadron, RAF. Together with Sergeant Thomas Gray, he was pilot in the leading Fairey Battle bomber that attacked the Albert Canal Bridge at Vroenhoven. This bridge had to be destroyed at all costs. As well as contending with enemy fighters, they met an inferno of anti-aircraft fire. Despite this, they pressed home the attack, dropping their bombs at low level. The plane then crashed into the village of Lanaken, both men being killed. British fighters in the vicinity reported that the target was obscured by bombs bursting on and in its vicinity. Only one bomber out of five returned home from this mission. Both men were awarded the VC.

Garland was the first of four brothers to be killed in the war. In 2005, to mark the 90th anniversary of 12 Squadron's foundation, an RAF Tornado GR4 made a fly-past; as a mark of respect, it bore the names of Flying Officer Garland and Sergeant Gray below the cockpit.

Sergeant THOMAS GRAY
ALBERT CANAL, Belgium 12 May 1940
He was 25 years old and serving in 12 Squadron, RAF. Together with Flying Officer

Donald Garland, he was in the leading Fairey Battle bomber that attacked the Albert Canal Bridge at Vroenhoven. This bridge had to be destroyed at all costs. As well as contending with enemy fighters, they met an inferno of anti-aircraft fire. Despite this, they pressed home the attack, dropping their bombs at low level. The plane crashed into the village of Lanaken, both men being killed. British fighters in the vicinity reported that the target was obscured by bombs bursting on and in its vicinity. Only one bomber out of five returned home from this mission. Gray was killed just five days short of his 26th birthday. Both men were awarded the VC.

In 2005, to mark the 90th anniversary of 12 Squadron's foundation, an RAF Tornado GR4 made a fly-past; as a mark of respect, it bore the names of Flying Officer Garland and Sergeant Gray below the cockpit.

Second Lieutenant RICHARD 'DICKIE' or 'JAKE' ANNAND

RIVER DYLE, Belgium 15/16 May 1940

He was 25 years old and serving in the 2nd Bn, Durham Light Infantry when his platoon was defending the river crossing. When a German bridging party came forward, he ordered an attack to drive them back. When the ammunition ran out, he advanced alone into the open and bombed them with grenades, causing many casualties. He was wounded, but after having his wounds dressed, he made another attack on the enemy. When ordered to pull back he withdrew his men, only to learn that his batman, Private Joseph Hunter, had been left behind. He went back and found him wounded, and brought him back in a wheelbarrow before collapsing from his wounds. Hunter was captured and died of his wounds.

Annand said of his VC: 'I would like you to know that there are others who ought to have the award as well as me. Every one of the men with me there deserves a medal. When I received this award my feelings were a communal satisfaction and not an individual one.'

Annand died on 24 December 2004.

Lieutenant CHRISTOPHER FURNESS

near ARRAS, France 17–24 May 1940

He was 27 years old and serving in the 1st Bn, Welsh Guards, in command of the carrier platoon, when he was ordered to cover the withdrawal of the battalion's transport to Douai. The enemy were advancing along the road towards the columns of vehicles, so Furness decided to attack. He reached the enemy position under heavy fire and when all the light tanks and carriers and their crews had become casualties, he engaged the enemy alone in hand-to-hand fighting until he was killed. His fight against hopeless odds made the enemy withdraw temporarily and allowed the other vehicles to get away. His body was never found.

Company Sergeant Major GEORGE GRISTOCK

RIVER ESCAUT, Belgium 21 May 1940

He was 35 years old and serving in the Royal Norfolk Regiment. His company was holding a position when the enemy succeeded in breaking through on the right flank. Having organised a party of eight men, Gristock led them forward, but realising that an enemy machine-gun was inflicting heavy casualties on his company, he went out with one man to put the gun out of action. He was severely wounded in both legs, but nevertheless killed the crew with well-aimed rapid fire. He then dragged himself back to the right flank position, from which he refused to be evacuated until contact was made with battalion.

He died from his wounds on 16 June 1940.

Lance Corporal HARRY NICHOLLS

RIVER ESCAUT, Belgium 21 May 1940

He was 25 years old and serving in the 3rd Bn, Grenadier Guards when his platoon was ordered to counter-attack. At the start of the advance Nicholls was wounded in the arm, but continued to lead his section forward. As the company came over a ridge, the enemy opened up heavy fire from machine-guns. Nicholls immediately grabbed a Bren gun, dashed forward and silenced no fewer than three enemy machine-guns, in spite of being wounded again. He then went up to higher ground and engaged the German infantry massed behind it, continuing to fire until he had used up all of his ammunition, causing many casualties. He had now been wounded four times, but still refused to give in. His company reached its objective, and the enemy fell back over the river.

Nicholls was reported to have been killed in action, but was in fact taken prisoner. He spent the rest of the war in Stalag XXB in Poland. On hearing he had been awarded the VC, the German Commandant of the camp presented him with a VC ribbon.

He died on 11 September 1975.

Captain HAROLD ERVINE-ANDREWS
DUNKIRK, France 31 May/1 June 1940
He was 28 years old and serving in the East Lancashire Regiment, when he was in command of a company defending over 1,000 yards of ground in front of Dunkirk. His line extended along the Canal de Bergues, and the enemy attacked at dawn. He held on for more than 10 hours under intense artillery, mortar and machine-gun fire, and in the face of vastly superior enemy forces. The enemy, however, succeeded in crossing the canal on both flanks; owing to the risk of one of his platoons being driven in, he called for volunteers to fill the gap and then went forward. Ervine-Andrews climbed on to the roof of a straw-roofed barn, from which he engaged the enemy with rifle and Bren gun fire. He personally accounted for at least 11 men with his rifle and many more with the Bren gun. When the barn was set on fire and his ammunition ran out, he sent the wounded back in the last remaining carrier. He then collected the remaining eight men and led them back, wading for over a mile in water, sometimes up to their chins.

He died on 30 March 1995, the last Irish VC to die.

Squadron Leader GEOFFREY CHESHIRE
GERMANY June 1940–July 1944
He was 22 years old and serving in the RAF Volunteer Reserve. From his first operational sortie on 9 June 1940 through to his 100th

mission in July 1944, he worked on the basis that there was no point in making a raid if you didn't hit the target. He soon became known for accepting extra elements of risk in order to guarantee success, and to make sure of a hit he would release his bombs from a much lower altitude than the textbooks dictated. On one occasion in November 1940 an anti-aircraft shell exploded inside his aircraft, blowing out one side and starting a fire, but he coolly proceeded to his target, bombed it and returned in one piece.

When his first tour finished in January 1941, he volunteered for a second, during which he survived missions over some of the major cities of the Reich. On his third tour, from August 1942 to March 1943, he received his first squadron command. His fourth tour was from October 1943 to July 1944, and is probably his most famous, flying with 617 (the Dam-Busters) Squadron. His immediate challenge was to devise a means of obtaining greater accuracy over smaller targets. He developed the 'Master Bomber' technique, whereby one aircraft would fly lower than the rest and act as a marker. This tactic was used against V1 sites in the Pas de Calais and against aircraft production sites in France. He flew the first raid using the 12,000-pounder bombs with himself as marker, the target being an aero engine factory at Limoges. He dropped his incendiary bombs from 200 feet and soon the factory was ablaze, providing an easy target for the main force. Of the five 12,000-pound bombs dropped, four hit the target, causing complete devastation.

On 20 April 1944 more than 250 aircraft took part in a raid on the railway marshalling yards at La Chapelle and, despite several delays and unforeseen glitches, the raid was successful. Two further raids in April were directed against crucial targets, but it was the second raid on 24 April over Munich that clinched Cheshire's award of the VC. A total of 265 aircraft took off and despite heavy defences, consisting of about 200 anti-aircraft guns, only ten aircraft failed to reach the target. Cheshire flew in at 700 feet and marked the target, along with three other Mosquitos. He then remained over the target directing the attack, despite his aircraft being hit and almost losing control due to the glare of a searchlight. Only when he was satisfied that he could do no more did he return home.

Bomber Command gave great support to the landings following D-Day, now using the 14,000-ton 'Tallboy' bombs which reached the ground travelling faster than the speed of sound. Cheshire orchestrated these operations with painstaking precision, achieving devastating results.

He was later posted to the USA, from where he flew in one of the B-29s which dropped the atomic bomb on Nagasaki on 9 August 1945. After the war he established the Cheshire Foundation Homes for the incurably ill. He is the author of several books, including *Bomber Pilot*, *Pilgrimage to the Shroud* and *The Face of Victory*.

He died from motor neurone disease on 31 July 1992.

Acting Leading Seaman JACK MANTLE
PORTLAND HARBOUR, England
4 July 1940
He was 23 years old and serving in the Royal Navy. He was manning the starboard 20mm pom-pom gun aboard HMS *Foylebank* during an air raid when his left leg was shattered by a bomb blast. He kept firing until the ship's electric power failed, but even then he stood fast at his gun. He was wounded many times and fell beside his gun. As *Foylebank* sank, he died from his wounds. His gallantry was noted by the captain.

Acting Captain ERIC WILSON
TUG ARGAN, Somaliland
11–15 August 1940
He was 27 years old and serving in the East Surrey Regiment, attached to the Somaliland Camel Corps, when he was in command of a machine-gun post on the key position of Observation Hill. When the enemy attacked on 11 August, Wilson and his Somali gunners beat off the attack and opened fire on the enemy troops attacking Mill Hill, another post within his range. He inflicted such heavy casualties

that the enemy became determined to put his guns out of action. They brought up a pack battery to within 700 yards, and scored two direct hits on his position, wounding him in the shoulder and eye, several of his men also being wounded. His guns were blown off their stands but he repaired and remounted them and, regardless of his wounds, carried on firing, even when his Somali sergeant was killed beside him. On the 12th and 14th the enemy again concentrated their artillery fire on Wilson's position, but he continued to man the guns, despite his wounds being untreated. On the 15th two of his gun posts were blown to pieces, yet Wilson still kept his own post in action, although he was now suffering from malaria in addition to his wounds. The enemy finally overran the position at 5pm on 15 August. Captain Wilson, fighting to the last, was believed to have been killed.

In fact he was taken prisoner, and learned that he had been awarded the VC 'posthumously' while a prisoner-of-war. He has the rare distinction of being personally awarded with his 'posthumous' VC.

He died on 23 December 2008.

Flight Lieutenant RODERICK LEAROYD
DORTMUND-EMS CANAL, Germany
12 August 1940
He was 27 years old and serving in 49 Squadron, RAF. Along with four other Hampden bombers, he attacked his target through a 'lane' of anti-aircraft guns. Two of the bombers were shot down and the other two badly damaged. Nevertheless, he pressed home his attack at 150 feet, his aircraft being repeatedly hit and large pieces torn away, but he dropped his bombs and subsequently brought his damaged aircraft home, landing without further damage to the plane or his crew.

He died from a heart attack on 24 January 1996.

Flight Lieutenant ERIC 'NICK' NICOLSON
SOUTHAMPTON, England
16 August 1940
He was 23 years old and serving in 249 Squadron, RAF when his Hurricane was fired

on by a Messerschmitt Me 110, wounding him in the eye and foot. His engine was damaged and the petrol tank set alight. As he struggled to leave the burning plane, he saw another Messerschmitt; managing to get back into his seat, he pressed the firing button and continued to fire until the enemy plane dived away to destruction. Not until then did he bale out, and was able to open his parachute in time to land safely. On his descent he was fired on by some over-excited Home Guard troops, who ignored his cries that he was an RAF pilot. On hearing of the award his only comment was 'Now I'll have to earn it.' He is the only Battle of Britain VC, and his VC action was in fact his first combat patrol. His VC was the only one awarded to an RAF fighter pilot.

He was killed on 2 May 1945, when the plane he was in caught fire and had to ditch into the sea. His body was never found.

Sergeant JOHN HANNAH
ANTWERP, Belgium 15 September 1940
He was 18 years old and serving in 83 Squadron, RAF when after a successful attack on German barges, the Handley Page Hampden bomber in which Hannah was the wireless operator/air gunner was subjected to intense anti-aircraft fire, starting a fire that spread quickly. The rear gunner and navigator had to bale out and Hannah could have done the same, but instead he remained to fight the fire, first with two fire extinguishers and then with his bare hands. He sustained terrible injuries, but succeeded in putting out the fire and the pilot was able to bring the bomber back safely.

Hannah is the youngest recipient of the VC for aerial operations.

He died on 15 June 1967.

Acting Captain EDWARD FEGEN
NORTH ATLANTIC 5 November 1940
He was 49 years old and serving in the Royal Navy, commanding the armed merchant cruiser *Jervis Bay*. He was escorting the 37 merchant ships of convoy HX-84 when they were attacked by the German pocket battleship *Admiral Scheer*. Fegen immediately engaged the enemy head on, placing his ship between the convoy and the enemy, thus giving the convoy time to scatter. Out-gunned and on fire, the *Jervis Bay* maintained the unequal fight for 3 hours, although the captain's right arm was shattered and his bridge was shot from under him. He went down with his ship, but due to his courageous action 31 ships of the convoy escaped.

1941

Second Lieutenant PREMINDRA SINGH BHAGAT
GALLABAT, Abyssinia
31 January–4 February 1941
He was 22 years old and serving in the Corps of Indian Engineers, Indian Army, attached to the Royal Bombay Sappers and Miners. During the pursuit of the enemy, he cleared fifteen Italian minefields. He covered 55 miles, was twice blown up in his universal carrier, each time suffering casualties among his men, and was ambushed, puncturing his ear drums. His actions over 96 hours ensured the safety of the column, relying on his speed and effort.

He died on 23 May 1975.

Subedar RICHHPAL (sometimes spelt RICHPAL) RAM
KEREN, Eritrea 7/8 February 1941
He was 41 years old and serving in the 6th Rajputana Rifles, Indian Army. As second-in-command of his company, he insisted on accompanying the lead platoon during an attack. When his company commander was wounded, he took over and led the attack. In the face of heavy fire, and with only 30 men, he rushed the objective with the bayonet and captured it. His party was now completely isolated but under his inspiring leadership managed to beat off six enemy attacks. By now the ammunition had run out, and Ram extricated his men and fought his way back to the battalion with just a handful of survivors.

He led another attack on the same position on 12 February, until his right foot was blown off. He continued to wave his men on with the words 'We'll capture this objective', before he was killed.

Flying Officer KENNETH CAMPBELL

BREST HARBOUR, France 6 April 1941
He was 23 years old and serving in 22 Squadron, RAF Volunteer Reserve. Due to horrendous weather conditions, he arrived at his target alone. Nevertheless he pressed home his attack through very heavy anti-aircraft fire and torpedoed the German battlecruiser *Gneisenau*, causing severe damage below the water line. His Beaufort was hit by anti-aircraft fire, causing it to crash in the harbour, killing him and his crew.

Corporal JOHN 'JACK' EDMONDSON

TOBRUK, Libya 13/14 April 1941
He was 27 years old and serving in the 2/17th (New South Wales) Bn, AIF when a large party of Germans broke though the wire defences and established themselves with numerous machine-guns, mortars and field pieces. Led by his officer, Edmondson and five men carried out a bayonet charge upon them under heavy fire. Although wounded in the neck and stomach, he not only killed one of the enemy, but went to the assistance of his officer, who was being attacked from behind while he was trying to bayonet another man who had seized him by the legs. Despite his wounds, Edmondson succeeded in killing both these Germans, thus undoubtedly saving the life of his officer. He later died of his wounds.

He was the first Australian to be awarded the VC in the Second World War.

Sergeant JOHN HINTON

KALAMAI, Greece 28/29 April 1941
He was 41 years old and serving in the 20th Bn (Canterbury Regiment), NZEF. His unit was waiting to embark from the beach when an enemy column came into view and the order was given to take cover. Hinton shouted: 'To hell with this, who'll come with me?' He ran to within a few yards of the nearest enemy gun and threw two grenades, which wiped out the crew. Then he charged with the bayonet,

followed by some of his men. The Germans retreated into two houses. He smashed the door open and dealt with them with the bayonet. He repeated this in the second house. When overwhelming German forces arrived, he fell with a wound to the abdomen and was taken prisoner.

Hinton was the first New Zealander to be awarded the VC in the Second World War.

He died on 28 June 1997, following a fall.

Petty Officer ALFRED SEPHTON

CRETE, Mediterranean Sea 18 May 1941
He was 30 years old and serving in the Royal Navy when his ship, HMS *Coventry*, went to the assistance of a hospital ship which was being attacked by dive-bombers. When *Coventry* came under attack, raked with machine-gun fire, Sephton was mortally wounded by a bullet that passed through him and injured another man beside him. Although in great pain and partially blinded, he stuck to his instruments and carried out his duties until the attack was over. Thereafter his valiant and cheerful spirit gave heart to the wounded.

He died of his wounds the next day.

Sergeant NIGEL LEAKEY

COLITO, Abyssinia 19 May 1941
He was 28 years old and serving in the 1/6th Bn, King's African Rifles. Two companies had established a bridgehead over the river when the enemy made a sudden counter-attack with light tanks. Leakey had been supporting the operation with 3-inch mortar fire, but had run out of ammunition. He went forward to see what he could do to help as the tanks were threatening to overrun the position and the men had no anti-tank weapons. Without regard for his personal safety, and in the face of heavy machine-gun fire, he leapt on to a tank, wrenched open the turret and shot all of the crew apart from the driver, whom he forced to drive to cover. Unable to get the gun to fire he dismounted, shouting: 'I'll get them on foot,' and charged across the open under machine-gun fire. He proceeded to stalk the other tanks which were threatening the position. He managed to jump on to another

tank and killed one of the crew before he was killed by fire from another tank. His superb courage was largely responsible for the Italian defeat.

Sergeant ALFRED HULME
CRETE, Greece 20–28 May 1941

He was 30 years old and serving in the 23rd Bn (Canterbury Regiment), NZEF. At Maleme airfield he personally led parties of men and destroyed the enemy who had established themselves in front of his position, from which they brought down heavy fire. He was continually going out either alone or in pairs to kill snipers. At Galatos the attack was held up by a large force occupying a school, but he drove them out with hand grenades, allowing the attack to continue. At Suda Bay he stalked and killed five snipers who had worked their way into the defence perimeter. Finally, on his own initiative he penetrated the enemy lines and killed the crew of a mortar that had been shelling the rearguard, and three snipers. He was wounded by a sniper shortly afterwards.

He died on 2 September 1982.

Second Lieutenant CHARLES 'PUG' UPHAM (VC action)
CRETE, Greece 22–30 May 1941

He was 33 years old and serving in the 20th Bn (Canterbury Regiment), NZEF when he commanded a platoon during an attack at Maleme and fought his way forward for 3,000 yards unsupported against a defence strongly organised in depth. During the operation his platoon destroyed numerous enemy posts. When his advance was held up by heavy fire from a machine-gun nest, he advanced to close quarters with pistol and grenades, so demoralising the Germans that his section was able to 'mop up' with ease. When another of his sections was held up by two machine-guns in a house, Upham went in and put a grenade through the window, killing the crew of one gun. The other gun was silenced by fire from his section. When they were held up again, he crawled to within 15 yards of a machine-gun post and killed the crew with a grenade. When his company had to withdraw from Maleme,

he helped to carry a wounded man out under fire, and together with another officer rallied men to help with the wounded. He was then sent to find a company that had become isolated. With a corporal, he went through 600 yards of enemy territory, killing two Germans on the way. He found the company and brought it back to the new battalion position. During the next two days his platoon occupied an exposed position on the forward slopes of a hill and was continuously under fire from the enemy. At one point Upham was blown off his feet by a mortar round, and wounded by another. He disregarded this wound and remained on duty. He was later wounded in the foot by a bullet, which was not removed until he was in Egypt, when he removed it himself.

On 25 May his platoon was heavily engaged and came under mortar and machine-gun fire. While his men stopped under cover he went forward, observed the enemy and brought the platoon forward when the enemy advanced. They killed over 40 Germans with small arms fire and grenades, the remainder being forced to retreat. When his platoon was ordered to retire, he sent them back with a sergeant and went on to warn the other troops they were being cut off. When he came back he was fired on by two Germans. He fell to the ground, then crawled into cover, resting his rifle in the fork of a tree as he could only use one arm. As the Germans came forward he shot them both, the second falling on to his rifle muzzle.

On 30 May at Sphakia his platoon was ordered to deal with a party of Germans who had advanced down a ravine towards the force HQ. Although in an exhausted condition, he climbed the steep ravine, placed his men in position on the slopes and went to the top with a Bren gun and two men. When an enemy party appeared, he opened fire at 500 yards' range, killing 22 and sending the rest running in panic.

During all of this time he was suffering from dysentery and was unable to eat very much. When told of his VC award, his first response was: 'It's meant for the men.'

(For his Bar action, see 14/15 July 1942.)

Lieutenant Commander MALCOLM 'WANKS' WANKLYN

SICILY, Mediterranean Sea 24 May 1941

He was 30 years old and serving in the Royal Navy, commanding HM Submarine *Upholder,* when he sighted a southbound enemy convoy with a strong destroyer escort. Due to the fading light, he was forced to make a surface attack. He positioned himself favourably and closed in to make sure of his target. By this time the whereabouts of the enemy destroyers could not be made out. Fully aware of the risk of being rammed, he pressed on. As he was about to fire, an enemy destroyer suddenly appeared out of the darkness and he only just avoided being rammed. As soon as he was clear he brought his sights to bear again and fired his torpedoes, sinking a large troopship. The enemy destroyers at once attacked, and during the next 20 minutes they dropped 37 depth-charges on *Upholder.* The failure of his listening gear made it hard for him to get away, but with great skill and coolness he finally got clear of the enemy and made it safely back to harbour. By the end of 1941 he had sunk nearly 140,000 tons of enemy shipping.

He was killed in action in the Gulf of Tripoli on 14 April 1942, when *Upholder* was sunk. His body was never recovered.

Lieutenant ARTHUR CUTLER

MERDJAYOUN-DAMOUR, Lebanon 19 June–6 July 1941

He was 25 years old and serving in the 2/5th Field Artillery, AMF when he was with a small party in a forward position. He went out under machine-gun fire and repaired a telephone wire, and then he called down artillery fire on enemy positions. The enemy attacked his outpost with infantry and tanks, killing two men, including the only other officer. Cutler manned the anti-tank rifle while another man used the Bren gun, driving the infantry back. The tanks continued the attack, but under constant fire from the anti-tank rifle and Bren gun they eventually withdrew. He then personally supervised the evacuation of the wounded. Undaunted, he pressed for a further advance.

He was ordered to establish an outpost from which he could observe the only road by which the enemy could enter the town. With another man he succeeded in establishing an outpost in the town itself. He knew the enemy were massing for a counter-attack and that he was in danger of being cut off. Nevertheless he carried on calling down artillery strikes on the road and other enemy targets. During the enemy counter-attack he was cut off and was forced to go to ground, but after dark he made his way back through enemy lines. His work in spotting enemy targets was a major factor in the enemy's defeat.

On the night of 23/24 June he was in charge of a 25-pounder gun sent forward to silence an enemy anti-tank gun that was holding up the attack. On 6 July, regardless of the danger, he went forward under heavy fire to lay a telephone wire, but was seriously wounded in the attempt. When he was recovered 26 hours later, his leg had to be amputated.

Cutler was Vice Chairman (Overseas) of the VC and GC Association (1986–91) and Deputy President (1991–2002).

He died on 21 February 2002.

Pilot Officer HUGHIE EDWARDS

BREMEN, Germany 4 July 1941

He was 26 years old and serving in 105 Squadron, RAF when he led fifteen Blenheim bombers in an attack against one of the most heavily defended towns in Germany. The attack took place in daylight, and the approach had to be made at less than 50 feet, passing under high tension cables, telegraph wires and through a formidable balloon barrage. On the way his formation was spotted by several enemy ships and he knew that the defences would be in a state of readiness. On reaching the target, he was met with a wall of fire; all his aircraft were hit and four of them went down. Nevertheless he made a most successful attack, and then managed to withdraw the surviving aircraft without further loss.

Edwards was ADC to the Queen (1960–63). He died on 5 August 1982.

Sergeant JAMES WARD
MUNSTER, Germany 7 July 1941

He was 22 years old and serving in the RNZAF, attached to 75 Squadron, RAF. He was the co-pilot of a Wellington bomber returning from a raid, when it was attacked by a nightfighter and received several hits from its cannon. The rear gunner was wounded and fire broke out near the starboard engine, fed by petrol from a split pipe. The fire quickly gained a hold and threatened to engulf the entire wing. The crew made a hole in the fuselage and made efforts to reduce the blaze with extinguishers and even coffee from their flasks, but without success. They were about to abandon the aircraft when Ward volunteered to climb out on to the wing to attempt to smother the flames with an engine cover. At first he wanted to discard his parachute, but was finally persuaded to take it with him. A rope was tied to him and he climbed through the astro-hatch. The wind pressure must have been incredible but he managed to break the fabric to make hand-holds where necessary, and made his way to the rear of the burning engine, although the slipstream nearly blew him off the wing. Lying in this position, he smothered the burning wing fabric and then tried to push the cover into the hole and on to the leaking pipe. But as soon as he removed his hand the terrific wind blew the cover out and he lost it when he tried again. There was now no danger of fire as there was no fabric nearby, and in due course the fire burnt itself out. Tired and burnt, he managed, with the navigator's help, to make it back into the aircraft. The bomber was able to fly back to its base and land safely.

He was killed in action over Hamburg on 15 September 1941, when his bomber was shot down.

Private JAMES GORDON
DJEZZINE, Syria 10/11 July 1941

He was 32 years old and serving in the 2/31st (Queensland & Victoria) Bn, AMF when his company was pinned down by intense machine-gun fire from a fortified position which completely dominated the area. Gordon, on his own initiative, crept forward alone. He succeeded in getting close to the enemy gun, and then charged it from the front and killed the four crew with the bayonet. His action so completely demoralised the enemy that the company was able to take the position.

He died on 24 July 1986.

Temporary Lieutenant Colonel GEOFFREY KEYES
BEDA LITTORIA, Libya
17/18 November 1941

He was 24 years old and serving in the Royal Scots Greys, Royal Armoured Corps (11th Scottish Commando) when he led a raid 250 miles behind enemy lines on a house used by Rommel. This attack, even if successful, meant almost certain death for the men who took part in it. Having dispatched the covering party to block the approaches to the house, he and two others crawled past the guards, through the fence and up to the house itself. Without hesitating, he and Captain Campbell banged on the door and demanded entrance in German. When the door was opened, it was impossible to overcome the sentry silently and it was necessary to shoot him. The noise naturally alerted the occupants of the house and Keyes, appreciating that speed was now the most important thing, took the lead and emptied his revolver into the first room, followed by Campbell throwing in a grenade. With great daring, Keyes entered the next room but was shot almost immediately and fell back into the passage mortally wounded. He died within minutes.

Second Lieutenant GEORGE GUNN
SIDI REZEGH, Libya 21 November 1941

He was 30 years old and serving in the 3rd Regiment, RHA when he was in command of four anti-tank guns that were part of a battery of 12 guns. At 1000 hours a probing force of enemy tanks was engaged and driven back, but an hour later the main attack developed with 60 enemy tanks. Gunn drove an unarmoured vehicle from gun to gun encouraging his men and reorganising his dispositions, as first one and then another gun was knocked out. Finally, when only two guns remained in action, they were under very heavy fire. One of these guns was destroyed and the portee of the other was set on fire, and the battery commander arrived and started to fight the flames. When Gunn saw this, he ran to his aid through heavy fire and got the gun on the burning portee back into action, sighting it himself. He fired between 40 and 50 rounds regardless of the enemy fire and the burning portee, which could have set off the ammunition at any moment. In spite of this, his shooting was so accurate at a range of 800 yards that at least two tanks were hit and set on fire, and several others were damaged, but he was shot through the head and killed shortly afterwards.

Rifleman JOHN BEELEY
SIDI REZEGH, Libya 21 November 1941
He was 23 years old and serving in the King's Royal Rifle Corps. When his company was attacking an airfield, the men were halted by short-range fire. All the officers of the company were wounded. On his own initiative, he ran forward over open ground, firing his Bren gun and at 20 yards' range put an anti-tank gun and two machine-guns out of action. He was killed but his actions inspired his company to further efforts to reach their objective, which was captured with 100 prisoners.

Acting Brigadier JOHN 'JOCK' CAMPBELL
SIDI REZEGH, Libya
21/22 November 1941
He was 47 years old and serving in the RHA, but commanding the 7th Armoured Division when his force was holding an area between the airfield and the ridge, and was repeatedly attacked by large numbers of enemy tanks supported by infantry. Wherever the situation was at its most difficult or the fighting at its hardest, he was to be seen with his forward troops. He carried out several reconnaissances for counter-attacks by tank units, whose senior officers were casualties. Standing in his open car, he would personally form up tanks under very heavy fire. The next day, when the enemy attacks intensified, he was in the forefront of

the fighting, encouraging his men, staging counter-attacks and personally controlling the fire of his guns. During the final enemy attack he acted as loader to one of the guns himself and in spite of being wounded refused to be evacuated, remaining with his command.

He died in a car accident on 26 February 1942.

Captain PHILIP 'PIP' GARDNER
TOBRUK, Libya 23 November 1941
He was 26 years old and serving in the Royal Tank Regiment when he took two tanks to rescue two armoured cars, which were out of action and under heavy fire. While one tank gave covering fire, Gardner dismounted and fixed a tow rope to one of the armoured cars. He also found a wounded officer who had had both his legs blown off, and lifted him on to the armoured car. The rope broke, so he returned to fix it but was wounded in the arm and leg. Despite his wounds, he carried the officer to his own tank and put him on the back and rode with him so he could hold on to him. On the return journey the tank was subjected to heavy anti-tank fire and the gun loader was killed.

Gardner was taken prisoner in 1942. He escaped from his Italian captors, but was caught by the Germans. He spent the rest of the war in a prisoner-of-war camp in Brunswick. During this time he collected money in the form of IOUs for the poor of London. After the war, he used the money to help set up the Brunswick Boys Club in Fulham.

He died on 15 February 2003.

Temporary Captain JAMES JACKMAN
TOBRUK, Libya 25 November 1941
He was 25 years old and serving in the 1st Bn, Royal Northumberland Fusiliers. During the assault on the El Duda ridge, as our tanks reached the crest of the rise they came under intense fire from a large number of guns. The fire was so heavy that it was doubtful whether the brigade could maintain its position. The tanks took up hull-down positions to engage the enemy. During this time Jackman rapidly pushed up the ridge leading his machine-gun trucks and saw at once that anti-tank guns were

firing into the flanks of our tanks, while rows of guns were engaging our tanks to the front. He immediately started to get his guns into action as calmly as if he were on manoeuvres, and so secured the right flank. Then, standing up in the front of his truck, with calm determination he led his trucks across the front between the tanks and the guns, there being no other way for them to get into action on the flank. Throughout he coolly directed his guns to their positions and pointed out targets to them, at times seeming to have a charmed life.

He was killed in action the next day.

Squadron Leader ARTHUR SCARF
SINGORA, Malaya 9 December 1941

He was 28 years old and serving in 62 Squadron, RAF when all available aircraft were ordered to make a daylight raid on the invading Japanese Army at Singora. Scarf had just taken off from his base when enemy aircraft swept in and destroyed or disabled all the other aircraft on the ground. Scarf circled the airfield and witnessed the disaster. He nevertheless decided to fly alone to his target. Despite attacks from roving fighters, he completed his bombing run and was on his way back when his Blenheim came under fire. The Blenheim was riddled with bullets and Scarf was severely wounded: his left arm was shattered, there was a large hole in his back, and he was drifting in and out of consciousness. Nevertheless, he managed to crash-land his aircraft at Alor Star without injury to any of his crew, and was rushed to hospital.

He died 2 hours later.

Company Sergeant Major JOHN OSBORN
MOUNT BUTLER, Hong Kong
19 December 1941

He was 42 years old and serving in the 1st Bn, Winnipeg Grenadiers, Canadian Army (Canadian Infantry Corps) when part of the company led by Osborn captured Mount Butler at the point of the bayonet and held it for 3 hours. When, owing to superior numbers of the enemy and fire on an unprotected flank, the position became untenable, Osborn with a small party of men covered the retreat, and when it was their turn to fall back he single-handedly engaged the enemy while the remainder successfully rejoined the company. He then had to run the gauntlet of heavy machine-gun and rifle fire. With no consideration for his own safety, he assisted and directed stragglers to the new company position and exposed himself to enemy fire to cover their retirement. Whenever danger threatened he was there to encourage his men.

During the afternoon the company was cut off from the battalion and completely surrounded by the enemy, who approached to within grenade-throwing range. Several grenades were thrown into the company position but Osborn calmly picked them up and threw them back. When another grenade landed in a position where it was impossible to pick it up, Osborn shouted a warning and then threw himself on to the grenade, which exploded, killing him instantly. His self-sacrifice undoubtedly saved many lives.

In life Company Sergeant Major John Osborn was an inspiring example to all throughout the defence which he assisted so magnificently in maintaining against an overwhelming enemy force for over 8½ hours, and in his death he displayed the highest qualities of heroism and self-sacrifice. He was the first Canadian to be awarded the VC in the Second World War.

1942

Lieutenant Colonel ARTHUR CUMMING
KUANTAN, Malaya 3 January 1942

He was 45 years old and serving in the 2nd Bn, 12th Frontier Force Regiment, Indian Army when the Japanese made a furious attack on his battalion and a strong force penetrated the position. He immediately led a counter-attack with a small party of men, and although all the men became casualties and he received two bayonet wounds to the stomach, he managed to restore the situation so that the major part of the battalion and its vehicles could be withdrawn. Later he drove in a carrier under heavy fire, to collect isolated detachments of men, and was again wounded. His gallant actions helped the brigade to withdraw safely.

He died on 10 April 1971. This VC action is of particular interest to me as it happened on my birthday, although not the same year of course!

Lieutenant Colonel CHARLES ANDERSON
MUAR RIVER, Malaya
18–22 January 1942
He was 44 years old and commanding the 2/19th (New South Wales) Bn, AMF when he was sent to restore a vital position. His force destroyed ten enemy tanks and later, although cut off, Anderson repelled persistent air and ground attacks on his position. He forced his way through 15 miles of enemy-held territory. When he was again surrounded, he was subjected to very heavy attacks, resulting in severe casualties. He personally led an attack with great gallantry on a bridge, and destroyed four guns. Throughout this fighting he protected his wounded and refused to leave them. He then attempted to fight his way through 8 miles of enemy-held territory. When this proved to be impossible, he was ordered to destroy his equipment and work his way around the enemy position. Throughout he set a magnificent example of leadership, determination and outstanding courage.

He died on 11 November 1988.

Lieutenant Commander EUGENE ESMONDE
STRAITS OF DOVER, English Channel
12 February 1942
He was 32 years old and serving in the Fleet Air Arm when he led a detachment of six Fairey Swordfish in an attack on the German battle-cruisers *Scharnhorst* and *Gneisenau* and the heavy cruiser *Prinz Eugen*, during the 'Channel Dash' (Operation Cerberus). When his orders came through, the enemy ships, with a strong escort of surface craft, were already entering the Straits of Dover. Esmonde waited as long as he could for a fighter escort, but eventually took off without it. Ten Spitfires of 72 Squadron met up with them shortly before they

were attacked by enemy fighters. Despite their planes being damaged and their escort being separated, the Swordfish continued on to the ships. The enemy destroyers were sending up large amounts of flak. Esmonde's plane received a direct hit that sheared off part of the port wing, but he continued to run-in towards his target, taking his flight right through the destroyer screen. He was still some 2,700 metres from his target when he was hit again; this time his plane burst into flames and crashed into the sea. He was killed. All of the planes were shot down, and only five crewmen survived, four of them wounded. Vice-Admiral Ramsay described the raid as 'One of the finest exhibitions of self-sacrifice and devotion to duty this war has yet witnessed.'

His great-uncle was Captain Thomas Esmonde VC.

Temporary Lieutenant THOMAS WILKINSON
JAVA SEA, Malaya 14 February 1942
He was 43 years old and serving in the Royal Naval Reserve aboard HMS *Li Wo*, which was carrying survivors from other ships and a few from the army and air force. Spotting two Japanese convoys, Wilkinson gathered his scratch crew together and told them he was going to attack and fight to the last in the hope of doing as much damage as possible. His decision drew resolute support from the crew. *Li Wo* was an old steamer armed with just one 4-inch gun and two machine-guns. The ship's battle ensign was raised and they headed straight for the enemy. In the action that followed, the machine-guns were used to good effect upon the crews of all ships in range and the volunteer crew that manned the 4-inch gun fought with such purpose that a transport ship was hit and set on fire. After an hour *Li Wo* had been badly damaged and was sinking. Wilkinson then decided to ram his principal target, the damaged transport ship that had been abandoned by her crew. But with all shells spent, and under heavy fire from an enemy cruiser, he finally gave the order to abandon ship. He himself remained aboard and went down with his ship. There were only about ten

Lieutenant PETER ROBERTS

MEDITERRANEAN SEA

16 February 1942

He was 41 years old and serving in the Royal Navy aboard HM Submarine *Thrasher*. After sinking a heavily escorted supply ship in daylight, the submarine was at once attacked with depth-charges and bombed by aircraft. When the submarine finally surfaced, two unexploded bombs were discovered in the gun casing. Lieutenant Roberts and Petty Officer Gould volunteered to remove the bombs, although they were of a type unknown to them. They removed the first without too much difficulty, but the second bomb was lying in a confined space and they had to lie full length to reach it. Gould took the bomb in his arms and Roberts pulled him for about 20 feet until it could be lowered over the side. Every time the bomb moved, there was a loud twanging noise, which did nothing for their peace of mind. This deed was even more gallant as *Thrasher*'s presence was known to the enemy, and the submarine was close to the enemy coast in frequently patrolled waters. There was every chance, and they knew it, that the submarine might have to crash-dive while they were in the casing, almost certainly drowning them. Both men were awarded the VC.

Roberts also served in Korea.

He died on 8 December 1979.

Petty Officer THOMAS 'NAT' GOULD (born WILLIAM THOMAS)

MEDITERRANEAN SEA

16 February 1942

He was 27 years old and serving in the Royal Navy aboard HM Submarine *Thrasher*. After sinking a heavily escorted supply ship in daylight, the submarine was at once attacked with depth-charges and bombed by aircraft. When the submarine finally surfaced, two unexploded bombs were discovered in the gun casing. Lieutenant Roberts and Petty Officer Gould volunteered to remove the bombs, although they were of a type unknown to them. They removed the first without too much difficulty, but the second bomb was lying in a confined space and they had to lie full length to reach it. Gould took the bomb in his arms and Roberts pulled him for about 20 feet until it could be lowered over the side. Every time the bomb moved, there was a loud twanging noise which did nothing for their peace of mind. This deed was even more gallant as *Thrasher*'s presence was known to the enemy, and the submarine was close to the enemy coast in frequently patrolled waters. There was every chance, and they knew it, that the submarine might have to crash-dive while they were in the casing, almost certainly drowning them. Both men were awarded the VC.

Gould died on 6 December 2001.

Commander ANTHONY 'CRAP' MIERS

CORFU HARBOUR, Greece

4 March 1942

He was 35 years old and serving in the Royal Navy, commanding HM Submarine *Torbay*. After following an enemy convoy into the harbour, he had to wait overnight to recharge his batteries and then attacked at dawn, torpedoing two 5,000-ton transports, both of which sank. He then faced a very hazardous withdrawal through a long channel with anti-submarine craft all round, and enduring 40 depth-charges on the way.

In November 1941 HMS *Torbay* had landed Lieutenant Colonel Keyes and 25 commandos for the attack on Rommel's HQ that earned Keyes the VC.

Miers died on 30 June 1985.

Lieutenant Colonel AUGUSTUS 'ACE' NEWMAN

St NAZAIRE, France 27/28 March 1942

He was 37 years old and serving in the Essex Regiment, attached to 2 Commando. He was in charge of the military forces during the assault on the harbour and, although he need not have landed himself, he was one of the first ashore. During the next 5 hours of bitter fighting, he personally entered several houses shot up the occupants and supervised the operations in the town, utterly regardless of his own safety, and he never wavered in his resolution to carry out the operation upon which so much depended. An enemy gun position on the roof of a U-boat pen was causing heavy casualties among the motor launches but Newman directed mortar fire on to it until it was silenced. Still fully exposed, he then brought machine-gun fire to bear on an armed trawler in the harbour, compelling it to withdraw. Under his brilliant leadership, the men fought magnificently and held vastly superior forces at bay until the demolition parties had successfully completed their work. By this time, most of the motor launches had been sunk or set on fire, and evacuation by sea was no longer possible. He now wanted to fight his way out into open country, but the only way was across an iron bridge covered by machine-guns. Although shaken by a German grenade that had exploded at his feet, he personally led the charge which stormed the position, and the small force fought its way through the streets to a point near open country. Only when all their ammunition was expended were they finally overpowered by the enemy.

He died on 26 April 1972.

Lieutenant Commander STEPHEN 'SAM' BEATTIE

St NAZAIRE, France 27/28 March 1942

He was 40 years old and serving in the Royal Navy, commanding HMS *Campbeltown*. Despite the intense fire that was directed at the bridge from point-blank range, and in the face of the blinding glare from numerous searchlights, he steamed *Campbeltown* into the dock gates in precisely the correct position. At dawn, senior German officers arrived to inspect the wreck, and as they were doing so 5 tons of explosives detonated, killing the Germans and two commando officers who had been captured and taken back to the ship. Although they were aware of the explosives, they kept silent and died in the blast.

This award was made in recognition not only of Beattie's valour but also that of the unnamed officers and men of a very gallant ship's company, many of whom never returned. The raid took place the day before Beattie's birthday.

He died on 24 April 1975.

Commander ROBERT 'RED' RYDER

St NAZAIRE, France 27/28 March 1942

He was 34 years old and serving in the Royal Navy, and was commanding the Naval Force aboard *MGB314* when HMS *Campbeltown* rammed the dock gates. He remained on the spot, conducting operations, evacuating men from *Campbeltown* and dealing with strongpoints and close-range weapons, while exposed to heavy fire for 1 hour and 16 minutes. He did not withdraw until it was certain that his motor gun boat could no longer be of any use. Now full of dead and wounded, the little boat withdrew through an intense barrage of close-range fire.

Ryder is author of *The Attack on St Nazaire* and *Coverplan*.

He died from a heart attack on 29 June 1986.

Sergeant THOMAS DURRANT

St NAZAIRE, France 27/28 March 1942

He was 23 years old and serving in the Corps of Royal Engineers, attached to 1 Commando, when he was in charge of a Lewis gun on Motor Launch 306, which came under heavy fire during the raid on St Nazaire. He engaged enemy gun positions and searchlights. During this action he was wounded in the arm, but refused to leave his gun. The launch was soon under attack from a German destroyer at 50–60 yards range, but he continued to fire into its bridge with great coolness and with complete disregard for the enemy's fire. The motor launch was illuminated by searchlights and he drew on to himself the attention of the enemy guns, and was wounded again. Despite these wounds, he still stayed at his post and fired his gun. After a time he was only able to support himself by holding on to the gun mounting. After a running fight, he was called on to surrender and answered with a long burst from his gun. Although he had no protection and had been wounded 14 times, he continued to fire until the launch was boarded and those who were still alive were taken prisoner. He

The Complete Victoria Cross

died of his wounds the next day, his last words being: 'Leave me, I'm finished.'

He is one of the very few men to receive their VC partly on the recommendation of an enemy officer, Kapitanleutnant F.K. Paul, commander of the German destroyer *Jaguar,* who singled Durrant out for his bravery.

Able Seaman WILLIAM SAVAGE
St NAZAIRE, France 27/28 March 1942

He was 29 years old and serving in the Royal Navy when during the raid on St Nazaire he was the gunlayer of the pom-pom gun aboard Motor Gun Boat 314. Completely exposed and under heavy fire, Savage engaged positions ashore with cool and steady accuracy. On the way out of the harbour he kept up the same accurate fire against the attacking ships, until he was killed at his gun.

This VC was awarded in recognition not only of the gallantry and devotion to duty of Able Seaman Savage, but also of the valour shown by many others, unnamed, in motor launches, motor boats and motor torpedo boats who carried out their duties in entirely exposed positions against enemy fire at very close range.

Squadron Leader JOHN NETTLETON
AUGSBURG, Germany 17 April 1942

He was 24 years old and was in command of 44 (Rhodesia) Squadron, RAF. He was leading one of two formations of Lancaster bombers on a daylight raid on a diesel factory when, soon after crossing into enemy territory, his formation was attacked by fighters. A running battle ensued and one by one the bombers were shot down until only two remained. The fighters were shaken off but the target was still a very long way away. With great spirit and now almost defenceless, Nettleton pressed on with the attack. As they neared the target, the anti-aircraft fire became very heavy. As the two bombers came in low over the roof tops, the other plane was hit and burst into flames, crashing nearby. Nettleton bombed his target amidst heavy anti-aircraft fire and managed to bring his bomber home, the only one to return out of the six that had set out.

He is one of only four South Africans to be awarded the VC in the Second World War, the others being Lieutenant Gerard Norton, Acting Major Edwin Swales and Sergeant Quentin Smythe. Nettleton was killed in action on 13 July 1943, when his bomber was shot down while returning from a raid on Turin. His body was never found.

Temporary Lieutenant Colonel HENRY 'FAIRY' FOOTE
LIBYA 27 May–15 June 1942

He was 37 years old and commanding the 7th Bn, Royal Tank Regiment when he displayed outstanding courage and leadership, always at the crucial point and at the right time. On 6 June he led his battalion in pursuit of a superior force. While charging from one tank to another, he was wounded in the neck but in spite of this he continued to lead his men from an exposed position on the outside of a tank. The enemy, who were holding a strong position with anti-tank guns, attacked his flank. As another tank was disabled, he continued on foot under intense fire, encouraging his men by example. By dusk, his leadership had enabled his men to defeat the enemy's attempt to encircle two divisions. On 13 June, when ordered to delay the enemy tanks so that the Guards Brigade could withdraw from encircle-ment, the first wave of British tanks having been destroyed, he reorganised the remaining tanks, going on foot from tank to tank to encourage the crews, while under intense artillery and anti-tank fire. As it was of vital importance that his battalion should not give ground, he placed himself in the lead tank so that he could be seen to be helping the men. This tank was badly damaged by shell fire and its gun rendered useless. Nevertheless, by his example the corridor was kept open and the Guards were able to get through.

Foote was Vice-Chairman (UK) of the VC and GC Association (1968–93).

He died on 11 November 1993.

Flying Officer LESLIE MANSER
COLOGNE, Germany 30/31 May 1942

He was 20 years old and serving in 5

Squadron, RAFVR when he was captain of a Manchester bomber. As he approached the target his aircraft came under intense accurate anti-aircraft fire, but he held his course and dropped his bombs on target. Then he set course for base, but his bomber had been damaged and was still under fire. Manser took evasive action but to no avail. The aircraft was hit repeatedly, the rear gunner was wounded and the cockpit was filling with smoke. Then the port engine started to overheat, and burst into flames. He ordered the crew to bale out. Someone offered him a parachute but he waved it away, saying he could only hold the aircraft for a few more seconds. While the crew were descending under their parachutes, they saw the bomber plunge to earth and crash in flames. By remaining at the controls for those extra few seconds, he preserved the lives of his crew, but sacrificed himself.

Temporary Captain John Randle VC was his brother-in-law.

Sergeant QUENTIN SMYTHE
ALEM HAMZA, Egypt 5 June 1942
He was 25 years old and serving in the Royal Natal Carabineers, SAF when during an attack on an enemy strongpoint, in which his commanding officer was severely wounded, Smythe took command of the platoon, despite being wounded himself. The strongpoint having been overrun, his men came under enfilade fire from an enemy machine-gun post. Realising the threat to his position, he person-ally stalked and destroyed the post with grenades, capturing the crew. Although weak from loss of blood, he continued to lead the advance, and on encountering an anti-tank position, he again attacked it single-handedly and again captured the crew. He was directly responsible for killing several of the enemy, shooting some and bayoneting another. After this, he consolidated the position, but due to the deterioration of the situation elsewhere, he was ordered to withdraw, which he did successfully, skilfully avoiding an attempt at encirclement.

He is one of only four South Africans to be awarded the VC in the Second World War, the others being Lieutenant Gerard Norton,

Acting Major Edwin Swales and Squadron Leader John Nettleton.

Smythe died from cancer on 22 October 1997.

Private ADAM WAKENSHAW
MERSA MATRUH, Egypt 27 June 1942
He was 28 years old and serving in the 9th Bn, Durham Light Infantry. He was manning a 2-pounder anti-tank gun when, shortly after dawn, the enemy attacked and heavy fire killed or wounded the entire crew. Wakenshaw's left arm was blown off above the elbow. However, he loaded the gun and fired five more rounds to considerable effect. A near-miss then killed his gun aimer and blew him away from the gun, wounding him again. Undeterred, he slowly crawled back to the gun, placed a round in the breech, and was preparing to fire when a direct hit on the ammunition caused a blast that killed him and destroyed the gun.

Captain CHARLES 'PUG' UPHAM
(Bar action)
LE RUWEISAT RIDGE, Egypt
14/15 July 1942
He was 34 years old and serving in the 20th Bn (Canterbury Regiment), NZEF. He was commanding a company in the Western Desert when he was wounded crossing open ground under fire to inspect his forward positions guarding the minefields. Again, after he had destroyed a truck-load of Germans with hand grenades, he insisted on remaining with his company to take part in the final assault. During the opening stages of the attack his company formed part of the reserve, but when communications with the forward troops broke down he was ordered to send an officer to report on the progress of the attack. He went himself, armed with a German machine-gun, and after several encounters with enemy machine-gun posts came back with the required information. Just before dawn the reserve was ordered forward, but when it had almost reached its objective it ran into heavy fire from a strongly defended enemy position, consisting of machine-guns and tanks. Without hesitation, he at once led his men in a

determined attack on the nearest two strong-points on the left flank. His voice could he heard above the din of battle cheering his men on, and despite the fierce resistance of the enemy the objective was taken. During this engagement Upham knocked out a tank and several guns and other vehicles with grenades, but was shot through the elbow and his arm broken. He went out again to bring in some of his men who had become isolated. He continued to dominate the situation until his men had beaten off an enemy counter-attack and consolidated the position. Exhausted and suffering from his wounds, he was removed to the aid post but as soon as his wounds were dressed he returned to his company, remaining with them all day long under heavy artillery fire, until the company had been reduced to just six survivors and he was wounded again. Now unable to move, he fell into the hands of the Germans when the position was overrun.

As a prisoner-of-war he started to live up to his nickname 'Pug' (short for Pugnacious), and made repeated escape attempts. Branded as 'dangerous' by the Germans, he was sent to the infamous Oflag IV-C prison, otherwise known as Colditz. After the war he took up farming, and it is said that he would not allow any German cars on to his land. He died on 22 November 1994, and 5,000 people lined the streets to watch his coffin pass. In 1995 the HMNZS *Charles Upham* was commissioned in his honour. A film portraying the life of Charles Upham is to be made, with the proposed title *Upham – Mark of the Lion*.

The other two men to be awarded the VC and Bar are Noel Chavasse and Arthur Martin-Leake. There are other links between these men: Martin-Leake was serving with the 46th Field Ambulance which brought Chavasse back to Brandhoeck, and Upham was a distant relation of Chavasse by marriage.

Sergeant KEITH ELLIOTT
RUWEISAT, Egypt 15 July 1942
He was 26 years old and serving in the 22nd Bn, NZEF. When leading his platoon in an attack under heavy machine-gun and mortar fire, he was wounded in the chest. Nevertheless he pressed on and led his men in a bayonet charge which resulted in the capture of four enemy machine-gun posts and an anti-tank gun. Seven of the enemy were killed and 50 taken prisoner. In spite of his wound, Elliott refused to leave his platoon until he had reformed them and handed over the prisoners, by now numbering 130.

He died on 7 October 1989.

Private ARTHUR GURNEY
TEL-EL-EISA, Egypt 22 July 1942
He was 33 years old and serving in the 2/48th (SA) Bn, AMF when during an attack his company was held up by heavy machine-gun fire. Numerous casualties were inflicted, including all the officers. Realising the serious-ness of the situation, he charged the nearest post and bayoneted three men. He then continued on to the next post, bayoneted two more men and captured another. Next he was knocked down by a grenade, but got up and charged the third post, again using his bayonet. He then disappeared from view. His body was found later by his comrades. By his single-handed action in the face of a determined enemy, he enabled his company to press forward to its objective.

Major CHARLES MERRITT
DIEPPE, France 19 August 1942
He was 33 years old and commanding the South Saskatchewan Regiment, CIC when his unit had to cross a bridge in Pourvill under heavy machine-gun fire. The first parties were mostly killed and the bridge was covered by their bodies. Waving his helmet, Merritt rushed forward, shouting: 'Come on over! There's nothing to worry about here.' He personally led the survivors across and quickly organised the men before leading them forward. When held up by enemy pillboxes, he again led rushes which succeeded in clearing them. Although twice wounded, he continued to direct operations with great vigour and determination. While organising the with-drawal, he stalked and killed a sniper, then coolly gave orders for the departure before announcing his intention to stay and hold off

and 'get even with' the enemy. He was last seen collecting weapons and preparing a defensive position to cover the withdrawal. He was captured along with many of the Canadians.

He died on 12 July 2000.

Honorary Captain JOHN FOOTE
DIEPPE, France 19 August 1942
He was 38 years old and serving in the Canadian Chaplains Service, attached to the Royal Hamilton Light Infantry, CIC, when during the Dieppe raid he helped tend to the wounded at the aid post on the beach. During the eight hours of the raid he time and again left the post, with utter disregard for his personal safety, and under very heavy fire tirelessly carried wounded men from the exposed beach into what little cover the aid post offered. He carried a number of wounded men down to the landing craft so they could be evacuated. He had the opportunity to embark himself on several occasions but returned to the beach to care for the wounded, eventually choosing to stay with the wounded as a prisoner-of-war.

He died from influenza on 2 May 1988.

Temporary Captain PATRICK PORTEOUS
DIEPPE, France 19 August 1942
He was 24 years old and serving in the Royal Regiment of Artillery when he was ordered to act as liaison officer between two detachments whose task was to assault the heavy coastal defence guns. While working with one detachment, he was shot through the hand at close range. Undaunted, he closed with his assailant and killed him with his own bayonet, thereby saving the life of a British sergeant on whom the German had turned his attention. In the meantime the other group had been held up, and the officers killed. Without hesitation, and in the face of heavy fire, he dashed across open ground to take command, rallying them. He then led them in a bayonet charge and carried the position, being wounded again, this time in the thigh. He continued to the final objective, eventually collapsing from loss of blood.

Porteous was Vice-Chairman (UK) of the VC and GC Association (1993–2000).

He died on 10 October 2000.

Private BRUCE KINGSBURY
ISURAVA, New Guinea
29 August 1942
He was 24 years old and serving in the 2/14th (Victoria) Bn, AMF when the enemy broke through his battalion's right flank, seriously threatening battalion HQ. Kingsbury's platoon had been overrun and he was one of the few survivors. However, he volunteered to join another platoon, which was ordered to counter-attack. He rushed forward shouting: 'Follow me! We can turn them back.' Firing his Bren gun from the hip, he succeeded in clearing a path through the enemy, sweeping the Japanese positions with fire and inflicting heavy casualties. Shortly afterwards he was shot dead by a sniper. His body was carried to the aid post by his best friend, Private Alan Avery.

Corporal JOHN FRENCH
MILNE BAY, New Guinea
4 September 1942
He was 28 years old and serving in the 2/9th (Queensland) Bn, AMF when during an attack the advance of his platoon was held up by machine-gun fire from three posts. Ordering his men to take cover, he attacked and silenced the first two posts with grenades. He then attacked the third post, firing his Tommy gun from the hip. He was seen to be hit but continued to advance. The enemy fire ceased and his section pushed on to find that the enemy in all three posts were dead, and French's body was lying in front of the last position. His supreme courage enabled his section to complete its task.

Sergeant WILLIAM KIBBY
MITEIRIYA RIDGE, Egypt
23–31 October 1942
He was 39 years old and serving in the 2/48th (SA) Bn, AMF when his platoon commander was killed and he took over command. No sooner had he done so than he was ordered to attack a strong enemy position that was holding up the advance. He dashed forward, firing his Tommy gun, and his rapid action resulted in the killing of three men and the capture of another 12, allowing his company to

The Complete Victoria Cross

continue the advance. On 26 October intense enemy artillery fire was directed on the battalion area, which was followed with counter-attacks by tanks and infantry. Throughout the attacks he moved from section to section, personally directing his men's fire and cheering them on. Several times under heavy fire he went out to repair the damaged communication line, thus allowing mortar fire to be brought down on the attacking enemy. During an attack on the night of 30/31 October, he went forward alone, throwing grenades to destroy enemy machine-gun posts that were only a few yards away. Just as success appeared certain, he was killed by a burst of machine-gun fire.

Private PERCIVAL GRATWICK
MITEIRIYA RIDGE, Egypt
25/26 October 1942
He was 40 years old and serving in the 2/48th (SA) Bn, AMF when his platoon met severe opposition from strong enemy positions, causing many casualties, his commanding officer and sergeant being among the dead. Grasping the seriousness of the situation, and acting on his own initiative, he charged the nearest post, destroying it with grenades. Then he charged another enemy machine-gun post under heavy fire, inflicting further casualties, and was within striking distance of it when he was killed by a burst of machine-gun fire. This action allowed his company to move forward and mop up its objective.

Temporary Lieutenant Colonel VICTOR TURNER
EL AQQAQIR, Egypt 27 October 1942
He was 42 years old and commanding the 2nd Bn, Rifle Brigade. After his battalion had taken its objective, he then organised his men for all-round defence. From 0530 to 0700 hours his unsupported battalion was attacked by no fewer than 90 tanks, which advanced in waves. All these attacks were repulsed with the loss to the enemy of 35 tanks destroyed and 20 immobilised. Throughout this action he went to each part of the front as it was threatened, at one point acting as loader for a 6-pounder gun as

most of the crew had been killed, knocking out five tanks.

Turner served with the Yeomen of the Guard from 1950 to 1967, and was Lieutenant of HM Body Guard from 1967 to 1970.

He died on 7 August 1972. His brother was Second Lieutenant Alexander Turner VC, and he is also related to Brevet Lieutenant Colonel Redvers Buller VC.

Acting Captain FREDERICK 'FRITZ' PETERS
ORAN, Algeria 8 November 1942
He was 43 years old and serving in the Royal Navy, commanding HMS *Walney,* when he led his force into Oran harbour through a boom and towards the jetty in the face of point-blank fire from shore batteries, a destroyer and a cruiser. He was blinded in one eye and he alone of the 17 men on the bridge survived. *Walney* reached the jetty disabled and ablaze, and went down with her colours still flying. Peters was captured and interrogated by a Vichy admiral, and released shortly afterwards.

He was killed in a flying boat crash on 13 November 1942. His body was never recovered.

Wing Commander HUGH MALCOLM
BIZERTA and CHOUGUI, Tunisia
17 November–4 December 1942
He was 45 years old and serving in 18 Squadron, RAF when he carried out a low-level formation attack, taking advantage of cloud cover. However, some 20 miles from the target the skies became clear. Knowing full well the danger of flying without a fighter escort, he carried on. Despite fierce opposition, all the bombs were dropped within the target area, while two enemy aircraft were shot down and many more were raked with machine-gun fire while still on the ground. On 28 November he again led his squadron of Blenheims against Bizerta airfield and bombed it from low altitude. The airfield this time was heavily defended, but after dropping their bombs, the Blenheims attacked again and again with machine-gun fire. On 4 December he received an urgent call to attack Chougui airfield. He

knew that such an attack without fighter escort would be almost suicidal, but believing it was necessary for the success of army operations, he decided to attack. After successfully bombing the target, his squadron was intercepted by an overwhelming force of enemy fighters. One by one his aircraft were shot down, and he himself was shot down in flames.

Flight Sergeant RAWDON MIDDLETON
TURIN, Italy 28/29 November 1942
He was 26 years old and serving in the RAAF, attached to 149 Squadron, RAF, when his Stirling bomber was hit many times before reaching the target, blinding him in the right eye and wounding two of the crew, including the co-pilot. Having dropped his bombs, he set course for home, now in great pain and suffering from loss of blood. Realising that he had insufficient fuel to reach his base, he flew over Kent so that his crew could bale out, but he knew that he would have little chance to save himself. After the rest of the crew had abandoned the bomber, he turned out to sea to avoid civilian casualties, and the Stirling crashed into the sea. His body was washed ashore near Dover on 1 February 1943.

Temporary Major HERBERT LE PATOUREL
TEBOURBA, Tunisia 3 December 1942
He was 26 years old and serving in the 2nd Bn, Hampshire Regiment when the enemy were holding an important feature. He took four volunteers and led them under heavy machine-gun fire to dislodge them. His party was heavily engaged, but managed to silence several machine-gun posts. Finally, when the remainder of his party were all either killed or wounded, he went forward alone with his pistol and grenades. He was thought to have been killed by the enemy, but in fact he had been wounded and captured.
He died on 4 September 1979.

Captain ROBERT SHERBROOKE
NORTH CAPE, Norway
31 December 1942
He was 41 years old and serving in the Royal

Navy aboard HMS *Onslow*. As senior officer in command of the destroyers, he was escorting a convoy bound for Russia when they made contact with a vastly superior enemy force, including the cruiser *Hipper* and the pocket battleship *Lutzow*. Undaunted, Sherbrooke led his destroyers into the attack and closed with the enemy. Four times the German ships tried to attack the convoy, but each time they were forced back behind a smokescreen and each time he pursued them and drove them away from the convoy. Early in the action he was wounded in the face and temporarily blinded; nevertheless he continued to direct his ships until more hits on his ship compelled him to withdraw. Only when the next senior officer assumed command did he agree to leave the bridge for medical attention, but he still insisted on receiving all reports of the action. By his actions the convoy was saved from destruction and brought safely to its destination.
He died on 13 June 1972.

1943

Havildar PARKASH SINGH
DONBAIK, Burma 6 and 19 January 1943
He was 29 years old and serving in the 8th Punjab Regiment, Indian Army. When two universal carriers had been put out of action, he drove forward in his own and rescued the two crews under heavy fire. They had used all their ammunition and the enemy were rushing the disabled carriers on foot. On 19 January three more carriers, one of which was carrying the survivors of another carrier as well as its own crew, were put out of action in an exposed area by anti-tank fire. On seeing what had happened, he went out in his own carrier and with complete disregard for his personal safety rescued the crews from one disabled carrier, together with the weapons from another. Then he went out again under heavy anti-tank and machine-gun fire, dismounted and connected a towing chain to a disabled carrier with two wounded men in it, and towed it back to safety.

He died on 23 March 1991, following an operation.

Flight Lieutenant WILLIAM 'BILL' NEWTON

SALAMAUA, New Guinea
16 and 18 March 1943

He was 24 years old and serving in 22 Squadron, RAAF when he led an attack on Salamaua in which his plane was repeatedly hit by anti-aircraft fire. In spite of this, he pressed on and dropped his bombs from low level on buildings and fuel dumps. He then managed to get his crippled plane back to base. On 18 March he made another attack on Salamaua with five other bombers and again hit his designated target, but this time his plane burst into flames. He managed to ditch into the sea, and he and his wireless operator, Flight Sergeant John Lyon, were seen swimming for shore.

They made contact with two friendly natives, but were soon captured by the Japanese and taken back to Salamaua, where they were interrogated before being moved to Lae, according to official Japanese records. They were interrogated by the military police, the Kempeitai. John Lyon was bayoneted to death shortly afterwards.

Newton was later returned to Salamaua and on 29 March 1943 he was beheaded by the Japanese officer who had captured him. In July 1948 the body of John Lyon was discovered near Lae airstrip. He was buried with full military honours near William Newton.

Temporary Lieutenant Colonel DEREK SEAGRIM

MARETH LINE, Tunisia
20/21 March 1943

He was 39 years old and serving in the 7th Bn, Green Howards (Alexandra, Princess of Wales's Own Yorkshire Regiment) when his battalion was ordered to capture an important objective on the left flank of the main attack. The position was very strongly defended, and protected by an anti-tank ditch some 12 feet wide and mined on both sides. From the start the battalion came under intense artillery and machine-gun fire. It looked as if the attack was going to fail, but Seagrim placed himself at the head of his men, who were suffering heavy casualties, and led them forward. He personally helped the team place a scaling ladder over the anti-tank ditch and was first to cross over it. He then led the attack, firing his pistol and throwing grenades, and personally assaulted two machine-gun posts which were holding up the advance. It is estimated that in this phase he killed or captured 20 Germans. This display of leadership and personal courage led directly to the capture of the objective. When daylight came, the battalion was firmly established on the position. The enemy made every effort to regain it. Every post was shelled and machine-gunned, and movement became practically impossible, but Seagrim was quite undeterred, moving from post to post organising and directing fire until the attackers were defeated.

He died on 6 April 1943 as a result of his wounds. His brother Hugh Seagrim was awarded the George Cross, giving these two men the distinction of being the only siblings to receive the VC and GC.

Second Lieutenant MOANA-NUI-A-KIWA NGARIMU

TEBAGA GAP, Tunisia 26/27 March 1943

He was 24 years old and serving in the 28th (Maori) Bn, NZEF when his platoon took part in an attack on a hill feature known as Point 209. His platoon was to take a lower part of the hill, forward of Point 209, which was held by the enemy in considerable strength. He led his men straight up the hill, undeterred by the intense machine-gun fire, which caused many casualties. He was the first man on to the crest of the hill, personally taking out at least two machine-gun posts. In the face of such a determined attack, the Germans fled. Further advance was not possible as the reverse slopes were swept by machine-gun fire from Point 209. Under cover of an artillery barrage, the enemy counter-attacked, and Ngarimu ordered his men to stand up and engage them man for man. This they did to such good effect that the attackers were mown down, Ngarimu personally accounting for several, although he was wounded in the shoulder and the leg.

Despite being urged by both his company and battalion commanders to go back, he refused, saying he would stay a little while with his men. Darkness found his platoon lying on the rocky face of the forward slopes, with the enemy on the reverse slopes only 20 yards distant. Throughout the night the enemy launched fierce attacks in an attempt to dislodge them, but each attack was beaten off. During one of these attacks the enemy, using grenades, succeeded in penetrating part of the line. Without hesitation, Ngarimu rushed to the threatened area. Those he did not kill he drove back with his Tommy gun, at one point even throwing stones at them. During another attack, part of the line broke. He rallied his men and led them in a fierce onslaught back into their old positions. Between each attack they were harassed by machine-gun and mortar fire. Morning found him still in possession of the hill, but with only two unwounded men left. The Germans attacked again, and he was killed. He died on his feet, defiantly facing the enemy with his Tommy gun at his hip. As he fell, he came to rest almost on top of those he had killed, the number of whom testified to his outstanding courage.

He was the first of two Maoris to be awarded the VC, the other being Corporal Willie Apiata in 2004.

Subadar LALBAHADUR THAPA

RASS-ES-ZOUAI, Tunisia 5/6 April 1943
He was 34 years old and serving in the 1st Bn, Gurkha Rifles, Indian Army when he was in command of two sections during a silent attack. First contact was made at the foot of a pathway winding up a narrow cleft. This position was well defended with a series of enemy posts. The men in the outer posts were all killed by the bayonet or kukri in the first rush, and then the enemy opened a very heavy fire straight down the narrow pathway. However, Thapa led his men on and fought his way up to the enemy position under heavy machine-gun fire, killing two with his revolver and two more with his kukri. Upon reaching the crest with just two other men, he killed another two men with his kukri and the rest

fled. He then covered his company's advance up to the crest. With the crest thus secured, an advance by the whole division was possible.
He died on 20 October 1968.

Temporary Lieutenant Colonel LORNE CAMPBELL

WADI AKARIT, Tunisia 6 April 1943
He was 40 years old and commanding the 7th Bn, Argyll and Sutherland Highlanders (Princess Louise's) when his battalion was given the task of breaking through the enemy minefield and anti-tank ditch in order to form a bridgehead. In spite of heavy machine-gun and shell fire, he successfully accomplished this and captured 600 prisoners. Later, he found that the gap which the Royal Engineers had made in the anti-tank ditch did not correspond with the cleared part of the minefield. In full daylight he made a reconnaissance which led to the establishment of a vehicle gap. This position then came under enemy counter-attacks, supported by tanks. By his sheer presence he inspired his men in the forefront of the fighting, cheering them on and rallying them, as he moved to where the fighting was heaviest. When one of his forward companies was forced to give ground, he went forward alone under a hail of fire and personally reorganised their position, remaining with them until the attack was beaten back. He was wounded in the neck but it was not until the battle had died down that he allowed his wound to be dressed. He still refused to be evacuated.
He died on 25 May 1991. His uncle was Commander Gordon Campbell VC.

Private ERIC ANDERSON

WADI AKARIT, Tunisia 6 April 1943
He was 27 years old and serving in the 5th Bn, East Yorkshire Regiment when a company had to withdraw under heavy fire to the crest of a hill. Seeing that wounded men were left behind, on his own initiative he went forward alone through intense fire, regardless of his personal safety, and carried a wounded man to a place of safety, where he could be given medical attention. Knowing more men were lying in the

open, he again went out, located a second wounded man and carried him to safety. He went out a third time and brought another wounded man back. On his fourth trip out he found a wounded man, but was killed while giving him first aid.

Company Havildar Major CHHELU RAM
DJEBEL GARCI, Tunisia
19/20 April 1943

He was 37 years old and serving in the 4th Rajputana Rifles, Indian Army when his company was held up by enemy machine-gun and mortar fire from high ground. Armed with a Tommy gun, he immediately rushed forward through intense fire and single-handedly killed three or four of the enemy, thus enabling the advance to continue. As they approached the next objective, the enemy brought down heavy fire which mortally wounded the company commander. Chhelu Ram went over to him and attended to his wounds, but was wounded himself. Despite this, he took command of the remnants of two companies, reorganising them. Almost immediately the enemy counter-attacked and his men ran short of ammunition. During the fierce hand-to-hand fighting that followed, his bravery and determination were beyond praise. He rushed to wherever the fighting was heaviest, rallying the men and driving the enemy back with cries of 'Jats and Mohammedans, there must be no withdrawal! We will advance! Advance!' He then led a counter-attack with the bayonet, and his men, inspired by his example, again drove the enemy back. He was mortally wounded during this attack, but refused to be carried back and remained in command until he died.

Captain CHARLES LYELL
DJ BOU ARADA, Tunisia
22–27 April 1943

He was 26 years old and serving in the 1st Bn, Scots Guards when he led his company under heavy mortar fire to repel a German counter-attack. On 23 April he captured the battalion's first objective and held it under heavy shell fire, personally using the radio to bring down artillery fire on enemy tanks and infantry. On 27 April his company was held up by heavy fire from a position that consisted of an 88mm gun and a machine-gun in separate pits. He collected four men together and led them in a rush towards the guns, he being a long way in front of the others. He threw a grenade into the machine-gun pit, killing the crew. Then, as one man gave him covering fire, he ran on to the 88mm gun pit and so quickly did he act that he was among the enemy with his bayonet before they had time to react. He killed a number of the gun crew before being overwhelmed and killed. The remaining gun crew fled, some being killed as they ran. His action allowed the company advance to continue.

Acting Major JOHN ANDERSON
LONGSTOP HILL, Tunisia 23 April 1943

He was 43 years old and serving in the 8th Bn, Argyll and Sutherland Highlanders (Princess Louise's) when his commander was killed. Taking command, he rallied the men and led the assault on the hill, during which he was wounded in the leg. In spite of this, he captured the hill with only 44 men remaining. The enemy fire had been so intense that the remainder of the battalion had been pinned down and unable to move until he had taken the objective. During the assault he personally led attacks on at least three machine-gun positions and a mortar pit containing four mortars and thirty Germans, he being the first into the pits. In all over 200 prisoners were captured.

He was killed in action at Termoli on 5 October 1943.

Lieutenant WILWARD SANDYS-CLARKE
GUIRIAT EL ATACH, Tunisia
23 April 1943

He was 24 years old and serving in the Loyal North Lancashire Regiment when, during an enemy counter-attack, his company had been almost wiped out. Already wounded in the head, he gathered a composite platoon together and volunteered to attack again. As soon as his platoon closed on the objective, it was met by heavy machine-gun fire. Ordering his men to cover him, he tackled the post single-handed, killing or capturing the crew. Almost at once the platoon came under fire from two more machine-gun posts. Sandys-Clarke again went forward alone, killing the crews or forcing them to surrender. He then led the platoon to the objective, where they came under sniper fire. Without hesitating, he advanced alone to clear the opposition, but was killed within a few feet of the enemy.

Lance Corporal JOHN KENNEALLY (real name LESLIE ROBINSON)
DJ BOU ARADA, Tunisia
28 and 30 April 1943
He was 22 years old and serving in the 1st Bn, Irish Guards when he saw around 100 Germans preparing to attack. Seizing the moment, he charged forward alone, firing his Bren gun from the hip. The enemy were completely thrown off guard and started to retreat in disarray. When the Germans formed up to attack again, Kenneally again charged with his Bren gun firing, routing them with many casualties. On 30 April he again charged a group of Germans as they were about to launch an attack, but was hit in the calf. Ignoring his wound, he hopped from one position to another, firing as the enemy advanced. He refused to give up his Bren gun and fought on all day until the enemy withdrew.

On hearing he had been awarded the VC he said: 'Now I'm bound to be rumbled,' in reference to his true identity. Kenneally also served in Palestine. His autobiography is called *Kenneally VC: The True Story of a Remarkable Life.*
He died on 27 September 2000.

Squadron Leader LEONARD TRENT
AMSTERDAM, Holland 3 May 1943
He was 28 years old and serving in the RNZAF, attached to 48 Squadron, RAF, when he led a formation of Ventura bombers in a daylight attack on a power station. One bomber was hit nearing the Dutch coast and had to turn back. Suddenly large numbers of enemy fighters appeared and the escorting fighters were hotly engaged, losing touch with the bombers. The Venturas closed up for protection and commenced their bomb run,

but they were at the mercy of 15 to 20 enemy fighters and within 4 minutes six bombers had been shot down. Trent continued on his course with the other three remaining aircraft. Although two more were shot down, Trent completed an accurate bombing run and even shot down an enemy fighter. After dropping his bombs, he turned away to see the bomber behind him shot down. Immediately afterwards his own aircraft was hit and went into a spin, breaking up. Trent and his navigator were thrown clear, but the rest of the crew were killed. He was sent to Stalag Luft III and took part in 'The Great Escape'.
Trent was ADC to the Queen (1962–65).
He died on 19 May 1986.

Wing Commander GUY 'GIBBO' GIBSON
MOHNE and EDER DAMS, Germany
16/17 May 1943
He was 24 years old and serving in 617 Squadron, RAF when he led the Dambuster Raid. Descending to within a few feet of the water, and bearing the full brunt of the anti-aircraft fire, he delivered his bouncing bomb with great accuracy. Afterwards, he circled low for 30 minutes to draw the enemy anti-aircraft fire on himself in order to give as free a run as possible to the following aircraft, which attacked the dam in turn. Then he led the remainder of his force to the Eder Dam, where again he flew low over the target to observe and was the last to leave the area. Both dams were breached.

As well as the VC he was awarded the DSO and Bar, and the DFC and Bar. His autobiography is called *Enemy Coast Ahead.* Gibson was killed in action near Bergen-op-Zoom on 19 September 1944. There is a blue plaque on his flat at 32 Aberdeen Place, London.

Havildar GAJE GHALE
CHIN HILLS, Burma 24–27 May 1943
He was 20 years old and serving in the 2nd Bn, 5th Royal Gurkha Rifles Regiment, Indian Army. He was in charge of a platoon of inexperienced men, engaged in attacking a strong Japanese position. Despite being wounded in the arm, chest and leg, he continued to lead

assault after assault, encouraging his men with the Gurkha's battle cry, 'Ayo Gurkha'. Spurred on by the irresistible will of their leader, the platoon finally stormed and captured the position, which Gaje Ghale then held and consolidated under heavy fire, refusing to go to the aid post until ordered.

He died on 28 March 2000.

Flying Officer LLOYD TRIGG

NORTH ATLANTIC 11 August 1943

He was 29 years old and serving in the RNZAF, attached to 200 Squadron, RAF. He was patrolling in a Liberator bomber when he sighted *U-468* on the surface. He prepared to attack but during his approach the aircraft took many hits from the submarine's anti-aircraft guns and burst into flames. He could have broken off and made a forced landing in the sea. However, he maintained his course despite the condition of his bomber and executed his attack, skimming over the U-boat at less than 50 feet with anti-aircraft rounds entering his open bomb doors. His bombs fell on and around the U-boat with devastating effect. The crippled aircraft then crashed into the sea. There were no survivors. The U-boat sank within 20 minutes and only seven of her crew survived. When picked up by the British, Oberleutnant Schamong recommended the pilot for his bravery. This is the only VC ever awarded solely on the evidence of the enemy.

Acting Flight Sergeant ARTHUR AARON

TURIN, Italy 12/13 August 1943

He was 21 years old and serving in 218 Squadron, RAFVR when his Stirling bomber was attacked and badly damaged. Three engines were hit, the windscreen was shattered, the front and rear turrets were both put out of action and the elevator control was damaged. One bullet hit Aaron in the face, breaking his jaw and tearing away part of his face. He also had a punctured lung and his right arm was useless. The navigator was killed and other members of the crew wounded. Despite these injuries, he managed to level the aircraft out at 3,000 feet, and then the bomb aimer took over control. Aaron was moved to the rear and

treated with morphia. After resting for some time, he insisted on returning to the pilot's cockpit. Although in great pain, he helped direct the bomb aimer in the task of landing the damaged aircraft in the dark with the undercarriage retracted. He died from his wounds 9 hours later. It is now known that they were fired on by another Stirling bomber from the same flight.

Private RICHARD KELLIHER

NADZAB, New Guinea 13 September 1943

He was 33 years old and serving in the 2/25th (Queensland) Bn, AMF when his platoon was pinned down by heavy machine-gun fire, which killed five and wounded three more. Without orders, he dashed downhill to within yards of the enemy position, throwing two grenades and killing some of the enemy. He then returned to his section to collect a Bren gun and once more charged, firing from the hip and silencing the position. Then, still under fire, he went forward and brought in his section leader, Corporal Richards, who had been severely wounded.

In 1942 he had been under investigation for 'failing to get into his allotted position with his section'. He was court-martialled in March 1943 and found guilty of 'misbehaving before the enemy in such a way as to show cowardice', and sentenced to 12 months in detention. In May 1943 an appeal resulted in the verdict and sentence being quashed.

He died from a stroke on 28 January 1963.

Lieutenant DONALD CAMERON

KAAFJORD, Norway 22 September 1943

He was 27 years old and serving in the Royal Naval Reserve, commanding midget submarine *X6*, when he carried out a most daring and successful attack on the German battleship *Tirpitz*, together with Lieutenant Place's *X7*. To reach the ship at all necessitated the penetration of an enemy minefield and a passage of 50 miles up the fjord, passing patrol boats, gun positions and listening posts. Having eluded all of these hazards and entered the anchorage, Lieutenant Cameron and Lieutenant Place worked their craft past the anti-submarine nets and placed the charges under the ship. Both submarines were scuttled under fire, and Cameron's crew were taken on board *Tirpitz* to await interrogation, trying to keep cool. When the charges went off, *Tirpitz* was badly damaged and put out of action for six months. Place and his crew were also captured. Both men were awarded the VC.

Cameron died on 10 April 1961.

Lieutenant BASIL PLACE

KAAFJORD, Norway 22 September 1943

He was 22 years old and serving in the Royal Navy, commanding midget submarine *X7* when he carried out a most daring and successful attack on the German battleship *Tirpitz*, together with Lieutenant Cameron's *X6*. To reach the ship at all necessitated the penetration of an enemy minefield and a passage of 50 miles up the fjord, passing patrol boats, gun positions and listening posts. Having eluded all of these hazards and entered the anchorage, Lieutenant Place and Lieutenant Cameron worked their craft past the anti-submarine nets and placed the charges under the ship. Both submarines were scuttled under fire and Cameron's crew were taken on board *Tirpitz* to await interrogation, trying to keep cool. When the charges went off *Tirpitz* was badly damaged and put out of action for six months. Place and his crew were also captured. Both men were awarded the VC.

Place also served in Korea. He was Chairman (UK) of the VC and GC Association (1971–94).

He died on 27 December 1994.

Company Sergeant Major PETER WRIGHT

SALERNO, Italy 25 September 1943

He was 27 years old and serving in the 3rd Bn, Coldstream Guards when his company was held up on the crest of a steep, wooded hill. Most of the officers having been killed, Wright took charge and single-handedly silenced three enemy machine-gun posts with grenades and the bayonet, and then led his men to consolidate the position. Next he beat off a counter-attack and, disregarding the heavy fire, brought up extra ammunition.

He died on 5 April 1990.

Acting Flight Lieutenant WILLIAM REID

DUSSELDORF, Germany

3 November 1943

He was 21 years old and serving in 61 Squadron, RAF when his Lancaster bomber was attacked while crossing the Dutch coast, shattering the windscreen, cockpit and both gun turrets. Reid was hit in the head and shoulder, and his face was cut by shards of Perspex from the windscreen. He pressed on regardless and was attacked again, this time killing the navigator and mortally wounding the wireless operator. Reid was wounded again. The hydraulics and oxygen system were also damaged. Aided by the flight engineer, Reid brought the bomber back under control. Any other pilot would have turned for home but Reid continued on to his target, dropped his bombs and finally headed home. Over the Dutch coast they came under anti-aircraft fire again, sending the Lancaster into a spin. Only his pilot's instinct saved him. Back at base, the undercarriage had to be lowered by hand but subsequently collapsed on landing, causing the plane to skid on its belly for 60 feet before coming to a halt.

Reid was later shot down and captured, being sent first to Stalag Luft III and later to Oflag IV-c, otherwise known as Colditz. When he married in 1952, he never even told his wife he had been awarded the VC, such was his modesty.

He died on 28 November 2001.

Sergeant THOMAS 'DIVER' DERRICK

SATELBERG, New Guinea

24 November 1943

He was 29 years old and serving in the 2/48th Bn, AMF when his battalion was ordered to outflank an enemy position on a cliff face, and then to attack a feature near the town of Satelberg. Due to the nature of the terrain, the only possible approach to the enemy position was through an open kunai patch directly beneath the top of the cliffs. For over 2 hours many attempts were made to clamber up the slopes to their objective, but each time they were met by intense machine-gun fire and grenades, and were forced to retire. It appeared that it was impossible to reach the objective or even to hold the ground already taken. Shortly before dark Derrick asked to be allowed to try one more time. Displaying dogged tenacity, he moved ahead of his platoon, personally destroying with grenades an enemy post that had been holding up the attack. He then ordered his second section around the flank. This move was met with heavy fire from six enemy outposts. Without regard for personal safety, he went forward well ahead of his men and hurled grenade after grenade, so completely demoralising the enemy that they fled, leaving their weapons behind. By this action alone the company was able to gain its first foothold. Not content with this, he took two sections to deal with the three remaining outposts in the area. On four occasions he dashed forward and threw grenades at a range of 6 to 8 yards until all of them were knocked out. In total, he took out ten enemy posts. Due to the taking of this ground, the rest of the battalion moved on to capture Satelberg the next morning.

He died of wounds received in action on 23 May 1945.

Captain PAUL TRIQUET
CASA BERARDI, Italy 14 December 1943
He was 33 years old and serving in the Royal 22nd Regiment, CIC when all the other officers and half the men in his company were killed or wounded. He went round reorganising the remainder and encouraging them. Finally, when the enemy infiltrated from all sides, he dashed forward shouting: 'There are enemy in front of us, behind us and on our flanks, there is only one safe place, that is on the objective,' and with his men following him he broke through the enemy resistance. In this action four enemy tanks were destroyed and several machine-gun posts silenced. In close co-operation with the tanks, they forced their way on until a position was held just short of the objective. By this time his force was reduced to fewer than 20 men. He set about organising a defensive perimeter around the tanks and

passed the 'mot d'ordre. Nous ne passerons.' The position was attacked by tanks and infantry, but ignoring the heavy fire Triquet was everywhere, encouraging the men and directing the defence. By using whatever weapons were to hand, he personally accounted for several of the enemy. He held out against several attacks until the remainder of the battalion relieved them.

He died on 8 August 1980.

1944

Lieutenant ALEC HORWOOD
KYAUCHAW, Burma 18–20 January 1944
He was 30 years old and serving in the 1/16th Bn, Queen's (West Surrey) Royal Regiment, attached to the 1st Bn, Northamptonshire Regiment, when he went forward and established an observation post. Throughout the day he lay in an exposed position under heavy fire. That night he came back with valuable information about enemy positions. On 19 January he moved forward and established an observation post on a ridge, from where he directed accurate mortar fire in support of two attacks, again under heavy fire. He also carried out a reconnaissance along the ridge, deliberately drawing enemy fire so that the enemy positions could be definitely located. On the night of 19/20 January he remained on the ridge and in the morning directed the mortar fire in support of another attack. Convinced the enemy would break, he volunteered to lead the attack planned for the afternoon. He led the men forward, and while standing up in the wire, directing the men, with complete disregard for his personal safety, he was mortally wounded.

Private GEORGE MITCHELL
DAMIANO RIDGE, Italy
23/24 January 1944
He was 32 years old and serving in the 1st Bn, London Scottish (Gordon Highlanders) when his company came under heavy machine-gun fire, killing or wounding most of the officers

and NCOs. He dropped the 2-inch mortar he was carrying, seized a rifle and charged alone up the hill through intense machine-gun fire. He reached the enemy position unscathed, jumped into the pit, shot one and bayoneted another, silencing the gun. Shortly afterwards, the advance was held up again by small arms fire. Realising that prompt action was necessary, he rushed forward, firing his rifle from the hip, completely oblivious of the bullets sweeping past him. The remainder of his section arrived in time to capture the position, in which six Germans were killed and 12 taken prisoner. As the men were reorganising, another machine-gun opened fire at close range. Once more, Mitchell rushed forward alone and bayoneted the crew. Now out of ammunition, and with small arms firing at him, he charged to the top of the hill, being the first man to enter the enemy position, and was largely instrumental in forcing the enemy to surrender. A few minutes later a German who had surrendered picked up a rifle and shot him dead.

Temporary Major WILLIAM SIDNEY
ANZIO, Italy 7/8 February 1944

He was 34 years old and serving in the 5th Bn, Grenadier Guards when some enemy infantry who had bypassed the forward company heavily attacked and took hold of a gulley. Sidney collected the crew of a 3-inch mortar and personally led an attack with submachine-guns and grenades, driving the enemy out of the gulley. He then sent the mortar crew back while he and a handful of men took up position on the edge of the gulley in order to beat off the enemy, who were now renewing their attack in some strength. They succeeded in keeping the majority of the enemy at bay, but a number reached a ditch 20 yards away, from which they could outflank his position. He dashed forward alone, in full view of the enemy, to a point from where he could engage them at point-blank range with his Tommy gun. As a result the enemy withdrew, leaving behind a number of dead. On returning to his position at the gulley, he kept two guardsmen with him and sent the rest back for more ammunition.

While they were away, the enemy attacked again. A grenade struck him in the face, but bounced off and then exploded, wounding him and one man, but killing the other man. Sidney, single-handedly, although wounded in the thigh, kept the enemy at bay until the ammunition party returned. Believing no more attacks would be made, he started to go back to have his wounds dressed, but before this could be done the enemy attacked again. He at once returned to his position and continued to engage the enemy for another hour, by which time the left of the battalion position was consolidated and the enemy finally driven off. Only then did he allow his wounds to be dressed. Now very weak from loss of blood, he was unable to be evacuated until after dark due to the close contact with the enemy. During this time, as before, he continued to encourage and inspire the men.

In later life, when asked where he had been shot, he would jocularly respond that he was shot in Italy. This was to conceal the fact that he had been shot in the buttocks. He was one of only a few VC holders who became MPs.

He died on 5 April 1991. His father-in-law was Lieutenant Colonel John Gort VC.

Temporary Major CHARLES HOEY
NGAKYEDAUK PASS, Burma
16 February 1944

He was 29 years old and serving in the 1st Bn, Lincolnshire Regiment when his company came under very heavy machine-gun fire. He personally led his men forward and, although wounded in the head and leg, seized a Bren gun. Firing from the hip, he was the first to enter the enemy position, where he killed all the occupants. Mortally wounded in this attack, he died the next day.

Acting Naik NAND SINGH
MAUNGDAW-BUTHIDAUNG ROAD,
Burma 11/12 March 1944

He was 29 years old and serving in the 1/11th Sikh Regiment, Indian Army. He was commanding the lead section of the attack when he was ordered to recapture a position taken by the enemy. Nand Singh led his men up a steep, knife-edged ridge under very heavy rifle and machine-gun fire, and although wounded in the thigh, captured the first trench. He crawled forward alone and was wounded again in the face and shoulder. He nevertheless captured the second and third trenches.

After the war he stayed in the Indian Army and took part in the Indo-Pakistani War of 1947. On 12 December 1947 he led his platoon in a desperate but successful attack to extricate his battalion from an ambush in the hills south-east of Uri. He was mortally wounded by a close-range burst of machine-gun fire, and was posthumously awarded the MVC, the second highest Indian decoration for gallantry. This makes Nand Singh unique in the annals of the VC. He is also the only VC holder to be killed in a post-Second World War conflict.

Lieutenant GEORGE CAIRNS
HENU BLOCK, Burma 13 March 1944
He was 30 years old and serving in the Somerset Light Infantry (Prince Albert's), attached to the South Staffordshire Regiment. During an attack on a hill-top position held by the Japanese, he was attacked by an officer who hacked off his left arm with his sword. Cairns killed the officer and picked up his sword. Still leading his men, he advanced, slashing left and right with the captured sword. He killed and wounded several of the enemy before he fell to the ground. His actions so inspired his men that the Japanese were completely routed, a very rare occurrence at this time. He later died from his wounds.

George Cairns' VC was the last to be gazetted for the Second World War. The original recommendation was with General Orde Wingate when he was killed in an air crash, and the information could not be retrieved until 1949.

Pilot Officer CYRIL BARTON
NUREMBERG, Germany
30/31 March 1944
He was 22 years old and serving in 578 Squadron, RAFVR. During a raid on Nuremberg his bomber was hit by enemy aircraft, losing an engine, while still 70 miles from the target. A misinterpreted signal resulted in three crew members baling out. With no navigator, bomb aimer or wireless operator, Barton pressed on with the attack, releasing the bombs himself. On the return journey he ran short of fuel and crash-landed, trying to avoid the houses and pit-head workings of the village of Ryhope, near Sunderland. Barton was killed, but the rest of the crew survived.

Jemadar ABDUL HAFIZ
IMPHAL, India 6 April 1944
He was 28 years old and serving in the 9th Jat Infantry, Indian Army when he was ordered to attack with two sections a position that was believed to be held by 40 Japanese. Before the attack he told his men they were invincible, and that all the enemy would be killed or routed. He so inspired his men that the attack proceeded with great dash; they charged up the slope with no cover into machine-gun fire and grenades. On reaching the crest Hafiz was wounded in the leg, but when he saw a machine-gun firing from the flank, he immediately rushed it and grabbed the barrel while another man killed the gunner. Then he took a Bren gun and advanced on the enemy, firing as he went, killing several of them. So fiercely did his men fight that the enemy, who were still in considerable numbers, fled. In the pursuit Hafiz was hit in the chest by a machine-gun firing from another position. Collapsing, he still tried to fire the Bren gun, shouting: 'Reorganise on the position and I will give covering fire.' He died shortly afterwards.

Lance Corporal JOHN HARMAN
KOHIMA, India 8/9 April 1944
He was 29 years old and serving in the 4th Bn, Queen's Own Royal West Kent Regiment when the enemy established a machine-gun post within 50 yards of his position, which soon became a menace. Owing to the nature of the ground, he was unable to bring fire down on to the position. Without hesitation he went forward alone and threw a grenade into the position, killing the crew, and returned with the gun. Early the next morning he recovered a

position on a forward slope 150 yards from the enemy in order to strengthen a platoon that had been attacked during the night. He then saw a party of the enemy digging in under cover of machine-gun and sniper fire. Ordering his Bren gunner to give covering fire, he charged them alone, shooting four and bayoneting another. As he was walking back he was hit by a burst of machine-gun fire and died shortly after reaching his own lines. His last words were: 'I got the lot – it was worth it.'

Sergeant NORMAN JACKSON
SCHWEINFURT, Germany
26/27 April 1944

He was 25 years old and serving in 106 Squadron, RAF. During a raid on Schweinfurt he had bombed his target when his plane was attacked by a night fighter and a fuel tank in the starboard wing caught fire. Jackson, already wounded, strapped on a parachute, took a fire extinguisher and climbed out on to the wing in order to put out the fire while the bomber was flying along at 200mph. The rushing wind blew his chute partially open, causing him to slip and fall into the fire. He sustained serious burns before falling 20,000 feet to the ground with a partially opened and burning parachute. He suffered further injuries upon landing, but managed to crawl to a nearby German village, where he was paraded through the street. He spent ten months recovering in hospital before being moved to Stalag Kc prisoner-of-war camp. He made two attempts to escape, the second of which was successful as he made contact with the US Third Army.

Jackson had in fact completed his tour of 30 missions before this flight, but one of those had been with another crew, and he wanted to fly once more so that he and his original crew could finish together. When he had first joined the RAF he greatly impressed his flight sergeant, who told him 'You know, boy, I'm convinced you will go a long way in this air force.' After the award of the VC the first telegram he received said: 'Well done, I knew I was right. Your ex-Flight Sergeant.'

He died on 26 March 1994.

Temporary Captain JOHN RANDLE
KOHIMA, India 4–6 May 1944

He was 26 years old and serving in the 2nd Bn, Royal Norfolk Regiment when he took over command after his commander was wounded. He continued to inspire his men by his initiative and courage until the company had captured and consolidated its objective, despite being wounded in the knee by grenade splinters. Then he went forward and brought in all the wounded men who were lying outside the perimeter. In spite of his wound he refused to be evacuated and insisted on carrying out a reconnaissance in moonlight on a position to be attacked. At dawn on 6 May the attack was led by Randle, and one platoon succeeded in reaching the crest of the hill held by the enemy. However, another platoon ran into heavy machine-gun fire from a bunker on the reverse slope. Realising the danger, he charged towards the bunker single-handedly with rifle and bayonet, and although wounded by machine-gun fire reached the position and threw a grenade inside. He then flung his body across the slit so that the aperture should be sealed. By his self-sacrifice he saved the lives of many men and the battalion captured its objective.

His brother-in-law was Flying Officer Leslie Manser VC.

Sepoy KAMAL RAM
RIVER GARI, Italy 12 May 1944

He was 19 years old and serving in the 3rd Bn, 8th Punjab Regiment, Indian Army when after crossing the river his company was held up by heavy machine-gun fire from four posts to the front and flanks. Ram volunteered to try to get around the rear of the post on the right. Crawling forward through wire, he attacked the post single-handed and shot the gunner; another German tried to seize the weapon but he killed him with the bayonet, and when an officer appeared from a trench, he shot him too. Still alone, he went on to the next post, where he shot the gunner and threw a grenade and the remaining enemy surrendered. With the help of a havildar, he also destroyed the third post. By his courage, initiative and disregard for personal safety, he enabled his company to secure the ground vital to establishing the bridgehead.

He died on 1 July 1982.

Temporary Captain RICHARD WAKEFORD

CASSINO, Italy 13/14 May 1944
He was 22 years old and serving in the 2/4th Bn, Hampshire Regiment. Accompanied by his orderly, and armed only with his revolver, he killed a number of the enemy and took 20 prisoners. On finding a house with a German officer and five men holding it, he made two attempts to approach it but was forced back. Finally he reached the house and threw in his grenades. Those who were not killed surrendered. When attacking a hill the following day his company became bogged down under heavy fire. Although wounded in the face and arms, he led his men up the hill, reaching the objective. He reorganised and consolidated the remainder of his men and reported to his commander before submitting to personal attention. During the several hours before stretcher-bearers could reach him, his unwavering high spirits encouraged the wounded men.

He died on 27 August 1972.

Fusilier FRANCIS JEFFERSON

MONTE CASSINO, Italy 16 May 1944
He was 22 years old and serving in the 2nd Bn, Lancashire Fusiliers when during an attack on the Gustav Line, his company had to dig in without protection. The enemy counterattacked with tanks opening fire at close range. On his own initiative Jefferson seized a PIAT gun and ran forward under a hail of bullets to fire on the lead tank. It burst into flames and all the crew were killed. He then reloaded and went forward again towards the next tank, but it withdrew before he could get within range. By now British tanks had arrived and the enemy counter-attack was smashed.

He threw himself under a train on 4 September 1982, while suffering from depression following the theft of his VC.

Major JOHN MAHONY

RIVER MELFA, Italy 24 May 1944
He was 32 years old and serving in the Westminster Regiment (Motor), CIC when he was ordered to establish a bridgehead across the river. He personally led his men across and directed each section into position. From 15:30 hours until 20:30 hours the company came under enemy attacks. Shortly after the bridgehead was established the enemy counter-attacked with tanks, SPGs and infantry but were beaten off by PIATs, 2-inch mortars and grenades. Mahony personally directed the fire of the PIATs throughout this action, encouraging and inspiring his men. By now the company strength had been reduced to 60 men, and most of the officers were wounded. An hour later enemy tanks and infantry formed up and launched another attack. Determined to hold the bridgehead at all costs, he went from section to section with words of encouragement, personally directing their fire. At one point a section was pinned down by accurate and intense machine-gun fire. Mahony crawled forward to its position, and by throwing smoke grenades succeeded in extricating the section with the loss of only one man. This second enemy attack was beaten off with the destruction of three SPGs and a tank. During the action he was wounded in the head and twice in the leg, but refused medical aid. Only when the remaining companies had crossed to support him did he allow his wounds to be dressed, but still refused to be evacuated.

He died on 16 December 1990, after a long battle with Parkinson's disease.

Sergeant MAURICE ROGERS

ANZIO, Italy 3 June 1944
He was 24 years old and serving in the 2nd Bn, Wiltshire Regiment when his carrier platoon was ordered to capture the final objective, supported by fire from the company and tanks. The platoon advanced through machine-gun and mortar fire until it reached the enemy's wire, just 70 yards from the objective, where it was checked by the fire of seven machine-guns, The men took what cover they could and returned fire. Rogers, without hesitation,

continued to advance alone, firing his Tommy gun. He got through the wire, ran across the minefield and accounted for two of the enemy posts with grenades and his Tommy gun. He was now 100 yards ahead of his platoon and 30 yards into the enemy position. He had drawn the fire of nearly all the enemy's machine-guns and thrown them into confusion. Inspired by his example, the platoon breached the wire and began the assault into the enemy position. Still alone, Rogers pushed deeper into the enemy position but while attempting to silence another machine-gun he was blown off his feet and wounded in the leg. Picking himself up and still firing, he ran on to the post, but was killed before he reached it.

Company Sergeant Major STANLEY HOLLIS
MONT FLEURY and CREPON, France
6 June 1944

He was 31 years old and serving in the 6th Bn, Green Howards (Alexandra, Princess of Wales's Own Yorkshire Regiment). After landing on Gold beach, his company pushed inland. Noticing that two pillboxes had been bypassed, he went with his company commander to deal with them; as they neared the first, they came under machine-gun fire. Hollis charged forward alone, firing his Sten gun into the slit, and then threw in a grenade, taking all but five of the occupants prisoner. Moving on to the next pillbox, he was gratified to receive the surrender of 26 Germans. Later his unit came up against a field gun position. Hollis led the attack on the gun, running forward and firing a Bren gun, putting the gun out of action and saving two of his men who were trapped.

He died on 8 February 1972.

Acting Sergeant HANSON TURNER
NINGTHOUKHONG, Burma
6/7 June 1944

He was 33 years old and serving in the 1st Bn, West Yorkshire Regiment (Prince of Wales's Own) when his platoon was forced to give ground. Turner at once reorganised his party and withdrew 40 yards. The Japanese made

determined and repeated attempts to dislodge them and a heavy fire was kept up on his men for 2 hours. All attacks were repelled and it was entirely due to his leadership that the position was held. It was now clear that the enemy were attempting to outflank his position. Determined to take the initiative, he went forward alone, armed with as many grenades as he could carry, and used them with devastating effect. When his supply ran out, he went back for more and returned to the offensive. In all he made five journeys to obtain further supplies of grenades and it was on the sixth occasion that he was killed while throwing a grenade.

Acting Captain MICHAEL ALLMAND
PIN HMI ROAD BRIDGE, Burma
11, 13 and 23 June 1944

He was 20 years old and serving in the Indian Armoured Corps, attached to the 3rd Bn, 6th Gurkha Rifles, Indian Army when his platoon came under very heavy machine-gun fire, forcing them to a halt with severe casualties. Allmand, however, charged on alone, throwing grenades into the enemy positions and killing three with his kukri. Inspired by his splendid example, the surviving men followed him and captured the objective. Now in command of the company, on 13 June he dashed 30 yards ahead of his men through marshy ground swept by machine-gun fire and personally killed a number of the enemy machine-gunners, and then led his men on to the high ground. In the final attack on the railway bridge on 23 June he moved forward alone, despite suffering from trench foot, through deep mud and shell-holes, to charge an enemy machine-gun nest. He was mortally wounded in this attack.

Rifleman GANJU LAMA (real name GYANTSO SHANGDERPA)
NINGTHOUKHONG, Burma
12 June 1944

He was 21 years old and serving in the 1st Bn, 7th Gurkha Rifles, Indian Army. His company was trying to stem the enemy's advance when it came under heavy machine-gun and tank fire. With complete disregard for his own safety, Ganju Lama took a PIAT gun and crawled forward. He succeeded in bringing the gun into action within 30 yards of the enemy tanks, knocking out two of them. Despite a broken wrist and serious wounds to his hands, he moved forward again and engaged the tank crews who were trying to escape. Not until he had accounted for all of them did he consent to having his wounds dressed.

His real name was Gyantso Shangderpa, but the clerk in the recruiting office wrote it down as Ganju, and the name stuck. He had little time for the niceties of military conduct: on his first day as batman to Major Roy Gribble he walked into his dug-out at 4am with a mess tin of tea and told the major to 'Get up!' There was no 'good morning' or 'Sir', but Gribble took to him at once.

Ganju Lama died on 30 June 2000.

Pilot Officer ANDREW MYNARSKI
CAMBRAI, France 12/13 June 1944

He was 27 years old and serving in 419 Squadron, RCAF when his Lancaster bomber was attacked by a nightfighter. Both port engines failed and fire broke out in the port wing and the rear of the fuselage. The captain ordered the crew to abandon the aircraft. Mynarski made his way to the escape hatch but then saw that the rear gunner was trapped in his turret. Without hesitation, he went through the flames in an attempt to reach him, but while doing so his clothing, including his parachute, caught fire. All his efforts to free the gunner were in vain. Eventually the gunner clearly indicated to him that there was nothing he could do and he should save himself. Reluctantly, he went back through the flames to the escape hatch, but before jumping he turned to the gunner, stood to attention and saluted. He was found by the French, but was so badly burned that he died from his injuries. The gunner had a miraculous escape when the bomber crashed, and subsequently testified that had Mynarski not attempted to save him, he could have left the aircraft in safety. He undoubtedly gave his life to help another man.

He was the first RCAF officer to be awarded the VC.

Corporal SEFANAIA SUKANAIVALU
BOUGAINVILLE, Solomon Islands 23 June 1944

He was 26 years old and serving in the 3rd Bn, Fijian Infantry Regiment, Fiji Military Forces when his platoon was ambushed. He crawled out twice to bring back two wounded men, then went out to try again. Despite machine-gun and mortar fire he got to another man. While returning, he was seriously wounded in the groin and thigh, leaving him unable to move his lower body. Several attempts were made to rescue him, but this only caused more casualties. He then called to his comrades, telling them not to try again as he was in too exposed a position. They replied that they would never leave him to fall into enemy hands. Realising his men would not withdraw as long as he was alive, and knowing that if they stayed many more men would be killed, he raised himself up in front of an enemy machine-gun and was riddled with bullets.

Rifleman TULBAHADUR PUN
MOGAUNG, Burma 23 June 1944

He was 21 years old and serving in the 3rd Bn, 6th Gurkha Rifles, Indian Army. His company was attacking the railway bridge when the enemy opened concentrated and sustained cross-fire from a position known as the Red House and a bunker 200 yards to the left of it. His company was pinned down and his section almost wiped out, only Pun, the CO and another man remaining. These three men charged forward but the CO was badly wounded. The other two continued the attack but when his comrade was wounded, Tulbahadur Pun seized the Bren gun, firing from the hip as he went, and continued the charge alone in the face of the most shattering concentration of machine-gun fire. He had to cross 30 yards of open ground, ankle deep in mud, to reach the Red House and close with the occupants. He killed three and put five to flight, capturing two machine-guns. He then gave supporting fire to the remainder of his platoon, enabling them to reach their objective.

He died on 20 April 2011.

Flight Lieutenant DAVID HORNELL
FAROES, Atlantic 24 June 1944
He was 34 years old and serving in 162 Squadron, RCAF when from his Catalina he sighted *U-1225* on the surface. He at once attacked, but was seen and the U-boat's anti-aircraft guns opened fire. Two large holes appeared in the starboard wing and oil began to pour from his starboard engine, which was on fire, as was the wing. Ignoring the enemy fire, he pressed home his attack with accuracy and determination; his depth charges straddled the submarine, which soon sank. The aircraft was now vibrating violently and very difficult to control, but he managed to land on the sea. After trial by fire came trial by water. There was only one four-man dinghy left serviceable so the crew took turns in the water. Two of the crew succumbed to exposure and by the time they were rescued they had been in the water for 24 hours. By this time Hornell was blind and completely exhausted and he died shortly after being picked up.

Acting Subadar NETRABAHADUR THAPA
BISHENPUR, Burma 25/26 June 1944
He was 28 years old and serving in the 2nd Bn, 5th Royal Gurkha Rifles, Indian Army when he was in command of a small isolated hill post known as 'Mortar Bluff'. This position was supported by 3-inch mortar fire from another post but was overlooked by the 'Water Piquet' post, which had been overrun by the enemy the previous night. A small relief party had made its way into the post by 18.30 hours. An hour later the enemy began to attack, firing a 75mm and a 37mm gun from Water Piquet. Shell after shell blasted into the position, and this barrage was followed by a determined attack by at least a company of Japanese infantry. A fierce fight ensued in which Netrabahadur Thapa's men held their ground due to his leadership. The enemy were driven back with heavy losses. During this attack he moved from post to post encouraging his young men, and tending the wounded. Under cover of night the enemy moved around to the jungle, from which they launched their next attack. Still in great strength and as determined as before, the

Japanese poured out from the jungle across the short space of open ground to the picket defences under cover from small arms and field guns. For a short time the Gurkhas held their ground, but when both their machine-guns jammed at the same time, greatly reducing their firepower, the enemy forced an entrance and overran two sections, killing or wounding most of the men. Having no reserve, Netrabahadur Thapa went forward himself and stemmed any further advance with grenades. With more than half his men injured, his ammunition stocks low and part of his perimeter occupied, he would have been justified in withdrawing, but in his next report to his CO he stated that he intended to hold on and asked for more ammunition and men. Not another yard was gained by the enemy, despite their best efforts. At 04.00 hours a section of eight men with grenades and ammunition came to his aid but all of them became casualties. Undismayed, he went out and retrieved the fresh ammunition, and then led his HQ platoon on the offensive with grenades and kukris until he was killed. His body was found the next day, kukri in hand and a dead Japanese soldier by his side.

Naik AGANSING RAI
BISHENPUR, Burma 26 June 1944
He was 24 years old and serving in the 2nd Bn, 5th Royal Gurkha Rifles, Indian Army. The enemy had overrun two posts, known as 'Water Piquet' and 'Mortar Bluff', and Rai's company was ordered to retake these positions. However, on reaching a false crest they were pinned down by heavy and accurate machine-gun fire from 'Mortar Bluff', and a 37mm gun firing from the jungle. Appreciating that any delay would only result in more casualties, Rai led his section forward under very heavy fire, and charged at 'Mortar Bluff', firing as he went and killing three of the machine-gun crew. Inspired by this act, the rest of the section surged forward and routed the garrison. This position now came under fire from the 37mm gun and from 'Water Piquet'. Again Rai advanced, this time on the 37mm gun, with his section following, but only four men reached the gun. Rai killed three of the crew himself.

While the rest of his platoon was forming up for the final assault on 'Water Piquet', heavy machine-gun fire was opened on them from an isolated bunker and once again Rai advanced alone, grenade in one hand and Tommy gun in the other. Through heavy fire, he reached the bunker and killed all of the occupants. The enemy were now completely demoralised by his actions and fled before the onslaught on 'Water Piquet'.

Agansing Rai also served in the Congo. He died on 27 May 2000.

Temporary Major FRANK BLAKER
TAUNGHI, Burma 9 July 1944

He was 24 years old and serving in the Highland Light Infantry, attached to the 3rd Bn, 9th Gurkha Rifles, Indian Army when his company was ordered to make an encircling movement across unknown ground, through dense jungle, to attack an enemy position on the summit of a hill. As he got his company into position, it came under fire from three machine-guns and the advance was halted. Blaker then advanced ahead of his men through very heavy fire, and in spite of a severe arm wound he located the guns and charged them single-handedly, but was hit by a burst of fire to the body. He continued to cheer his men on while lying on the ground. His fearless courage so inspired the men of his company that they captured the position while the enemy fled into the jungle.

He died from his wound while being evacuated. He was known as 'Blanket Sahib' by his men, Peter by his family and Jim by his fellow officers.

Naik YESHWANT GHADGE
UPPER TIBER VALLEY, Italy
10 July 1944

He was 22 years old and serving in the 5th Maratha Light Infantry, Indian Army when his rifle section came under heavy machine-gun fire at close range which killed or wounded all except the commander. Without hesitation, Ghadge rushed the gun position, first throwing a grenade which knocked out the gun and gunner, and then shooting one of the crew.

Finally, having no time to change his magazine, he clubbed to death the two remaining crew members. He fell mortally wounded, shot by an enemy sniper.

Flying Officer JOHN CRUICKSHANK
North Atlantic 17/18 July 1944

He was 24 years old and serving in 210 Squadron, RAF. When a U-boat was sighted on the surface, he at once turned to the attack. In the face of heavy anti-aircraft fire he manoeuvred into position and attacked, but his depth charges failed to release. He was well aware that the failure of his first attack had lost him the advantage of surprise. Nevertheless, he climbed and turned to come in for a second attack. This time the aircraft was met by intense fire and was repeatedly hit, the bomb aimer being killed, and the co-pilot and two other crew wounded. Cruickshank himself was wounded 72 times, receiving two serious wounds to his lungs and ten penetrating wounds to his lower limbs. His Catalina was badly damaged and filled with smoke, but he pressed home his attack and released the depth charges himself, straddling the *U-347* and sinking her. He then collapsed and the co-pilot took over. Recovering shortly afterwards, Cruickshank insisted on resuming command, despite his wounds, until he was satisfied that the aircraft was under control, that a course had been set for base and that all the necessary signals had been sent out. Only then did he have his wounds dressed. He refused morphia in case it prevented him from carrying on. During the return journey he lapsed into unconsciousness several times. Each time, when he came to, his first thoughts were for the safety of his aircraft and crew. The damaged aircraft eventually reached its base, but it was clear that landing would be a hazardous task for the wounded and less experienced co-pilot. Although he was only able to breathe with great difficulty, Cruickshank insisted on being carried forward and propped up in the co-pilot's seat, in spite of the pain this caused him. For an hour he refused to bring the aircraft down until the conditions of light and sea made it possible without undue risk. With his assistance the aircraft was landed safely on the water. He then directed the taxiing and beaching of the Catalina. When the medical officer went on board, Cruickshank collapsed and had to be given a blood transfusion before he could be taken to hospital.

He said years later: 'When they told me that I was to get the VC it was unbelievable. Decorations didn't enter my head. The citation said "showed great courage" and all that nonsense, but a lot of people would have done that in the same circumstances.' At the time of going to press, he is one of the 10 surviving VC holders.

Acting Squadron Leader IAN BAZALGETTE
TROSSY ST MAXIMIN, France
4 August 1944

He was 25 years old and serving in 635 Squadron, RAFVR. He was the master-bomber of a Pathfinder squadron when, on nearing the target, his Lancaster bomber came under heavy anti-aircraft fire. Both starboard engines were put out of action and fire broke out in the fuselage. The bomb aimer and mid-upper gunner were also badly wounded. Despite the appalling conditions in his burning aircraft, he pressed on to his target, marking and bombing it accurately. That the attack was successful was due entirely to his magnificent effort. The aircraft then went into a dive and only through his expert airmanship did he regain control, but then the port inner engine failed. He ordered the unwounded crew to bale out, but refused to do so himself and attempted to land the burning aircraft in a field. Upon landing, however, it exploded, killing Bazalgette and the two wounded crew members who were still aboard.

Corporal SIDNEY BATES
SOURDEVAL, France 6 August 1944

He was 23 years old and serving in the Royal Norfolk Regiment when his unit was heavily attacked by the 10th SS Panzer Division. The attack developed quickly and 60 of the enemy were soon on top of his position. He seized a Bren gun and charged forward through a hail of bullets, firing from the hip. He was almost immediately wounded and fell to the ground, but recovered. Continuing his advance, spraying bullets as he went, he was wounded again. However, he staggered once more to his feet and moved forward again, still firing. The enemy started to withdraw but at this moment he was hit by a mortar blast. Falling to the ground, he kept firing until his strength failed. This was not, however, until the enemy had withdrawn and the situation had been restored. He died shortly afterwards.

Captain DAVID JAMIESON
GRIMBOSQ, France 7/8 August 1944

He was 23 years old and serving in the Royal Norfolk Regiment. His company had established a bridgehead over the Orne river, and the enemy made seven counter-attacks on this position, during which he was wounded. But throughout 36 hours of bitter and close fighting, Jamieson's company didn't give in. These attacks included Tiger and Panther tanks that shot up the tanks supporting the Norfolks. Jamieson at one point mounted a British tank under enemy fire to talk to the commander. He dismissed it as anything heroic, saying that he had to as the telephone link didn't work. The image of him riding a tank while under attack from enemy tanks was immortalised in a painting.

He died on 5 May 2001.

Lieutenant TASKER WATKINS
BARFOUR, France 16 August 1944

He was 26 years old and serving in the 1/5th Bn, Welch Regiment when his company had to cross open cornfields in which booby traps had been placed. The company came under heavy machine-gun fire from posts within the cornfield and from an 88mm anti-tank gun, causing many casualties and halting the advance. Watkins, as the only officer left, placed himself at the head of his men and charged two posts in succession, personally killing or wounding the occupants with his Sten gun. As he reached an anti-tank gun his Sten gun jammed, so he threw it at the German gunner and shot him with his pistol before he could recover. His company was

The Complete Victoria Cross

now down to only 30 men but he led a bayonet charge against 50 Germans, practically wiping them out. It was now dusk and the battalion was ordered to withdraw but these orders did not reach Watkins' company as the wireless had been destroyed. Finding themselves alone and surrounded, Watkins decided to rejoin his battalion by passing round the flank of the enemy position through which he had advanced. He ordered his men to scatter and personally charged an enemy machine-gun post, silencing it. He then led the remnants of his company back to his battalion.

His VC action was in fact his first combat action. Watkins was Deputy President of the VC and GC Association from 2002 until 2007.

He died on 9 September 2007.

Major DAVID CURRIE

FALAISE, France 18–20 August 1944

He was 32 years old and commanding a battle group of tanks from the South Alberta Regiment, and infantry and artillery from the Argyll & Sutherland Highlanders of Canada when he was ordered to cut off one of the Germans' main escape routes out of the Falaise pocket, where the remnants of two German armies were trapped. He led an attack on the village of St Lambert-sur-Dives and consolidated a position halfway inside. He repulsed repeated attacks over the next day and a half. Despite heavy losses, his battle group destroyed 7 tanks, 12 88mm guns and 40 other vehicles, and killed 300 men, wounded 500 and captured 1,100. He personally used a rifle to deal with enemy snipers.

Currie's is the only VC to be awarded to a Canadian for the Normandy campaign and the only one ever awarded to the Royal Canadian Armoured Corps. A photo, held by the National Archives of Canada, shows Major Currie accepting the surrender of German troops at St Lambert-sur-Dives. Uniquely, this photo depicts some of the actions for which he was awarded the VC. Currie was Vice-Chairman (Overseas) of the VC and GC Association from 1968 to 1986. He died from a heart attack on 24 June 1986. The Lieutenant Col. D.V. Currie VC Armoury is named in his honour.

Lieutenant GERARD NORTON

MONTE GIDOLFO, Italy 31 August 1944

He was 28 years old and serving in the Kaffrarian Rifles, SAF when his platoon was pinned down by heavy fire. On his own initiative and with complete disregard for his own safety, he advanced alone and attacked the first machine-gun emplacement, killing the crew of three. He then went on to the second position which contained two more machine-guns and 15 men; he took out both machine-guns, and killed or took prisoner the remainder. Throughout these attacks he was under continuous fire from a self-propelled gun. While still under fire from this SPG, he went on to clear a house, taking several prisoners and putting many more men to flight. Although wounded and weak from loss of blood, he continued to lead his men up the valley to capture the remaining enemy positions.

He is one of only four South Africans to be awarded the VC in the Second World War, the others being Sergeant Quentin Smythe, Acting Major Edwin Swales and Squadron Leader John Nettleton.

Norton died on 29 October 2004.

Lieutenant JOHN GRAYBURN

ARNHEM, Holland 17–20 September 1944

He was 26 years old and serving in the Parachute Regiment (Army Air Corps) when he and his platoon managed to get to the main bridge. He was ordered to lead an attack across the bridge to capture the southern end, but was met by a hail of fire from two 20mm flank guns and an armoured car. Almost at once he was wounded in the shoulder but although there was no cover he pressed forward with great dash and determination until heavy casualties forced him to withdraw. Grayburn directed the withdrawal personally and was himself the last man to leave. His men were ordered to occupy a house which was vital to the defence of the bridge. Throughout the 18th the enemy made ceaseless attacks with infantry, mortars, machine-guns, tanks and SPGs. The building was very exposed and difficult to defend and the fact that it did not fall to the Germans was entirely due to his inspiring leadership. He constantly exposed himself to the enemy while moving about his platoon, and seemed oblivious to danger.

On the 19th the enemy renewed the attack with increased intensity but all attacks were repulsed until the house was set on fire and had to be abandoned. He then took command of elements of all arms, including the remainder of his company. He spent the night organising a defensive position to cover the approach to the bridge. On 20 September he extended his defences by a series of fighting patrols preventing the enemy gaining access to the houses near the bridge. This forced them to bring up tanks which put his men under such heavy fire that he was compelled to move further north. He was again wounded, this time in the back, but he refused to be evacuated. Finally, when an enemy tank approached so close that his position became untenable, he stood up and personally directed the withdrawal to the main defensive perimeter to which he had been ordered. He was killed that night.

Rifleman SHERBAHADUR THAPA
SAN MARINO, Italy
18/19 September 1944
He was 22 years old and serving in the 1st Bn, 9th Gurkha Rifles when his battalion was fighting its way forward against bitter German opposition from prepared positions dominating the river valley. Together with his section commander, he charged an enemy post, killing a machine gunner and putting the rest to flight. Almost immediately another party of Germans attacked the two men, and the section commander was badly wounded by a grenade. Without hesitation, Sherbahadur Thapa rushed at the attackers and fired his Bren gun into them. He then lay in the open under a hail of bullets, firing his gun at the enemy. In this manner he silenced several machine-guns and checked a number of Germans who were trying to infiltrate the ridge. After 2 hours both forward companies had exhausted their ammunition and as they were by then practically surrounded, they were ordered to withdraw. Sherbahadur Thapa covered the withdrawal as they crossed the

open ground to a position in the rear and he remained alone until his ammunition ran out. Then he dashed forward under accurate fire and rescued two wounded men lying between him and the advancing Germans. While returning the second time he was killed by a hail of bullets.

Captain LIONEL QUERIPEL
ARNHEM, Holland 19 September 1944
He was 24 years old and serving in the Royal Sussex Regiment, attached to 10th Parachute Bn, when he was acting as commander of a company of men from three battalions. As they advanced along a main road on an embankment towards Arnhem they came under continuous machine-gun fire. At one point the fire became so heavy that the company was split on either side of the road and suffered considerable casualties. Queripel immediately reorganised his men, crossing and recrossing the road under heavy fire from a strongpoint consisting of a captured British anti-tank gun and two machine-guns. While carrying a wounded sergeant to the aid post he was himself wounded in the face. Having reorganised his force, he personally led a party of men against the strongpoint that was holding up the advance. Despite the extremely heavy fire directed at him, he succeeded in killing the machine-gun crews and recapturing the anti-tank gun, thus enabling the advance to continue. Later Queripel was ordered to defend some woodland near the Wolfheze level crossing, which was vital to the British advance. By this time he had received further wounds to both arms. Cut off with a small party of men, he took up position in a ditch. Disregarding his wounds and the heavy mortar and machine-gun fire, he continued to inspire his men to resist with grenades, pistols and the few remaining rifles with ammunition. On at least one occasion he picked up a German grenade which had landed in the ditch and threw it back. As the enemy pressure increased, Queripel decided that it was impossible to hold his position any longer and ordered the remaining men to withdraw. Despite their protests, he insisted on covering the with-

The Complete Victoria Cross

drawal himself with only his pistol and a few grenades. He was never seen alive again.

Flight Lieutenant DAVID LORD
ARNHEM, Holland 19 September 1944
He was 30 years old and serving in 271 Squadron, RAF when the starboard wing of his C-47 Dakota was twice hit by anti-aircraft fire, setting the engine on fire. He would have been justified in turning back, but on learning that none of his crew was injured and that the drop zone was only 3 minutes away, he decided to complete his mission as he knew the men on the ground were in dire need of the supplies his aircraft was carrying. By now the starboard engine was burning furiously. He came down to 900 feet and on reaching the drop zone he kept his aircraft on a straight and level course while dropping supplies. At the end of the run he was told that two containers remained on board. Although he must have known that his starboard wing could fail at any time, he duly made a second run. This took 8 minutes in all and the Dakota was under anti-aircraft fire for the whole time. Once the second run was completed, he ordered his crew to bale out. A few seconds later the wing collapsed and the aircraft fell to the ground in flames. The only survivor was Pilot Officer Harry King, who was taken prisoner and only told his story of the incident after the war. This is the only VC awarded to a member of Transport Command.

Temporary Major ROBERT CAIN
ARNHEM, Holland
19–25 September 1944
He was 35 years old and serving in the Royal Northumberland Fusiliers, attached to the South Staffordshire Regiment, 1st Airborne Division, when his company was cut off from the rest of his battalion and during the next six days was closely engaged with enemy tanks, SPGs and infantry. The Germans made repeated attempts to infiltrate into the company position, and had they succeeded the safety of the whole of the airborne forces would have been jeopardised. Due to his outstanding leadership, he was to a large extent personally responsible for saving a vital sector from

falling into enemy hands. On the 20th a tank approached his company position and Cain went out alone to deal with it, armed only with a PIAT. Taking up position he held his fire until the tank was only 20 yards away. When he opened fire the tank halted and turned its guns on him, shooting away the corner of the house near where he was lying. Although wounded by machine-gun fire and hit by falling masonry, he continued to fire until he had scored several hits, immobilising the tank, and then supervised the bringing up of a 75mm howitzer which completely destroyed it. Only then did he allow his wounds to be dressed. The next morning he drove off three more tanks by use of the PIAT, on each occasion leaving cover and taking up a position in the open with complete disregard for his personal safety. During the following days he was everywhere that danger threatened, moving among his men and encouraging them to hold out by his fearless example. He refused rest or medical aid in spite of his many wounds, including a perforated eardrum. On the 25th the enemy attacked with infantry and flame-throwers, but by this time the last PIAT had been put out of action. Cain armed himself with a 2-inch mortar, and by skilful use of this weapon and his daring leadership of his few remaining men, he completely demoralised the enemy, who, after a 3-hour engagement, withdrew in disorder.

He died from cancer on 2 May 1974. His son-in-law is the TV presenter Jeremy Clarkson.

Lance Sergeant JOHN BASKEYFIELD
ARNHEM, Holland 20 September 1944
He was 21 years old and serving in the 2nd Bn, South Staffordshire Regiment at Oosterbeek near Arnhem when his 6-pounder anti-tank gun came under attack from tanks and self-propelled guns. He allowed the tanks to come within 100 yards before opening fire, and duly knocked out three tanks. He was badly wounded in the leg and the rest of his crew were either killed or wounded, but he refused to go to the first aid post. After a brief respite, he came under a heavy artillery and tank attack but he did not cower. He crawled to another

gun, which he manned alone. firing three rounds and knocking out an SPG. He was killed by supporting enemy tank fire.

In 1981 Dutch workmen found a body at the site of his VC action, which was buried as 'unknown'.

Corporal JOHN HARPER
DEPOT DE MENDICITE, ANTWERP, Belgium 29 September 1944

He was 28 years old and serving in the 4th (Hallamshire) Bn, York and Lancaster Regiment. During an attack on a position surrounded by an earth dyke and a waterway, he led his section across 300 yards of open ground under a hail of fire from small arms and mortars. Leading his men straight up to the dyke, he killed or captured the enemy holding the near side. His platoon commander was wounded and he took over. He climbed to the top of the dyke alone and threw grenades at the enemy on the far side, forcing them to retire. He shot several and took four prisoners as they fled. Then he again crossed the dyke to find out whether it was possible for his platoon to cross the waterway, but found it was too deep. Receiving orders to establish his platoon on the enemy side of the dyke, he crossed it for the third time and found some German weapon pits. Providing covering fire, he urged his men to climb the dyke and cross the open ground. Subsequently finding a ford, he went back to direct his company commander to the crossing-point but was fatally wounded.

Private RICHARD BURTON
MONTE CECO, Italy 8 October 1944

He was 21 years old and serving in the 1st Bn, Duke of Wellington's (West Riding) Regiment when an attack on a vital position was held up by machine-gun fire. Burton rushed forward and engaged the first machine-gun position with his Tommy gun, killing the crew of three. When held up again by fire from two machine-guns, he again showed complete disregard for his personal safety and dashed forward, firing his Tommy gun until his ammunition was exhausted. Then he picked up a Bren gun and killed the crews of both machine-gun posts.

The enemy immediately counter-attacked, but although most of his comrades were killed or wounded, Burton once again dashed forward, firing his Bren gun with such accuracy that the enemy retired, leaving the position firmly in British hands. When another counter-attack was made by the enemy on an adjoining platoon, he brought such accurate fire to bear on them that this attack was also beaten back.

He died on 11 July 1993.

Acting Sergeant GEORGE EARDLEY
OVERLOON, Holland 16 October 1944

He was 32 years old and serving in the 4th Bn, King's Shropshire Light Infantry when strong opposition was met from well-sited machine-gun posts. The platoon sent forward to clear the way was halted 80 yards from its objective by machine-gun fire. This fire was so heavy that it appeared impossible for anyone to remain unscathed by it. Eardley spotted one of the posts and moved forward, firing his Sten gun, and then killed the occupants with a grenade. A second machine-gun opened fire and he at once charged 30 yards and silenced it. The attack was continued but was soon held up again by another machine-gun, and the section sent in to deal with it was beaten back. Ordering his section to take cover, Eardley crawled forward alone and destroyed the gun with a grenade.

He died on 11 September 1991.

Private ERNEST 'SMOKEY' SMITH
SAVIO RIVER, Italy 21/22 October 1944

He was 30 years old and serving in the Seaforth Highlanders of Canada, CIC when his unit was in the spearhead of the attack. In torrential rain they crossed the river and captured their objectives. The rain had caused the river to rise 6 feet and the soft banks made it impossible to bridge it and bring over tanks or guns. As the right forward company was consolidating the position it was suddenly attacked by two SPGs and 30 infantry, and the situation appeared hopeless. Under heavy fire, Smith led his PIAT team of two men across an open field to a position from which the PIAT could best be used. Leaving one man with the weapon, he crossed the road with another man and got another PIAT. Almost immediately an enemy tank came down the road firing its machine-guns along the line of ditches. His comrade was wounded, but at a range of just 30 feet, and exposed to the enemy, Smith fired at the tank, putting it out of action. Ten German infantrymen jumped off the back and charged him. Without hesitation he moved out on to the road and opened fire on them at point-blank range, killing four and forcing the rest back. Another tank then opened fire and more infantry closed in on him. He steadfastly held his position, protecting his wounded comrade and fighting the enemy until they finally with-drew in disorder. Yet another tank then swept the area with fire from long range. Smith, still showing utter contempt for the enemy fire, helped his wounded comrade to cover and obtained aid for him. He then returned to his position beside the road to await further attacks. No more attacks came and the bridge-head was consolidated.

An independent and strong-willed man who frequently questioned authority, Smith had been promoted to corporal nine times and demoted nine times, before his VC action. He re-enlisted for the Korean War but was consid-ered too valuable an icon to risk in combat.

He died on 3 August 2005.

Acting Subadar RAM SARUP SINGH
KENNEDY PEAK, TIDDIM, Burma
25 October 1944

He was 25 years old and serving in the 2nd Bn, 1st Punjab Regiment, Indian Army when his section and another section were ordered to attack the flank of an enemy position, which was well defended with machine-guns sited in bunkers. The attack was so sudden that the enemy were bewildered and fled from their positions. He was wounded in both legs but took no notice of his wounds. As they were consolidating the position, the enemy counter-attacked in three waves. It seemed that the position would be overrun, but Ram Sarup Singh got a machine-gun into position and then led a charge into the advancing enemy, bayoneting four himself. Although badly

wounded in the thigh, he again went for the enemy shouting encouragement to his men. He bayoneted one and shot another, but was mortally wounded by a burst of machine-gun fire to the neck and chest.

Rifleman THAMAN GURUNG
MONTE SAN BARTOLO, Italy
10 November 1944

He was 20 years old and serving in the 1st Bn, 5th Royal Gurkha Rifles, Indian Army. Acting as a scout, he was sent on a reconnaissance mission with another man, and they skilfully reached the German position undetected. Seeing that the enemy were preparing to fire on the leading section, and knowing they would suffer heavy casualties, Thaman Gurung leapt to his feet and charged. Completely taken by surprise, the Germans surrendered without firing a shot. Then he crept forward to the summit of the position, from where he could see a party of well-dug-in Germans preparing to throw grenades at the leading section. He moved across the summit and fired on them with his Tommy gun, allowing the section to reach the summit without further loss. When the platoon was ordered to withdraw due to heavy fire, Gurung covered the withdrawal with bursts of fire from his Tommy gun until the ammunition ran out. Then he threw the two grenades he had with him and went back for more, throwing them on his return to the summit and enabling all but the leading section to withdraw. Then he seized a Bren gun, stood up on the summit and fired on the enemy posi-tions, shouting to the remaining section to withdraw. It was not until he had emptied two magazines and the remaining section was well on its way down the slope that he was killed.

Sepoy BHANDARI (aka BANDARI) RAM
EAST MAYU, ARAKAN, Burma
22 November 1944

He was 25 years old and serving in the 16th Bn, 10th Baluch Regiment, Indian Army when his platoon was climbing a precipitous slope. As they neared the top they came under heavy machine-gun fire from a strongly held bunker position. Bhandari Ram was wounded in the shoulder and leg. The platoon was now pinned down, and he crawled forward to within 15 yards of a machine-gun post. The enemy threw grenades at him, seriously wounding him in the face and chest. Undeterred, he crawled to within 5 yards and threw a grenade, killing three crew. Inspired by his example, the platoon rushed forward and captured the position. It was only then that he allowed his wounds to be dressed.

In a 1999 interview, he explained his action thus: 'It was all to do with wanting to please [the] commanding officer by doing a good job.' He died on 19 May 2002.

Temporary Captain JOHN BRUNT
FAENZA, Italy 9 December 1944
He was 22 years old and serving in the Sherwood Foresters, Nottinghamshire and Derbyshire Regiment, attached to the 6th Bn, Lincolnshire Regiment, when his platoon was holding a vital sector of the line. At dawn the German 90th Panzer-Grenadier Division attacked with tanks and infantry, destroying the house occupied by his platoon. He rallied and moved his men to another position, continuing to hold the enemy infantry, although outnumbered at least 3 to 1. He personally killed about 14 of the enemy with a Bren gun. On receiving an order to withdraw, he remained to give covering fire. When his Bren gun ran out of ammunition, he used a PIAT and then a 2-inch mortar. This aggressive defence caused the enemy to pause, so he took a party back to his previous position and, although engaged by small-arms fire, he managed to carry away the wounded who had been left behind. When another attack was put in by the enemy, he went around his forward positions rallying his men. Then he leapt on to a Sherman tank and ordered the commander to drive from one position to another while he stood on the turret, directing their fire at the advancing enemy, under a hail of bullets. When small parties of the enemy armed with anti-tank weapons tried to approach around the flank he jumped off, seized a Bren gun and stalked them, killing some and forcing the rest to withdraw.

Brunt was killed in action the next day. The John Brunt VC pub was named in his honour, and St Andrew's Church has a VC window dedicated to him. Both are at Paddock Wood, Kent.

Havildar UMRAO SINGH
KALADAN VALLEY, Burma
15/16 December 1944
He was 24 years old and serving in the 30th Mountain Regiment, Indian Army when his battery was in an advanced position. After enduring a 90-minute sustained bombardment from the Japanese, his position was attacked by at least two companies of Japanese infantry. He used a Bren gun and also directed the rifle fire of his gunners to hold off the assault, during which he was wounded by grenades. A second wave of attackers killed all but Singh and two of his men, but were also beaten off. The three men had only a few bullets remaining and these were rapidly used in the initial stages of the third attack. Undaunted, Singh picked up a 'gun bearer' and used it as a weapon in hand-to-hand fighting. He was seen to strike down three enemy infantrymen before succumbing to a rain of blows.

Some 6 hours later, after a counter-attack, he was found alive but unconscious near his gun. He was almost unrecognisable, having suffered a head injury, but was still clutching his gun bearer. Ten Japanese soldiers lay dead nearby. His field gun was back in action later that day.

During the celebrations for the 50th anniversary of VE-Day in London in 1995, he was almost turned away from the VIP tent because his name was not on the right list, but Brigadier Tom Longland, who organised the event, saw his VC and gave orders to admit him. After the event, Singh complained to the Prime Minister John Major about the meagre pension of £100 per year paid to the then ten living Indian VC holders. The amount had been fixed since 1959, but John Major subsequently arranged for the pension to be raised to £1,000 per year. In spite of personal hardship and although he received a number of substantial offers, Singh refused to sell his medal during his lifetime, saying that selling it would 'stain the honour of those who fell in battle'. It is therefore very sad to see that his medal is now in private hands.

He died of prostate cancer on 21 November 2005.

Squadron Leader ROBERT PALMER
COLOGNE, Germany 23 December 1944
He was 24 years old and serving in 109 Squadron, RAFVR when he led a formation of Lancaster bombers in a daylight raid. His task was to mark the target, but he came under heavy anti-aircraft fire some minutes before reaching it. Two engines were set on fire and smoke filled the nose and bomb bay. Enemy fighters now attacked in force, but he was determined to complete the run and provide an accurate aiming point for the other bombers. Immense effort was needed to keep the aircraft on a straight course. Nevertheless he made a perfect approach and his bombs hit the target. His aircraft was last seen spiralling to earth in flames.

1945

Flight Sergeant GEORGE THOMPSON
DORTMUND-EMS CANAL, Germany 1 January 1945
He was 24 years old and serving in 9 Squadron, RAFVR when after dropping bombs from his Lancaster bomber the aircraft was hit by heavy anti-aircraft fire. Fire broke out and smoke filled the fuselage, then the nose was hit and the inrush of air cleared the smoke, revealing a scene of utter devastation. Most of the nose compartment had been shot away, gaping holes had been torn in the canopy above the pilot's head, the intercom wiring was cut, there was a large hole in the floor and one engine was on fire. Thompson then saw that the mid-upper turret gunner was unconscious and his turret on fire. Without hesitation he went down the fuselage through the fire and pulled the man out; carrying him away from the flames, he put out the gunner's burning clothes

with his bare hands, being burned himself on the face, hands and legs. Then he noticed that the rear gun turret was also on fire. Despite his own injuries he went to help the rear gunner, whose clothes were on fire. With great difficulty he extricated the helpless gunner and carried him clear, again using his bare hands to put out the flames. By now he was almost completely exhausted but felt it was his duty to report the fate of the crew to the captain. He made the perilous journey back through the burning fuselage, clinging to the sides to get across the hole in the floor. The flow of cold air caused him great pain and frostbite. So pitiful was his condition that the captain failed to recognise him. He was given such medical aid as was possible until a crash landing was made 40 minutes later. Only one of the gunners survived

Thompson died from his wounds on 23 January 1945.

Fusilier DENNIS DONNINI
between the ROERS and MAAS RIVERS, Germany 18 January 1945
He was 19 years old and serving in the 4/5th Bn, Royal Scots Fusiliers when his platoon was ordered to attack the village of Stein. As they left their trench they came under heavy fire from a house and Donnini was hit in the head. After coming round, he charged 30 yards down the open road and hurled a grenade though the nearest window, whereupon the enemy fled, pursued by Donnini and the survivors of his platoon. Under heavy fire at 70 yards' range he crossed an open space and reached the cover of a wooden barn. Just 30 yards from the enemy, he went into the open again under close-range fire and carried one of his wounded companions back to the barn. Taking a Bren gun, he went out yet again. He was wounded a second time but recovered and went on firing until a third bullet hit one of his grenades, which exploded, killing him. His superb bravery and self-sacrifice drew the enemy's fire away from his platoon and on to himself, thus allowing his comrades to overcome an enemy twice their own number.

Lance Naik SHER SHAH
KYEYEBYIN, Burma 19/20 January 1945
He was 27 years old and serving in the 7th Bn, 16th Punjab Regiment, Indian Army. He was in command of the left forward section of his platoon when at 19.30 hours an enemy platoon attacked his position. Realising that the enemy would overrun and destroy his section, he crawled forward alone and fired into the rear of the Japanese, breaking up their attack. He killed the platoon commander and six men, and after their withdrawal he crawled back to his post. At 00.15 hours the Japanese troops, now reinforced with a company, started to form up for another attack. He heard their officers giving orders and bayonets being fixed prior to the assault. Again he crawled forward alone, until he could see the officers and men grouped together. He fired into this group at close range and they ran away in disorder. While on his way back he was hit by a mortar bomb, which shattered his right leg. Despite this, he made it back to his section and propped himself against the side of a trench, from where he continued firing and encouraging his men. When asked if he was hurt, he replied that it was only slight. Some time afterwards it was discovered that his leg was missing. The Japanese again started forming up for another attack. In spite of his severe wounds and considerable loss of blood, he once again crawled forward, firing into them at point-blank range. He continued firing until the attack was broken up, when he was shot in the head, an injury from which he subsequently died. In all 23 dead and 4 wounded men, including an officer, were found at daybreak immediately in front of his position. His indomitable courage undoubtedly saved his platoon from being overrun, and was the deciding factor in defeating the Japanese attacks.

The 7/16th Punjab Regiment, now part of the Pakistan Army, is proudly known as the 'Sher Shah Battalion'.

Lance Corporal HENRY HARDEN
BRACHTERBEEK, Holland
23 January 1945
He was 33 years old and serving in the Royal

Army Medical Corps, attached to 45 Royal Marine Commando, when he ran across 100 yards of open ground under a hail of bullets to get to some wounded men. With great coolness he remained in the open and tended their wounds. He carried one back to safety, being wounded himself. He was ordered not to go out again, but he insisted on going forward. With a volunteer stretcher party he succeeded in bringing back another badly wounded man. He then went out again with the stretcher-bearers, and had started back with a wounded man when he was hit and killed.

He is the only member of the RAMC to be awarded the VC during the Second World War.

Lieutenant GEORGE KNOWLAND
KANGAW, Burma 31 January 1945
He was 32 years old and serving in the Royal Norfolk Regiment, attached to 1 Commando, when he was commanding the forward platoon of 24 men, positioned on a hilltop. His platoon was heavily shelled and then repeatedly attacked, yet he moved about his men keeping them alert and encouraging them. When the enemy, some 300 strong, attacked they concentrated all their efforts on his platoon, but in spite of the ferocity of the fighting he continued to move about distributing ammunition. He fired his rifle and threw grenades, often from exposed positions. Later, when one of his Bren gun crew had been wounded, he manned the gun himself, standing up and firing at a range of just 10 yards and successfully keeping the enemy back so a medical orderly could remove the wounded men behind him. When a new attack came in he manned a 2-inch mortar and stood up firing it from the hip, killing six of the enemy with his first bomb. He held his position until mortally wounded. Such was his inspiration that although 14 of his 24 men became casualties, and six of his positions were overrun, his men held on for 12 hours until reinforcements arrived.

Jemadar PRAKASH SINGH
KANLAN YWATHIT Burma
16/17 February 1945
He was 31 years old and serving in the 4/13th

Frontier Force Rifles, Indian Army when his platoon was attacked by overwhelming numbers of the enemy, supported by artillery, mortars and machine-guns. He was wounded in both ankles early in the attack, so his company commander relieved him of command and brought him back to company HQ. When his second-in-command was also wounded, Prakash Singh crawled back to his platoon and again took command. He was propped up by his batman, who had also been wounded, and started firing a 2-inch mortar. He was shouting encouragement to his men and directing the fire of his platoon. Having fired off all his mortar ammunition, he crawled around collecting ammunition from the dead and wounded, and this he distributed himself. As one section of his platoon had all became casualties, he took over their Bren gun and held the sector alone until reinforcements were rushed forward by the company commander. He fired his Bren gun from a position in the open as he was unable to stand in the trenches. He was again wounded in both legs, above the knees. In spite of his pain he continued firing his gun and dragging himself from one section to another by the use of his hands, as his legs were now completely smashed. At this time he continued to encourage and direct his men, regrouping them around him so that they held up a fierce Japanese charge. Being wounded for the third time, again in the leg, he was now unable to move, but he was lying on his side facing the enemy and directing the action of his men. Although it was obvious he was dying, he shouted out the Dogra war cry, which was taken up by the whole company. His example and leadership so inspired the company that the enemy were finally driven off, but Singh was wounded again, this time in the chest by a grenade. He died a few minutes later, after telling his company commander not to worry about him for he could look after himself.

Acting Major EDWIN SWALES
PFORZHEIM, Germany 23 February 1945
He was 29 years old and serving in 582 Squadron, RAF. He was flying as the master-bomber for a force of 367 Lancasters and 13 Mosquitos. Soon after he reached the target area he was engaged by an enemy Me110 (possibly flown by Hauptmann Gerhard Freidrich) and one of his engines was put out of action. His rear guns also failed, leaving his crippled aircraft easy prey to further attacks. Unperturbed, he carried on with his task, clearly and precisely issuing aiming instructions to the main force. Meanwhile he was attacked again by the same fighter, and a second engine was put out of action. Almost defenceless, he stayed over the target area issuing his aiming instructions until he was satisfied that the attack had achieved its purpose. It is known that 83 per cent of the target was destroyed.

His aircraft was badly damaged, and its speed so reduced that it was difficult to keep it in the air. The blind-flying instruments were no longer working. Nevertheless, determined to prevent his aircraft and crew from falling into enemy hands, he set course for home. The aircraft became more and more difficult to control, and was losing height steadily, but finally made it back to friendly territory. Realising that the situation was desperate, he ordered his crew to bale out. It required all his exertion and skill to keep the aircraft steady while each of his crew moved into position and parachuted to safety. Hardly had the last man jumped when the aircraft plunged to earth. Swales was found dead at the controls. He did his duty to the last, giving his life so that his comrades might live.

Although he is often referred to as a captain he was in fact an acting major. Air Chief Marshal Sir Arthur Harris wrote to Swales' mother, saying in part: 'On every occasion your son proved himself to be a determined fighter and resolute Captain of his crew; his devotion to duty and complete disregard for his own safety will remain an example and inspiration to us all.' He is one of only four South Africans to be awarded the VC in the Second World War, the others being Lieutenant Gerard Norton, Sergeant Quentin Smythe and Squadron Leader John Nettleton.

Sergeant AUBREY COSENS

MOOSHOF, Holland 25/26 February 1945
He was 23 years old and serving in the 1st Bn, Queen's Own Rifles of Canada, CIC when his platoon, supported by tanks, attacked a number of enemy strongpoints, twice being beaten back. Then they were counter-attacked and the platoon commander killed. Cosens at once took command of the only other four survivors of his platoon, whom he placed in a position to give him covering fire. He then ran across open ground under heavy fire to the one remaining tank, where he took up an exposed position in front of the turret to direct its fire. After another enemy counter-attack had been repulsed, Cosens ordered the tank to attack while the rest of his men followed in support. After the tank had rammed a building he entered alone, killing several Germans and taking the rest prisoner. Single-handedly, he then entered the next two buildings and personally killed or captured the occupants. Moments later he was shot and killed by a sniper. The outstanding leadership and gallantry of this NCO, who personally killed 20 of the enemy and took as many prisoners, resulted in the capture of a position which was vital to the success of future operations.

Acting Major FREDERICK TILSTON

HOCHWALD FOREST, Germany
1 March 1945
He was 48 years old and serving in the South Essex Regiment, CIC when he led his company through 500 yards of flat open country in the face of intense machine-gun fire. He kept his men dangerously close to the supporting artillery fire in order to get the maximum cover. Although wounded in the head, he continued to lead his men forward through 10 feet of wire and into the enemy trenches, shouting orders and encouraging the men. When the platoon to his left came under heavy machine-gun fire he dashed forward and silenced it with a grenade. Tilston was the first to reach the enemy position and took the first prisoner. He then pressed on to the second line of defence, but as he approached he was wounded in the hip. Shouting to his men to carry on without him

and urging them to get into the enemy position, he struggled to his feet and rejoined them. Despite his wounds, he showed an unyielding will to close with the enemy, setting a magnificent example to his men, overrunning two German HQs and inflicting many casualties on them. So savage was the fighting that his company was reduced to only 26 men. During repeated enemy counter-attacks he moved from platoon to platoon in the open, quickly reorganising their defences and directing their fire towards the advancing enemy. He made six trips to a company on his flank to bring up ammunition under heavy fire, and on the last of these he was wounded in the leg. He would not submit to medical attention until he had given instructions as to the defence of the position. He fired his men with such determination that the position was held.

Tilston lost both his legs. He was lying in bed when an over-zealous Red Cross lady came fussing down the ward, asking each man what was wrong with him. When she reached Tilston, he answered: 'A bad case of athlete's foot, madam, both feet.'

He died on 23 September 1992.

Private JAMES STOKES

KERVENHEIM, Germany 1 March 1945
He was 30 years old and serving in the 2nd Bn, King's Shropshire Light Infantry when his platoon came under intense rifle and machine-gun fire from a farm building, and was pinned down. Stokes got up and rushed forward, firing from the hip, and was seen disappearing into the building. The enemy fire stopped and he reappeared with 12 prisoners. He had been wounded in the neck but refused to go to the aid post. On approaching the next objective, the platoon again came under heavy fire from a house. Again he rushed the house alone, firing from the hip. He was seen to drop his rifle and fall to the ground wounded. However, he got up again, picked up his rifle and continued to advance, despite the intense fire. He entered the house and all firing from it stopped. When he rejoined his platoon he had five more prisoners. At this time the company was forming up for its assault on the final objective, a group

of buildings that had been turned into a strong-point. Although severely wounded, he once again rushed forward alone across the remaining 60 yards to the strongpoint, still firing from the hip as he struggled through intense fire. He fell mortally wounded 20 yards from the enemy position, firing his rifle to the last, and as the rest of the company passed him in the final charge he raised his hand and shouted goodbye. He was found to have eight wounds to the body. His magnificent courage, devotion to duty and splendid example inspired all those around him, and ensured the success of the attack at a most critical moment. Moreover, his self-sacrifice saved his platoon many casualties.

Naik GIAN SINGH

KAMYE-MYINGYAN ROAD, Burma
2 March 1945

He was 24 years old and serving in the 15th Punjab Regiment, Indian Army when two companies successfully carried out an encir-cling movement and established themselves in the rear of the enemy position. They then attacked a village with the aid of tanks, Gian Singh being in command of the leading section. Ordering his Bren gunner to cover him, he rushed forward alone, firing his Tommy gun. He was met by a hail of bullets and was wounded in the arm, but despite this he continued his advance, throwing grenades and killing several Japanese soldiers. By this time the tanks had moved up in support and came under fire from a cleverly concealed anti-tank gun. Seeing the danger, he again rushed forward alone, killed the crew and captured the gun. His men followed him and he led them down a lane, clearing all the enemy positions. After this action the company reformed to take the enemy positions to the rear. Singh was ordered to the aid post but refused to go, and led his section until the whole action was over. There is no doubt that his acts of gallantry saved the platoon many casualties.

He died on 6 October 1996.

Acting Naik FAZAL DIN

MEIKTILA, Burma 2 March 1945

He was 23 years old and serving in the 7th Bn 10th Baluch Regiment, Indian Army when during an attack his section was held up by machine-gun fire from enemy bunkers. He rushed the nearest bunker alone and silenced it. Then he led his men against the other bunkers. Suddenly six men led by two officers wielding swords rushed at them. Fazal Din was run through the chest by one of the officers, but as the sword was withdrawn he tore it from the officer's hand and killed him with it. He then attacked another man and killed him also. Seeing one of his men struggling with an enemy soldier, he went to his assistance, killing the assailant with the sword. Then, waving the sword in the air, he continued to encourage his men, and then staggered to platoon HQ to make his report. He collapsed and died soon after reaching the aid post. His action was seen by almost the whole platoon, and the men undoubtedly inspired by his gallantry, took advantage of the enemy's bewilderment and annihilated the garrison.

Lieutenant WILLIAM WESTON

MEIKTILA, Burma 3 March 1945

He was 21 years old and serving in the Green Howards (Alexandra, Princess of Wales's Own Yorkshire Regiment). He was commanding a platoon which, together with the rest of the company, had been ordered to clear the enemy from Meiktila from the north to the water's edge in the south, some 1,600 yards, the last half of which was supported by bunkers. Weston's platoon was leading the attack. By 13.30 hours they had 800 yards to go to reach the water. Almost none of Weston's men had seen action before, but he led them superbly. As the advance continued, the already deter-mined opposition increased to a fanatical level. Each bunker had to be dealt with, and he was often the first one in to each bunker. The fighting throughout the day was at very close quarters. Without thought for his own safety he personally led his men into bunker after bunker, killing the enemy wherever he found them. At 17.00 hours, and within sight of the water's edge, they were held up by a very strong bunker position. Knowing that he had to clear his final position before nightfall, he led a party with bayonets and grenades to eliminate the enemy. At the entrance he fell wounded. As he lay on the ground, he realised that his men would not be able to capture the position without heavy casualties so he coolly pulled the pin from one of his grenades and deliberately blew himself up, together with the occupants of the bunker. Throughout the final 3 hours of the battle Weston had set an example that could not have been equalled.

Rifleman BHANBHAGTA GURUNG
TAMANDU, Burma 5 March 1945
He was 23 years old and serving in the 3rd Bn, 2nd Gurkha Rifles, Indian Army when his section was pinned down by heavy machine-gun and sniper fire. Being unable to fire from a lying position, he stood up fully exposed to the heavy fire and calmly shot the sniper. Then he dashed forward alone, killing the occupants of one foxhole with grenades and those in another with the bayonet. Two further enemy foxholes were bringing fire down on his section and again he dashed forward and cleared them with grenades and the bayonet. During this time he was under fire from a machine-gun in a bunker. He went forward alone under fire and leapt onto the roof, from where he threw two smoke grenades into the slit. Two Japanese ran out and he killed them with his kukri. He then went into the bunker and killed the machine-gunner, capturing the gun. The enemy could be seen forming up for a counter-attack, so he took two riflemen and a Bren gunner and took up position in the bunker. Under his direction the counter-attack was repelled with heavy losses to the enemy. His courageous clearing of five enemy positions single-handedly was in itself decisive in capturing the objective and was an inspiring example to his company.

His three sons also served in the 2nd Gurkha Rifles.

He died as a result of asthma on 1 March 2008.

Lieutenant KARAMJEET SINGH JUDGE
MEIKTILA, Burma 18 March 1945
He was 21 years old and serving in the 4th Bn,

15th Punjab Regiment, Indian Army when his platoon was leading an attack. Time and again the attack was held up by machine-gun fire from bunkers not seen by the supporting tanks. On each occasion, with complete disregard for his own safety, he went forward to call up the tanks by means of a telephone. He pointed out the bunkers to the tanks and then personally led the infantry in to finish them off, being the first to reach each one. On one occasion two Japanese suddenly rushed him and he killed them at a range of only 10 yards. He had cleared some ten bunkers in this fashion when a nest of three bunkers was located. He directed a tank to within 20 yards of the first bunker and threw a smoke grenade to help the tank see it. After a few shots he asked the tank to cease firing and he led a few men in to mop up. When he was within 10 yards of the bunker a machine-gun opened fire, mortally wounding him in the chest.

Lieutenant CLAUD RAYMOND
TALAKU, Burma 21 March 1945
He was 21 years old and serving in the Royal Corps of Engineers when he was second-in-command of a patrol. Moving across a stretch of open ground, they came under heavy fire from a strongly entrenched enemy position on a jungle-covered hill. He at once charged towards the position and was wounded in the right shoulder. Ignoring his wound, he charged on, firing his rifle from the hip, but had advanced only a few yards further when he was wounded in the head by a grenade blast. He fell but almost immediately picked himself up again, and in spite of his wounds continued to lead his men on. He was then hit a third time, his wrist being shattered, but he never wavered and carried on into the enemy position. In the sharp action that followed he was largely responsible for capturing the position. Several other men had been wounded and he refused medical aid until all the other casualties had been treated. His outstanding gallantry, endurance and leadership were an inspiration to everyone and a major factor in the capture of the strongpoint.

He died from his wounds the next day.

Corporal REGINALD RATTEY
BOUGAINVILLE, Solomon Islands
22 March 1945
He was 26 years old and serving in the 25th Bn, AMF when his battalion was met with very heavy fire from three bunkers. He dashed forward, firing his Bren gun from the hip, and neutralised the enemy bunkers. On reaching the first bunker, he threw in a grenade, silencing it. With no more grenades, he went back to his section under heavy fire, obtained two more, then rushed back and silenced both bunkers, killing seven of the enemy. The advance continued but soon came under heavy machine-gun fire. Without hesitation, Rattey rushed the gun and killed the crew with his Bren gun.
He died on 10 January 1986.

Corporal FREDERICK 'TOPPY' TOPHAM
RHINE CROSSING, Germany
24 March 1945
He was 27 years old and serving as a medical orderly in the 1st Canadian Parachute Bn, Canadian Army when he heard a cry for help from a wounded man in the open. Two orderlies had just been killed in trying to reach the man, but Topham went forward without hesitation through intense fire. As he worked on the casualty he was shot through the nose. In spite of this, he never faltered in his task. Having completed his first aid, he carried the man steadily and slowly back through continuous fire to shelter. During the next 2 hours he refused all offers of medical help, working devotedly to bring in the wounded. Only when all the other casualties had been cleared did he consent to his own wound being treated. His immediate evacuation was ordered but he refused to go. On his way back to his company he came across a burning carrier with its ammunition exploding; seeing three wounded men inside, he went over to it, despite being warned by an officer not to, and rescued them. One died but the other two undoubtedly owe their lives to him.
He died on 31 May 1974.

Lieutenant ALBERT CHOWNE
DAGUA, New Guinea 25 March 1945
He was 24 years old and serving in the 2/2nd (New South Wales) Bn, AMF when the leading platoon came under heavy fire from concealed machine-gun positions. One man was killed and nine wounded, including the platoon commander. Without orders, Chowne, whose platoon was in reserve, rushed forward. Running up a steep, narrow track he threw grenades which took out two enemy machine-gun positions. Then he called on his men to follow him, charging forward firing his sub-machine-gun. Although he was wounded twice in the chest, his charge carried him 50 yards into the enemy position. He accounted for two more of the enemy before he was killed. His superb courage and self-sacrifice resulted in the capture of this strongly held position.

Corporal EDWARD CHAPMAN
DORTMUND-EMS CANAL, Germany
2 April 1945
He was 25 years old and serving in the 3rd Bn, Monmouthshire Regiment when his section came under heavy machine-gun fire, suffering many casualties. He ordered his men to take cover and went forward alone with a Bren gun, firing from the hip. He killed several men and forced the remainder to retire in disorder. Later his section became isolated and the enemy began to close in, making determined charges with the bayonet. On each occasion he rose with his Bren gun to meet the assault and halted the enemy advance. Running low on ammunition, he shouted to his men to bring up more and covered them while they did so. The Germans made every effort to eliminate him with grenades, but with a reloaded weapon he closed with them and once again drove them back with heavy losses. His company commander was wounded during the withdrawal and was left lying in the open. Chapman went out alone under withering fire and carried him for 50 yards to comparative safety, only to find he had been hit again and killed. Chapman was also wounded while carrying him, but he refused to be evacuated and went back to his

company until the position was restored 2 hours later.

He died on 3 February 2002.

Temporary Corporal THOMAS HUNTER
LAKE COMACCHIO, Italy
2 April 1945

He was 22 years old and serving in No. 43 Commando, attached to Special Service Troops, in charge of a Bren gun section. Advancing in the open, he saw the enemy were holding a group of houses. Realising his men were too good a target to be missed, he rushed forward alone to draw the enemy fire. He attracted most of the machine-gun fire, but so determined was his charge and so accurate his firing from the hip that the enemy became demoralised. Showing complete disregard for the enemy fire, he ran through the houses, clearing them. Six Germans surrendered and the remainder fled. His men now became the target for enemy machine-gun fire. Again offering himself as a target, he lay in full view of the enemy and fired at the concrete pill-boxes. He again drew most of the fire, but by now the greater part of his troop had made it to the safety of cover. Calling for more magazines, he continued to engage the enemy until he was killed by a burst of machine-gun fire. Throughout the action his magnificent courage, leadership and cheerfulness had been an inspiration to his comrades.

He is the only Royal Marine to be awarded the VC during the Second World War.

Temporary Captain IAN LIDDELL
LINGEN, Germany 3 April 1945

He was 25 years old and serving in the 5th Bn, Coldstream Guards when he was ordered to capture the bridge over the River Ems. The bridge was covered by an enemy strongpoint as well as three 88mm guns and two 20mm guns. It had also been prepared for demolition with 500lb bombs. Having got his two leading platoons into a cover position, he ran forward alone and climbed the 10-ft-high road-block, dashed across the bridge under intense fire, disconnected the charges on the far side, then ran back and cut the wires on the near side. He

then discovered there were charges under the bridge and cut these too. In full view of the enemy he climbed on to the road-block and signalled to his leading platoon to advance. Thus alone, without cover and under heavy fire, he achieved his objective as the bridge was taken intact.

He was killed in action at Rothenburg on 21 April 1945.

Temporary Major ANDERS LASSEN
LAKE COMACCHIO, Italy
8/9 April 1945

He was 24 years old and attached to the Special Boat Service, 1st SAS Regiment when he was commanding a 19-man raid. His task was to cause as many casualties and as much confusion as possible to give the impression of a major landing. No previous reconnaissance was possible and the party found itself on a narrow road flanked by water. Covered by two scouts, he led his men along the road towards a town, but they were challenged. An attempt to allay suspicion by answering that they were fishermen returning home failed. Fire was opened on them by the sentry and from two unseen positions. Lassen himself attacked with grenades, annihilating the first position. Ignoring the hail of bullets sweeping the road, he raced forward to engage the second position under covering fire from his men. Throwing in a grenade, he silenced this position. By now his force had suffered casualties and its firepower was considerably reduced. Still under fire he rallied and reorganised his men and brought fire to bear on the third position. He then went forward and threw in a grenade, which produced a cry of 'Kamerad'. He ordered the enemy out to take their surrender. While shouting to them, he was hit by a burst of machine-gun fire and fell mortally wounded, but still managed to throw in a grenade, allowing his men to finish off the occupants. He refused to be evacuated as he said it would impede the withdrawal and endanger his men. His magnificent leadership and utter disregard for personal safety achieved his objective.

As well as the VC, he was awarded the MC and two Bars.

Sepoy ALI HAIDAR
SENIO RIVER, Italy 9 April 1945

He was 31 years old and serving in the 13th Frontier Force Rifles, Indian Army. His platoon was crossing the river when it came under very heavy machine-gun fire from two posts. He was one of only three men to get across. Leaving the other two men to cover him, he charged the nearest post and threw a grenade into it, at the same time being wounded in the back by a grenade thrown at him by the enemy. The post was destroyed and four Germans surrendered. With complete disregard for his personal safety, he then charged the next post and was again wounded, this time in the right arm and leg. Undeterred, he crawled forward and threw in a grenade and then charged, finding two wounded and two men surrendering. The rest of the men of his company were now able to cross the river and establish a bridgehead. His action undoubtedly saved many lives.

He died on 15 July 1999.

Sepoy NAMDEO JADHAO
SENIO RIVER, Italy 9 April 1945

He was 23 years old and serving in the 5th Mahratta Light Infantry, Indian Army. When crossing the river his company came under fire from three machine-gun posts and his commander was one of several men killed or wounded. He immediately carried one wounded man through the deep water, up the precipitous slope on the east bank and across a mine-belt to safety. He then went back to help another of the wounded men. Both times he was under heavy fire. Determined to avenge his dead comrades and eliminate the machine-gun posts that were still pinning down the battalion, he crossed the exposed east bank a third time and dashed at the nearest enemy post, silencing it with his Tommy gun. He was, however, wounded in the hand and was no longer able to use his gun so he threw it away and resorted to hand grenades. With these he charged and destroyed two more enemy posts, at one point crawling to the top of the bank to resupply his stock of grenades from comrades on the reverse slope. Having silenced all the machine-gun fire from the east bank, he stood in the open shouting the Mahratta war cry and waving the rest of the companies on across the river. This sepoy not only saved the lives of the men he rescued, but his outstanding personal bravery enabled the battalion to secure a deeper bridgehead, which in turn led to the collapse of German resistance in the area.

He died on 2 August 1984.

Guardsman EDWARD CHARLTON
WISTEDT, Germany 21 April 1945

He was 24 years old and serving in the 2nd Bn, Irish Guards as the co-driver of a tank which had taken the village of Wistedt. The Germans attempted to retake the village with a force that largely consisted of officer cadets under the command of their very experienced officers, supported by several SPGs. Charlton's tank was out of action before this attack started and the crew were ordered to take the Browning machine-gun from it and support the infantry. As the Irish Guards were in danger of being overrun by the Germans, Charlton, on his own initiative, advanced in full view of the attacking enemy, firing from the hip as he did so. He inflicted heavy casualties, halting the lead company and allowing the rest of the Guards a brief respite to retire and reorganise. He continued his attack even when he was wounded in the left arm. Charlton managed to rest the machine-gun on a fence, from where he launched a further attack before his arm was shattered by enemy fire. With just one arm, he carried on with his astonishing attack until he was wounded again and collapsed, dying of his wounds. His courageous and selfless disregard for his own safety helped save the precarious situation that the Guards faced. Unusually much of the citation for his award is based on German accounts of the fighting, as most of the action was not witnessed by any of the surviving Guardsmen.

This was the last VC to be awarded for the European Theatre in the Second World War.

Corporal JOHN MacKEY
TARAKAN ISLAND, North Borneo
12 May 1945

He was 22 years old and serving in the 2/3rd Pioneer Bn, AMF. His section was advancing along a narrow spur, scarcely wide enough for more than one man at a time, when it came under fire from three well-sited positions. Mackey charged the first machine-gun, bayoneting one gunner, and then charged straight on to the next, killing the crew with grenades. Exchanging his rifle for a submachine-gun, he charged the last position but was killed by a burst of machine-gun fire, although not before he had killed another two of the enemy. He was responsible for killing seven Japanese and silencing two machine-guns, which enabled his platoon to capture its objective.

His action took place just four days before his 23rd birthday.

Rifleman LACHHIMAN GURUNG
TAUNGDAW, Burma 12/13 May 1945

He was 27 years old and serving in the 4th Bn, 8th Gurkha Rifles, Indian Army. His unit was manning the most forward post when over 200 Japanese assaulted the position, the brunt of the attack being borne by his section. Before the assault the enemy hurled large numbers of grenades at the position from close range. One landed on the lip of his trench and he at once grabbed it and threw it back at the enemy. Almost immediately another fell in his trench and again he threw it back. When a third grenade fell just in front of his trench, he picked it up but it exploded in his hand, blowing off his fingers, shattering his right arm and severely wounding him in the face, body and right leg. His two comrades were also badly wounded and lay helpless in the bottom of the trench. The enemy, screaming and shouting, now rushed forward in an attempt to take the position by sheer weight of numbers. Despite his wounds, Gurung loaded and fired his rifle with his left hand, maintaining a steady rate of fire. Repeated attacks were thrown in by the enemy and all were repulsed with heavy losses. For 4 hours he remained at his post alone, calmly waiting for each attack,

which he met with point-blank fire from his rifle, determined not to give an inch of ground. Of the 87 enemy dead counted in the immediate area, 31 lay in front of his trench, the key to the whole position. Had the enemy taken his trench the whole of the reverse slope would have been completely overrun. By his magnificent example he inspired his comrades to resist the enemy to the last; although surrounded and cut off for three days and two nights, they held on and smashed back every attack. His outstanding gallantry and extreme devotion to duty in the face of overwhelming odds were the main factors in the defeat of the enemy.

He died from pneumonia on 12 December 2010.

Private EDWARD KENNA
WEWAK, New Guinea 15 May 1945

He was 25 years old and serving in the 2/4th Bn (New South Wales), AMF when his platoon was ordered to deal with an enemy machine-gun bunker, so that the company operation could proceed. His section moved forward in order to harass the enemy, so an attack could be launched from a flank. When the attacking sections came into view they immediately came under heavy machine-gun fire from a previously concealed position. Casualties were suffered and the attacking sections could not move closer. Kenna tried to get his Bren gun into a firing position but was unable to do so because of the nature of the ground. On his own initiative and without orders he stood up in full view of the enemy, who were less than 50 yards away, and engaged the bunker, firing his gun from the hip. The enemy machine-gun immediately returned fire, with such accuracy that bullets actually passed between his arms and his body. Undeterred, he remained completely exposed and continued to fire until his magazine was empty. Still making a target of himself, he seized a rifle and with great coolness killed the gunner with his first shot. A second machine-gun then opened fire on him and another man tried to take over the dead gunner's position, but he remained standing and killed him with his next shot. The result of his magnificent bravery in the face of such concentrated fire was that the bunker was taken without further loss and the company attack proceeded to a successful conclusion. There is no doubt that the success was due entirely to his magnificent courage and complete disregard for his own safety.

He died on 8 July 2009.

Private LESLIE STARCEVICH
BEAUFORT, North Borneo
25 May 1945

He was 27 years old and serving in the 2/43rd (South Australia) Bn, AMF. During an approach along a thickly wooded spur the leading section came under fire from two Japanese machine-gun posts and suffered casualties. Starcevich moved forward and assaulted each post in turn, firing his Bren gun from the hip, killing five men and putting the rest to flight. The advance progressed until the section came under fire from two more machine-gun posts, which halted progress temporarily. He again advanced fearlessly, ignoring the hostile fire and still firing his gun from the hip, and captured both posts single-handedly, killing seven of the enemy. The track on which this action took place was later renamed Victoria Cross Road.

He died on 17 November 1989.

Private FRANK PARTRIDGE
BOUGAINVILLE, Solomon Islands
24 July 1945

He was 20 years old and serving in the 8th (Victoria) Bn, AMF when his section came under heavy machine-gun fire from a bunker. He was wounded in the arm and thigh, while his section Bren gunner was killed and two others severely wounded. Despite his wounds, and with complete disregard for his personal safety, he rushed forward and retrieved the Bren gun, giving it to another man to cover him. Then he rushed the bunker and threw in a grenade, following up a few seconds later and killing with his knife the only occupant left. He then attacked another bunker, but loss of blood compelled him to stop and he told his

section commander he was unable to continue. With the way clear, the platoon moved forward and established a defensive perimeter, but heavy fire soon made this position untenable. Partridge rejoined the fight and withdrew with the platoon's casualties.

He died on 23 March 1964, following a road traffic accident.

Lieutenant IAN 'TICH' FRASER
STRAITS OF JOHORE, Singapore
31 July 1945

He was 24 years old and serving in the Royal Naval Reserve in command of HM Midget Submarine *XE3* when it attacked the heavy cruiser *Takao* at her moorings. During the long approach he deliberately left the safe channel and entered mined waters in order to avoid hydrophone posts. The target was found to be partly aground and Fraser tried for 40 minutes to push *XE3* under the cruiser before finally succeeding. Acting Leading Seaman James Magennis left the submarine to place limpet mines on the cruiser. This was done with great difficulty due to the presence of barnacles, which he had to clear with his bare hands. Fraser then tried to drop his side-charges, but one failed to release. Although exhausted, Magennis volunteered to go out again to release it rather than allow a less experienced diver to undertake the task. After several minutes of nerve-racking work he succeeded in freeing the side-charge. Fraser then experienced difficulty in extricating *XE3* from under the cruiser, but the submarine finally came free and commenced the long journey out to sea. The courage and determination shown by Fraser and Magennis is beyond praise. Any man not possessed of Fraser's relentless determination would have dropped the side-charges alongside the target instead of persisting until he had forced his submarine right under the cruiser. The approach and withdrawal covered 80 miles of water which was mined by both the enemy and the Royal Navy, past hydrophone posts and through an anti-submarine boom. Both men were awarded the VC.

Fraser died on 1 September 2008.

Acting Leading Seaman JAMES 'MICK' MAGENNIS
STRAITS OF JOHORE, Singapore
31 July 1945
He was 25 years old and serving in the Royal Navy when he left the midget submarine *XE3* to place limpet mines on the heavy cruiser *Takao* at her moorings. This was done with great difficulty due to the presence of barnacles, which he had to clear with his bare hands. He returned to the submarine to find that one of the side-charges would not release. Although exhausted, Magennis volunteered to go out again to release it rather than allow a less experienced diver to undertake the task. After several minutes of nerve-racking work he succeeded in freeing the side-charge. Fraser then experienced difficulty in extricating *XE3* from under the cruiser, but finally the submarine came free and commenced the long journey out to sea. The courage and determination showed by Fraser and Magennis is beyond praise. The approach and withdrawal covered 80 miles of water which was mined by both the enemy and the Royal Navy, past hydrophone posts and through an anti-submarine boom. Both men were awarded the VC.

Magennis was the only native of Northern Ireland to receive the VC in the Second World War.

He died on 11 February 1986.

Temporary Lieutenant ROBERT GRAY
ONAGAWA BAY, HONSHU, Japan
9 August 1945
He was 27 years old and serving with the Royal Canadian Naval Volunteer Reserve, with 1841 Squadron, Fleet Air Arm, when in the face of anti-aircraft fire from shore batteries and ships he pressed home his attack on the destroyer *Amakusa*, flying very low in his Corsair in order to ensure success. He scored at least one hit, sinking the destroyer. He was wounded in the attack and his aircraft crashed into the sea in flames. His body was never recovered.

Chapter Thirteen

THE POST-WAR PERIOD, 1950–2015

The Korean War, 1950–53 (4 VCs)

After the end of the Second World War Korea was divided in two, by American and Soviet agreement, into the communist Democratic People's Republic of Korea in the north and the pro-West Republic of Korea in the south. On 25 June 1950 the North Korean Army invaded the south and the United Nations Security Council summoned the aid of all member nations in halting the attack. Four Victoria Crosses were awarded for this campaign.

Major KENNETH MUIR
HILL 282, SONGJU 23 September 1950
He was 38 years old and serving in the Argyll and Sutherland Highlanders. Two companies had taken Hill 282, but some difficulty was experienced in evacuating the wounded from the position. At about this time the position came under mortar fire and shelling. Small parties of the enemy started to infiltrate the left flank, making it necessary to reinforce the forward position. For an hour the infiltration and the shelling increased, causing more casualties. Due to the reinforcing of the left flank and the provision of men to help with the wounded, both companies became inextricably mixed and it was obvious that they needed to come under one command. Although he was only visiting the position, Muir took over command and with complete disregard for his own safety started to move around the forward elements, cheering and encouraging the men to greater efforts, despite the fact that ammunition was running low. He was continually

under fire, but refused to take cover despite pleas from officers and men alike. When an air strike was called in the aircraft hit the company's position instead of the enemy, causing more casualties and necessitating a withdrawal to a position 50 feet below the crest. A complete retreat from the hill would have been fully justified at this time, with only 30 fighting men remaining and ammunition very low. However, Muir realised that the enemy had not taken immediate advantage of the air strike and that the crest of the hill was unoccupied, although it was still under fire. With the three remaining officers, he immediately formed a small force of all ranks and personally led a counter-attack on the crest, retaking it. From this moment on his actions were beyond all praise as he was determined the wounded would have adequate time to be evacuated and that the enemy would not take the crest. Muir moved about his men, distributing the fast-diminishing ammunition, and when his own weapon ran out of ammunition he took over a 2-inch mortar, which he used to good effect. While firing the mortar he was still shouting encouragement and advice to his men. Finally he was hit by two bursts of automatic fire which mortally wounded him, but he retained consciousness and was still determined to fight on. His last words were: 'The gooks will never drive the Argylls off this hill.' The effect of his splendid leadership on the men was nothing short of amazing and it was entirely due to his magnificent courage and example that all the wounded were evacuated from the hill and very heavy casualties were inflicted on the enemy.

Lieutenant Colonel JAMES 'FRED' CARNE
IMJIN RIVER 22/23 April 1951

He was 51 years old and commanding the 1st Bn, Gloucestershire Regiment when his battalion was heavily attacked, suffering numerous casualties. The battalion was incessantly engaged by vastly superior numbers of the enemy, who repeatedly launched mass attacks that were only stopped at close quarters. The battalion was completely cut off from brigade, but remained an effective fighting unit in the face of almost continual onslaughts from a determined enemy trying to overrun it. At all times Carne's manner remained coolness itself; via the radio, the only link with brigade, he repeatedly assured his commander that all was well and that his battalion could hold on, and that everyone was in good heart. Throughout this entire action he showed a complete disregard for his personal safety, moving around the whole battalion under very heavy machine-gun and mortar fire, inspiring the men and giving them the will to resist the enemy. On two occasions, armed with rifle and grenades, he personally led assault parties that drove back the enemy and saved important situations. His example of courage, coolness and leadership was felt not only by his battalion but by the whole brigade. He fully realised that his flanks had been turned, but he also knew that the abandonment of the position would clear the way for the enemy to make a breakthrough, and this would have endangered the corps. At last it became apparent that his battalion would not be relieved, and on orders from brigade he organised his battalion into small officer-led groups who then broke out from the position. He himself was captured while in charge of a party trying to fight its way out.

He died on 19 April 1986, following a fall.

Lieutenant PHILIP CURTIS
'CASTLE HILL', IMJIN RIVER
22/23 April 1951

He was 26 years old and serving in the Duke of Cornwall's Light Infantry, attached to the 1st Bn, Gloucestershire Regiment when the enemy secured a footing on his unit's position. His company counter-attacked, led by Curtis, and under the covering fire of machine-guns the attack gained initial success but was eventually held up by heavy fire. The enemy just below the crest raced to reinforce the position and a fierce firefight developed. Curtis ordered his men to give covering fire and rushed the position, being severely wounded by a grenade as he did so. His men crawled out to him and pulled him back under cover, but when he recovered he insisted on trying again. Breaking free from the men who were trying to restrain him, he made another charge, throwing grenades as he went, but was killed by a burst of automatic fire when within a few yards of his objective. Although the immediate objective of this counter-attack was not achieved, it had a great effect on the outcome of the battle. The enemy had gained a foothold on a position that was vital to the defence of the whole company area, but their advance here had been met with such ferocity that they made no further attempt to exploit it. If they had done so, the withdrawal of the company might well have proved impossible.

Private WILLIAM 'BIG BILL' SPEAKMAN (name changed to SPEAKMAN-PITTS)
UNITED HILL 4 November 1951

He was 24 years old and serving in the Black Watch, later the Royal Highland Regiment, attached to the 1st Bn, King's Own Scottish Borderers, when a Chinese attack was launched in three waves, the first wave being little more than 'cannon fodder' intended to flatten the wire. The section holding the left flank of the company's position had been seriously depleted and was almost overrun by the second wave. Speakman, on his own initiative, collected six men and led a series of counter-charges. He broke up several enemy attacks, causing heavy casualties, and in spite of being wounded in the leg and shoulder continued to lead charge after charge. When the ammunition ran out he started throwing stones and bottles and anything else he could get his hands on. The position was in danger of being overrun, and he was ordered to withdraw. Instead, he went forward again to clear the hill and save the wounded. He was then ordered off the hill to get his wounds dressed, but when the medical orderly was hit Speakman went forward again and kept the enemy at bay long enough to enable his company to withdraw safely. In total he led some fifteen charges, until he fell unconscious.

Press reports of the time said that Private Speakman began throwing beer bottles at the enemy after running out of grenades, and hence became known as 'the beer bottle VC.' When asked about it, he at first denied it but later said there may have been a few bottles involved. Although his award was approved by King George VI, Speakman's was the first VC to be presented by Queen Elizabeth II. At the time of going to press he is one of the 10 surviving VC holders.

The Malaysia-Indonesia Confrontation, 1963–66 (1 VC)

In 1963 the Federation of Malaysia was officially recognised, and it was agreed that the continued presence of British armed forces would be allowed. Indonesia saw this as a thinly disguised attempt to continue colonial rule in the area. The so-called 'Confrontation' began when small parties of Indonesians began to cross into Malaysia, but by late 1963 regular units were involved. One Victoria Cross was awarded for this campaign.

Lance Corporal RAMBAHADUR LIMBU
GUNONG TEPOI, Sarawak
21 November 1965
He was 26 years old and serving in the 2nd Bn, 10th Gurkha Rifles (Princess Mary's) when his company was attacking a position on top of a jungle-covered hill, the only approach being along a knife-edge ridge. As he led his group forward, he could see the nearest trench, with a sentry and machine-gun. Determined to gain first blood, he inched his way towards it but he was spotted only 10 yards away and the machine-gun opened fire, wounding the man to Limbu's right. He rushed forward and in seconds had killed the sentry, thereby gaining a foothold on the ridge. The enemy were now fully alerted and from their positions brought

down heavy automatic fire on the attackers. Knowing that he could not carry out his task from this position, he left the comparative safety of his trench and, completely disregarding the hail of bullets directed at him, led his group to a better fire position some way forward. He now attempted to indicate his intentions to his platoon commander by hand signals but could not make himself understood, so he again went out into the open and reported personally, despite the danger of being hit by both friend and foe. At this point he saw that both men in his little group had been wounded, and he knew full well their only chance was to be evacuated for immediate first aid. Using what little cover he could find, he crawled forward in full view of at least two machine-gun posts which opened fire on him. For 3 minutes he inched forward, but was driven back by the intense automatic fire when he was almost able to reach the first man. After a pause he again started to crawl forward but soon realised that only speed would give him the cover he needed. Rushing forward, he threw himself on the ground next to one of the wounded men and, calling for support from two machine-guns which had by now come up to his right, he picked up the man and carried him down the hill to safety. Without hesitation, he immediately returned to the top of the hill determined to complete his self-imposed task of rescuing those for whom he felt personally responsible. It was clear from the increased fire being concentrated on the approach to the remaining casualty that the enemy were doing all they could to prevent any further attempts at rescue. Despite this, Limbu again moved out into the open and eventually reached the wounded man following a series of short rushes, despite having been pinned down for some time by machine-gun fire, when bullets could be seen striking the ground all round him. Picking up the wounded man, he carried him back as fast as he could through a hail of bullets. For all but a few seconds of the 20 minutes it took him to complete this gallant action and the events leading up to it, he was moving in full view of the enemy and under continuous automatic fire.

That he was able to achieve this against such overwhelming odds without being hit was miraculous. His outstanding bravery, complete disregard for his own safety and determination to save the lives of his men set an incomparable example and inspired all who saw him. Rejoining his section on the left flank of the attack, he was able to recover the machine-gun abandoned by the wounded and with it won his revenge, being responsible for killing four of the enemy as they attempted to escape across the border. This hour-long battle, which had been fought at point-blank range and with the utmost ferocity by both sides, was won. At least 24 of the enemy are known to have been killed, at a cost of three killed and two wounded in the attacking force. His achievement in this engagement stands out as one of the most important of any VC actions and there is no doubt that but for his inspired conduct at a most vital stage much less would have been achieved and greater casualties suffered.

When he came to London to receive his VC he stopped off at the Stock Exchange, where he was recognised. Almost to a man, everyone stopped trading and applauded him for 3 minutes. Never before had one of the world's premier financial markets stood still for so long, and it was solely so that those present could pay tribute to an incredibly brave man. His autobiography is called *My Life Story*. At the time of going to press, he is one of the 10 surviving VC holders.

The Vietnam War, 1965–73 (4 VCs)

In August 1962 Australian army advisers arrived in South Vietnam to work with US planners in training the South Vietnamese army, but they had no mandate to take part in combat. By 1965 100 Australians were working with the US advisory team. When the first US combat soldiers arrived in March, the Australian premier committed a force of 1,100 men to the conflict, working in counter-insurgency operations. Four Victoria Crosses were awarded for this campaign.

Warrant Officer Class II KEVIN 'DASHER' WHEATLEY

TRA BONG VALLEY 13 November 1965
He was 28 years old and serving in the Australian Army Training Team Vietnam (known as 'The Team') when he was with the right-hand platoon in a search and destroy operation. At 13.40 hours Wheatley reported contact with the enemy. The Viet Cong resistance increased in strength and Wheatley called for assistance. Captain Fazekas immediately organised the centre platoon to help and personally led it towards the area of action. They were on their way when he received another radio message from Wheatley saying that Warrant Officer Swanton had been hit in the chest, and requesting an air strike and a helicopter to evacuate the casualties. At about this time the right-hand platoon broke in the face of heavy Viet Cong fire and began to scatter. Although told by the medical assistant that Swanton was dying, Wheatley refused to abandon him. He discarded his radio to enable him to half-drag, half-carry the wounded man, under heavy machine-gun and automatic rifle fire, out of the open rice paddies and into the comparative safety of a wooded area, some 200 metres away. He was assisted by Private Dinh Do, who, when the Viet Cong were only some 10 metres away, urged him to leave his dying comrade. Again he refused, and was seen to pull the pins from two grenades as he calmly awaited the Viet Cong, holding one grenade in each hand. Shortly afterwards two explosions were heard, followed by several bursts of small arms fire. The two bodies were found lying together at first light the next morning, after the fighting had ceased. Both had died from gunshot wounds.

Warrant Officer Wheatley displayed magnificent courage in the face of an overwhelming Viet Cong force, which was estimated at more than a company. He had the clear choice of abandoning a dying comrade and saving himself, or of staying with Swanton and thereby facing certain death. His act of heroism, determination and unflinching loyalty in the face of the enemy will always stand as an example of the true meaning of valour. In addition to his VC, he was awarded the US Silver Star, the South Vietnamese Knight of the National Order of the Republic of Vietnam, the Military Merit Medal and the Vietnamese Gallantry Cross with Palm.

Major PETER BADCOE (spelt BADCOCK before 1961)
PHU TU/QAING DIEN/HUONG TRA
23 February, 7 March and 7 April 1967

He was 33 years old and serving in the Australian Army Training Team Vietnam (known as 'The Team') when he was monitoring a radio transmission which stated that the sub-sector adviser, an American officer, had been killed and his body was within 50 metres of an enemy machine-gun position. An American medic had also been wounded and was in danger from the enemy. Badcoe, with complete disregard for his own safety, moved alone 600 metres under fire and reached the wounded man, tended his wounds and ensured his safety. Then he led a platoon towards the enemy position. His personal leadership and encouragement in the face of the enemy led to a successful assault on the machine-gun post, where he personally killed the gunners directly to his front. He then picked up the dead officer and carried him back, still under fire, to the command post. On 7 March he led his company in an attack over open ground to assault a heavily defended enemy position, turning defeat into victory by preventing the enemy from capturing the district HQ. On 7 April the company came under heavy small arms fire during an advance and withdrew to a cemetery. This left him and his radio operator 50 metres in front of his men, under mortar fire. Seeing the withdrawal, he ran back and through his encouragement and example got the men moving forward again. He then moved to the front to lead them on. The company stopped again under heavy small arms fire, but he continued on and prepared to throw a grenade. When he rose to throw it his radio operator pulled him back down as heavy fire was being brought to bear on them. He later got up again to throw a grenade and was killed by a burst of machine-gun fire. Soon after-

wards artillery fire was called in and the position taken. He was known as 'The Galloping Major'.

Warrant Officer Class II RAYENE SIMPSON
KONTUM PROVINCE
6 and 11 May 1969

He was 43 years old and serving in the Australian Army Training Team Vietnam (known as 'The Team'). He was commanding the 232nd Mobile Strike Force Company of the 5th Special Forces Group on a search and clear mission near the Laotian border when one of his platoons became heavily engaged with the enemy. Simpson led the rest of the company to its assistance, placing himself at the head of his men and thus becoming the focal point of enemy fire, and personally leading the assault on the left flank of the enemy position. As the company moved forward a warrant officer from one of his platoons was seriously wounded and the attack began to falter. Simpson, at great personal risk and under heavy fire, went to the wounded man and carried him to a place of safety. He then returned to his company where he crawled forward to within 10 metres of the enemy and threw grenades into their position. As darkness fell they were still unable to break into the enemy position, and Simpson ordered his men to withdraw. He then threw smoke grenades and, carrying a wounded platoon commander, covered the withdrawal of the company together with five South Vietnamese soldiers. On 11 May, during the same operation, his battalion commander was killed and a warrant officer wounded, along with several of his men. In addition, another warrant officer who had been separated from the main body was contained in an area by enemy fire. Simpson quickly organised two platoons of South Vietnamese with several advisers and led them forward under very heavy fire. All but a few fell back. Disregarding his own safety, he moved forward in the face of accurate machine-gun fire in order to cover the initial evacuation of the casualties. The wounded were moved out of the line of fire, which had been directed at

Simpson from close range. At the risk of almost certain death he made several attempts to move towards his battalion commander's body, but each time he was stopped by heavy fire. Realising the position was becoming untenable and that priority should be given to removing the other casualties as quickly as possible, he single-handedly covered the withdrawal by placing himself between the wounded and the enemy. From this position he fought on and through his outstanding courage was able to prevent the enemy's advance until the wounded were removed from danger. His gallant action and his coolness under fire were instrumental in the successful evacuation of the wounded to the helicopter pad.

In addition to the VC and DCM, he was awarded the US Silver and Bronze Star.

He died from cancer on 18 October 1978.

Warrant Officer Class II KEITH PAYNE
BEN HET, KONTUM PROVINCE
24 May 1969
He was 35 years old and serving in the Australian Army Training Team Vietnam (known as 'The Team'). He was commanding the 212th Company of the 1st Mobile Strike Force Battalion when the two leading companies, including his own, became isolated and were under attack from an NVA force of superior numbers. Under heavy mortar and rocket fire, and attacked from three sides, his men began to give ground. Directly exposing himself to the enemy's fire, he temporarily held off the attackers by alternately firing his weapon and running from position to position collecting grenades and throwing them at the enemy. At this time he was wounded in the hands and arms. Despite his outstanding efforts, his men gave way under the enemy's increased pressure and the battalion commander, several advisers and a few soldiers withdrew. Despite his wounds, and still under very heavy fire, Payne covered the withdrawal by throwing more grenades and firing his weapon at the enemy who were attempting to follow up. Still under fire he ran across exposed ground to head off his own men who were withdrawing in disorder. He stopped them and by

nightfall had organised the remnants of the two companies into a defensive perimeter. On his own initiative and at great personal risk he went out of the perimeter alone to look for wounded men and stragglers. Although the enemy were still occupying the previous position, with complete disregard for his personal safety he crawled back to the position and extricated several wounded men. With the enemy moving about he continued to search the area for some 3 hours, finally collecting 40 men, some of whom were wounded, and returned with this group to the defensive perimeter, only to find the remainder of the battalion had moved back. Undeterred by this, and helping a seriously wounded American soldier, he led the group back through the enemy to the safety of the new battalion position. His sustained and heroic efforts in this action were outstanding and undoubtedly saved many lives.

He had also served in Korea, Malaya and Papua New Guinea. As well as the VC, he was awarded the Australian Order of Merit, the US Silver Star and Distinguished Service Cross and the Vietnamese Cross for Gallantry. When I wrote to him in 2008, he wrote back saying 'I'm coming to London, let's meet.' I could hardly believe my good luck. We spent a very pleasant afternoon together in the Union Jack Club. At the time of going to press, he is one of the 10 surviving VC holders.

The Falklands War, 1982 (2 VCs)

After the British Government had decided to scrap HMS *Endurance*, the Argentinian Junta, who needed something to restore their fast-deteriorating popularity at home, believed the British were weak and would not fight to keep the Falkland Islands. But when some Argentinian scrap-metal merchants were landed on South Georgia, the British sent marines to the island. Then Buenos Aires replaced the scrap-metal workers with a force of marines. A small engagement followed and the British surrendered. Argentina then invaded the Falkland Islands on 2 April 1982.

Two Victoria Crosses were awarded for this campaign.

Lieutenant Colonel HERBERT 'H' JONES
GOOSE GREEN 28 May 1982

He was 42 years old and commanding the 2nd Bn, Parachute Regiment when he was ordered to attack enemy positions in and around the settlements of Darwin and Goose Green. The enemy were well dug in with mutually supporting positions sited in depth, and during the attack the battalion was held up just south of Darwin by a particularly well-prepared and resilient enemy position of at least eleven trenches on an important ridge. A number of casualties were taken. In order to read the battle fully and to ensure that the momentum of his attack was not lost, Jones took forward his reconnaissance party to the foot of a re-entrant which a section of his battalion had just secured. Despite persistent, heavy and accurate fire the reconnaissance party gained the top of the re-entrant, at approximately the same height as the enemy positions. From here Jones directed his battalion mortar fire, in an effort to neutralise the enemy positions. However, these had been well prepared and continued to pour effective fire on to the battalion advance, which had already been held up for over an hour and was in danger of faltering under increasingly heavy artillery fire. In his efforts to gain a good viewpoint, Jones was now at the very front of his battalion. It was clear to him that desperate measures were needed in order to overcome the enemy position and rekindle the attack, and that unless these measures were taken promptly the battalion would sustain increasing casualties and the attack perhaps even fail. It was time for personal leadership and action. Calling on those men around him to follow, Jones immediately seized a sub-machine-gun and, with total disregard for his own safety, charged the nearest enemy position. This action exposed him to fire from a number of trenches. As he charged up a short slope at the enemy position he was seen to fall and roll backwards downhill. He immediately picked himself up and again charged the enemy trench, firing his submachine-gun and seem-ingly oblivious to the intense fire directed at him. He was hit by fire from another trench which he outflanked, and fell dying only a few feet from the enemy he had assaulted. A short time later a company of the battalion attacked the enemy, who quickly surrendered, Jones's display of courage having completely undermined their will to fight on. Thereafter the momentum of the attack was rapidly regained, Darwin and Goose Green were liberated, and the battalion released the local inhabitants unharmed and forced the surrender of some 1,200 of the enemy. The achievements of the Paras at Darwin and Goose Green set the tone for the subsequent land victory on the Falklands. The British achieved such a moral superiority over the enemy in this first battle that, despite the advantages of numbers and selection of battle-ground, the Argentinian troops never thereafter doubted either the superior fighting qualities of the British troops or the inevitability of their defeat. This was an action of the utmost gallantry by a commanding officer whose dashing leadership and courage throughout the battle were an inspiration to all about him.

The award of the posthumous VC to Jones was controversial at the time because some military experts considered that, despite his undoubted courage, he had failed as a leader, losing sight of the overall battle picture and failing to allow his sub-unit commanders to exercise Mission Command, before his fatal attempt to lead A Company forward from the position where they had become bogged down.

Sergeant IAN McKAY
MOUNT LONGDON 12 June 1982

He was 29 years old and serving in the 3rd Bn, Parachute Regiment when his battalion mounted an attack on an enemy position. After the initial objective had been secured, his platoon was ordered to clear the northern side of the long east–west ridge held by the enemy. By now the enemy were fully alerted and resisting fiercely. As his platoon continued to advance, it came under increasingly heavy fire from well-sited machine-gun positions on the ridge. Realising that no further advance was possible, the platoon commander ordered a move to cover, where they met another platoon. The enemy fire was still both heavy and accurate, and the two platoons' position was becoming increasingly hazardous. The platoon commander then took McKay and a few other men forward to reconnoitre the enemy positions but he was hit in the leg and command fell to McKay. It was clear that instant action was needed if the advance were to continue, and he decided to convert reconnaissance into attack in order to eliminate the enemy positions. He was in no doubt of the enemy's strength, but taking three men with him he broke cover and charged. The attack was met by a hail of bullets, with one man killed and two wounded. Despite this, McKay charged on alone and on reaching the position he dispatched the enemy with grenades, thus relieving the beleaguered platoons, who could now redeploy in relative safety. McKay was, however, killed at the moment of victory, falling on the enemy bunker. Without doubt his action saved a most dangerous situation and was instrumental in ensuring the success of the attack. His was a coolly calculated attack and he acted with outstanding selflessness and courage. With complete disregard for this own safety, he displayed courage and leadership of the highest order and was an inspiration to all those around him.

McKay was a talented football player and was offered terms by Doncaster Rovers, but he turned down this opportunity to join the army. He had also served in Northern Ireland.

IRAQ, 2003–09 (1 VC)

After the 1991 Gulf War, when Iraq had occupied Kuwait and the US/UK-led coalition had forced them out, it was hoped that the Iraqi people would rise up and overthrow Saddam Hussein, but the uprising was brutally put down. On 19 March 2003, on the pretext of seeking weapons of mass destruction, another US/UK-led coalition attacked Iraq, occupied the country and removed Saddam Hussein from power. Although the initial fighting was

over very quickly, the occupying troops continued to face resistance from insurgents. One Victoria Cross has been awarded for this campaign.

Private JOHNSON 'BEE' BEHARRY
AL-AMARAH 1 May and 11 June 2004

He was 24 years old and serving in the 1st Bn, Princess of Wales's Royal Regiment when his company was ordered to replenish an isolated Coalition Forces outpost. He was driving a Warrior armoured personnel carrier. His platoon was the company reserve force and was placed on immediate notice to move. As the main elements of his company were moving into the city to carry out the replenishment, they were retasked to fight through a series of enemy ambushes in order to extract a foot patrol that had become pinned down under sustained small arms and heavy machine-gun fire, and improvised explosive devices and RPGs. His platoon was tasked over the radio to come to the assistance of the remainder of the company, which was attempting to extract the foot patrol. As his platoon passed a roundabout en route to the pinned-down patrol, they became aware that the road to the front was empty of all civilians and traffic, an indicator of a potential ambush ahead. The platoon commander ordered the vehicle to halt, so that he could assess the situation, and the Warrior was immediately hit by multiple RPGs. Eyewitnesses report that the vehicle was engulfed in a number of violent explosions, which physically rocked the 30-tonne Warrior.

As a result of this ferocious initial volley of fire, both the platoon commander and the vehicle's gunner were incapacitated by concussion and other wounds, and a number of the men in the rear of the vehicle were also wounded. Due to damage sustained in the blast to the vehicle's radio systems, Beharry had no means of communication with either his turret crew or any of the other Warriors around him. He did not know if his commander or crewmen were still alive, or how serious their injuries might be. In this confusing and dangerous situation, and on his own initiative, he closed the driver's hatch and moved forward through the ambush position to try to establish some form of communications, halting just short of a barricade placed across the road.

The vehicle was hit again by sustained RPG attack from insurgent fighters in the alleyways and on rooftops around his vehicle. Further damage to the Warrior from these explosions caused it to catch fire and fill with thick smoke. Beharry opened up his hatch cover to clear his view and orientate himself. He still had no radio communications, and was now acting on his own initiative as the driver of the lead vehicle of a six-Warrior convoy in an enemy-controlled area of the city at night. He assessed that his best course of action to save the lives of his crew was to push through and out of the ambush. Accordingly, he drove his Warrior directly through the barricade, not knowing if there were mines or improvised explosive devices placed there to destroy the vehicle. By doing this he was able to lead the Warriors towards safety.

As the smoke in his driver's tunnel cleared, he was just able to make out the shape of another RPG in flight heading directly towards him. He pulled the hatch down with one hand, while still controlling his vehicle with the other. However, the overpressure from the explosion wrenched the hatch out of his grip, and the flames and force of the blast passed directly over him, down the driver's tunnel, further wounding the semi-conscious gunner in the turret. The impact of this rocket destroyed his periscope, so he was forced to drive through the remainder of the ambush route, some 1,500 metres, with his hatch open and his head exposed to enemy fire, all the time with no communications with any other vehicle. During this long surge through the ambush the vehicle was again struck by RPGs and small arms fire. With his head remaining out of the hatch to enable him to see the route ahead, he was directly exposed to much of this fire, and was himself hit by a 7.62mm bullet, which penetrated his helmet and remained lodged on its inner surface.

Despite this harrowing weight of incoming fire, he continued to push through the extended ambush, still leading his platoon until he broke

clear. He then visually identified another Warrior from his company and followed it through the streets to the outside of the Cimic House outpost, which was receiving small arms fire from the surrounding area. Once he had brought his vehicle to a halt, without thought for his personal safety, he climbed on to the turret of the still burning vehicle and, seemingly oblivious to the incoming fire, manhandled his wounded platoon commander out of the turret, off the vehicle and into the safety of a nearby Warrior. He then returned once again to his vehicle and again mounted the exposed turret to lift out the gunner and move him to a position of safety. Exposing himself yet again to enemy fire, he returned to the rear of the burning vehicle to lead the disorientated and shocked men and casualties to safety. Remounting his vehicle for the last time, he drove it through the complex chicane and into the security of the defended perimeter, thus denying it to the enemy. Only then did he pull the fire extinguisher handles, immobilising the engine, dismount and move himself into the relative safety of the back of another Warrior. Once inside, he collapsed from sheer physical and mental exhaustion from his efforts and was subsequently evacuated himself.

On 11 June his Warrior was part of a quick reaction force tasked to attempt to cut off a mortar team that had attacked a Coalition Force base. As the lead vehicle of the platoon he was moving rapidly through the dark streets towards the suspected firing point when his vehicle was ambushed by the enemy from a series of roof-top positions. During this initial heavy weight of enemy fire, an RPG detonated on the vehicle's frontal armour, just 6 inches from Beharry's head, resulting in a serious head injury. Other RPGs struck the turret and sides of the vehicle, incapacitating his commander and injuring several of the crew. Despite the blood from his head obscuring his vision, he managed to control his vehicle and forcefully reversed out of the ambush area. The vehicle continued to move until it struck the wall of a nearby building and came to rest. Beharry then lost consciousness as a result of his wounds. By moving the Warrior out of the enemy's chosen killing area he enabled other Warrior crews to extract his crew with a greatly reduced risk from incoming fire. Despite his serious head injury, his level-headed actions in the face of heavy and accurate fire at short range again almost certainly saved the lives of his crew and provided the conditions for their safe evacuation to medical treatment.

Beharry displayed repeated extreme gallantry and unquestioned valour, despite intense direct attacks, personal injury and damage to his vehicle in the face of relentless enemy action. He had also served in Kosovo. At a press conference he was asked what was going through his mind during the engagement. Johnson, without thinking, answered 'An RPG.' When the Queen pinned the VC to his chest she said to him: 'It's been rather a long time since I've awarded one of these.'

I had the great pleasure of meeting Johnson in 2006. Asked what he did to earn his VC, he says: 'I have no memory of it, only what I have been told I did.' He is one of the most modest men I have ever met, and does not believe that he did anything other than his duty. The men of his platoon would not agree with him, and neither do I. Grenada is planning to declare an annual 'Beharry Day' in his honour. His autobiography is called *Barefoot Soldier*. At the time of going to press, he is one of the 10 surviving VC holders.

Afghanistan, 2000–2015

As part of the West's 'War on Terror', US/UK forces occupied Afghanistan to remove the Taliban from power. This was done very quickly, but the occupying troops continue to face resistance from insurgents. So far eight Victoria Crosses have been awarded for this campaign.

Lance Corporal WILLIE 'MUDGUTS' APIATA
between March and October 2004
He was 35 years old and serving in the 1st New Zealand Special Air Service Group when he was part of a troop which had laid up in a

defensive formation for the night. At approximately 03.15 hours the troop was attacked by about twenty enemy fighters, who had approached by stealth. RPGs struck two of the troop vehicles, destroying one and immobilising the other. The strike was followed by dense and persistent machine-gun and automatic rifle fire from close range. The initial attack was directed at the vehicle where Apiata was stationed and he was blown off the bonnet by the impact of the RPGs striking the vehicle. He was dazed but not injured. The two other vehicle crew members had been wounded by shrapnel, and one of them, Corporal 'D', was in a serious condition. Illuminated by the burning vehicle and under sustained, accurate enemy fire, the three men took what little cover was available. Corporal 'D' was discovered to have sustained life-threatening wounds. The other two men immediately began applying basic first aid. Lance Corporal Apiata assumed command of the situation, as he could see that his superior's condition was deteriorating rapidly. By this time, however, their exposed position was coming under increasingly intense enemy fire. Corporal 'D' was now suffering from serious arterial bleeding and was lapsing in and out of consciousness.

Apiata concluded that his comrade urgently required medical attention, or he would likely die. Pinned down by the enemy, in the direct line of fire between friend and foe, he also judged that there was almost no chance of help reaching his position. With no thought of abandoning his colleague to save himself, he took a decision of the highest order of personal courage under fire. Knowing the risks involved in moving to open ground, Lance Corporal Apiata decided to carry Corporal 'D' single-handedly to the relative safety of the main Troop position, which afforded better cover and where medical treatment could be given. He ordered his other colleague, Trooper 'E', to make his own way back to the rear.

In total disregard for his own safety, he stood up and lifted his comrade. He then carried him across 70 metres of broken, rocky and fire-swept ground, fully exposed to heavy enemy fire and into the face of returning fire from the main position. That neither of them was hit was miraculous. Having delivered his wounded companion to relative safety, he then rearmed himself and rejoined the fight in counter-attack. The troop could now concentrate entirely on winning the firefight. After an engagement lasting approximately 20 minutes, the assault was broken up and the numerically superior attackers were routed with significant casualties, with the troop in pursuit. Lance Corporal Apiata had contributed materially to the operational success of the engagement.

A subsequent medical assessment confirmed that Corporal 'D' would probably have died from loss of blood and shock had it not been for Lance Corporal Apiata's selflessly courageous act. At the 2008 VC and GC Association meeting he was asked about his VC action, and replied simply, 'You look after your friends.' The exact date of this VC action is still classified, as is the name of the soldier whose life Apiata saved. But I wrote to the NZSAS and was given 'between March and October'. His is the first VC for New Zealand since that country introduced its own award in 1991. At the time of going to press, he is one of the 10 surviving VC holders.

Corporal BRYAN BUDD

SANGIN, Helmand Province
27 July and 20 August 2006

He was 29 years old and serving in the 3rd Bn, Parachute Regiment when his section was on patrol and identified and engaged two enemy gunmen on the roof of a building in the centre of Sangin. Without regard for his personal safety, he led an assault where the enemy fire was heaviest. His gallant action allowed a wounded soldier to be evacuated to safety for life-saving treatment. On 20 August, when he was located in the town of Sangin, Budd and his platoon were holding a small isolated coalition outpost (known as a Platoon House) to protect engineers blowing holes in a compound 500 metres away. The site was subject to almost daily Taliban attacks. There were three sections on patrol, spread out in a head-high cornfield around the compound. Budd spotted four Taliban approaching at a distance of 50

metres. Using hand signals, he led his section in a flanking move to try to cut them off, but they were seen and the Taliban opened fire. A further group of enemy then opened fire from a wall further back. The British soldiers took heavy fire as they knelt or lay down trying to take cover. One soldier was hit in the shoulder and another was shot in the nose. Realising his section was taking heavy fire and the men were likely to be killed, Budd got up and rushed straight through the corn in the direction of the Taliban, now just 20 metres away. He opened up on them in fully automatic mode with his rifle, and contact was immediately lost, but the enemy fire lessened, allowing the rest of the section to withdraw to safety so the casualties could be treated.

After the withdrawal Budd was declared missing in action and most of A Company was sent back to find him. Apache and Harrier air support was called in to beat the Taliban back. An hour later Budd was found beside three dead Taliban. It was clear he had killed them, but he was badly wounded and had no pulse. The company sergeant major recovered his body on a quad bike, but he was declared dead on arrival at the Platoon House. Ballistics has since shown that he was killed by a NATO round. He had also served in Yugoslavia, Sierra Leone, Macedonia and Iraq.

Trooper MARK DONALDSON

Oruzgan Province 2 September 2008

He was 29 years old and serving in the 3rd Australian Special Air Service Squadron. He was travelling in a combined Afghan, US and Australian convoy when it was engaged by a numerically superior, well-entrenched and coordinated enemy. The ambush was initiated by a high level of sustained machine-gun fire coupled with the effective use of RPGs. Such was the effect of the heavy fire that the patrol suffered numerous casualties, completely losing the initiative and becoming suppressed. Donaldson reacted spontaneously to regain the initiative. He moved rapidly between alternate positions of cover engaging the enemy with 66mm and 84mm anti-tank weapons as well as his M4 rifle. During the early stages of the ambush he deliberately exposed himself to enemy fire in order to draw attention to himself and away from the wounded men. This selfless act bought enough time for the wounded to be moved to a position of relative safety.

As the enemy had employed a rolling ambush, the convoy was forced to conduct numerous vehicle manoeuvres, under intense Taliban fire, over a distance of approximately 4 kilometres to escape from the engagement area. As the wounded were taking up most of the available space in the vehicles, those who had not been wounded, including Donaldson, were left with no option but to run alongside the vehicles throughout. During this time a severely wounded coalition force interpreter was inadvertently left behind. Without orders and on his own initiative, Donaldson, with complete disregard for his own safety, moved alone on foot across 80 metres of exposed ground to recover the wounded interpreter. His movement, once identified by the enemy, drew intense and accurate machine-gun fire from entrenched positions. Upon reaching the wounded man, he picked him up and carried him back to the relative safety of the vehicles and then provided immediate first aid before returning to the fight.

On subsequent occasions during the action Donaldson administered medical aid to other wounded men, while continually engaging the enemy. Trooper Donaldson's acts of exceptional gallantry in the face of accurate and sustained enemy fire ultimately saved the life of the interpreter and ensured the safety of the other members of the convoy. He had also served in East Timor and Iraq. His is the first VC for Australia since that country introduced its own award in 1991. At the time of going to press, he is one of the 10 surviving VC holders.

Corporal BENJAMIN 'RS' or 'ARSE' ROBERTS-SMITH

TIZAK, Kandahar Province 11 June 2010
He was 32 years old and serving in the Australian Special Air Service Squadron when he was circling the battle in a Blackhawk helicopter, providing sniper support to the force on the ground. Immediately upon the heli-copter insertion, the troop was engaged by machine-gun and RPG fire from multiple positions. Two men were wounded and the troop pinned down by fire from three machine-guns in an elevated fortified position. Under cover of close support, Roberts-Smith's patrol manoeuvred to within 70 metres of the enemy in order to neutralise the machine-guns and regain the initiative. His patrol fought their way to within 40 metres and the weight of enemy fire prevented further forward movement. Roberts-Smith then noticed some nearby cover provided by a small building which he moved up to; at this point he spotted an insurgent engaging his patrol. Roberts-Smith engaged this insurgent and killed him.

With members of his patrol still pinned down, Roberts-Smith exposed himself to draw fire away from the pinned men, which enabled them to bring fire to bear on the enemy. With two men Roberts-Smith ended up in front of the enemy machine-guns and the three Diggers crawled to within 20 metres of the insurgents, when grenades were thrown and an SAS soldier knelt to engage the enemy until his gun jammed. The third man was under such withering fire that he could not even raise his head, so Corporal Roberts-Smith realised it was up to him. In his own words, 'I saw my mates getting ripped up so I decided to move forward; I wasn't going to sit there and do nothing.' He got to a wall and silenced the first gun before moving forward 9 metres to the second enemy gun, which he also silenced. Within seconds his comrades were right next to him and they decided to push the advantage while they had it; they killed a number of insurgents before the position was consolidated. Roberts-Smith's act of selfless valour directly enabled his troop to go on and clear the village. The action lasted for six hours, by the end of which 60 insurgents were killed. This decisive engagement subsequently caused the remaining Taliban in the Shah Wali Kot District to retreat from the area. Ben said of it all; 'I saw a lot of brave men do a lot of brave things that day. I just hope that everyone would understand that I'm wearing it for the unit.' Sergeant 'P' was awarded the Star of Gallantry for the same action.

Roberts-Smith has also served in East Timor, Fiji and Iraq. He has also been awarded the Medal for Gallantry. At the time of going to press, he is one of the 10 surviving VC holders.

Corporal DANIEL 'PRINCE HARRY' KEIGHRAN
DERAPET Uruzgan Province
24 August 2010

He was 27 years old and serving in the 6th Battalion, Royal Australian Regiment when he was a member of a fighting patrol with men of the Afghan National Army. They were engaged by a numerically superior and coordinated enemy attack from multiple positions. The attack was initiated by a high level of sustained and accurate machine-gun and small arms fire which pinned down the combined forces and caused a loss of momentum.

Realising that the forward elements of the patrol needed effective fire support, Keighran and another man moved to an exposed ridge-line to identify enemy positions to direct the return fire of both Australian and Afghan machine-guns. This was done under heavy fire.

On reaching this position and with complete disregard for his own safety, Keighran moved over the ridgeline in order to identify targets for the support troops. After identifying some targets he, still under persistent enemy fire continued to lead his team and move around the ridge to both direct fire and to move them to more effective positions.

As the intensity of enemy fire grew, Keighran returned to the crest to identify targets and adjust the fire of Australian light armoured vehicles. His actions resulted in the suppression of the enemy, which assisted in turning the fight in favour of the combined patrol. Keighran deliberately and repeatedly again exposed himself to heavy enemy fire to assist in target identification and marking of the forward line of troops for fire support while simultaneously engaging the enemy.

Realising that the new position was a better location for the patrol's joint fire controller, he moved over 100 metres across exposed parts of the ridgeline under fire to relocate the fire controller to the new position. Keighran then rose from cover to expose his position four times in order to assist in target identification of a further three enemy firing points, all the time under fire.

During one of these occasions, Lance-Corporal Jared MacKinney became a casualty; Keighran left his position to deliberately draw fire away from the team treating the wounded man. Keighran remained in an exposed position under fire in order to direct suppressing fire and then to assist in the clearance of the landing zone to enable evacuation of the casualty. MacKinney later died of his wounds.

These deliberate acts of courage were instrumental in permitting the withdrawal of the combined patrol with no further casualties.

Keighran also served in East Timor and Iraq. Of the award he said, 'It was not so much brave as very stupid. I wouldn't be here today if it wasn't for the boys with me that day; it's as much theirs as mine.' He is known as 'Prince Harry' due to his flaming red hair. At the time of going to press, he is one of the 10 surviving VC holders.

Lance-Corporal JAMES ASHWORTH
NAHR-E-SARAJ Helmand Province 13 June 2012

He was 23 years old and serving in the 1st Battalion, The Grenadier Guards when two aircraft landing the Reconnaissance Platoon were hit by enemy fire as they came in to land. Unflustered, Ashworth – an inexperienced NCO – raced 300 metres with his fire team into the heart of the insurgent-dominated village. While two insurgents were killed and two sniper rifles recovered, an Afghan Police follow-up attack stalled when a patrolman was killed by the fleeing enemy. Called on to press-on the attack, Ashworth insisted on moving to the front of his fire team to lead the pursuit. Approaching the entrance to a compound under enemy machine-gun fire, he stepped over the body of the dead patrolman, threw a grenade and surged forward. Breaking into the compound, Ashworth quickly drove the insurgent back and into an out-building from where he made his last stand.

By now the compound was being pressed on a number of fronts by insurgents desperate to relieve their sniper team. Realising the stalemate had to be broken quickly, Ashworth identified a low wall that would provide him with enough cover to get close to his target to accurately post his final grenade. As he started to crawl behind the wall towards the enemy a fierce fire-fight broke out but, undaunted by the danger, he grimly continued his advance. After three minutes of crawling he had edged forward 15 metres and then crawled out of cover to get a better throwing angle. By now enemy rounds were tearing up the ground around him. Then, as he threw the grenade, he was hit by enemy fire and killed. Despite the ferocity of the insurgent's resistance, Ashworth refused to be beaten. His total disregard for his own safety in ensuring that his grenade was posted accurately was the gallant act of a soldier who had willingly placed himself in the line of fire and deserves the highest recognition.

Corporal CAMERON 'CAM' BAIRD
KHOD VALLEY Uruzgan Province
22 June 2013
He was 32 and serving in the 4th Battalion, 2nd Royal Australian (Commando) Regiment when during Operation Slipper his team conducted a helicopter assault into the village of Ghawchak and came under small arms fire from several enemy positions. Baird seized the initiative, leading his team to take out the positions, killing six of the enemy and enabling the assault to continue. Shortly afterwards another team came under heavy fire, resulting in the commander being badly wounded. Baird led his team to provide support. En route his team again came under machine-gun fire from a number of enemy positions. Baird charged at these positions, supported by his team. On nearing the enemy they came under fire from the flank. Baird immediately took out this new threat while his team continued the attack on the prepared positions. Again Baird came under machine-gun fire; he moved to cover and suppressed this new threat, enabling his team to close on the entrance to the prepared positions.

On three separate occasions Baird charged an enemy-held building within the prepared compound. On the first he charged the door, followed by another team member. Despite heavy fire, Baird pushed forward while firing into the building but was forced to withdraw due to a malfunction with his weapon. Once the stoppage was cleared, he again advanced on the door under fire. He engaged the enemy through the door but was unable to suppress the position and took cover to reload. For the third time Baird selflessly drew the enemy fire away from his team and assaulted the doorway. Enemy fire was seen to strike the ground and walls around him until dust obscured visibility. The enemy was neutralised but Corporal Baird was killed in the effort.

Baird had also served in East Timor and Iraq. He was also a recipient of the MG.

Lance Corporal JOSHUA LEAKEY
Helmand Province, 22 August 2013
He was 25 years old and serving in the 1st Battalion, The Parachute Regiment, when he took part in a combined UK/US assault on a Taliban stronghold. The force came under accurate machine-gun and RPG fire, resulting in the Command Group being pinned down on the exposed slope of a hill. The team tried to extract the Command Group from the killing zone for a hour, resulting in US Marine Captain Brandon Bocian being wounded and their communications being put out of action.

Lance Corporal Leakey, positioned in the lee of the hill, realised the seriousness of the situation and with complete disregard for his own safety he dashed across the open hillside, which was being raked by machine-gun fire. As he crested the hill, the full severity of the situation became apparent: some twenty Taliban had surrounded two friendly MG teams and a mortar section, rendering their fire support ineffective.

Undeterred by the danger, Leakey moved down the slope and gave first aid to Captain Bocian. Despite being the most junior NCO, Leakey took control and initiated the casualty evacuation. Realising that the initiative was still in the hands of the enemy, he set off back up the hill under fire to get one of the suppressed MGs into action. With bullets impacting all around him, Leakey moved the gun to another position and began to engage the enemy. This action spurred those around him back into the fight; nonetheless heavy enemy fire continued. In full knowledge of the danger, Leakey ran down the hill again, picked up the second MG and brought it up to the top of the hill. Drawing much enemy fire, he overcame his fatigue to re-site the gun, and returned fire. This proved the turning point. Inspired by Leakey's actions, and with MGs now at their disposal, the force began to fight back with renewed ferocity. Leakey then handed over the MG and led the extraction of Captain Bocian to a point from where he could be evacuated.

During this assault 11 of the Taliban were killed and 4 wounded. Lance Corporal Leakey single-handedly regained the initiative and prevented considerable loss of life. Asked about his valour, Leakey simply said, 'The only thing I was scared of was letting my cap badge down.' He is second cousin twice removed of Nigel Leakey VC. At the time of going to press, he is one of 10 surviving VC holders.

Chapter Fourteen

BURIAL LOCATIONS

Here I have listed each country, followed by each cemetery, in alphabetical order. Where two cemeteries have the same name, I have also given the town name, in *italics*. These entries are in turn followed by each recipient's number, in **bold**, taken from the chronological list. Anyone wishing to visit any VC holder's grave can see at a glance how many are buried in any given cemetery. Full cemetery addresses can be found in the chronological list. Note that St Mary's RC Cemetery and Kensal Green Cemetery are at the same location, as are St Mary's and Charlton Cemeteries, Dover. Not all cemeteries are open to the public so visitors should check before travelling. This list does not include those buried at sea, those with no known grave, cremations (unless the ashes are buried in a cemetery or churchyard), or those buried in a lone grave not in a cemetery.

AFGHANISTAN
Seah Sang Cemetery **326**; Sherpur Cantonment Cemetery **344**.

ALGERIA
Bone War Cemetery **1251**.

AUSTRALIA
Albury Presbyterian Cemetery **1019**; Allonah Cemetery **887**; Balmoral Cemetery **428**; Bendigo General Cemetery **262**; Botany Cemetery **798**; Bowral Cemetery **120**; Brighton Cemetery **884**, **1085**; Brighton Lawn Cemetery **1043**; C of E Cemetery **46**; Cornelian Bay Cemetery **749**; East Brighton General Cemetery **792**; Esperance Public Lawn Cemetery **1339**; Fawkner Cemetery **609**; Frankston Cemetery **1114**; General Presbyterian Cemetery **260**; Hamilton Lawn Cemetery **1338**; Karrakatta Cemetery **650**, **745**, **835**, **1087**, **1191**; Lawn Cemetery **1348**; Longreach Town Cemetery **1057**; Macksville Cemetery **1340**; Melbourne General Cemetery **13**, **335**; Mount Duneed Cemetery **824**; Myrtleford Cemetery **1059**; Norwood Cemetery **975**; Pinaroo Lawn Cemetery **1052**; Reedycreek Baptist Churchyard **1362**; Rookwood Cemetery **217**, **795**; St James' Churchyard **488**; St Kilda Cemetery **622**; St Matthew's Anglican Churchyard **1062**; South Head Cemetery **1190**; Springvale Cemetery **831**, **1107**; Springvale Lawn Cemetery **1252**; Stirling District Cemetery **736**; Stirling North Garden Cemetery **532**; Toowong Cemetery **315**; Tower Hill Cemetery **228**; West Terrace AIF Cemetery **735**, **789**, **877**, **1015**; West Wyalong Cemetery **1326**; Woronora Cemetery **647**.

BAHAMAS
Nassau War Cemetery for United Nations Airmen **717**.

BELGIUM
Bedford House Cemetery **664**; Birr Cross Road Cemetery **853**; Blankenberg Town Cemetery **993**; Brandhoek New Military Cemetery **744/854**; Bruges Town Cemetery **86**; Brussels Town Cemetery **1310**; Canada Farm Cemetery **850**; Essex Farm Cemetery **840**; Grooterbreek Cemetery **613**; Heverlee War Cemetery **1166**, **1167**, **1216**; Hooge Crater Cemetery **888**; La

Brique Military Cemetery **683**; Leopoldsburg War Cemetery **1300, 1316**; Lijssenthoek Military Cemetery **644**; Mendinghem Military Cemetery **842**; Menin Road South Military Cemetery **843**; Oxford Road Cemetery **891**; Perth Cemetery **539, 879**; Railway Dugouts Burial Ground **839**; St Symphorien Military Cemetery **523**; Stacegham Communal Cemetery **1131**; Tyne Cot Cemetery **893, 903, 916**; Vlamertinghe Military Cemetery **529**; Vlamertinghe New British Cemetery **867**; Westoutre British Cemetery **983**; White House Cemetery **581**; Ypres Reservoir Cemetery **465**; Zantvoorde British Cemetery **548, 1100**.

BELIZE
Belize City Military Cemetery **328**.

BERMUDA
St George's Methodist Cemetery **603**.

BURMA
Taukkyan War Cemetery **1262, 1264, 1277, 1285, 1314, 1322, 1325**; Yay Way Cemetery **179**.

CANADA
Anglican Cemetery **1125**; Cranberry Lake Cemetery **1105**; Eastnor Township Cemetery **279**; Elnora Cemetery **1033**; Field of Honour Cemetery **1117**; Forest Lawn Memorial Park **940**; Greenwood Cemetery **828, 907, 1292**; Hantsport Baptist Church Cemetery **225**; Hillside Cemetery **590**; Holy Sepulchre Cemetery **132**; Holy Trinity Cemetery **912**; Lougheed Cemetery **911**; Masonic Cemetery **871**; Moosomin South Side Cemetery **910**; Mount Hermon Cemetery **493**; Mount Hope Cemetery **1318**; Mount Pleasant Cemetery **1095, 1137**; Mount Royal Cemetery **592, 1053, 1074**; Mountain View Cemetery **470, 756, 860, 906, 923**; Notre Dame de Lourdes Cemetery **872**; Oakland Cemetery **793**; Ocean View Memorial Park **1222**; Pine Cemetery **1031**; Pine Hill Cemetery **620**; Prospect Cemetery **295, 915, 1075**; Royal Oak Burial Park **1006**; St Alban's Cemetery **1024**; St Andrew's Presbyterian Churchyard **1223**; St James' Cemetery **492**; St Mark's Church Cemetery **586**; St Michael's Cemetery **155**; Sanctuary Park Cemetery **1327**; Snider Mountain Baptist Church Cemetery **1098**; Union Cemetery **788, 1049**; West Korah Cemetery **1109**; Winnipeg Presbyterian Cemetery **972**; York Cemetery **563**.

CHANNEL ISLANDS
Mont a L'Abbe Cemetery **284**; St Saviour's Churchyard **989**.

CHINA
Bubbling Road Cemetery **991**.

CORFU
British Cemetery **105**.

CYPRUS
Kyrenia British Cemetery **339**.

DENMARK
Garnisons Kirkegaard Cemetery **642**; Horsholm Cemetery **1037**.

EGYPT
Cairo War Memorial Cemetery **1197**; El Alamein War Cemetery **1218, 1221, 1227, 1228**; Hadra War Memorial Cemetery **543**; Halfaya Sollum War Cemetery **1099**; Kantara War Memorial Cemetery **1077**.

ENGLAND
Abney Park Cemetery **201**; Acklam Cemetery **1275**; Acton Parish Churchyard **99**; Aldershot Military Cemetery **289, 1135, 1354**; All Saints' Cemetery **747**; All Saints' Chapel **708**; All Saints' Church, *Selsley* **401**; All Saints' Church, *Swallowfield* **33**; All Saints' Churchyard, *Ashbocking* **1255**; All Saints' Churchyard, *Branksome Park* **322**; All Saints' Churchyard, *Crondall* **777**; All Saints' Churchyard, *Hordle* **776**; All Saints' Churchyard, *Leamington Spa* **1148**; All Saints' Churchyard, *Maidenhead* **300**; All Saints' New Cemetery **1155**; All Souls' Cemetery **180**; All Souls' Churchyard **340**; Allerton Cemetery **447, 836**; Alton Cemetery **1152**; Ardington Church **7**; Ardwick Cemetery **166**; Arksey Cemetery **797**; Arnos Vale Cemetery **100, 1121**; Bardwell Parish Churchyard **291**; Barrow-in-Furness Cemetery **347**; Basingstoke Old Cemetery **636**; Bath Abbey Cemetery **2**; Bear Road Cemetery **775, 1170**; Beckenham Cemetery **740**; Bells Hill Cemetery **459**; Belper Cemetery **954**; Blackley Jewish Cemetery **781**; Boarshaw New Cemetery **1010**; Bradden Cemetery **1298**; Bretby Churchyard **961**; Brighton Extra-Mural Cemetery **50, 1002**; Brompton Cemetery **11, 22, 77, 98, 128, 147, 213, 224, 264, 290, 395, 627**; Brookwood Cemetery **6, 150, 186, 371, 435, 460, 516, 547, 695, 919, 1041, 1093**; Burlington Priory Churchyard **69**; Burngreave Cemetery **461**; Burnham Norton Churchyard **1290**; Cadeby Churchyard **530**; Cadley Churchyard **72**; Camberwell Old Cemetery **28, 998**; Cambridge City Cemetery **239, 491**; Canford Cemetery **405, 502**; Canterbury City Cemetery **430**; Carisbrooke Cemetery **140**; Cavendish Churchyard **1173**; Chadderton Cemetery **550**; Charing Cemetery **832**; Charlton Cemetery **499**; Cheltenham Cemetery **9, 64, 317, 987**; Cheriton Road Cemetery **37, 110, 143**; Chesterton Parish Churchyard **131**; Chislehurst Cemetery **655**; Christ Church Churchyard **1143**; Christchurch Cemetery, *Brentwood* **31**; Christchurch Cemetery, *Southbourne* **283**; Christchurch Churchyard **577**; Church of the Holy Cross Churchyard **108**; City of London Cemetery **84, 599**; City of Westminster Cemetery **39**; Colchester Cemetery **365**; Coleford Cemetery **693**; Coniston Churchyard **1001**; Corton Denham Churchyard **1254**; Cranham Churchyard **1345**; Denbury Churchyard **1012**; Dewsbury Cemetery **805**; Dorking Cemetery **946**; Earnley Cemetery **748**; East Cemetery **233**; East Sheen Cemetery **370**; East-the-Water Cemetery **78, 341**; Ecclesall Churchyard **858**; Edgerton Cemetery **892**; Egremont Cemetery **677**; Epsom Cemetery **439**; Eston Cemetery **996**; Exeter Higher Cemetery **134**; Exwick Cemetery **278**; Fairfield Road Cemetery **337**; Falmouth Town Cemetery **1213**; Ford Cemetery **137**; Ford Park Cemetery **38, 306**; Gorton Cemetery **780**; Grange Cemetery **931**; Great Malvern Cemetery **181**; Greenbank Cemetery **863**; Harberton Parish Churchyard **243**; Harehills Cemetery **674**; Hastings Borough Cemetery **231**; Heaton Cemetery **425**; Hendon Park Cemetery **310, 467**; Heywood Cemetery **44**; Highgate Cemetery **174, 182**; Highland Road Cemetery **29, 66, 79, 241, 254, 313, 324, 396**; Hillingdon Churchyard **977**; Hills Street Cemetery **249**; Holy Cross Churchyard, *Crediton* **362**; Holy Cross Churchyard, *Newton Ferrers* **1206**; Holy Trinity Churchyard, *Claygate* **618**; Holy Trinity Churchyard, *Hoylake* **1126**; Holy Trinity Churchyard, *Sunningdale* **1035**; Holy Trinity Churchyard, *Tunbridge* **841**; Holy Trinity Parish Churchyard **169**; Hulbert Road Cemetery **453**; Hunslet Cemetery **855**; Hunton Churchyard **917**; Ilkley Cemetery **829**; Inghamite Burial Ground **852**; Ipswich Old Cemetery **672**; Kensal Green Cemetery **12, 23, 59, 113, 115, 204, 240, 299, 325, 408, 409, 411, 480**; Kibworth Harcourt Parish Churchyard **301**; Kings Langley Cemetery **785**; Kingston Cemetery, *Kingston-upon-Thames* **1265**; Kingston Cemetery, *Portsmouth* **82**; Kirkdale Cemetery **138**; Lambeth Cemetery **192, 237**; Lansdown Cemetery **261**; Laventie British War Cemetery **1014**; Leigh Cemetery **1130**; Liverpool Cemetery **75, 123, 145**; Locksbrook Cemetery **168, 170, 280**; Lockwood Cemetery **807**; London Road Cemetery, *Coalville* **510**; London Road Cemetery, *Coventry* **466**; London Road Cemetery, *Maldon* **397**; Longborough Churchyard **501**; Maidstone Road Cemetery **95**; Manchester Southern Cemetery **40, 763**; Manor Park Cemetery **706**; Margravine Road Cemetery **80, 282**; Marlow Parish Churchyard **250**; Medstead Churchyard **474**; Mill Hill Cemetery **570**; Milton Cemetery **391, 873**; Morden Cemetery **200**; Mousehole Old School Cemetery **89**; Netherbury Churchyard Cemetery **359**; New Hall Cemetery **684**; New Monkland (Landward) Cemetery **874**; New Wortley Cemetery **985**; Newport Cemetery **616**; Nocton Churchyard **679**; Norham Churchyard **661**; North Cemetery

Leckenham **151**; St Peter's Churchyard, *Peterchurch* **356**; St Peter's Churchyard, *Rodmarton* **364**; St Peter's Churchyard, *Shambrook* **515**; St Peter's Parish Churchyard, *Clearwell* **1132**; St Peter's Parish Churchyard, *Ightham* **152**; St Stephen's Parish Churchyard **297**; St Swithun's Parish Church **276**; St Thomas of Canterbury Churchyard **441**; St Thomas's Churchyard **823**; St Veep Parish Churchyard **772**; Shire Lodge Cemetery **1361**; Shorncliffe Military Cemetery **199**, **257**, **393**; Spittal Cemetery **55**; Sprowston Cemetery **794**; Stapleford Cemetery **611**; Stockport Borough Cemetery **932**; Stoke Cemetery **442**; Streatham Cemetery **812**; Streatham Park Cemetery **968**; Swinton Cemetery **506**; Temple Road Cemetery **406**; Thorntree Cemetery **825**; Tiverton Cemetery **897**, **967**; Tottenham Cemetery **486**; Touchen End Cemetery **640**; Tower Hamlets Cemetery **116**; Undercliffe Cemetery **73**; Upper and Lower Wortley Cemetery **865**; Wandsworth Cemetery **386**; Wardsend Cemetery **149**; Warstone Lane Cemetery **331**; Warsop Cemetery **845**; Watling Street Burial Ground **419**; Wells Cemetery **329**, **404**; Weaste Cemetery **51**; West Hampstead Cemetery **950**; West Hill Cemetery **212**, **574**; Western Cemetery **769**; Westminster Abbey **32**; Weston-super-Mare Cemetery **107**; Whalley New Road Cemetery **455**; Wheatley Hill Cemetery **678**; Whitwick Cemetery **388**; Wilford Hill Cemetery **680**, **1171**; Willow Grove Cemetery **898**; Wilton Cemetery **628**; Wimborne Road Cemetery **431**; Windsor Town Cemetery **177**, **673**; Witton Cemetery **448**, **662**; Woodhouse Lane Cemetery **652**; Woodlands Cemetery **330**, **1154**, **1204**; Woolwich Cemetery **83**, **286**; Wych Hill Cemetery **403**; York Cemetery **71**.

ERITREA
Senafe Military Cemetery **17**.

FALKLAND ISLANDS
Blue Beach War Cemetery **1353**.

FRANCE
Abbeville Communal Cemetery **625**; Adanac Military Cemetery **764**, **1046**; AIF Burial Ground **958**; Annoeullin Communal Cemetery **813**; Arras Road Cemetery **653**; Auberchicourt British Cemetery **1141**; Aubigny Communal Cemetery **1064**; Bailleul Communal Cemetery **770**; Bancourt British Cemetery **750**; Barlin Communal Cemetery **804**; Bayeux War Cemetery **1289**; Beinvillers Military Cemetery **555**; Bellicourt British Cemetery **1102**; Berles New Military Cemetery **790**; Bethune Town Cemetery **560**; Beuvry Communal Cemetery **1039**; Boulogne Eastern Cemetery **629**; Bouzincourt Ridge Cemetery **960**; Braine Communal Cemetery **544**; Brest (Kerfautras) Cemetery **1182**; Brown's Copse Cemetery **802**; Caen Protestant Cemetery **215**; Carnieres Communal Cemetery **1118**; Choques Military Cemetery **670**; Cimetiere de Caucade **196**, **471**; Cimetiere Protestant du Grand-Jus **314**; Cojeul British Cemetery **801**, **810**; Contalmaison Chateau Cemetery **742**; Corbie Communal Cemetery **729**; Couin New British Cemetery **1021**; Crouy British Cemetery **1025**; Cuinchy Guards Cemetery **473**; Dartmoor Cemetery **741**; Delville Wood Cemetery **738**; Dernancourt Communal Cemetery **1030**; Dominion Cemetery **1069**; Douchy-les-Ayette British Cemetery **876**; Dourlers Communal Cemetery **937**; Dud Corner Cemetery **654**, **657**; Escoublac-la-Baule War Cemetery **1212**; Estaires Communal Cemetery **517**; Etaples Military Cemetery **535**; Etretat Churchyard **752**; Fillievres British Cemetery **699**; Flatiron Copse Military Cemetery **585**; Foncquevillers Military Cemetery **718**; Fouquescort British Cemetery **1028**; Gordon Dump Cemetery **728**; Gorre British and Indian Cemetery **941**; Hangard Wood British Cemetery **1026**; Heath Cemetery **1023**, **1034**; Hem Farm Cemetery **1061**; Hem Hill Military Cemetery **782**; Hermies Hill British Cemetery **762**, **1083**; La Chaudiere Military Cemetery **800**; Le Cateau Military Cemetery **953**; Lichfield Crater Cemetery **796**; Lilliers Communal Cemetery **538**, **690**; Longuenesse Souvenir Cemetery **579**; Lonsdale Cemetery **721**; Mailly Wood Cemetery **1048**; Marfaux British Cemetery **1020**; Masnieres British Cemetery **1096**; Mazingarbe Communal Cemetery **666**; Meharicourt

Communal Cemetery **1279**; Metz-en-Couture Cemetery **934**; Moeuvres Communal Cemetery **806**; Mory Abbey Military Cemetery **1040**; Namps-au-Val British Cemetery **976**; Naves Communal Cemetery **1123**; Nery Communal Cemetery **536**; Neuvilly Communal Cemetery **1120**; Niagara Cemetery **1119**; Noeux-les-Mines Communal Cemetery **864**, **866**; Norfolk Cemetery **716**, **1150**; Ors Communal Cemetery **1144**, **1147**; Peronne Communal Cemetery **1063**; Peronne Road Cemetery **966**; Pozieres Military Cemetery **739**; Queant Communal Cemetery **1094**; Queant Road Cemetery **787**; Querrieu British Cemetery **962**; Rocquigny-Equancourt Road British Cemetery **900**; Roisel Communal Cemetery **951**; Romeries Cemetery **1076**; Royal Irish Rifles Churchyard **714**; Sablonnieres New Communal Cemetery **437**; St Sever Cemetery **978**; Ste Marie Cemetery **1086**; Sanders Keep Military Cemetery **1097**; Senantes Churchyard **1288**; Unicorn Cemetery **1072**; Vadencourt British Cemetery **556**; Vailly British Cemetery **527**; Vaulx Hill Cemetery **1054**; Vertigneul Churchyard **938**; Vieille-Chapelle New Military Cemetery **980**, **981**; Villers-Bretonneux Military Cemetery **1027**; Villers-Faucon Communal Cemetery **837**, **870**; Vracourt Copse Cemetery **1045**; Wanquentin Communal Cemetery **1011**; Warlencourt British Cemetery **754**; Wavans British Cemetery **943**; Y Farm Military Cemetery **626**.

GERMANY
Becklingen War Cemetery **1331**, **1335**; Berlin South-Western Cemetery **531**; Hamburg Cemetery **927**, **1192**; Niederzehren Cemetery **963**; Reichswald Forest War Cemetery **1319**; Rheinberg War Cemetery **1309**.

GIBRALTAR
North Front Cemetery **203**.

HOLLAND
Arnhem Oosterbeek War Cemetery **1294**, **1296**, **1297**, **1299**; Groesbeek Canadian War Cemetery **1317**; Nederweert War Cemetery **1313**; Sittard War Cemetery **1311**; Steenbergen-en-Kruisland RC Churchyard **1248**.

INDIA
Agra Cemetery **206**; Allahabad Cemetery **8**; Artillery Cemetery **164**; Artillery Lines Cemetery **121**; Bandel Churchyard **189**; Barrackpore New Cemetery **126**; Bolandsharh Cemetery **160**; Dehra Dun Cemetery **117**; Dehra Ismail Khan Cemetery **312**; Dharmsala Churchyard **412**; Ferozepore Civil Cemetery **118**; Fort Ruhya Cemetery **270**; Funchal British Cemetery **67**; Guides Cemetery **1161**; Gwalior Cemetery **165**; Harley Street Cemetery **146**; Imphal Indian Army War Cemetery, **1276**; Imphal War Cemetery **1266**; Kashmir Cemetery **342**; Kohat Cemetery **238**; Kohima War Cemetery **1267**, **1269**; Madras Cemetery **292**; Miranshar Cemetery **569**; Mooltan Cemetery **221**; New Cantonment Cemetery **349**; Old British Cemetery **14**, **188**, **190**; Old Delhi Military Cemetery **119**, **129**, **161**, **304**; Rakli Cemetery **518**; St John's Cemetery **130**, **227**; St Mary's Churchyard **112**; St Patrick's Churchyard **334**; St Thomas's Cathedral **103**; St Thomas's Churchyard **1127**; Saugor New Cemetery **288**; Secunderadad Cemetery **20**; Simla Churchyard **202**; Taujore Cemetery **223**; Umballa Cemetery **252**.

IRAQ
Amara War Cemetery **694**, **771**; Basra War Cemetery **583**.

IRELAND
Aghada Cemetery **159**; Arbour Hill Cemetery **229**; Ballymore RC Churchyard **144**; Castletown Church of Ireland Churchyard **637**; Christchurch Church of Ireland Cemetery **456**; Clongem Churchyard **372**; Clouleigh Churchyard **54**; Cobh Old Church Cemetery **633**; Conwal Cemetery **944**; Cornamagh RC Cemetery **234**; Dean's Grange Cemetery **990**; Derrinlogh English

Churchyard **320**; Donaghmore RC Churchyard **193**; Duleek Churchyard **319**; Glasnevin Cemetery **57**, **81**, **185**, **258**, **390**; Gorey Churchyard **226**; Grangegorman Cemetery **1068**; Killinardrish Church of Ireland Churchyard **725**; Lockeen Churchyard **230**; Mount Jerome Cemetery **24**, **114**, **343**; Newbridge Cemetery **26**; Old Bloomfield Cemetery **751**; Roscrea RC Cemetery **875**; St James Churchyard **305**; St John's Churchyard **277**; St Keman's Church of Ireland Churchyard **632**; St Mary's Churchyard **434**; St Mary's Church of Ireland Churchyard **183**; St Patrick's Cemetery **156**; Sligo Town Cemetery **1124**; Upper Aghada Cemetery **608**; Westport Old Cemetery **124**.

ISRAEL
Beersheba War Cemetery **511**, **908**, **914**; Gaza War Cemetery **935**; Khayat Beach War Cemetery **1136**.

ITALY
Alassio English Cemetery **521**; Argenta Gap War Cemetery **1330**, **1332**; Beach Head War Cemetery **1274**; Bordighera English Cemetery **171**; Faenza War Cemetery **1307**; Giavera British Cemetery **1013**; Grienze Churchyard **361**; Minturno War Cemetery **1260**; Pallanza New Cemetery **136**; Rimini Gurkha War Cemetery **1295**, **1305**; Sangro River War Cemetery **1244**; Staglieno Commonwealth War Graves Cemetery **689**.

JAMAICA
Up Park Military Cemetery **25**, **410**.

JAPAN
Yokohama War Cemetery **1351**.

KENYA
Voi Cemetery **651**.

KOREA
United Nations Memorial Cemetery **1344**, **1346**.

LIBYA
Benghazi War Cemetery **1194**; Knightsbridge War Cemetery **1195**, **1196**; Tobruk War Cemetery **183**, **1199**.

MALAYSIA
Labuan War Cemetery **1257**, **1336**; Taiping War Cemetery **1200**; Terendak Garrison Camp Cemetery **1350**.

MALTA
Msida Bastion Cemetery **88**; Ta Braxia International Cemetery **102**.

NEPAL
Bharse Gulmi **984**; Paklihawa Camp Cemetery **1239**.

NEW ZEALAND
Alexandra Redoubt Commemorative Park Cemetery **308**; Andersons Bay Soldiers' Cemetery **21**, **449**; Auckland Cemetery **638**; Dudley Cemetery **1187**; Golders Cemetery **1058**; Hokitika Municipal Cemetery **15**; Karori Soldiers' Cemetery **498**; Levin RSA Cemetery **849**; Masterton Cemetery **191**; Otahuhu Old Cemetery **309**; Paraparaumu Cemetery **1220**; Purewa Cemetery **90**;

The Complete Victoria Cross

Ruru Lawn Cemetery **1184**; St Paul's Churchyard **1188/1219**; Servicemen's Cemetery **1079**; Taita Servicemen's Cemetery **833**; Terrace End Cemetery **307**; Waikumete Memorial Park Soldiers' Cemetery **1106**; Waikumete Cemetery **1050**.

NORTHERN IRELAND
Bannagh RC Churchyard **256**; Belfast City Cemetery **176**, **236**; Billy Parish Protestant Cemetery **723**; Broughshane Presbyterian Churchyard **375**; Cammoney Cemetery **880**; Creggan Presbyterian Cemetery **687**; Donagh Cemetery **163**; Friar's Bush RC Cemetery, **263**; St Mark's Church of Ireland Churchyard **220**.

NORWAY
Ballangen New Cemetery **1164**.

PAKISTAN
Bannu Cemetery **1157**; Jandola Cemetery **1158**; Lahore Cemetery **383**; Quetta English Cemetery **387**; Rukham Village Cemetery **552**; St Alban's Churchyard **421**; Shahu Khel **1333**; Takhti Village Cemetery **698**; Warsak Road Cemetery **607**.

PAPUA NEW GUINEA
Lae War Cemetery **1236**, **1328**; Port Moresby War Cemetery **1225**, **1226**; Rubual War Cemetery **1280**.

RUSSIA
Archangel Allied Cemetery **1156**.

SCOTLAND
Ayr Cemetery **668**; Balbeggie Churchyard **265**; Bennochy Road Cemetery **400**; Bothwell Park Cemetery **271**; Castlewood Cemetery **1129**; Comrie Cemetery **830**; Culross Abbey Cemetery **184**; Dalberth Cemetery **209**; Dunfermline Cemetery **1081**; Eastern Cemetery **135**; Eastern Necropolis **5**, **42**, **219**; Eastwood New Cemetery **925**; Elgin Cemetery **173**; Forglen Cemetery **424**; Graigdunin Cemetery **216**; Grange Cemetery **245**; Holy Trinity Churchyard **623**; Kilmarnock Churchyard **1145**; Kirkmichael Churchyard **49**; Kirktown Cemetery **826**; Kirriemuir Cemetery **808**, **1301**; Knadgerhill Cemetery **541**; Lairg Cemetery **384**; Lerwick New Cemetery **1282**; Lesmahagow Cemetery **222**; Moffat Cemetery **930**; New Cemetery **851**; North Merchiston Cemetery **267**, **495**; Old Carlton Cemetery **303**; Oronsay Priory **316**; Piershill Cemetery **58**, **542**; Portobello Cemetery **438**; Riddrie Park Cemetery **546**; Rosmarkie Churchyard **336**; St Andrew and St Michael's Churchyard **1256**; St Kentigern's Cemetery **294**, **378**, **766**; St Mary's Church **211**; St Mary's Churchyard **63**; St Michael's Churchyard **18**; St Monance Cemetery **525**; St Peter's Cemetery **85**; Southern Necropolis **275**; Tomnahurich Cemetery **420**, **1208**; Towie Churchyard **255**; Tranent Parish Churchyard **127**; Trinity Churchyard **154**; Upper Largo Churchyard **614**; Warriston Cemetery **1240**; Wellshill Cemetery **266**; Western Necropolis **60**; Woodside Cemetery **43**.

SOUTH AFRICA
Belfast Cemetery **497**; Braamfontein Cemetery **783**; Chively War Cemetery **446**; Driefontein Cemetery **457**; Ermelo Cemetery **746**; Fugitive's Drift **345**, **346**; Gladstone Cemetery **302**; Grahamstown Old Cemetery **436**; Gruisbank British Cemetery **458**; King William's Town Cemetery **373**; Kokstad Cemetery **389**; Krugersdorp Cemetery **478**; Ladysmith Cemetery **381**, **452**; Mafeking Cemetery **1029**; Maitland Road No. 1 Cemetery **558**; Maitland Road No. 4 Cemetery **468**; Molteno Cemetery **429**; Newcastle Town Cemetery **500**; Old Anglican Cemetery **153**; Old Cemetery **440**; Ossuary Gardens of Remembrance **36**; Plumstead Cemetery **368**; Russe

Road RC Cemetery **351**; St Andrew's Churchyard **21**; St Mary's Cemetery **97**; Stella Wood Cemetery **1108**; Waggon Hill Cemetery **454**; Woltermade Cemetery **369**.

SWEDEN
Kviberg Cemetery **705**.

SWITZERLAND
Clarens Cemetery **366**.

TANZANIA
Morogoro Cemetery **557**.

TUNISIA
Beja War Cemetery **1231**; Bone War Cemetery **1251**; Massicault War Cemetery **1243**, **1245**; Sfax War Cemetery **1237**, **1238**, **1241**, **1242**.

TURKEY
Lala Baba Cemetery **427**; Lancashire Landing Cemetery **601**; Twelve Tree Copse Cemetery **685**; V Beach Cemetery **605**.

USA
Arlington Cemetery **1151**; Bayside Cemetery **1071**; Evergreen Cemetery **323**; Highland Memorial Park **733**; Laurel Hill Cemetery **333**; Rosehill Cemetery **1066**; Sandhill Cemetery **1022**.

URUGUAY
Montevideo British Cemetery **139**.

WALES
Amlwch Cemetery **834**; Brecon Cathedral Churchyard **101**; Caio Churchyard **141**; Ebbw Vale Cemetery **1116**; Llanbadarn Churchyard **890**; Monmouth Cemetery **352**; Oystermouth Cemetery **540**; Pant Cemetery **913**; Pantag Cemetery **1329**; Rhyl Cemetery **1051**; St Katherine's Cemetery **765**; St Mary's Churchyard **475**; St Michael's Churchyard **34**, **357**; St Woolo's Cemetery **47**.

YEMEN
Maala Christian Cemetery **505**.

ZIMBABWE
Bulawayo Town Cemetery **413**, **414**; Gwelo Cemetery **509**; Harare Anglican Cathedral **415**; Pioneer Cemetery **731**.

Chapter Fifteen

ALPHABETICAL LIST OF
VICTORIA CROSS HOLDERS

The following is a complete alphabetical list of all Victoria Cross holders. Each entry starts with the recipient's rank or position. (All ranks are as at the time of the VC action.) Although used extensively locally, the terms Trooper and Rifleman did not officially come into being until 1923. The rank is followed by the recipient's full name, and then their position in the chronological list, and finally the relevant page number in the 'Campaigns' section.

Acting Flight Sergeant ARTHUR LOUIS AARON (1251), 326
Jemadar ABDUL HAFIZ (1266), 320
Private ALFRED ABLETT (96), 98
Temporary Captain HAROLD ACKROYD (853), 242
Private ABRAHAM ACTON (567), 188
Reverend JAMES WILLIAM ADAMS (380), 145
Brevet Lieutenant Colonel ROBERT BELLEW ADAMS (417), 160
Private HENRY ADDISON (291), 131
Chaplain WILLIAM ROBERT FOUNTAINE ADDISON (695), 212
Temporary Second Lieutenant TOM EDWIN ADLAM (760), 224
Naik AGANSING RAI (1284), 335
Lieutenant AUGUSTUS WILLINGTON SHELTON AGAR (1152), 298
Lieutenant FREDERICK ROBERTSON AIKMAN (240), 123
Lieutenant ROBERT HOPE MONCRIEFF AITKEN (135), 105
Trooper HERMAN ALBRECHT (454), 167
Major ERNEST WRIGHT ALEXANDER (528), 182
Private JOHN ALEXANDER (87), 97
Lieutenant WALLACE LLOYD ALGIE (1119), 291
Sepoy ALI HAIDAR (1333), 352
Captain WILLIAM BARNSLEY ALLEN (748), 222
Corporal WILLIAM WILSON ALLEN (aka ALLAN), (352), 148
Acting Captain MICHAEL ALLMAND (1277), 333
Lance Corporal WILLIAM AMEY (1148), 296
Private CHARLES ANDERSON (287), 131
Lieutenant Colonel CHARLES GROVES WRIGHT ANDERSON (1203), 313
Private ERIC ANDERSON (1241), 323
Acting Major JOHN THOMPSON McKELLAR ANDERSON (1244), 324
Corporal WILLIAM ANDERSON (578), 190
Acting Lieutenant Colonel WILLIAM HERBERT ANDERSON (966), 263
Corporal LESLIE WILTON ANDREW (849), 241
Temporary Captain HENRY JOHN ANDREWS (1157), 299
Lance Corporal WILLIAM ANGUS (628), 200

Second Lieutenant **RICHARD WALLACE ANNAND (1168)**, 303
Captain **AUGUSTUS HENRY ARCHIBALD ANSON (196)**, 117
Lance Corporal **WILLIE HENRY APIATA (1355)**, 365
Sapper **ADAM ARCHIBALD (1149)**, 296
Gunner **THOMAS ARTHUR** (real name **McARTHUR), (72)**, 95
Private **THOMAS ELSDON ASHFORD (388)**, 146
Lance Corporal **JAMES ASHWORTH (1361)**, 368
Sergeant **ALFRED HENRY ATKINSON (458)**, 167
Lieutenant **HAROLD AUTEN (1022)**, 273
Lance Corporal **THOMAS LESLIE AXFORD (1016)**, 272
Captain **FENTON JOHN AYLMER (407)**, 156

Major **WILLIAM BABTIE (442)**, 164
Major **PETER JOHN BADCOE** (spelt **BADCOCK** before 1961)**, (1350)**, 360
Ressaidar **BADLU SINGH (1089)**, 285
Corporal **CAMERON BAIRD (1362)**, 369
Lieutenant **CHARLES GEORGE BAKER (283)**, 130
Temporary Captain **ALBERT BALL (813)**, 234
Private **VALENTINE BAMBRICK (272)**, 128
Captain **EDWARD BAMFORD (991)**, 267
Cornet **WILLIAM GEORGE HAWTRY BANKES (251)**, 125
Private **EDWARD BARBER (580)**, 190
Acting Major **WILLIAM GEORGE BARKER (1137)**, 294
Private **THOMAS BARRATT (840)**, 240
Lieutenant **JOHN CRIDLAN BARRETT (1090)**, 285
Corporal **COLIN FRASER BARRON (915)**, 253
Private **JOHN BARRY (497)**, 173
Company Sergeant Major **FREDERICK BARTER (619)**, 198
Pilot Officer **CYRIL JOE BARTON (1265)**, 330
Lance Sergeant **JOHN DANIEL BASKEYFIELD (1299)**, 340
Corporal **CYRIL ROYSTON GUYTON BASSETT (638)**, 202
Corporal **SIDNEY BATES (1289)**, 337
Lieutenant **ARTHUR HUGH HENRY BATTEN-POOLL (711)**, 215
Second Lieutenant **EDWARD FELIX BAXTER (699)**, 213
Trooper **FRANK WILLIAM BAXTER (414)**, 158
Acting Squadron Leader **IAN WILLOUGHBY BAZALGETTE (1288)**, 337
Private **THOMAS BEACH (42)**, 90
Temporary Commander **DANIEL MARCUS WILLIAM BEAK (1041)**, 276
Temporary Second Lieutenant **ERNEST FREDERICK BEAL (956)**, 261
Private **ROBERT MATTHEW BEATHAM (1034)**, 275
Lieutenant Commander **STEPHEN HALDEN BEATTIE (1210)**, 315
Acting Captain **ANDREW FREDERICK WEATHERBY BEAUCHAMP-PROCTOR** (born
    PROCTOR), (1029), 274
Rifleman **JOHN BEELEY (1196)**, 311
Private **WILLIAM BEES (510)**, 174
Private **WILLIAM BEESLEY (1005)** 270,
Corporal **HARRY CHURCHILL BEET (470)**, 169
Private **JOHNSON GIDEON BEHARRY (1356)**, 363
Lance Sergeant **DOUGLAS WALTER BELCHER (618)**, 198
Private **DAVID BELL (330)**, 140
Temporary Second Lieutenant **DONALD SIMPSON BELL (728)**, 218

Captain **EDWARD WILLIAM DERRINGTON BELL (4)**, 84
Temporary Captain **ERIC NORMAN FRANKLAND BELL (719)**, 217
Lieutenant **FREDERICK WILLIAM BELL (502)**, 173
Lieutenant **MARK SEVER BELL (340)**, 142
Squadron Commander **RICHARD BELL-DAVIES (681)**, 210
Lieutenant **EDWARD DONALD BELLEW (590)**, 192
Lieutenant **EUGENE PAUL BENNETT (767)**, 225
Temporary Lieutenant Colonel **PHILIP ERIC BENT (889)**, 249
Drummer **SPENCER JOHN BENT (553)**, 186
Captain **WILLIAM LESLIE DE LA POER BERESFORD (372)**, 151
Private **JAMES BERGIN** (spelt **BERGEN** in cemetery register)**, (334)**, 141
Sergeant **JOHN BERRYMAN (19)**, 86
Temporary Lieutenant Colonel **BERTRAM BEST-DUNKLEY (842)**, 240
Rifleman **BHANBHAGTA GURUNG (1323)**, 349
Sepoy **BHANDARI** (aka **BANDARI**) **RAM (1306)**, 342
Commander **EDWARD BARRY STEWART BINGHAM (704)**, 214
Second Lieutenant **FREDERICK BIRKS (879)**, 247
Trooper **JOHN HUTTON BISDEE (488)**, 171
Captain **WILLIAM AVERY BISHOP (828)**, 237
Lieutenant **WILLIAM DAVIDSON BISSETT (1135)**, 294
Temporary Lieutenant **ARCHIBALD BISSETT-SMITH (784)**, 229
Second Lieutenant **ARTHUR SEAFORTH BLACKBURN (735)**, 220
Captain **JAMES BLAIR (154)**, 109
Lieutenant **ROBERT BLAIR (190)**, 116
Temporary Major **FRANK GERALD BLAKER (1285)**, 336
Captain **WILLIAM ANDERSON BLOOMFIELD** (born **BROOMFIELD**)**, (746)**, 222
Lieutenant **ANDREW CATHCART BOGLE (148)**, 108
Lieutenant **GUY HUDLESTON BOISRAGON (408)**, 157
Lieutenant **CHARLES GEORGE BONNER (856)**, 243
Colour Sergeant **ANTHONY CLARKE BOOTH (360)**, 150
Sergeant **FREDERICK CHARLES FRANCIS BOOTH (775)**, 227
Lieutenant **ALBERT CHALMERS BORELLA** (name changed to **CHALMERS-BORELLA** in 1939)**, (1019)**, 272
Lieutenant Colonel **ARTHUR DRUMMOND BORTON (917)**, 254
Second Lieutenant **STANLEY HENRY PARRY BOUGHEY (935)**, 257
Lance Corporal **ABRAHAM BOULGER (144)**, 107
Sergeant **WILLIAM EWART BOULTER (730)**, 219
Lieutenant **CLAUD THOMAS BOURCHIER (48)**, 91
Lieutenant **ROWLAND** (sometimes spelt **ROLAND**) **RICHARD LOUIS BOURKE (1006)**, 270
Second Lieutenant **GEORGE ARTHUR BOYD-ROCHFORT (637)**, 201
Midshipman **DUNCAN GORDON BOYES (321)**, 138
Lieutenant Commander **EDWARD COURTNEY BOYLE (610)**, 197
Captain **EDWARD KINDER BRADBURY (536)**, 183
Lieutenant Commander **GEORGE NICHOLSON BRADFORD (993)**, 267
Temporary Lieutenant Colonel **ROLAND BOYS BRADFORD (762)**, 225
Driver **FREDERICK HENRY BRADLEY (509)**, 174
Private **JOSEPH BRADSHAW (61)**, 93
Assistant Surgeon **WILLIAM BRADSHAW (183)**, 115
Bombardier **JOSEPH CHARLES BRENNAN (257)**, 126
Acting Corporal **ALEXANDER PICTON BRERETON (1033)**, 275
Lieutenant **JEAN BRILLANT (1027)**, 274

Captain WALTER LORRAIN BRODIE (**555**), 186
Lieutenant GONVILLE BROMHEAD (**349**), 147
Temporary Major CUTHBERT BROMLEY (**591**), 192
Lieutenant JAMES ANSON OTHO BROOKE (**548**), 185
Company Sergeant Major EDWARD BROOKS (**814**), 235
Lance Sergeant OLIVER BROOKS (**673**), 208
Sergeant DONALD FORRESTER BROWN (**754**), 223
Major EDWARD DOUGLAS BROWN (later **BROWN-SYNGE-HUTCHINSON**), (**490**), 171
Lieutenant FRANCIS DAVID MILLEST BROWN (**212**), 119
Private HARRY W. BROWN (**864**), 244
Trooper PETER BROWN (**369**), 152
Corporal WALTER ERNEST BROWN (**1018**), 272
Lieutenant EDWARD STEVENSON BROWNE (**366**), 151
Captain SAMUEL JAMES BROWNE (**281**), 130
Lieutenant WILLIAM ARTHUR McCRAE BRUCE (**564**), 188
Temporary Captain JOHN HENRY COUND BRUNT (**1307**), 343
Lance Corporal THOMAS BRYAN (**797**), 231
Second Lieutenant JOHN CRAWFORD BUCHAN (**951**), 260
Temporary Captain ANGUS BUCHANAN (**693**), 212
Private WILLIAM HENRY BUCKINGHAM (real name **BILLINGTON**), (**573**), 189
Temporary Corporal ALEXANDER HENRY BUCKLEY (**1063**), 280
Lieutenant CECIL WILLIAM BUCKLEY (**67**), 94
Deputy Assistant Commissary of Ordnance JOHN BUCKLEY (**116**), 102
Sergeant MAURICE VINCENT BUCKLEY (aka **GERALD SEXTON**), (**1085**), 284
Corporal BRYAN BUDD (**1357**), 366
Private PATRICK JOSEPH BUGDEN (**888**), 249
Brevet Lieutenant Colonel REDVERS HENRY BULLER (**362**), 150
Temporary Lieutenant Colonel DANIEL BURGES (**1082**), 283
Lieutenant HUGH TALBOT BURGOYNE (**65**), 93
Sergeant WILLIAM FRANCIS BURMAN (**881**), 247
Lieutenant NATHANIEL GODOLPHIN BURSLEM (**298**), 133
Corporal ALFRED ALEXANDER BURT (**667**), 207
Corporal ALEXANDER STEWART BURTON (**645**), 203
Private RICHARD HENRY BURTON (**1301**), 341
Lieutenant Colonel CHRISTOPHER BUSHELL (**962**), 262
Lieutenant JOHN FITZHARDINGE PAUL BUTLER (**557**), 186
Lieutenant THOMAS ADAIR BUTLER (**242**), 124
Private WILLIAM BOYNTON BUTLER (**855**), 242
Sergeant ROBERT JAMES BYE (**845**), 240
Private JAMES BYRNE (**258**), 126
Private JOHN BYRNE (**47**), 91
Private THOMAS BYRNE (**430**), 161
Lieutenant JOHN BYTHESEA (**2**), 83

Lieutenant THOMAS CADELL (**127**), 104
Captain WILLIAM MARTIN CAFE (**264**), 127
Private JOHN CAFFREY (**680**), 210
Temporary Major ROBERT HENRY CAIN (**1298**), 340
Lieutenant GEORGE ALBERT CAIRNS (**1264**), 330
Sergeant HUGH CAIRNS (**1141**), 295
Sergeant THOMAS CALDWELL (**1140**), 295

Captain ALEXANDER STANHOPE COBBE (**515**), 177
Lieutenant HUGH STEWART COCHRANE (**254**), 125
Lieutenant HAMPDEN ZANE CHURCHILL COCKBURN (**492**), 172
Private WILLIAM COFFEY (**55**), 92
Temporary Brigadier General CLIFFORD COFFIN (**841**), 240
Lieutenant NEVILL JOSIAH AYLMER COGHILL (**346**), 147
Sergeant JOHN COLEMAN (**94**), 98
Acting Sergeant HAROLD JOHN COLLEY (**1048**), 277
Second Lieutenant JOSEPH HENRY COLLIN (**980**), 265
Acting Lieutenant Colonel JOHN STANHOPE COLLINGS-WELLS (**960**), 262
Acting Corporal JOHN COLLINS (**913**), 253
Gunner JAMES COLLIS (**386**), 146
Lance Corporal WILLIAM HAROLD COLTMAN (**1113**), 290
Private HERBERT GEORGE COLUMBINE (**959**), 262
Second Lieutenant HUGH COLVIN (**880**), 247
Lieutenant JAMES MORRIS COLQUHOUN COLVIN (**420**), 159
Acting Captain THOMAS RIVERDALE COLYER-FERGUSSON (**843**), 240
Lieutenant ROBERT GRIERSON COMBE (**819**), 236
Commander JOHN EDMUND COMMERELL (**110**), 100
Captain WALTER NORRIS CONGREVE (**443**), 165
Major WILLIAM LA TOUCHE CONGREVE (**729**), 219
Gunner WILLIAM CONNOLLY (**138**), 106
Private JOHN CONNORS (**105**), 100
Lieutenant JOHN AUGUSTUS CONOLLY (**24**), 87
Captain JOHN COOK (**344**), 144
Private WALTER COOK (**293**), 131
Private THOMAS COOKE (**737**), 220
Lieutenant Commander EDGAR CHRISTOPHER COOKSON (**669**), 207
Sergeant EDWARD COOPER (**862**), 244
Boatswain HENRY COOPER (**68**), 94
Private JAMES COOPER (**331**), 140
Corporal FREDERICK GEORGE COPPINS (**1032**), 274
Private FREDERICK CORBETT (real name **DAVID EMBLETON**), (**397**), 154
First Class Boy JOHN (aka **JACK**) TRAVERS CORNWELL (**706**), 214
Sergeant AUBREY COSENS (**1317**), 347
Corporal WILLIAM COSGROVE (**608**), 196
Lieutenant EDMOND WILLIAM COSTELLO (**416**), 159
Acting Corporal WILLIAM REGINALD COTTER (**690**), 211
Colour Sergeant CORNELIUS COUGHLAN (aka **COGHLAN**), (**124**), 104
Lieutenant GUSTAVUS HAMILTON BLENKINSOPP COULSON (**503**), 173
Private JACK THOMAS COUNTER (**989**), 267
Second Lieutenant GABRIEL GEORGE COURY (**743**), 221
Sergeant CHARLES HENRY COVERDALE (**892**), 250
Lieutenant Commander CHARLES HENRY COWLEY (**700**), 213
Private CHRISTOPHER AUGUSTUS COX (**785**), 229
Colour Sergeant JAMES CRAIG (**97**), 99
Second Lieutenant JOHN MANSON CRAIG (**830**), 238
Private HARRY GEORGE CRANDON (**506**), 174
Captain O'MOORE CREAGH (**370**), 145
Surgeon Captain THOMAS JOSEPH CREAN (**512**), 175
Private JAMES CRICHTON (**1106**), 288

Surgeon JOHN CRIMMIN (**404**), 156
Skipper THOMAS CRISP (**859**), 243
Private JOHN BERNARD CROAK (or CROKE), (**1026**), 273
Lance Corporal ARTHUR HENRY CROSS (**968**), 263
Second Lieutenant JOHN JAMES CROWE (**988**), 267
Lieutenant JOSEPH PETRUS HENDRICK CROWE (**153**), 109
Flying Officer JOHN ALEXANDER CRUICKSHANK (**1287**), 336
Private ROBERT EDWARD CRUICKSHANK (**1003**), 269
Lieutenant VICTOR ALEXANDER CHARLES CRUTCHLEY (**999**), 269
Lieutenant WILLIAM GEORGE CUBITT (**133**), 105
Lieutenant Colonel ARTHUR EDWARD CUMMING (**1202**), 312
Corporal JOHN CUNNINGHAM (**804**), 232
Private JOHN CUNNINGHAM (**769**), 226
Lieutenant WILLIAM JAMES MONTGOMERY CUNNINGHAME (**49**), 91
Private WILLIAM MATTHEW CURREY (**1060**), 280
Major DAVID VIVIAN CURRIE (**1292**), 338
Private ALBERT EDWARD CURTIS (**459**), 168
Boatswains Mate HENRY CURTIS (**82**), 96
Sergeant HORACE AUGUSTUS CURTIS (**1128**), 292
Lieutenant PHILIP KENNETH EDWARD CURTIS (**1346**), 357
Lieutenant ARTHUR RODEN CUTLER (**1190**), 309

Assistant Commissary JAMES LANGLEY DALTON (**351**), 148
Driver HENRY DALZIEL (**1017**), 272
Trooper JOHN DANAHER (or DANAGHER), (**391**), 153
Private FREDERICK GEORGE DANCOX (**902**), 251
Midshipman EDWARD ST JOHN DANIEL (**15**), 85
Company Sergeant Major HARRY DANIELS (**576**), 190
Captain HENRY CECIL DUDGEON D'ARCY (**373**), 151
Temporary Lieutenant WILBUR (born WILLIAM THOMAS) TAYLOR DARTNELL (**651**), 204
Naik DARWAN SINGH NEGI (**559**), 187
Lieutenant JOHN CHARLES CAMPBELL DAUNT (**198**), 117
Corporal PHILIP DAVEY (**1015**), 272
Corporal JAMES LLEWELLYN DAVIES (**850**), 241
Corporal JOHN THOMAS DAVIES (**965**), 263
Corporal JOSEPH JOHN DAVIES (**732**), 219
Captain GRONOW DAVIS (**100**), 99
Private JAMES DAVIS (real name KELLY), (**267**), 127
Corporal JAMES LENNOX DAWSON (**675**), 209
Lieutenant GEORGE FIOTT DAY (**107**), 100
Corporal SIDNEY JAMES DAY (**873**), 246
Acting Sergeant JOHN BRUNTON DAYKINS (**1129**), 292
Temporary Lieutenant DONALD JOHN DEAN (**1091**), 285
Lieutenant PERCY THOMPSON DEAN (**995**), 268
Lieutenant MAURICE JAMES DEASE (**523**), 180
Lieutenant RAYMOND HARVEY LODGE JOSEPH de MONTMORENCY (**429**), 161
Private DENIS DEMPSEY (**155**), 109
Lieutenant FRANK ALEXANDER de PASS (**560**), 187
Sergeant THOMAS CURRIE DERRICK (**1257**), 327
Second Lieutenant EDMUND de WIND (**952**), 260

Sergeant SAMUEL FORSYTH (**1046**), 277
Lieutenant GEORGE VINCENT FOSBERY (**311**), 135
Captain CHARLES CALVELEY FOSS (**574**), 190
Corporal EDWARD FOSTER (**812**), 234
Private EDMUND JOHN FOWLER (**365**), 150
Major CHARLES CRAUFORD FRASER (**290**), 131
Lieutenant IAN EDWARD FRASER (**1341**), 354
Private JOHN FREEMAN (**201**), 118
Corporal JOHN ALEXANDER FRENCH (**1226**), 319
Temporary Lieutenant Colonel BERNARD CYRIL FREYBERG (**768**), 226
Lance Corporal SAMUEL FRICKLETON (**833**), 239
Acting Captain CYRIL HUBERT FRISBY (**1093**), 286
Lance Corporal WILFRED DOLBY FULLER (**577**), 190
Lance Corporal WILLIAM CHARLES FULLER (**540**), 184
Lieutenant CHRISTOPHER FURNESS (**1169**), 303
Private JAMES HENRY FYNN (born **FINN**), (**697**), 212

Lieutenant ALFRED EDWARD GABY (**1023**), 273
Havildar GAJE GHALE (**1249**), 325
Rifleman GANJU LAMA (real name **GYANTSO SHANGDERPA**), (**1278**), 333
Sergeant GEORGE GARDINER (**54**), 92
Captain PHILIP JOHN GARDNER (**1198**), 311
Colour Sergeant WILLIAM GARDNER (**271**), 128
Corporal CHARLES ERNEST GARFORTH (**526**), 181
Flying Officer DONALD EDWARD GARLAND (**1166**), 302
Colour Sergeant STEPHEN GARVIN (**131**), 105
Second Lieutenant BENJAMIN HANDLEY GEARY (**586**), 191
Temporary Captain ROBERT GEE (**928**), 256
Naik GIAN SINGH (**1320**), 348
Wing Commander GUY PENROSE GIBSON (**1248**), 325
Lieutenant EDRIC FREDERICK GIFFORD (**337**), 142
Sergeant ALBERT GILL (**738**), 220
Sergeant Major PETER GILL (**121**), 103
Driver HORACE HENRY GLASOCK (**468**), 169
Lance Corporal WILLIAM GOATE (sometimes spelt **GOAT**), (**241**), 123
Rifleman GOBAR SING NEGI (**572**), 189
Lance Dafadar GOBIND (spelt **GOVIND** on later records) **SINGH** (**936**), 257
Private SIDNEY FRANK GODLEY (sometimes spelt **GODLY** prior to 1909), (**524**), 181
Corporal HERMAN JAMES GOOD (**1024**), 273
Lieutenant CHARLES AUGUSTUS GOODFELLOW (**296**), 132
Brevet Major GERALD LITTLEHALES GOODLAKE (**30**), 88
Lance Corporal BERNARD SIDNEY GORDON (**1052**), 278
Private JAMES HEATHER GORDON (**1193**), 310
Captain WILLIAM EAGLESON GORDON (**477**), 170
Corporal WILLIAM JAMES GORDON (**410**), 157
Captain HENRY GEORGE GORE-BROWNE (**157**), 110
Temporary Lieutenant ROBERT VAUGHAN GORLE (**1108**), 289
Seaman JAMES GORMAN (**46**), 90
Acting Lieutenant Colonel JOHN STANDISH SURTEES PRENDERGAST VEREKER GORT
(**1092**), 285
Sergeant WILLIAM GOSLING (**791**), 230

[389]

Captain THOMAS DE COURCY HAMILTON (**64**), 93
Lieutenant WALTER RICHARD POLLOCK HAMILTON (**367**), 144
Captain ARTHUR GEORGE HAMMOND (**382**), 145
Sergeant HARRY HAMPTON (**483**), 171
Private THOMAS HANCOCK (**128**), 104
Company Sergeant Major ROBERT HILL HANNA (**871**), 246
Sergeant JOHN HANNAH (**1178**), 306
Captain PERCY HOWARD HANSEN (**642**), 202
Lance Corporal HENRY ERIC HARDEN (**1313**), 345
Farrier Major WILLIAM JAMES HARDHAM (**498**), 173
Gunner ISRAEL HARDING (**396**), 154
Chaplain THEODORE BAILEY HARDY (**978**), 265
Lieutenant HASTINGS EDWARD HARINGTON (**206**), 118
Lance Corporal JOHN PENNINGTON HARMAN (**1267**), 330
Corporal JOHN WILLIAM HARPER (**1300**), 341
Sergeant THOMAS JAMES HARRIS (**1030**), 274
Lieutenant Commander ARTHUR LEYLAND HARRISON (**994**), 268
Leading Seaman JOHN HARRISON (**224**), 121
Second Lieutenant JOHN HARRISON (**820**), 236
Lieutenant REGINALD CLARE HART (**359**), 144
Pensioned Sergeant HENRY HARTIGAN (**126**), 104
Surgeon Major EDMUND BARRON HARTLEY (**371**), 152
Major FRANCIS JOHN WILLIAM HARVEY (**703**), 213
Lieutenant FREDERICK MAURICE WATSON HARVEY (**788**), 230
Private JACK HARVEY (**1073**), 282
Private NORMAN HARVEY (**1136**), 294
Private SAMUEL HARVEY (**672**), 208
Lieutenant HENRY MARSHAM HAVELOCK (later **HAVELOCK-ALLAN**), (**146**), 108
Captain LANOE (sometimes misspelt **LANCE**) GEORGE HAWKER (**634**), 201
Private DAVID HAWKES (**247**), 125
Bugler ROBERT HAWTHORNE (**166**), 112
Acting Captain REGINALD FREDERICK JOHNSON HAYWARD (**955**), 261
Major CHARLES HEAPHY (**315**), 137
Lieutenant ALFRED SPENCER HEATHCOTE (**120**), 103
Private WILLIAM EDWARD HEATON (**485**), 171
Private MICHAEL WILSON HEAVISIDE (**823**), 236
Temporary Lieutenant FREDERICK WILLIAM HEDGES (**1134**), 293
Acting Captain ARTHUR HENDERSON (**810**), 234
Temporary Lieutenant Colonel EDWARD ELERS DELAVAL HENDERSON (**771**), 226
Captain GEORGE STUART HENDERSON (**1159**), 300
Trooper HERBERT STEPHEN HENDERSON (**413**), 158
Captain CLEMENT HENEAGE-WALKER (later known as **WALKER-HENEAGE**), (**276**), 129
Sergeant ANDREW HENRY (**38**), 89
Temporary Second Lieutenant ALFRED CECIL HERRING (**964**), 262
Lieutenant WILLIAM NATHAN WRIGHTE HEWETT (**29**), 88
Lance Corporal JAMES HEWITSON (**1001**), 269
Second Lieutenant DENNIS GEORGE WYLDBORE HEWITT (**844**), 240
Lance Corporal WILLIAM HENRY HEWITT (**883**), 248
Lieutenant ALAN RICHARD HILL (later **HILL-WALKER**), (**392**), 153
Private ALBERT HILL (**733**), 219
Sergeant SAMUEL HILL (**227**), 121

Lieutenant JAMES JOHN McLEOD INNES (**239**), 123
Second Lieutenant GILBERT STUART MARTIN INSALL (**679**), 209
Private REGINALD ROY INWOOD (**877**), 247
Private CHARLES IRWIN (**220**), 120
Sepoy ISHAR SINGH (**1160**), 299

Lance Corporal ALBERT JACKA (**621**), 199
Temporary Captain JAMES JOSEPH BERNARD JACKMAN (**1199**), 311
Sergeant HAROLD JACKSON (**958**), 261
Sergeant NORMAN CYRIL JACKSON (**1268**), 331
Lance Corporal THOMAS NORMAN JACKSON (**1097**), 286
Private WILLIAM (born **JOHN**) JACKSON (**712**), 215
Temporary Captain MANLEY ANGELL JAMES (**949**), 260
Second Lieutenant WALTER HERBERT JAMES (**630**), 200
Captain DAVID AULDGO JAMIESON (**1290**), 337
Corporal GEORGE JARRATT (**821**), 236
Lieutenant HANSON CHAMBERS TAYLOR JARRETT (**288**), 131
Lance Corporal CHARLES ALFRED JARVIS (**525**), 181
Surgeon JOSEPH JEE (**175**), 113
Fusilier FRANCIS ARTHUR JEFFERSON (**1272**), 332
Captain CLARENCE SMITH JEFFRIES (**903**), 251
Rough Rider EDWARD JENNINGS (**207**), 119
Private JOERGAN (sometimes spelt **JORGEN**) CHRISTIAN JENSEN (**789**), 230
Captain HENRY EDWARD JEROME (**261**), 126
Lieutenant ALAN JERRARD (**977**), 265
Acting Lieutenant Colonel DUDLEY GRAHAM JOHNSON (**1143**), 295
Temporary Second Lieutenant FREDERICK HENRY JOHNSON (**656**), 205
Second Lieutenant JAMES BULMER JOHNSON (**1122**), 291
Sergeant WILLIAM HENRY JOHNSON (**1111**), 289
Captain ROBERT JOHNSTON (**434**), 163
Captain WILLIAM HENRY JOHNSTON (**539**), 184
Stoker WILLIAM (enlisted and served as **JOHN**) JOHNSTONE (**3**), 83
Lieutenant ALFRED STOWELL JONES (**125**), 104
Sergeant DAVID JONES (**750**), 222
Captain HENRY MITCHELL JONES (**70**), 94
Colonel HERBERT (known as 'H') JONES (**1353**), 362
Commander LOFTUS WILLIAM JONES (**705**), 214
Temporary Lieutenant RICHARD BASIL BRANDRAM JONES (**702**), 213
Private ROBERT JONES (**356**), 149
Private THOMAS ALFRED JONES (**757**), 224
Private WILLIAM JONES (**355**), 149
Captain EUSTACE JOTHAM (**569**), 189
Lieutenant WILLIAM DONOVAN JOYNT (**1043**), 276
Sergeant REGINALD STANLEY JUDSON (**1050**), 278

Corporal JOSEPH KAEBLE (**1011**), 271
Sepoy KAMAL RAM (**1270**), 331
Lieutenant KARAMJEET SINGH JUDGE (**1324**), 349
Rifleman KARANBAHADUR RANA (**984**), 266
Civilian THOMAS HENRY KAVANAGH (**203**), 118
Major RICHARD HARTE KEATINGE (**249**), 125

Corporal DANIEL KEIGHRAN **(1360)**, 368
Boatswain Third Class JOSEPH KELLAWAY **(95)**, 98
Private RICHARD KELLIHER **(1252)**, 326
Lance Corporal ROBERT KELLS **(192)**, 116
Temporary Second Lieutenant HENRY KELLY **(763)**, 225
Private WILLIAM STEPHEN KENEALLY (spelt **KENEALY** on headstone), **(601)**, 195
Private EDWARD KENNA **(1338)**, 353
Captain PAUL ALOYSIUS KENNA **(427)**, 161
Lance Corporal JOHN PATRICK KENNEALLY (real name **LESLIE ROBINSON**), **(1246)**, 325
Private CHARLES THOMAS KENNEDY **(495)**, 172
Private HENRY (cremated under the name **HARRY**) EDWARD KENNY **(658)**, 206
Private JAMES KENNY **(221)**, 121
Private THOMAS KENNY **(678)**, 209
Private THOMAS JAMES BEDE KENNY **(798)**, 231
Drummer WILLIAM KENNY **(547)**, 185
Lieutenant WILLIAM DAVID KENNY **(1158)**, 299
Lieutenant ALLAN EBENEZER KER **(950)**, 260
Lieutenant GEORGE FRASER KERR **(1095)**, 286
Private JOHN CHIPMAN KERR **(756)**, 223
Lieutenant WILLIAM ALEXANDER KERR **(143)**, 107
Temporary Lieutenant Colonel GEOFFREY CHARLES TASKER KEYES **(1194)**, 310
Private LEONARD MAURICE KEYSOR (sometimes spelt **KEYZOR**), **(639)**, 202
Lance Corporal LEONARD JAMES KEYWORTH **(624)**, 200
Sepoy KHUDADAD KHAN **(552)**, 182
Sergeant WILLIAM HENRY KIBBY **(1227)**, 319
Captain ARTHUR FORBES GORDON KILBY **(653)**, 205
Private BRUCE STEEL KINGSBURY **(1225)**, 319
Private CECIL JOHN KINROSS **(911)**, 253
Corporal FRANK HOWARD KIRBY **(472)**, 169
Second Lieutenant JAMES KIRK **(1147)**, 296
Private JOHN KIRK **(123)**, 104
Sergeant ALFRED JOSEPH KNIGHT **(882)**, 248
Acting Sergeant ARTHUR GEORGE KNIGHT **(1069)**, 281
Corporal HENRY JAMES KNIGHT **(484)**, 171
Lieutenant GEORGE ARTHUR KNOWLAND **(1314)**, 345
Temporary Second Lieutenant CECIL LEONARD KNOX **(957)**, 261
Sergeant JOHN SIMPSON KNOX **(9)**, 84
Acting Corporal FILIP KONOWAL **(872)**, 245
Rifleman KULBIR THAPA **(660)**, 206

Rifleman LACHHIMAN GURUNG **(1337)**, 353
Major ALEXANDER MALINS LAFONE **(908)**, 252
Piper DANIEL LOGAN LAIDLAW **(661)**, 206
Lance Naik LALA **(688)**, 211
Subadar LALBAHADUR THAPA **(1239)**, 323
Sergeant Major GEORGE LAMBERT **(149)**, 108
Private THOMAS LANE **(302)**, 134
Acting Captain ARTHUR MOORE LASCELLES **(937)**, 257
Temporary Major ANDERS FREDERICK EMIL VICTOR SCHAU LASSEN **(1332)**, 351
Private DAVID ROSS LAUDER **(648)**, 204

Gunner THOMAS LAUGHNAN (**208**), 119
Sergeant HARRY JOHN LAURENT (**1079**), 283
Sergeant BRIAN TURNER TOM LAWRENCE (**482**), 170
Lieutenant SAMUEL HILL LAWRENCE (**139**), 106
Private EDWARD LAWSON (**425**), 161
Captain EDWARD PEMBERTON LEACH (**361**), 144
Second Lieutenant JAMES EDGAR LEACH (**549**), 185
Private JOHN LEAK (**736**), 220
Lance Corporal JOSHUA MARK LEAKEY (**1363**), 369
Sergeant NIGEL GRAY LEAKEY (**1186**), 307
Acting Major OKILL MASSEY LEARMONTH (**866**), 245
Flight Lieutenant RODERICK ALASTAIR BROOK LEAROYD (**1176**), 305
Major WILLIAM KNOX LEET (**363**), 150
Colour Sergeant PETER LEITCH (**80**), 96
Lieutenant JAMES EDGAR LEITH (**255**), 126
Corporal WILLIAM JAMES LENDRIM (aka **LENDRUM**), (**52**), 91
Lieutenant WILBRAHAM OATES LENNOX (**50**), 91
Lieutenant EDMUND HENRY LENON (**299**), 134
Temporary Major HERBERT WALLACE LE PATOUREL (**1233**), 321
Surgeon FERDINAND SIMEON LE QUESNE (**405**), 156
Corporal FRANK LESTER (**1120**), 291
Private HUBERT (aka **HERBERT**) WILLIAM LEWIS (**765**), 225
Lance Corporal LEONARD ALLAN LEWIS (**1088**), 285
Temporary Captain IAN OSWALD LIDDELL (**1331**), 351
Captain JOHN AIDEN LIDDELL (**636**), 201
Senior Subaltern ROBERT JAMES LINDSAY (later **LOYD-LINDSAY**), (**7**), 84
Commander JOHN WALLACE LINTON (**1162**), 301
Ensign EVERARD ALOYSIUS LISLE-PHILLIPPS (**119**), 103
Sergeant JOSEPH LISTER (**898**), 251
Surgeon Major OWEN EDWARD PENNEFATHER LLOYD (**411**), 157
Gunner ISAAC LODGE (**467**), 169
Private ARNOLD LOOSEMORE (**858**), 243
Flight Lieutenant DAVID SAMUEL ANTHONY LORD (**1297**), 340
Temporary Major STEWART WALKER LOUDOUN-SHAND (**716**), 216
Sergeant ALBERT DAVID LOWERSON (**1059**), 279
Boatswains Mate CHARLES DAVIS LUCAS (**1**), 83
Colour Sergeant JOHN LUCAS (**305**), 133
Driver FREDERICK LUKE (**534**), 183
Captain CHARLES LUMLEY (**101**), 99
Major FREDERICK WILLIAM LUMSDEN (**790**), 230
Lieutenant GRAHAM THOMSON LYALL (**1099**), 287
Captain CHARLES ANTHONY LYELL (**1243**), 324
Private JOHN LYNN (**613**), 197
Private JOHN LYONS (**74**), 95
Lieutenant HENRY LYSONS (**364**), 150
Lieutenant HARRY HAMMON LYSTER (**273**), 128

Sergeant JOHN McAULAY (**925**), 255
Lieutenant WILLIAM McBEAN (**245**), 124
Lance Corporal ROBERT GORDON McBEATH (spelt **MacBEATH** on his headstone)**, (923**), 255

Lieutenant **LAWRENCE DOMINIC McCARTHY (1044)**, 277
Private **CHARLES McCORRIE** (aka **McCURRY**)**, (88)**, 97
Surgeon **JOHN FREDERICK McCREA (389)**, 153
Temporary Captain **JAMES THOMAS BYRFORD McCUDDEN (943)**, 258
Private **JOHN McDERMOND** (spelt **McDIARMID** in cemetery register)**, (43)**, 90
Colour Sergeant **HENRY MacDONALD (60)**, 93
Civilian **WILLIAM FRASER McDONELL (151)**, 108
Private **JOHN McDOUGALL (303)**, 134
Sergeant **STANLEY ROBERT McDOUGALL (975)**, 264
Captain **THAIN WENDELL MacDOWELL (793)**, 230
Private **WILLIAM FREDERICK McFADZEAN (715)**, 216
Lance Sergeant **SAMUEL McGAW (339)**, 142
Sergeant **LEWIS McGEE (893)**, 250
Private **JOHN McGOVERN** (aka **McGOWAN**)**, (132)**, 105
Lieutenant **DAVID STUART McGREGOR (1131)**, 293
Temporary Captain **JOHN MacGREGOR (1105)**, 288
Private **RODERICK McGREGOR (63)**, 93
Acting Sergeant **LOUIS McGUFFIE (1100)**, 287
Sergeant **JAMES McGUIRE** (sometimes spelt **MAGUIRE**)**, (163)**, 111
Private **PATRICK McHALE (199)**, 117
Gunner **HUGH McINNES (209)**, 119
Private **GEORGE IMLACH McINTOSH (851)**, 242
Temporary Lieutenant **DAVID LOWE MacINTYRE (1047)**, 277
Major **DONALD MacINTYRE (336)**, 141
Private **HUGH McIVER (1045)**, 277
Private **DAVID MacKAY (222)**, 121
Sergeant **IAN McKAY (1354)**, 362
Lance Corporal **JOHN FREDERICK MacKAY (471)**, 169
Lieutenant **GEORGE BURDON McKEAN (1002)**, 269
Sergeant **JAMES McKECHNIE (5)**, 84
Colour Sergeant **EDWARD McKENNA (307)**, 136
Able Seaman **ALBERT EDWARD McKENZIE (998)**, 268
Lieutenant **HUGH McDONALD McKENZIE (909)**, 252
Private **JAMES MacKENZIE (566)**, 188
Sergeant **JOHN MacKENZIE (473)**, 176
Corporal **JOHN BERNARD MacKEY (1336)**, 353
Lieutenant **DONALD MacKINTOSH (802)**, 232
Lieutenant **HECTOR LACHLAN STEWART MacLEAN (418)**, 160
Second Lieutenant **ALAN ARNETT McLEOD (972)**, 264
Private **PETER McMANUS (187)**, 115
Assistant Surgeon **VALENTINE MUNBEE McMASTER (176)**, 113
Temporary Lieutenant **ERIC ARCHIBALD McNAIR (689)**, 211
Sergeant **WILLIAM McNALLY (1138)**, 294
Lieutenant **FRANK HUBERT McNAMARA (786)**, 229
Corporal **JOHN McNAMARA (1076)**, 282
Lieutenant Colonel **JOHN CARSTAIRS McNEILL (316)**, 137
Lance Sergeant **FREDERICK McNESS (755)**, 223
Lieutenant **HERBERT TAYLOR MacPHERSON (179)**, 114
Colour Sergeant **STEWART McPHERSON (184)**, 115
Corporal **JAMES McPHIE (1123)**, 291
Private **BERNARD McQUIRT** (spelt **McCOURT** in cemetery register)**, (236)**, 123

Acting Captain **ALLASTAIR** (spelt **ALASTAIR** on early records) **MALCOLM CLUNY**
   McREADY-DIARMID (formerly **DREW**), **(933)**, 257
Private **ROBERT MacTIER (1061)**, 280
Sergeant **WILLIAM McWHEENEY** (aka **MAWHINNEY**), **(16)**, 86
Sergeant Major **AMBROSE MADDEN (25)**, 87
Acting Leading Seaman **JAMES JOSEPH MAGENNIS (1342)**, 355
Drummer **MICHAEL MAGNER** (aka **BARRY**), **(335)**, 141
Sergeant **PATRICK MAHONEY (172)**, 113
Major **JOHN KEEFER MAHONY (1273)**, 332
Surgeon **WILLIAM JOB MAILLARD (431)**, 162
Wing Commander **HUGH GORDON MALCOLM (1231)**, 320
Lieutenant **JOHN GRANT MALCOLMSON (113)**, 101
Lieutenant **GEORGE ALLEN MALING (655)**, 205
Midshipman **WILFRED ST AUBYN MALLESON (600)**, 195
Lance Sergeant **JOSEPH MALONE (21)**, 86
Civilian **ROSS LOWIS MANGLES (150)**, 108
Assistant Surgeon **WILLIAM GEORGE NICHOLAS MANLEY (317)**, 137
Lieutenant **JOHN MANNERS-SMITH (409)**, 157
Major **EDWARD MANNOCK (1014)**, 271
Captain **CONWYN MANSEL-JONES (462)**, 168
Flying Officer **LESLIE THOMAS MANSER (1216)**, 316
Acting Leading Seaman **JACK FOREMAN MANTLE (1174)**, 305
Private **WILLIAM MARINER** (aka **WILLIAM WIGNALL**), **(623)**, 199
Lieutenant **PERCIVAL SCROPE MARLING (401)**, 155
Acting Lieutenant Colonel **JAMES NEVILLE MARSHALL (1144)**, 295
Quartermaster Sergeant **WILLIAM THOMAS MARSHALL (400)**, 155
Lieutenant **CYRIL GORDON MARTIN (575)**, 190
Sergeant **HORACE ROBERT MARTINEAU (449)**, 166
Surgeon Captain later Lieutenant **ARTHUR MARTIN-LEAKE (514)** & **(551)**, 175, 185
Private **RICHARD GEORGE MASTERS (982)**, 266
Lieutenant **JAMES EDWARD IGNATIUS MASTERSON (453)**, 167
Captain **FRANCIS CORNWALLIS MAUDE (177)**, 113
Brevet Lieutenant Colonel **FREDERICK FRANCIS MAUDE (98)**, 99
Second Lieutenant **THOMAS HAROLD BROADBENT MAUFE (829)**, 238
Lieutenant **FRANCIS AYLMER MAXWELL (465)**, 168
Lieutenant **JOSEPH MAXWELL (1112)**, 289
Private **HENRY MAY (546)**, 185
Lieutenant **LESLIE CECIL MAYGAR (511)**, 174
Midshipman **ARTHUR MAYO (233)**, 122
Lance Sergeant **TOM FLETCHER MAYSON (848)**, 241
Corporal **SAMUEL MEEKOSHA** (name changed to **INGHAM** in 1939), **(682)**, 210
Sergeant **JOHN MEIKLE (1020)**, 273
Captain **MATTHEW FONTAINE MAURY MEIKLEJOHN (435)**, 163
Chaplain **EDWARD NOEL MELLISH (692)**, 212
Captain **CHARLES JOHN MELLISS (489)**, 176
Lieutenant **TEIGNMOUTH MELVILL (345)**, 147
Private **CHARLES MELVIN (808)**, 233
Sergeant **WILLIAM MERRIFIELD (1109)**, 289
Major **CHARLES CECIL INGERSOLL MERRITT (1222)**, 318
Lance Corporal **WILLIAM HENRY METCALF (1071)**, 281
Captain **GODFREY MEYNELL (1161)**, 300

Lieutenant Commander **MARTIN ERIC NASMITH** (later **DUNBAR-NASMITH), (622)**, 199
Lieutenant **PHILIP NEAME (565)**, 188
Private **SAMUEL NEEDHAM (1077)**, 282
Corporal **THOMAS NEELY (1096)**, 286
Sergeant **DAVID NELSON (538)**, 183
Captain **RANDOLPH COSBY NESBITT (415)**, 158
Acting Subadar **NETRABAHADUR THAPA (1283)**, 335
Squadron Leader **JOHN DERING NETTLETON (1214)**, 316
Private **ROBERT NEWELL (252)**, 125
Captain **JAMES ERNEST NEWLAND (792)**, 230
Lieutenant Colonel **AUGUSTUS CHARLES NEWMAN (1209)**, 314
Flight Lieutenant **WILLIAM ELLIS NEWTON (1236)**, 322
Second Lieutenant **MOANA-NUI-A-KIWA** (spelt **KIWI** on headstone) **NGARIMU (1238)**, 322
Private **HENRY JAMES NICHOLAS (938)**, 257
Lance Corporal **HARRY NICHOLLS (1171)**, 303
Lieutenant **WILLIAM HENRY SNYDER NICKERSON (469)**, 169
Flight Lieutenant **ERIC JAMES BRINDLEY NICOLSON (1177)**, 305
Acting Corporal **CECIL REGINALD NOBLE (579)**, 190
Private **WILLIAM NORMAN (51)**, 91
Lieutenant **GERARD ROSS NORTON (1293)**, 338
Second Lieutenant **JOHN NORWOOD (437)**, 164
Private **CLAUDE JOSEPH PATRICK NUNNEY (1064)**, 280
Corporal **GEORGE EDWARD NURSE (447)**, 166

Sergeant **JAMES OCKENDON** (spelt **OCKENDEN** on his VC), **(894)**, 250
Sergeant **LUKE O'CONNOR (10)**, 84
Leading Seaman **WILLIAM ODGERS (297)**, 133
Private **TIMOTHY O'HEA (327)**, 139
Acting Captain **CHRISTOPHER PATRICK JOHN O'KELLY (905)**, 252
Lance Corporal **MICHAEL JOHN O'LEARY (570)**, 189
Captain **WILLIAM OLPHERTS (178)**, 114
Private **MARTIN O'MEARA (745)**, 221
Sergeant **JOHN O'NEILL** (or **O'NIELL) (1126)**, 292
Lance Corporal **GEORGE ONIONS (1042)**, 276
Sergeant **JOHN WILLIAM ORMSBY (805)**, 233
Private **MICHAEL JAMES O'ROURKE (860)**, 244
Company Sergeant Major **JOHN ROBERT OSBORN (1201)**, 312
Private **JAMES OSBORNE (394)**, 154
Captain **GERALD ROBERT O'SULLIVAN (631)**, 201
Sergeant **EDMUND O'TOOLE (374)**, 151
Corporal **JAMES OWENS (31)**, 88
Corporal **WILLIAM OXENHAM (134)**, 105

Private **ANTHONY PALMER (44)**, 90
Lance Sergeant **FREDERICK WILLIAM PALMER (776)**, 227
Squadron Leader **ROBERT ANTHONY MAURICE PALMER (1309)**, 344
Gunner **JAMES PARK (210)**, 119
Sergeant **JOHN PARK (8)**, 84
Havildar **PARKASH SINGH (1235)**, 321
Sergeant **CHARLES EDWARD HAYDON PARKER (466)**, 169
Lance Corporal **WALTER PARKER (611)**, 197

Private SAMUEL (aka GEORGE) PARKES (22), 87
Mercantile Marine Master FREDERICK DANIEL PARSLOW (633), 201
Lieutenant FRANCIS NEWTON PARSONS (457), 167
Temporary Second Lieutenant HARDY FALCONER PARSONS (870), 245
Private FRANK JOHN PARTRIDGE (1340), 354
Acting Captain GEORGE PATON (934), 257
Sergeant JOHN PATON (217), 120
Private JOHN GEORGE PATTISON (800), 232
Warrant Officer Class II KEITH PAYNE (1352), 361
Private GEORGE STANLEY PEACHMENT (659), 206
Acting Major GEORGE RANDOLPH PEARKES (912), 253
Sergeant SAMUEL GEORGE PEARSE (1156), 299
Private JAMES PEARSON (259), 126
Private JOHN PEARSON (279), 129
Lieutenant Colonel CYRUS WESLEY PECK (1065), 280
Captain WILLIAM PEEL (14), 85
Lance Corporal WALTER PEELER (884), 248
Lieutenant HENRY SINGLETON PENNELL (423), 160
Colonel HENRY HUGH MANVERS PERCY (32), 88
Sapper JOHN PERIE (spelt PIRRIE in cemetery register), (85), 97
Acting Captain FREDERICK THORNTON PETERS (1230), 320
Temporary Lieutenant ROBERT EDWIN PHILLIPS (772), 227
Major EDMUND JOHN PHIPPS-HORNBY (464), 168
Lieutenant ARTHUR FREDERICK PICKARD (314), 136
Petty Officer ERNEST HERBERT PITCHER (857), 243
Lieutenant HENRY WILLIAM PITCHER (312), 135
Private JAMES PITTS (455), 167
Lieutenant BASIL CHARLES GODFREY PLACE (1254), 327
Second Lieutenant ALFRED OLIVER POLLARD (816), 235
Corporal JAMES DALGLEISH POLLOCK (668), 207
Lieutenant CHARLES POPE (806), 233
Temporary Captain PATRICK ANTHONY PORTEOUS (1224), 319
Private FREDERICK WILLIAM OWEN POTTS (649), 204
Private ARTHUR POULTER (985), 266
Jemadar PRAKASH SINGH (1315), 345
Second Lieutenant PREMINDRA SINGH BHAGAT (1180), 306
Lieutenant HARRY NORTH DALRYMPLE PRENDERGAST (232), 122
Corporal JOHN PRETTYJOHNS (sometimes spelt PRETTYJOHN), (40), 89
Lieutenant LLEWELLYN ALBERIC EMILIUS PRICE-DAVIES (508), 174
Captain of the Afterguard THOMAS PRIDE (322), 138
Captain DIGHTON MacNAUGHTON PROBYN (115), 102
Private ARTHUR HERBERT PROCTER (708), 215
Private JOSEPH PROSSER (75), 95
Chief Petty Officer GEORGE PROWSE (1067), 281
Acting Captain THOMAS TANNATT PRYCE (986), 266
Private JOHN PURCELL (129), 105
Sergeant Major CHARLES COLQUHOUN PYE (228), 122

Captain LIONEL ERNEST QUERIPEL (1296), 339
Private ROBERT QUIGG (723), 217

Lieutenant HENRY JAMES RABY (**79**), 96
Acting Subadar RAM SARUP SINGH (**1304**), 342
Sergeant HENRY RAMAGE (**26**), 87
Lance Corporal RAMBAHADUR LIMBU (**1349**), 358
Trooper HORACE EDWARD RAMSDEN (**450**), 166
Temporary Captain JOHN NEIL RANDLE (**1269**), 331
Captain HARRY SHERWOOD RANKEN (**544**), 184
Private WILLIAM RATCLIFFE (**836**), 239
Corporal REGINALD ROY RATTEY (**1326**), 350
Private GEORGE RAVENHILL (**448**), 166
Private WALTER LEIGH RAYFIELD (**1075**), 282
Lieutenant CLAUD RAYMOND (**1325**), 349
Acting Sergeant JOHN CRANSHAW RAYNES (**674**), 208
Lieutenant WILLIAM RAYNOR (**118**), 103
Captain ANKETELL MOUTRAY READ (**654**), 205
Surgeon HERBERT TAYLOR READE (**168**), 112
Private JOHN READITT (**780**), 228
Captain HAMILTON LYSTER REED (**444**), 165
Sergeant IVOR WILMOT BRABAZON REES (**847**), 241
Temporary Major LIONEL REES (**717**), 216
Able Seaman THOMAS REEVES (**41**), 89
Captain OSWALD AUSTIN REID (**783**), 229
Acting Flight Lieutenant WILLIAM REID (**1256**), 327
Bandsman THOMAS EDWARD RENDLE (**558**), 187
Lieutenant WILLIAM RENNIE (**173**), 113
Lieutenant GEORGE ALEXANDER RENNY (**170**), 113
Captain DOUGLAS REYNOLDS (**535**), 183
Captain HENRY REYNOLDS (**878**), 247
Surgeon Major JAMES HENRY REYNOLDS (**350**), 148
Private WILLIAM REYNOLDS (**6**), 84
Lance Sergeant JOHN HAROLD RHODES (**900**), 251
Second Lieutenant WILLIAM BERNARD RHODES-MOORHOUSE (born **MOORHOUSE**),
    (**606**), 196
Sergeant ALFRED JOSEPH RICHARDS (**596**), 194
Sergeant ARTHUR HERBERT LINDSAY RICHARDSON (**476**), 170
Private GEORGE RICHARDSON (**295**), 131
Piper JAMES CLELAND RICHARDSON (**764**), 225
Subadar RICHHPAL (sometimes spelt **RICHPAL**) RAM (**1181**), 306
Quartermaster WILLIAM THOMAS RICKARD (**111**), 101
Private THOMAS RICKETTS (**1125**), 292
Captain RICHARD KIRBY RIDGEWAY (**377**), 152
Sergeant FREDERICK CHARLES RIGGS (**1110**), 289
Corporal JOHN RIPLEY (**614**), 197
Commander HENRY PEEL RITCHIE (**561**), 187
Drummer WALTER POTTER RITCHIE (**724**), 217
Private JACOB RIVERS (**582**), 191
Gunner JOHN ROBARTS (**66**), 94
Acting Lieutenant Colonel FRANK CROWTHER ROBERTS (**961**), 262
Lieutenant FREDERICK HUGH SHERSTON ROBERTS (**446**), 165
Lieutenant FREDERICK SLEIGH ROBERTS (**235**), 123
Private JAMES REYNOLDS ROBERTS (**195**), 117

Temporary Second Lieutenant **JOHN SCHOFIELD (981)**, 265
Seaman **MARK SCHOLEFIELD (45)**, 90
Captain **ANDREW SCOTT (342)**, 143
Private **ROBERT SCOTT (456)**, 167
Sergeant **ROBERT GEORGE SCOTT (368)**, 152
Captain **FRANCIS ALEXANDER CARRON SCRIMGER (592)**, 193
Temporary Lieutenant Colonel **DEREK ANTHONY SEAGRIM (1237)**, 322
Lance Corporal **ERNEST SEAMAN (1103)**, 288
Seaman **WILLIAM HENRY HARRISON SEELEY (323)**, 138
Lance Corporal **GEORGE SELLAR (384)**, 146
Petty Officer **ALFRED EDWARD SEPHTON (1185)**, 307
Lieutenant **CECIL HAROLD SEWELL (1054)**, 279
Naik **SHAHAMAD KHAN (698)**, 212
Lieutenant **ROBERT SHANKLAND (906)**, 252
Acting Corporal **CHARLES RICHARD SHARPE (616)**, 198
Corporal **JOHN DAVID FRANCIS SHAUL (440)**, 164
Captain **HUGH SHAW (324)**, 137
Private **SAMUEL** (aka **SAME** or **JOHN**) **JAMES SHAW (274)**, 128
Lieutenant **ROBERT HAYDON SHEBBEARE (162)**, 111
Private **ALBERT EDWARD SHEPHERD (924)**, 255
Boatswains Mate **JOHN SHEPPARD** (or **SHEPHERD**), **(92)**, 98
Rifleman **SHERBAHADUR THAPA (1295)**, 339
Captain **ROBERT ST VINCENT SHERBROOKE (1234)**, 321
Lance Naik **SHER SHAH (1312)**, 345
Acting Lieutenant Colonel **JOHN SHERWOOD-KELLY (919)**, 254
Corporal **ROBERT SHIELDS (103)**, 99
Private **WILLIAM HENRY SHORT (742)**, 221
Captain **ALFRED JOHN SHOUT (643)**, 203
Temporary Major **WILLIAM PHILIP SIDNEY (1261)**, 329
Lance Sergeant **ELLIS WELWOOD SIFTON (796)**, 231
Quartermaster Sergeant **JOHN SIMPSON (265)**, 127
Warrant Officer Class II **RAYENE STEWART SIMPSON (1351)**, 360
Private **JOHN JOSEPH SIMS (84)**, 96
Lance Corporal **JOHN SINNOTT (200)**, 118
Captain **JOHN ALEXANDER SINTON (687)**, 211
Company Sergeant Major **JOHN KENDRICK SKINNER (867)**, 245
Corporal **MICHAEL SLEAVON** (spelt **SLEVIN** on his death certificate), **(256)**, 126
Gunner **ALFRED SMITH (403)**, 155
Second Lieutenant **ALFRED VICTOR SMITH (685)**, 210
Lieutenant **CLEMENT LESLIE SMITH (521)**, 179
Lance Sergeant **EDWARD BENN SMITH (1039)**, 276
Private **ERNEST ALVIA SMITH (1303)**, 341
Corporal **FELIX PHILIP SMITH (81)**, 96
Captain **FREDERICK AUGUSTUS SMITH (319)**, 137
Lance Corporal **HENRY SMITH (165)**, 112
Acting Corporal **ISSY SMITH** (born **ISHROULCH SHMEILOWITZ**), **(609)**, 196
Corporal **JAMES SMITH (422)**, 159
Private **JAMES ALEXANDER GLENN SMITH** (born **GLENN**), **(568)**, 188
Sergeant **JOHN SMITH (164)**, 111
Private **JOHN SMITH (223)**, 121
Lieutenant **JOHN GEORGE SMYTH** (sometimes spelt **SMYTHE**), **(620)**, 198

Private ROSS TOLLERTON (**541**), 184
Major HENRY TOMBS (**140**), 106
Lance Corporal JOSEPH HARCOURT TOMBS (**620**), 198
Corporal FREDERICK GEORGE TOPHAM (**1327**), 350
Private JAMES TOWERS (**1115**), 290
Lieutenant EDGAR THOMAS TOWNER (**1057**), 279
Captain ERNEST BEACHCROFT BECKWITH TOWSE (**441**), 164
Acting Captain ALFRED MAURICE TOYE (**967**), 263
Corporal CHARLES WILLIAM TRAIN (**940**), 258
Colonel JAMES TRAVERS (**136**), 106
Sergeant RICHARD CHARLES TRAVIS (born **DICKSON CORNELIUS SAVAGE**), (**1021**), 273
Sergeant WILLIAM BERNARD TRAYNOR (**499**), 173
Squadron Leader LEONARD HENRY TRENT (**1247**), 325
Major WILLIAM SPOTTISWOODE TREVOR (**325**), 138
Seaman JOSEPH TREWAVAS (**89**), 97
Flying Officer LLOYD ALLAN TRIGG (**1250**), 326
Captain PAUL TRIQUET (**1258**), 328
Lieutenant FREDERICK HAROLD TUBB (**644**), 203
Rifleman TULBAHADUR PUN (**1281**), 334
Sergeant JAMES YOULL TURNBULL (**721**), 217
Second Lieutenant ALEXANDER BULLER TURNER (**670**), 208
Acting Sergeant HANSON VICTOR TURNER (**1276**), 333
Lieutenant RICHARD ERNEST WILLIAM TURNER (**493**), 172
Private SAMUEL TURNER (**130**), 105
Temporary Lieutenant Colonel VICTOR BULLER TURNER (**1229**), 320
Private THOMAS GEORGE TURRALL (**726**), 218
Lieutenant JOHN ADAM TYTLER (**238**), 123

Havildar UMRAO SINGH (**1308**), 343
UNKNOWN AMERICAN SOLDIER of WWI (**1151**), 297
Captain EDWARD UNWIN (**593**), 193
Second Lieutenant CHARLES HAZLITT UPHAM (**1188**) & (**1219**), 308, 317
Corporal JAMES UPTON (**615**), 197

Captain JOHN FRANCIS VALLENTIN (**554**), 186
Acting Lieutenant Colonel BERNARD WILLIAM VANN (**1102**), 288
Private THEODORE WILLIAM HENTY VEALE (**734**), 219
Private ARTHUR VICKERS (**662**), 206
Temporary Captain CHARLES GEOFFREY VICKERS (**676**), 209
Private SAMUEL VICKERY (**426**), 161
Captain WILLIAM JOHN VOUSDEN (**383**), 146

Lieutenant RICHARD WADESON (**147**), 108
Captain RICHARD WILLIAM LESLIE WAIN (**920**), 254
Temporary Captain RICHARD WAKEFORD (**1271**), 332
Private ADAM HERBERT WAKENSHAW (**1218**), 317
Captain GARTH NEVILLE WALFORD (**605**), 196
Lieutenant MARK WALKER (**37**), 89
Captain WILLIAM GEORGE WALKER (**519**), 178
Temporary Lieutenant SAMUEL THOMAS DICKSON WALLACE (**930**), 256

Lieutenant GEORGE WALLER (**169**), 112
Private HORACE WALLER (**801**), 232
Lieutenant WILLIAM FRANCIS FREDERICK WALLER (**280**), 129
Sergeant GEORGE WALTERS (**39**), 89
Lieutenant Commander MALCOLM DAVID WANKLYN (**1189**), 309
Captain BERNARD ARMITAGE WARBURTON WARBURTON-LEE (**1164**), 302
Private CHARLES BURLEY WARD (**475**), 169
Private HENRY WARD (**181**), 114
Sergeant JAMES ALLEN WARD (**1192**), 310
Sergeant JOSEPH WARD (**277**), 129
Corporal SIDNEY WILLIAM WARE (**694**), 212
Lance Sergeant WILLIAM HERBERT WARING (**1086**), 284
Major BLAIR ANDERSON WARK (**1104**), 288
Flight Sub Lieutenant REGINALD ALEXANDER JOHN WARNEFORD (**626**), 200
Private EDWARD WARNER (**612**), 197
Private SAMUEL WASSALL (**347**), 147
Acting Major ARNOLD HORACE SANTO WATERS (**1146**), 296
Lieutenant TASKER WATKINS (**1291**), 337
Lieutenant JOHN WATSON (**205**), 118
Acting Lieutenant Colonel OLIVER CYRIL SPENCER WATSON (**973**), 264
Lieutenant THOMAS COLCLOUGH WATSON (**421**), 159
Skipper JOSEPH WATT (**826**), 237
Lance Corporal HENRY WEALE (**1051**), 278
Second Lieutenant FRANK BERNARD WEARNE (**838**), 239
Temporary Corporal LAWRENCE CARTHAGE WEATHERS (**1072**), 282
Lance Corporal JAMES WELCH (**817**), 235
Sergeant HARRY WELLS (**657**), 205
Captain FERDINAND MAURICE FELIX WEST (**1035**), 275
Acting Lieutenant Colonel RICHARD ANNESLEY WEST (**1040**), 276
Lieutenant WILLIAM BASIL WESTON (**1322**), 348
Private FRANCIS WHEATLEY (**11**), 85
Warrant Officer Class II KEVIN ARTHUR WHEATLEY (**1348**), 359
Major GEORGE CAMPBELL WHEELER (**779**), 228
Major GEORGE GODFREY MASSY WHEELER (**583**), 191
Private FREDERICK WHIRLPOOL (born **CONKER** but later changed to **JAMES**), (**260**), 126
Surgeon Captain HARRY FREDERICK WHITCHURCH (**412**), 158
Sergeant ALBERT WHITE (**827**), 237
Temporary Captain ARCHIE CECIL THOMAS WHITE (**761**), 224
Lieutenant Commander GEOFFREY SAXTON WHITE (**945**), 259
Major GEORGE STUART WHITE (**375**), 145
Private JACK WHITE (**781**), 228
Temporary Second Lieutenant WILLIAM ALLISON WHITE (**1084**), 284
Private HAROLD WHITFIELD (**947**), 259
Private THOMAS WHITHAM (**852**), 242
Sergeant JOHN WOODS WHITTLE (**795**), 231
Lance Corporal ALFRED WILCOX (**1080**), 283
Private ALFRED ROBERT WILKINSON (**1130**), 293
Bombardier THOMAS WILKINSON (**71**), 94
Temporary Lieutenant THOMAS WILKINSON (**1205**), 313
Temporary Lieutenant THOMAS ORDE LAUDER WILKINSON (**727**), 218
Private JOHN WILLIAMS (real name **FIELDING**), (**357**), 149

Company Sergeant Major JOHN HENRY WILLIAMS (1116), 290
Seaman WILLIAM WILLIAMS (834), 239
Able Seaman WILLIAM CHARLES WILLIAMS (602), 195
Captain RICHARD RAYMOND WILLIS (594), 193
Captain HENRY WILMOT (244), 124
Captain ARTHUR KNYVET WILSON (399), 155
Acting Captain ERIC CHARLES TWELVES WILSON (1175), 305
Private GEORGE WILSON (542), 184
Corporal HARRY BLANSHARD WOOD (1121), 291
Lieutenant (christened **HENRY) EVELYN WOOD (289)**, 131
Captain JOHN AUGUSTUS WOOD (112), 101
Private WILFRED WOOD (1139), 294
Lance Sergeant JOSEPH EDWARD WOODALL (990), 267
Private THOMAS WOODCOCK (876), 247
Sergeant CHARLES WOODEN (27), 87
Second Lieutenant SIDNEY CLAYTON WOODROFFE (635), 201
Private JAMES PARK WOODS (1087), 285
Second Lieutenant GEOFFREY HAROLD WOOLLEY (587), 192
Private ALEXANDER WRIGHT (53), 92
Company Sergeant Major PETER HAROLD WRIGHT (1255), 327
Captain THEODORE WRIGHT (527), 182
Lieutenant WALLACE DUFFIELD WRIGHT (516), 177
Lance Corporal GEORGE HARRY WYATT (530), 182
Lieutenant GUY GEORGE EGERTON WYLLY (487), 171

Major CHARLES ALLIX LAVINGTON YATE (531), 182
Naik YESHWANT GHADGE (1286), 336
Second Lieutenant FREDERICK YOUENS (839), 239
Lieutenant JOHN SCOTT YOULL (1013), 271
Sergeant Major ALEXANDER YOUNG (507), 174
Second Lieutenant FRANK EDWARD YOUNG (1083), 284
Private JOHN FRANCIS YOUNG (1074), 282
Private THOMAS YOUNG (real name **MORRELL), (969)**, 263
Lieutenant THOMAS JAMES YOUNG (215), 120
Private WILLIAM YOUNG (684), 210
Captain DAVID REGINALD YOUNGER (478), 170

Sergeant RAPHAEL LOUIS ZENGEL (1031), 274

BIBLIOGRAPHY

Adkin, Mark, *The Last Eleven?* (Pen & Sword, Barnsley, 1991)

Arthur, Max, *Symbol of Courage. The Men Behind the Medal* (Sidgwick & Jackson, London, 2004)

Ashcroft, Michael, *Victoria Cross Heroes* (Headline Book Publishing, London, 2006)

Bancroft, James, W., *Local Heroes: Boer War VCs* (The House of Heroes, 1994)

Barthrop, Michael, *Heroes of the Crimea* (Blandford, London, 1991)

Barthrop, Michael, *The Zulu War* (Blandford, London, 1992)

Batchelor, Peter F. and Christopher Matson, *VCs of the First World War: The Western Front 1915* (Wrens Park Publishing, 1999)

Beharry, Johnson, *Barefoot Soldier* (Sphere, London, 2006)

Best, Brian (ed.), *The Journal of the Victoria Cross Society* (Editions 1–12, The Victoria Cross Society)

Biggs, Maurice, *The Story of the Gurkha VCs* (Winchester, Gurkha Museum, 2001)

Billiere, Gen. Sir Peter de la, *Supreme Courage: Heroic Stories from 150 Years of the Victoria Cross* (Little, Brown, London, 2004)

Bowyer, Chaz, *For Valour: The Air VCs* (William Kimber, London, 1978)

Cooksley, Peter G., *VCs of the First World War: The Air VCs* (Wrens Park Publishing, 1999)

Crook, M.J., *The Evolution of the Victoria Cross* (Midas Books, in association with Ogilby Trusts, Tunbridge Wells, 1975)

Frayn Turner, John, *VCs of the Second World War* (Pen & Sword, Barnsley, 2004)

Glanfield, John, *Bravest of the Brave. The Story of the Victoria Cross* (Sutton Publishing, Stroud, 2005)

Gliddon, Gerald, *VCs of the First World War: 1914* (Budding Books, 1997)

Gliddon, Gerald, *VCs of the First World War: The Somme 1916* (Budding Books, 1997)

Gliddon, Gerald, *VCs of the First World War: Spring Offensive 1918* (Sutton Publishing, 1997)

Gliddon, Gerald, *VCs of the First World War: Arras & Messines 1917* (Wrens Park Publishing, 2000)

Gliddon, Gerald, *VCs of the First World War:*

The Final Days 1918 (Sutton Publishing, 2000)

Gliddon, Gerald, *VCs of the First World War: The Road to Victory 1918* (Sutton Publishing, 2000)

Harvey, David, *Monuments to Courage. Victoria Cross Headstones & Memorials* (K. & K. Patience, 1999)

Haydon, A.L., *The Book of the VC* (Andrew Melrose, 1906)

Little, Matthew Grant, *The Royal M the Victoria Cross* (Royal Marines Museum, Southsea, 2002)

Little, Paul, *Willie Apiata VC* (Penguin Group, 2008)

Littlewood, Arthur, *Indian Mutiny & Beyond. The Letters of Robert Shebbeare VC* (Pen & Sword, Barnsley, 2007)

Morris, Donald R., *The Washing of the Spears* (Book Club Associates, 1966)

Mulholland, John, and Jordan, Alan, *Victoria Cross Bibliography* (Spink & Son, 1999)

North, John, *Gallipoli: The Fading Vision* (Faber & Faber, London, 1936)

Percival, John, *For Valour* (Methuen, London, 1985)

RAMC, *The Medical Victoria Crosses* (Arrow Press, Aldershot, 1983)

Register of the Victoria Cross (This England Books, 3rd edn, Cheltenham, 1997)

Roe, Gordon E., *The Bronze Cross. A Tribute to Those who Won the Supreme Award for Valour in the Years 1940–45* (P.R. Gawthorn, London, 1945)

Smyth, Sir John, *The Story of the Victoria Cross, 1856–1963* (Frederick Muller, London, 1963)

The VC and DSO Book: The Victoria Cross 1856–1920 (ed. the late Sir O'Moore Creagh and E.M. Humphris, The Naval & Military Press)

Tidey, Iain W., *Sidney Frank Godley VC* (unpublished, 1999)

Toomey, T. E., *Heroes of the Victoria Cross* (Geo. Newnes, 1895)

Turner, John Frayn, *VCs of the Air* (Harrap, 1960)

Wilkins, Philip, *The History of the Victoria Cross* (Constable, London, 1904)

Winton, John, *The Victoria Cross at Sea* (Joseph, London, 1978)